Expository Discourses on First Epistle of the Apostle Peter

Volume II of II

Expository Discourses on First Epistle of the Apostle Peter

Three Volumes In Two
Volume II of II

John Brown of Edinburgh

Senior Minister of the United Presbyterian Congregation, Broughton Place, Edinburgh, and Professor of Exegetical Theology to the United Presbyterian Church

Sovereign Grace Publishers, Inc.
P.O. Box 4998
Lafayette, IN 47903

Expository Discourses on the First Epistle of the Apostle Peter
Volume II of 2 Volumes, Paperback Edition
Copyright © 2000
By Jay P. Green, Sr.
All Rights Reserved

ISBN: 1-58960-133-5

Printed in the United States of America
By Lightning Source, Inc.

NOTE: THIS VOLUME CONTAINS THE FIRST VOLUME OF THE ORIGINAL THREE
VOLUME SET
And
THE FIRST HALF OF THE ORIGINAL VOLUME II OF THE THREE VOLUME SET

THE PAGE NUMBERS HAVE NOT BEEN RENUMBERED FROM THE PAGINATION OF THE
ORIGINAL SET
THEREFORE THIS VOLUME CONTAINS TWO PAGE 241'S THROUGH PAGE 436

CONTENTS - VOLUME II

SECOND HALF OF ORIGINAL VOLUME II NOW APPENDED TO BEGINNING OF THIS VOLUME

DISCOURSE XV.

DUTIES OF CHRISTIANS, IRRESPECTIVE OF THEIR CIVIL AND DOMESTIC RELATIONS.

CHAPTER III. 8-17, pp. 241-376.

PART I. Duties of Christians to each other, page 247. § 1. To cultivate and manifest union of sentiment, 248. § 2. To cultivate and manifest union of feeling, 257. § 3. To cultivate and manifest brotherly kindness, 259. PART II. Duties of Christians to mankind generally, 265.   § 1. To "be pitiful," 265.   § 2. To "be courteous," 279. PART III. Duties of Christians under persecution, 298.   § 1. Abstinence from all resentful retaliation, and meeting injury and reproach by kindness, both in conduct and language, 298.   (1.) The duty explained, 299.   (2.) The duty enforced, 304.   § 2. Guarding against the fear of man by cultivating the due fear of God, 316.   § 3. Readiness at all times to give an answer to every one that asketh them a reason of the hope that is in them, 331.   § 4. Maintaining "a good conscience" and "a good conversation," 351.   Conclusion, 366. NOTES, 372.

DISCOURSE XVI.

THE SUFFERINGS OF CHRIST (THEIR NATURE, DESIGN, CONSEQUENCES) AN ENCOURAGEMENT TO CHRISTIANS SUFFERING FOR HIS CAUSE.

CHAPTER III. 18-22, pp. 377-497.

PART I. The Sufferer, page 381.   § 1. Christ, 381.   § 2. The just One, 384.   PART II. His sufferings, 388.   PART III. The nature of his sufferings, 396.   § 1. Penal, 397.   § 2. Vicarious, 399.   § 3. Expiatory, 403.   PART IV. The design of his sufferings, "to bring men to God," 409.   § 1. To bring men to the knowledge of God, 411.   § 2. To bring men to favour with God, 424.   § 3. To bring men to likeness to God, 437.   § 4. To bring men to fellowship with God, 443.   PART V. The consequences of his sufferings, 449.   § 1. He became dead in the flesh, quickened in the Spirit, and went and preached to the spirits in prison, 453.   § 2. He rose from the dead, ascended to heaven, sits at the right hand of God; angels, and authorities, and powers, being made subject to him, 475.   (1.) His resurrection, 476.   (2.) His ascension to heaven, 481.   (3.) He is "on the right hand of God," 484.   (4.) Angels, authorities, and powers, are made subject to him, 487. PART VI. The tendency of these truths respecting the sufferings of Christ to support and encourage Christians suffering for his cause, 490.

APPENDIX TO DISCOURSE XVI.

FACTS IN ANTEDILUVIAN HISTORY REFERRED TO BY THE APOSTLE, AND THEIR BEARING ON HIS OBJECT.

Pp. 498-528.

PART I. Facts in antediluvian history referred to by the apostle, page 502.   PART II. Object of the apostle in referring to these facts, 509. NOTES, 523.

II. TABLE FOR FINDING OUT THE EXPOSITION OF ANY VERSE OR CLAUSE OF THE EPISTLE IN THIS VOLUME.

CHAPTER II.

Ver.
16. As free, 1, 19; and not using your liberty for a cloak of maliciousness,
17. 37; but as the servants of God, 13, 53. Honour all men, 75; love the brotherhood, 94; fear God, 115; honour the king, 125. Ser-
18. vants, be subject to your own masters, 144; with all fear, 148; not
19. only to the good and gentle, but also to the froward, 150. For this is thankworthy, if a man for conscience toward God endure grief,
20. suffering wrongfully, 151. For what glory is it, if, when ye be buffeted for your faults, ye shall take it patiently, 152; but if, when ye do well, and suffer for it, ye take it patiently, this is
21. acceptable with God, 153. For even hereunto were ye called, 158, 168, 175; because Christ also suffered for us, 160; leaving us an
22. example that ye should follow his steps, 166. Who did no sin,
23. neither was guile found in his mouth, 161. Who, when he was reviled, reviled not again; when he suffered, he threatened not, 163;
24. but committed himself to him who judgeth righteously, 164. Who his own self bare our sins in his own body on the tree, 176; that we, being dead to sins, 182; should live to righteousness, 182; by
25. whose stripes ye were healed, 185. For ye were as sheep going astray, 186; but ye are now returned unto the Shepherd and Bishop of your souls, 187.

CHAPTER III.

1. Likewise, ye wives, be in subjection to your own husbands, 195; that if any obey not the word, 208; they may, without the word,
2. be won by the conversation of the wives, 211; when they behold
3. your chaste conversation coupled with fear, 199; whose adorning, let it not be that outward adorning of plaiting the hair, and of
4. wearing of gold, or of putting on of apparel, 200; but let it be the hidden man of the heart, in that which is not corruptible, 203; even the ornament of a meek and quiet spirit, which is in the sight of
5. God of great price, 206. For after this manner, in the old time, the holy women also who trusted in God, adorned themselves,
6. being in subjection to their own husbands, 215; even as Sarah obeyed Abraham, calling him Lord, 216; whose daughters ye are as long as ye do well, and are not afraid with any amazement, 217.
7. Likewise, ye husbands, dwell with them according to knowledge, 223, 225; giving honour unto the wife, as unto the weaker vessel, 229; and as being heirs together of the grace of life, 231; that
8. your prayers be not hindered, 235. Finally, 245; be ye all of one mind, 248; having compassion one of another, 257; love as bre-
9. thren, 259; be pitiful, 265; be courteous, 279. Not rendering evil for evil, nor railing for railing, 299; but contrariwise blessing, 302;

Ver.	
	knowing that ye are thereunto called, 304 ; that ye should inherit
10.	a blessing, 308. For he that will love life, and see good days, let him refrain his tongue from evil, and his lips that they speak no
11.	guile, 306. Let him eschew evil, and do good, 307 ; let him seek
12.	peace and ensue it, 308. For the eyes of the Lord are over the righteous, and his ears are open to their prayers, 308 ; but the face
13.	of the Lord is against them who do evil, 308. And who is he that will harm you, 308 ; if ye be followers of that which is good ? 310.
14.	But 'and if ye suffer for righteousness' sake, happy are ye, 312 ;
15.	and be not afraid of their terror, neither be ye troubled, 316. But sanctify the Lord God in your hearts, 316, 321 ; and be ready always to give an answer, 341; to every man that asketh you, 342 ; a reason of the hope, 331 ; that is in you, 337 ; with meekness,
16.	346 ; and fear, 347. Having a good conscience, 351 ; that whereas they speak evil of you as of evil-doers, they may be ashamed, 365 ;
17.	that falsely accuse your good conversation in Christ, 361, For it is better, if the will of God be so, that ye suffer for well-doing, than
18.	evil-doing, 366. For Christ, 381 ; also hath once, 380 ; suffered, 388; for sins, 397, 403 ; the just, 384 ; for the unjust, 399 ; that he might bring us to God, 409 ; being put to death in the flesh,
19.	459 ; but quickened by the Spirit, 460. By which also he went
20.	and preached unto the spirits in prison, 461 ; which sometimes were disobedient, 462 ; when once the long-suffering of God waited in the days of Noah, while the ark was a preparing, wherein few,
21.	that is, eight souls, were saved by water, 502, 509. The like figure whereunto even baptism does now save us, 513 ; not the putting away of the filth of the flesh, 515 ; but the answer of a good conscience towards God, 515 ; by the resurrection of Jesus Christ, 518.
22.	Who is gone into heaven, 481 ; and is on the right hand of God, 484 ; angels, and authorities, and powers, being made subject to him, 487.

END OF CONTENTS FOR ORIGINAL VOLUME II

CONTENTS FOR ORIGINAL VOLUME III
ON NEXT PAGE

DISCOURSE XV.

DUTIES OF CHRISTIANS, IRRESPECTIVE OF THEIR CIVIL AND DOMESTIC RELATIONS.

"Finally, be ye all of one mind, having compassion one of another; love as brethren, be pitiful, be courteous: not rendering evil for evil, or railing for railing; but contrariwise blessing: knowing that ye are thereunto called, that ye should inherit a blessing. For he that will love life, and see good days, let him refrain his tongue from evil, and his lips that they speak no guile; let him eschew evil, and do good; let him seek peace, and ensue it. For the eyes of the Lord are over the righteous, and his ears are open unto their prayers; but the face of the Lord is against them that do evil. And who is he that will harm you, if ye be followers of that which is good? But and if ye suffer for righteousness' sake, happy are ye: and be not afraid of their terror, neither be troubled; but sanctify the Lord God in your hearts: and be ready always to give an answer to every man that asketh you a reason of the hope that is in you with meekness and fear; having a good conscience; that, whereas they speak evil of you, as of evil-doers, they may be ashamed that falsely accuse your good conversation in Christ. For it is better, if the will of God be so, that ye suffer for well-doing, than for evil-doing."—1 PET. iii. 8-17.

"LET not your good be evil spoken of," says the Apostle Paul to the Christians of Rome; and the injunction is equally applicable to, equally obligatory on, Christians of all countries and ages.

The religion of Christians is emphatically their "good thing," their most precious treasure, their most valuable possession. Christianity, viewed not merely as exhibiting a perfect system of religious and moral truth, and prescribing a complete course of religious and moral discipline, but considered also as "the ministration of the Spirit"— of truth, and purity, and happiness—to ignorant, deluded, depraved, miserable men,—the appointed and the only medium through which God, the Author of all good, will bestow on mankind forgiveness, sanctification, and eternal life,—" the power of God unto salvation,"—is plainly inexpressibly, inestimably excellent and valuable. "It cannot be valued with the gold of Ophir, with the precious onyx, or the sapphire. The gold and the crystal cannot equal it, and the exchange of it shall not be for jewels of pure gold. No mention shall be made of coral or of pearls; for its price is above rubies. The topaz of Ethiopia shall not equal it, neither shall it be valued with pure gold."

To him who cordially embraces it, it is an abundant, perennial fountain of the most precious blessings. It is in him "a well of living water, springing up unto everlasting life;" it gives peace to his conscience, and purity to his heart; it guides him in perplexity, sustains him in weakness, defends him in danger, and comforts him in sorrow; it quells his fears and animates his hopes; it stimulates his indolence, and directs his activity; it sweetens the cup of death, and brightens the prospect of eternity. And even with regard to those who neglect or oppose it, when brought within the sphere of its indirect influence, though by increasing their responsibilities it increases their hazards, it yet materially adds both to the number and security of their comforts. How much happier is the state of society in Britain than in any heathen country, and how much of this favourable difference is to be traced to Christianity! How much do those who neglect, those who would destroy Christianity, owe to it!

It is strange that so good a thing should be evil spoken of. Of it, as of its Author, it may well be asked, "Why, what evil has it done?" Yet so it is; in all countries and ages this incomparably good thing has been evil spoken of. Its doctrines have been misstated, and its tendencies misrepresented. Its divine origin has been called in question and denied; and its effects both on the character and happiness of mankind, both in their individual and social capacities, have been represented as in a high degree injurious. In no case have names been more misapplied and things confounded than here. Sweet has been termed bitter; light, darkness; and good, evil.

To expect to render unadulterated Christianity, all excellent as it is, admired by, or even palatable to, a world sunk in ignorance and sin, "lying under the wicked one," without a radical revolution in their sentiments and habits, is a most unreasonable anticipation. Men will prefer darkness to light while their deeds are evil. But though it be impossible, while worldly and wicked men and the religion of Christ continue what they are, to extinguish malignant feeling and silence reproachful speeches in reference to the gospel; yet it is most true that the sphere of these calumnies would be considerably narrowed, the plausibility of these misrepresentations greatly lessened, and of consequence their probable mischievous effect much diminished, were it not for the improprieties and imprudences of the professed, and even of the real friends of Christianity. The behaviour of false disciples has frequently drawn not only much deserved reproach on themselves, but also much unmerited odium on the cause for which they had no true regard; and, what is still more to be deplored, the temper and conduct of those to whom that cause was really dear, have been too often such as to make their good evil spoken of.

Nor will this fact, however much to be lamented, appear difficult to be accounted for by any one who is acquainted with the very imperfect state of even regenerated human nature in this world. Through inadvertency, want of experience, error in judgment, unexpected temptation, and other evils inseparable from our present condition, persons whose prevailing chief desire is, "to adorn the doctrine of God our Saviour in all things," are in constant hazard, by something in their sentiments or dispositions, or language, or conduct, of giving strength to the prejudices of worldly men against Christianity, and plausibility to the false and calumnious misrepresentations to which those prejudices give origin. To guard against this evil seems the great object of the Apostle Peter, in that section of his epistle, part of which forms the subject of the present discourse.

That section commences with the 12th verse of the second chapter, and terminates with the 17th verse of the third. Its theme is, "Have your conversation honest," that is, honourable, "among the Gentiles; that whereas they speak against you as evil-doers, they may, by your good works which they behold, glorify God in the day of visitation." In other words, "Provide things honest in the sight of all men." "Let not your good be evil spoken of." In the peculiarities of the faith and experience of the Christian, in the peculiar doctrines of the gospel, and in the inner life of him who believes it, there is much, when brought strongly out, to excite the astonishment and even the disgust of an ungodly world; and though, to prevent this, the Christian must neither conceal the one nor disavow the other, nor be ashamed of either, yet, if he would avoid the evil of bringing reproach on his religion, and gain the good of constraining even enemies to feel its power and acknowledge its excellence, he must endeavour to make stand out in strong relief those parts of the Christian system and character, of which even an unregenerate man is, to a considerable extent, a judge; and which, approving themselves to his understanding and conscience and affections, are fitted to allay his prejudices against the system of which they form an essential part.

In accordance with this principle, the apostle, in order to the gaining of the end in view, exhorts Christians to a scrupulously exact discharge of the duties which rise out of the relations of civil and domestic society, especially in cases where the persons with whom they were connected in these relations were not Christians. He calls upon them, as members of civil society, to yield a cheerful obedience to the commands, and a ready submission to the arrangements, of the constituted authorities, whether supreme or subordinate, so far as compliance with these would not compromise their allegiance to the absolutely Supreme Ruler: "Submit to every institution of man for the punishment of evil-doers, and the praise of them who do well;" and, while showing a peculiar regard to the Christian society of which they were members, to manifest a proper respect for every human being, whatever might be his religious opinions or his place in civil society, thus "honouring all men." He calls on Christian servants, who were generally slaves, to be subject to their own masters, who were generally heathens; and warns them against allowing the unreasonableness and severity of the treatment which they might receive so to influence their minds as to induce them to neglect their duties, or to be negligent in performing them. He calls on Christian wives to be subject to their own husbands, even when unconverted men; and he calls on Christian husbands to be equally conscientious in the discharge of their duties to their wives. He then "finally," in the passage of which the text is a part, thus closing this series of exhortations, lays before them a variety of injunctions of a more general nature, obligatory, not on particular classes, but on the whole body of Christians.

These injunctions naturally range themselves under three heads, as they refer to the temper and conduct which Christians should cherish and exemplify towards each other, towards mankind at large, and towards their persecutors, or those who treated them injuriously on account of their religion. Within the limits of the Christian society they were to be distinguished by a community of views and feelings, the characteristic views and feelings of the society, and by cherishing and displaying brotherly love. " Be of the same mind; have compassion one of another,"—or rather, have the same feelings; be united in heart as well as in mind; " love as brethren." Within and without these limits, they were to manifest " pitifulness," that is, mercifulness, kind-heartedness; and " courtesy," that is, affability and kindliness; or, according to another reading very generally adopted, humility, " be pitiful, be humble-minded." And with regard to those who persecuted and despitefully used them, they were not to resent such treatment, but to meet it by a display of the directly opposite sentiments: they were to guard against an undue fear of their persecutors by cultivating the supreme fear due to God; and they were always to be ready to give an account of their faith and hope, and of the grounds on which these rested, to those who called them in question for them, maintaining at once "a good conscience" and "a good conversation." Some of these injunctions are given without any motive being urged but the general one, that this was necessary in order to have their conversation honest among the Gentiles; while others, especially those belonging to the last class, are enforced by a variety of appropriate considerations.

It is always desirable to look at a passage of Scripture not only in itself, but in its connection. When we act otherwise, we not only are all but sure to lose much of its beauty and force, but in many cases we are in danger of entirely misapprehending its reference and mistaking its meaning. When, as in the case before us, we can distinctly see to what particular class of persons injunctions are addressed, and what is the object in addressing such injunctions to such a class, we can the more readily discover the practical improvement we ought to make of them, and are the more likely to find that particular portion of "Scripture given by inspiration of God, profitable to us for doctrine and reproof, for correction and instruction in righteousness," that as Christian men we may be made "perfect, thoroughly furnished to every good work."

I. DUTIES OF CHRISTIANS TO EACH OTHER.

Let us then, in the first place, turn our attention to those injunctions which refer to the temper Christians should cherish, and the conduct they should pursue, in reference to each other. These injunctions are three: "Be all of one mind; having (or have) compassion one of another; love as brethren." Strictly speaking, all the terms here employed are descriptive of internal habits and dispositions; but these terms are here, like similar terms both in the Scriptures and common language, used to signify not only the inward sentiment, but the outward expression of it. When we say "Be kind," we mean not merely 'cherish benevolent feelings, be kindly affected,' but 'manifest this by friendly behaviour, by using the language and performing the offices of kindness.' So when the apostle says, "Be of one mind; be united in your affections; love as brethren," he means, 'Be and appear to be united in your views and feelings; cherish and manifest brotherly love toward each other.'

The external manifestations of unity and love, apart from the internal principle, do not fulfil the apostle's injunction.

They are worse than valueless; they are criminal. They are a beautiful body dead, or, if animated, animated by the demon of deceit. But, on the other hand, these principles, excellent as they are, unless embodied in suitable actions and habits, would not at all serve the purpose which the apostle has in view,—the making an impression favourable to Christianity and to Christians, on the minds even of unconverted men.

§ 1. *To cultivate and manifest union of sentiment.*

Keeping this general remark in view, let us proceed to the consideration of the first of these injunctions, "Be ye all of one mind."[1] We have the same, or a very similar, injunction repeatedly given by the Apostle Paul. "Be of one mind," says he to the Roman churches, "one towards another;" "Be like-minded towards one another, according to Christ Jesus, that ye may with one mind and one mouth glorify God, even the Father of our Lord Jesus Christ." To the Corinthians he says, "Brethren, I beseech you that ye be perfectly joined in the same mind and in the same judgment;" "Brethren, be of one mind." And to the Philippians, "Be like-minded, having the same love, being of one accord, of one mind; stand fast in one spirit, with one mind."[2] An injunction so frequently repeated, so warmly urged, by men who wrote as they were moved by the Holy Ghost, must be important. Let us endeavour distinctly to apprehend its meaning; for if we do not distinctly understand it, we are not likely accurately to obey it.

The term "mind" is frequently, perhaps usually, employed in Scripture to signify the whole inner man, including both the intellect and the affections; what we call

[1] Πάντες ὁμόφρονες.
[2] Rom. xii. 16, xv. 5, 6; 1 Cor. i. 10; 2 Cor. xiii. 11; Phil. i. 27, ii. 2.

figuratively both the head and the heart. To "have the mind of Christ in us," is to think and feel as Christ did, to have the same views of truth as he had, and to be similarly affected by these views. To "mind the things of the flesh," is to make present sensible things, "things seen and temporal," the great subjects of our thoughts, and the great objects of our affections. "To mind the things of the spirit," is to make the realities of the invisible and future world, "the things unseen and eternal"—for our knowledge of which we are entirely indebted to the Spirit—the great subjects of our thoughts, and the great objects of our affections.[1]

When, however, the term is used along with, and, as it were, in contradistinction to, some other term descriptive of affection and feeling, it is to be viewed as denoting sentiment or opinion. This is the case here. The union of feeling, the common affections by which Christians should be characterized, are enjoined in the second clause of the verse, which may be justly rendered, "have the same feelings."[2] We therefore consider the injunction before us as equivalent to, 'have, and show that you have, the same sentiments.'

"Be of one mind" does not mean, 'Have the same sentiments on all subjects,' or even, 'Have the same sentiments on all subjects connected with religion.' Compliance with such an injunction is impossible, so long as the measure of mental faculty and the means of information are different

---

[1] Phil. ii. 3; Rom. viii. 5.

[2] Συμπαθεῖς, similiter affecti. This is one of the ἅπαξ λεγόμενα. The cognate verb occurs Heb. iv. 15, x. 34. Raphelius furnishes a fine illustration of the meaning of the word, in a passage from Polybius: "Certainly, if Scipio was peculiarly fitted by nature for anything, it was for this, that he should inspire confidence in the minds of men." Καὶ συμπαθεῖς ποιῆσαι τοὺς παρακαλουμένους, 'and transfuse his own feelings into those whom he addressed.'—*Raph. Obs.* vol. ii. p. 760.

in some degree or other in every individual. If a man honestly exercise his mind on the subject brought before it, that is, if he really have a mind of his own, that mind will be in some respects different from every other man's mind.

But it does mean, 'Be united, be entirely united in those views, both doctrinal and practical, the possession of which is essential to the very being of genuine Christianity.' There are such principles; and notwithstanding all the ingenious and perplexing discussions which have taken place respecting fundamental and non-fundamental principles in religion, there is little practical difficulty in determining what are the views in which Christians must be united in mind and judgment.

With regard to doctrines, they are such as the following: As to man's natural estate, that it is one of guilt, and depravity, and helplessness: As to God's character and government, that He is most holy and benignant, and that it is most wise and righteous; that "He is the rock, his work is perfect, all his ways are judgment, a God of truth and without iniquity, just and right is he;" "His law is holy, just, and good:"[1] As to Jesus Christ, that he is the divinely appointed, the divinely qualified, the divinely accredited, the divine Saviour from guilt, and depravity, and misery; that "his blood cleanseth from all sin;" that "he is able to save to the uttermost them that come to God by him;" that he will never "cast" out any who come to him; that he was "given for our offences, and raised again for our justification;" that "he is Lord and Judge of all;" that he is the one Master of all his disciples, the only Lord of their consciences:[2] As to the Holy Spirit, that he is the Divine Author of all that is spiritually right and

[1] Deut. xxxii. 4; Rom. vii. 12.
[2] 1 John i. 7; Heb. vii. 25; John vi. 37; Rom. iv. 25; Acts x. 36.

good in the views and affections and conduct of mankind, and that in his enlivening, and enlightening, and sanctifying, and consoling influence, he is shed forth abundantly on all who believe on Christ Jesus, as the earnest of their inheritance, as the seal of God on them till the day of final and complete redemption. These are a specimen of the kind of doctrinal principles referred to by the apostle.[1]

As to practical principles, in which Christians must be all of one mind, they are such as the following: that "we ought to obey God rather than man;" that "things unseen and eternal" are to be preferred to "things seen and temporal;" that we must "deny ourselves, take up the cross, and follow Christ," wherever he leads us; that the greatest suffering is to be chosen before the least sin; that we must become as little children, in order to enter into the kingdom of God; that "it is more blessed to give than to receive;" that we should "live not to ourselves, but to him who died for us, and who rose again."[2] With regard to these principles, and such principles as these, Christians must be of one mind. He who is otherwise minded, he who is oppositely minded, is not, and cannot be, a Christian.

The unity of mind which the apostle requires on such subjects can be secured only in one way. The desired and desirable oneness of mind is neither to be obtained by the great mass of Christian men, of moderate intellectual faculties and attainments, implicitly submitting to the decisions of a few master minds; nor by individual Christians making mutual compromises of sentiment: it is to be obtained by all Christians seeking to have in them the mind of their Master, Christ.[3] The union of mind they are to seek is

---

[1] Eph. i. 13, 14.
[2] Acts v. 29; Matt. xvi. 24, xxviii. 3; Acts xx. 35; 2 Cor. v. 15.
[3] The Apostle Paul exhorts the Philippians (ii. 2) τὸ αὐτὸ φρονεῖν—εἶναι

union in the truth, in "the truth as it is in Jesus." The mind of Christ is in his word. His Spirit is promised to enable us to understand his word. The man who studies that word in a dependence on that Spirit will be made to know and believe the truth which it contains, so far as this is necessary to salvation; and in the degree in which he does so, Christ's mind will become his mind. All who follow this course will, in proportion to the simplicity, and ardour, and perseverance with which they prosecute it, be successful; and in being conformed to the mind of Christ, they will come all to have one mind in reference to each other. And so indeed it is, and always has been, and ever will be. All true Christians, amid all their differences of opinion, are of one mind in reference to the great doctrinal and practical principles of their holy faith,—the principles which pacify the conscience, and purify the heart, and guide the conduct,—the principles by which they live, in which they find the life of their souls, the spring of their spiritual activity, the source of their spiritual comfort.

As to the points on which they differ, so far as they act in character, it will be found that it is their union of mind on the one great principle, that "One is our Master, even Christ,"[1] which leads to a difference of mind respecting those points, uniformly of minor importance. Those Christians who differed in their judgments as to the propriety of observing certain days, were of one mind as to the duty of Christians to yield implicit obedience to the seen will of their common Lord: "He that observed the day observed it to the Lord; and he who did not observe the day, to the Lord he did not observe it."[3] And giving each other credit for acting with a good conscience "as to the Lord," they

σύμψυχοι, τὸ ἓν φρονοῦντες; and (ver. 5) he shows them how to secure this, τοῦτο γὰρ φρονείσθω ἐν ὑμῖν ὃ καὶ ἐν Χριστῷ Ἰησοῦ.

[1] Matt. xxiii. 8. [2] Rom. xiv. 6.

felt more united by their common mind that the Lord was to be obeyed, than divided by the diversity of their opinions, as to what in such a case was obedience to him.

With regard to the great principles above referred to, the apostolic rule is, "Let us who are perfect be *thus* minded"— " of one mind," " perfectly joined in the same judgment :" having attained to this, " let us walk by the same rule, let us mind the same thing."[1] And with regard to the minor points referred to, the rule is, "Let every man be fully persuaded in his own mind," and, " Let no man judge his brother in such matters."[2] And this is our comfort, that if we walk together, in the great things in which we are of one mind, we are likely ere long to become of one mind too with regard even to the minor points on which we do not agree; "for," says the apostle, "if in anything we" who are of one mind in Christ " be differently minded from each other, God shall reveal even that to us."[3]

It should be the constant care of those who are called on to watch over the communion of the Christian Church, that none be admitted into it but those who appear to be of one mind, even " the mind of Christ," on the essentials of Christian doctrine and practice, and that none be continued members of that Church who give evidence that on these points they are differently minded from him. Yet great care must be taken not to insist on a greater extent of union of mind than the Master has insisted on. It has been no uncommon thing for men, even good men, in insisting that all applying for admission should be entirely of one mind with them on points on which the will of the Lord is revealed with comparative obscureness, or, it may be, not revealed at all, to exclude men who were obviously of the same mind with their Lord; and to admit men who, though they professed, and it may be truly, that they were of the

[1] Phil. iii. 15.   [2] Rom. xiv. 5, 10, 15.   [3] Phil. iii. 15.

same mind with *them* as to their sectarian peculiarities, made it very evident that they were not of the same mind with *Him* with regard to those saving principles which transform the character. Few things have done greater harm to the Church than this attempt to make the mind of a man, or body of men, rather than the mind which was in Christ, the test of that *one mind* which is the true term of Christian communion.

This is just a peculiar form of the pride and selfishness which are natural to all men, and are not extinguished even in good men. It is the wish to have men of my way of thinking, or of the way of thinking of my denomination, instead of the wish to have both them and myself of the one mind which God gives us, when he by his Spirit puts his laws, the revelation he has made of his mind and will, in the heart, and writes them on the inward parts. It has been beautifully said, " There is naturally, in every man's mind, and most in the shallowest, a kind of fancied infallibility in themselves, which makes them as earnest about agreement in the smallest punctilio as in the highest article of faith. Stronger spirits are usually more patient of contradiction, and less violent, especially in doubtful things; and they that see furthest are least peremptory in their determinations. The apostle to Timothy speaks of 'the spirit of a sound mind.' It is a good sound constitution of mind not to feel every blast either of seeming reason, to be taken with it; or of cross opinion, to be offended at it."[1]

This oneness of mind which Christians are to seek in a common conformity of their minds to the mind which is in Christ, should be manifested in their common profession, defence, and practice of the truth which they all know and believe. They are together " to hold fast," and

[1] Leighton.

together to "hold forth," the word of life; to "strive together for the faith of the gospel;" to walk together "in all the ordinances and commandments of the Lord, blameless." When, instead of this, professed Christians strive and dispute among themselves; when, instead of appearing to be "perfectly joined in the same mind and in the same judgment," there are "divisions and contentions;" when, instead of "with one mind and one mouth glorifying God, even the Father of our Lord Jesus Christ," they, in effect, excommunicate one another, and treat each other as heathen men and publicans: the conversation of Christians is not "honest among the Gentiles." Great discredit has thus been cast on the cause of Christ: great obstacles have been thrown in the way of the conversion of unbelievers, and the name of God and his Son have been blasphemed. Woe, woe has been to the world because of these stumbling-blocks. The controversies among Christians have far more effectually impeded the progress of the gospel than the controversies against Christianity.

When Christians shall more consistently manifest the Christian mind, which already exists in all who deserve the name, in the united exhibition of the truth in their profession and conduct, the word of the Lord will have free course; "it will run, and be" more illustriously "glorified." It will "grow and be multiplied."[1] It was so in the beginning of the gospel. When "the multitude of them that believed were of one heart and of one soul," and "continued with one accord stedfastly in the apostles' doctrine and fellowship, and in breaking of bread, and in prayers," they had "favour with all the people;" "the people magnified them;" "multitudes were added to the Church, both of men and women;" "there were daily added to the Church such as should be saved;" "the word of God in-

[1] 2 Thess. iii. 1; Acts xii. 24.

creased, the number of disciples multiplied in Jerusalem greatly, and a great company of the priests were obedient to the faith."[1] If Christians had taken but half the pains to show the world how completely they are united in mind and judgment on the great points, that they have taken to make it acquainted with the minute and sometimes impalpable differences which exist among them (the former is fitted to do themselves and their Master honour, and the world good; the latter casts discredit not only on themselves, but on the cause they support, and throws stumbling-blocks in the world's way); and had they exhibited more of the noble, liberal character which the contemplation of the great points of union is fitted to form, than of the contracted selfish temper which those controversies about minor points engender and nourish, how much higher would both Christianity and Christians have stood in the estimation of mankind at large, and how much nearer would the Christian Church have been to the full possession of her goodly heritage, the peopled earth! Could we indulge, to borrow Robert Hall's language, the hope "that such a state of things was likely soon to establish itself, we should hail the dawn of a brighter day, and consider it as a nearer approach to the ultimate triumph of the Church, than the annals of time have yet recorded. In the accomplishment of our Lord's prayer, that all his people may be one, men would behold a demonstration of the divinity of his mission, which the most impious could not resist; and behold in the Church a peaceful haven, inviting them to retire from the tossings and perils of this unquiet ocean, to a sacred enclosure, a sequestered spot, which the storms and tempests of the world were not permitted to invade."[2]

[1] Acts iv. 32, 33, ii. 42, 47, vi. 7.
[2] On terms of communion.—*Works*, ii. 168.

§ 2. *To cultivate and manifest union of feeling.*

The second injunction of the apostle, bearing on this temper and conduct of Christians among themselves, as given by our translators, is, " Have compassion one of another." This version is justly considered by interpreters generally as very unduly limiting the meaning of the apostolic injunction. It confines it to sympathy with fellow-Christians under suffering; whereas the word, even supposing our translation to be substantially right in the meaning given to it, refers to fellow-feeling generally, and includes rejoicing with Christian brethren when they rejoice, as well as weeping with them when they weep. It is plain, however, that this sympathizing temper is one variety, a particular aspect, of the disposition enjoined in the next clause, " Love as brethren;" and though this fact would not be a good reason for giving the word before us an unauthorized or even a very uncommon signification, yet if the proper and common meaning of the word brings out a sense different from that of the succeeding clause, a sense true and important in itself, and peculiarly suitable to the connection in which it stands, there can be no doubt that that sense ought to be preferred.

Now this, we apprehend, is a correct statement of the case. The words literally signify, " Have common feelings." They are the counterpart of the first clause : that says, ' Be of one mind;' this, ' Be of one heart:' that says, ' Think alike;' this, ' Feel alike :' that says, ' Hold the same truth;' this, ' Cherish the same dispositions.' Be all animated by the same affections. To unfold the sentiment a little : ' Cherish every one of you the same reverence and trust in God; the same sense of insignificance as creatures, of demerit as sinners, of obligation as saved sinners; the same love and gratitude to the Saviour; the same dependence on, and fear of grieving, the Holy Spirit; the same hatred of sin and love of holiness; the same holy contempt of the present evil world; the same moderation in prosperity, and patience in adversity; the same zeal for the divine glory; the same brotherly kindness; the same charity. Let not merely the articles of your faith be the same, but also the features of your character.'

This injunction is very closely connected with that which precedes it. This can be complied with only by those who have obeyed that. We must have the one mind, in order to our having the one heart; and if we really have the one mind, we certainly shall have the one heart. We are "transformed by the renewing of the mind." The doctrine delivered to us, to use the apostle's figure, is the mould in which the new creature is cast;[1] the various principles of the truth as it is in Jesus being as it were the various parts of this mould, each intended and fitted to produce some portion of that image of God in the soul of man of which the Holy Spirit is the wondrous author. His influence and the divine word are equally necessary in their own places to the production of the desired effect. The word will not do it alone, for without his influence it will not be understood and believed; and whatever divine influence might do—and he would be equally unwise and impious who should set limits to Omnipotence—we have no reason to expect that that influence will produce its effects in any other way than that which equally corresponds with the constitution of man, the work of God's hand, and the declarations of Scripture, the word of his mouth, through means of the truth understood and believed.

He, then, who would comply with the apostle's injunction, to have those common feelings which ought to characterize all Christians, must study the Bible, in its meaning and

[1] Rom. xii. 2, vi. 17. Εἰς ὃν παρεδόθητε τύπον διδαχῆς.

evidence; he must "let the word of Christ," which contains his mind, "dwell in him richly;"[1] and he must at the same time yield up his mind to the influence of the good Spirit, beseeching him to guide him into the truth, to open his understanding to understand the Scriptures, and to open his heart to receive the love of the truth, that he may be saved, by being sanctified by it.

This common mode of feeling ought to be, and indeed where it exists must be, manifested in a corresponding conduct. And when a Christian does habitually exhibit the feelings, disposition, and temper which the truth believed naturally produces, the effect is " a conversation honest," honourable, "among the Gentiles." When the piety, and humility, and self-denial, and brotherly kindness, and patience, and public spirit of the gospel are displayed, the men of the world have not only no evil thing to say, but are involuntarily impressed with a reverence both for the man and for his principles. The Christian who acts thus will make it impossible that any man who narrowly observes him should despise either him or his religion ; while, on the other hand, the want of a manifestation of such feelings as a Christian profession gives the world a right to expect in an individual, and still more the manifestation of an opposite kind of feeling, excites suspicion both with regard to the man and his principles, leading to the conclusion either that he is a hypocrite, or, if he be not, that the system that he professes must either be a bad one, as making him a bad man, or at any rate a powerless one, as not having been able to make him a good man.

§ 3. *To cultivate and manifest brotherly kindness.*

The third injunction of the apostle, referring to the temper which Christians should cherish, and the conduct

[1] Col. iii. 16.

they should pursue towards each other, is, "Love as brethren." This injunction may be and has been rendered, 'Be lovers of the brethren;'[1] that is, cherish and display the peculiar affection which Christians ought to bear to Christians. When illustrating the concluding paragraph of the first chapter of this epistle, I had an opportunity of explaining at considerable length the foundation, the nature, and the appropriate manifestations of this principle.[2]

The order of the apostle's injunctions here deserves well to be noted: "Be of one mind, be of one heart." Hold and profess the same principles, cherish and manifest the same feelings,—in other words, be brethren in Christ, be spiritual brethren,—and then love the brethren: "love as brethren." The foundation of the peculiar love which Christians should cherish to Christians, lies in their common faith and experience as Christians. They love one another "in the truth, for the truth's sake which is in them." Just in the degree that I am a true Christian, do I become capable of loving those who are true Christians; and just in the degree in which they are true Christians, are they, can they be, the objects of my Christian affection.

The idea suggested by the words as rendered by our translators is slightly different, yet well worthy of illustration: "Love as brethren;" that is, either love one another, seeing ye are brethren; or, let your love correspond to the intimacy and permanency of the relation in which ye stand to one another—love as brothers love each other. The first idea I illustrated fully in the discourse already referred to. I shall now attempt briefly to unfold the second. Let your love to your fellow-Christians resemble the love which one brother bears, or ought to bear, to another. True Christian love resembles the love of brothers in various respects, to a few of which I shall shortly advert.

[1] Φιλάδελφοι, i.e. ἔστε.   [2] Discourse VI.

They may both be considered as partaking very much of the nature of instincts. It is a part of my constitution as a man to love my brother. Not to love a brother is felt to be something unnatural as well as improper, monstrous as well as wrong. It is a part of my constitution as a new creature to love all my spiritual brethren. If I love my Father, how can I but love his children? He who makes me a member of the family, in so doing gives me the feelings of a child and a brother. Christians are "thus taught of God,"[1] not only in the word, but as it were in the instincts of their new nature, to love one another. "As touching brotherly love," says the Apostle Paul, "ye need not that I write unto you; for even ye yourselves are taught of God to love one another."

The affection of a brother to a brother is sincere and disinterested. When first developed, the habit of duplicity is unknown; and the child, in loving his brother, thinks of nothing less than mercenary advantage: he loves him just because he is his brother. The love of Christians to Christians should be "without dissimulation;" "unfeigned;" "love out of a pure heart."[2]

The affection of a brother to a brother is warm and tender. When David would express the peculiar ardour of his attachment to Jonathan, he calls him brother: "I am distressed for thee, my brother Jonathan;"[3] and it is proverbial to say of one friend strongly attached to another, He loves him as if he were his brother. The affection which Christians should bear to Christians should be a strong affection, capable of producing much forbearance, much exertion, much sacrifice, much suffering; a love which many waters cannot quench, which the floods cannot drown.

The love of brothers is forbearing and forgiving. A brother will forbear with and forgive in a brother what he

[1] Θεοδίδακτοι, 1 Thess. iv. 9. [2] 1 Tim. i. 5. [3] 2 Sam. i. 26.

would consider as insufferable and unpardonable in a stranger; and a dutiful, affectionate brother, when differences do arise in the family, throws a veil over them, seeks to keep them within the sacred domestic circle; and even when dissatisfied with a brother, does not think of proclaiming his brother's injustice and faults, and his own injuries, to a stranger. And thus, too, Christians, "with all lowliness and meekness," are to "forbear one another in love," "putting away from them all bitterness, and wrath, and anger, and clamour, and evil-speaking, with all malice; and being kind one to another, tender-hearted, forbearing one another in love, and forgiving one another, if any have a quarrel against any, even as God for Christ's sake has forgiven them;" forgiving "not only seven times, but seventy times seven." [1]

The love of a brother to a brother is active. It is chiefly manifested in habitual kindliness of behaviour, and in doing its object good as opportunity occurs. It is love, "not in word and in tongue, but in deed and in truth." And so it ought to be with the Christian. If a brother or sister be naked, and destitute of daily food, the Christian brother must not content himself with saying, Depart in peace, may you be warmed and filled; he must give him the things which are necessary for the body. If he have "this world's goods, and seeth his brother have need," he must not "shut up his bowels of compassion from him." If he do, it is a proof that neither the love of God nor of the brethren dwells in him.[2]

Few things have a greater tendency to recommend Christianity to worldly unbelieving men than the habitual exemplification of this precept; and, on the other hand, few things have done more to injure that religion, and to prevent its progress, than the angry debates, the unseemly animosi-

---

[1] Eph. iv. 31, 32; Matt. xviii. 22.
[2] James ii. 15, 16; 1 John iii. 17.

ties, the virulent quarrels, which have so often taken place among its professors. These " cause the way of truth to be evil spoken of," and " give occasion to the adversary to speak reproachfully." Proceedings of this kind should lead to great searchings of heart among those who indulge in them: for surely there is reason to fear that they are not really, but only nominally, among the disciples of HIM who says, " By this shall all men know that ye are my disciples, if ye have love one to another;" and were their ears but open to discipline, they could scarcely help hearing *Him* indignantly saying to them, " Why call ye me Lord, Lord, and do not the things that I say to you?" " A new commandment I give unto you, that ye love one another, as I have loved you." " Ye are my friends, if ye do whatsoever I command you." " But if ye bite and devour one another," if ye hate and revile one another, what are ye? " He that saith he is in the light, and hateth his brother, is in darkness even until now. He that loveth his brother abideth in the light, and there is none occasion of stumbling in him; but he that hateth his brother is in darkness, and walketh in darkness, and knoweth not whither he goeth, because the darkness hath blinded his eyes. In this the children of God are manifest, and the children of the devil. Whosoever loveth not his brother is not of God. He who loveth his brother, hath passed from death to life. He that loveth not his brother abideth in death. If a man say, I love God, and hateth his brother, he is a liar; for he that loveth not his brother whom he hath seen, how can he love God whom he hath not seen?"[1]

Such is a short illustration of those general injunctions contained in the text that refer to the temper which Christians should cherish, and the conduct they should

[1] John xiii. 34, 35; Luke vi. 46; John xv. 14; 1 John ii. 9-11, iii. 10, 14, iv. 20.

exemplify, in reference to one another. They are to hold and profess the same principles; they are to cherish and manifest the same feelings; and they are to cultivate and display that love to one another which naturally grows out of this community of sentiment and feeling,—loving the brethren because they are brethren,—cherishing and manifesting towards them an affection which, in its spontaneousness, and warmth, and steadiness, and active influence, resembles the affection of brother to brother; and they are to do all this, that their conversation may be "honest among the Gentiles," and that thus they may adorn the doctrine of God their Saviour. I conclude this part of the discourse with the prayer that the good Spirit would write these golden maxims on our hearts, and enable us to exhibit a fair copy of his writing on these fleshly tablets, in our habitual temper and behaviour: "Be of one mind: be of one heart: love as brethren." And "now may the God of patience and consolation grant us to be likeminded one towards another, according to Christ Jesus, that we may with one mind and one mouth glorify God, even the Father of our Lord Jesus Christ; and that there be no division among us, but that we be perfectly joined together in the same mind, and in the same judgment;"[1] so that the unbelieving world, beholding the effects of our union of mind and heart, in our common hearty efforts in the cause of our common Lord, and in bearing one another's infirmities, and relieving one another's wants, may be constrained to say, as of old, "Behold how these Christians love one another!" and that we ourselves, feeling the holy delights of such union and communion, may sing in our hearts, making melody to the Lord: "Behold, how good and how pleasant a thing it is for brethren to dwell together in unity! It is as the dew of

[1] Rom. xv. 5, 6; 1 Cor. i. 10.

Hermon, the dew that descended on the mountains of Zion; for there the Lord commands the blessing, even life for evermore."

II. DUTIES OF CHRISTIANS TO MANKIND GENERALLY.

Let us now consider those injunctions respecting disposition and conduct, which refer not only to the Christian brotherhood, but to all mankind. "Be pitiful, be courteous." Let us attend to these two injunctions in their order.

§ 1. *To "be pitiful."*

The first injunction is, "Be pitiful." The command contained in these words is substantially the same as that of our Lord: "Be ye merciful, as your Father in heaven is merciful;" and those of his holy Apostle Paul, "Be kindly affectioned; be kind, tender-hearted; put on bowels of mercies, kindness, meekness, long-suffering."[1]

Mercy, properly speaking, is kindness to the miserable, benignity as manifested towards the suffering. To be merciful or pitiful, is to cherish and manifest kind feeling towards those who are in distress. The mercy or pitifulness which is the subject of injunction, is something very different from a naturally kind temper. That is a mere instinctive feeling, and, though amiable and useful, is no proper object of moral approbation. Some very bad men have a large portion of it; while some very good men, if not destitute of it altogether, are by no means distinguished for it. In its movements there is no reference to divine authority; and it is often, as we have just remarked, found in conjunction with principles and habits most decidedly condemned by the divine law.

The mercy here enjoined has no doubt its basis, as all

[1] Luke vi. 36; Rom. xii. 10; Eph. iv. 32.

emotions have, in that part of our physical-mental constitution, which we call the affections. Had we no affections, we could not be subjects of Christian mercy. But Christian mercy is the result of the truth as it is in Jesus, understood and believed, acting on that part of our constitution. It is the feeling which in man, a being capable of affection, is naturally and necessarily developed when he believes that truth, and in the degree in which he believes it. It is the feeling which a man who knows and believes that, in the exercise of sovereign kindness on the part of God, he is, through the mediation of Jesus Christ, who, under the influence of divine pity, took and bore all his responsibilities to divine justice, delivered from evils infinite in their number, immense in their magnitude, eternal in their duration,—evils to which he had rendered himself liable by his unprovoked and innumerable violations of a law most holy, just, and good;—it is the feeling which such a conscious debtor to divine mercy naturally cherishes towards men who are involved in suffering, especially in that worst species of suffering from which he, through divine goodness and pity, has obtained security. This is a feeling which can be awakened in the human heart only by the Divine Spirit, leading the individual to believe the great love wherewith God hath loved us, and which he has commended to us, in not sparing his Son for our sakes, and in sparing and blessing us for his sake. Till there is this faith, there cannot be this feeling; and where this feeling is not, the very soul of Christian mercy is absent.

The essence of the disposition required is kind feeling towards the miserable, and its natural manifestation is the use of the means in our power to prevent and to relieve misery. It is the direct opposite, not merely of cruelty, but of insensibility; a compassionate tenderness of heart, which makes us weep with them who weep, or who, though they do not weep, being ignorant of or insensible to their wretchedness, have on that ground the greater cause to weep.

This Christian pity has a wide range. It looks at man in both the constituent parts of his nature. It regards both the souls and the bodies of men. It is drawn out both by their spiritual and their bodily miseries; by evils feared as well as felt; by evils not feared, but sure to be felt if not feared; by the evils of eternity as well as of time. It ought to be exercised to all men who are in misery, though connected with us by no tie but that of a common nature; and the limits of its practical manifestation are to be prescribed by our means of preventing and relieving misery, and a wise judgment as to how those means can be most effectually employed in gaining the end in view—the prevention, the relief, the extinction of suffering.

The regard which Christian pity shows in reference to the miseries of man, as a being connected with God and destined to immortality, is one of the features by which it is chiefly distinguished from that instinctive kindness to which I have been adverting. The good-natured, generous man of the world, pities and relieves the temporal wants and miseries of his fellow-men; but he thinks not of their spiritual state, their everlasting prospects. He has a tender sympathy, he exerts a generous activity, in reference to disease and destitution, and such varieties of ignorance and vice as produce misery and disorder to the individual and society; but he has no pity for a soul dead in sin, far from God, destitute of hope, doomed to destruction. Indeed, this could not reasonably be expected. How should he feel for others in reference to such subjects, who has in that respect no feeling for himself? The foundation of such feelings is wanting in him, in a just abiding conviction of the realities of the unseen and eternal world. Though professing, as many such persons do, to hold the views Scripture presents on these subjects, there does appear a monstrous absurdity in being so exceedingly concerned about the alleviation or removal of the sufferings of a few short years, and altogether careless about the prevention of the intolerable miseries of eternity. The pitifulness which the apostle enjoins is not thus inconsistent. The Christian looks on mankind chiefly in their relation to God and eternity. In his estimation, he is poor who is not rich towards God; he is blind who is ignorant of the way of salvation; he is naked who is destitute of the robe of righteousness; he is diseased who is covered with the leprosy of sin. No loss appears to him worthy of being compared with the loss of the soul; no death deserving the name but the second death; no agonies like the pangs of remorse and the torments of hell.

In this respect, Christian pitifulness resembles the divine mercy, in the faith of which it originates. The God whose nature as well as name is love, pities all the miseries of man; but it is immortal man, the sinner, who is emphatically the object of divine mercy. He thought of us in our low estate of guilt, and condemnation, and depravity, for " his mercy endureth for ever." It stretches onwards to eternity, and manifests its greatness in delivering from "the lowest hell." In like manner, the Christian should and will regard with peculiar pity his fellow-men, viewed as immortal beings labouring under spiritual disease, in danger of eternal death.

It has been justly said, " The sins of men, and the danger of their everlasting ruin by them, will awaken a lively concern and grief in every Christian mind," in every heart in which the love of God shed abroad by the Holy Ghost has produced genuine love to man. " He has the truest and justest compassion for his neighbour, who cannot without a tender sorrow see him provoking the great God to jealousy, throwing away his immortal soul, living under the power of a fell mortal distemper, and laying up in store for a dreadful account, 'heaping up wrath for the day of wrath, and revelation of the righteous judgment of God.' Whoever believes that religion is a reality, must be more deeply, if not more sensibly, affected with such a melancholy sight, than with seeing the bodily wants or consuming diseases of men, or with hearing their most dismal groans and mournful complaints occasioned by worldly loss or corporeal suffering; for he knows the soul is more valuable than the body, hell is worse than death, and time is shorter than eternity." In a world full of suffering, "the transgressor" is the fittest object of the deepest commiseration. "I beheld the transgressors, and was grieved;" "Rivers of water,"—the tears of pity for self-destroying man, as well as of regret for injury done to the holy character and law of God,—" Rivers of water run down mine eyes, because the wicked keep not thy law."[1]

But while chiefly affected by the miseries of men as sinners, by their ignorance, and error, and guilt, and obduracy, and depravity, in their endlessly varied forms, and by the fearful, unavoidable, remediless state of wretchedness which awaits impenitent men in the future world, the pitifulness of the Christian is drawn forth by misery of every kind, by suffering in every form.

The Christian, when he acts like himself, is far from being insensible to those calamities and wants of man which are limited to the present state. He cherishes a tender sympathy with " all the evils to which men are exposed in their bodies, in their minds, in their connection with each other, in their external circumstances, from whatever cause they may originate,—whether from the

[1] Ps. cxix. 158, 136.

immediate visitation of God, from the injustice and cruelty of their fellow-men, or from their own folly and crime."[1] He pities suffering in every form. Wherever he sees misery, he feels compassion. Like Job, he "weeps for all who are in trouble, and his soul is grieved for the poor."

But the apostolic injunction looks to the appropriate manifestation of this feeling, as well as to its existence. When he says, "Be pitiful," he means, Show by your conduct that you are pitiful. Christian pity is essentially an operative principle. It is not "a well shut up, a fountain sealed;" it is a copious source of streams of blessing.

Pity for the spiritual miseries of men must be manifested in appropriate, wise, vigorous, persevering endeavours for relief. We must not stand by the self-erected pile on which the sinner is about to offer himself in sacrifice to the powers of evil, bemoaning his folly. We must "pull him out of the fire." It were well if Christians would ponder more deeply those words of awful import: "If thou forbear to deliver them that are drawn to death, and those that are ready to be slain; if thou sayest, Behold, we knew it not; doth not he that pondereth the heart consider it? and he that keepeth thy soul, doth he not know it? and shall he not render to every man according to his works?"[2] And those words, too, so full of encouragement: "He that converteth a sinner from the error of his ways, shall save a soul from death, and shall hide a multitude of sins."

Every Christian is bound personally to perform such acts of mercy within his own sphere of activity, and by his influence and property to give support to all scriptural plans for alleviating and removing the spiritual miseries of men both at home and abroad. Our pity should take the form of constant persevering prayer, for the work is more God's than man's; but it should take the form, too, of

---

[1] Wardlaw.   [2] Prov. xxiv. 11, 12.

cheerful, liberal, regular contribution, and personal exertion, for the work is man's work as well as God's; and God's work by man, God being the primary agent, man the active instrument. That man surely has no bowels of compassion for perishing men, no Christian pitifulness, who can see thousands of them falling over the precipice into perdition, without shedding a tear over their hopeless misery, and thousands more rushing onwards towards that precipice, without attempting to arrest their course. Were Christians as pitiful as they should be, as they might reasonably be expected to be, there would be no want of Christian missionaries either for home or foreign service, and no want of funds for their support.

Pity for the bodily wants and miseries of men must also be manifested in appropriate, wise, vigorous, persevering endeavours for their relief. The Christian's sympathy must not remain hidden in his bosom, a source merely of painful or pleasant excitement to himself. It must not expend itself in words of commiseration. It must take the form of sacrifice and exertion. He must not content himself with saying to the houseless, ill-clad, shivering object of his compassion, "Be ye warmed and filled;" he must, if it be in his power, give him "the things which are needful for the body." This is the pity which characterized the patriarch Job: "When the ear heard me, then it blessed me; and when the eye saw me, it gave witness to me; because I delivered the poor that cried, and the fatherless, and him that had none to help him. The blessing of him that was ready to perish came on me; and I caused the widow's heart to sing for joy. I was eyes to the blind, and feet was I to the lame. I was a father to the poor, and the cause which I knew not I searched out."[1] This is the pity of which the divine approbation is so strikingly declared

[1] Job xxix. 11-16.

by the prophet Isaiah. The Lord promises to "guide continually," and to bless abundantly, the man who "deals his bread to the hungry, and brings the poor who are cast out to his house; who, when he sees the naked, covers them, and hides not himself from his own flesh: who draws out his soul to the hungry, and satisfies the afflicted soul."[1] And this is the pity which will meet with the solemn approval of the Supreme Judge, when from his great white throne in the heavens he pronounces the sentences which are to fix the eternal state of men and angels: "Then shall the King say to them on the right hand, Come, ye blessed of my Father, inherit the kingdom prepared for you from the foundation of the world: for I was an hungered, and ye gave me meat; I was thirsty, and ye gave me drink; I was a stranger, and ye took me in; naked, and ye clothed me; I was sick, and ye visited me; I was in prison, and ye came unto me. Inasmuch as ye have done it unto one of the least of these my brethren, ye have done it unto me."[2]

It is thus only that Christian pitifulness can have that character which our Lord requires when he says, "Be ye merciful, as your Father in heaven is merciful," for HIS pity was active pity. "For the great love wherewith he loved" miserable men, he "spared not his own Son," devoted him for us as a victim, gives him to us as a Saviour, and gives us all things with him, "blessing us in him with all heavenly and spiritual blessings." It is thus only that Christian pity can form a part of that resemblance to our Lord in which true Christian holiness consists. HE, as well as his divine Father, not only pitied, but saved; and saved at what an expenditure of sacrifice, and toil, and suffering! "Though in the form of God, he humbled himself," laid aside the glories of that form, took on him the nature of a man, the form of a servant, the likeness of a sinner, be-

[1] Isa. lviii. 7, 10.   [2] Matt. xxv. 34-36.

coming " obedient unto death, even the death of the cross." With what indefatigable activity, with what disinterested self-denial, with what patient endurance, did he seek to relieve the wants, to remove the miseries of men! It was his meat to do the benignant will of his Father in heaven, in showing mercy to the miserable. "He went about doing good." This was his "Father's business," about which he was always to be found engaged. He embraced every opportunity of manifesting his pity, showing mercy; and not contented with answering applications made to him, he often went in quest of objects of compassion, to comfort and relieve them. In their measure Christians must thus be pitiful; for it is only thus that they can have evidence that the mind which was in Christ is in them, and that they are His, having his Spirit dwelling in them.

There are two principles on this subject which must be held with equal firmness. The one is, that external acts of beneficence in supplying want and relieving distress, though in themselves good and useful, if disjoined from the faith of the gospel, and the pity which it uniformly excites, and which it alone can excite, are no evidences of Christian character, and cannot be accepted of God as a part of the living sacrifice, with which, with which alone, for Christ's sake, he is well pleased. The other is, that wherever the principle of Christian pity exists, it will manifest itself by producing its appropriate effects. Where the ability and opportunity to do good exist, and yet no good is done, professions of sympathy with human misery, however fervent, must be hypocritical; and however they may impose on man, which they do to a far less extent than they who deal in them seem to suppose, must be regarded with abhorrence by him who "desireth truth in the inward part."

It scarcely needs to be remarked, that the form and

degree of the manifestation of that Christian temper which is enjoined in the text, must depend on the circumstances in which the individual who cherishes it is placed. A kind look, a soothing word, a compassionate tear, "a cup of cold water," are sometimes both more genuine expressions of Christian pity, and more effectual means of gaining its object, the alleviation of suffering, than the most costly pecuniary offerings.

This pitiful, compassionate disposition is not to be limited to any particular class of sufferers. It is not to be confined to relations or friends, to fellow-Christians or fellow-citizens. Wherever there is misery, there should be commiseration; and wherever there is the power to relieve, there should be relief. "Christian pity is a prime lineament of the image of God; and the more absolute and disengaged it is in regard to those towards whom it acts, the more is it like unto God; looking upon misery as a sufficient incentive of pity and mercy, without the ingredient of any other consideration. It is merely a vulgar piece of goodness to be helpful and bountiful to friends, or to such as are within appearance of requital. It is a trading commerce that; but pity and bounty which need no inducements but the meeting a fit object to work upon, where it can expect nothing save only the privilege of doing good, which is in itself so sweet, is Godlike indeed,—like HIM, who is rich in bounty, without any necessity, yea, or possibility of return from us; for we have neither anything to confer upon him, nor hath he need of receiving anything, who is the spring of goodness and of being."[1]

At the same time, it must not be forgotten, that while Christian pity leads those under its influence to compassionate and relieve all the indigent and wretched as they have opportunity, it impels them with peculiar force to

[1] Leighton.

relieve the wants of those with whom they are most intimately connected. The man who speculates and talks of universal philanthropy, and even makes exertions in behalf of a benevolent object, if it be but on a sufficiently magnificent scale, while, in the circle of his family or neighbourhood, he does little or nothing to relieve suffering and supply want, may without breach of charity be set down as a pretender to a character that does not belong to him; and the consistency of his Christian profession may well be questioned, whatever we may think of its sincerity, who, while manifesting zeal for diminishing the sufferings and promoting the improvement of the inhabitants of distant lands, is inattentive to the distress and destitution with which he is surrounded; who, while he professes to feel for Negroes and Tartars, Turks and Jews, seems to have no bowels of compassion for his countrymen who are destitute of the necessaries of life, or are perishing for lack of knowledge.

Such, then, is the Christian pitifulness which the apostle enjoins as a part of "a conversation honest among the Gentiles;" a means of constraining those who "spoke evil of them" ignorantly and falsely, "as of evil-doers," to form a more favourable opinion both of them and of their religion; a means of "putting to silence the ignorance of such foolish men," of winning those without the word who will not obey the word, of making those ashamed who falsely accused their good conversation in Christ.

It requires but little reflection to perceive, that the cultivation and display of this amiable temper are well fitted to gain these ends. The efforts of Christian piety, in the way of attempts to relieve the spiritual wants of mankind, not unfrequently excite the resentment of those who are their immediate objects, and draw forth the ridicule of ungodly observers. Yet even these, when obviously springing from genuine, though, in the estimation of unconverted men, misguided benevolence, produce on the whole a favourable impression both of their authors and of their religion; while, on the other hand, apathy and inaction on the part of professed Christians in reference to the removal of evils, which, if there be any truth in the Bible, are the greatest of all man's miseries, necessarily awaken in the mind of reflecting infidels doubts with regard to their sincerity, and give plausibility to the suggestion that Christianity does not possess the power which it lays claim to, as a transformer of the character and director of the conduct.

Few things are more fitted to soften prejudices against, and produce a disposition fairly and favourably to consider the claims of, Christianity, than Christian individuals and societies cheerfully and liberally and laboriously supporting every probable scheme that is brought forward for lessening the mass of human suffering, in the form of poverty and disease, and for increasing the sum of human health and enjoyment. These are subjects in which men of the world can take an interest, and of which they can form a just judgment. Of the excellence of peculiar doctrines of Christianity, of the internal holiness which the faith of these doctrines is intended to produce, and actually does produce, they can form no just estimate, and "they speak evil of things which they know not." But to feed the hungry, to clothe the naked, to console the distressed, to provide means of recovery for the bodily or mentally diseased, appear to them "things good and profitable unto men;" and when they perceive Christians discovering a readiness to make sacrifices, to expend time and property and labour to gain such objects, in a degree far superior to that of men not possessed of Christian principles, the natural effect is, to lead them to inquire into the cause of the difference; and finding, what Christians should never be backward to avow, that such exertions are the result of their peculiar views and feelings as Christians, their prejudices are softened, and they are furnished with a motive to examine into what these principles are, and are placed in more favourable circumstances for entering on such an examination, and conducting it to a desirable issue. This consideration of itself ought to be felt by every Christian as a powerful motive to comply with the injunction in the text, "Be pitiful."

I conclude this division of the discourse by two quotations: the one the words of the Apostle Paul, the other the words of our Lord Jesus: the first placing in a strong light the peculiar reasons which urge Christians to be pitiful and kind; the second, the absolutely monstrous character of the opposite disposition, in all who live under such a dispensation of mercy as is revealed in the word of the truth of the gospel: "Be gentle, showing all meekness unto all men: for we ourselves also were sometimes foolish, disobedient, deceived, serving divers lusts and pleasures, living in malice and envy, hateful, and hating one another. But after that the kindness and love of God our Saviour towards man appeared, not by works of righteousness which we have done, but according to his mercy he saved us, by the washing of regeneration, and the renewing of the Holy Ghost, which he shed on us abundantly, through Jesus Christ our Saviour; that being justified by grace, we should be made heirs according to the hope of eternal life. This is a faithful saying: and these things I will that thou affirm constantly, in order that they who have believed in God may be careful to maintain good works:" among the rest, the works of Christian mercy. "These things are good and profitable unto men."[1]

[1] Tit. iii. 2-8.

So much for the words of the holy apostle. Now for the words of his and our Lord: "Therefore is the kingdom of heaven likened unto a certain king, which would take account of his servants. And when he had begun to reckon, one was brought unto him which owed him ten thousand talents. But forasmuch as he had not to pay, his lord commanded him to be sold, and his wife and children, and all that he had, and payment to be made. The servant therefore fell down and worshipped him, saying, Lord, have patience with me, and I will pay thee all. Then the lord of that servant was moved with compassion, and loosed him, and forgave him the debt. But the same servant went out, and found one of his fellow-servants, which owed him an hundred pence; and he laid hands on him, and took him by the throat, saying, Pay me that thou owest. And his fellow-servant fell down at his feet, and besought him, saying, Have patience with me, and I will pay thee all. And he would not; but went and cast him into prison, till he should pay the debt. So when his fellow-servants saw what was done, they were very sorry, and came and told unto their lord all that was done. Then his lord, after that he had called him, said unto him, O thou wicked servant, I forgave thee all that debt, because thou desiredst me: shouldest not thou also have had compassion on thy fellow-servant, even as I had pity on thee? And his lord was wroth, and delivered him to the tormentors, till he should pay all that was due unto him."[1] Thus, he that shows no mercy shall have judgment without mercy.

How powerful, how persuasive, are these motives! Let us lay open our hearts to their influence. Let us be pitiful; pitiful to our relations, to our neighbours, to strangers, to enemies, to our fellow-Christians, our fellow-citizens, our

[1] Matt. xviii. 23-34.

fellow-men: pitiful to their bodies, pitiful to their minds, pitiful to their souls; pitiful in reference to the interests of time; above all, pitiful in reference to the interests of eternity. Let us "be merciful, as our Father who is in heaven is merciful."

§ 2. *To "be courteous."*

The second injunction in reference to the Christian's behaviour to mankind at large, " Be courteous," comes now to be considered. This injunction is certainly not " the first and great commandment" of the Christian law. It is not even one of " the weightier matters of that law." But it is a part of that law; and the fact that it is so, is an illustration of the divine statement, that that law is exceeding broad. It may be considered as included in the second commandment of that law which is like the first: " Thou shalt love thy neighbour as thyself." It is, indeed, an injunction of one of the minor manifestations of that love which is " the fulfilling of the law." It belongs to that class of commandments of which our Lord says, that he who breaks them, and teaches men so, shall be called the least in the kingdom of heaven; while he who does and teaches them shall be called great in the kingdom of heaven.

That it forms, then, a proper subject of occasional illustration and enforcement by the Christian minister, cannot be doubted by any one who believes that it is the Christian pastor's duty to teach those under his care " to observe *all* things whatsoever the Master has commanded;" and to " stir up" the purest-minded of them, " by way of remembrance, that they may be mindful of the commandments of the apostles of the Lord and Saviour:" I say a proper subject of *occasional* illustration; for he would ill deserve the appellation of a good minister of Jesus Christ, who should give to such topics as this the principal, or even a very prominent, place in his public or private teaching. "The grace of God," and the godliness, righteousness, and sobriety which it alone can effectually teach, should form the staple matter of our ministry. Pulpit instruction should consist habitually of the exposition of the doctrines and the inculcation of the duties, the belief and practice of which are essential to the formation of the Christian character and the realization of the Christian hope. What we are chiefly to testify is, "the gospel of the grace of God;" "repentance towards God, and faith towards our Lord Jesus Christ." But we must never forget that "every word of God is pure;" "all Scripture is profitable;" and he who would be "perfect, thoroughly furnished to every good work," must consider with attention and receive with meekness "every word which has proceeded out of the mouth of God." The Christian minister is not to shun to declare to his people "all the counsel of God:" he is not to "keep back anything which may be profitable unto them." Whatever has appeared to God worthy of suggestion by his Spirit, and inscription by an apostle in that book which is intended to be the permanent revelation of his mind and will, and the permanent guide of our faith and conduct, must be deserving of our considerate attention.[1]

The original term[2] which appears in the received text is capable of, and has received, different renderings. By our translators it is rendered courteous; by others not inferior to them in learning and judgment, it has been translated friendly-minded, obliging. This, too, is one of the comparatively few places where there is some uncertainty as to what is the genuine reading. In most of the critical editions of the New Testament, instead of the word which signifies courteous or friendly-minded, we have a word which signifies humble or modest.[3] As there is thus some

[1] 2 Tim. iii. 16, 17; Acts xx. 20, 27.   [2] φιλόφρονις.   [3] ταπεινόφρονις.

uncertainty as to the precise idea which the inspired writer expresses here, and as courtesy and friendliness and humility are all of them tempers which, according to the Christian law, Christians should cherish and exercise in reference to all mankind, and the display of which is well fitted to secure the object which the apostle has in view,—the protection of Christianity from the misapprehensions and misrepresentations of an unbelieving world, and the recommending of it to their respectful notice and favourable consideration,—instead of attempting to fix which of these three closely connected senses is the meaning of the apostle, I shall shortly advert to them all, as any of them *may* be, as one of them *must* be, his meaning.

I remark, then, in the first place, that the apostle may be considered as here enjoining courtesy. The English words courtesy and courteousness are derived from the term court, and are used in their primitive sense to describe that polish and refinement of manners which prevail in the palaces of princes, and distinguish the intercourse of the great, just as that rudeness of manner which is opposed to these is termed rusticity,—a word which primarily denotes the characteristic manner of the inhabitants of the rural districts, who for the most part belong to the humbler and less educated part of the community, and whose means of intercourse even with each other, and still more with the polished portion of society, are necessarily circumscribed. This is the origin of the term, though there is abundant foundation for the remark of the poet—

" Courtesy,
Which oft is sooner found in lowly sheds,
With smoky rafters, than in tapestry halls
And courts of princes, where at first 'twas nam'd,
And yet is most pretended."[1]

---

[1] Milton, *Comus.*

I do not know that the subject of the apostle's injunction, in this view of it, can be better described than as a disposition, with its appropriate manifestations, to treat with becoming respect all with whom we are brought in connection, either occasionally or permanently, in the ordinary intercourse of social life; and to avoid everything in manner, language, and conduct, which may unnecessarily wound their feelings or interfere with their enjoyment. It is, indeed, nothing else than enlightened benevolence manifesting itself in reference to little things. It supposes a capacity of entering into the feelings of others, and judging rightly as to what would gratify and what would wound their feelings; and a disposition to act towards them on the principle, "Whatsoever ye would that men should do to you, do ye even so to them."[1] As no man would be unjust or cruel, so few would be discourteous, if they habitually acted according to this golden rule.

Courtesy in general is opposed both to unsociableness and moroseness, the indisposition to mingle with our fellow-men, and the disposition, when we mingle with them, to make them uncomfortable. The courteous man finds a pleasure in the society of his fellow-men; and when in their society, discovers his satisfaction by endeavouring to make all around him happy. The particular form which courtesy assumes, depends on the relation the courteous person stands to the object of his courtesy. If he is his superior, he regards and treats him with deference and respect; avoiding, on the one hand, all impertinence and presumption, and uncalled-for obtrusive display of independence, and, on the other, all man-worship, all cringing obsequiousness. If he is his inferior, he treats him with condescension and civility, like one who, in by far the most important points of view, stands on a level with himself; not coldly indifferent to nor

[1] Matt. vii. 12.

cruelly negligent of his feelings, but disposed to respect his rights and to promote his happiness. If he is his equal, he treats him with affability; he is not morose, but conciliatory, —not sullen, but cheerful. He is attentive; ready to give, ready to receive, the tokens of mutual respect. He is disposed to please and to be pleased, not fretful or quarrelsome or contemptuous, ever ready to put the best construction on words and actions; indisposed to take, and careful not to give, offence.

The courtesy which the apostle enjoins in the text must not be confounded with that artificial polish of manners which marks the higher classes of society. Christian courtesy may be combined with this artificial politeness; and the combination is beautiful, a gem richly set, "apples of gold in pictures of silver," a fair body with a fairer soul; but they are often to be found separate. Many who are distinguished by this artificial politeness are entire strangers to Christian courtesy; and many are habitually and thoroughly courteous who have had no opportunity of acquiring even the first elements of this artificial politeness. In very many cases artificial politeness is systematic hypocrisy: it is a mask concealing truth and exhibiting falsehood; the not appearing to be what we are, or the appearing to be what we are not. Sentiments and feelings are often strongly expressed, when they exist only in a very inferior degree, or, it may be, where they do not exist at all, or where sentiments and feelings of a directly opposite kind exist. Under a pretence of studying the feelings of others, the most malignant selfishness often seeks gratification: under the guise of the most courteous demeanour and language, the most unkind and contemptuous feelings are frequently cherished and expressed; and he who is studiously courteous to certain individuals and classes, according to the laws and usages of a conventional politeness, may be, and not uncommonly is, characterized by an utter disregard, an entire want of respect, for the feelings of other individuals and classes.

Christian courtesy, like all Christian social virtues, originates in that love of man which flows from the love of God, and grows out of the knowledge and belief of the truth. The Christian regards all men as the children of God; endowed with reason, destined to immortality, capable of being, through the atoning blood and sanctifying Spirit of Jesus Christ, made fit for the most intimate fellowship with God in knowledge, and holiness, and blessedness. He regards the arrangements of society as the result of divine appointment and agency; and hence learns that respect for all men, that honour for all in authority, and that cordial sympathy with all in the humbler stations of society, which naturally express themselves in a courteous demeanour.[1]

While there may be conventional politeness where there is no true courtesy, and true courtesy where there is little conventional politeness, yet it deserves to be remarked, that, so far as the established forms of intercourse in society are innocent, consistent with truth and integrity, Christian courtesy will induce its possessor to conform to them. Wherever these forms imply falsehood, a higher law than that of custom or fashion, the law of God, forbids compliance. He must not use "flattering words:" he must not express sentiments which he does not believe, nor simulate affections which he does not feel; but that eccentricity which leads a man to disregard innocent social usages may commonly be traced to pride and selfishness, principles the

---

[1] "This is affability of the heart as well as of the demeanour: this is Christian civility; as many degrees above modish civility as to serve another effectually is better than to be *his most obedient servant*."— JORTIN.

very reverse of those from which true Christian courtesy springs.

This courtesy should be commensurate with our social relations. We should be courteous to all. It should regulate the intercourse of kindred: no intimacy of relation can be sustained as a reason for dispensing with it. Husbands and wives, parents and children, masters and servants, ought to treat one another courteously, with respect as well as with kindness. This greatly adds to the order and happiness of a family, and serves in some measure as a security for the performance of the higher duties. The manner in which the apostle enjoins the duty on servants is very striking: "Let as many servants as be under the yoke, count their own masters worthy of all honour; and they that have believing masters, let them not despise them, because they are Christian brethren."[1] It should be manifested in the Church of God. The pastors and elders should conduct themselves courteously to the humbler members of the flock; and the members of the congregation should, in their turn, cherish respectful sentiments, and express them in their language and conduct, towards those that are over them in the Lord. This courtesy should also mark the conduct of the Christian in all his intercourse with the world. He is to show all courtesy, as well as "all meekness, to all men." But there is the less necessity for my dwelling on this part of the subject, that I have already had an opportunity of going somewhat into detail in the illustration of it, when explaining the injunction, "Honour all men."

It may be proper to notice here that Christian courtesy, as it does not require, nor indeed permit, the use of language or the performance of acts inconsistent with truth and integrity; so neither does it forbid the statement of sentiments and the performance of actions which duty

[1] 1 Tim. vi. 1, 2.

requires, however unpleasant they may be to the persons more immediately concerned, though it secures that such sentiments shall be stated and such actions performed in such a way as shall give no needless offence. "Neither is it to be supposed," to use the words of a living author, "that courtesy to others implies a forgetfulness of what we owe to ourselves, or a just sense of what others owe to us. Our Lord, who was the perfect example of courtesy, as of every other excellence, more than once evaded interrogatories which were intended to entrap him; and Paul, at Philippi, asserted his political rights as a Roman citizen, by refusing liberty when offered, unless granted in the manner in which it became him to receive it."

The illustration of Christian courteousness by Archbishop Leighton well deserves quotation: "This courteousness which the apostle recommends is not satisfied with what goes no deeper than words and gestures. That is sometimes the upper garment of malice, saluting him aloud in the morning whom they are undermining all the day; and sometimes, though more innocent, it may be troublesome, merely by the vain affectation and excess of it; and even this becomes not a wise man, much less a Christian: an over-studying or acting of this is a token of emptiness, and is below a solid mind. Nor is it that graver and wiser way of external plausible deportment which fully answers this word. That is the outer half indeed; but the thing itself is a radical sweetness in the temper of the mind that spreads itself into a man's words and actions, and this not merely natural (a gentle, kind disposition, which is indeed a natural advantage which some have), but spiritual, from a new nature descended from heaven; and so in its original nature it far excels the other, supplies it where it is not, and doth not only increase it where it is, but elevates it above itself, renews it, and sets a more excellent stamp upon it."

To the cultivation of this courtesy Christians are urged by most powerful motives. It is explicitly enjoined by the highest authority. He who commands us to be holy, commands us to be courteous. It is one way of fulfilling the great law of love, and it is among "the things which are honest, honourable, lovely, and of good report," which Christians are called to "think on," in order to their practising them. It deserves notice, that we find the law of God under the former dispensation breathing the same spirit. What are the commands, "When thou shalt lend thy brother anything, thou shalt not go into his house to fetch his pledge;" "Thou shalt rise up before the hoary head, and honour the face of the old man: I am the Lord. Thou shalt not curse the deaf; Thou shalt not put a stumbling-block before the blind;"—what are all these precepts, inculcating, as they do, regard to the feelings and respect for the persons and situations of others, but instances of the endless variety of particular injunctions that are all bound up in the one brief law, "Be courteous?"

Besides, courteousness is taught and enforced not only by precept, but by example. He who is our great Exemplar has set us an example of courtesy. There was nothing stern or boisterous in his language and demeanour. He did not "strive or cry." Little incidents mark character. "He," we are told, "prayed," that is, courteously requested, the crew of a boat in which he sat, "to put a little away from the land;" and there is a dignified courteousness as well as an unparalleled meekness in his behaviour to his enemies: "Friend," said he to Judas, "wherefore art thou come?" And to those who smote him on the cheek he said, "If I have spoken evil, bear witness of the evil; but if well, why smitest thou me?" It deserves notice, too, that he mildly reproved, for want of courtesy, Simon the Pharisee, who entertained him at dinner: "Thou gavest me no water to wash my feet; thou gavest me no kiss; mine head with oil thou didst not anoint."

Some of the most distinguished of the saints whose lives are recorded in Scripture, were distinguished for their courtesy. We shall select an example from each of the volumes of inspired truth. First in this class stands Abraham, the father of the faithful, and the friend of God. What beautiful pictures of true politeness are presented to us in the following incidents of his history! "And the Lord appeared unto him in the plains of Mamre: and he sat in the tent-door in the heat of the day; and he lift up his eyes and looked, and, lo, three men stood by him: and when he saw them, he ran to meet them from the tent-door, and bowed himself toward the ground, and said, My lord, if now I have found favour in thy sight, pass not away, I pray thee, from thy servant. Let a little water, I pray you, be fetched, and wash your feet, and rest yourselves under the tree: and I will fetch a morsel of bread, and comfort ye your hearts; after that ye shall pass on: for therefore are ye come to your servant. And they said, So do as thou hast said. And Abraham hastened into the tent unto Sarah, and said, Make ready quickly three measures of fine meal, knead it, and make cakes upon the hearth. And Abraham ran unto the herd, and fetched a calf tender and good, and gave it unto a young man: and he hasted to dress it. And he took butter and milk, and the calf which he had dressed, and set it before them; and he stood by them under the tree, and they did eat."[1]

The next incident is still more striking and affecting: "And Sarah was an hundred and seven and twenty years old: these were the years of the life of Sarah. And Sarah died in Kirjath-arba; the same is Hebron in the land of Canaan: and Abraham came to mourn for Sarah, and to

[1] Gen. xviii. 1-8.

weep for her. And Abraham stood up from before his dead, and spake unto the sons of Heth, saying, I am a stranger and a sojourner with you: give me a possession of a burying-place with you, that I may bury my dead out of my sight. And the children of Heth answered Abraham, saying unto him, Hear us, my lord: Thou art a mighty prince among us; in the choice of our sepulchres bury thy dead: none of us shall withhold from thee his sepulchre, but that thou mayest bury thy dead. And Abraham stood up, and bowed himself to the people of the land, even to the children of Heth. And he communed with them, saying, If it be your mind that I should bury my dead out of my sight, hear me, and entreat for me to Ephron, the son of Zohar, that he may give me the cave of Machpelah, which he hath, which is in the end of his field: for as much money as it is worth he shall give it me, for a possession of a burying-place amongst you. And Ephron dwelt among the children of Heth. And Ephron the Hittite answered Abraham in the audience of the children of Heth, even of all that went in at the gate of his city, saying, Nay, my lord, hear me: The field give I thee, and the cave that is therein, I give it thee; in the presence of the sons of my people give I it thee: bury thy dead. And Abraham bowed down himself before all the people of the land. And he spake unto Ephron, in the audience of the people of the land, saying, But if thou wilt give it, I pray thee, hear me: I will give thee money for the field; take it of me, and I will bury my dead there. And Ephron answered Abraham, saying unto him, My lord, hearken unto me: The land is worth four hundred shekels of silver; what is that betwixt me and thee? bury therefore thy dead. And Abraham hearkened unto Ephron; and Abraham weighed to Ephron the silver, which he had named in the audience of the sons of Heth, four hundred shekels of silver, current money with the merchant. And the field of Ephron, which was in Machpelah, which was before Mamre, the field, and the cave which was therein, and all the trees that were in the field, that were in all the borders round about, were made sure unto Abraham for a possession, in the presence of the children of Heth, before all that went in at the gate of the city."[1]

Our other example is the Apostle Paul; the most extraordinary merely human personage the New Testament makes us acquainted with. "Paul," it has been well said, " was the most distinguished for zeal as an apostle, the most remarkable for courtesy as a man. His language in some of his letters, and his conduct on certain occasions, are a perfect model of polite and courteous phraseology, of bland and beautiful address." Take, as a specimen, his address to Felix, and view in contrast with it the fulsome flattery of Tertullus the orator: " And after five days, Ananias the high priest descended with the elders, and with a certain orator named Tertullus, who informed the governor against Paul. And when he was called forth, Tertullus began to accuse him, saying, Seeing that by thee we enjoy great quietness, and that very worthy deeds are done unto this nation by thy providence, we accept it always, and in all places, most noble Felix, with all thankfulness. Notwithstanding, that I be not further tedious unto thee, I pray thee that thou wouldest hear us of thy clemency a few words. For we have found this man a pestilent fellow, and a mover of sedition among all the Jews throughout the world, and a ringleader of the sect of the Nazarenes: who also hath gone about to profane the temple; whom we took, and would have judged according to our law: but the chief captain Lysias came upon us, and with great violence took him away out of our hands, commanding his accusers to come unto thee: by examining of whom thyself mayest

[1] Gen. xxiii. 1-18.

take knowledge of all these things whereof we accuse him. And the Jews also assented, saying that these things were so. Then Paul, after that the governor had beckoned unto him to speak, answered, Forasmuch as I know that thou hast been of many years a judge unto this nation, I do the more cheerfully answer for myself: because that thou mayest understand that there are yet but twelve days since I went up to Jerusalem for to worship. And they neither found me in the temple disputing with any man, neither raising up the people, neither in the synagogues, nor in the city: neither can they prove the things whereof they now accuse me. But this I confess unto thee, that after the way which they call heresy, so worship I the God of my fathers, believing all things which are written in the law and in the prophets; and have hope toward God, which they themselves also allow, that there shall be a resurrection of the dead, both of the just and unjust. And herein do I exercise myself, to have always a conscience void of offence toward God, and toward men."[1]

Even still more striking is the conversation between Paul and the Roman judge and king Agrippa. How far does the prisoner exceed the judge in dignified courtesy! "And as he thus spake for himself, Festus said with a loud voice, Paul, thou art beside thyself; much learning doth make thee mad. But he said, I am not mad, most noble Festus; but speak forth the words of truth and soberness. For the king knoweth of these things, before whom also I speak freely: for I am persuaded that none of these things are hidden from him; for this thing was not done in a corner. King Agrippa, believest thou the prophets? I know that thou believest. Then Agrippa said unto Paul, Almost thou persuadest me to be a Christian. And Paul said, I would to God, that not only thou, but also all that hear me

[1] Acts xxiv. 1-16.

this day, were both almost and altogether such as I am, except these bonds."[1]

What a beautiful instance of courteousness have we in the first chapter of the Epistle to the Romans, where, after having expressed a wish to go to Rome, that he might impart to the Christians there "some spiritual gift;" lest their feelings should be hurt, as if he thought all the advantage was to be on their side, he adds, "that I may be comforted together with you, by the mutual faith both of you and me!" And what a delicate touch of Christian courtesy, as well as kindness, is to be found in the way in which he sends his affectionate remembrance to the mother of Rufus, at the 13th verse of the sixteenth chapter of that epistle: "His mother and mine!"

The Epistle to Philemon stands, in relation to this subject, as a composition, unrivalled and alone, both for its sentiments and language. Read it carefully, and say if the apostle does not appear a perfect master of the trains of thought and forms of expression most indicative of eminence in this Christian grace of courtesy.

Few things tend more to make a Christian conversation "honest," that is, honourable, "among unbelievers," than the culture and display of courtesy; while its absence, and still more the presence of opposite tempers and habits, gives occasion to those who are seeking occasion, both to think and speak unfavourably of Christianity and of Christians. The want of courtesy has often more than neutralized the influence of great talents and great excellence; and the possession of it has rendered men of but moderate talents or endowments greatly useful in promoting the Christian cause. It is very justly remarked by a Christian moralist: "If religious but coarsely-mannered persons, however safe they may be as to their own state,

[1] Acts xxvi. 24-29.

could be made aware how much injury their want of prudence and delicacy is doing to the minds of the polished and discriminating, who, though they may admire Christianity in the abstract, do not love it so cordially as to bear with the grossness of some of its professors, nor understand it so intimately as to distinguish between what is essential and what is extrinsic; if they could conceive what mischief they do to religion by the associations which they lead the refined to combine with it, so as to lead them inseparably to connect piety with vulgarity, they would endeavour to correct their own taste, from the virtuous fear of shocking that of others."[1] It is greatly to be deprecated, thus to throw additional obstacles in the way of Christianity getting justice done to it, and of unbelievers becoming Christians. It is treating it unjustly, and then unkindly. Let no one then say of courtesy, it is a small matter thus to make so much of. It is a small matter compared with righteousness, mercy, temperance, and fidelity; but it is one of the matters of the Christian law; and let us remember who it is who says, "These things ye ought to do, and not to leave the others undone."[2]

[1] Hannah More.
[2] What a beautiful picture of courtesy is given in Matthew Henry's Life of his father! "It may not be improper to observe, what was obvious as well as amiable to all who conversed with him,—that he had the most sweet and obliging air of courtesy and civility that could be; which some attributed in part to his early education at court. His mien and carriage were always so very decent and respectful, that they could not but win the hearts of all he had to do with. Never was any man further from that rudeness and moroseness which some scholars, and too many that profess religion, either wilfully affect or carelessly allow themselves in, sometimes to the reproach of their profession. It is one of the laws of our holy religion, exemplified in the conversation of this good man, to 'honour all men.' Sanctified civility is a great ornament to Christianity. It was a saying he often used, 'Religion doth not destroy good manners;' and yet he was very far from anything like vanity in apparel or formality of compliment in address: but his conver-

Having gone so fully into the illustration and enforcement of Christian courtesy, I must confine myself to a very few observations on the two other views which may be taken of the inspired injunction now before us.

I observed in the second place, that it may be considered as requiring a friendly or obliging temper or behaviour. This, rather than "courtesy" strictly so called, is considered by many as the import of the original term. Christians should cherish and manifest a kind and obliging disposition to all. They are not only to be pitiful to sufferers, but kind and obliging to all; disposed to do good to *all* as they have opportunity. This Christian temper and habit is opposed to that disposition of which Nabal[1] is the type, which prevents a man almost from speaking peaceably to his neighbour. There are men who can scarcely speak without saying, who can scarcely act without doing, something disobliging and displeasing to their fellow-men, "so churlish is their nature."

But it is opposed not only to this most unlovely temper, but also to that retiredness of mind and temper which leads a man to shut himself up in himself, and his own immediate interests. Such a man may be peaceable and harmless, but he is not obliging and useful. He will neither say nor do an unkind or injurious thing, but the law of kindness is not on his lips; and his hand, though not wielding the weapons of warfare against his neighbour, is not employed in promoting his happiness. The Christian,

---

sation was all natural and easy to himself and others, and nothing appeared in him which even a severe critic could justly call affected. This temper of his tended very much to the adorning of the doctrine of God our Saviour; and the general transcript of so excellent a copy would do much toward the healing of those wounds which religion hath received in the house of her friends."—*Account of the Life and Death of Mr Philip Henry*, p. 4. London, 1712.

[1] 1 Sam. xxv. 17.

in reference to all with whom he comes in contact, should discover a disposition to oblige and serve them.

This greatly tends to soften men's prejudices against religion, while an opposite temper and behaviour on the part of professors are as powerfully calculated to harden their prejudices, and to give occasion to the adversaries to reproach Christians, and blaspheme Christianity and its Author.

I observed in the third place, that the apostle may be considered as enjoining here humility or modesty. In many of the most ancient manuscripts, the reading is, "Be humble." Christians are not to think of themselves "highly," but "soberly." If they are Christians, they must believe their insignificance as creatures, and their demerit as sinners. They must believe that they are in their natural state thoroughly depraved; deeply, inexcusably guilty; righteously condemned; hopelessly wretched; and that if their state is altered, if their characters are transformed, if their prospects are improved, it is all owing to sovereign divine kindness operating through the mediation of Jesus Christ, and by the influence of the Holy Spirit. The native tendency of such views is to make a man humble and lowly in spirit; to make him feel that pride was not made for him. This should be the habitual temper of the Christian, and should give a decided character to his habitual demeanour and behaviour. He should be "clothed with humility:" "in lowliness of mind esteeming others better than himself."[1]

He should carefully avoid all kinds of pride as absurd and criminal, but especially spiritual pride. His conduct should never be such as to say to those about him, "Stand by thyself; come not near to me, I am holier than thou." He must not "mind high things;" he must "condescend

[1] 1 Pet. v. 5; Phil. ii. 3.

to men of low estate;" he must not "be wise in his own conceit."[1]

The cultivation and display of humility are recommended by very numerous and powerful motives. It is the most reasonable of all things. Pride in a creature, in a sinner, is absolutely monstrous. Humility is very often enjoined in Scripture: "Walk worthy of the vocation wherewith ye are called with all lowliness. Let nothing be done through vainglory. Put on, as the elect of God, humbleness of mind."[2] No temper is more highly eulogized in Scripture; and to the possession of none are made promises more exceeding great and precious. "He hath showed thee, O man, what is good; to walk humbly with thy God. Though the Lord be high, he hath respect to the lowly. Blessed are the poor in spirit. Whosoever shall humble himself like this little child, the same is greatest in the kingdom of heaven. God forgetteth not the cry of the humble. He resisteth the proud, but giveth grace to the humble. He that humbleth himself shall be exalted. Thus saith the high and lofty One that inhabiteth eternity, whose name is holy: I dwell in the high and holy place, with him also who is humble and of a contrite spirit, to revive the spirit of the humble, and to revive the heart of the contrite ones."[3]

Humility formed one of the distinguishing ornaments of the character of our Lord. It was emphatically "the mind which was in Him,"[4] who was meek and lowly; who humbled himself, and came not to be ministered to, but to minister. And, finally, it is greatly fitted to lessen the prejudices of the world against Christianity, and to shut the mouths of those who calumniate it, as calculated to make

---

[1] Rom. xii. 16.   [2] Eph. iv. 1, 2; Phil. ii. 3; Col. iii. 12.
[3] Mic. vi. 8; Ps. cxxxviii. 6; Matt. v. 3, xviii. 4; Ps. ix. 12; James iv. 6; Luke xiv. 11; Isa. lvii. 15.
[4] Phil. ii. 3-11.

men self-conceited, and despisers of all who do not embrace their opinions.

It is worthy of remark, that the last two Christian tempers we have been illustrating are, as it were, the elements of the first. Kindliness and humility naturally, necessarily produce courtesy. Everything by which courtesy is violated may be traced either to selfishness, the reverse of kindliness, or to pride, the reverse of humility.

Thus have I shortly considered the tempers and conduct in reference to mankind at large, which the apostle enjoins on believers, in order that their conduct might be "honest among the Gentiles." I cannot conclude this department of the subject without remarking what a wonderful book is the Bible! and what a universal remedy is Christianity for all the evils of man! There is nothing too great, nothing too little, for the Bible. It unfolds the principles which guide the government of the universe, and it gives directions for the regulation of man's every-day tempers and manners. It provides for the highest interests of the soul through eternity, and yet descends to point out the way, with wondrous minuteness of detail, in which most happiness may be attained by man during his short sojourn in the present state.[1] Christianity not only transforms the character, but improves the manners. It is the greatest tamer of savage man, as well as the only purifier of depraved man. There are, indeed, men, we confess it with regret, rude with it, but they would have been brutal without it.

Let us show our regard to the Bible by making the intended use of all its revelations. Let us show our regard to Christianity as a universal remedy, by submitting the whole frame of our natures, intellectual and active, to its healing influence. Let us see to it, that this portion of Scripture given by inspiration be indeed profitable to *us*. It

[1] Binney.

will be so only in the degree in which we are what it commands us to be—courteous, kindly, and humble. "Wherefore, lay apart all filthiness and superfluity of naughtiness, and receive with meekness the ingrafted word, which is able to save your souls. But be ye doers of the word, and not hearers only, deceiving your own selves. For if any man be a hearer of the word and not a doer, he is like unto a man beholding his natural face in a glass: for he beholdeth himself and goeth his way, and straightway forgetteth what manner of man he was. But whoso looketh into the perfect law of liberty," one of whose precepts we have been expounding, and "continueth therein, he being not a forgetful hearer, but a doer of the work, that man shall be blessed in his deed."

III. DUTIES OF CHRISTIANS UNDER PERSECUTION.

It is now time for us to turn our attention to the third class of duties enjoined by the apostle,—the duties of Christians in reference to their persecutors, viewed with a particular reference to the influence which the performance of these duties is calculated to have on the character both of Christianity and of Christians among unbelieving men.

§ 1. *Abstinence from all resentful retaliation, and meeting injury and reproach by kindness both in conduct and language.*

The first duty, then, which the apostle enjoins on Christians in reference to their persecutors, is abstinence from all resentful retaliation, and the meeting of injury and reproach by kindness, both in conduct and language. The injunction and enforcement of this duty occupy the greater part of the paragraph, from ver. 9 down to the middle of ver. 14. The duty, and the motives by which it is enforced, are then successively to be considered. The duty is thus described: "Not rendering evil for evil, or railing for railing, but contrariwise blessing." The motives are four: 1. Christians are "called" to the discharge of this duty, ver. 9. 2. They are called to this, "that they may inherit a blessing," ver. 9. These two motives are illustrated by a quotation from the Old Testament Scriptures, vers. 10-12. 3. This is really the way to escape with the least possible suffering, ver. 13; and 4. If their peaceable, kind conduct does not produce its proper result on others, still, in thus suffering, Christians are blessed or happy, ver. 14. Let us attend to these topics in their order.

(1.) *The duty explained.*

The duty enjoined is abstinence from all resentful retaliation, and the meeting of injury and reproach by kindness, both in action and words: "Render not evil for evil, nor railing for railing, but contrariwise blessing." This injunction plainly goes on the assumption that they to whom it was addressed were exposed to injurious treatment and contumelious reproach. Their Lord and Master, when he was on earth, was most injuriously and unkindly treated, and his character and conduct were the objects of the most malignant misrepresentation and cruel obloquy. He was denied not only what—as an immaculately innocent, an absolutely perfect man, the greatest, the most disinterested, the most unwearied, the most successful of all philanthropists and public benefactors, a fully accredited divine messenger, an Incarnation of the Divinity—he had the strongest claims to; he was denied the common rights of humanity, and was represented as a demoniac and blasphemer, a teacher of error, and a stirrer up of sedition, "a glutton and wine-bibber, a friend of publicans and sinners." And he distinctly warned his followers that they should meet with similar usage: "The servant," said he, "is not greater than his lord. They have persecuted me; they will also persecute you. In the world ye shall have tribulation. They have called the master of the house Beelzebub; how much more them of his household? Ye shall be hated of all men for my name's sake. Men shall hate you, and shall separate you from their company, and shall reproach you, and shall cast out your name as evil for the Son of man's sake."[1]

These predictions were fulfilled to the letter in the case of the apostles and many of the primitive Christians. They were "despised and buffeted, reviled and defamed, made as the filth of the world, and the offscouring of all things." "They were troubled, perplexed, and persecuted." "They endured a great fight of affliction; they were made a gazing-stock both by reproaches and afflictions." Some were "tortured; others had trials of cruel scourgings; yea, moreover, of bonds and imprisonment. They were stoned, they were sawn asunder, were tempted, were slain with the sword; they wandered about in sheep-skins and goat-skins, being destitute, afflicted, tormented; they wandered in deserts and in mountains, and in dens and caves of the earth."[2] They were everywhere spoken against as despisers of the gods, haters of the human race, and perpetrators of the most shocking impurities and barbarities.

In succeeding ages, comparatively few Christians have been exposed to such extremity of ill-usage; yet in every age the apostle's declaration has been verified, "They that *will* live godly"—are determined to act out the principles and precepts of Christianity—"*must* suffer persecution."[3] No consistent Christian passes through this world without

[1] John xv. 20, xvi. 33; Matt. x. 25, xxiv. 9.
[2] 1 Cor. iv. 9-13; 2 Cor. iv. 8, 9; Heb. xi. 36, 37.
[3] 2 Tim. iii. 12.

personal experimental evidence that "this world is not his friend, nor this world's law;" and he who has never suffered in any way for his religion, who is an entire stranger to "the reproach of Christ," has some reason to read with alarm the words of our Lord: "If ye were of the world, the world would love its own; but because ye are not of the world, but I have chosen you out of the world, therefore the world hateth you."[1]

Whatever be the degree of ill-usage, whatever the measure of opprobrious language to which the Christian may be exposed, his duty is not "to render evil for evil, or railing for railing." There is nothing inconsistent with Christian principle and feeling in endeavouring, by using such means as law warrants, to disarm the man who has already wounded me, and who shows a disposition to repeat the injury,—to shut the mouth which has already calumniated me, and seems ready to pour forth additional torrents of abuse. Regard to society, and indeed to the poor infatuated individual himself, even more than a due respect to my own interests and feelings, may make this even my duty. But I must not seek to injure him. I must not inflict undeserved, nor even unnecessary suffering. Restraint, even punishment, may not be evil,—it may be benefit to the individual as well as to society; but even in securing this, I must avoid resentful feeling. I must not seek to avenge myself. And as to railing, reproachful, contumelious language, I may, in many cases I ought to, rebut false charges, which, if credited, might injure my reputation and lessen my usefulness; and in doing this, it may be absolutely necessary to state and substantiate what will necessarily lower the character of the railer; but I must make no statement, however true, of a disadvantageous kind, which self-defence or public duty does not require; and in making such statements, I must

[1] John xv. 19.

keep at the greatest distance from everything like abuse. I must not speak angrily, contemptuously, reproachfully, spitefully, provokingly.

There are some men who seem to think that they have done their duty in this respect, when they have refrained from injuring those who have never injured them—from speaking evil of those who have never spoken evil of them; but that injury warrants injury, and evil-speaking sanctions evil-speaking in return. But as the good Archbishop says, "One man's sin cannot procure privilege to another to sin in that or the like kind. If another has broken the bonds of allegiance to God and charity to thee, yet thou art not the less tied by the same bonds still."[1] Besides, to act thus is a trenching on the divine prerogative, as well as a violation of the divine commands. "Dearly beloved, avenge not yourselves, but rather give place to wrath: for it is written, Vengeance is mine; I will repay, saith the Lord."[2]

But this is only the one part, and the least part, of the Christian's duty to him who, unprovoked, injures and maligns him: "Contrariwise render blessing." To "bless" is frequently significant of kindness generally—kindness embodied in deeds as well as in words. It is the duty of the Christian to render benefit for injury, blessing for railing. He is to "do good to those who hate him,"—to do whatever lies in his power to promote their real welfare, to go out of his way to do them a service; and, not satisfied with his own efforts to advance their happiness, he is to call in the aid of infinite power, and wisdom, and kindness, by the prayer which has power with God. You are to "pray for them who despitefully use you and persecute you."[3] To "bless" here, however, does not seem to mean either generally to do good or to invoke the divine blessing, though to do both, as

---

[1] Leighton. [2] Rom. xii. 19. [3] Matt. v. 44.

we have seen, is the Christian's duty to his enemy. It is the opposite of railing; it denotes the Christian's duty to speak courteously and kindly to, and, as far as truth will admit, well of, the railers.

The duties here enjoined are just various modes of expressing that love to enemies which our Lord requires from all his disciples. Without this love, they cannot be performed. With this love, this command will not be found a grievous one; for love can intentionally do no harm to its object; love naturally prompts to do all practicable good to its object. I may pity, I may blame, I may even punish the object of my love; but I cannot do what is intended, what in my view is calculated, to injure him.

There is nothing unreasonable, nothing impracticable, in the requisitions before us. We are not required to regard the wicked with the sentiments of complacent esteem with which we regard the good. We are not required to regard the man who has injured us with the same feelings of grateful affection with which we regard our friends and benefactors. But we are required to cherish towards our enemies, however wicked and depraved and malicious, a sentiment of genuine good-will; to be sincerely desirous of their real welfare and happiness; never to lift up the hand against them, except self-defence or the public good require it; to forbid so much as a finger to move, a wish to stir against them at the instigation of malice; to have no pleasure in any of their sufferings; to feel no joy when they stumble; to be ever ready to relieve them when in a situation which makes them the fit objects of rational benevolence; and not to be more backward to show towards them the offices of kindness, which man owes to man, than to those who have never done us an injury.

If such is the conduct and the language by which a Christian should be characterized in reference to his worst enemies, those who hate and persecute him because of his religion, what are we to say of those professors of Christianity, who treat those whom they call brethren with injustice and unkindness, and scourge them, unoffending and uncondemned, with malignant insinuations, railing accusations, and contemptuous abuse? The least we can say is, with Archbishop Leighton, to remark, that they are an "unchristian kind of Christians;" to warn them to beware what spirit they are of; to bid them remember this is not the spirit of Him who, even "when reviled, reviled not again;" and ponder the weighty truths, that "he who has not the Spirit of Christ is none of his;" and that for brethren to "bite and devour one another," for one servant to beat his fellow-servants, is neither becoming nor safe. The Great Judge obviously accounts such conduct immoral in no ordinary degree. When he is setting in order the sins of the forgetters of God, next after companionship with thieves and adulterers, he charges them with this: "Thou sittest and speakest against thy brother, thou slanderest thine own mother's son."[1]

(2.) *The duty enforced.*

This injunction is enforced by powerful motives. To this mode of conduct Christians are "called:" to this mode of conduct they are called, in order "that they may inherit a blessing." This mode of conduct is of all others the best fitted to secure from suffering. And finally, in cases in which, after all, Christians are exposed to suffering, they are blessed in *thus* suffering. Let us shortly explain these statements, and show their force as motives.

(1.) Christians are called to the course of conduct which the apostle has been recommending. "Hereunto ye are called." To no duty are Christians more explicitly called.

[1] 1 Pet. ii. 23; Rom. viii. 9; Ps. l. 19.

Hear the words of our one Master in heaven: "Ye have heard that it has been said, Thou shalt love thy neighbour, and hate thine enemy." This was the doctrine of the scribes, and it was but too fully acted out in the conduct of their disciples, the Pharisees. But hear the law of the kingdom: "I say unto you, Love your enemies, bless them who curse you, do good to them who hate you, and pray for them who despitefully use you, and persecute you; that ye may be the children of your Father which is in heaven: for he maketh his sun to rise on the evil and on the good, and sendeth rain on the just and on the unjust. For if ye love them that love you, what reward have ye? do not even the publicans the same? Be ye therefore perfect, as your Father who is in heaven is perfect."[1]

The call of his word is seconded by the call of his example. He has left us a pattern, that we should follow his steps. He has fully exemplified his own precept; and his call, in reference to this height of moral excellence, is not, 'Go up yonder,' but, 'Come up hither.' When reviled, he reviled not again; when injured, with power to punish, he went on to bless. "Father," said he with his dying lips, in reference to his murderers, "Father, forgive them; for they know not what they do." "When we were ungodly, sinners, enemies, in due time he died for us."[2]

The call is repeated by one of his apostles, who had drunk deep into his spirit: "Recompense to no man evil for evil: bless them that curse you; bless, and curse not. Dearly beloved, avenge not yourselves, but rather give place unto wrath: for it is written, Vengeance is mine; I will repay, saith the Lord. Therefore if thine enemy hunger, feed him: if he thirst, give him drink: for in so doing thou shalt heap coals of fire on his head," which may

[1] Matt. v. 43-48. [2] Luke xxiii. 34; Rom. v. 6, 8, 10.

melt his cold heart into ingenuous shame and grateful affection. "Be not overcome of evil, but overcome evil with good."[1]

Paul's conduct, like that of his Master, corresponded with his words. How did he labour and pray for the salvation of his worst enemies! It is in reference to those who sought his life, and would have rejoiced in his ruin, that he says: "My heart's desire and prayer for them is, that they may be saved. I have great heaviness and continual sorrow of heart. I could wish myself accursed from Christ for my brethren, my kinsmen according to the flesh." It was in reference to those who reviled him that he says: "I bear them record that they have a zeal of God, but not according to knowledge."[2]

But the call not to render evil for evil, railing for railing, but contrariwise blessing, is to be found in the Old Testament as well as in the New. It comes from David as well as from his Son and Lord; from Solomon as well as from Paul. Acting on the principles laid down by his beloved brother Paul, that "all Scripture is given by inspiration of God," and that "whatsoever things were written beforetime were written for our instruction," Peter here quotes a passage from the book of Psalms, in illustration of both parts of the complex motive, "Hereunto were ye called, that ye might inherit a blessing." The passage is to be found in the thirty-fourth Psalm; and as the words before us do not exactly correspond in words either to the Hebrew text or the Greek translation, though in meaning it exactly agrees with both, it is probable that the apostle quoted from memory, under the inspiration of the Holy Spirit. The words are: "For he that will love life and see good days, let him refrain his tongue from evil, and his lips that they speak no guile; let him eschew evil, and do good; let him

[1] Rom. xii. 14, 17, 19-21.   [2] Rom. ix. 1-3, x. 1, 2.

seek peace, and pursue it: for the eyes of the Lord are on the righteous, and his ears are open to their prayers; but the face of the Lord is against them that do evil." In these words we have evidence that Christians are called not to render evil for evil, nor railing for railing. They are required to "refrain their tongue from evil, and their lips that they speak no guile; to eschew evil, and do good; to seek peace, and pursue it." And we have also evidence that they are called to this in order that they may inherit a blessing. It is thus that they are to escape a curse; "for the face of the Lord is against them who do evil:" and it is thus they are to obtain the life they love, and the good days they desire. It is thus that they are to secure the complacent eye and the propitious ear of God. It is to the illustration of the first motive, "Hereunto are ye called," that I am now inviting your attention.

"Hereunto are ye called;" for what says the Scripture? "Refrain thy tongue from evil, and thy lips that they speak no guile." "Evil" is here injury, wrong; and the whole injunction is equivalent to, 'Neither by open calumny, abuse, or railing, nor by secret, guileful, deceitful surmisings, injure any man.' The command is universal in its reference, and therefore includes enemies as well as others. It is no reason why I should injuriously speak evil, whether openly or secretly, of a man, that he is my enemy. If I am called to refrain my tongue from evil, then I am called, too, not to render railing for railing.

"Eschew evil, and do good." When we look at the connection, we cannot doubt that evil here, as in the former clause, is wrong or injury. Carefully abstain from doing any injury to any human being. As the Apostle Paul explains this very expression, "Abhor that which is evil."[1] Regard every act of injury with abhorrence. But the

[1] Rom. xii. 9.

Psalmist calls on us not only to do no harm to any, but to do good to all. Do good. Good is here *benefit;* as in the precept, "Do good to all men, as ye have opportunity."[1] Make it your business to make men happy.

"Seek peace, and pursue it." Never quarrel with those with whom you are connected; and if they discover a disposition to quarrel with you, leave off such contention before it be meddled with. If they strike one blow, do not you, by returning it, give them an excuse for striking a second. "Pursue peace," even when it seems about to fly away; "follow peace with all men;" "as much as lieth in you, live peaceably with all men."[2]

There may be something fanciful in Leighton's remark, but it is beautiful and just: "We may pursue peace among men, and not overtake it; we may use all good means, and fall short: but pursue it up as far as the throne of grace; seek it by prayer, and that will overtake it,—that will be sure to find it in God's hand, 'who stilleth the waves of the sea and the tumults of the people.' 'If he give quietness, who can give trouble?'" So much for the first motive, Ye are "called" to this mode of conduct. No part of the Christian's call is more explicit; few parts of it more frequently repeated.

(2.) The second motive is: Ye are called to this mode of conduct, in order that in following it "ye may inherit a blessing."[3] God does not mean, by requiring you to deny and mortify your resentful feelings, and submit to unavenged wrong, that you are to be ultimate losers. If you "refrain your lips from evil;" if you "eschew evil, and do good;" if you "seek peace, and pursue it," you will obtain the life you love, you will "see good days." "God's eye will be on you; God's ear will be open to your prayers." While, on the other hand, "the face of the Lord will be against

[1] Gal. vi. 10.   [2] Heb. xii. 14; Rom. xii. 18.   [3] Gal. iii. 13.

the ill-doer," the injurious man.¹ He can have no token of his complacency and approbation, for he does not possess it. Life is happiness; good days are happy days. Happiness consists in enjoying God's favour. His favour is life, his loving-kindness better than life. To have his eye resting complacently on us, to be objects of his love and care, to have his ear open to our prayers; to have him, infinitely powerful, wise, and good, always ready to listen to our petitions and supply our need,—this is life, this is happiness: while, on the other hand, to have his face set against us, to have his countenance covered with frowns, to have him looking at us as he did out of the pillar of cloud on the Egyptians struggling with the billows of the Arabian Gulf, —this is misery.

Our obedience cannot, indeed, deserve this inheritance of blessing, though our disobedience well deserves the corresponding curse; but by God's appointment, and in the very nature of the case, while the benefits bestowed on men are "the gift of God through Jesus Christ,"—the result of sovereign kindness, manifesting itself in consistency with justice, through the mediation of our Lord,— they can be enjoyed only in a state of conformity of mind and heart to the will of God, discovering itself in a cheerful obedience to his commandments. "In the keeping of his commandments there is great reward;" and it is through "a constant continuance in well-doing" that the full enjoyment of the inheritance of blessing is to be reached. It is in "adding to faith virtue, and knowledge, and temperance, and patience, and godliness, and brotherly kindness, and charity," that we are to enjoy the earnest of the inheritance; and it is in persevering in this course that we are to look at last for "an abundant entrance into the everlasting

---

¹ Ira totam faciem—πρόσωπον commovet: amor oculos ὀφθαλμοὺς tingit.—BENGEL.

kingdom of our Lord and Saviour Jesus Christ,"—the inheritance itself, "incorruptible, undefiled, and that fadeth not away, laid up in heaven" for all who, through faith and patience, are followers of those who have already entered on its possession.

(3.) The course recommended is of all others the best fitted to secure from suffering: "Who will harm you if ye be followers of that which is good?"[1] The phraseology here requires some explanation. The phrase rendered "that which is good," may, viewed by itself, with at least equal propriety, be rendered 'Him who is good.'[2] The word "followers" signifies imitators; and in every case in which it is used in the New Testament, has a reference to persons.[3] *Good* is here, as throughout the passage, equivalent to *kind*. If the rendering adopted by our translators be the true one, then a follower of that which is good is one who imitates what is kind in the character and conduct of others. If the rendering 'Him who is good' be preferred, then it refers either to God, who is, by way of eminence, the good or benignant One; and in this case it puts us in mind of what our Lord says, "Do good to them that

---

[1] 1 Cor. iv. 16, xi. 1; Eph. v. 1; 1 Thess. i. 6, ii. 14; Heb. vi. 12.

[2] Ἐὰν τοῦ ἀγαθοῦ μιμηταὶ γίνησθε.

[3] "It should be read *imitators*: so the word signifies; and so, whereas *following* is either of a *pattern* or of an *end*, the former must be meant here, by the natural importance of that word. And hence, by *that which is good*, is not to be understood *created goodness;* for it is not enough to *imitate* that goodness, for so we must *be* good, but the words are capable of being read *him that is good*, or, which is all one, *the good*, as Plato and his followers used the expression τ' ἀγαθὸν fully according to the sense of Matt. xix. 17. And so it is the *increate good*, the blessed God himself, formally considered under the notion of good. Nothing can harm you if you be like God: that is the plain sense of the scripture. A person truly like God is secure from any external violence, so far as that it shall never be able to invade his spirit. He is in spirit raised above the tempestuous stormy region, and converses where winds and clouds have no place."—HOWE: *Bless. of the Right.* chap. vii.

hate you, that ye may be the children of your Father in heaven;" and of what the apostle says, "Be followers of God as dear children;" or it may refer to our Lord, who, in not reviling when reviled, in not threatening when he suffered, set his people an example that they should follow his steps; and who, both in the preceding and succeeding context, is represented by the apostle as our great exemplar.[1]

The meaning in all these various modes of exposition is substantially the same: If you in your character manifest that benignity, even toward enemies, which characterizes the divine administration, and which so remarkably distinguished the words and actions of him who was "God manifest in flesh;" if ye are thus characterized by harmlessness, and quiet unresisting suffering, "who," says the apostle, "will harm you?"

The meaning of this interrogation is not, 'No one will harm you;' for the greatest harmlessness and forbearance and patience will not in every case protect from even very severe suffering; but the meaning is, 'If anything can protect you, this will.' If, discovering these tempers, you yet suffer; were you discovering opposite ones, you would suffer still more. It is justly remarked, "that there are virtues which are apt, in their own nature, to prevent injuries and affronts from others. Humility takes away all occasion of insolence from the proud and haughty; it baffles pride, and puts it out of countenance. Meekness pacifies wrath, and blunts the edge of injury and violence. Patient suffering, and the returning of good for evil, is apt to allay and extinguish enmity, to subdue the roughest disposition, and to conquer even malice itself. Besides, the providence of God usually watches over the interests of those who, instead of seeking to avenge themselves,

[1] Matt. v. 48; Eph. v. 1; 1 Pet. ii. 21-23.

commit themselves in patience and well-doing to 'Him who judgeth righteously.' 'When a man's ways please the Lord, he,' often in a very remarkable manner, 'maketh his enemies to be at peace with him.' It is true of more than the patriarchs during their wanderings, that God 'suffers no man to do them wrong.'"[1]

The words may with equal propriety be rendered, Who *shall* harm you? as who *will* harm you? God is with them; who can be effectually against them? who can really harm them? "He that dwelleth in the secret place of the Most High, shall abide under the shadow of the Almighty. Surely he shall deliver thee from the snare of the fowler, and from the noisome pestilence. He shall cover thee with his feathers, and under his wings shalt thou trust; his truth shall be thy shield and buckler." "He shall deliver thee from six troubles; yea, in seven, there shall no evil touch thee. In famine he shall redeem thee from death, and in war from the power of the sword. Thou shalt be hid from the scourge of the tongue, neither shalt thou be afraid of destruction when it cometh." "Fear not then the reproach of men, neither be afraid of their revilings: for the moth shall eat them up like a garment, and the worm shall eat them like wool; but my righteousness shall be for ever, and my salvation from generation to generation."[2]

(4.) The last motive to the course of conduct recommended is, that should they, as was not unlikely, notwithstanding their harmlessness and patience, be exposed to suffering for righteousness' sake, for the sake of the righteous cause of their Lord, still they should be blessed. "But and if ye suffer for righteousness' sake, happy are ye." It is great honour to suffer shame and injury in such a cause. The peculiar aids of the good Spirit are secured to such

[1] Scott.   [2] Ps. xci.; Job v. 19-21; Isa. li. 7, 8.

sufferers. "If ye be reproached for the name of Christ, happy are ye; for the Spirit of God and of glory resteth on you."[1] Such sufferings identify those who are exposed to them, as to character and prospects, with the holy men who, in former ages, through much tribulation have entered into the kingdom; and to them are given peculiar, exceeding great, and precious promises, well calculated to make them "count it all joy when brought into such trials." "It is a faithful saying, If we suffer with him, we shall also reign with him." "Blessed are they who are persecuted for righteousness' sake;[2] for theirs is the kingdom of heaven. Blessed are ye when men shall revile you, and persecute you, and shall say all manner of evil against you falsely, for my sake. Rejoice, and be exceeding glad; for great is your reward in heaven: for so persecuted they the prophets which were before you." "Verily I say unto you, There is no man that hath left houses, or brethren, or sisters, or father, or mother, or wife, or children, or lands, for my sake and the gospel's, but he shall receive an hundred-fold now in this time, houses, and brethren, and sisters, and mother, and children, and lands, with persecutions, and in the world to come life everlasting."[3]

And we find that in fact it has been so. Most wonderfully has God enabled his people to magnify his faithfulness, by showing how happy they were in the midst of their sufferings. Oh, how happy were the Apostles Peter and John, after being threatened by the Sanhedrim, when,

[1] 1 Pet. iv. 14.
[2] There can be no reasonable doubt that Peter directly refers to this passage in the Sermon on the Mount. It is as if he had said, 'Your Lord has pronounced you blessed, blessed for this very reason,—not only *although*, but *because*.' The reference is obscured by the use of the word 'happy;' it should have been 'blessed.'
[3] James i. 2; 2 Tim. ii. 11, 12; Matt. v. 10, 12; Mark x. 30.

being "let go, they went to their own company," and "lifted up their voice to God with one accord, and said, Lord, thou art God, who hast made heaven, and earth, and the sea, and all that in them is; who by the mouth of thy servant David hast said, Why did the heathen rage, and the people imagine vain things? The kings of the earth stood up, and the rulers were gathered together against the Lord, and against his Christ. For of a truth, against thy holy child Jesus, whom thou hast anointed, both Herod and Pontius Pilate, with the Gentiles and people of Israel, were gathered together, to do whatsoever thy hand and counsel determined before to be done. And now, Lord, behold their threatenings; and grant unto thy servants, that with all boldness they may speak thy word, by stretching forth thine hand to heal; and that signs and wonders may be done by the name of thy holy child Jesus."[1] Yes, they were happy. "The Spirit of God and glory rested on them." How happy were Paul and Silas, though they had many stripes laid on them, and been thrust into the inner prison, and had their feet made fast in the stocks, when, through the overpowering force of divine joy, they "at midnight prayed and sang praises to God, so that the prisoners heard them!"[2] Many such sufferers have gloried in their tribulation, "knowing that tribulation worketh patience; and patience, experience; and experience, hope: and hope maketh not ashamed; for the love of God was shed abroad in their hearts by the Holy Ghost given to them."[3]

In addition to these particular motives to the conduct recommended, there is the general one, which equally applies to all the duties here enjoined in the paragraph: its tendency to reflect credit on their religion and Lord. But I shall have an opportunity of considering this, after I have

[1] Acts iv. 23-30.   [2] Acts xvi. 25.   [3] Rom. v. 3-5.

illustrated the other injunctions which the apostle gives, respecting the conduct of Christians in reference to their persecutors.

The temper which we have been illustrating and recommending—a forbearing, forgiving disposition—is by worldly men very generally underrated, and even despised, as indicating meanness of spirit, and a want of force of character. But such an estimate is owing to ignorance of this temper, arising in many cases out of a moral incapacity to form a just idea of it. This temper springs from enlightened moral principles; it is consistent with, and indeed expressive of, true magnanimity. A Christian forbears to retaliate on his enemy, not because he fears him, but because he does not fear him. The calmness with which he receives injuries and insults has no more connection with fear, than the tranquillity and silence of Heaven when insulted by the voice of human blasphemy.

"Let the world account it a despicable simplicity; seek you still more of this dovelike spirit, the spirit of meekness and of blessing. It is a poor glory to vie in railings, to contest in the power of resenting wrong: the most abject persons have abundance of that great spirit, as foolish, low-minded persons account it. The true glory of man is to pass by a transgression. This is the noblest victory. And to excite us to aspire after it, we have the highest example. God is our pattern here. Men esteem much more some other virtues which make more show, and trample on love, compassion, and meekness. But though these violets grow low, and are of a dark colour, yet they are of a very sweet and diffusive smell. They are odoriferous graces. And the Lord propounds himself as our example in them. To love them that hate you, and bless them that curse you, is to be truly 'the children of your Father who is in heaven, who maketh his sun to rise on the evil and the good.'

Be you like that sun: however men behave themselves, keep on your course, and let your benignant influence rest on all within your sphere. Jesus Christ, too, sets in himself these things before us. 'Learn of me,' says he, not to heal the sick or to raise the dead, but 'to be meek and lowly in heart;' to forbear and forgive; to repay injury with benefit, execration with benediction. If you are his followers, this must be your way, for 'hereunto ye are called,' and you have much to encourage you to walk in it; for this is the end of it, 'the inheritance of a blessing.'"[1] Of this inheritance of blessings you have already the rich earnests, the sweet foretastes; and yet a little while, when a few more years are come, the possession, in all its inestimable preciousness, in all its immeasurable dimensions, shall be yours for ever. And then will it be made to appear, that "faithful is He who hath called you," that the inheritance was safely laid up for you, and you safely kept for it; and that the afflictions of the present state were light in comparison to the weight of its glory, and but for a moment in comparison of the eternity of its endurance.

§ 2. *Guarding against the fear of man by cultivating the due fear of God.*

I proceed now to the consideration of the second injunction laid on Christians exposed to persecution; and that is, to guard against the undue fear of man, by cultivating the due fear of God. While they were not to provoke their persecutors, they were not to quail before them. They were not to seek to obtain their favour, or escape their displeasure, by denying the truth or neglecting their duty. The injunction is contained in these words, "Be not afraid

[1] Leighton.

of their terror, neither be ye troubled; but sanctify the Lord God in your hearts."[1]

In these words the apostle obviously refers to a passage in the prophecies of Isaiah: "For the Lord spake thus to me with a strong hand, and instructed me, that I should not walk in the way of this people, saying, Say ye not, A confederacy, to all them to whom this people say, A confederacy; neither fear ye their fear, nor be afraid. Sanctify the Lord of hosts himself, and let him be your fear, and let him be your dread; and he shall be for a sanctuary."[2] In this passage, as it stands in the prophet's oracle, there can be little doubt that the fear of the unbelieving king and people of Judah, against which Jehovah warns the prophet and the pious Jews, is the fear which they entertained,—a fear of the allied powers of idolatrous Syria and apostate Israel, leading them to distrust Jehovah, and seek after a forbidden alliance with the idolatrous kingdom of Assyria.[3] Instead of fearing Rezin and Pekah, and trusting in Sennacherib, he calls on them to fear and trust in Him as the Lord of hosts; and to manifest this fear and trust by avoiding whatever he forbade, and doing whatever he commanded, notwithstanding all the hazards to which their obedience might seem to expose them.

In the passage, as quoted and applied by the apostle to the state of the Christians to whom he was writing, the expression "their terror," that is, plainly, the terror of those who persecuted them for righteousness' sake, does not seem so much to refer to the terror which these persons felt, or to the objects exciting that terror, as to the terror which they endeavoured to strike into the victims of their malignity, and the objects which they held out to them to excite that terror. It seems just equivalent to the expression of the Apostle Paul, in his Epistle to the Philippians, "And"

---

[1] See note A. [2] Isa. viii. 11-13. [3] 2 Kings xvi. 5-9.

be "in nothing terrified by your adversaries." Let not the fear of any evil they can inflict on you induce you to deny your Lord, and make shipwreck of your faith.

The slight diversity of meaning in the words as originally employed by Isaiah, and as here employed by Peter, needs neither excite surprise nor give offence. Wherever a passage of Old Testament scripture is quoted in the New, to give evidence to a fact or principle, or to give authority to a precept, it must bear the same sense in the place where it is quoted as in the place where it originally occurs. Were it otherwise, just reason would be afforded for suspecting the inspiration, if not the honesty, of the writer employing the quotation. But when the words of the Old Testament are merely alluded to, employed by the New Testament writer to express his own ideas, the precise force of the words is to be gathered from the connection in which they are introduced; and there is nothing either to wonder at or to be offended by, though the thought clothed in them be somewhat different from that which they were originally employed to express.[1] The judicious application of this principle will free from all difficulty a variety of passages which have afforded plausible ground for cavil to infidels, and occasioned perplexity to inquirers and believers.[2]

Indeed, in the case before us, the object of fear to the Christian's persecutors was substantially the same thing as the object of fear which they held up to the minds of the

---

[1] That there is allusion, not proper quotation, here, will appear more manifest if the true reading be as Lachmann, Theile, Tischendorf, and Tregelles, following the ancient MSS., hold, κύριον δὲ τὸν Χριστόν. If the apostle had not held the proper deity of Jesus Christ among τὰ πεπληροφορημένα (Luke i. 1), it is utterly inconceivable that, even in the way of accommodation, he should apply to him what the prophet says of "*Jehovah* TSEBAOTH."

[2] See note B.

Christians, in order to terrify them into apostasy. They themselves considered the loss of worldly good, the infliction of worldly evil, as the things above all other things to be feared; and therefore, judging of others by themselves, it was by presenting these to the minds of Christians, as the necessary consequence of their maintaining their faith and profession, that they sought to trouble them, and make them "fall from their stedfastness." The loss of property, the loss of reputation, the loss of friends, the loss of ease, the loss of life,—poverty, reproach, imprisonment, torture, death in its most frightful forms,—were presented before the mind of the Christian for the purpose of terrifying him into an abandonment of his Lord, and a compliance with the will of his enemies.

These, no doubt, were altogether very frightful objects. But, says the apostle, "Be not afraid of their fear." Show them that what would dismay them does not dismay you. Show them that no evil, however alarming, which they can threaten or inflict, can so trouble you as to induce you to deny the truth or dishonour the Saviour.

This seems a hard saying, a difficult command; but it is not an unreasonable one. The persons addressed are supposed to be partakers of "like precious faith" with the apostles; to have laid hold of the hope set before them in the gospel, the hope of "an inheritance incorruptible, undefiled, and that fadeth not away, laid up in heaven" for them, to which they are kept by the mighty power of God unto salvation. It is to very little purpose to call on mere professors of Christianity—men who "have a name that they live, but are dead," men who, being strangers to the faith of the gospel, must be strangers to the hope of the gospel—to make sacrifices for the cause of Christ, to remain unterrified amid such alarms, stedfast and immoveable in the face of such danger. But to a genuine Christian it may well be said, "Who art thou, that thou shouldest be afraid of a man that shall die, or the son of a man who shall be made as grass?" Thou needest not fear what man can do to thee. "Should such a one as thou flee?"[1]

Of how little good comparatively can man deprive *him!* How little evil comparatively can he inflict on *him!* How short is the season during which he can deprive him of blessings, or inflict on him sufferings! He may deprive him of his worldly substance; but he "knows in himself that he has in heaven a more enduring substance." He may make him "poor in this world;" but he remains "rich in faith," "rich towards God," an inheritor of "the true riches." He may deprive him of civil liberty; but he cannot take from him the liberty wherewith Christ has made him free. He may enslave his body; but he cannot enthral his spirit. The oppressor may hold

> "His body bound, but knows not what a range
> His spirit takes, unconscious of a chain;
> And that to bind him is a vain attempt,
> Whom God delights in, and in whom he dwells."[2]

He may shut him out from intercourse with his friends; but he cannot deprive him of the guardianship of angels, of the fellowship of God. The Christian needs not fear banishment from one part of the earth to another; for wherever he is, he is a pilgrim and stranger while here: "his citizenship is in heaven." He needs not fear death, but should rather welcome it, for that will convey him home to that better country, his true fatherland. Why should he fear man, "who, after he hath killed the body, has no more that he can do?" Besides, "all things shall work together for his good;" and "his light afflictions, which are but for a moment, will assuredly work out for him a far

[1] Isa. li. 12; Neh. vi. 11.   [2] Cowper, *Task*, 5.

more exceeding and an eternal weight of glory." Well, then, may the address be made to persecuted Christians, "Hearken unto me, ye that know righteousness, the people in whose heart is my law; fear ye not the reproach of men, neither be ye afraid of their revilings: for the moth shall eat them up like a garment, and the worm shall eat them like wool; but my righteousness shall be for ever, and my righteousness shall not be abolished."[1] And well may they reply, "We will not fear though the earth be removed, though the mountains be cast into the midst of the sea; though the waters thereof roar and be troubled, though the mountains shake with the swelling thereof. The Lord of hosts is with us; the God of Jacob is our refuge."[2]

Such, we apprehend, is the meaning of the apostle's first exhortation, though it may be right to state, before going further, that some interpreters have considered this terror of the Christians' persecutors as a phrase to be interpreted in the same way as the expression, "the fear of Isaac,"—an appellation used by Jacob for Jehovah as the object of his worship, the God of his fathers,—"the God of Abraham, and the fear of Isaac;"[3] in which case Christians are cautioned against fearing the false deities of their heathen persecutors, and are called to fear, not them, but the only living and true God, Jehovah. This use of the expression is, however, very rare, and the context seems plainly to lead to the interpretation we have adopted.

The only way in which a Christian can rise to this noble superiority to the fear of man, is by having his mind habitually occupied with God.[4] We are delivered from the undue power of what is seen and temporal, when the

[1] Isa. li. 7, 8.
[2] Luke xii. 4; Rom. viii. 28; 2 Cor. iv. 17; Ps. xlvi. 2, 3, 11.
[3] Gen. xxxi. 42.
[4] Je crains Dieu, cher Abner, et je n'ai point d'autre crainte.—RACINE.

eye of the mind is opened to see Him who is invisible, and that which is eternal. That Christians, exposed to persecution, may be enabled to comply with the injunction, "Be not afraid of their terror, neither be ye troubled," the apostle calls on them to "sanctify the Lord God in their hearts."

The primary idea expressed by the word generally rendered SANCTIFY, both in the Old and New Testaments, seems to be separation, especially separation or setting apart for a religious purpose.[1] Objects of worship, places of worship, instruments of worship, and worshippers, are represented as sanctified and holy; and as, under the Old Testament, things and persons set apart or consecrated were ceremonially pure, and as, under the New Testament dispensation, persons set apart by the Lord for himself, by the "sanctification of the Spirit, and the belief of the truth," are set apart that they may be spiritually pure, "holy and without blame before God," holy comes often to be used as equivalent to free from moral impurity, possessed of spiritual moral excellence; and "sanctify" is used as equivalent to make thus holy, when used to denote what God does to man, or to declare to be holy, or to treat as holy, when used to denote what man does to God. It is not very easy to say with certainty, whether the word is here to be considered as used in its primary or in its secondary signification. In either case the injunction is full of important meaning; and, indeed, the meaning in both cases is substantially the same.

God is, by way of eminence, the "Holy, holy, holy" One, the separate One,[2] "dwelling in the light which is

---

[1] Ἁγιάζω. קדש.

[2] "Holiness in the Scriptures comprehends majesty, as well as holiness in the limited sense. God is holy, inasmuch as he is separated from every created and finite being, and lifted above them, particularly above

inaccessible and full of glory;" not only completely removed from all defect and fault, from all that is weak and all that is wicked, but free from that defectibility which belongs to created being; possessed of an infinity of all the excellences of which we see traces among his creatures; full of being, of intelligence, of power, of righteousness, of benignity; distinguished by eternal, immutable, absolute perfection,—by a grandeur and an excellence, of which the highest conception we can form of grandeur and excellence comes infinitely short. His is being underived; liberty absolute; power unlimited and illimitable; knowledge intimate and infinite; wisdom unsearchable and unerring. And all this "excellent greatness," this "glorious majesty," is beautified by absolute moral perfection. His is a purity before which the holiness of angels waxes dim; and his a benignant tenderness, of which the yearning of a mother's heart is but a feeble figure. He is one who neither can be, purpose, say, nor do, anything that is not infinitely wise, just, and good. This is the holy, separated One.

This is what he is in himself. Let this be what he is to thee. Sanctify him in thy heart. Think of him as the Holy One. Separate from him in thy conceptions all that is imperfect, human, evil, capricious, changeable, malignant. Feel towards him as the Holy One. Let thy heart be, as it were, his temple; and there let Him dwell alone in its inmost shrine, esteemed and loved, feared and trusted, in a manner altogether different from that in which any created being, however excellent, is esteemed and loved, feared and trusted. To give to any created being the kind or degree of esteem, or affection, due to Him, is to profane his name,

sin, which can establish its seat only within the domain of finite beings. Isa. lvii. 15, xl. 25, 26; Hab. iii. 3; Ps. xcix. 3, cxi. 9. The signification of purity, so far from being the only one of קדש, cannot be considered even as the fundamental one."—HENGSTENBERG on Ps. xxii. 3.

to desecrate his temple, by introducing idols there. Treat him as what he is, and do this in thine heart,—not only with thy lips by praise and prayer, not only in external acts of homage and obedience, but in thine heart, with thy whole intelligent, affectionate nature; really, not in profession merely, but worshipping Him who is a spirit, in spirit and in truth.

"Beware of an external, superficial sanctifying of God, for he takes it not so; he will interpret that a profaning of him and of his name. Be not deceived, he is not mocked: he looks through all visages and appearances, in upon the heart; sees how *it* entertains him, and stands affected to him, if it be possessed with reverence and love more than either thy tongue or carriage can express; and if it be not so, all thy seeming worship is but injury, and thy speaking of him is but babbling, be thy discourse never so excellent; and the more thou hast seemed to sanctify God, while thy heart has not been chief in the business, thou shalt not by such service have the less, but the more fear and trouble in the day of trouble, when it comes upon thee. No estate is so far off from true consolation, and so full of horrors, as that of the rotten-hearted hypocrite. His rotten heart is sooner shaken to pieces than any other. If you would have heart's peace in God, you must have this heart-sanctifying of him. It is the heart that is vexed and troubled with fears. The disease is there; and if the prescribed remedy reach not there, it will do no good; but let your hearts sanctify him, and then he will fortify and establish your hearts."[1]

There are two illustrations given of this sanctification of Jehovah, in the passage in the prophecy of Isaiah to which the apostle refers. He who thus sanctifies the Lord of hosts, Jehovah himself, or, as the apostle has it, the Lord

[1] Leighton.

God in his heart, makes him "his fear and his dread," and he finds him "a sanctuary;" and he is thus enabled not to be afraid of the fear of his persecutors, neither to be troubled. He who sanctifies the Lord in his heart, "makes him his fear and his dread;" that is, he fears him, and he supremely fears him. When the truth about the divine character really dwells in the mind, the individual cannot but fear him. A holy awe fills the heart; not the fear that has torment, not the terrible apprehension of God as an omnipotent, omniscient, all-wise enemy, determined to destroy us; but such a veneration of his infinite greatness, and such an esteem of his infinite excellence, as are necessarily accompanied with a deep-seated conviction that his favour is happiness, his displeasure misery, and that it is madness to forfeit his approbation for any conceivable earthly good,—madness to incur his displeasure, in order to avoid any conceivable earthly evil. And this fear is supreme. He makes HIM his fear and dread. HE seems to him the only being in the universe that is "worthy" *thus* "to be feared." Nothing in the wide compass of real or possible being is, in his estimation, so terrible as HIS frown, the loss of his favour, the incurring of his disapprobation.

But he who sanctifies the Lord God in his heart, not only makes him his "fear and dread,"—cherishes a supreme reverence for him; but he finds him "a sanctuary,"— cherishes a supreme confidence in him. He in whose mind God is the object only of fear, has not sanctified God in his heart. He has not "seen God, neither known him;" for it is just as certain that none can know him without trusting in him, as it is that none can know him without fearing him. "They that know his name, put their trust in him."[1] They who really sanctify him in their heart, find in him a sanctuary, a place of refuge and security.

[1] Ps. ix. 10.

They see that He, He alone, is a suitable upmaking portion to their soul; that from his infinite perfection, as manifested in the person and work of his incarnate Son, he is at once able and disposed to make them happy, in all the extent of their nature, up to their largest capacity of enjoyment, during the entire eternity of their being. What more is necessary to make one happy, happy for ever, than infinite power, regulated by infinite wisdom, and influenced by infinite benignity?

The manner in which the sanctification of God in the heart, leading thus to supreme veneration for, supreme confidence in, Him, operates in raising the persecuted Christian above all the power of worldly fears to dishearten him in, or terrify him out of, the onward path of faith, and profession, and obedience, is obvious. Fearing God, the Christian knows no other fear. "That fear, as greatest, overtops and nullifies all lesser fears. The heart possessed by this fear has no room for the others. It resolves the man, in point of duty, what he should and must do: that he must not offend God by any means. It lays down that as indisputable, and so eases the mind of doubtings and debates of that kind, whether I shall comply with the world and deny truth, or neglect duty, or commit sin, to escape reproach or persecution." He who, sanctifying God in his heart, has made him his fear and his dread, sees very clearly, feels very strongly, that he "ought to obey God rather than man;" and that the question is an equally clear one, whether viewed as a question of duty or a question of interest. "It seems to him immeasurably best to retain His favour, though, by taking the course that is necessary to secure this, he should displease the most respected and considerable person he knows. He holds it as absolutely certain that it is better, in every view of the case, to choose the universal and highest displeasure of the world for ever, than his smallest disapprobation, even for a moment. One thing appears to him as self-evident, that the only indispensable necessity to him is to cleave to God, and obey him."[1]

We have some striking instances of the power of the fear of God to subdue, to annihilate the fear of man, recorded in Scripture. When Moses' parents by faith sanctified Jehovah in their heart, making him their "fear and dread," they at all hazards disobeyed the wicked edict requiring them to murder their son, and "were not afraid of the king's commandment;" and their illustrious son, under the influence of the same principle, "forsook Egypt, not fearing the wrath of the king."[2] The fear of God annihilated in the minds of the three Hebrew youths the fear of the fury of the Babylonian tyrant, and of the flames of his fiery furnace; and in the mind of Daniel, the fear of the loss of high station, and all the horrors of the den of lions.[3] It enabled the Christian apostles to set at nought all the threats of their persecutors. It enabled their and our Lord, with all the shame and agony of the cross full in his view, to confess the truth, and "finish the work which the Father had given him to do." This holy fear, with its kindred holy confidence, led him to "give his back to the smiters, and his cheeks to them that plucked off the hair; to hide not his face from shame and spitting. For the Lord God," says he, "will help me; therefore shall I not be confounded: therefore have I set my face like a flint, and I know that I shall not be ashamed. He is near that justifieth me; who will contend with me? let us stand together: who is mine adversary? let him come near to me. Behold, the Lord God will help me; who is he that shall condemn me? lo, they shall wax old as doth a garment; the moth shall eat them up."[4] And he calls on all his

[1] Leighton. [2] Heb. xi. 23, 27. [3] Dan. iii. 6. [4] Isa. l. 7-9.

followers to follow in his steps: when exposed to suffering, to fear the Lord, to trust in the name of the Lord, and stay upon his God. This fear leads directly to this conclusion, and enables the Christian to hold it fast at all hazards: 'It is not necessary to have the favour of the world; but it is necessary to have the favour of God: it is not necessary that I should live in comfort, nor indeed that I should live at all; but it is necessary that I hold fast the truth, that I should obey God, that I should honour HIM in life and in death.'

That confidence in God, which, equally with fear of him, is the result of sanctifying him in the heart, naturally also raises the persecuted Christian above the fear of man. He who knows God, and who believes that he has said, "I will never leave thee, I will never forsake thee," may boldly say, will boldly say, "The Lord is my helper, I will not fear what man can do to me;" "God is my refuge and my strength, a very present help in trouble: therefore I will not fear;" "God is my rock and my salvation; he is my defence; I shall not be moved. In him is my salvation and my glory: the rock of my strength, and my refuge, is in God. Trust in him at all times; ye people, pour out your hearts before him: God is a refuge for us. Surely men of low degree are vanity, and men of high degree a lie: to be laid in the balance, they are altogether lighter than vanity. God hath spoken once; twice have I heard this, that power belongeth to God. Also to thee, O Lord, belongeth mercy."[1] How reasonable, then, is it to trust in him! How unreasonable to fear them; and how powerfully is trust in him calculated to put down fear of them![2]

Thus have I endeavoured shortly to illustrate the second injunction given by the apostle to Christians as to their so conducting themselves under persecution, as that even their

[1] Ps. lxii. 1, 2, 5-12.   [2] See note C.

enemies might be compelled to honour both them and their religion: "Be not afraid of their terror, but sanctify the Lord in your hearts."

Sanctifying the Lord in the heart, and making him our fear and our confidence, is the duty of the Christian, not only when exposed to persecution for righteousness' sake, but at all times and in all circumstances; and it is the true and effectual antidote to all the fears and troubles of whatever kind that he is exposed to in the present state. The Christian is often harassed with fears in reference to his external circumstances. Let him sanctify the Lord in his heart; realize the truth respecting Him; fear Him; trust in Him; and he will thus learn to "be careful," that is, anxious, "about nothing."[1] When David sanctified God in his heart, he was delivered from all his fears; and this is his advice and encouragement to all who, like him, are involved in such perplexities, to fear and trust in the Lord: "O fear the Lord, all ye his saints: for there is no want to them who fear him. The young lions may lack, and suffer hunger; but they that seek the Lord shall not want any good thing. The righteous cry, and the Lord heareth, and delivers them out of all their troubles. The Lord redeemeth the soul of his servants; and none that trust in him shall be desolate."[2]

But the Christian is liable to fears and perplexities of a more painful kind still. The troubles of remorse, the fears of hell, sometimes agitate him. "The sorrows of death compass him; the pains of hell get hold of him. He has found trouble and sorrow." He feels as if his unseen foes were about to triumph over him, and that continued resistance is hopeless. But let him sanctify the Lord in his heart. Let him so realize the truth about HIM, as, while trembling at his word and standing in awe of his judgments, he at

[1] Phil. iv. 6. [2] Ps. xxxiv. 9, 10, 17, 22.

the same time trusts in his mercy and hopes in his promise; and he will be reassured and comforted. Let him contemplate at once the awful and amiable glories of his character as the God who cannot clear the guilty, and yet, through the propitiation he has set forth in the blood of his Son, pardons iniquity, transgression, and sin, blotting them out for his own sake as " a just God and a Saviour," "just, and the justifier of him who believeth in Jesus;"[1] and he will find security and peace amid all the fightings without and the fears within.

The way to have true rest in the heart is to have God there, through the knowledge and faith of the truth respecting him; and to sanctify him there, to cherish towards him those affections of supreme reverence and confidence to which he is entitled.

> " He is the source and centre of all minds,
> Their only point of rest.
> From him departing, they are lost, and rove
> At random, without honour, hope, or peace."[2]

You, then, who would " dwell at ease, and be quiet from the fear of evil," seek to have the Lord God in your heart; seek to sanctify him there, by making him at once your fear and confidence.

It is thus that the sinner as well as the saint is to get rid of his fears. We say to the sinner, as well as to the saint, " Acquaint thyself with God, and be at peace; thereby good shall come to thee."[3] Know that his nature as well as his name is holy love. Let both these letters of his name be impressed on your heart—holiness and grace; and learn so to fear his holiness and justice and power as to cease to oppose him, under a deep conviction that it is equally wicked and unwise, criminal and ruinous. O learn

---

[1] Ps. cxvi. 3; Isa. xlv. 21; Rom. iii. 26.
[2] Cowper.   [3] Job xxii. 21.

so to trust his grace and faithfulness, as gladly and gratefully to receive what, in the word of the truth of the gospel, he sincerely and urgently offers thee, sinner as thou art—a free forgiveness, a full salvation.

To all, then, whether saint or sinner, we proclaim as the only means of obtaining true composure of spirit and permanent peace in this region where there is so much to terrify and trouble, "Sanctify the Lord in your heart; let him be your fear and dread, and he will be to you a sanctuary." Happy those who, by complying with the command, enter into peace. But oh! what will become of those who refuse this divine call, who set at nought this divine counsel? What will become of them "when their fear cometh as desolation, and their destruction as a fire that burneth; when distress and anguish come upon them?" "*Now* is the accepted time; *now* is the day of salvation." *Then* will be the time of reckoning; *then* will be the day of vengeance. Then there can be no peace to these wicked ones. Then will be at once the realization of their worst fears; and fears of greater evils still, the prospect of eternally accumulating misery. Sinner, "if thou be wise, thou shalt be wise for thyself; but if thou scornest, thou alone shalt bear it."[1]

§ 3. *Readiness at all times to give an answer to every one that asketh them a reason of the hope that is in them.*

The third injunction given to Christians, as exposed to persecution, is, to "be always ready to give an answer, to every one who should ask them a reason of the hope that was in them, with meekness and fear."

The inspired injunction obviously takes for granted that Christians are distinguished by the possession of a peculiar hope—they have "a hope in them;" that this hope is not a groundless one—a reason can be given for it, it can be

[1] Prov. ix. 12.

defended; that this hope ought not, and cannot, be concealed; and that for this hope Christians may be, are likely to be, called on to give an account;—and it calls on Christians, in these circumstances, to give an answer to every one that asks them a reason of their hope: in other words, to state and defend the grounds of their hope; to be always prepared to do this; and finally, to do this, whenever it is done, with meekness and fear. These are, as it were, the elementary parts into which the injunction naturally resolves itself, and I shall briefly direct your attention to them in their order.

Christians are distinguished by the possession of a peculiar hope. They have a hope in them. It is not the possession of hope generally that distinguishes Christians from the rest of mankind; for it would not be easy to fix on any characteristic that more certainly belongs to the whole race, than the capacity and disposition to anticipate with desire and delight future good. Unbelieving men are indeed said to "have no hope," but it is the same way in which they are said to be "without God."[1] They have hopes many, as they have gods many; though strangers to the true God, and to the hope which maketh not ashamed. Human suffering would be often intolerable, were it not for the hope of deliverance. There is truth as well as beauty in the adage, "If it were not for hope, the heart would break;" and, even when happiest, it will be found that a very considerable portion of man's enjoyment arises, not from what he has, but from what he hopes for.

> "Hope springs eternal in the human breast;
> Man never is, but always to be blest."[2]

But as, while all men believe as well as the Christian, he has his peculiar belief, which distinguishes him from all

[1] Eph. ii. 12.   [2] Pope.

other men; so, while all men hope, the Christian has his peculiar hope, which equally distinguishes him from all other men,—a hope of which he was once destitute, and of which he obtained possession, when, by the faith of the truth, he became a Christian in the only true and proper sense of that word.[1]

That hope thus obtained, is variously described in the New Testament. It is termed "the hope of salvation;" "the hope of eternal life;" "the hope of the glory of God;" "the hope of the righteousness," or justification, "by faith."[2] Each of these terms is full of meaning.

It is "the hope of salvation;" that is, of deliverance from evil, both physical and moral, in all its forms and degrees, for ever. It is "the hope of eternal life;" that is, not merely of immortal existence, but of an eternity of what constitutes the life of life, true happiness,—a happiness suited to all our various capacities of enjoyment, filling these capacities to an overflow,—a happiness pervading the whole nature throughout unending duration.

It is "the hope of the glory of God." The glory of God in this expression seems equivalent to the approbation of God. Men have sinned, and lost God's approbation. They are not, they cannot be, the objects of his approbation. They are the objects of his judicial displeasure, of his deep moral disapprobation. Little as sinful men think of it, this is the sum and substance of their misery; and the removal of this, and restoration to his favour, are at once absolutely necessary and completely sufficient to make them happy. The Christian's hope is a hope that he shall ultimately be just what God would have him to be, perfectly holy, perfectly happy, in intimate relation, in complete conformity, to God; that the eye of his Father in heaven

---

[1] Eph. i. 12, 13. Trusted; margin, hoped.
[2] 1 Thess. v. 8; Tit. iii. 7; Rom. v. 2; Gal. v. 5.

shall yet rest on him with entire moral complacency, and his word pronounce him, as a part of his completed new creation, very good.

It is "the hope of the righteousness," or justification, "by faith;" that is, not the hope of obtaining justification by faith, for justification by faith is, as it were, the fundamental blessing of Christianity, not a benefit to be conferred at some future period. It is something that the Christian possesses already. It is not one of the blessings of salvation of which the apostle speaks, when he says, "We are saved by hope;" that is, our salvation is yet future—ours, not in possession, though in sure prospect. The hope of the justification by faith is the hope that grows out of justification by faith; the hope which only the justified by faith can cherish. "Being justified by faith, we have peace with God through our Lord Jesus Christ; by whom also we have access by faith to this grace wherein we stand, and rejoice in hope of the glory of God."[1]

Such are some of the scriptural designations of this hope. Let us now inquire a little more particularly what are its objects?

The Christian is "confident that he who has begun the good work" in him, "will perform it until the day of Jesus Christ;" that he will "preserve him from every evil work, unto his heavenly kingdom;" that he will "make his grace sufficient for him;" that he will "strengthen him with all might, unto all patience and long-suffering, with joyfulness;" that he will "supply all his need according to his glorious riches;" that he will "never leave him, never forsake him;" that he will make "all things work together for his good," and even his afflictions, however severe and long-continued, to "work out for him a far more exceeding and eternal weight of glory." He hopes that "Christ will

[1] Rom. v. 1, 2.

be magnified in his body, whether by life or by death."[1] And he has hope in death, hope after death. He hopes that, when his spirit becomes "absent from the body," it will become "present with the Lord;" being with him where he is, and, beholding and sharing his glory, mingling with "the innumerable company of angels, and with the spirits of the just made perfect;" being "before the throne of God, and serving him day and night in his temple; while he who sits on the throne dwells among them, and they hunger no more, neither thirst any more, neither does the sun light on them, nor any heat; for the Lamb, who is in the midst of the throne, shall feed them, and lead them to fountains of living waters; and God shall wipe away all tears from their eyes."[2] His "flesh also rests in hope." His hope is the hope of the resurrection to life; "the blessed hope of the glorious appearing of our Lord Jesus Christ." He looks for Him from heaven, "to change his vile body, and fashion it like unto his own glorious body." He hopes that "this corruptible shall put on incorruption, this mortal shall put on immortality; that what is sown in corruption, shall be raised in incorruption; what is sown in dishonour, shall be raised in glory; what is sown in weakness, shall be raised in power; what is sown a natural body, shall be raised a spiritual body." He is looking for Him to come "the second time without sin unto salvation;" and his hope is, that "when He shall appear, he shall appear with Him in glory;" being "like Him, seeing Him as He is." He is hoping for this "manifestation of the sons of God,"—this "adoption, the redemption of the body;" and his final hope is that, body and soul, "he shall ever be with the Lord."[3]

---

[1] Phil. i. 6, iii. 19; Col. i. 11; Heb. xiii. 5; Rom. viii. 28; 2 Cor. iv. 17.
[2] 2 Cor. v. 6-8; John xvii. 24; Heb. xii. 22, 23; Rev. vii. 15-17.
[3] Ps. xvi. 9; Tit. ii. 13; Phil. iii. 21; 1 Cor. xv. 42-44, 53; Heb. ix. 28; 1 John iii. 2; Rom. viii. 19, 23; 1 Thess. iv. 17.

Such is the hope of the Christian with regard to himself; and he cherishes the same hope in reference to all his brethren in Christ. He hopes that Christ, who loved the Church, will, after having purified her by the washing of water through the word, "present her to himself" as a bride adorned for her husband, "a glorious Church, not having spot or wrinkle, or any such thing." He hopes for a "gathering together" of all the faithful at the coming of the Lord; he hopes that when the Lord descends from heaven, all the dead in Christ shall rise, all the living in Christ shall be changed, and that they shall "together be caught up in the clouds, to meet the Lord in the air," and shall "together be made perfect."[1]

The Christian, too, has characteristic hopes concerning the cause and kingdom of his Lord. He hopes for its ultimate triumph over all its opposers, all the powers of darkness, all the forms of evil, ignorance, error, superstition, fanaticism, idolatry, in all their endless diversities of false principles and depraved dispositions, which counterwork its benignant tendencies, and have hitherto rendered its progress so slow, and its influence so limited. He hopes for a period when the idols shall be utterly abolished, when "the earth shall be filled with the knowledge of the Lord," when "the kingdoms of this world shall become the kingdom of our Lord and of his Christ," when "men shall be blessed in Him, and all nations call him blessed."[2] Such is the Christian's hope.

And this hope is not groundless; it is no airy dream, no uncertain probability. It rests on the power and wisdom and faithfulness and benignity of God, pledged in a plain, well-accredited revelation of his will. It has come to him

---

[1] Eph. v. 25-27; 2 Thess. ii. 1; 1 Thess. iv. 16, 17; Heb. xi. 40. Οὗτοι πάντες—μὴ χωρὶς ἡμῶν.

[2] Isa. xi. 9; Rev. xi. 15; Ps. lxxii. 17.

by "the word of the truth of the gospel,"[1] to understand and believe and love which, his mind and heart have been opened by the effectual working of the good Spirit. He has formed these expectations not in consequence of following cunningly devised fables, but in consequence of believing that word, which brought along with it powerful demonstration that it was "not the word of man, but, as it is in truth, the word of God, which worketh effectually in them believing it;"[2] tranquillizing the mind, pacifying the conscience, purifying the heart, transforming the character.[3] Thus he knows whom he has believed, and in whom he hopes. His hope is in God. Jehovah is the hope of his people. They hope in his mercy; they hope in his word. "Our Lord Jesus himself, and God, even our Father, who hath loved us, hath given us everlasting consolation, and good hope through grace."[4]

These hopes dwell in the heart of the Christian. There seems emphasis in the expression, "the hope that is in you." It has not merely been "set before" you; it has been embraced by you. It is not a mere professed hope; it is a real hope, a living, not a dead hope.

But though it dwells in the heart, it does not, it should not, it cannot, remain concealed. From its very nature, it must manifest itself both in words and in actions: "Out of the abundance of the heart the mouth speaketh." "Knowing," says the apostle, referring to one leading object of the Christian hope, "that he who raised up the Lord Jesus shall raise up us also by Jesus, and shall present us with

---

[1] Col. i. 5.   [2] 1 Thess. ii. 13.

[3] "It is certain there is no hope without some antecedent belief that the thing hoped for may come to pass; and the strength and stedfastness of our hope is ever proportioned to the measure of our faith."—BENTLEY.

[4] 2 Thess. ii. 16.

you; we also believe, and therefore speak." Christians cannot but speak of the things which they hope for; and "every one who hath this hope in Him purifieth himself, even as He is pure," whom they are hoping to see, and to whom they are hoping to be conformed when he appears.[1] No; Christian hope cannot be concealed. What fills the mind to an overflow, must become manifest. Even the Old Testament believers " declared plainly that they were seeking a country, and confessed that they were strangers and pilgrims on the earth." [2]

The profession of hope on the part of the Christian is, moreover, matter of positive obligation. It is expressly commanded. It is necessarily implied in the duty of confessing Christ, and is requisite to our performance of our highest duties to our fellow-men. "Let us hold fast the profession of our hope" (hope, not faith, is the genuine reading), says the apostle, " without wavering, for he is faithful that hath promised;"[3] and he assures us that this is the proof of our belonging to " the house," the family of Christ, that " we hold fast the confidence "—that is, the free, fearless avowal of—" and the rejoicing of," the glorying in, "the hope of the gospel, firm to the end." [4] The Christian acts very unworthily who behaves as if he was ashamed of his hope—ashamed of a hope which will never make ashamed any who really cherish it. The avowal of the Christian's hope is necessarily implied in that confession of the mouth which the apostle represents as, equally with faith in the heart, requisite in order to salvation. A Christian cannot declare his faith without avowing his hope; and he cannot neglect the declaration of his faith without exposing himself to that tremendous denunciation: "Whosoever shall deny me before men, him will I deny before

---

[1] 2 Cor. iv. 13, 14; 1 John iii. 3.   [2] Heb. xi. 13, 14.
[3] Heb. x. 23.   [4] Heb. iii. 6. Τὴν παῤῥησίαν καὶ τὸ καύχημα τῆς ἐλπίδος.

my Father who is in heaven. He that is ashamed of me, and of my words, before this adulterous and sinful generation, of him shall the Son of man be ashamed, when he cometh in the glory of his Father with the holy angels."[1]

It has been justly said, "To all who deliberately hold the truth captive, we are bound to declare that they do not possess the truth, or rather that the truth does not possess them—does not dwell in them richly. Religious conviction, which refuses to express itself, is disowned by that very act."

Those doctrines which embody the Christian's hope are the saving truth. That every one who is in possession of that truth should make it known to others, is the first duty which the second great commandment of the law, "Thou shalt love thy neighbour as thyself," binds on the conscience. In presenting it to their belief, he must avow his own; and he cannot, as we have seen, avow his faith without professing his hope. "We are debtors of religious truth to our brethren," says one of the greatest writers of our age, "so soon as we ourselves become possessed of it;" "we are debtors in the strictest sense of the term, for, properly speaking, the truth is not the exclusive property of any one. Every good which may be communicated by its possessor without impoverishing himself, cannot remain exclusively his own. If this proposition be not true, morality falls to the ground. How much more does this hold good of a blessing which is multiplied by division, of a spring which becomes more abundant as it pours out its waters?"[2] The hope of the gospel is necessary to true comfort here, to perfect happiness hereafter. I am bound then to communicate, so far as man can do it, this hope to those who are destitute of it. How can I do this but by telling them what I hope for, and why I hope for it; showing them how that hope became mine, and how it may become theirs?

[1] Matt. x. 33; Luke xii. 8.   [2] Vinet.

For the Christian to keep his hope to himself, were it possible, would be to deny the bread of life to those who are perishing of hunger. Almost every denial may find some excuse but this. We are not bound to give bread to all men in all circumstances; but we do owe to all men, in all circumstances, the communication of saving truth.

Even though the Christian were disposed to conceal his hope, he would find it difficult to do so; for he is likely, as the apostle intimates, to be called to give an account of it: a reason of his hope is likely to be demanded of him. Such inquiries may originate in various and opposite causes. Some, who are honestly inquiring after truth and happiness, having discovered that the hopes which the world offers to its votaries are liable to be disappointed, and even when realized cannot confer true permanent enjoyment, may ask a reason of the hope that is in the Christian, that they may see whether it meets the exigencies of their case, and, if it does so, that they may find how they may become partakers of it; others may make such inquiries merely for the purpose of cavilling at and casting ridicule on the Christian and his hope; and others, armed with civil power, may call him in question for his hope and faith, and for his conduct as influenced by this hope and faith. In the primitive age, and in other ages too, the faith and hope of the gospel have often led their possessors to refuse compliance with what custom and law required, and to follow certain courses which custom and law condemned and proscribed; and Christians have, in consequence of this, often been " called before governors and kings, magistrates and powers," as their Lord forewarned them, to give an account of that hope which distinguished them from those among whom they lived, and of the grounds on which it rested. When the connection of the passage is carefully attended to, it can scarcely be doubted that it is to this last species of inquisition into the nature and ground of the Christian's hope that the apostle directly refers.

Whatever may be the motives of the inquirers, it is the duty of the Christian, in ordinary circumstances, "to give an answer to every one who asketh him a reason of the hope that is in him." What the apostle calls on Christians to do, is to *defend* their hope to those who called on them to give an account of it, for that is the force of the word rendered *answer:*[1] apology, in the sense in which the word is used in reference to the Apologies of the Fathers for Christianity, the publication of which was indeed just a specimen of obedience to the apostle's injunction,—a defence of the faith and hope of the gospel, by a statement of their grounds to those Roman magistrates who persecuted them. Every Christian, when called on to give an account of his hope, is to defend it. He is to do this, first, by distinctly stating what it is; by giving a plain account of what are the objects of his hope: and this of itself, if candidly listened to, will go far to answer all the purposes of defence. But he must do more than this: he must be ready to show, that what he hopes for is really promised in the Scriptures, and that these Scriptures are indeed "given by inspiration of God,"—an infallible and authoritative revelation of the divine mind and will, for the regulation of the religious sentiments and conduct of mankind, and therefore a solid foundation for his hope. He must show that his hope is no mere imagination, but is founded on the most certain truth; and that in performing the duties, making the sacrifices, cherishing the expectations, which naturally flow from its admission, he is acting a reasonable, the only reasonable part, and that to abandon his hope, or to do anything inconsistent with it, were to act the part of a fool and a madman. And the Christian is to do this, not only where it

[1] Ἀπολογία.

may be done without inconvenience or hazard, but in the face of the greatest dangers, though sure to draw down on himself ridicule, scorn, contumely, torture, death. "Consequences should be accounted for nought in the discharge of this duty, which is of an absolute nature; or, if considered at all, should be regarded only as motives and additional inducements to its fulfilment."[1]

There are, however, cases in which a formal defence of the Christian's hope, even when he is called in question for it, could serve no good purpose. The command of our Lord is not superseded by, for it is not inconsistent with, that of his apostle: "Give not that which is holy to the dogs, neither cast your pearls before swine, lest they trample them under their feet, and turn again to rend you."[2] It has been justly observed, "that the truth is not to be scattered at random like contemptible dust: it is a pearl which must not be exposed to be trodden under foot by the profane. To protect it by an expressive silence, is sometimes the only way we can testify our own respect for it, or conciliate that of others. He who cannot be silent respecting it, under certain circumstances, does not sufficiently respect it. Silence is on some occasions the only homage truth expects from us. This silence has nothing in common with dissimulation; it involves no connivance with the enemies of truth; it has no other object than to protect it from needless outrage. This silence, in a majority of instances, is a language; and when, in the conduct of those who maintain it, everything is consistent with it, the truth loses nothing by being suppressed. Or, to speak more correctly, it is not suppressed: it is vividly, though silently, pointed out; its dignity and importance are placed in relief; and the respect which occasioned this silence, itself imposes silence on the witnesses of its manifestation."[3] The greatest

[1] Vinet.   [2] Matt. vii. 6.   [3] Vinet.

of all witnesses to the truth, who, in delivering his testimony, set his face as a flint, not fearing the cross, despising the shame, maintained on some occasions a dignified silence even when questioned; but it was only where the truth had already been declared by Him, and when a renewed declaration of it could have served no good purpose. His object was not to shelter himself, but the truth, from unnecessary insults. Generally, his conduct corresponded with the prophetic oracle concerning him: "I have preached righteousness in the great congregation: lo, I have not refrained my lips, O Lord, thou knowest. I have not hid thy righteousness within my heart; I have declared thy faithfulness and thy salvation: I have not concealed thy loving-kindness and thy truth from the great congregation."[1]

But though Christians may not be required in every case to give an answer, even when questioned, respecting their hope, they must always hold themselves "ready" to do so when called on. To be "ready," is to be prepared, when called on, to state and defend the Christian hope. For this purpose it is necessary that the Christian should be constantly giving all diligence towards maintaining the full assurance of hope in his own heart; that he should be familiarly acquainted with the objects of his hope, as these are stated in the Holy Scriptures; and with the manner, too, in which those things, which it would seem at first sight to be folly and presumption in man to hope for, have become the object, the reasonable object, of his hope, and may become the reasonable object of the hope of every man who, like him, believes in Jesus. He must be able to show how he once cherished false hopes; and how he was made ashamed of these hopes; and how he was, when destitute of all hope, led, in the faith of the truth of the

[1] Ps. xl. 9, 10.

gospel, to lay hold on the hope there set before him. He must be able to show how the free grace of God, manifested in a consistency with his righteousness, through the mediation of his Son Jesus Christ, when apprehended in the statements and promises of the gospel, lays a solid foundation for all the great and glorious expectations which he entertains. And as such a statement can be satisfactory only on the supposition that the Bible is indeed a divine revelation, he must be prepared to show, that in giving credit to its declarations, and grounding his hope on them, he has acted a reasonable part; because it is indeed given by the inspiration of that God who cannot lie, who cannot be deceived, and who cannot deceive.

The importance of an accurate and extensive knowledge of the evidence of Christianity can scarcely be overrated, if it be not substituted in the place of an experimental knowledge of Christianity itself. It is of vital importance to the individual Christian's peace and improvement. It is intimately connected with the vigour of his graces and the abundance of his consolations. I do not say that a man is not a Christian who cannot give a distinct account of the evidence of the divinity of the religion which he professes to believe; but in proportion to the imperfection and indistinctness of his views on this subject, will be the deficiency and insecurity of his attainments, both in holiness and in comfort. These are weighty words of Richard Baxter: "I take it to be the greatest cause of coldness in duty, weakness in grace, boldness in sinning, and unwillingness to die, that our faith in the divine authority of the Scriptures is either unsound or infirm. Few Christians among us have anything better than an implicit faith on this point. They have received it by tradition. Godly ministers and Christians tell them so: it is impious to doubt it, and therefore they believe it. And this worm lying at the root, causeth the languishing and decaying of the whole. Faith in the verity of the Scriptures would be an exceeding help to the joy of the saints. For myself," adds that wonderful man, " if my faith in this point had no imperfection, if I did as verily believe the glory to come as I do believe that the sun will rise again when it is set, oh, how would it raise my desires and my joys! What haste would I make! How serious should I be! How should I trample on these earthly vanities, and even forget the things below! How restless should I be till I was assured of the heavenly rest; and then how restless till I did possess it! How should I delight in the thoughts of death, and my heart leap at the tidings of his approach!"

If such a knowledge of the evidences of revelation be of importance to the healthy state of the Christian life generally, it is absolutely necessary to the discharge of that particular function of it of which we are speaking. How can a Christian, with very limited and confused ideas on this subject, give a reason for his hope, or defend it? It is, then, of great importance that Christians should not satisfy themselves with any confidence or persuasion unless they have such clear and rational grounds thereof, as do not only convince themselves, but admit of being stated in a distinct manner to others.

If we would " be ready to give an answer to every one that asketh us a reason of the hope that is in us," we must attend to the wise man's declaration, " The heart of the wise *studieth* to answer."[1] We must give ourselves to reading, we must meditate on these things, and thus lay up in store what we may turn to account when called on to state and defend our hope. To be ready for the discharge of this duty, we must further habitually seek and cherish the influence of the good Spirit, who is the author of faith and

[1] Prov. xv. 28.

hope; who takes the things of Christ and shows them to us; who brings truth seasonably to remembrance; and who was "a mouth and wisdom" to the primitive Christians, when called to state and defend their hope. He who has his mind full of truth and its evidence, and his heart filled with humble, confiding dependence on the teaching and guidance of the good Spirit; he whose habitual prayer is, "Uphold me according to thy word, and let me not be ashamed of my hope;"[1] he, he alone, is "always ready" to discharge the duty here enjoined in a manner creditable to his religion, calculated to convince the candid, and to "put to silence the ignorance of foolish men." Such a man, if called to it, will ." speak of God's testimonies before kings, and not be ashamed."[2]

It only remains that a word or two be said respecting the manner in which this duty to our religion and its Author, and to our fellow-men, is to be performed. Christians are to "give an answer to those who ask them a reason of the faith that is in them with meekness and fear."[3]

The truth is to be stated and defended in its own spirit— the spirit not only "of power," but "of love;" not only of a "sound mind," but of a tender heart. The conduct of those who call them to give an account of their faith may be, often has been, most unreasonable and provoking. But the Christian confessor must possess his soul in patience. "The servant of the Lord must not strive, but in meekness instruct those who oppose themselves," "showing all meekness to all men."[4] "He must not bluster and fly into

---

[1] Ps. cxix. 116.   [2] Ps. cxix. 46.

[3] "*Meekness* towards those who give occasions for entering into the defence of our religion ; and *fear*, not of them, but of God—that reverential fear which the nature of religion requires, and which is so far from being inconsistent with, that it will inspire proper courage towards men."—BISHOP BUTLER: *Charge.*

[4] 2 Tim. ii. 25 ; Tit. iii. 2.

invectives, because he has the better of it, against any man who questions him of his hope, as some think themselves authorized to use rough speech because they plead for truth. On the contrary, so much the rather should he study meekness for the glory and advantage of the truth. It needs not the service of passion; yea, nothing so disserves it as passion when set to serve it. The spirit of truth is withal the spirit of meekness—the dove that rested on that great champion of truth, who is truth itself; and this spirit is from him derived to the lovers of truth, and they ought to seek the participation of it. Imprudence, want of meekness, rashness, or harshness, makes some kind of Christians lose much of their labour in speaking for religion, and drives those further off whom they would draw into it."[1]

The pleader for religion cannot be too earnest; but it must be the earnestness of conviction as to the truth, the earnestness of compassion as to those who oppose it. As an able writer says, "His voice may well falter from emotion; but it must not be the emotion of anger. Energy may give emphasis to his words, and cause them to vibrate, but passion never."[2]

This duty is to be performed not only with meekness, but "with fear;" that is not, as some have supposed, with due respect to the heathen magistrates before whom Christians were called to defend their hope; but with religious reverence, with holy fear, with a sense of the infinite importance of the subject, and its close connection with the eternal interests both of those who question and of him who answers. "Divine things ought never to be spoken in a light, perfunctory way, but with a reverent, grave temper of spirit; and for this reason some choice should be made (when we have it in our power) of time and persons. The confidence that is in this hope makes the believer not fear

[1] Leighton.   [2] Vinet.

men to whom he answers; but still he fears God, for whom he answers, and whose interest is chief in the things he speaks of. The soul that has the deepest sense of spiritual things, and knowledge of God, is most afraid to miscarry in speaking of him; most tender and wary how to acquit itself when engaged to speak of and for God."[1] There is something very shocking in an irreverent defence of the solemn verities of the Christian revelation. It almost necessarily induces a suspicion of the depth, if not of the reality, of the conviction of the apologist. The man who regards as real the glorious objects of the Christian hope, must be filled with a heartfelt joy and a solemn awe, both equally incompatible with every approach to irreverence. He will rejoice, but he will " rejoice with trembling."

Thus have I endeavoured briefly to illustrate this interesting passage. Of the mode of conduct which it recommends, we have a fine specimen in the conduct of the Apostles Peter and John before the Jewish Sanhedrim, as recorded in the fourth chapter of the Acts of the Apostles, and of the Apostle Paul in his defence of himself before Festus and King Agrippa. What clear statements, what powerful reasons, what a readiness in giving them, what meekness, what fear, characterize their speeches! How well fitted were they to compel respect both for the cause and its advocates, even from the most prejudiced judges!

I cannot conclude this part of the discourse without calling on all my hearers seriously to examine whether they have any hope in them in reference to eternity; and whether the hope they have in them be the hope of the gospel. There are not a few who have no hope with regard to eternity. They have no faith, no solid belief, on such subjects, and therefore they can have no hope. Others

[1] Leighton.

have a kind of faith as to eternity, of which they would very willingly get rid; but it is a faith which produces, not the hope which gives peace, but the fear that has torment. Others have hope, it may be strong hope; but they can give no satisfactory reason for their hope. It rests on no solid basis, but on false views of God and of themselves. If you have no hope for eternity, be assured you have not believed the gospel; and if your hope rests on anything but the free grace of God, manifested in consistency with his justice in the atonement of Christ, apprehended by you in the faith of the truth of the gospel, be assured that that hope will fail you in the day of trial, and make you "ashamed and confounded, world without end."

How sad is it to think that so many are without hope, so many without good hope; while there is hope, good hope, set before every sinner to whom the gospel comes! "This is a faithful saying, that God is in Christ reconciling the world to himself. The blood of Jesus Christ, God's Son, cleanseth us from all sin. He came to save sinners, even the chief. He is able to save to the uttermost all coming to God by him. Whosoever believeth in him shall not perish, but shall have everlasting life." This is the very truth most sure. This great salvation was spoken to us by the Son of God, and has been confirmed to us by them who heard him; and God has given witness to it by divers signs, and miracles, and gifts of the Holy Ghost, according to his own will, and especially by raising Christ from the dead, and giving him glory, that our faith and hope might be in him.[1]

Let those who, through the faith of this truth, have hope, good hope, in them, prove its reality by purifying themselves as he in whom they hope is pure; and let them seek

[1] 1 Tim. i. 15; 2 Cor. v. 19; 1 John i. 7; Heb. vii. 25; John iii. 16; Heb. ii. 4; 1 Pet. i. 21.

to grow in hope that they may grow in holiness; and seek to grow in holiness that they may grow in hope; and seek to grow in faith that they may grow both in hope and holiness. Let them " show all diligence, to the full assurance of hope to the end: that they be not slothful, but followers of them who through faith and patience inherit the promises." Let them prove themselves to be the family of Christ, by " holding fast the confidence and rejoicing of their hope stedfast to the end." Let them hold forth the word of life, the ground of their hope, in a meek and reverent confession of the truth, and attest and adorn that confession by " a conversation becoming the gospel"—a holy, happy, useful life. Let them " not cast away their confidence, which has great recompense of reward." Let them persevere in faith and hope and holiness; that, " after having done the will of God, they may receive the promise."[1]

It is but a little while, and faith shall be converted into vision, hope into enjoyment; that which is in part shall pass away, and that which is perfect shall take its place. They who are " looking for the blessed hope, the glorious appearing of him who is the great God and our Saviour," shall not look in vain. " He that shall come will come, and will not tarry." Meanwhile let us live by faith; let us persevere in the belief and profession and practice of the truth; knowing that, "if any man turn back, God's soul has no pleasure in him." Oh, may all of us, who profess to have the faith and hope of the gospel in us, be found at last, not among " them who draw back unto perdition, but among them who believe to the saving of the soul."[2]

[1] Heb. vi. 11, 12, iii. 6, x. 35, 36. [2] Heb. x. 37-39.

§ 4. *Maintaining " a good conscience" and " a good conversation."*

It only remains to consider the last injunction laid on Christians as exposed to persecution. They are exhorted to " have a good conscience; that, whereas they spoke evil of them, as of evil-doers, they might be ashamed who falsely accused their good conversation in Christ." In the remaining part of the discourse, I shall first inquire what the apostle calls on the calumniated Christians to do; and second, why he requires them to do this. He requires them to do two things: the one in express terms; the other by necessary implication. He requires them to "have," or hold, "a good conscience," and to maintain "a good conversation," in Christ; and he requires them to do this, that their calumniators may be made ashamed of their false accusations.

In considering the first part of our subject, I shall, in succession, endeavour to explain to you what it is to have a good conscience, and what it is to maintain a good conversation in Christ; and then show how these are mutually connected, how they act and react on each other.

There are few subjects on which more has been written and spoken to little or no, or worse than no purpose, than conscience. " Here," as Leighton justly says, " are many fruitless, verbal debates; and, as in other things that most require solid and useful consideration, the vain mind of man feedeth on the wind, and loves to be busy to no purpose. How much better is it to have the good conscience than dispute about its nature; to experience its power than to understand its definition !" Yet it is very desirable that we should have distinct and accurate ideas on this subject. If we do not know what conscience is, how can we understand what is meant by a good conscience? and if we do not know what a good conscience is, how can we employ the appropriate means of obtaining it if we are destitute of it, or of retaining it if we are so happy as already to possess it?

Conscience may be described as that part of our mental constitution which makes us the proper subjects of religious and moral obligation and responsibility; or, in other words, the human mind in its relations to God and duty. It is a part of the constitution of man, that as he makes, and cannot but make, a distinction between propositions as true and false, so he makes, and cannot but make, a distinction between dispositions and actions as right and wrong; and as he cannot but count what he thinks to be true to be worthy of belief, and what he thinks to be false to be worthy of disbelief, so he cannot but count what he thinks right worthy of approbation and reward, and what he thinks wrong worthy of disapprobation and punishment; and he cannot do what he knows to be right without the pleasurable feeling of self-approbation, nor can he do what he knows to be wrong without the painful feeling of self-disapprobation. These seem to be the acts of states of the mind to which we give the general name of conscience. It is, as the apostle expresses it, the having "the work," the office[1] of law so "written in the heart," so inwoven into his nature, as that without a written law he is as a law to himself, his thoughts accusing or excusing one another. It seems to be this part of our constitution to which Solomon refers, when he says, that "the spirit of a man is the candle of the Lord, searching all the inward parts of the belly." It is this peculiar endowment of the human soul more than anything else, more than all things else taken together, that raises it above the animating principle of the brutes.[2]

[1] Τὰ τοῦ νόμου. Τὸ ἔργον τοῦ νόμου.—Rom. ii. 14, 15.
[2] See Bishop Butler's *Three Sermons on Human Nature*—the most valuable treatise on the philosophy of morals in existence.

The conscience is good when the mind exercises all the functions referred to, in a way fitted to promote the religious and moral excellence, the holiness and the happiness, both of the individual and of all with whom he is connected. It is absolutely good when it gains this end in the highest degree; and it is good or evil just in the degree in which it gains these ends, or comes short of them, or conduces to ends of an opposite kind.

Man, when he came from the hand of his Creator, was, as a being possessed of conscience, as in every other view that can be taken of his nature, very good. He had a good conscience. He clearly perceived what was right, and strongly felt what was good. He thought, and felt, and acted, in entire coincidence with his convictions of right. His heart condemned him not, and he had confidence towards God, arising from the consciousness that, in mind and heart, he was entirely conformed to His will.

Had this state of things continued, sin and misery had never been known; and in a growing acquaintance with what is holy, just, and good, and a corresponding disposition to conform himself in all the faculties of his nature to it, a foundation was laid for illimitable progress in moral excellence and happiness.

But man's conscience became evil, and "that which was ordained to life became death"—the fruitful source both of sin and of misery. The conscience, under malignant spiritual influence, became evil, morally depraved, hesitating in a case where there was no room for hesitation; doubting as to the absolute authority of a distinctly uttered announcement of the mind of God, and as to the necessary connection between sin and punishment. Had conscience maintained its superiority over desire, Satan might have tempted, but man would not have fallen. But conscience betrayed its trust, and delivered man up to the influence of curiosity and ambition, inflamed by the false representations of the great deceiver; and no sooner had he, yielding to temptation, violated the divine law, than, incapable of changing its nature, the inward witness and judge instantly became evil, in the sense of being productive of misery. It having first deceived him, then slew him. It repeated the declaration of the Lawgiver in a most terrific form: "Thou hast eaten, thou must die: thou art a sinner, thou art miserable." It filled him with remorse and the fear which has torment; and made him flee from what had been the source of his happiness, but now was the object of his terror—"the presence of the Lord."[1]

Man, the sinner, is exposed, under the penal arrangements of the divine government, to the operation of causes both of depravity and of wretchedness without himself; but the principal sources both of his ever-growing sin and misery are within himself, in his own depraved nature. He is his own perverter and his own tormentor. All the faculties of his nature have become "instruments of unrighteousness unto sin;" and they all, too, "bring forth fruit unto death." All his faculties, originally good, are now evil: evil—influenced by depravity; evil—productive of misery. Conscience, the master faculty, is thus emphatically evil.

Conscience, influenced by ignorance and error and cri-

---

[1] Prima est hæc ultio, quod se
Judice, nemo nocens absolvitur. . . .
     Cur tamen hos tu
Evasisse putes, quos diri conscia facti
Mens habet attonitos et surdo verbere cædit
Occultum quatiente animo tortore flagellum?
Pœna autem vehemens, ac multo sævior illis
Quas et Cædicius gravis invenit, aut Rhadamanthus,
Nocte dieque suum gestare in pectore testem.
—JUVENAL, xiii.

minal inclination, pronounces false judgments; calls evil good, and good evil; and says "Peace, peace, where there is no peace." It approves what it should condemn, and condemns what it should approve. It is fitful and uncertain, and inconsistent and unreasonable; sometimes, at the same time it may be, reproving and punishing severely for the neglect of some superstitious usage, and permitting, or even enjoining, the perpetration of the greatest crimes. It is sometimes absurdly and most vexatiously sensitive and scrupulous, and at other times "seared as with a hot iron." This is the very core of man's depravity and wretchedness. When the mind and the conscience are defiled, nothing can be pure. When the light which is in man is darkness, "how great is that darkness!"

Even when conscience, in the unchanged, unpardoned sinner, performs its most legitimate function, *condemnation*, it is *evil*,—productive of depravity as well as of misery. Its condemnation irritates, instead of destroying or even weakening, the sinful principle which is condemned. It awakens into more exasperated fury, enmity against Him who forbids and who punishes what the sinner loves. It makes the sinner "run, as it were, on the Almighty's neck, on the thick bosses of his buckler;" or, paralyzing the sinews of dutiful exertion, makes him say there is no hope, and yield himself up an unresisting victim to the powers of evil. And the most fearful scenes of suffering that are witnessed on this side death, out of the prison-house from which there is no discharge, are those which originate in the inflictions of a guilty, awakened, unenlightened conscience. This is the most adequate representation we can have of "the worm that dieth not, and the fire that cannot be quenched."

Behold a picture drawn from the life, of a sinner conscience-struck:—

> "Alas! how changed! Expressive of his mind,
> His eyes are sunk, arms folded, head reclined.
> Those awful syllables—hell, death, and sin!
> Though whisper'd, plainly tell what works within:
> That conscience there performs her proper part,
> And writes a doomsday sentence on his heart.
> Forsaking and forsaken of all friends,
> He now perceives where earthly pleasure ends.
> Hard task for one who lately knew no care;
> And harder still, as learned beneath despair!
> His hours no longer pass unmark'd away—
> A dark importance saddens every day:
> He hears the notice of the clock, perplexed,
> And cries—Eternity perhaps comes next!
> Sweet music is no longer music here,
> And laughter sounds like madness in his ear;
> His grief the world of all her powers disarms—
> Wine has no taste, and beauty has no charms."[1]

Out of this darkness God can bring light; but its natural consummation is "the blackness of darkness for ever."

The question is a most important one, How is conscience in man, the sinner, to become good, the source of holiness and happiness, a well of living water in him, springing up unto everlasting life? The true answer is, the conscience must be brought under the saving operation of "the redemption that is in Christ Jesus." It must be sprinkled by the blood of his atoning sacrifice; it must be enlightened by his word; it must be influenced by his Spirit. It is thus, thus alone, that any sinner can have a good conscience.

"The blood of Christ, who through the eternal Spirit offered himself without spot unto God, purges the conscience from dead works, to serve the living God."[2] The heart is thus "sprinkled from an evil conscience." The evil conscience becomes good. The sprinkling of the blood

---
[1] Cowper. [2] Heb. ix. 14.

of the atoning sacrifice of Jesus Christ on the conscience of the sinner makes it clean, "good;" converts it from a source of misery and sin into a source of peace and of holiness. But what is meant by this sprinkling of the blood of Christ on the heart or conscience; and how does it produce such wonderful, such delightful results? The best way of answering the first of these interesting questions is, perhaps, by asking another. The sprinkling of the blood of the sin-offering was necessary, in order to its being effectual to the removal of the guilt of those for whom it was offered. What, in the Christian economy of redemption, answers to this part of "the patterns of the heavenly things?"[1] There can be but one reply: the faith of the truth respecting the atoning sacrifice of Christ, produced by the Holy Spirit. It is this which brings home the saving results of the atonement to the individual sinner.

Now, how does this faith of the truth respecting Christ as the great atonement deliver from the evil conscience, and bring us under the power of a good conscience? Till this truth is understood and believed, conscience condemns, cannot but condemn, the sinner, and produce in his mind and heart the natural consequences of this condemnation, fear and dislike of God. But when, in the faith of the truth, conscience sees God setting forth his Son a propitiation in his blood, and hears him declaring that he is the Lamb of God, who has borne, and borne away, the sin of the world; who, though he knew no sin, has been made sin for men, wounded for their transgressions, bruised for their iniquities; and who thus has magnified the law and made it honourable, and brought in an everlasting righteousness; and that He, the righteous Judge, is well pleased for that righteousness' sake, and while the just God is the Saviour, "just, and the justifier of him that believeth in Jesus;"—

---

[1] Heb. ix. 23. 'Υποδείγματα τῶν ἐπουρανίων.

conscience, seeing and hearing all this, and echoing as formerly the voice of God, proclaims, "It is finished:" God is satisfied, and so am I; he justifies, and I absolve: "There is no condemnation to them who are in Christ Jesus."[1] Believing in him, thou art justified from all things, accepted in the Beloved. Thy sin is more condemned than ever through his flesh; but thou, thou art justified. Who shall lay anything to thy charge? God justifies; who shall condemn? Christ has died, the just in the room of the unjust.

And as the condemning conscience naturally filled the mind with dislike and fear of God; so the absolving, the justifying conscience casts out the jealousies of unforgiven guilt, fills the heart with confidence and love, fitting the man to yield a living service to the living God. In this way, in this way alone, can the conscience of man be made good, or kept good, by bringing it and keeping it under the pacifying, purifying power of the blood of atonement.

This is indeed "a good conscience." It makes its possessor at once happy and holy. Let him who has heard its testimony, tell how it does so:

> " 'Tis Heaven, all Heaven, descending on the wings
> Of the glad legions of the King of kings:
> 'Tis more; 'tis God, diffused in every part,
> 'Tis God himself, triumphant in the heart." [2]

The conscience that is thus sprinkled by Christ's blood is enlightened by Christ's truth. The Christian is "not unwise, but understands what the will of the Lord is." His conscience is not a blind impulse. Regulating him, it is itself regulated by "the perfect law of liberty," "the good, and perfect, and acceptable will of the Lord." It is

[1] Rom. viii. 1.   [2] Cowper.

not guided in its decisions by his own caprice, or his own reason, or the opinions of other men; but by "what is good, by what the Lord hath required."

And while sprinkled by the blood of Christ's sacrifice, and enlightened by the truth of Christ's law, it is guided in its operation by the influence of Christ's Spirit. He enables it wisely and honestly to make the precepts and motives of the Christian law bear on the varying circumstances of the Christian's inner and outer life: on his transactions with God, and his transactions with men. A conscience which allows its possessor no quiet of mind, while known duty is neglected or known sin is indulged, and makes him habitually feel the need of repairing to the fountain opened for sin and for uncleanness, and at once inclines and enables him to "walk at liberty," while he keeps God's law, and to "serve God without fear, in righteousness and holiness, all the days of his life,"[1] is the good conscience, to possess which is one of the Christian's highest privileges, and to maintain and improve which is one of his principal duties.

It is but right, however, before closing this part of the subject, to remark, that the phrase " a good conscience" is sometimes used in the New Testament in a more restricted sense, to signify that state of the mind when the conscience bears witness "in the Holy Ghost" to the individual, that his conduct in any particular case is in accordance with what he knows and believes to be the will of God: an approving conscience. To this the apostle refers when he says, " Our rejoicing is this, the testimony of our conscience, that in simplicity and godly sincerity, not by fleshly wisdom, but by the grace of God, we have our conversation in the world;" and again, "Herein do I exercise myself to maintain a conscience void of offence towards God and towards

[1] Ps. cxix. 44, 45; Luke i. 74, 75.

man;" and again, "Pray for us, for we trust we have a good conscience, willing in all things to live honestly."[1] The question whether the apostle here uses the phrase in its more extended or more restricted sense, will meet us before we close the discourse.

Having thus illustrated the apostle's express injunction, to have a good conscience, I must pass more lightly over his implied one, to maintain a good conversation in Christ. The word "conversation" here, as uniformly in its biblical sense, does not mean, as in common usage, colloquial intercourse, but character and conduct, disposition and behaviour. Conversation in Christ is Christian character and conduct; though, when the phrase "in Christ" is used, as it very often is in this way, as equivalent to an adjective, it has a great deal more meaning than we commonly attach to the word Christian. A conversation in Christ, is such a frame of disposition and tenor of conduct, as becomes persons who are placed in a relation so close to Jesus Christ, that all the most intimate unions known among men are employed to shadow forth its closeness. They are in him as the branches are in the vine, and the members in the body; they are so in him as that they died, and were buried, and rose again, in his death, burial, and resurrection; so one with him as that what he did was considered as done by them, and what he deserved is bestowed on them; so one with him as that his Father is their Father, his God their God, and his inheritance their inheritance; they are animated by his Spirit, having the same mind in them that was in him; thinking as he did, willing as he did, feeling as he did, choosing as he did; they acknowledge him as their one Teacher, Saviour, and Lord; they are "under law" in religious matters to him, to him alone; they are "in the world as he was in the world," his animated images,

[1] 2 Cor. i. 12; Acts xxiv. 16; Heb. xiii. 18.

his " living epistles, seen and read of all men." Such a character and conduct must have in them something very peculiar.

There are men calling themselves Christians, and who would not be very well pleased with any one who questioned their right to that appellation, who think, feel, and act just as if there never had been such a person as Jesus Christ, and whose life is anything rather than " a life by the faith of the Son of God." Their conversation is not in Christ; his sacrifice is not the ground of their hope; his Spirit not the source of light, and life, and energy, and peace, and joy to them; his law is not the rule of their duty; his example not the pattern of their imitation; his authority and grace not their motives to duty; his glory not the end of their conduct. In a word, their conversation is not " such as becomes the gospel of Jesus Christ."

The maintenance of such " a conversation in Christ" ought to be a main object with every Christian. He must habitually endeavour to comply with the exhortation of Leighton, " Seek this as the only way to have thy soul and thy ways righted : to be in Christ, and then to walk in him. Let thy conversation be in Christ. Study him, and follow him. Look on his way, in his graces, his obedience, humility, and meekness, till, looking on them, they make the very idea of thee new, as the painter doth of a face he would draw to the life. So behold his glory, that thou mayest be transformed from glory to glory; but, as it is there added, this must be ' by the Spirit of the Lord.' Do not, therefore, simply look on him as an example without thee, but a life within thee. Having received him, walk not only 'like him, but in him. Let your conversation be not only according to him, but in him;" animated by his Spirit as well as regulated by his law.

Such a Christian conversation will of necessity be " a

good conversation." It is to "walk as He also walked;" the "holy, harmless" One; "separate from sinners;" "who did no sin, neither was guile found in his mouth;" "who went about doing good."[1] A conversation in Christ must, just because it is a conversation in Christ, include in it every species, every degree of excellence.

The apostle had obviously a particular purpose to serve, in giving this epithet to the Christian conversation which he intimates is expected from those to whom he wrote. It suggests the thought, 'If you Christians were characterized by an evil conversation, then not they who speak of you as evil-doers, but you, would have cause to be ashamed; but if your conversation be the good conversation, which it must be if it be a conversation in Christ, then the reality in your character and conduct will so strikingly, so grotesquely, contrast with their calumnious misrepresentations, they will be so plainly in the wrong, that they must be shamed into silence.'

The mutual relation of the apostle's two injunctions—the one express, relating to a good conscience; and the other implied, relating to a good conversation—requires now to be attended to. The relation is different, according as you consider the good conscience as bearing the wide or the more limited sense in which I explained the phrase in the preceding part of the discourse.

If you understand it in the wide sense, then the good conversation is the result of the good conscience; and the exhortation is, 'Hold a good conscience, that you may maintain a good conversation in Christ.' Seek to have your conscience habitually sprinkled by Christ's blood, enlightened by Christ's truth, influenced by Christ's Spirit, that you may exemplify all the graces of the Christian character, and perform all the duties of the Christian life.

[1] 1 John ii. 6; Heb. vii. 26; 1 Pet. ii. 22; Acts x. 38.

In this view, the words embody one of the most important maxims of practical religion.

If, on the other hand, you understand having or holding a good conscience to mean, seeking to maintain the approving smile of our own mind in a consistency with the truth of the case, then the good conscience is the result of the good conversation; and the exhortation is, 'Let your temper and behaviour as Christians be habitually such, as that, whatever calumniators may say, you shall have the approving testimony of "the man within the breast;" that you shall have "a conscience void of offence towards God and towards men."' This is another important maxim of practical religion.

The conversation cannot be made good but by having the conscience made good. The conscience cannot be kept good but by the conversation being kept good. To attempt, as some do, to get the conversation good, while the conscience is not good, is "to be still putting the handle of the clock right with your finger, which is a continual business, and does no good."[1] And to try, as others do, while not maintaining a good conversation, to keep a good opinion of themselves, and think this the testimony of a good conscience, by cherishing antinomian dogmas, mystical dreams, or enthusiastic raptures, is like a person attempting by the use of narcotic medicines to preserve peace of mind, when, through indolence and mismanagement, his affairs are in disorder, and ruin is at hand, and poverty about to come on him as an armed man.

The particular object for which the apostle addresses these injunctions to the persecuted Christians comes now shortly to be noticed. Have a good conscience and a good conversation in Christ, "that they who speak evil of you as evil-doers, and accuse you, may be ashamed."

[1] Leighton.

Christians cannot gratify their calumniators more than by being induced, under the irritating influence of their false accusations, to do anything inconsistent with a good conversation in Christ, which would, of course, interfere with the testimony of a good conscience. Even the slightest deviation of a Christian, not only from what is right in the estimation of a lax worldly morality, but from what is right according to the principles of spiritual Christianity, gives countenance to the slanders, and enables their authors to say, 'You see he is not what his profession requires him to be; and he only needs to be better known to be found out to be, indeed, the very bad person we represent him.'

On the other hand, uniform, consistent good conduct, as it is often the only, so it is always in the long run the most effectual, method of putting down calumny, and putting to shame calumniators. "A lying tongue is but for a moment."[1] Men cannot continue to believe without evidence, and in opposition to evidence. A uniform course of Christian behaviour secures, that if the accusations are taken up and inquired into, they will be found not true. They will be found to be not even plausible; they will be found to be false, entirely false, obviously, malignantly false. Such was the result in the case of our Lord, when the attempt was made to substantiate the calumnies of his enemies. "I find no fault in him," said a judge certainly by no means predisposed in his favour. And such, too, was the result in the case of Paul, when he was spoken evil of as an evil-doer, and falsely accused. Claudius Lysias, the Roman commander, after inquiry, declared that, notwithstanding all the calumnies of his enemies, he had done nothing worthy of death or of bonds; and Festus the governor, and King Agrippa, came to the same conclusion; thus covering his calumniators with shame. Even where

[1] Prov. xii. 19.

no formal investigation of calumnies takes place, a blameless holy life effectually refutes them.

When our hope is called in question, in all ordinary cases we should defend it; but defend it with meekness and fear. Silence in such a case is often, is usually, injustice to truth. But when our character is calumniated, in very many instances it is the wisest course to allow it to vindicate itself. In such a case, to use Archbishop Leighton's beautiful figure, "the integrity of a Christian conquers, as a rock unremoved breaks the waters that are dashing against it. This is not only a lawful, but a laudable way of revenge; shaming calumny out of its malignant lies; punishing evil-speakers by well-doing; showing by facts, not words, how false is the accusation brought against us." This is the most effectual apology, the most triumphant refutation. It is like the reply which was given to the sophist, who denied the possibility of motion, and fortified his denial by many very ingenious reasons. His antagonist, without speaking a word, rose and walked. The most elaborate refutation would not more satisfactorily have exposed the absurdity, or so effectually have put the sophist to shame.

It is also a very weighty consideration, that without this good conscience and conversation, any defence we can make of our religion is not likely to have much influence. One unchristian action on the part of a professor of Christianity, will cast more discredit on his religion than the largest and best-framed speeches in its behalf can compensate. Religion has never permanently suffered from calumnies cast on consistently religious men; and the objects of such calumnies have seldom been permanent sufferers. When they "trust in the Lord and do good," when they "delight themselves in him," and "commit their way to him," he often, in a manner that amazes themselves and confounds their enemies, "brings forth their righteousness as the light, and their judgment as the noon-day."¹

The apostle closes his exhortations to Christians under persecution, by directing their attention to a view of affliction calculated at once to afford support and direction, consolation and guidance: "For it is better, if the will of God be so," or since it is the will of the Lord, "that ye suffer for well-doing than for evil-doing;" literally, "that ye suffer as well-doers rather than evil-doers."²

These words do not seem to have any peculiarly close connection with the verse which immediately precedes them. They are connected with the whole paragraph, occupied as it is with an account of the duties of Christians exposed to persecution. The force of the connective particle seems to be, 'You ought to submit to suffering, and you ought to act in this manner under suffering; "for it is better, since such is the will of God, to suffer; and it is better to suffer doing well than doing evil."'

It is better, since such is the will of God, that Christians should suffer. Suffering is not in itself desirable. Abstractly considered, it is not better to suffer than not to suffer. But, taking into consideration the whole circumstances of the case, it is much better that Christians should suffer than that they should not suffer. "It is needful" that they be "in heaviness through manifold trials."³ A life of ease would not be the suitable means of forming them to that character which is essential to their complete and final happiness. They all are made to see this in a good measure; and to say, "It has been good for me that

---

¹ Ps. xxxvii. 3-6.
² Κρεῖττον γὰρ ἀγαθοποιοῦντας (εἰ θέλει τὸ θέλημα Θεοῦ) πάσχειν, ἢ κακοποιοῦντας.
³ 1 Pet. i. 6.

I have been afflicted. I know, O Lord, that thy judgments are right, and that thou in faithfulness hast afflicted me." [1] The occurrence of the affliction is proof enough that it is the "will of the Lord." "Shall there be evil in a city, and the Lord hath not done it?" [2] Every affliction " comes forth from him who is wonderful in counsel and excellent in working." And the undoubted fact, that these sufferings are the will of God, is to Christians undoubted evidence that it is better for them to suffer. For does not God love them? is he not infinitely wise? has he not promised to give them what is good, and to make all things work together for their good? Whatever, then, may be the form, whatever the degree, whatever the continuance of the affliction, there can be no reasonable doubt that this is the will of God concerning us; and as little doubt that that will is good. Nature may, nature often does, say, 'It were better that I did not suffer;' but faith reproves nature, and bids reason school her into a better mind. 'It is the will of the Lord that I suffer, that I suffer thus; and can anything be better, better for me, than the will of my Father in heaven, my almighty, all-wise, infinitely righteous, infinitely benignant, unchanging Friend?'

There is to every rational being a strong argument for submission under affliction, in the sentiment, 'Such is the will of God.' For "what is, what can be, gained by our reluctances and repinings, but pain to ourselves? He doth what he wills, whether we consent or no. Our disagreeing doth not prejudice his purpose, but our peace. If we will not be led, we must be drawn; we must suffer if he will: but if we will what he wills, even in suffering that makes it sweet and easy when our mind goes along with his, and we willingly move with the stream of providence, which will carry us with it, though we row against it, and we still have

[1] Ps. cxix. 71, 75.   [2] Amos iii. 6.

nothing but toil and weariness for our pains. And why should we not will what he wills, when we know this is his will, even our sanctification, our salvation; and that when he wills our sufferings, he wills them in order to these?"[1]

But the words before us not only intimate that it is better, since such is the will of God, that Christians suffer, but it is better that they suffer doing well than doing evil. The sentiment which our translation brings out of the words is a just one, "It is better to suffer for well-doing than for evil-doing." 'Take heed,' as if he had said, 'that your enemies never have occasion to punish you for real crimes; " let none of you suffer as a murderer, or as a thief, or as an evil-doer, or as a busybody in other men's matters"—that would be disgraceful to yourselves, disgraceful to your cause; but if any man suffer as a Christian, for righteousness' sake, because he will not deny his Lord or renounce his faith, " let him not be ashamed." It is far better to suffer in this last way than in the first way. Your characters will be improved, your religion will be honoured, by such sufferings. The other sort of suffering is calculated to disgrace both.'[2]

At the same time, the words do seem naturally to express a somewhat different and an equally important and appropriate sentiment. It is better to suffer the trials to which as Christians you are exposed, doing well than doing evil. It is better to bear them in a right spirit than in a wrong spirit; to act properly under them than to act improperly. It is better, for example, that you should for injury and insult render blessing, than that you should resentfully retaliate; better that you should entirely rise above the fears of your adversary, than in any degree sink under

---

[1] Leighton.

[2] "It is inconsiderately said by many, 'If I had deserved such usage, I could have borne it:' as if suffering without sin were not a lighter burden than sin and suffering for it."—BAXTER.

them; better that you should meekly and piously meet the demands of your enemies for an account of your faith, than manifest either cowardice in shrinking from, or bad temper in conducting, your defence; better quietly live down the calumnies of your enemies, than be hurried by resentment of them into anything inconsistent with the holding a good conscience, or maintaining a good conversation. It is not enough that Christians, when they suffer, should suffer, not for doing ill, but for doing well; but further, that they should do well, and not do ill, in suffering. They should be good sufferers in a good cause. It is not the mere suffering that is to do us good; it is the manner in which we think, and feel, and act under suffering. It is much better, when called to suffer, to suffer in the manner the apostle recommends, than in an opposite way. How much more comfortable, how much more advantageous to ourselves, how much more honourable to God, how much more creditable to religion, to bear the afflictions laid on us, especially those which come in the form of persecution, in a quiet, resigned, pious, cheerful, humble, patient, meek spirit, than in a different, than in an opposite temper! "Wherefore, let them that suffer according to the will of God, commit the keeping of their souls to him, in well-doing, as unto a faithful Creator." Then will "tribulations work patience, and experience, and hope, that makes not ashamed." "The chastisement," though "not for the present joyous, but grievous," will yield "the peaceable fruits of righteousness unto them who are exercised thereby;" and their "light affliction, which is but for a moment, will work out for" them "a far more exceeding and an eternal weight of glory."[1]

I cannot conclude without taking notice of the illustra-

[1] Rom. v. 3, 5; Heb. xii. 11; 2 Cor. iv. 17.

tion which the subject of discourse gives, of what Tertullian calls "the adorable fulness of the Holy Scriptures." They are indeed full, full to an overflow, of the mind and spirit of Christ, of light and love, of truth and grace. All that man needs to know in reference to his relations to God and eternity, to make him wise, and good, and happy, is to be found there. There is no question respecting the divine character and government, the solution of which is necessary to human duty or happiness, which is not there satisfactorily settled; and, amid the immense variety of circumstances in which a human being may be placed, there is not one situation to which there is not to be found, in the Holy Scriptures, appropriate warning, direction, or consolation. Their fulness, as a practical directory, must often have struck with wonder and awe, as well as gratitude and delight, the intelligent Christian. When the ear of his mind is opened to discipline, the Holy Spirit, bringing to remembrance his own oracles, makes him often in the hour of perplexity, in a way which astonishes himself, hear as it were a word behind him, "This is the way, walk in it." Not merely are there to be found in them wide-reaching principles of duty, which admit of easy application to an endless number and variety of particular cases, but there are comparatively few combinations of circumstances, even the most extraordinary, in which the diligent, humble, pious student of the Scriptures will not find himself furnished there with information and directions, as suited even to the minute peculiarities, or it may be, as he is apt to think it, the absolute singularities of his case, as if these had been immediately before the mind of the inspired writers. He is there taught how to employ all his faculties; how to regulate all his desires; how to behave himself to God and man, to relatives and strangers, to friend and enemy; in retirement and in society; in his own house and in the house of

God; in prosperity and in adversity; in youth, in middle life, and in old age; how to think and feel; how to speak and act; how to live and how to die. How so much particular, easily applicable, practical instruction, could, without any appearance of unnatural constraint, be brought within the compass of so moderate a sized volume as the Bible, is indeed extraordinary; and he who is best acquainted with that divine Book, and has been most in the habit of taking it as a "lamp to his feet and a light to his path," will be readiest to say with Tertullian, " I adore the fulness of the Holy Scriptures."

This train of thought is naturally suggested by observing how much varied, important, particular, readily available instruction, on the interesting subject of the duties of Christians when exposed to persecution on account of their religion, is crowded into the short paragraph with which the subject of this discourse concludes. We have here not a general exhortation to patience and constancy; but directions are given suited to the various forms which persecution might assume. Injuries and insults might be heaped on them : how were they to act in this case? They were not to "render evil for evil, but contrariwise, blessing." Prospects the most appalling might be presented to them for the purpose of shaking their faith: how were they to act in this case? They were not to be afraid of the terror of their enemies, neither were they to be troubled, but to " sanctify the Lord God in their hearts," as the object both of supreme fear and confidence. They might be called on publicly to state and defend the religion on which rested all their hopes : how were they to act in this case? They were to " be always ready to give an answer to every one who asked them a reason of the hope that was in them with meekness and fear." They might be exposed to a sort of attack from which it is peculiarly difficult to defend either themselves or their cause—systematic calumniation; men might " speak evil of them, and falsely accuse them as evil-doers:" how were they to act in this case? They were to hold " a good conscience," and to maintain " a good conversation in Christ." And what a persecuted Christian must have found in this portion of Scripture, given by inspiration of God, every Christian, if he is but careful enough to search the Scriptures, will find in some portion of it that which is fitted to make him, as a " man of God, perfect, thoroughly furnished " for work and for warfare.

Note A. p. 317.

The present division of the Holy Scriptures into chapters and verses is not of divine origin, but is a human invention of comparatively late date, intended chiefly to facilitate reference to any particular portion of the sacred oracles. With the exception of the book of Psalms—the particular poems in which, as separate compositions, given forth at different times and on various occasions, were from the beginning divided from each other—all the books, both in the Old Testament and the New, were originally written as so many continued discourses; not only without paragraphs, but with the clauses, and even sentences, undivided by such notes as we call points, and the words themselves not separated by any sensible distance from each other.

The division first made of the Old Testament writings is considerably ancient; probably not much, if at all, posterior to the days of Ezra. The different books were divided into large paragraphs, and into verses; which last were, however, merely marked by a point, not numbered. This division was probably made for the convenience of their synagogue worship. Pure Hebrew, in which the Old Testament books are written, ceased to be the vernacular language of the Israelites after the Babylonian captivity. After the return from Babylon, when the sacred writings were read in the synagogue, they were first read in the original, and then interpreted into the Chaldaic or Syro-Chaldaic dialect, which was commonly used by the people. To this mode of reading the Holy Scriptures, it is generally supposed there is a reference, Neh. viii. 8, where it is said that the Levites " read in the book, in the law of the Lord, distinctly, and gave the sense, and caused them to understand the reading." As this was done period by period, it became necessary to adopt some notation to mark the beginning and end of the periods.

The division of the Bible into the chapters with which we are familiar, is comparatively a modern invention. It was made, about the middle of the thirteenth century, by a cardinal of the Roman Church, Hugo de St Caro, who formed the first concordance of the Latin Vulgate translation of the Scriptures, for the obvious purpose of facilitating reference to any particular word or passage. This division was adopted by a learned Jew, Rabbi Isaac Nathan, who, about the middle of the fifteenth century, published the first concordance of the Hebrew Scriptures; and, in addition, he numbered the verses into which the sacred text had been anciently divided.

About a century later, a learned French printer, Robert Stephens, divided the New Testament into verses; and his division, with few exceptions and with very slight variations, has been generally adopted in the editions of the original text, and in the translations of the Scriptures which have been since published throughout the Christian world.

This division of the sacred text is convenient for the purpose of reference; and, had it been always judiciously made and accommodated to the different kinds of composition of which the sacred books are made up, might have contributed materially to the more important purpose of interpretation. Like all human works, however, it bears abundant evidence of the imperfection of its authors, and has been productive of some bad as well as of some good consequences. The division, whether of chapters or of verses, is not always judicious: where there is no pause in the discourse, no division in the thoughts, we often find a division in the words; while, on the other hand, where the sense requires such a division, it is not always to be found.

To no part of the sacred writings does the division into chapters and verses less happily apply, than to the epistolary writings of the New Testament. Both from their argumentative character and their epistolary form, it becomes almost impossible to break them down into such short sections as our verses, without materially impairing their beauty and obscuring their meaning. It would be a considerable help towards the understanding of the apostolical epistles, if the chapters and verses were merely marked on the margin, while the epistle itself was printed as a continuous discourse, broken down only into such paragraphs as it naturally resolves itself into; and indeed we are persuaded nobody will ever make very satisfactory progress in the study of these most interesting portions of sacred writ, who does not get into the habit of reading them with an almost total disregard of the ordinary divisions.

We have an illustration of these remarks in the words which form the subject of the first division of the third part of this discourse. They form a part of a series of injunctions laid by the apostle on the Christians to whom he wrote, respecting their duty so to behave themselves towards their persecutors as that no discredit should be reflected either on their religion or themselves; but that, on the contrary, the doctrine of God their Saviour might be adorned, and their adversaries have no evil thing to say with truth of its professors. The first injunction is, to abstain from all resentful retaliation, and to meet injury and reproach by kindness both in conduct and in language. This injunction is contained in the 9th verse; and with the illustration and enforcement of this injunction, the apostle is engaged down to the middle of the 14th verse. Here there is a pause in the discourse, a division in the thought. He proceeds to a second injunction; calling on them to guard against the undue influence of fear, and prescribing a due regard to God as the best means of preventing an undue regard to man. But you will notice there is in our common Bibles no division of the words here. You would suppose the second part of the verse just a following out the thought contained in the first; when, in reality, it is what in a discourse we would call entering on the illustration of a new particular. And as we have here no division where the sense required one, so, at the close of the verse, we have a division where the sense requires there should be none: for the first part of the 15th verse is just the conclusion of the sentence begun in the last part of the 14th,—a part, indeed, of the same quotation from an Old Testament writer. And then again a third and entirely distinct injunction is given in the remaining part of the 15th verse,—an injunction to be always ready to give an account of their religion, and its grounds, to all who should call them in question for them. Here again we have a distinct division in the thoughts, unmarked by any corresponding division in the words.

These may appear to some very minute and unimportant remarks, and comparatively they are so; but nothing should be considered as trifling or useless which goes to remove obscurity or pointlessness from an inspired declaration or precept; or to give it, even in a slight degree, additional clearness or force.

Note B. p. 318.

"Observandum est, duo esse in Novo Testamento e veteri citationum genera. Quædam enim, imo pleraque omnia loca quæ e veteri proferuntur in Novo Testamento ejus modi sunt, ut, juxta mentem consilium et scopum Scriptoris ex quo depromuntur, adducantur ad doctrinæ evangelicæ confirmationem. Sed et alia sunt nonnulla in quibus a Novi Testamenti Scriptoribus, non tam spectatur mens consilium et scopus, quam Scriptoris verba duntaxat, quæ quoniam aliquam habent cum iis de quibus loquuntur similitudinem et significationis convenientiam, iis utuntur, non tanquam testimonio et auctoritate, qua velint dictum suum communire, sed per allusionem duntaxat. Cujus modi ferme sunt illa quæ vulgo Noemata seu Gnomas Rhetores vocant, dicta nimirum quædam sententiosa ex poeta aliquo—Virgilio puta vel Homero deprompta, quæ nos solemus ad rem et propositum nostrum accommodare, non quod hoc velimus, poetam idipsum spectasse et in animo habuisse quod nos cum ejus verba usurpamus, sed id grata quadam 'accommodatione' duntaxat a nobis fit, quod allusionibus libenter et impense soliti sint homines delectari."—Matt. xiii. 34; Ps. xlix. 2; Rom. x. 18; Ps. xix. 5; 2 Cor. viii. 15; Ex. xvi. 13.—L. CAPELLUS.

Note C. p. 328.

"Should the empress," says Chrysostom, in his epistle to Cyriacus, "determine to banish me, let her banish me; 'the earth is the Lord's, and the fulness thereof.' If she will cast me into the sea, let her cast me into the sea; I will remember Jonah. If she will throw me into a burning fiery furnace; the three children were there before me. If she will throw me to the wild beasts; I will remember that Daniel was in the den of lions. If she will condemn me to be stoned; I shall be the associate of Stephen, the proto-martyr. If she will have me beheaded; the Baptist has submitted to the same punishment. If she will take away my substance; 'naked came I out of my mother's womb, and naked shall I return to it.'"

DISCOURSE XVI.

THE SUFFERINGS OF CHRIST (THEIR NATURE—DESIGN—CONSEQUENCES) AN ENCOURAGEMENT TO CHRISTIANS SUFFERING FOR HIS CAUSE.

" For Christ also hath once suffered for our sins, the just for the unjust, that he might bring us to God, being put to death in the flesh, but quickened by the Spirit: By which also he went and preached unto the spirits in prison ; which sometime were disobedient, when once the long-suffering of God waited in the days of Noah, while the ark was a preparing, wherein few, that is, eight souls, were saved by water. The like figure whereunto even baptism doth also now save us (not the putting away of the filth of the flesh, but the answer of a good conscience toward God), by the resurrection of Jesus Christ: who is gone into heaven, and is on the right hand of God ; angels, and authorities, and powers, being made subject unto him."—1 PET. iii. 18-22.

IN studying Christianity, as developed in the inspired writings of the New Testament, few things are more fitted to strike the mind than the intimate, the indissoluble connection which exists between its principles and its laws, its doctrinal statements and its practical requirements. Its doctrines are such as, if really believed, necessarily lead to the discharge of its duties; and its duties are such as cannot be discharged without a knowledge and belief of its doctrines. They are connected together as the two constituents of human nature, body and soul. The doctrines are embodied in the duties, and the duties are animated by the doctrines.[1]

---

[1] " La religion chrétienne est toute d'une piece. Elle ne presente pas sur deux lignes paralleles et distinctes des dogmes d'une part, et des devoires de l'andre. Un lien spirituel reunit les uns avec les autres d'une maniere inseparable, en sort qu'il est egalement impossible de croire sans pratiquer, et de pratiquer sans croire."—VINET.

This is true, even of those doctrines which, at first view, seem to partake most of the nature of abstract principles; such as the doctrine of the expiation of human guilt, and the accomplishment of human salvation, through the penal, vicarious, expiatory sufferings of the incarnate Son of God. This doctrine, which to many seems a point of mere speculation, having little or nothing to do with the formation of character or the guidance of conduct, is brought forward in the New Testament as the grand motive to Christian obedience generally, and to all the various parts of Christian obedience. Are Christians exhorted to universal holiness? this is the motive, "Ye are bought with a price; therefore glorify God in your body and in your spirit, which are God's." Are they exhorted to "walk in love?" the motive is, "Christ also hath loved us, and hath given himself for us, an offering and a sacrifice to God, for a sweet-smelling savour." Are they exhorted to mutual forgiveness? the motive is, "God, for Christ's sake, hath forgiven us." Are they exhorted to a complying, self-denying spirit? the motive is, "Christ pleased not himself." Are they exhorted to public spirit, in opposition to selfishness? the motive is drawn from "the mind which was in Christ," and which manifested itself in his emptying and abasing himself, in his labouring, and suffering, and dying for the salvation of men. Are they exhorted to make pecuniary sacrifices for the relief of their poor brethren? the motive is, "Ye know the grace of our Lord Jesus, in that though he was rich, yet for your sakes he became poor, that ye through his poverty might be rich." Are husbands urged to love their wives? the motive is, "Christ also loved the Church," his spouse, "and gave himself for her." And not to multiply examples, are Christians, in the passage which I have read as the subject of discourse, called on cheerfully and patiently to endure suffering in the cause of Christ? the motive is,

"Christ also once suffered for us, the just for the unjust, that he might bring us to God, being put to death in the flesh, and quickened by the Spirit; by which also he went and preached to the spirits in prison; which aforetime were disobedient: and having risen from the dead, is gone into heaven, and is on the right hand of God; angels, and authorities, and powers, being made subject to him."

In the immediate context, as you are aware, the apostle has been instructing those to whom he was writing how to behave themselves when exposed to persecution on account of the religion of Christ, so as to reflect honour on Him, on it, and on themselves; and to reconcile them to such sufferings, and induce them to conduct themselves properly under them, he suggests the thought, that divinely appointed suffering in a good cause, rightly sustained, is not to be considered as an evil. "If ye suffer for righteousness' sake, happy are ye." "It is better, since such is the will of God, that ye doing well suffer:" better not only that ye should suffer doing well, "rather than doing evil;" but better in these circumstances that ye should suffer than ye should not suffer.

It is in illustration and proof of this principle, I apprehend, that the apostle introduces the example of our Lord, the Prince of sufferers. His sufferings were divinely appointed sufferings; sufferings in the best of all causes; sufferings sustained in the best possible manner; and sufferings terminating in such a way, as very strikingly to show that divinely appointed suffering in a good cause, rightly sustained, is rather to be chosen and embraced as a good, than dreaded and shunned as an evil. Such seems to me the general import of the interesting paragraph I have read, excluding from consideration at present the 20th and 21st verses, which, being plainly parenthetical, may be left out without at all interrupting the train of thought, and which, being involved in considerable difficulties, may with greater advantage be afterwards made a subject of separate examination.

In suffering " for righteousness' sake," you may well account yourselves happy. It is better, since such is the will of God, that you doing well should suffer; for *even*[1] (that is the force of the particle rendered *also*) the Lord Christ, all excellent and glorious as he is, even HE ONCE suffered, though now and henceforth he suffers no more—is completely and for ever exempt from suffering of every kind, in every degree, the ends of his sufferings being completely gained. He suffered, even to the death, "for sins;" not his own, for he had none, but for those of others; of course, then, by the will of God, the express appointment of the supreme Judge, " in the stead of sinners;" and he suffered doing well, being and appearing to be " the just One," though " in the room of the unjust." And these sufferings were for a most holy and benignant object, that he might restore sinful and miserable men to holiness and happiness by bringing them to God. These sufferings, though they ended in a most violent death (for he was put to death, or became dead " in the flesh," or bodily), led to a vivification, a quickening "in the Spirit," or spiritually, which manifested itself in his going and preaching to the spirits in prison, whatever that may mean, and to a bodily resurrection too, which was followed by ascension to heaven, where, in the nature in which he had endured so much suffering, he sits " at the right hand of God; angels, and authorities, and powers, being made subject to him." Is there not abundant reason here why Christians, the followers of that illustrious sufferer, the Captain of salvation, thus made perfect through suffering, when exposed to suffering for his sake, should count it all joy to be subjected to mani-

[1] Καὶ.

fold trials while he is conducting them to glory; should reckon themselves happy because they thus endure; should consider it better, since such is the will of God, that they doing well should suffer?

For the further illustration of this most interesting and instructive passage of Scripture, I shall call your attention, first, to the illustrious sufferer, "Christ the just One;" secondly, to his sufferings,—he suffered, suffered even to death; thirdly, to the nature of his sufferings,—they were penal, vicarious, expiatory, for sins, in the room of the unjust; fourthly, to the design of his sufferings,—to bring men to God; and fifthly, to the consequences of his sufferings,—" Being quickened in the Spirit, he went and preached to the spirits in prison; and having risen from the dead, he went into heaven, where he is on the right hand of God; angels, and authorities, and powers, being made subject to him." After having illustrated under these heads the important principles contained in this passage, I shall endeavour to show how they are fitted to serve the purpose for which they are brought forward by the apostle: to reconcile Christians to suffering; to give them both support and direction under their sufferings.

I. THE SUFFERER.

Let us then, first, inquire into the import of the two descriptive appellations here given to the illustrious Sufferer. He is Christ, the just One.

§ 1. *Christ.*

First, He is Christ. This is not, strictly speaking, the proper name of Him who bears it. It is one of his official designations, and in this way stands in the same class as Mediator, Redeemer, Saviour. Jesus was his proper name;

and Jesus Christ, or rather Jesus the Christ, is not, like Simon Peter or John Mark, a double name, but, like John the Baptist or Herod the king, a proper name and a descriptive appellation conjoined. Christ is a Greek word,[1] corresponding in meaning to the Hebrew word Messiah, and the English word Anointed.

The Christ, then, is just the Anointed One. Anointing seems, from a very early period, to have been the emblem of consecration—the setting apart of a person or thing to a particular and sacred purpose;[2] and it appears that, among the Jews, consecration to the three sacred offices, the prophetical, priestly, and kingly, was indicated by anointing.[3] In the Old Testament Scriptures, the great Deliverer, who had been promised almost immediately after man by his sin had brought himself into circumstances which made a deliverer necessary, is spoken of as God's Anointed One, with a reference to all the three sacred offices. David speaks of him as Jehovah's Anointed King, Isaiah as his Anointed Prophet, and Daniel as his Anointed Priest.[4] During the period which elapsed from the close of the prophetic canon till the birth of Jesus, no appellation for the promised Deliverer seems to have been so commonly employed as this, The Messiah; and this is still the name which the Jews ordinarily use when they speak of Him whom they hope for, as "the glory of God's people Israel."

Our Lord is termed *The* Christ, or Anointed One, as standing apart, by himself, far elevated above all other anointed persons; just as he is, amid the countless millions of the sons of men, termed *The* Son of man.

The appellation Christ naturally called up to the mind

---

[1] Χριστός. [2] Gen. xxviii. 18, xxxi. 13, xxxv. 14.
[3] 1 Sam. xxiv. 6; 2 Sam. xxiii. 1; Lam. iv. 20; Lev. iv. 3.
[4] Ps. ii. 3, xx. 6, xlv. 7; Isa. xli. 1; Dan. ix. 24-26.

of a believing Jew,—and such were all the writers of the New Testament, as well as most of its original readers,—much important and interesting truth respecting Him who bore it. The Christ, as they thought of him, was a person in whom all the varied predictions respecting the great promised Deliverer had found, or were to find, their accomplishment: the seed of the woman who was to bruise the head of the serpent; the seed of Abraham, in whom all the families of the earth were to be blessed; the great Prophet like unto Moses, whom all men were required to hear and obey; the Priest after the order of Melchizedek; the Priest on his throne; the Root out of the stem of Jesse; the Branch of Jehovah; the Angel of the covenant; the Lord of the temple; the wonderful Counsellor; the mighty God; the Father of the future age; the Prince of peace; Immanuel, God with us; Jehovah-Tsidkenu, the Lord our Righteousness, our Justification, our Justifier.[1] While the name Christ naturally calls up all the truth respecting Him who bears the name, it brings him especially before the mind as Prophet, Priest, and King; the anointed Prophet, Priest, and King: the Prophet,—the great revealer of truth respecting the divine character and will; the Priest,—the only expiator of human guilt, and reconciler of man to God; the King,—the supreme and sole legitimate ruler over the minds and hearts of mankind. And he not only fills these offices and performs these functions, but he has been anointed to do so; that is, in figurative language, he has been divinely appointed, divinely qualified, divinely commissioned, and divinely accredited: divinely appointed, —" set up from everlasting," God's " elect" one; divinely qualified,—the Spirit of the Lord was given him not by measure; divinely commissioned,—" called of God as was

[1] Gen. iii. 15, xxii. 18; Deut. xviii. 15; Ps. cx. 4; Zech. vi. 13; Isa. ix. 6, xi. 1-10, vii. 14, iv. 2; Jer. xxiii. 6; Mal. iii. 1.

Aaron," "the Father sent him to be the Saviour of the world;" and divinely accredited,—the Father who sent him bears witness of him, "both with signs and wonders, and divers miracles, and gifts of the Holy Ghost, according to his own will."[1] So full of meaning is the appellation CHRIST, a word which I am afraid we often use without having any very definite idea in our minds; a word in which, however, is folded up the whole saving truth, so that he who, in the true, full import of the words, "believes that Jesus is the Christ," believes the saving truth, and has the privilege conferred on him of being a son of God.[2]

§ 2. *The just One.*

The second appellation given to the glorious Sufferer spoken of in the text is, the just, or the righteous One. "The just One," as well as the anointed One, is an appellation given to the great promised Deliverer in the writings of the Old Testament prophets. In the last prophetic words of David, he speaks of his Son and Lord under this name. "The just One ruleth among men;" for so do the best Scripture critics render the words translated in our version, "He that ruleth among men must be just." It is of him of whom it was predicted that "a bone of him should not be broken,"—that it is said by the same inspired writer, "Many are the afflictions of the righteous" or just One. The prophet Isaiah speaks of him as Jehovah's "righteous Servant;" and the prophet Zechariah, congratulating the Church on his appearance, exclaims, "Behold, thy King cometh. He is just, having salvation."[3]

---

[1] Prov. viii. 23 ; Isa. xlii. 1 ; Heb. v. 4 ; Isa. xi. 2-4, xlix. 6 ; Acts ii. 22 ; John v. 37.

[2] 1 John v. 1.

[3] 2 Sam. xxiii. 3 ; Ps. xxxiv. 19, comp. with 20 ; Isa. liii. 11 ; Zech. ix. 9.

In obvious allusion to such passages, we find the appellation not unfrequently given by the New Testament writers to our Lord Jesus. "Your fathers," says Stephen, "have slain them who spake before of the coming of the just One." "Ye denied," says the Apostle Peter to his countrymen, "the Holy One, and the just." "The God of our fathers," said Ananias to Saul of Tarsus, "hath chosen thee to see that just One, and to hear the words of his mouth." "Ye have condemned and killed the just One," says the Apostle James to his unbelieving countrymen. "We have an advocate with the Father," says the Apostle John, "Jesus Christ the righteous."[1]

The appellation is most accurately descriptive, both personally and officially, of Him who wears it. Personally our Lord is absolutely free from sin, and in heart and life completely conformed to the requisitions of the holy, just, and good law of God. The man Christ Jesus came into the world free from every taint or tendency to evil; and if the questions be asked, in reference to him, "What is man, that he should be clean? or he who is born of a woman, that he should be righteous? Who can bring a clean thing out of an unclean?"—the evangelist will answer them: "The Holy Ghost came upon" his virgin mother, "and the power of the Highest overshadowed her;" and that which was born of her was a "Holy thing," and was "called," and was indeed, "the Son of God."[2] This original purity was never in the slightest degree stained. Though exposed to the assaults of the great author of evil, that adversary did not prevail against, that son of mischief did not overcome him. Though in a world full of temptation and sin, he remained untainted; though tried both by its smiles and its frowns, its terrors and its allurements, he never in the

---

[1] Acts vii. 32, iii. 14, xxii. 14; James v. 6; 1 John ii. 1.
[2] Job xv. 14, xiv. 4; Luke i. 35.

slightest degree imbibed its spirit or imitated its manners. He kept himself "unspotted from the world," being "in it, not of it;" and he died, as he lived, a stranger to guilt and depravity. No action, no word, ever escaped from him, no thought, no desire, ever arose in his bosom, inconsistent with the requisitions or with the spirit of the divine law. He left this world as he entered it, "holy, harmless, undefiled, and separate from sinners."[1]

But the character of our Lord was not merely free from faults; it was distinguished by every possible moral excellence. Every holy principle in absolute perfection reigned in his mind; and his conduct was a uniform tenor of perfect obedience to that law which was in his heart. He fulfilled the law in both of its great requisitions. "He loved the Lord his God with all his heart, and soul, and strength, and mind; and he loved his neighbour as himself." He "did justly, loved mercy, and walked humbly with his God." He fully did all that God required, and cheerfully suffered all that God appointed. In principle, in extent, in continuance, his obedience completely answered the demands of the holy law, which is spiritual and exceeding broad. "His meat was to do the will of him who sent him, and to finish his work."[2] All excellences were found in him, and found in their due proportion; and they wrought together in uninterrupted harmony. "He was all fair; there was no spot in him."

"The just One" is an appellation equally applicable to him in his official administration as in his personal character; no less applicable to him as the Christ, than as the man Jesus. He is "faithful to Him who appointed him." He was appointed to glorify God in the salvation of an innumerable multitude of mankind; and in the accomplishment of this great work, "righteousness has been the

[1] Heb. vii. 26.   [2] John iv. 34.

girdle of his loins, and faithfulness the girdle of his reins." He has shown in every part of his work, that "he loves righteousness and hates iniquity." As a Prophet, he has faithfully delivered the message he has received from his Father; he has "declared him whom no man hath seen at any time;" he has "manifested his name." His "mouth spoke truth; wickedness was an abomination to his lips." " All the words of his mouth were in righteousness; there was nothing froward or perverse in them." As a Priest, he has "fulfilled all righteousness." He has fully satisfied all the demands of the divine law on those in whose room he stood. When exaction was made, he answered it. There was not one requisition of the law, but he readily and completely met it. He obeyed the whole precept; he bare the entire penalty of the violated law. He "finished transgression, made an end of sin, brought in an everlasting righteousness." He " gave himself for us, an offering and a sacrifice to God, for a sweet smelling savour;" and thus "magnified the law and made it honourable." And as a King, he " reigns in righteousness," and rules in judgment. "Justice and judgment are the habitation of his throne." "The sceptre of his kingdom is a right sceptre." He is the true Melchizedek, the King of righteousness, as well as the Prince of peace. " In majesty he rides prosperously in the cause of truth, and meekness, and righteousness." His administration in reference to his own people is an administration of pure grace, but it is " grace reigning through righteousness unto everlasting life;" and ruling, as he does, in the midst of his enemies, his royal style and appellation is "FAITHFUL AND TRUE, and in righteousness he doth judge and make war."[1]

[1] Heb. iii. 2; Isa. xi. 5; Ps. xlv. 7; John i. 18, xvii. 6; Prov. viii. 7, 8; Matt. iii. 15; Isa. liii. 7, Lowth; Dan. ix. 24; Eph. v. 2; Isa. xlii. 21, xxxii. 1; Ps. lxxxix. 14, xlv. 6, 4; Rom. v. 21; Rev. xix. 11.

While it is obvious, from these remarks, that the appellation, the just One, is admirably descriptive both of the personal character and the official administration of our Lord, there can be but little doubt that the great design of the inspired writer in using it here, is to fix our minds on the facts, that our Lord Jesus Christ, of all the sons of Adam, is the only just One—all the rest are unjust; and that, from the spotlessness of his nature, the perfection of his obedience to the preceptive part of the law, and the cheerfulness of his submission to its sanctionary enactments, all infinitely dignified by that divine nature which was in personal union with the human nature in which he obeyed and suffered,—there is in the sacrifice which by the appointment of his Father he offered up, an infinity of merit or righteousness, which, for all the purposes of law and justice, more than compensates for all the demerit and unrighteousness of those innumerable offences in the innumerable multitude of unjust ones in whose room he stood; so that HE, the righteous One, "who knew no sin," having been "made sin" for them, they who were nothing but sin "might be made the righteousness of God in him." The just One here is just equivalent to Isaiah's "Jehovah's righteous Servant, who justifies many, having borne their iniquities;" or Jeremiah's "Jehovah our righteousness," in whom, in whom alone, any unrighteous sinner can find righteousness; in whom every sinner, however unrighteous, will assuredly find righteousness, believing in Him.[1]

II. HIS SUFFERINGS.

Having thus shortly illustrated the two descriptive appellations here given to the illustrious Sufferer, let us now, in the second place, turn our attention to his sufferings. "Christ,

[1] 2 Cor. v. 21; Isa. liii. 11; Jer. xxii. 6.

the just One, suffered; being put to death in the flesh." The exalted personage to whom these appellations belong, existed from before all ages in a state of the most perfect blessedness: "He was in the beginning with God," "in the bosom of the Father," enjoying glory with him before the foundation of the world, delighting in him, and delighted in by him. A state of suffering was not, then, his original condition.[1]

But when, in order to gain the great objects of his eternal appointment, he, in the fulness of the times, took on him the nature of men in its present humbled state,—a state resulting from their violation of the divine law,—"the likeness of sinful flesh," he, of course, became a sufferer: for "man born of a woman is of few days, and full of trouble; he comes forth as a flower, and is cut down; he flees as a shadow, and continues not." He is "born to trouble as the sparks fly upward."[2]

It is obvious, however, that by divine appointment, Christ, the just One, was a sufferer far beyond the ordinary lot of mankind. His sufferings commenced with his birth. Unfurnished with the accommodations which the humblest ordinarily enjoy in entering into life, his birthplace was a stable, his cradle a manger. While yet an infant, his life was endangered by the unprincipled and cruel jealousy of a tyrant; and he was exposed to the hazards and fatigues of a hurried flight into a foreign country. At an early age he felt the pressure of the "primal curse," "In the sweat of thy brow shalt thou eat thy bread," and engaged in the toilsome labours of mechanical industry. We have no reason to believe that our Lord was ever affected by disease, but he experienced all the other sinless infirmities of our nature. He was hungry, and thirsty, and weary; felt the inconveniences of the extremes of cold and heat; and was

[1] John i. 1, 18, xvii. 5.   [2] Rom. viii. 3; Job xiv. 1, v. 7.

no stranger to disappointment, vexation, and sorrow, and the pangs of unrequited kindness and violated friendship. Destitute of the conveniences and comforts, he was but scantily and precariously furnished with the necessaries, of life. He seems often to have been indebted for a supply of these to the hospitality of others; and while "the foxes had holes, and the birds of the air nests, he had not where to lay his head."[1] Though followed and admired by multitudes, he was the object of the contempt and hatred of by far the greater part of his countrymen of all classes. He was the butt of the great man's scorn, and the poor man's contumely. He was represented as a mover of sedition and a speaker of blasphemy, an impostor or a madman, a glutton and a drunkard, an emissary of Satan, a friend and companion of the basest of men.

Nor were his sufferings limited to those inflicted by his fellow-men. He was exposed to temptations to sin from malignant spiritual beings, which to his holy mind must have been productive of the most poignant anguish. On one occasion, for forty successive days, in a desolate wilderness, he was subjected to these attacks; and we read that, when his infernal tormentor left him, he did so only "for a season." We know that, in the time of the deepest complication of the Saviour's sufferings, he returned. That was his hour when "the power of darkness" especially exerted itself.[2] The degree of suffering occasioned to a being so holy and so benignant, by witnessing the empire of the evil one in the depravity and wretchedness of mankind, can be very inadequately conceived of by even the holiest and most benevolent of imperfect men.

The severest of all his sufferings, however, were those which came immediately from the hand of God as the manifestation of the divine righteous displeasure at the sins

[1] Matt. viii. 20; Luke iv. 13.   [2] Matt. iv. 1-11; Luke xxii. 53.

of those in whose room he stood. These sufferings of his soul were the soul of his sufferings. There is something in the inspired description of them, that excites amazement rather than communicates definite information : " A horror of great darkness" comes over his mind; " he begins to be sorrowful, to be sore amazed, and to be very heavy;" he " becomes suddenly possessed with fear, horror, and amazement; encompassed with grief and overwhelmed with sorrow; pressed down with consternation and dejection of mind; tormented with anxiety and disquietude of spirit."[1] Under his intolerable load of anguish, he pours out his heart in supplication to his Father: "And, being in an agony, he prayed more earnestly; and his sweat was as it were great drops of blood falling down to the ground." Again and again, he, with strong crying and tears, repeats the same prayer, and an angel is sent to strengthen him. He was " poured out like water, his heart was like wax; it was melted in the midst of his bowels."[2]

But the sufferings of Christ, the just One, were not yet completed. The awful solemnities of Gethsemane, its preternatural sufferings and consolations, were broken in on by a band of ruffians led on by a traitor disciple. Deserted by his friends, who had lately assured him of inviolable fidelity, he was dragged as a felon before the tribunal of the high priest, and there accused of the foulest crimes, and subjected to the vilest indignities. He was reviled and insulted in all the forms which wanton vulgar malignity could invent. They spat in his face, and buffeted him with the palms of their hands. And while thus abused by his enemies, he was basely denied with oaths and execrations by one of his followers, who had lately drawn his sword in his defence,

---

[1] The student will do well to consult the learned note in *Pearson on the Creed*, Art. iv. p. 190, fol. 1676.

[2] Luke xxii. 44; Ps. xxii. 14.

and declared that, though he should die with him, he would never deny him. With an impious mockery of justice under the form of law, he was condemned as worthy of death for imposture and blasphemy. Hurried before the judgment-seat of the Jewish procurator, he was there accused of the state crimes of sedition and treason; and though declared innocent of them, his dastardly judge delivered him up to the will of his inveterate foes, sentencing him first to the scourge and then to the cross. The barbarous soldiery who were entrusted with carrying the unrighteous sentence into execution, robed him in the garments of mock royalty, and wreathed a garland of thorns round his temples, in savage mockery of his claims to be a king. On his lacerated, bleeding, enfeebled body, he bore the ponderous instrument of torture and death to the place of execution; and, stripped of his raiment, he was there affixed to the cross, amid the sarcasms of the chief priests and the shouts of the populace. To add to his ignominy, two notorious malefactors were crucified along with him, and the middle cross was assigned him as the vilest criminal of the three. While hanging on the cross in agony, his enemies continued to insult him by their contemptuous speeches; and instead of water to quench his thirst, they offered him vinegar mixed with gall. To crown his sufferings, a dark cloud was interposed between him and his Father: the comforts of sensible intercourse with HIM, the source of his happiness, were withdrawn; and those words, so big with anguish, came forth from a breaking heart, "My God, my God! why hast thou forsaken me?" Such were the sufferings of Christ, the just One.

The sufferings were sufferings to death. When he suffered, he was "put to death in the flesh." After hanging on the cross for a number of hours, "he bowed the head, and gave up the ghost." His death was a violent death;

and of all violent deaths, that probably which inflicted most pain on the sufferer. During these tedious hours he suffered every moment more than the agonies of an ordinary death. It was of all modes of punishment, too, the most ignominious. No Roman citizen, however foul his crime, could be legally crucified. It was the punishment appropriated to felonious slaves. In being nailed to the cross, our Lord was exhibited as an outcast from society, a man who had no rights, a person unworthy of being treated as an ordinary human criminal; "a worm, and no man." It was also a death, in consequence of a Jewish law which required the dead bodies of criminals who had suffered capital punishment to be hung on a tree, as a token of their having suffered the vengeance of the law, which marked the peculiar character of his sufferings. It intimated that he died accursed, condemned of God as the victim of human transgression; "As it is written, Cursed is every one that hangeth on a tree."[1] Surely well then may we, with all the emphasis that can be given to the term, pronounce that "even Christ, the just One, suffered."

What his sufferings were, none knew, none can ever know, but he who endured and he who inflicted them. We know he endured the adequate penalty of sin; but what that is, who can tell? We know it is the displeasure of God; but "who knoweth the power of His anger? According to his fear, so is his wrath." The most dreadful apprehension comes infinitely short of the more dreadful reality. Never was there a sufferer like Christ, the just One. He was, in a far higher sense than the weeping prophet, "the man who saw affliction by the rod of God's wrath." He was "the man of sorrows, and acquainted with grief." "Behold, and see, all ye that pass by, if there be any sorrow like unto the sorrow wherewith the Lord afflicted him in the

[1] Gal. iii. 13.

day of his fierce anger."¹ To borrow the words of an old divine, "If hunger and thirst, if revilings and contempt, if sorrows and agonies, if stripes and buffetings, if condemnation and crucifixion, be suffering, Jesus suffered. If the infirmities of our nature, if the weight of our sins, if the malice of man, if the machinations of Satan, if the hand of God, could make him suffer, our Saviour suffered." And of this wonderful fact we have the most abundant evidence: "If the annals of the times, if the writings of his apostles, if the death of his martyrs, if the confessions of the Gentiles, if the scoffs of the Jews, be testimonies, Jesus suffered."²

Such views of the Saviour as have now been presented to you, are intended and calculated to have an important practical influence on our hearts and lives. If he is the divinely appointed, qualified, commissioned, accredited revealer of the will of God, let us " hear him," him alone, as the authoritative teacher of religious truth. His word is the word of Him that sent him. Let us not disregard it, let us not reject it, let us not mutilate it, let us not adulterate it. Let us believe and obey his word, and humbly submit our minds to the teaching of his Spirit.

If he is the divinely appointed, qualified, commissioned, accredited expiator of human guilt, let us rely with unsuspecting confidence on the great sacrifice which, through the Eternal Spirit, he offered without spot and blemish to the Supreme Judge, and on the all-prevalent intercession which, on the ground of that sacrifice, he ever lives to make for all coming to God by him.

If he is the divinely appointed, qualified, commissioned, accredited King over God's holy hill of Zion, let us seek to know his laws and ordinances; and knowing them, let us walk in them all blameless, confiding in his power to protect us amid, and to save us from, all our enemies.

[1] Ps. xc. 11; Isa. liii. 3; Lam. iii. 1, i. 12.   [2] Pearson.

If he is the righteous One, let us receive him as "of God, made to us righteousness."[1] Let us, instead of going about to "establish our own righteousness," seek to "be made the righteousness of God in him;" seek to "win him, and to be found in him;" and, deeply feeling that "all our righteousnesses are as filthy rags," let us gladly and gratefully say, "Surely in the Lord have I righteousness: in the Lord I am justified, and in the Lord I glory." And let us not forget that, as the righteous One, he is not only the ground of our acceptance, but the pattern for our imitation. Let us seek to be "righteous even as he was righteous." Let it be our desire to be "in the world as he was in the world," having his mind in us, and having "his life manifested in our mortal flesh."[2]

Did Christ, the righteous One, suffer, and so suffer, for us? How inconceivably malignant must sin be, which made such sufferings of such a glorious person necessary to its expiation and pardon; and how inconceivably strong must his love be, which made him willingly undergo such sufferings, rather than that we should be exposed to the tremendous consequences of unexpiated, unforgiven iniquity!

Oh, how should we hate sin! Oh, how should we love the Saviour! Nothing is better fitted to animate and strengthen these two master principles of Christian holiness, the hatred of sin and the love of the Saviour, than the believing contemplation of his sufferings for sin in the room of sinners. Under the influence of the truth now stated, let each of us say in his heart, "Herein is love, not that I loved him, but that he loved me, and gave himself to be a propitiation for my sin." I would put that to death in my flesh, which put Him to death in the flesh. I would mortify my members which are on the earth; I would crucify the flesh, with its

[1] 1 Cor. i. 30; Rom. x. 3; 2 Cor. v. 21; Phil. iii. 8, 9; Isa. lxiv. 6.
[2] Isa. xlv. 24, 25; 1 John iii. 7, iv. 17; Phil. ii. 5; 2 Cor. iv. 11.

affections and lusts; and forasmuch as He has suffered for me in the flesh, borne my sin in his own body to the tree, that I, being dead to sin, might live unto righteousness, I will arm myself with the same mind, that I no longer live the rest of my time in the flesh to the lusts of men, but to the will of God; and taught by the grace of God in Christ his Son, the righteous One suffering for my sins in my stead, I will " deny ungodliness and worldly lusts, and live soberly, righteously, and godly in the present world; looking for the blessed hope, the glorious appearance of the great God and our Saviour Jesus Christ;" "who gave himself for us, that he might redeem us from all iniquity, and purify unto himself a peculiar people, zealous of good works."[1]

III. THE NATURE OF HIS SUFFERINGS.

We proceed now to call your attention to the account contained in the text, of the nature of these sufferings of " Christ the just One." They were sufferings " for sins," " for the unjust;" on account of sins, in the room of sinners. These two expressions seem plainly to intimate that our Lord's sufferings were PENAL, VICARIOUS, and EXPIATORY; in other and plainer words, that they were the manifestation of the divine displeasure against sin, against the sin of men, and were intended and are found effectual to render the pardon of sin and the salvation of sinners consistent with, and gloriously illustrative of, the perfections of the divine character and the principles of the divine government. That is what we mean, when we say these sufferings were penal, vicarious, and expiatory. Let us shortly look at these three distinct but inseparably connected characters of our Lord's sufferings.

[1] 1 John iv. 10; Col. iii. 5; Gal. v. 24; 1 Pet. iv. 1, 2; Tit. ii. 12-14.

§ 1. *Penal.*

First, then, the sufferings of our Lord were penal sufferings. This was their grand, their leading characteristic. They were not disciplinary; intended to perfect his character. This is the view which is consistently enough taken of them by those who deny his divinity, and consider him as a man of our own order, the son of Joseph and Mary; and to which, with less consistency, some countenance has been given by men who held a purer faith. He was, throughout his whole course, holy, harmless, undefiled. His character was perfect from the beginning. He was, in every stage of his mortal life, just what he should have been—entirely conformed to the will of God. His life was not the acquirement, but the manifestation, of excellence. Being perfect in a moral sense, he needed not to be perfected.

He indeed " learned obedience by the things which he suffered;"[1] but that does not mean that he was disciplined by his sufferings into obedience. "The rod and reproof" were not necessary to teach him to obey. His Father's law was in his heart; and to obey was as natural to him as to breathe. Neither does it mean, he learned by his sufferings how painful and difficult a thing obedience is; for it was just because it was obedience that suffering, otherwise intolerable, was readily borne by him. It was "his meat to do the will of him who sent him, and to finish his work."[2] It means, that by his sufferings he became practically acquainted with the full amount of the obedience, "obedience unto death," which was required of him as the Redeemer of man, and by which he was "perfected," became fully accomplished, as to merit authority and sympathy for the discharge of all his functions as " the Captain

[1] Heb. v. 8.   [2] John iv. 34.

of salvation, leading many sons to glory;" "the Author of eternal salvation to all who obey him."[1]

Nor was the great design of our Lord's sufferings to give evidence of his divine mission, nor to afford opportunity for that display of the suffering virtues which was necessary to his being a perfect example to his followers. Both these ends have been gained by his sufferings; but the first of these ends might have been gained without suffering at all; and if the second had been the only or the chief end in view, suffering in degree more like that to which the bulk of mankind are exposed, we are ready to think, would have better served that purpose. There is much, very much, in the nature and in the extremity of our Lord's sufferings, which both these hypotheses leave utterly unaccounted for.

The primary object of these sufferings was to manifest the displeasure of God against sin. They were "for sins." They were the very evils which, by divine appointment, are the result of the violation of his holy, just, and good law. Christ was treated just as if he had been a sinner, a very great sinner, the greatest of sinners. In the kind and degree of his sufferings, there was something that, even to his unreflecting countrymen, marked him as "stricken of God,"[2] a doomed person.

Nor are we to think of these evils as merely the natural result of the appearing of such a being as the incarnate Son of God in a world peopled by guilty, depraved men, suffering under the partial infliction of the curse which their disobedience has incurred. This character of our Lord's sufferings was the result of express divine appointment. "God sent forth his Son, made of a woman, made under the law." "The Lord made to meet on him the iniquity of us all;" so that exaction was made, and he

[1] Heb. v. 9.   [2] Isa. liii. 4.

answered it. Though he knew no sin, he was "made sin;" constituted liable to sufferings expressive of God's displeasure against sin. Though he deserved nothing but blessings, he "was made a curse;" that is, he was doomed, divinely doomed, to suffering on account of sin.[1]

The peculiar manner of his death marked, and was intended to mark, the penal nature of the whole course of suffering of which it was the close. In the Mosaic law it was provided, that the bodies of all who were put to death, by whatever means, for crime, should be exposed on a gibbet: "Cursed is every one that hangeth on a tree." Every one whose body was hung on a tree was thus publicly declared to have paid his life as a forfeit to justice.[2] To the enlightened eye, there is found on the cross another inscription besides that which Pilate ordered to be written there: THE VICTIM OF GUILT; THE WAGES OF SIN. But how is this? How does, how can, the just One thus die for sins? How is the innocent, the perfect, God-man treated as if he were a sinner, the chief of sinners?

§ 2. *Vicarious.*

The answer to this question is to be found in the second character of his sufferings. When the just One died "for sins," he died "for the unjust," in the room of the unjust; in other words, his sufferings were vicarious. By divine appointment he suffered what sinners deserved, that provision might be made for their being delivered from the sufferings which they had merited, and to which they were doomed. "Messiah was cut off, but not for himself." The just One suffered "for sins," but it was "in the room of the unjust."[3]

There is no possibility of reconciling the penal sufferings

[1] Gal. iv. 4; Isa. liii. 6, margin; 2 Cor. v. 21; Gal. iii. 13.
[2] See note A.   [3] Dan. ix. 26.

of the just One with the wisdom, benignity, or justice of the divine character and government, but on this supposition. The difficulty is great, even if you take the lowest ground that can be taken, the ordinary Socinian ground; for how are you to account for the benignant and righteous Governor of the world treating, or permitting to be treated, as a sinner, as a great sinner, an innocent and perfect man? But just as you elevate, in your conception, the sufferer in the scale of being, the difficulty increases, till, when the truth is stated, it swells beyond all possibility of being grasped by any created mind: the Son of God in human nature, all excellent, and infinitely beloved of his Father, is treated as if he were a sinner! "Wonder, O heavens: Be astonished, O earth!"

On the supposition that he was the substitute of guilty men,—that he voluntarily took their place in accordance with the benignant will of his Father, and, standing in their place, met with their desert,—the darkness which covers this part of the divine procedure is in some measure dispelled. We deserved to endure every kind and degree of suffering. We deserved to die accursed. He, standing in our room, met not with what he personally deserved, but with what we deserved.

This account of the matter, it may be said, removes one difficulty, but it is only by creating another. And it is true there is a difficulty, and a great one: How came he to occupy our place? But this difficulty is of a totally different character from that which we have just been considering. In the former case we were perplexed with an apparent want of wisdom, righteousness, and benignity in the divine dispensation; but admit, what cannot well be denied, that the Son of God had complete power over that human nature which he had taken into union with his divinity, and all foundation for accusing the divine government of injustice, for treating him according to the character which he had voluntarily assumed, is obviously removed: and take into consideration the immeasurable glory which was to accrue to the character and government of God, in the prevention of an accumulation of sin and misery through all eternity, which baffles all power of imagination to estimate, and the securing of a corresponding accumulation of holy happiness, which this strange dispensation is fitted to secure,—which, so far as we know, could not have been secured in any other way,—which we are sure could not have been secured in any other way so well,—then, instead of an apparent want, there is an obvious superabundance, of wisdom and benignity in it. We do not cease to wonder, —if possible, we wonder more than ever; but the expression of our wonder is not, "Doth God pervert judgment? Doth the Almighty pervert judgment?" It is, "O the depth of the riches both of the divine knowledge and wisdom, and righteousness and grace. How unsearchable are his counsels, and his ways past finding out!"[1] The difficulty now is, not to reconcile incompatibilities, but to comprehend infinities. There is still a mystery; but it is a bright, not a dark one. It is the mystery of divine holiness and kindness; and its contemplation at once awes and delights, as we fear Jehovah and his goodness. "Thy mercy is in the heavens, Holy, Holy, Holy One. How excellent is thy loving-kindness! Is this the manner of man, O Lord God?"

The doctrine of our Lord's substitution has plainly, then, at least this proof of truth—that it, and it alone, accounts satisfactorily for the facts of the case, and leaves the subject free from all difficulties, except such as necessarily arise out of its nature. But this is but a small part of the evidence in its support.

[1] Job viii. 3; Rom. xi. 33.

The doctrine of the vicarious, as well as penal, nature of our Lord's sufferings, is implied in all those passages of Scripture, and they are very numerous, in which he is represented as having been a sacrifice for sin. The circumstance that the term "sin" is often used in the Hebrew Scriptures to signify a sin-offering, is a very strong proof that the victim was considered as standing in the room of the sinner; and how could the fact be more plainly stated than in the words of the Jewish legislator: "Aaron shall lay his hand on the head of the live goat, and confess over him all the iniquities of the children of Israel, and all their transgressions in all their sins, putting them on the head of the goat?" When Christ, then, is said to "have had his soul made," or "to have made his soul a sacrifice for sin;" when he is said to be "a propitiation," that is, a propitiatory sacrifice, "in his blood;" when he is said to be "sacrificed for us as our passover;" when he is said to put away sin by the sacrifice of himself; when he is said to have been "offered to bear the sins of many,"—we are plainly taught that he stood in our room, and bore the penal consequences of our violation of the divine law.[1]

But the doctrine is not only requisite to account for the facts of the case, and necessarily implied in all those passages of Scripture where Christ is represented as a victim, and his death as a sacrifice; but it is frequently stated in the most explicit language in the Holy Scriptures. I shall quote a few passages. Speaking of Jehovah's righteous servant, Isaiah says, "We esteemed him stricken, smitten of God, and afflicted,"—we reckoned him a person punished signally for his own great, though unknown crimes: "but he was wounded for our transgressions, he was bruised for our iniquities; the chastisement of our peace was on him.

---

[1] Lev. xvi. 21; Isa. liii. 10; Rom. iii. 25. Θῦμα, not ἐπίθεμα, is the proper supplement to ἱλαστήριον.—1 Cor. v. 7; Heb. ix. 26, 28.

The Lord laid on him the iniquities of us all." Exaction was made, and he became answerable. "My righteous servant, by his knowledge, shall justify many; for he shall bear their iniquities. Numbered with the transgressors, he bore the sins of many." "Christ died *for* the ungodly" in the way in which some would dare to die for a good man, that is, to undergo death in his stead. "Christ bare our sins in his own body on the tree," or "to the tree."[1] These statements are so very explicit, that one is disposed to say, if the vicarious nature of our Lord's sufferings be not revealed in them, it is impossible that it should be revealed; for language furnishes no terms more clear and unequivocal for this idea than those which have been already employed.

§ 3. *Expiatory.*

The third idea which the language of the text conveys respecting the nature of our Lord's sufferings is, that they were expiatory. When he suffered in the room of sinners those evils which were the manifestations of the divine displeasure against their sins, it was in order to expiate or make atonement for their sins; or, in other words, to render the pardon of their sins consistent with the perfections of the divine character, the honour of the divine law, and the stability of the divine government; and as this was the design of his sufferings, so it has been completely gained by them.

This was the design of our Lord's sufferings. The prophet Daniel informs us that a great event was to take place at a fixed period, even that "Messiah was to be cut off, but not for himself." And what was to be the object of this? "To finish the transgression, to make an end of sin, to make reconciliation for iniquity, to bring in everlasting righteousness." John the Baptist describes our Lord as

[1] Isa. liii. 5-7, 11, 12; Rom. v. 6-8; 1 Pet. ii. 24.

"the Lamb of God, who taketh away the sins of the world." Our Lord himself says that he came to "give himself a ransom for many." The apostle informs us that "he came in the end of the age to put away sin by the sacrifice of himself," and that "God made him to be sin for us, that we might be made the righteousness of God in him." Indeed, what could be the object of vicarious endurance of penal evil but expiation?[1]

This end our Lord's sufferings have completely gained. "The blood of Jesus Christ, God's Son, cleanseth us from all sin." We are redeemed by this price, so "much more precious than silver and gold." "In him, we have redemption through his blood, the forgiveness of sins." "He is set forth a propitiation for our sins, through faith in his blood." "He is the propitiation for our sins; and not for our sins only, but also for the sins of the whole world."[2]

In this glorious truth, that the vicarious sufferings of our Lord have made full expiation for our sins, we ought joyfully to acquiesce, even though we were utterly incapable of perceiving how the means employed were fitted to gain the end. God, who knew what the expiation of sin required, appointed his incarnate Son to be the victim of human guilt, making to meet on him the iniquities of us all; and he has expressed, in the most unequivocal manner, that he is well pleased with the sacrifice which has been presented. "I have finished the work thou gavest me to do," said the Saviour. "Now, O Father, glorify thou me with thine own self with the glory which I had with thee before the world was." And the Father heard him and answered him. He raised him from the dust of death, and placed him at his own right hand, and gave him all power in heaven and in earth, that he might give eternal

---

[1] Dan. ix. 24-26; John i. 29; Matt. xx. 28; 2 Cor. v. 21; Heb. ix. 26.
[2] 1 John i. 7; 1 Pet. i. 18; Eph. i. 7; Rom. iii. 25; 1 John ii. 2.

life to all coming to the Father by him; that in expecting pardon and salvation on the ground of his expiatory sacrifice, "our faith and hope might be in God."[1]

But when we look at the whole wondrous dispensation as unfolded in Scripture, we cannot help saying, "It *became* him for whom are all things, and by whom are all things,"[2] *thus* to dispense pardon and salvation. There is more honour done to the divine law by the incarnate Son of God yielding, in the room of the guilty, a holy obediential submission to its penal sanction, than could have been done it by their everlasting destruction. We wonder how the Father should not spare his Son, but deliver him up to be the victim of human guilt. We wonder how "the brightness of the Father's glory, and the express image of his person," the Creator and Lord of the universe, should have in human nature made himself a sacrifice; but we do not wonder that the Father was propitiated by that sacrifice, we do not wonder that by that sacrifice the Son "purged our sins." We wonder that "he, by whom and for whom all things were created, that are in heaven and on earth, visible and invisible, whether they be thrones or dominions, or principalities or powers," who is before them all, and by whom they all subsist, should, "in fashion as a man," shed his blood on a cross; but we do not wonder that "through that blood we should have redemption, even the forgiveness of sins." We not only believe it because God says it; but we see that, if HE has been the propitiation for our sins, God is just, that he is "the just God" as well as "the Saviour, while he justifies the ungodly, the sinner believing in Jesus;" and we feel the conclusiveness of the apostle's noble argument: "For if the blood of bulls and of goats, and the ashes of an heifer sprinkling the unclean, sanctifieth to the purifying of the flesh; how much more shall the

[1] John xvii. 4, 5; 1 Pet. i. 21.   [2] Heb. ii. 10.

blood of Christ, who through the eternal Spirit offered himself without spot to God, purge your conscience from dead works, to serve the living God? And for this cause he is the mediator of the new covenant, that by means of death, for the redemption of the transgressions that were under the first covenant, they which are called might receive the promise of eternal inheritance."[1]

These remarks on the nature of our Lord's sufferings as penal, vicarious, and expiatory, force on our minds the reflection,—How fearful are the state and prospects, how certain and dreadful will be the destruction, of those sinners who are not by the faith of the truth savingly interested in the penal, vicarious, expiatory sufferings of Jesus Christ! "If these things were done in the green tree, what shall be done in the dry?"

"Had it been possible for sin to be pardoned, and for sinners to be saved, without the atonement made by the sufferings and death of the Son of God, we may be sure that these sufferings and that death would never have been endured." No. God would have spared his Son. He would not have given him up for us, could sin have been pardoned without being expiated, or could it have been expiated at a less cost, by a less noble victim. We argue this on the ground of divine wisdom, justice, and goodness. That wisdom does nothing in vain; that justice could not afflict the guiltless but with his own consent, and for an adequate end; that goodness could inflict no needless suffering, especially on one who was worthily the object of his entire complacency, his infinite delight. If it had been possible that the salvation of a guilty world could have been effected without atonement, without such an atonement, Christ had not died. Nothing presents to the mind more strikingly than this, the impossibility of sin being

[1] Heb. i. 3; Col. i. 14-16; Rom. iii. 25, 26; Heb. ix. 13-15.

pardoned, or the sinner saved, without a personal participation in the expiatory efficacy of the one great sacrifice. "There is not a surer proof of the reality of hell than the cross; not one clearer evidence of the certainty of future vengeance than the means provided for averting it. Had the punishment of iniquity not been under the divine government a sure and settled thing, we should never have heard of such an atonement, or any atonement being made for it. Calvary confirms the sentences of Sinai. What justice thundered from Sinai, mercy, though with tearful eye, yet with unfaltering voice, whispers from Calvary, and the announcement is more fearful in the whisper than in the thunder."[1] The soul that has sinned, and puts away from it the blood of the only atoning sacrifice, must die, die the second death. "Without shedding of blood there is no remission." "His blood cleanseth from all sin;" but if you put it away from you as "a common thing," your blood must be shed, the life of your souls must answer for it: and yet there can be no remission, there is no atonement in your sufferings, there can be none; for there is no adequate satisfaction to the demands of law and justice.

And the destruction of the neglecter, the despiser, of the blood of the Son, by whom alone there is expiation, will be as dreadful as it is certain. If we form our judgment of the amount of the penalty from the amount of the expiation, no light thought of it will for a moment lodge within us. Nowhere is the lesson, "It is a fearful thing to fall into the hands of the living God,"[2] more alarmingly uttered than from the cross. The wrath of God is on the unpardoned

---

[1] These sentences within inverted commas, in this paragraph, and many of the thoughts in it and the following one, are borrowed from one to whose valuable writings the author owes ampler and heavier obligations—his esteemed and beloved brother and friend, Dr Wardlaw.

[2] Heb. x. 31.

sinner, and it must abide on him if he lay not hold of the hope set before him in the gospel,—if, by the faith of the truth, he do not become one with him who suffered, the just in the room of the unjust. Who knoweth the power of this wrath? Look to the cross, and find there the most adequate answer that can be given to this dreadful question. He who hangs there knows the power of this wrath. Think on what He suffered; and learn to think justly of the evil of sin, and of what awaits the obstinate unbelieving sinner. If God spared not his Son, standing in the room of sinners, shall he spare the sinner who madly insists on keeping his own place, and refuses to seek shelter under the overshadowing wings of the angel of the covenant? No: there is no salvation without pardon; no pardon without atonement; no atonement without satisfaction; no satisfaction but in the atonement of Christ Jesus. No: "there remaineth no more sacrifice for sin;" and to him who rejects it, "there remaineth nothing but a certain fearful looking for of judgment and fiery indignation, to devour the adversaries."[1]

I cannot close this section of the discourse with these tremendous words. No. Unbelieving, impenitent sinner, thou art yet within the sphere, throughout which the infinite atonement is shedding its saving influence. Once more, it may be only once more, thou hearest the sincere affectionate call of "God in Christ, reconciling the world to himself, not imputing to men their trespasses:" "Be reconciled." He who knew no sin, has been made sin in the room of men, that they may be made the righteousness of God in him. "Turn ye, turn ye, from your evil ways; for why will ye die?" "Behold the Lamb of God bearing, and bearing away, the sin of the world." "Be it known to you, men and brethren, that through this man is preached

[1] Heb. x. 26, 27.

to you the forgiveness of sin." "This is a faithful saying, and worthy of all acceptation, that Christ Jesus came into the world to save sinners," even the chief; that he came to "give his flesh for the life of the world;" that "his blood cleanseth us from all sin;" and that "he is able to save them to the uttermost that come to God by him."[1] Believe, and live. Persist in unbelief, and absolutely certain, inconceivably dreadful, must be your perdition. The divine decree, confirmed by an oath, "The unbeliever shall not enter into my rest," is unrepealed, unrepealable.

But, blessed be God, not less surely established in the heavens is that faithful saying, "God so loved the world that he gave his only-begotten Son, that WHOSOEVER"—whosoever, though his sins in number be infinite, and in heinousness and aggravation beyond all created power to estimate—whosoever, however frequently he has, in resisting the command to believe, and in refusing the offer of mercy, called God a liar, and trampled under foot equally his authority and his grace—WHOSOEVER "believeth in him shall not perish, but have everlasting life."[2]

IV. THE DESIGN OF HIS SUFFERINGS, "TO BRING MEN TO GOD."

We are now prepared to proceed with our illustration of the apostle's statement of the design of the penal, vicarious, expiatory sufferings of Christ, the just One. They were intended "to bring us, to conduct us, to God." The phrase, to "bring men to God," is obviously figurative. But, though figurative, it is not obscure. It obviously indicates some change in man's relations and dispositions and actions

[1] 2 Cor. v. 20; Ezek. xxxiii. 11; John i. 29; Acts xiii. 18; 1 Tim. i. 5; John vi. 51; 1 John i. 7; Heb. vii. 25.
[2] John iii. 16.

—his state and character and conduct in reference to God. This change is represented under the image of bringing a person near to another, from whom previously he had been at a distance. Such ideas as distance, nearness, and motion, borrowed from physical objects, must, when applied to moral subjects, be understood figuratively; and such expressions as that before us communicate no real information to the mind, till the idea, stripped of its metaphorical dress, stands before us in its naked reality. Then the figure will be of use in illustrating the thing signified. Till this is done, there is nothing in the mind but a confused jumble of material images and moral truths.

Distance of one person from another, when the phrase is used figuratively, is descriptive of ignorance, enmity, dissimilarity, and non-intercourse; want of acquaintance, want of friendship, want of resemblance, want of fellowship. When men, then, are represented, as they often are in Scripture, as far from God, the meaning is, they are ignorant of his character and will; they are in a state of enmity against him, and the objects of his displeasure; they are very unlike God, indeed directly opposed to him in the general features of their moral character; and they are estranged from him, having no favourable intercourse and fellowship with him. And when men are said to be brought to God, it is intimated to us that their state and character in reference to God are materially and most beneficially altered; that from a state of ignorance and error, they are brought to the true knowledge of his character and will; that from a state of mutual hostility, they are brought into a state of reconciliation; that from a state of moral dissimilarity, they are brought into a state of moral resemblance; and that from a state of estrangement and non-intercourse, they are brought into a state of habitual and friendly fellowship. You see, then, the meaning of the figurative expression in the text, the bringing men to God; and thus you may clearly perceive the object to which all the succeeding illustrations will be directed—to make it evident to you that the great design of the penal, vicarious, expiatory, sufferings of the incarnate Son of God, the appointed Saviour of men, was to lead men to just views of the divine character and will, to reconcile them to God, to make them like God, and to establish a friendly intercourse between them and God—to show that they have effected this design, and to show, too, how they have effected it. This must be kept steadily in view by all who would wish fully to understand the subsequent part of our illustration of this vitally important subject.

§ 1. *To bring men to the knowledge of God.*

I observe, then, in the first place, that it was a design of the sufferings of Christ for sins, and in the room of sinners, to bring men to the true knowledge of the character and will of God. In this respect, as indeed in every phase of meaning which belongs to the figurative expression, man was originally *near* God. Man was originally made, as it has been happily expressed, "receptive of a Deity."[1] He was endowed with faculties capable of apprehending the signatures of divinity impressed on all the works of the divine hand, whether in creation or providence; and with a disposition to exercise these faculties—a taste for the high and holy satisfaction growing out of the mental contemplation of boundless power, regulated by perfect wisdom and righteousness, and influenced by perfect benignity; and he was moreover blessed with direct communications from heaven of what, in reference to his own relations and duties to God, it was most desirable for him to know. He was made "in God's image, after his likeness;" and we

[1] Howe.

know that that image consists "in knowledge" as well as "in righteousness and holiness."[1]

When Adam sinned, we are not to suppose, that immediately on his transgression he lost, as by a miracle, all such information respecting the divine character and will as he had previously possessed, or that he was deprived of those rational faculties by which he was made capable of acquiring such information: But becoming an object of the divine judicial displeasure, necessarily from his becoming a sinner, two things followed, which most materially affected the state of his knowledge: he ceased to be the subject of that holy divine influence, the communication of which is the strongest manifestation of the divine favourable regard, which makes those intelligent beings over whom it exerts its benignant power count all knowledge worthless in comparison of "the excellent knowledge" of God; and the Divine Being having now become an object of dread and aversion to guilty and depraved man, it must have become a desirable thing with man "not to retain God in his knowledge," to dismiss him as much as possible from his mind, to guard against the entrance of thoughts about Him, as calculated to interfere with his favourite pursuits, to poison his chosen enjoyments.[2]

The natural operation of these two circumstances would very soon have led to the utter extinction of all true knowledge of God among mankind, even keeping out of view the influence of him who is the prince of darkness, and who, as he led them first away from God, seeks to alienate them from Him more and more, by shutting out the truth respecting God from their minds, and filling them with false views of his character. The religious knowledge of the parents of the human race would soon have been lost. It

---

[1] Gen. i. 27; Col. iii. 10; Eph. iv. 24.
[2] Rom. i. 28. Οὐκ ἐδοκίμασαν τὸν Θεὸν ἔχειν ἐν ἐπιγνώσει.

would in a great measure have died with them; and succeeding generations born ignorant of it,—not destitute, indeed, of faculties to acquire it, but placed in circumstances in which they had few facilities for acquiring it; with no supernatural revelation, which, in the supposed case, could not exist; destitute of all inward impulse towards the acquisition of such knowledge, nay, positively indisposed to its pursuit; exposed to a powerful influence, the object of which is to prevent the entrance of such knowledge into the mind, and to produce false views on its subjects,—must have been almost entirely unacquainted with, must have become fearfully misinformed in reference to, the divine character and will. This, I say, would have been the state of all mankind, had things been left to their natural, or rather unnatural, course, which, blessed be God, they were not; and even as it is, with all the preventive means he has employed, such is nearly the actual state of a very large portion of the human race, "the nations who know not God:" and, indeed, with regard to every human being, however largely furnished with the means of information, his natural state is a state of ignorance and error respecting the divine character and will. Now, what is required to bring such men to the knowledge of the truth on these all-important subjects?

There are obviously two things that are absolutely necessary for this purpose: First, a revelation of the truth with regard to the divine character and will, couched in intelligible language, and attended with sufficient evidence; and, secondly, an influence sufficiently powerful to counteract man's indisposition, man's antipathy, towards such knowledge, and to fix the attention of the mind on this revelation and its evidence, and keep it fixed, till its meaning and authority are so perceived as that it is understood and believed. There is no other conceivable way of communicating the true knowledge of God to a man unacquainted with the divine character, and indisposed to seek knowledge, strongly disposed to eschew it, but that which I have just described. The revelation is not enough without the influence; nor the influence without the revelation. Both are necessary; and, when they are united, they are sufficient to serve the purpose. Accordingly, we find such is the method which God has adopted, to prevent the utter extinction of all true knowledge of himself in the world, and is employing, to make the true knowledge of himself universal in the world. The revelation of his character and will in the Holy Scriptures, attended by the influence of his Spirit, leading men to understand and believe them, is the grand means of bringing men from darkness to light, from the slavery of Satan to the service of God, by putting them in possession of that eternal life which is implied in the true knowledge of the only true God, and of Jesus Christ whom he hath sent.

But some of you are probably disposed to say, " All this is very true, and very important; but apparently not very much to the purpose. You began with asserting the influence of Christ's penal, vicarious, and expiatory sufferings, on men's being brought to the true knowledge of God; and you have only shown us that the Word of God and the Spirit of God are necessary and sufficient for this purpose." I have not, however, finished my illustration. When I have shown, as I am just about to do, that but for the penal, vicarious, and expiatory sufferings of Christ, there could have been no such divine revelation, no such divine influence, as we have been speaking of, it will appear with sufficient clearness, that ignorant deluded man's restoration to the knowledge of God is closely connected with, is necessarily dependent on, those sufferings for sin in the room of the unjust.

What would have been the situation of mankind in the present state, had the atonement not formed a part of the divine arrangement, it is not very easy fully and distinctly to bring before the mind: it is, however, very evident that but for this we could have had no Bible, and no divine influence to enable us to understand and believe the Bible, and of course we could have had no true knowledge of God. God, in consistency with his moral perfections, can bestow directly no spiritual blessing on the objects of his righteous condemnation. Whatever good of this kind he does to man, he does through the mediation of his Son; and whatever he does through the mediation of his Son, he does with a reference to his atoning sacrifice. Had it not been that Christ, as the victim of human guilt, the ransom of human beings, "the Lamb of God who taketh away the sins of the world," was "fore-ordained before the foundation of the world,"[1] no revelation of the truth respecting the character of Jehovah, as the God of holiness and love, justice and mercy, could ever have reached our earth, nor could a divine influence have found its way to the heart of condemned, depraved man, to render that revelation effectual.

Indeed, what is the revelation of God which serves this purpose but the revelation of "his glory in the face of his Son,"[2] that is, in his person and in his work? What man needs is "repentance towards God;"[3] a change of mind respecting God. It were endless to detail all the erroneous views of men with regard to the divine character; but there are two mistakes universally prevalent among men, in their unconverted state, on this subject. They do not believe God to be the holy Being he really is; they do not believe him to be the benignant Being he really is. These were

[1] 1 Pet. i. 20. [2] 2 Cor. iv. 6.
[3] Μετάνοια εἰς τὸν Θεόν. Acts xx. 21.

the original false views which the father of lies infused into the mind of man. It is in the atonement of Jesus, the incarnate only-begotten of God, that the immaculate holiness and the inconceivable kindness, the inflexible justice and the transcendent mercy of the Divine Being, are most gloriously and affectingly displayed. That exhibition of the divine character forms the great subject of the scriptural revelation. Everything is subordinated to the bringing of this out in strong relief; and it is, indeed, just in proportion as men understand and believe the truth on this subject that they really know God.

God is not truly known, though we may be acquainted with many of his attributes and works, till he is known as "God in Christ, reconciling the world to himself, not imputing to men their trespasses; seeing he has made him sin for us, who knew no sin, that we might be made the righteousness of God in him."[1] "No man has seen," no man can see, "God; the only-begotten of the Father, who was in his bosom, He has declared him."[2] In his work primarily, and then in his word, which is the record of his work, he has disclosed the mingled glories of divine holiness and grace, and the unfathomable depth of divine wisdom, and the exceeding greatness of divine power, in the formation and execution of that wondrous scheme, of which his atoning death was, as it were, the foundation and centre. Hence, in the estimation of the apostle, the most direct way of bringing men, sunk in ignorance and error, to the knowledge of God, was to preach Christ, Christ crucified. "Here shine spotless justice, incomprehensible wisdom, and infinite love, all at once. None of them darkens or eclipses the other: every one of them gives a lustre to the rest. They mingle their beams, and shine with united eternal splendour; the just Judge, the merciful Father, and the

[1] 2 Cor. v. 19, 21. [2] John i. 18.

wise Governor. Nowhere does justice appear so awful, mercy so amiable, or wisdom so profound."[1]

And as there could be no such revelation of the divine character as is necessary to bring man to a right knowledge of God, without these penal, vicarious, expiatory sufferings of the Son of God, so without these sufferings there could have been no such divine influence as the depravity of man makes necessary to secure that that revelation, however clear and well accredited, shall serve its purpose. It is with a reference to this atonement that all saving divine influence is put forth. The Holy Spirit, in his renewing influence, is "shed forth abundantly through Jesus Christ the Saviour;" and redemption from the curse lays the foundation for our receiving "the promised Spirit through believing."[2]

In order that God may be known by fallen man, there must be a revelation of God—a suitable revelation of God. The giving of that revelation goes on the supposition that God has been propitiated by an atonement; and the atonement by which God is propitiated is the great subject of the revelation, and makes it what it is,—a revelation fitted to give fallen men just views of the divine character. To the knowledge of God by fallen man, a divine influence is necessary to dispose him to receive, to make him understand and believe, this revelation; and but for the sufferings of Jesus Christ, no such influence could have been put forth. Thus, we trust, we have made it clear to the understandings of all, that to lead men into the knowledge of the divine character by a revelation not only confirmed, but merited, by his sufferings,—and which is a revelation of God chiefly because it is an account of those sufferings in which the character of God is unfolded,—and by a divine influence not only dispensed, but procured, by him, is one design

[1] M'Laurin.   [2] Tit. iii. 5, 6; Gal. iii. 13, 14.

which the Saviour had in view when, according to the benignant good pleasure of his Father, He, as the just One, suffered for sins in the room of the unjust.

On allowing the mind to rest on such views, the reflection naturally rises, How highly should we value our Bibles! How highly should we value them, when we think what they have cost! How highly should we value them, when we think what they contain! How highly should we value them, when we think what end they are intended and fitted to serve!

How much have our Bibles cost? They have not cost us much. Though there once was a time when, even in this country, a single copy of the Scriptures was a possession to which only the wealthy and noble could aspire,[1] yet, ever since any of us can recollect, the Bible was to be obtained at a moderate price; and we have great cause to rejoice that now the best of books is the cheapest of books.[2] If any one in our country is without a Bible, the reason must be sought somewhere else than in the scarceness or the dearness of the inspired volume. Yet the Bible, which costs us so little, cost some very dear, through whose instrumentality it comes to us. Our English Bible cost William Tyndale his life; and many others "bonds and imprisonments." Indeed, it were difficult to estimate the amount of labour and suffering which our English Bible has cost;[3] still more difficult to estimate the expense of toil

---

[1] In England, in 1274, the price of a Bible, with a commentary, fairly written, was L.30; the equivalent of fifteen years' work of a labourer, whose wages were then 1½d. a day. In 1429, Wiclif's New Testament sold for L.2, 16s. 8d., equal to L.30 of our money.—*Le Bas' Wiclif*, and *Townley's Biblical Anecdotes*.

[2] See note B.

[3] My ancient and much esteemed friend, the Rev. Christopher Anderson, in his elaborate and valuable *Annals of the English Bible from 1524 to 1844*, has, at a great expense of time and toil, furnished British

and sacrifice at which, since the beginning, the preservation and transmission of the sacred books have been secured. All these considerations go to enhance the value of our Bibles; but they are all as nothing in comparison with the consideration which the subject of our discourse brings before the mind. Looking at our Bibles, we may well say, "They were not gotten for gold, neither was silver weighed for their price. They cannot be valued with the gold of Ophir, with the precious onyx, or the sapphire. No mention shall be made of the coral, or pearls; for their price is above rubies. The topaz of Ethiopia cannot equal them, neither can they be valued with fine gold." They were not purchased for us by "such corruptible things as silver and gold;" nay, not by such things even as the travail of men's minds, or the sacrifice of men's lives, but "by precious blood, as of a lamb without blemish and without spot—the blood of Christ."[1] Our Bibles are blood-bought Bibles! Surely, then, we should value them, and show our value for them by rightly using them. He who neglects the Bible pours contempt on the blood of the incarnate Son of God.

Our regard to the Bible should be strengthened by the consideration of what it contains. It is the record of those sufferings of which it is one of the many precious results. It tells us, of what it never could have entered into the heart of man to conceive, that He who was "God manifest in the flesh," died, died as a victim, in our room, for our salvation. It tells us how He who "was in the form of God, and thought it not robbery to be equal with God, humbled himself;" took on him the nature of a man, the form of a servant, the likeness of a sinner; and, having had our sins

---

Christians with the means of forming a just judgment on the topics referred to in the text; and they will not act with wisdom and gratitude if they do not avail themselves of these means.

[1] Job xxviii. 15-19; 1 Pet. i. 18, 19.

made to meet on him, became "obedient unto death, even the death of the cross." What are the events of history, what are the wonders of nature, what are the inventions of art, what are the discoveries of research, what are the demonstrations of science, compared with this! "Into these things angels desire to look;"[1] and shall we, we who have so much deeper an interest in them, turn away from them with indifference or disgust?

Another consideration calculated to increase our regard to our Bible, which our subject brings before the mind, is the end for which it is designed. It is the design of the penal, vicarious, expiatory sufferings of Christ, by means of the Bible, to bring us to God; to make us acquainted with him "whom to know is life eternal," and acquaintance with whom is at once necessary and sufficient to secure true peace to the mind; to restore us to his favour "whose favour is life, and whose loving-kindness is better than life;" to conform us to his image who is the perfection of intellectual and moral beauty; and to introduce us to intercourse with him whose fellowship is the highest honour and the highest blessedness of the highest order of intellectual beings. Let us then value our Bibles; we cannot overvalue them. Let us show our sense of their worth by applying them to the purpose for which they have been given to us; and let us show our love to our fellow-men, by exerting ourselves, that all of them may be put in possession of a gift so costly and so advantageous.

The same considerations which should lead us to value the divine word, should lead us to value the divine influence. Both are necessary to our salvation. Neither could have been ours, but for the penal, vicarious, expiatory sufferings of the Son of God. Let those of us who have obtained the Spirit through believing, "having obeyed the truth by the

[1] 1 Pet. i. 12.

Spirit," seek larger measures of his influence for ourselves. We obtained it when we were not seeking it, when from our ignorance and unbelief we could not seek it; but now that we know its reality and its value, let us seek a more abundant effusion of it. Jesus has died, Jesus has been glorified, that the Spirit may be poured down from on high. "Ask, and ye shall receive; seek, and ye shall find; knock, and it shall be opened to you: for every one that asketh receiveth, and he that seeketh findeth, and to him that knocketh it shall be opened. If ye, being evil, know how to give good gifts to your children, how much more shall our Father in heaven give" good gifts, give his "Holy Spirit, to them who ask him!" And let us not confine our prayers to ourselves, but extend them to those who are yet "sensual, and have not the Spirit." Let us say, "Come from the four winds, O Spirit of the Lord, and breathe upon these slain, that they may live."[1] He could, He alone could, bring us to God. He can, He alone can, bring them to God. Let us bless the Son, to whose meritorious sufferings we owe the word of life and the Spirit of life; and let us bless the Father, to whom we owe the Son, and all the blessings he procures and bestows; in bringing us back to him, in drawing nearer and nearer to whom, through eternal ages, consists "the whole" of man,[2] the whole of his holiness, honour, and happiness.

The subject we have been considering naturally suggests an important question in which we all have a very deep interest. Has this end of the penal, vicarious, expiatory sufferings of Jesus Christ, the bringing men to the true knowledge of God,—has this end been answered in us as individuals? Have we thus been brought to God? Do we know God? Do we really understand and believe the truth with regard to the divine character? This is far from being a common attainment, even in this nominally Chris-

[1] Luke xi. 9-13; Ezek. xxxvii. 9.   [2] Eccles. xii. 13.

tian country. It is far from being a universal attainment, even among members of Christian churches. Many are called by the name of the true God. Many externally call on that name who do not know it, who are entire strangers to that knowledge of the only true God which is eternal life. No man has this knowledge naturally. No man can acquire it without divine teaching. Brother may say to brother, Know the Lord; but the knowledge of God is "a good gift that cometh down from above." "The Lord giveth" this "wisdom; out of his mouth cometh knowledge and understanding."[1] Are we in possession of this knowledge of God, this knowledge which brings us near God, which makes us habitually dwell as in his presence? He who thus knows God, trusts in him. "They that know thy name will put their trust in thee."[2] He that knows God as he ought, loves God. He who knows God follows on to know him, "counting all things loss" in comparison of this excellent knowledge; yet "not counting himself to have attained, neither to be already perfect," but "following after to apprehend that for which also he has been apprehended of God." He that knows God is "strong, and does exploits" in the spiritual warfare. He who is thus acquainted with God, is "at peace,"—at peace with God, at peace with himself, at peace with all the world. He who knows God is transformed by his knowledge, "changed into the same image, from glory to glory."[3] Are we in possession of this knowledge? And is it in the school of the cross that we have learned it? Are the penal, vicarious, expiatory sufferings, the mirror in which we with open face have seen the unveiled glories of the divine character?

If this is indeed the case, happy are we. We "walk in the light of his countenance;" we "rejoice in his name all

[1] Prov. ii. 6.   [2] Ps. ix. 10.
[3] Phil. iii. 3-12; Job xxii. 21; 2 Cor. iii. 18.

the day," and we "are exalted in his righteousness." We are near him, and we shall yet be nearer him. " We know in part;" ere long " we shall know even as we are known." We shall be brought very near him, even to the light which is his dwelling-place; "and in his light we shall see light."[1]

But if we have not been thus brought to God, by being made truly to understand, really to believe, the truth respecting him, especially as manifested in the penal, vicarious, expiatory sufferings of his incarnate Son; though in words we should profess to know Him, living and dying in these circumstances, we shall find our place among " them who know not God, and obey not the gospel of our Lord Jesus Christ." And we know that when He comes, it will be " in flaming fire, to take vengeance" on all such. To those who never knew him in truth, though they professed to know him, he will say, "I never knew you: depart from me."[2] And then they shall never, never know God, but as a God of righteous vengeance; never so know Him as to have life eternal in the knowledge of Him. Far from him now, they shall everlastingly go further and further from the light of life into the blackness of darkness, never to find their way back to Him, the Sun of the universe, the Fountain of knowledge, purity, and happiness. But now they may. To them who are furthest from Him in ignorance and in error, and in alienation through that ignorance and error that are in them, God still proclaims, " Acquaint yourself now with ME, and be at peace." " No man hath seen," no man can see me; but " the Only-Begotten has declared" me. " He that hath seen the Son hath seen the Father." Look to Jesus, then, if you would know God. " How long, ye simple ones, will ye love simplicity; how long, ye fools, will ye hate knowledge?" "Turn ye at his

---

[1] Ps. lxxxix. 15-17; 1 Cor. xiii. 12; Ps. xxxvi. 9.
[2] 2 Thess. i. 7, 8; Matt. vii. 23.

reproof: behold, he will pour out his Spirit unto you, he will make known his words to you;" he will give you "an understanding heart," and "ye shall know he is the Lord."[1]

§ 2. *To bring men to favour with God.*

A second view of the object of the penal, vicarious, expiatory sufferings of Christ is, that they were designed to bring men from a state of enmity into a state of reconciliation with God. The original state of man in reference to God was one of cordial friendship. It was the state of a dutiful child in the well-regulated family of a wise and affectionate parent; it was the state of a loyal subject under the government of a wise and benevolent prince: the happiness of the child was in accordance with, and secured by, the good order of the family; the happiness of the subject was accordant with, and secured by, the good government of the state. The Father, the Sovereign, regarded the dutiful child and subject with complacent approbation and kindness; and the dutiful child and subject regarded the wise and righteous and benignant Father and Sovereign with veneration, love, and confidence.

The introduction of sin necessarily revolutionized all this. The order of the family made it necessary that the undutiful child's conduct should be distinctly marked with the Father's displeasure. The well-being of the community made it necessary that the rebel subject should be adequately punished. Man, when he became a sinner, became, necessarily became, the object of the judicial displeasure and of the moral disapprobation of God. His happiness became opposed to the honour of the divine character, and to the stability and well-being of the divine government. No change took place in God. He is Jehovah; he cannot change. He is "the Father of lights, with whom there is

[1] Job xxii. 21; John i. 18, xiv. 9; Prov. i. 22, 23; Jer. xxiv. 7.

no variableness, neither shadow of turning." The change had taken place in man; and his changed moral state necessarily produced a change in his moral relations to the unchanged One,—produced such a change just because He was the unchanged, the unchangeable One. Had there been no such change, God must have changed; he must have ceased to be holy and just, to love righteousness, and to hate iniquity. Man, the safe happy child and subject, has thus become the disowned outcast, the condemned rebel; and dislike, suspicion, and fear have in his heart taken the place of affectionate esteem and humble confidence.

Thus man, the sinner, in both these respects, is far from God; and the natural course of things is, that he should go further and further from God, sink deeper and deeper in guilt, become more and more hardened in alienation and enmity. "God is," and cannot but be, "angry with the wicked every day." "He will," he can, "by no means clear the guilty."[1] If the sinner *will* continue to break the holy, just, and good law, that holy, just, and good law *must* continue to sentence him to merited adequate punishment. God cannot deny himself. His will, his nature, cannot change with man's wayward inclinations. And the sinner becomes every day, by the indulgence of forbidden dispositions, and the perpetration of forbidden crimes, more and more an alien and an enemy. He knows God is displeased with him, and that He has reason to be so. He hates the law, which he cannot but abstractly approve; and he regards the Author and Executor of that law with mingled fear and aversion. "The carnal mind is enmity against God; it is not subject to the law of God, neither indeed can be."[2]

The inquiry, Is it a possible thing that man, in this aspect of his moral state and religious relations, as far from God, should be brought near to him? is a question which,

---

[1] Ps. vii. 11; Ex. xxxiv. 6.   [2] Rom. viii. 7.

if proposed to the unfallen angels, would certainly not have been answered in the affirmative. With their high adoring sentiments of the unfathomable wisdom, and unbounded power, and infinite benignity of God, they would not have, with the rashness men often manifest in treating similar questions, pronounced such a consummation absolutely impossible. But the probabilities must have appeared to them fearfully against it. The angels who sinned perished irremediably. Would he who spared not sinning angels, ministers of light, spare sinning men, the children of the dust? And how could he spare them, without tampering with justice and violating faithfulness? If it be possible, it must be in some way which reconciles apparent incompatibilities; for God cannot deny himself. Had the question been proposed to those wise and holy beings, their reply would probably have been, "O Lord, THOU knowest:" and had it then been announced to them that the event was not only possible, but certain; and that in the depth of the divine counsels lay a plan for its accomplishment; and had they been called to conjecture what were the means which God had devised, that "his banished should not be expelled from him,"[1] they would have been as much at a loss as ever. They would have answered, "Such knowledge is too wonderful for us: it is high, we cannot attain to it." Most certain it is that the truth could never have entered into their mind, that this end was to be gained by the penal, vicarious, expiatory sufferings of the Only-Begotten of God, "the brightness of his Father's glory, and the express image of his person." Yet so it is; and though this method of bringing God and man into a state of reconciliation could never have suggested itself to the mind of man or angel, yet now that it has been developed in the incarnation, and life, and death, and resurrection, and exaltation of the divine

[1] 2 Sam. xiv. 14.

Saviour, as described in the word of the truth of the gospel, we cannot help perceiving how admirably fitted it is to accomplish its mighty purposes, in making the pardon and salvation of man consistent with the perfections of the divine character and the principles of the divine government; in destroying the natural enmity of the depraved human heart, and in again making God and man the objects of most complacent mutual regards.

We do not here ask what was necessary to make God willing that self-ruined man should be ultimately happy. Nothing was necessary to this but his essential infinite benignity. He has "no pleasure in the death of him that dieth."[1] Should the whole sinning universe perish, it is not for want of love in him who is love. The question here is, What could reconcile the exercise of mercy to man with the claims of the divine justice, with the declarations of the divine law, with the stability of the divine government, with the well-being of the great moral family of God? It was necessary that something should be done which would place the excellence of the divine law, which had been violated, in a point of view at all events no less clear than the unswerving obedience of the human race as unfallen, or the everlasting destruction of the human race as fallen, would have done. To all created wisdom, it must have appeared a hopeless inquiry, What can do this?

Yet this has been accomplished, fully accomplished, by the penal, vicarious, expiatory sufferings of the incarnate Son of God. He who was "in the form of God" became a man; was "made under the law" which man had violated; had the iniquities of man laid on him by the Supreme Judge; yielded an obedience to the law, absolutely perfect as to principle, extent, and continuance; "was made a curse" for man; endured the very evils which are the

[1] Ezek. xxxiii. 11.

manifestation of the displeasure of God against man's sin, the result of his violation of the holy, just, and good law; and became obedient unto death, even to the death of the cross. The law was more honoured in the obedience of its precepts and endurance of its sanctions by him who is "God manifest in the flesh," than it had been dishonoured by the sin of man. "The Lord was well pleased for his righteousness' sake," because by it "he magnified the law, and made it honourable." He "put away sin by the sacrifice of himself." He "finished transgression, made an end of sin, and brought in everlasting righteousness."[1] On the ground of what he has done and suffered, the just in the room of the unjust, the just God is the justifier of the ungodly believing in him. It has become a righteous thing with God to forgive the sin and save the sinner.[2] Thus we see how the penal, vicarious, expiatory sufferings of our Lord, make the pardon of sin and the salvation of sinners consistent with the perfection of the divine character and the principles of the divine government.

But the atonement is intended and fitted not only to remove the judicial displeasure, but the moral disapprobation, of God from those who are interested in its saving efficacy. By the atonement, according to the arrangements of the "covenant ordered in all things and sure," is secured to the chosen of God the communication of that divine influence which is necessary to transform the character, and make him who is the proper object of God's moral disapprobation the object of his holy complacency. "Christ hath redeemed us from the curse of the law," that we might receive not only the blessing of Abraham, a free and full justification by faith, but also that we might receive the promised Spirit by believing.[3] And still further, it is

---

[1] Isa. xlii. 21; Heb. ix. 26; Dan. ix. 24.
[2] 1 John i. 9.   [3] Gal. iii. 14, 15.

the exhibition of the divine character, made in the penal, vicarious, expiatory sufferings of Christ, as this is brought before the mind in a plain, well-accredited revelation, that is the grand instrument, in the hand of the divine Spirit, in creating men anew in Christ Jesus unto good works; in bringing them into a mode of thinking, and feeling, and acting, that is in accordance with his mind and will, and therefore the object of his complacent approbation. As the restoration of man to the friendship of God, in the sense of his becoming the object of the divine moral complacency, is the result of his restoration to the image of God, it is enough to have generally referred to the subject here. Its more full illustration will naturally come to be attended to under some of the subsequent divisions of our subject.

It is time now that we observe that the reconciliation between God and man must be mutual. The sinner's enmity against God must be removed, as well as God's judicial displeasure against the sinner; and while God regards the saved sinner with complacent approbation, he must be made to cherish reciprocal affections of supreme veneration, esteem, love, and confidence towards God. The penal, vicarious, expiatory sufferings of our Lord are intended, are calculated, and are found, in fact, to be effectual for gaining these ends. Man was led away from God by the suspicion infused into his mind by the father of lies, that God did not wish to make him as happy as he might be,—that by the commands and threatenings of his law he threw obstructions in the way of his being free and happy; and now, in his guilty and depraved state, the knowledge that God condemns him on account of sin, and the deep feeling that the requisitions of his law, though just, are in direct opposition to the strongest propensities of his nature, lead him to regard God with settled aversion. Nothing can change this state of mind but a just view of the divine character, especially of the holy benignity of that character. I must know and believe the love of God before I can cordially love him. I must see him to be lovely, I must see him to be kind. No manifestation of the divine character will serve this purpose but that which is made in the atonement of Christ. There is no power but the power of Christ's death, which can bring home a human heart to God. "Common mercies of God, though they have a *leading* faculty to repentance, yet the rebellious heart will not be led by them. The judgments of God, public or personal, though they should drive us to God, yet the heart unchanged runs the further from him. Do we not see it by ourselves and other sinners about us? They look not at all towards him that smites, much less do they return; or if any more serious thoughts of returning arise upon the surprise of an affliction, how soon do they vanish! either the stroke abating, or the heart by time growing hard and senseless under it. Indeed, where it is renewed and brought in by Christ, then all other things have a sanctifying influence, according to their quality, to stir up a Christian to seek after fuller communion, closer walk, and nearer access to God. But leave out Christ, Christ crucified, and all other means work not this way: neither the works nor the word of God sounded in his ear, 'Return, return,' will bring him near. Let the rod speak too, to make the cry louder, still the wicked will do wickedly; will not hearken to the voice of God; will not see the hand of God, though lifted up; will not be persuaded to lay aside enmity, or seek for reconciliation."[1] No, till they are made to see HIM on the cross as a high altar, "lifted up" as the victim of human guilt, bearing and bearing away the sins of the world, they will never be drawn to God. Whenever they are made in the

[1] Leighton.

faith of the truth to see that "in this was manifested the love of God, in that God sent his only-begotten Son into the world, that," through his being the propitiation for our sins, "we should live through him," then, and not till then, they learn to "love him who first loved them," who thus loved them.[1] They cannot doubt the kindness of Him who "spared not his own Son, but delivered him" up as a sacrifice in their room. The weapons of rebellion drop out of their hand, the jealousies of guilt are banished from their heart; and as enmity is destroyed by the view of the divine character given in the atonement, when apprehended in the faith of the truth, so it is principally by the same exhibition of the divine character being brought more fully and kept habitually before the mind, that all the holy affections of divine friendship on the part of the reconciled sinner are excited and strengthened so as to become leading constituents of the character, every-day principles of action.

Our illustration of this part of the subject would be defective, did we not add that the destruction of the enmity, and the cultivation of this holy friendship, is not only effected chiefly by the instrumentality of the faith of the truth respecting the penal, vicarious, expiatory death of Christ; but, as we have already had occasion to remark, that that divine influence which gives to this instrumentality all its efficacy, is an influence which never could have found its way to the corrupted human heart, but for the atonement of Christ, and the communication of which to all the chosen of God is secured by that atonement.

Let us here again pause for a little, and inquire, Have we *thus* been brought to God? Have we from a state of hostility been brought into a state of reconciliation? The question is not, Has an atonement which lies at the foundation of a reconciliation been made? That is beyond all

---

[1] 1 John iv. 9, 19.

question. The substance of all the typical shadows of the legal atonement is to be found in the sacrifice of Christ: "Christ, our paschal lamb," "the Lamb of God," "has been sacrificed for us." There is no need of asking if that sacrifice of atonement be an adequate one. "If the blood of bulls and goats, and the ashes of an heifer sprinkling the unclean, sanctified to the purifying of the flesh; how much more shall the blood of Christ, who through the eternal Spirit offered himself to God without spot, purge the conscience from dead works, to serve the living God?" The only fit judge of its adequacy has most explicitly declared his satisfaction with it, by raising the self-devoted victim from the dust of earth, and setting him on the throne of the universe, "giving him glory, that our faith and hope might be in God."[1] The "seventy weeks" have long ago been accomplished; and reconciliation has been made for iniquity, by full satisfaction being yielded to the requisitions of the offended justice and violated law of God.

There is no need of asking if this reconciliation be intended for me. Who shall enjoy the saving results of this reconciliation is known only to God, can be known only to God, except in the case of those who make their election sure by making sure their calling; who, by accepting the reconciliation, obtain experimental evidence that they are reconciled. But nothing is plainer than that this reconciliation, and the blessings flowing from it, were intended to be, and are in fact, freely offered to all who hear the gospel; and who that knows anything of the character of him who makes the offer, dare express or even harbour a doubt as to that offer being a most sincere and unequivocal one? The satisfaction made was perfect satisfaction. The law could demand no more. The atonement is an infinite atonement: Christ, the incarnate, only-

---

[1] 1 Cor. v. 7; Heb. ix. 13, 14; 1 Pet. i. 21.

begotten, "suffered for sin, the just One in the room of the unjust." For every human being then, however guilty and depraved, to whom the gospel comes, there is reconciliation through Christ, if he will but gladly and gratefully receive what is freely given him of God.

Men have foolishly and impiously made questions on these points; but there is no room—blessed be God that it is so!—no room for rational doubts here. If there were, where, oh where, were the hopes of any of the children of men? Were not an all-perfect atonement, a complete reconciliation in the word of the truth of the gospel, held out for the acceptance of "mankind-sinners as such," as our fathers of the Secession loved to say, that gospel would be anything rather than "glad tidings of great joy to all people." Yes, "God is in Christ reconciling the world to himself, not imputing their trespasses to them; for he hath made him to be sin for us who knew no sin, that we might be made the righteousness of God in him."[1]

But it is a question, and a most important one,—let us, every one of us, endeavour to resolve it in reference to himself,—Have we received the reconciliation? It is absolutely certain that Christ has "made peace by the blood of his cross;" but have we through this pacification, as individuals, been brought into a state of peace with God? Have we reason to believe that the blood of our paschal Lamb has been so sprinkled on us, as that the destroying angel shall not touch us? Have we reason to believe that we are delivered from the curse through him having been made a curse for us? We are, questionless, in this most desirable state, if we have believed the truth as it is in Jesus. And with equal certainty may it be affirmed, we are not in this state if we have not believed the truth as it is in Jesus: "He that believeth in him is

[1] 2 Cor. v. 21.

not condemned ;" he shall never come into condemnation : "he that believeth not is condemned already," and, continuing an unbeliever, "the wrath of God abideth on him."[1]

But how am I to know if I believe the truth, the faith of which savingly interests me in the reconciling efficacy of the penal, vicarious, expiatory sufferings of Jesus Christ? To this question many satisfactory answers might be given, affording the individual the means of resolving the awfully important question; but I content myself with that which grows out of our subject. If you are in your minds no more enemies to God through wicked works, but, on the contrary, have his love shed abroad in your hearts; if you love God, and love him just because he is God,—that is, holy love, infinitely excellent, infinitely kind; if you cordially acquiesce in, if you supremely approve and admire, the divine method of salvation, "grace reigning through righteousness unto eternal life;"[2] if you are reconciled to the divine law, accounting it in all things to be right, "holy, just, and good,"—esteeming entire conformity to it, as exemplified in the character and conduct of our Lord, as your highest honour and happiness as well as duty; if you are reconciled to the divine providential arrangements, however opposite to your natural inclinations, saying, "Good is the will of the Lord,"—Lord, what thou wilt, when thou wilt, how thou wilt; if there is a distinctly begun and steadily progressive conformity of your mind and will to the mind and will of God; then have you reason to conclude, not only that reconciliation has been made for iniquity, but that you have received that reconciliation.

And if we have thus received the reconciliation, what a debt of gratitude do we owe to Him who has reconciled us to himself by Christ Jesus; to Christ Jesus, who hath thus brought us to God; and to the good Spirit, who in our

[1] John iii. 18, 36. [2] Rom. v. 21.

case has rendered the ministration of reconciliation effectual, and has saved us from the fearful consequences of receiving this grace of God in vain! Let this gratitude manifest itself in leading us habitually to cherish the sentiments and pursue the conduct which becomes us as restored prodigal children, pardoned rebel subjects. Let us, constrained " by the mercies of God, present ourselves to Him as living sacrifices, holy and acceptable, which is our reasonable service, our rational worship." Let us serve him without fear, "in holiness and righteousness, all the days of our lives;" "walking at liberty, keeping his commandments;" serving him "in newness of spirit," and "not in the oldness of the letter;" making it evident, from the manner in which we do and suffer his will, that we are not slaves, but sons; that "we have not received the spirit of bondage again to fear, but the spirit of adoption, whereby we cry, Abba, Father." Let us show that we really do "know the joyful sound, by walking in the light of the divine countenance, rejoicing in God's name all the day, being exalted in his righteousness."[1]

If there be any here who have not received the reconciliation, what shall I say to them? I cannot bid them hope, remaining in their present circumstances. No; there is, there can be, neither happiness nor hope in a state of enmity with God. I might represent to them the horrors of their condition, the still greater horrors of their prospects, and expostulate with them on the shocking unnaturalness as well as inconceivable sinfulness of their conduct, in being enemies of the most excellent and amiable and benignant of beings. But, instead of doing this, I shall at once urge them to "lay hold on the hope that is set before even them in the gospel." To the human being within these walls

[1] Rom. xii. 1; Luke i. 74, 75; Ps. cxix. 45; Rom. vii. 6, viii. 15; Ps. lxxxix. 15, 16.

most characterized by enmity against God, most under the influence of the carnal mind, God is now proclaiming, "Acquaint thyself with ME, and be at peace; so shall good come to thee." Behold me! Behold me! I am glorious in holiness; but I am rich in mercy. I can by no means clear the guilty; but I have set forth Christ Jesus a propitiation, through faith in his blood. I am a just God; but I am the Saviour. I am just; but I am the justifier of him who believes in Jesus. As I live, I have no pleasure in the death of him who dieth. Return to me; I have redeemed you. Return, return. I, even I, am he who blotteth out your transgression for my own sake, and I will not remember your sin. Be reconciled to God. Oh, be persuaded, that remaining far from him you must perish! Oh, be persuaded, that it is good for you to draw near to God![1]

And say not, "Wherewith shall I come before the Lord?" Who shall bring me near before him? How can I stand before thee, Holy Lord God? Behold "one like unto the Son of man," but in reality the Son of God; yet your brother, your kinsman-Redeemer. He has "engaged his heart to approach to Jehovah" in your name, and has opened a way by which you may come into his favourable presence. Hear him proclaiming, "I am the way, the truth, and the life: no man can come to the Father but by me." "His blood cleanseth us from all sin." He is "able to save to the uttermost them that come to God by him;" and "him that cometh to Him he will in nowise cast out." He is "the power of God unto salvation." He is "the arm," "the strength of Jehovah." Lay hold of him, and "make peace with Jehovah, and he will make peace with you." Receive the message of mercy, and you will find that he is

[1] Heb. vi. 18; Job xxii. 21; Ex. xv. 11; Eph. ii. 4; Ex. xxxiv. 7; Rom. iii. 25; Isa. xlv. 21; Rom. iii. 27; Ezek. xviii. 32, xxxiii. 11; Isa. xliv. 22, xliii. 25; 2 Cor. v. 20; Ps. lxxiii. 27, 28.

"pacified towards you for all the iniquities which you have done;" that he is waiting to be gracious, and ready to bless you "with all heavenly and spiritual blessings in Christ Jesus."[1] Persist in your enmity, and you are undone, utterly undone, undone for ever.

§ 3. *To bring men to likeness to God.*

I proceed now to remark, in the third place, that it was a design of the penal, vicarious, expiatory sufferings of Christ, to bring men from a state of moral dissimilarity into a state of moral resemblance to God. Man in his primeval state, as he had just views of the divine character and will, and enjoyed the favour of God, regarding him with sentiments of supreme veneration, confidence, and love, was also, in the great lineaments of his moral character, assimilated to God. "God created man in his own image, in the likeness of God created he him;" and we know that image consists "in knowledge, righteousness, and holiness."[2] His mind was in entire accordance with the mind of God, his will with the will of God, so far as they were made known to him. He had no views inconsistent with the mind of God, which is truth; no inclinations opposed to the will of God, which is righteousness.

It is altogether otherwise with man the sinner. He is not only ignorant of God, and in a state of enmity with him; but the whole frame of his sentiments and feelings is in direct contrariety to the divine mind and will; he being the image, not of his Father in heaven, but of his fallen earthly father. "God is light, and in him there is no darkness at all;" but "the eyes of the understanding" of irregenerate man "are darkened," nay, he is "darkness,"—

---

[1] Mic. vi. 6; 1 Sam. vi. 20; Jer. xxx. 21; John xiv. 6; 1 John i. 7; Heb. vii. 25; John vi. 37; Isa. xxvii. 5; Ezek. xvi. 63; Eph. i. 3.

[2] Gen. i. 27; Eph. iv. 24; Col. iii. 10.

by ignorance alienated from, opposed to, God. "God is love," but mankind are "hateful," "full of hatred," hating God, and hating each other. God is holy, but they are unholy. God is true and faithful, but they are the children of him who is a liar as well as a murderer from the beginning.[1] And this opposition of character is manifested in the conduct of irregenerate men. They are continually engaged in an attempt to counterwork God, following a rule, seeking an end, entirely different from, entirely irreconcilable with, the rule and end of him, "of whom, and through whom, and to whom are all things."

It is the purpose of God from among the ruins of the fall to create anew a "peculiar people," to form a people for himself, that they may show forth his praise. It is his design to restore in them that moral image of himself which sin has defaced; and the grand means for gaining this end are the penal, vicarious, expiatory sufferings of his own Son.

That the atonement was intended to secure, and has indeed secured, to all who are by faith interested in its saving efficacy, sanctification as well as justification, restoration to the divine image as well as to the divine favour, is a doctrine very clearly revealed in Scripture. "God condemned sin in the flesh, by sending his Son in the likeness of sinful flesh, and for sin"—that is, as a sacrifice for sin. God thus condemned sin, "which the law could not do, in that it was weak through the flesh;" and the consequence is, "the righteousness of the law is fulfilled in us believers, walking not after the flesh, but after the Spirit."[2] "Our old man was crucified with Christ, that we should no longer be the slaves of sin."[3] "For this cause," says the Saviour, "I sanctify myself, that they also may be sanctified through

---

[1] 1 John i. 5; Rom. i. 21; Eph. iv. 18, v. 8; John viii. 44.
[2] Rom. viii. 3, 4.   [3] Rom. vi. 6.

the truth."¹ "He gave himself for us, that he might redeem us from all iniquity, and purify unto himself a peculiar people, zealous of good works."² "Christ loved the Church, and gave himself for her; that he might sanctify and cleanse her by the washing of water through the word; that he might present her to himself a glorious Church, without spot, or wrinkle, or any such thing."³ "Ye know that ye were not redeemed by such corruptible things as silver and gold, from your vain conversation received by tradition from your fathers; but with the precious blood of Christ, as of a lamb without blemish and without spot. He his own self bare our sins in his own body on, or rather to, the tree, that we, being dead to sin, might live to righteousness."⁴ There can be no doubt of the fact, then; but how the penal, vicarious, expiatory sufferings of Christ were necessary for, how they are effectual to, the gaining this end, is an important and interesting subject of inquiry. To understand in theory the influence of the atonement on sanctification, is no inconsiderable attainment in Christian theology; to know it in experience, is the very essence of Christian godliness.

In the few observations I am about to make on the subject, I shall endeavour equally to avoid rash speculation as to the mode of the efficacy of the atonement—an "intruding into those things which men have not seen," cannot see, for God has not revealed them,—and that "voluntary humility" which prevents an explicit avowal of what Scripture does reveal, from a fear of opposing the prejudices or exciting the dislike of the wise men of this world. The whole truth, we apprehend, on the subject may be stated in the three following propositions. By the atonement, as satisfaction to divine justice for sin, and the

[1] John xvii. 19. [2] Tit. ii. 14.
[3] Eph. iv. 25-27. [4] 1 Pet. i. 18, 19, ii. 24.

meritorious ground of the Redeemer's exaltation, obstacles otherwise insurmountable are removed out of the way of the sinner being restored to the divine image; by the atonement, in connection with covenant engagements, or the purpose of mercy, the communication of a divine influence necessary and sufficient for this purpose is secured; and by the atonement, as the subject of a divine revelation, an appropriate instrumentality is furnished for accomplishing this end.

The condemning sentence of the divine law was one obstacle in the way of the restoration of the divine image, insurmountable by all human, all created means. No man, no angel, could make satisfaction to divine justice for sinful man. Till this is made, it consists not with the wisdom, holiness, justice, and faithfulness of God, to bestow on the sinner that sanctifying influence, the communication of which to any created being is the highest proof that he is the object of the kind regard of Him who confers it. Christ giving himself for us as a sacrifice, according to the benignant will of his Father, by which the law was magnified and made honourable, makes it a righteous thing for God to give us, through him and for his sake, all good things; and among these good things, that greatest of all spiritual blessings, being indeed the sum and substance of them all—the good, sanctifying, transforming Spirit.

The power of Satan is another obstacle in the way of the restoration of the sinner to holiness, in restoration to the image of God,—an obstacle which no created agency could have removed. That power is destroyed, and could only have been destroyed, by our Lord, the stronger Man, who "enters the house of the strong man and spoils him of his goods." This work is accomplished in the exercise of Christ's mediatorial power and authority. That power and authority were conferred on him as the reward of that obedience unto death, in which he accomplished the work of atonement. Christ, the just One, having suffered to death for sins in the room of sinners, went to heaven, sat down on the right hand of God, principalities and powers, fallen and unfallen, being put under him, so that the prey may now be taken from the mighty, and the captive of the terrible one be delivered.

But this is not all. By the atonement, in connection with the purpose of mercy, is secured to all the chosen of God, the communication of that divine influence which is at once absolutely necessary and completely sufficient to restore man to the divine image. Such an influence is absolutely necessary to the production of true holiness in the human heart. " It is the Spirit that quickeneth." " We are sanctified by the Spirit of our God."[1] The connection of the communication of the Spirit with the atonement is stated in such passages as the following:— " The Spirit was not yet given, for Jesus was not yet glorified." " It is expedient that I go away: for if I go not away, the Comforter will not come unto you; but if I go away, I will send him." " Christ hath redeemed us from the curse of the law, by being made a curse for us, that we might receive the promise of the Spirit by faith." The Spirit is the Spirit of faith, and "it is given" to men " on the behalf of Christ to believe in his name." It belongs to him as the perfected Captain of our salvation, the Prince and the Saviour, in virtue of the promises made before the world began, to " give" to his redeemed ones "repentance," the new mind,—just another word for the restored image of God,—as well as " the remission of sins." [2]

Finally, by the atonement securing the scriptural revelation of the divine character and will, and being itself indeed

[1] John vi. 63; 1 Cor. vi. 11.
[2] John vii. 39, xvi. 7; Gal. iii. 13, 14; Phil. i. 29; Acts v. 31.

the great subject of that revelation, an appropriate instrumentality is furnished for the sanctification of man, or, in other words, bringing him to God, by restoring him to the divine image. It is by the truth about God, known and believed, that men are conformed to God's image. They are "sanctified by the truth." They "are transformed by the renewing of the mind."[1] In a former part of this discourse, I showed how, without the atonement, no such revelation of the divine character as would transform man could have been given to man. The view given us of the character and will of God in the atonement, the great subject of divine revelation, is such as, just in the degree in which it is apprehended in its meaning and evidence, just in the degree in which it is understood and believed, must conform us to God. "He gave himself for his Church, that he might purify and cleanse her by the word;"[2] of which word his giving himself is the great subject; and it is this which gives it its aptitude for cleansing and renewing the human heart. "Let any person," it has been justly said, "be brought to understand correctly, and to believe cordially, that part of the divine testimony; as a necessary consequence his soul must experience a most momentous moral transformation. He will learn to love God, and to confide in him, as his reconciled Father; he will feel emotions of unfeigned and fervent gratitude for such a marvellous manifestation of kindness; and he will feel sincerely desirous to testify his gratitude, by putting on that moral image of God which in absolute perfection was manifested in his incarnate Son, now seen and felt to be the beauty and dignity of the soul, and by obeying the divine law, which he now sees and feels to be indeed 'holy, just, and good.'"

[1] John xvii. 17; Rom. xii. 2.   [2] Eph. v. 26.

§ 4. *To bring men to fellowship with God.*

I proceed now to remark, in the fourth place, that the penal, vicarious, expiatory sufferings of Christ were designed to bring men from a state of alienation and non-intercourse into a state of habitual favourable fellowship with God. Fellowship with God is a phrase to which I am afraid many attach very indefinite, confused, incorrect ideas. The term fellowship indicates either common possession or mutual intercourse. In the first sense, fellowship with God means the thinking, willing, choosing, and enjoying in common with God, and is, in fact, just what we have been speaking of under the name of conformity to God's image. In the second sense, fellowship with God means intercourse with God—interchange of thoughts and sentiments; intercourse maintained on his part by his communication of gracious influence and saving blessings, and on the part of man, by the exercise of devout affections.

When the Christian is enabled firmly to believe the truth as it is in Jesus, confidently to rely on the Saviour, humbly to hope for the grace that is to be brought to him at the coming of our Lord Jesus, patiently to bear affliction, triumphantly to conquer temptation, it is in consequence of divine communications. Good and perfect gifts come down to him from above; and the reception of these gifts draws out from the heart of the Christian holy aspirations of gratitude and desire, which find their expression in thanksgiving and prayer. These bring down new supplies of celestial influence; and these influences, in their turn, excite more enlarged wishes for spiritual blessings, stimulating the very appetite which they gratify. There is thus an ever-growing interchange of influences and desires, and of prayers and blessings.[1]

[1] Balmer.

This is the sense in which we use the word fellowship with God in the present remarks.

Man, in his original condition, lived in this state of intercourse with God. Adam, as well as Enoch, " walked with God;" and though we have but a few fragments of paradisaical history, we cannot doubt that, still more than in the case of Moses, God spake to Adam " as a man to his friend." Sin interrupted this intercourse. Man's guilt made it inconsistent with God's holiness, and justice, and truth, to have intercourse with man as his friend; and man's depravity equally unfitted and indisposed him for acceptable intercourse with God. The language of the human heart in its unchanged state is, " Depart from me, I desire not the knowledge of thy ways." " What have I to do with thee, thou Holy One?"

To re-open this intercourse, and to lay a foundation for its permanent maintenance, is one great purpose of the atonement of our Lord. And it is obviously well fitted to gain this object. It has gained it in the case of all who, through believing, have obtained a personal interest in its saving effects.

We have already, in effect, shown how this is accomplished. It is by producing reconciliation and resemblance that the atonement opens up the way for communion. "Between parties at variance there can be no agreeable or affectionate intercourse without reconciliation. Between persons whose principles and tastes, whose dispositions and pursuits, have no congeniality, there cannot exist an intimate or permanent friendship; and even their casual intercourse must be comparatively heartless and joyless. 'Can two walk together except they be agreed?'"[1] We have seen how " God is in Christ, reconciling the world to himself, not imputing to them their trespasses; seeing that he has made him to be sin for us who knew no sin, that we might

[1] Balmer.

be made the righteousness of God in him;" how he brings men, naturally afar off, nigh by the blood of the cross; how he "abolishes the enmity thereby;" how the sprinkling of the blood of Jesus Christ on the conscience purifies the heart, and sheds abroad there the love of God, and all its blessed holy fruits.[1]

Our heavenly Father, regarding his adopted, regenerated children with ineffable, complacential delight, cannot but take pleasure in giving them tokens of his love; and they, on the other hand, cannot be happy if their fellowship be not with the Father, and with his Son Jesus Christ. He comes to them through the mediation of his Son. They go to him through the same mediation. He, "for the great love wherewith he loves them, blesses them with heavenly and spiritual blessings in Christ Jesus; and they, "by one Spirit through him, have access to the Father," in the full assured belief that "his blood cleanseth from all sin," and that "he, ever living to make intercession for them, is able to save them to the uttermost." Knowing that they "have a great High Priest for them passed into the heavens," they habitually "come boldly to the throne of grace, that they may obtain mercy, and find grace to help in the time of need."[2]

This intercourse is chiefly maintained through the instituted means of Christian worship, secret, private, and public. It is in reference to these that Jehovah promises to come to his people, and bless them, and supply their need; and it is in reference to these that they say, "We will go into his tabernacles, we will worship at his footstool;" "then will I go to the altar of God, to God my exceeding joy;" in Bethel, in his own house, God Almighty met with me and blessed me; "it is good for me to draw near to God."[3]

[1] 2 Cor. v. 19, 21; Col. i. 20; Eph. ii. 15; Heb. ix. 14.
[2] Eph. ii. 18; John i. 7; Heb. ii. 25, iv. 15, 16.
[3] Ps. cxxxii. 7, xliii. 4, lxxiii. 28; Gen. xlviii. 3.

We have thus seen, that the great design of the penal, vicarious, expiatory sufferings of Jesus Christ, is to bring men to God; from a state of ignorance and error into a state of true knowledge; from a state of enmity into a state of friendship; from a state of dissimilarity into a state of resemblance; from a state of non-intercourse into a state of fellowship. We have seen that the atonement actually does all this; and we have seen too, in some measure, *how* it does all this.

This glorious design it gains to a certain extent, in the case of every believer, even in the present world. This glorious design it will gain in absolute perfection, with regard to every believer, with regard to the whole company of believers, in the heavenly state. Having given himself for them, and having purified them by his Spirit, through his word and providential dispensations, he will collect them all together (there is to be "a gathering together at his coming"), and present them to God, his Father and their Father, his God and their God, "a glorious Church, without spot, or wrinkle, or any such thing;" saying, "Behold me, and the children thou hast given me;" "not one of them is lost." Then will it appear how careful the good Shepherd has been of his charge; "how faithful to Him who appointed him." They are all raised up at the last day, near, very near to God; so far as the difference of nature admits, "holy as he is holy, perfect as he is perfect;" even their bodies fashioned like unto the glorious body of him who is God manifest in flesh. Then shall be fulfilled, in all its extent of meaning, that promise which cheered the heart of the Saviour amid the toils and sorrows, the agony and blood of the great work of expiation: " Since he has made his soul a sacrifice for sin, he shall see his seed, he shall prolong his days, and the pleasure of the Lord shall prosper in his hand. He shall see of the travail of his soul, and shall be satisfied; by his knowledge shall my righteous servant justify many, for he has borne their iniquities. Therefore will I give him the great for his portion, and he shall have the strong for his spoil, because he poured out his soul to death, and was numbered with the transgressors; and he bare the sin of many, and made intercession for the transgressors." With gladness and rejoicing shall his redeemed ones be brought; they shall enter into the King's palace, " and there they shall abide." They shall be for ever with the Lord; like him, seeing him as he is; beholding, and, as far as it is possible, sharing his glory and his blessedness. And all this is the result of Christ the just One suffering for sins in the room of sinners.[1]

And now let us once more, each for himself, seriously propose the question, Have I thus, through the atoning death of Christ, been brought to God? Have I been conformed to his image? Have I been introduced into his fellowship? Have I been delivered from this present evil world through Christ giving himself for me? Have I been redeemed from my vain conversation received by tradition from my fathers? Have I indeed been born again? Have I received " a divine nature?" Have I become " a new creature?" Is my mind conformed to God's mind—my will to God's will? And is my conformity to God increasing? Am I growing in knowledge, and purity, and love? Am I becoming more and more a partaker of his holiness? Am I daily receiving spiritual benefits from God, and rendering daily to him the expressions of a grateful mind, a loving heart? And can I say, " Truly my fellowship is with the Father, and with his Son Jesus Christ; my conversation is in heaven; my affections are set on things above?"

The person who is a stranger to the state and exercises of mind described in these expressions, whatever profession

[1] Eph. v. 27; Isa. viii. 18; Heb. ii. 13; Isa. liii. 10-12.

he may make, has not received the atonement. As yet Christ has died in vain, so far as he is concerned. He is not yet brought to God. Let all of us beware of resting short of this conformity to, this fellowship with, God. Let us beware of resting in speculation, in profession, in formal worship, in external obedience. Let us especially put far away from us the monstrous thought, that we can be enjoying the divine favour and fellowship through the atonement of Christ, while living in sin. To expect this is to expect an utter impossibility; is to impose on ourselves by a damnable delusion. " What fellowship hath righteousness with unrighteousness? What communion hath light with darkness? What concord has Christ with Belial?" "If we say that we have fellowship with God, and walk in darkness, we lie, and do not the truth; but if we walk in the light, as he is in the light, we have fellowship one with another"—that is, he and we have indeed communion,—" and the blood of Jesus Christ his Son cleanseth us from all sin."[1]

Let the conviction be every day deepened, that coming to God in the way of assimilation and fellowship is absolutely necessary to our true and final happiness; and that this conformity to, this communion with God, can be obtained only " through the redemption that is in Christ Jesus." Yes, my brethren, it is in the faith of the truth respecting the great atonement that the sinner finds " redemption from all his iniquities." There is no possibility of being conformed to God till we are reconciled to God: it is at the cross that the pilgrim loses his burden; and there is no being reconciled to God without being conformed to Him.

Let all those who, through the power of the atonement, and by the faith of the truth, have obtained some measure of conformity to God, and of favourable intercourse with him, seek larger and still larger measures of those spiritual

[1] 2 Cor. vi. 14, 15; 1 John i. 6, 7.

blessings from the same source, through the same channel. Let them never forget that they must owe their sanctification as well as their justification, their new character as well as their new state, to God sending his Son in the likeness of sinful flesh, a sacrifice for sin,—to Christ the just One suffering for sins in the room of the unjust. Christ, "Christ crucified," is all in all. "All things are of God," through his Son. "Of God are we in Christ Jesus, who of God is made to us wisdom, and righteousness, and sanctification, and redemption."[1] To him be all the glory.

V. THE CONSEQUENCES OF HIS SUFFERINGS.

The consequences of our Lord's penal, vicarious, expiatory sufferings come now to be considered. They are thus stated by the apostle: "Christ the just One, having suffered for sins in the room of the unjust, that he might bring them to God," was "put to death in the flesh, but quickened by the Spirit; by which also he went and preached to the spirits in prison, who sometime were disobedient; and having risen from the dead, he went into heaven, where he is on the right hand of God; angels, and authorities, and powers, being made subject to him."

The Bible has often been represented as a book full of obscurities and difficulties; by infidels, who wish to disprove its divine origin; by Roman Catholics, who need an argument to prove the necessity of tradition on which their system rests, and an apology for their apparently impious and paradoxical conduct, in withholding a confessedly divine revelation from the unrestrained perusal of the common people, and endeavouring to keep it covered by the veil of a dead language; and by mere nominal Christians among Protestants, who equally need an excuse for their habitual

[1] Col. iii. 11; 2 Cor. v. 18; 1 Cor. i. 30.

neglect of a volume which they admit to be of divine authority, and profess to regard as the ultimate rule of religious faith and moral duty. And if the Bible were really so full of obscurity and difficulty, if it were the ambiguous and unintelligible book it has been represented, neither the careless Protestant nor the cautious Catholic would be much to be blamed, except for inconsistency. And even with this minor fault the infidel would not be justly chargeable; for if he can make out his premises, that the Bible is an unintelligible book, there can be little difficulty in admitting his conclusion, that it is not a divine one. A book full of darkness cannot come from Him who "is light, and in whom there is no darkness at all;" and it is certainly useless to read what it is impossible to understand.

But it is not true that the Holy Scriptures are full of obscurities and difficulties. The Bible, generally speaking, is a very plain book. It would not be easy to find a book of its size, on its subjects, where there is so much level to the apprehension of ordinary understandings. No person who sits down to the study of it with an honest wish to apprehend its statements, will find any great difficulty in discovering what are the doctrines it unfolds, or what are the duties it enjoins. "The commandment of the Lord is *pure*,"[1] that is, clear as the light of heaven, "and it enlightens the eyes." But though the Bible is not *full* of obscurities and difficulties, there are obscurities and difficulties in it. It is with the great light of the moral as of the natural world,—the whole of its disc is not equally lustrous. There are spots in the sun; but he must be very blind, or very perverse, who should on that account maintain that the sun is not a luminous body at all, and insist that it gives no light, and that, if it rays forth anything, it rays forth darkness.

[1] Ps. xix. 8. "Clarum, dilucidum."—ROSENMÜLLER.

On the other hand, he who insists that there are no spots on the sun, and he who insists that there are no difficulties in the Bible, equally prove that they are very superficial observers or very prejudiced judges. That in writings so ancient as the Hebrew Scriptures, published originally in a state of society so different from that which at present prevails, among a people whose language has long ceased to be spoken, and whose laws and customs and manners have little resemblance to ours, there should be difficulties, was naturally to be expected; and indeed this could not have been prevented without a miracle. But these obscurities attach themselves to comparatively but few passages; and the difficulties to which they give origin are gradually diminishing and disappearing as the knowledge of the sacred languages, antiquities, and criticism makes progress; and with regard to those which remain, there are two considerations that deserve remark: the first, that in no case is there uncertainty cast on any of the leading facts or doctrines or laws of revelation by these obscurities and difficulties; and the second, that in almost every case, though in some passages there may be words or phrases, the precise import or reference of which it may be difficult or impossible to determine with certainty, these passages are found notwithstanding replete with important instruction.

These remarks are applicable to the passage of Scripture to which our attention has for some time been directed. The observation of the Apostle Peter respecting his "beloved brother Paul," is applicable to himself. In his epistles "there are some things hard to be understood, which the unlearned and the unstable wrest to their own destruction,"[1] and this is one of them. Few passages have received a greater variety of interpretations; and he would prove more satisfactorily his self-confidence than his wisdom, who

[1] 2 Pet. iii. 15, 16.

should assert that *his* interpretation was undoubtedly the true one.[1] Yet, though we should not be able to determine with absolute certainty who those spirits in prison are, and when, and where, and how, and for what purpose, Christ went and preached to them; and whatever opinion we may adopt as most probable on these subjects, no Christian doctrine, no Christian duty, is affected by our uncertainty or by our opinion. Even were we holding, what appears to us the least probable one, that the words teach us that our Lord, during his disembodied state, went to the region of separate souls, and made a communication of some kind to its inhabitants, either to such of them as were "in safe keeping," in paradise, or "in prison," in Gehenna, they would give no countenance to the delusive dreams either of the Roman Catholic respecting purgatory, or of the Universalist concerning the possibility of favourably altering the condition of men after they have left the present state: they would merely state an insulated fact, nowhere else referred to in Scripture, and from which no legitimate consequence can be deduced at all inconsistent with any other portion of revealed truth; and though we should never obtain satisfactory information on the points referred to, how replete with truth and holy influence is the sentence (vers. 18-22), of which one or two clauses are to us obscure, perhaps unintelligible, "how profitable for doctrine, for reproof, for correction, and for instruction in righteousness!" It would be very presumptuous to expect that I should be able to remove entirely difficulties which have baffled the attempts of the ablest interpreters. Yet I believe that patient, careful, honest, persevering, prayerful study of any portion of God's word, is never unproductive of some good effect; and I must say, after the experience of forty years'

[1] "The passage is indeed extremely obscure; and I have seen no explanation of it that is free from objection."—ARCHBISHOP WHATELY.

study of the Bible, that in inquiring into the meaning of Scripture, " darkness has often been made light before me, crooked things straight, rough places plain."[1]

The consequences of the penal, vicarious, expiatory sufferings of our Lord, plainly divide themselves into two classes. First, such as took place *not* in heaven; for that is all that we yet consider ourselves as warranted to say of them; whether on the earth or under the earth, may perhaps appear in the course of our illustrations: " He was put to death in the flesh, but quickened by the Spirit; he by it went and preached to the spirits in prison, who sometime were disobedient;"—and secondly, such as took place in heaven: " Having risen from the dead, he went into heaven, and is on the right hand of God; angels, and authorities, and powers, being made subject to him."

§ 1. *He became dead in the flesh, quickened in the Spirit, and went and preached to the spirits in prison.*

Let us attend to these two classes of the consequences of our Lord's penal, vicarious, expiatory sufferings in their order; and first, of those which took place not in heaven.

Some interpreters consider only the words rendered " put to death in the flesh, but quickened by the Spirit," as descriptive of the consequences of our Lord's penal, vicarious, expiatory sufferings. What follows they consider as referring to something which he did in or by the same Spirit by which he was quickened, on another occasion altogether, at a former period, so long gone by as the antediluvian times. They interpret the words descriptive of the consequences of our Lord's sufferings for sins in the room of sinners thus: He was violently put to death, in his body, or in his human nature; but he was quickened, restored to life, by the Spirit,—that is, either by the Holy Ghost, the third

[1] See note C.

person of the Holy Trinity, or by his divine nature, the spirit of holiness, according to which he is the Son of God, in contradistinction to his being the son of David according to the flesh,—that Spirit by which he was justified,—that eternal Spirit through which he offered himself to God, a sacrifice without spot or blemish. And the remaining part of the statement they consider as equivalent to, By the Holy Spirit inspiring Noah as a preacher of righteousness, or in his divine nature, through the same instrumentality, he in the antediluvian times "went and preached,"—either a pleonastic expression for preached, or intimating that he came from heaven in his divine influence and operation, as he came to paradise in the cool of the day, came down to see the tower of Babel, came down on Mount Sinai at the giving of the law,—made known the will of God to the men of that generation, who were *then* " spirits in prison," condemned men, doomed to punishment for their sins, and kept as in a prison till the time of execution, when the flood came ; or who are *now* spirits in the prison of hell, kept along with the evil angels,."under chains of darkness, to the judgment of the great day."

The sense thus brought out of the words is self-consistent, and not incompatible with any of the facts or doctrines of revelation ; but this mode of interpretation seems to us liable to great, and indeed insurmountable, objections. The words flesh and spirit are plainly opposed to one another. The prepositions *in* and *by* are not in the original. The opposed words[1] are in the same case: they stand plainly in the same relation respectively to the words rendered put to death and quickened,[2] and that relation should have been expressed in English by the same particle.[3] If you give

---

[1] Σαρκὶ—πνεύματι. Hæc verba pro ἐν σαρκὶ ἐν πνεύματι et quidem pro adjectivis (adverbiis ?) posita videntur.—STORR.

[2] Θανατωθεὶς. Ζωοποιηθεὶς.   [3] See note D.

the rendering, "put to death *in* the flesh," you must give the corresponding rendering, " quickened *in* the spirit;" which would bring out the sense, either ' quickened in his human spirit or soul,' a statement to which it is difficult to attach a distinct meaning, for the soul is not mortal, Christ's spirit did not die, and to continue alive is not the meaning of the original word; or ' quickened in his divine nature,' a statement obviously absurd and false, as implying that He who is " the life," the living One, can be quickened, either in the sense of restored from a state of death, or endowed with a larger measure of vitality. On the other hand, if you adopt the rendering of our translators in the second clause, " quickened *by* the Spirit," then you must render in accordance with it the first clause, ' put to death *by* the *flesh*.' If by the Spirit you understand the divine nature of our Lord, by the flesh you must understand the human nature, which makes the expression an absurdity. On the other hand, if you understand by the Spirit the Holy Ghost, then by flesh you must understand " mankind,"—put to death by men, but restored to life by God the Spirit. This interpretation, though giving a consistent and true sense, —the sense so forcibly expressed in Peter's words to the Jews, " whom *ye* crucified; whom *God* raised from the dead,"—is forbidden by the usage of the language. Then there can be no doubt that there does appear something very unnatural in introducing our Lord, in the midst of what is plainly a description of the results of his atoning sufferings, as having in the Spirit, by which he was quickened after he had been put to death, gone many centuries before, in the antediluvian age, to preach to an ungodly world; and there is just as little doubt that the only meaning that the words will bear without violence being done them is, that it was when he had been put to death in the flesh, and quickened in the Spirit, or by the Spirit, whatever that may mean, he went and preached; and that "the spirits," whoever they be, were "in prison," whatever that may mean, when he preached to them.

These are not all the difficulties connected with this interpretation, which may be termed the common Protestant interpretation of the passage; but they are quite sufficient to convince us that it is untenable, and to induce the apprehension that it would never have been resorted to but from its supposed necessity to destroy the shadow of support which another mode of interpretation gives to some of the errors of Popery, which have, by that "deceivableness of unrighteousness" which characterizes the system, been turned to great account in fettering the minds and plundering the property of the unhappy victims of that masterpiece of imposture and superstition; or to the soul-endangering dream of Universalism, that there are means of grace of which those who die unforgiven may avail themselves in the separate state, so as to avert the natural results of their living and dying in unbelief and impenitence.

Another class of interpreters consider the whole statement before us as referring to what happened subsequent to, and consequent on, our Lord's penal, vicarious, expiatory sufferings.[1] Some of these consider the event referred to in the words, "He went and preached to the spirits in prison," as having taken place during the interval between our Lord's death and resurrection; others, as having taken place after his resurrection. The first consider the words rendered "having been put to death in the flesh, but quickened by the Spirit," as equivalent to—"having become dead as to his body (a very fair rendering of the words), but continuing alive as to his soul (a sense which the original words will not bear), he in that soul went to the region of separate souls, Hades, the invisible state, and there preached

[1] See note E.

to the spirits in prison, who before were disobedient." The second consider the words referred to as equivalent to—"Being put to death in his human nature, but restored to life by his divine nature, or by the Holy Ghost, he in his resurrection body, which they conceive was not subject to the ordinary laws of matter, or in his new life, went down to the region of separate souls, and there preached to the spirits in prison."

These two classes of interpreters, holding in common that our Lord went down to Hades, are considerably divided as to what was his object in going there, as described or hinted at in the passage before us: one class holding that he went to hell (Gehenna), the place of torment, to proclaim to the fallen angels, who are kept there under chains of darkness, as the spirits in prison (though how *they* could be said to be disobedient in the days of Noah does not appear; and besides, these spirits seem plainly to belong to the same class of beings as "the souls" that were saved, ver. 20),—to proclaim throughout that dismal region his triumph over them and their apostate chief; another class holding that he went to this place of torment to announce his triumph over the power of darkness, and to offer salvation through his death to those human spirits who had died in their sins; a third class holding that he went to purgatory to release those who had been sufficiently improved by their disciplinary sufferings, and to remove them to paradise; and a fourth class, who translate the "spirits in prison,"[1] "the spirits in safe keeping," holding that he went to paradise, the residence of the separate spirits of good men, to announce to them the glad tidings, that the great salvation which had been the object of their faith and hope was now completed.

Each of these varieties of interpretation is attended with

[1] Τοῖς ἐν φυλακῇ πνεύμασι.

its own difficulties, which appear to me insuperable. Some of them go upon principles obviously and demonstratively false; and all of them attempt to bring much out of the words which plainly is not in them. To state particularly the objections against them would occupy a good deal of time, and I am afraid would afford little satisfaction and less edification to my hearers. There are, however, common difficulties bearing on them all which seem quite sufficient to warrant us to set them all aside, and which may be stated in a sentence or two. It seems incredible, if such events as are darkly hinted at rather than distinctly described in these words thus interpreted had taken place, that we should have no account of them, indeed no certain allusion to them, in any other part of Scripture.[1] It seems quite unaccountable why the separate spirits of those who had lived in the days of Noah, and perished in the deluge, are specially mentioned as those, among the inhabitants of the unseen world, to whom the quickened Redeemer went and preached; the much greater multitude who, before that time, and since that time, had gone down to the land of darkness, being passed by without notice. And what will weigh much with a judicious student of Scripture is, that it is impossible to perceive how these events, supposing them to have taken place, were, as they are represented by the construction of the language to be, the effects of Christ's suffering for sins in the room of sinners, and how these statements at all serve to promote the apostle's practical object, which was to persuade persecuted Christians patiently and cheerfully to submit to sufferings for righteousness' sake, from the

---

[1] "They that think Christ's soul and godhead preached to spirits while his body lay in the grave, suppose that those spirits knew it whom it concerned. But if it had been necessary for us to know not only Christ's preaching to ourselves but to them, he would surely have more clearly told it us."—RICHARD BAXTER.

consideration exemplified in the case of our Lord, that suffering in a good cause and in a right spirit, however severe, was calculated to lead to the happiest results. No interpretation, we apprehend, can be the right one, which does not correspond with the obvious construction of the passage, and with the avowed design of the writer.

Keeping these general principles steadily in view, I proceed now to state, as briefly and as plainly as I can, what appears to me the probable meaning of this difficult passage: " A passage," as Leighton says, " somewhat obscure in itself, but as it usually falls, made more so by the various fancies and contexts of interpreters aiming or pretending to clear it."

The first consequence of those penal, vicarious, expiatory sufferings which Christ, the just One, endured by the appointment of his Father, the righteous Judge, for sins, in the room of the unjust, noticed here is, that he " was put to death in the flesh."[1] The unjust, in whose room he stood, were doomed to death; and he, in bearing their sins, submitted to death, to a violent death, to a form of violent death which, by a divine appointment, marked him as the victim of public justice.[2] He was with wicked hands crucified, hanged on a tree; and he that was hanged on a tree was declared to be accursed, or to have died as a victim of sin by the hand of public justice. The idea here, however, seems not to be so much the violent nature of the infliction, as its effect, the entire privation of life, and consequently of power. The word seems used as in Rom. vii. 4, " Ye are become dead."[3] He became dead in the flesh, he became bodily dead.[4] He lay an inanimate, powerless corpse in the sepulchre.

---

[1] Θανατωθεὶς μὲν σαρκί. Morte affectus, quoad corpus.—KUTTNER.
[2] Deut. xxi. 23 ; Gal. iii. 13.
[3] Ἐθανατώθητε τῷ νόμῳ—not " ye have been put to death by the law."
[4] Σαρκικῶς.

But his becoming thus bodily dead and powerless was not more certainly the effect of his penal, vicarious, expiatory sufferings, than the second circumstance here mentioned, his "being quickened in the Spirit." If this refer to his resurrection, we must render it quickened by the Spirit; but we have already seen that, without misinterpretation, it cannot be so rendered. Besides, the resurrection is expressly mentioned in the 21st verse, in connection with the ascension to heaven. To be quickened in the Spirit is to be quickened spiritually, as to be put to death in the flesh is to become dead bodily. This interpretation is quite warranted.[1] The word rendered to be quickened,[2] literally signifies to be made alive or living. It is used to signify the original communication of life, the restoration of life to the dead, and the communication of a larger measure of life to the living. A consequence of our Lord's penal, vicarious, expiatory sufferings was, that he became spiritually alive and powerful, in a sense and to a degree in which he was not previously, and in which but for these sufferings he never could have become—full of life to be communicated to dead souls, "mighty to save." He was thus spiritually quickened. "The Father gave him to have life in himself, that he might give eternal life to as many as the Father had given him"—"to all coming to the Father through him." "All power," even the power of God, "was given to Him," who had been "crucified in weakness;" and by this power he lives and gives life. "The second Adam" thus became "a quickening spirit." He became, as it were, the receptacle of life and spiritual influence, out of which men

---

[1] Thus, poor in spirit, πτωχοὶ τῷ πνεύματι, i.e. πνευματικῶς.—Matt. v. 3. Waxed strong in spirit, ἐκραταιοῦτο πνεύματι, i.e. πνευματικῶς.—Luke i. 80. Rejoiced in spirit, ἠγαλλιάσατο τῷ πνεύματι, i.e. πνευματικῶς, etc.—Luke x. 21.

[2] Ζωοποιεῖσθαι.

were to "receive, and grace for grace." As a divine person, all life, all power, necessarily inhered in his nature; but as Mediator, that spiritual life and energy which make him powerful to save, are gifts bestowed on him by the Father, as rewards of his obedience to death, and as the means of gaining the ultimate object of his atoning sufferings. He asked of the Father this life, and he gave it him. It was the consequence of his penal, vicarious, expiatory sufferings, on which his intercession is based. It is to this that he refers when he says, "Except a corn of wheat fall to the ground and die," or rather, fall into the ground, being dead, "it abideth alone; but if it die," if it be dead, "it bringeth forth much fruit." Had Christ not died as the victim of sin bodily, he could never have "lived for ever" as an all-successful Intercessor, "able to save us to the uttermost"— for ever.[1] "If I," said he, "be lifted up," lifted up on the cross ("for this he said, signifying what death he should die"),—"I, if I be lifted up, will draw all men to me."[2] "The Captain of salvation was perfected by suffering." "Because he humbled himself, God highly exalted him, and gave him" all "power over all flesh," all "power in heaven and earth."

The spiritual life and power conferred on the Saviour as the reward of his disinterested labours in the cause of God's honour and man's salvation, were illustriously manifested in that wonderful quickening of his apostles by the communication of the Holy Ghost on the day of Pentecost; and in communicating through the instrumentality of their ministry spiritual life, and all its concomitant and following blessings, to multitudes of souls dead in sins.[3]

It is to this, I apprehend, that the apostle refers, when

---

[1] Εἰς τὸ παντελές, Heb. vii. 25.   [2] John xii. 24, 32.
[3] Πορευθεὶς postquam in cœlum ascendit ut mox, com. 12.—John xiv. 2, 3, 12, 28, xvi. 7, 28. Dicitur Christus predicasse gentibus, quia Apostoli

he says, *by which*, or *whereby*, by this spiritual quickening,—or *wherefore*,[1] being thus spiritually quickened,—" he went and preached to the spirits in prison, who beforetime were disobedient." If our general scheme of interpretation is well founded, there can be no doubt as to who those "spirits in prison" are. They are not human spirits confined in bodies like so many prisons, as a punishment for sin in some previous state of being,—that is a heathenish doctrine, to which Scripture rightly interpreted gives no sanction,—but sinful men righteously condemned, the slaves and captives of Satan, shackled with the fetters of sin. These are the captives to whom Messiah, " anointed by the Spirit of the Lord,"—that is just, in other words, "quickened in the Spirit,"—was to proclaim liberty, the bound ones to whom he was to announce the opening of the prison. This is no uncommon mode of representing the work of the Messiah. "Thus saith the Lord God, he that created the heavens, and stretched them out; he that spread forth the earth, and that which cometh out of it; he that giveth breath unto the people upon it, and spirit to them that walk therein: I the Lord have called thee in righteousness, and will hold thy hand, and will keep thee, and will give thee for a covenant of the people, for a light to the Gentiles; to open the blind eyes; to bring out the prisoners from the prison, and them that sit in darkness out of the prison-house."[2] "He said unto me, Thou art my servant, O Israel, in whom I will be glorified. Then I said, I have laboured in vain, I have spent my strength for nought, and in vain; yet surely my judgment is with the Lord, and my work with my God. And now, saith the Lord that formed

---

id ejus nomine et virtute fecerunt.—2 Cor. v. 20; Acts xiii. 47; Rom. xv. 16; Gal. ii. 8; Eph. ii. 17.—GROTIUS.

[1] Ἐν ᾧ. Τοῦτο ΕΝ Ὡι ἀντὶ τοῦ ΔΙΟ κεῖται αἰτιολογικῶς.—ŒCUMENIUS.

[2] Isa. xlii. 5, 7.

me from the womb to be his servant, to bring Jacob again to him, Though Israel be not gathered, yet shall I be glorious in the eyes of the Lord, and my God shall be my strength. And he said, It is a light thing that thou shouldest be my servant, to raise up the tribes of Jacob, and to restore the preserved of Israel; I will also give thee for a light to the Gentiles, that thou mayest be my salvation unto the end of the earth. Thus saith the Lord, the Redeemer of Israel, and his Holy One, to him whom man despiseth, to him whom the nation abhorreth, to a servant of rulers, kings shall see and arise, princes also shall worship, because of the Lord that is faithful, and the Holy One of Israel, and he shall choose thee. Thus saith the Lord, In an acceptable time have I heard thee, and in a day of salvation have I helped thee: and I will preserve thee, and give thee for a covenant of the people, to establish the earth, to cause to inherit the desolate heritages: that thou mayest say to the prisoners, Go forth; to them that are in darkness, Show yourselves: they shall feed in the ways, and their pastures shall be in all high places. They shall not hunger nor thirst; neither shall the heat nor sun smite them: for he that hath mercy on them shall lead them, even by the springs of water shall he guide them. And I will make all my mountains a way, and my highways shall be exalted. Behold, these shall come from far; and, lo, these from the north and from the west; and these from the land of Sinim."[1]

It is not unnatural, then, that guilty and depraved men should be represented as captives in prison; but the phrase "spirits in prison" seems a strange one for spiritually captive men. It is so; but the use of it, rather than the word *men* in prison, or prisoners, seems to have grown out of the previous phrase, quickened in spirit.[2] He who was

[1] Isa. xlix. 3-12. [2] "Congruens sermo."—BENGEL.

quickened in the Spirit had to do with the spirits of men, with men as spiritual beings. This seems to have given a colour to the whole passage: the eight persons saved from the deluge are termed eight *souls*.[1]

But then it seems as if the spirits in prison, to whom our Lord, quickened in spirit, is represented as coming and preaching, were the unbelieving generation who lived before the flood,—"the spirits in prison, who aforetime were disobedient, when once the long-suffering of God waited in the days of Noah." This difficulty is not a formidable one: this stumbling-block may easily be removed. "Spirits in prison" is a phrase characteristic of men in all ages. We see nothing perplexing in the statement, 'God sent the gospel to the Britons, who in the days of Cæsar were painted savages:' the persons to whom God sent the gospel were not the same individuals who were painted savages in the days of Cæsar, but they belonged to the same race. Neither should we find anything perplexing in the statement: Jesus Christ came and preached to spiritually captive men, who were hard to be convinced in former times, especially in the days of Noah.[2] The reason why there is reference to the disobedience of men in former times, and especially in the days of Noah, will probably come out in the course of our future illustrations.

Having endeavoured to dispose of these verbal difficulties, let us now attend to the sentiment contained in the words,

---

[1] Πνεύματα hic in genere denotant homines quemadmodum paullo post ψυχαὶ ἐν φύλακι. Judæi sub jugo legis—Gentiles sub potestate Diaboli—Illos omnes Christus liberavit, prædicationem verbi sui ad ipsos mittens, et continuans, et Apostolos divina virtute instruens.—SCHŒTGENII. *Horæ Heb.* p. 1043.

[2] Grotius's note is worth quoting: *Quales* animi olim Noæ temporibus non obtemperarunt. Loquitur quasi iidem fuisent: et fuerunt *iidem*, spiritus, sive animi—iidem non ἀριθμῷ, ut Aristoteles loquitur, sed genere.

'Jesus Christ, spiritually quickened, came and preached to the spirits in prison, who in time past were disobedient.' The coming and preaching describe not what our Lord did *bodily*,[1] but what he did *spiritually*;[2] not what he did personally, but what he did by the instrumentality of others. The Apostle Paul has explained the meaning of the Apostle Peter, when, in the second chapter of the Epistle to the Ephesians, he represents Christ as, after " having abolished in his flesh the enmity, coming and preaching peace to them who were afar off, and to them who were nigh;" that is, both to Gentiles and to Jews. Another very satisfactory commentary may be found in the Gospels. " All power is given unto me," said our Saviour after being quickened in the spirit,—" All power is given to me in heaven and in earth. *Go ye* therefore, and teach all nations, baptizing them in the name of the Father, and of the Son, and of the Holy Ghost; teaching them to observe all things whatsoever I have commanded you: and, lo, I am with you always, even to the end of the world. So, then, after the Lord had spoken to them, he was received into heaven, and sat on the right hand of God. And they went forth, and preached everywhere, the Lord working with them, and confirming the word with signs following."[3] To the apostle, who was born as one out of due time, the commission was, " I send thee to the Gentiles, to open their eyes, to turn them from darkness to light, and from the power of Satan to God, that they may receive the forgiveness of sins, and an inheritance among them which are sanctified by faith that is in Christ;" and whatever Paul did effectually in the discharge of that commission, it was not *he*, but *Christ* by him.[4] Thus, then, is Christ, quickened

---

[1] Σαρκικῶς, or σωματικῶς.   [2] Πνευματικῶς.
[3] Eph. ii. 13-17 ; Matt. xxviii. 18, 19 ; Mark xvi. 19, 20.
[4] Acts xxvi. 16-18 ; Rom. xv. 18.

in consequence of his suffering, the just One in the room of the unjust, going and preaching to the spirits in prison.

There are two subsidiary ideas in reference to this preaching of Christ quickened in the Spirit, to the spirits in prison, that are suggested by the words of the apostle; and these are—the success of his preaching, and the extent of that success. These spirits in prison had "aforetime been disobedient." Christ had preached to them not only by Noah, but by all the prophets, for the spirit in the prophets was "the Spirit of Christ;" but he had preached in a great measure in vain. He had to complain in reference to his preaching by his prophets, and in reference to his own personal preaching, previously to his suffering the just in the room of the unjust: "I have laboured in vain, I have spent my strength for nought, and in vain. All day long I have stretched out my hands to a stiffnecked and rebellious people." "Who hath believed our report?" But now, Jesus Christ being quickened by the Spirit, and quickening others by the Spirit, the consequence was, "the disobedient were turned to the wisdom of the just;" and "the spirits in prison" appeared "a people made ready, prepared for the Lord." The word, attended by the Spirit, in consequence of the shedding of the blood of the covenant, had free course and was glorified, and "the prisoners were sent forth out of the pit wherein there was no water." "The prey" was "taken from the mighty," the captive of the terrible one was delivered. The sealed among the tribes of Israel were "a hundred forty and four thousand;" and the converted from among the nations, the people taken out from among the Gentiles, to the name of Jehovah, formed an innumerable company, "a multitude which no man could number, out of all nations, and kindreds, and people, and tongues." It was not then "as in the days of Noah, when few, that is, eight souls, were saved." Multitudes heard and knew the joyful sound; the shackles dropped from their limbs, and they walked at liberty, keeping God's commandments. And still does the fountain of life spring up in the quickened Redeemer's heart, and well forth, giving life to the world. Still does the great Deliverer prosecute his glorious work of spiritual emancipation. Still is he going and preaching to the "spirits in prison;" and though all have not obeyed, yet many already have obeyed, many are obeying, many more will yet obey.

The connection of Christ's penal, vicarious, expiatory sufferings, with this increased spiritual life and vigour in Him as the Redeemer and Saviour of men, and its blessed consequences in the extensive and effectual administration of the word of his grace, is stated here, but not here only. It is often, as I have already had occasion to remark, brought forward in Scripture: " Christ has redeemed men from the curse of the law, having become a curse in their room, that the blessing of Abraham," a free and full justification, " might come upon the Gentiles, and that men might receive the promised Spirit through believing." "It is expedient for you that I go away: for if I go not away, the Comforter will not come; but if I depart, I will send him to you." The Spirit is given because Jesus is glorified; and Jesus is glorified, for he has " finished the work which the Father had given him to do," in laying down his "life for his sheep," and in giving his " flesh for the life of the world."

This connection between the atoning death of Christ, and his being quickened, and the quickening of men by him, may be easily understood. The truth respecting it may be stated in a sentence or two. The power of dispensing divine influence formed an important part of our Lord's mediatorial reward, and it was impossible to conceive of any reward more suitable to his holy, benevolent character; and there was an obvious propriety that the work should be accomplished before the reward was conferred. Besides, the truth respecting Christ suffering and dying, the just in the room of the unjust, is the grand instrument which the Holy Spirit employs for converting men, for quickening dead souls. This is the great subject of efficient preaching. Till the atonement was made, the revelation of it could be but obscure. It was meet that the great Preacher should have a clear, full message to proclaim, before he came and preached to every nation under heaven; and that the great spiritual agent should be furnished with the fittest instrumentality for performing all the moral miracles of the new creation. Such appears to me the probable meaning of this much disputed passage.

This view of the subject has this additional advantage, that it preserves the connection of the passage, both grammatical and logical. The words of the apostle, thus explained, plainly bear on his great practical object: 'Be not afraid, be not ashamed of suffering in a good cause, in a right spirit. No damage comes from well-doing, or from suffering in well-doing. Christ, in suffering the just for the unjust, that he might bring us to God, suffered for well-doing; and though his sufferings ended in his dying bodily, they ended also in his being spiritually quickened, and, through the effectual manifestation of the truth, becoming the "author of eternal salvation to all who obey him." Nor is this all. Even his mortal body has, in consequence of these sufferings, been raised from the grave, and in that body he is "gone into heaven, and has sat down on the right hand of God; angels, and authorities, and powers, being made subject to him."'

I am further confirmed in this view of the passage, by observing that in one very important part of it I have the support of Archbishop Leighton. In the text of his commentary, he interprets the passage according to the usual

Protestant mode of exposition; but in a note he observes: "Thus I then thought, but do now apprehend another sense as more probable. The mission of the Spirit, and the preaching of the gospel by it, after his resurrection: preaching to sinners, and converting them according to the prophecy which he first fulfilled in person, and after more amply in his apostles; that prophecy, I mean, Isa. lxi.: The Spirit was upon him, and was sent from him to his apostles, to preach to spirits in prison, to preach liberty to the captives, captive spirits, and therefore called *spirits* in prison, to illustrate the thing the more by opposition to that Spirit of Christ, the Spirit of liberty, setting them free; and this to show the greater efficacy of Christ's preaching than of Noah's: though he was a signal preacher of righteousness, yet only himself and his family, eight persons, were saved by him, but multitudes of all nations by the Spirit and preaching of Christ in the gospel."

What a striking light does this representation cast on the deplorable condition of fallen men! "Spirits in prison;" "dead souls." There is something monstrous here. Nothing naturally so free as spirit; nothing so full of life as *souls*. How deplorable to see bondage and death, where there originally was nothing but liberty and life! We may be disgusted, but we are not surprised, at seeing a loathsome reptile crawling on the earth. But we are at once amazed and shocked, when we see the bird of the sun, with blinded eyes, and broken pinions, and soiled feathers, moving with awkward difficulty along the ground, instead of "sailing with supreme dominion through the azure deep of air,"[1] "unscaling his sight at the fountain of radiance."[2] Alas, what a captivity! Condemned—waiting the hour of the execution of the sentence—no possibility of effecting their escape! Nor man nor angel can open the door of their

[1] Gray.   [2] Milton.

prison-house. Yet are they, blessed be God, prisoners of hope. There is a Saviour, and a great one: Jesus, who "saves his people from their sins," and who, in doing so, "delivers them from the wrath to come."

How well fitted is He for performing all the functions of a deliverer! This is a second reflection suggested by our subject. He has become "perfect through sufferings." He has all the merit, all the power, both as to external event and internal influence, all the authority, all the sympathy that is necessary to enable him effectually to liberate the prisoners of divine justice, the captives of infernal power. He has suffered for sins, the just for the unjust, so as to become dead, as the victim of human transgression; and the atonement made by these sufferings is an atonement of infinite value. And he has been spiritually quickened: endowed with such a superabundance of life as to enable him to give eternal life to innumerable dead souls; and endowed with an infinity of energy, so that he can vanquish the enslavers, level the prison walls, loose the fetters of innumerable "spirits in prison."

Prisoners of hope, turn the eye of faith and desire towards your all-accomplished Deliverer. Remember, now is the accepted time. Yet a little longer, and you will be prisoners more than ever, but no longer prisoners of hope. To borrow the earnest expostulations of a pious divine, "Oh, do not destroy yourselves! You are in prison; he proclaims your liberty. Christ proclaims you liberty; and will you not accept it? Think, though you may be pleased with your present thraldom and prison, it reserves you (if you come not forth) to another prison, which will not please you. These chains of spiritual darkness in which you now are, unless ye be by him freed, will be exchanged, not for freedom, but for the chains of everlasting darkness, wherein the hopeless prisoners are kept to the judgment of the great day."[1] Accept his offer of deliverance, life, liberty. The eternal life which was with the Father gives you life: receive it, and you have life; you have it abundantly. Blessedness is yours, yours for ever. "The Son makes you free, and ye are free indeed."

In what a dignified light does this passage represent the ministry of divine truth! It is the work of the perfected Saviour. Having suffered to the death for sins, in the room of the unjust, and having been spiritually quickened, he comes and preaches to the spirits in prison. He preaches "peace to you who were afar off, and to them who were nigh." The voice is on earth, the speaker is in heaven. "God, who at sundry times and in divers manners spake to the fathers by the prophets, hath in these last days spoken unto us by his Son, whom he hath appointed heir of all things, by whom also he made the worlds; who, being the brightness of his glory, and the express image of his person, and upholding all things by the word of his power, when he had by himself purged our sins, sat down on the right hand of the Majesty on high, being made so much better than the angels, as he hath received by inheritance a more excellent name than they." He that neglecteth and despiseth the word of reconciliation, despiseth not man, but God—"God in Christ, reconciling the world to himself:" wonderful, most wonderful! beseeching men to be reconciled to Him. Surely we should see that we "refuse not Him that speaketh thus to us from heaven." Surely we should "give the more earnest heed to the things which we have heard," which we now hear from him, "lest at any time we should let them slip: for if the word spoken by angels was stedfast, and every transgression and disobedience received a just recompense of reward, how shall we escape if we neglect so great salvation; which at the first began to be spoken by the

[1] Leighton.

Lord, and was confirmed unto us by them who heard him; God also bearing witness, both with signs and wonders, and with divers miracles and gifts of the Holy Ghost, according to his own will?"

The exalted Redeemer is the great, the only effectual preacher. His ministers preach with effect only when he speaks and works *in* them and *by* them. It is an advice full of wisdom as well as of piety, which the good Archbishop gives to those who are anxious to derive saving advantage from the ministry of the word: "Ye that are for your own interest, be earnest with this Lord of life, this fountain of spirit, to let forth more of it upon his messengers in these times. You would receive back the fruit of your prayer. Were ye living this way, you would find more life and refreshing sweetness in the word of life, how weak and worthless soever they were that brought it. It would descend as sweet showers upon the valleys, and make them fruitful."

"Brethren, for your own sakes as well as ours, pray for us, that the word of the LORD may have free course and be glorified." *His* word is quick and powerful. It is "spirit and life;" it "converts the soul; it makes wise the simple; it rejoices the heart; it enlightens the eyes; it endureth for ever." It is as powerful now as in the primitive age. It still "brings down high imaginations;" and while it emancipates the imprisoned spirit from the thraldom of depraved principle, satanic power, and human authority, "it brings into captivity every thought to the obedience of Christ." Oh that through *his* preaching many may be thus at once emancipated and made captive, freed from the fetters of earthliness and sin, bound in the chains of holy principle and divine love; may at once cease to be "spirits in prison," and become inhabiters of that "high tower, that impregnable fortress," in which all obedient to his call are "kept by the power of God through faith unto salvation!"

The subject we have been considering in this section of the discourse brings also before the mind, in a very striking form, some of the great motives and encouragements to missionary exertion. The state of the unenlightened part of mankind, as spirits in prison, calls for our sympathy; and since their imprisonment is not hopeless, it calls for our exertions to procure their emancipation. Had there been no atoning sacrifice, no quickening Spirit, it would have been godlike to mourn their servitude and condemnation, but it would have been madness to have attempted their deliverance.

But there has been an all-perfect, an infinitely valuable atoning sacrifice offered up. Christ, the just One, has died in the room of the unjust, for the express purpose that enslaved, condemned man may be brought to forgiveness and liberty, by being brought to God. No legal bar lies in the way of the emancipation of the spirits in prison, for the offered sacrifice has been accepted. The righteous Judge is well pleased with it, and is ready to demonstrate that he is just in justifying the ungodly who believe in Jesus. He has shown this, by bringing from the dust of death, and seating on his right hand, Him who gave himself a ransom for many. And as there is a law-satisfying atonement, so there is a powerful quickening Spirit, who gives life and liberty. He who was put to death in the flesh is spiritually quickened by that Spirit. And having that Spirit given him without measure, he, in the word of the truth of the gospel, not only proclaims liberty to the captive, but, going forth by the Spirit, he actually unlooses their fetters, and gives them at once that power and the disposition to walk at liberty, keeping the commandments of God. Yes, He who died, the just in the room of the unjust,—He who, to make atonement for sin, was "crucified in weakness," and "became dead in the flesh," having been "quickened in the Spirit," lives by the power of God, and has come preaching to the spirits in prison, making the perverse willing in the day of his power, and "turning the disobedient to the wisdom of the just."

The great work of the emancipation of the spirits in prison is not, then, a hopeless one. Many have been delivered, multitudes more will be delivered. Jesus Christ has not died in vain. The life which the Father has given him to have in himself shall not remain dormant and inoperative. It was so ordained that he might be a fountain of life to spiritually dead man, and might quicken whom he would. This great work of the emancipation of spirits in prison is, strictly speaking, the work of the *Divine* Deliverer. He only could make atonement; He only can give the Spirit.

But he has most kindly and wisely so arranged the method of emancipation, that a place is afforded for the active willing services of those whom he has delivered, in accomplishing the actual enfranchisement of their brethren who still remain "spirits in prison." The gospel which announces the atonement, and in connection with which the Spirit is given, is to be diffused, not by miraculous means, not by angelic agency, but by the voluntary exertions of spiritually emancipated men. It is by their exertions, as the helpers of the Lord, that the chariot in which the Redeemer "rides forth prosperously, because of truth and meekness and righteousness," taking captive captivity, wresting his slave from the mighty, his prey from the terrible one, moves on. They are that angel by which the "everlasting gospel is to be preached to them who dwell on the earth, and to every nation, and kindred, and tongue, and people." It is in the gospel thus propagated that we are to look for him who is quickened in the Spirit to preach effectually to the spirits in prison. Let, then, the considerations, that mankind, the great body of our race, are in a state of condemnation and spiritual slavery; that an all-perfect atoning sacrifice has been offered up, suited to them all, sufficient for them all, offered to them all; that by that sacrifice an honourable channel has been opened for the life-giving, liberty-giving Spirit; that a plain, well-accredited record has been given into our hands, a record fitted and intended to be the Spirit's instrument of putting the individual sinner in possession of the saving results of the atonement, and of filling his heart with the energies and joys of spiritual life and liberty, and that this record is put into *our* hands for the purpose of being universally made known, that wherever there are spirits in prison, liberty may be proclaimed to them ;—let these considerations make their due impression on us; and then, instead of becoming weary in well-doing, allowing our zeal to abate or our exertions to diminish, we shall be "stedfast and immoveable, always abounding in this work of the Lord," counting it a high honour that we are permitted to take a part, however humble, in carrying forward towards complete accomplishment the mighty enterprise in which God makes known the depth of his wisdom, the greatness of his power, and the riches of his grace, and for which his incarnate Son died on earth and reigns in heaven.

§ 2. *He rose from the dead, ascended to heaven, sits at the right hand of God; angels, and authorities, and powers, being made subject to him.*

The second statement in reference to the consequences of our Lord's penal, vicarious, expiatory sufferings, comes now to be considered. "Having been raised from the dead, he went into heaven,[1] where he is on the right hand of God; angels, and authorities, and powers, being made subject to him." Our Lord's resurrection; his ascension or entrance

[1] Without any authority from existing Greek MSS., the Vulgate adds here, "Deglutiens mortem, ut vitæ æternæ heredes efficeremur." It is difficult to account for such an interpolation. It seems to be a *scholion*

into heaven; his session at the right hand of God; and the subjection of angels, and authorities, and powers, to him; all viewed as the consequences of his penal, vicarious, expiatory sufferings: these are the interesting topics to which your attention is now to be directed.

(1.) *His resurrection.*

I remark, then, that as the result of his penal, vicarious, expiatory sufferings, our Lord was raised from the dead. He not only, by laying down, as the victim of human guilt, his natural life as a man, obtained for himself that spiritual life and vigour, in the exercise of which he subdued multitudes of the hardened race which had stood out against former attempts to reclaim them; but he also, after a short season, resumed the life which he had laid down. The body of Jesus, after he had on the cross given up the ghost, was taken down and laid in a sepulchre, and his parted spirit went to paradise.[1] The two constituent parts of his human nature were completely separated, disjoined from each other, though neither of them was disunited from his divinity, and remained in a state of separation for a season, from the evening of the sixth to the morning of the first day of the week; a season sufficiently long, in connection with the circumstances of his crucifixion, to prove that his death was not seeming, but real.

Our Lord had repeatedly assured his disciples that he would rise again, rise again on the third day; though it seems plain they attached very indistinct ideas to these words till events made them plain. Rumours respecting these statements had got abroad, and the Jewish authorities

---

brought into the text; but it must have been so at a very early period, as, with the exception of *two*, or perhaps *three*, it appears in all the MSS. of the Vulgate.

[1] Luke xxiii. 43.

thinking, or pretending to think, that his disciples would attempt to steal his body, and turn his empty grave in connection with these statements to account, in support of their Master's claim to Messiahship, took every precaution to secure the sepulchre from violation till after the specified period had elapsed. But how vain these counsels, how fruitless these attempts to defeat the purposes of God, to falsify the declarations of his Son! He that sat in the heavens laughed at them. Jehovah held them and their endeavours in derision. These endeavours to render impossible the proof of Jesus' Messiahship, ended in furnishing the most convincing demonstration of that great fact, on which, above all others, the evidence of that truth rests.

"In the end of the Sabbath," we are informed by the sacred historian, "as it began to dawn towards the first day of the week, there was a great earthquake: for the angel of the Lord descended from heaven, and came and rolled away the stone from the door of the sepulchre, and sat upon it. His countenance was like lightning, and his raiment white as snow: and for fear of him the keepers did shake, became as dead men," and precipitately retreated from a scene so full of terror.[1] It was amid these awful appearances of nature, meet accompaniments of a transaction so inappreciably important, that the Son of God exercised his power, in taking up again that life which no man could have taken from him, but which he had laid down of himself; and that the Father, "according to the working of his mighty power," fulfilled his ancient promise, that the soul of his Holy One should not be left in the separate state, and that his body should not see corruption.[2]

The resurrection of our Lord in the body in which he lived and died, as it is the fact on which, above all others, rests his claims and our hopes, is established by the most in-

[1] Matt. xxviii. 1-4.   [2] John x. 17, 18; Eph. i. 19; Ps. xvi. 10.

fallible proofs, the most abundant evidence. The sepulchre was found empty on the morning of the third day. That is an indubitable fact; and the only satisfactory, the only plausible account that ever has been given of that fact, is the resurrection. The only other account of it which the ingenuity of ancient and modern infidels has been able to devise, is the self-contradictory story—a story which bears collusion on the face of it—which was put into the mouths of the Roman soldiers, "that the disciples came by night and stole him away while they slept."[1]

The resurrection makes all things plain. It suits with all that went before and all that followed. On the supposition that it did not take place, the history of the life and death of Jesus, and the history of his religion, are alike riddles and mysteries, involved in inextricable difficulties. No human ingenuity can in this case reconcile the authenticated facts with the ordinary principles of human nature, and the established laws of the moral world.

Nobody can doubt that the resurrection of Christ was taught by his original followers: "Jesus and the resurrection" were their great themes. This, supposing that he had not risen from the dead, could only originate either in fraud or in enthusiasm. If fraud had existed, it must have been detected. There was no want of power, or disposition, or opportunity, to detect it. Besides, the character of the apostles; their previous views and conduct; their personal toils, hazards, and sufferings, in a cause which, if not the cause of truth, could do nothing for them, but, on the contrary, entail ruin on them in both worlds; their making the propagation of this fact, and of others connected with it, their great business through life, and then cheerfully sealing their testimony by their blood;—all these make it as certain as anything of the kind can be, that there was no

[1] Matt. xxviii. 13.

imposture in the case. And if they did not deceive, it is just as plain they were not, they could not be, deceived. They were intimately acquainted with Jesus previously to his death; they often saw him during the six weeks he continued on earth after his resurrection. "It was not one person, but many, that saw him: they saw him not only separately, but together; not only at night, but by day; not at a distance, but near; not once, but several times. They not only saw him, but touched him, conversed with him, ate with him, and examined his person to satisfy their doubts."[1] Well might the evangelical historian say, that "to the apostles whom he had chosen, he showed himself alive after his passion, by many infallible proofs."[2]

The proofs of the resurrection of Christ should be most familiar to our minds; for it is the very corner-stone of Christian evidence. "If Christ be not risen, our preaching is vain, our faith is vain;" the apostolic testimony is falsehood; "we are yet in our sins," and all our hopes of pardon and eternal life are delusive dreams. And viewed in connection with the doctrine that "Christ died for our sins, according to the Scriptures," the statement that he "rose again on the third day according to the Scriptures," forms an essential part of that gospel which has been preached to us by the apostles, which we also have received, and wherein we stand, by which we shall be saved, if we keep in memory what has been preached to us; for "this is the word of faith which we preach," says the apostle, "that if thou shalt confess with thy mouth the Lord Jesus, and shalt believe in thine heart that God hath raised him from the dead, thou shalt be saved."[3]

The resurrection of our Lord owes its peculiar importance to the fact of its being the result of his penal, vicarious, expiatory sufferings. It is the evidence that the

[1] Paley. [2] Acts i. 3. [3] 1 Cor. xv. 1-4, 14-17; Rom. x. 8-10.

Supreme Judge is satisfied with these sufferings as an adequate compensation for the injuries done to his law and government by the sins of men. "It is finished," said the Saviour from the cross; and from out the empty sepulchre comes, to the ear of enlightened faith, the echo of these words, "It is finished:" for God, as "the God of peace," the reconciled Divinity,—he who was angry at the sins of men, but whose anger is turned away,—"has brought again from the dead our Lord Jesus, that great Shepherd of the sheep, through the blood of the everlasting covenant."[1] Because that blood, by which the everlasting covenant was to be ratified, has been shed, therefore "hath God raised him up from the dead, and given him glory, that our faith and hope might be in God,"[2] as well pleased *with* him, well pleased with us *in* him. Having fully answered all the demands of that law under which he was made, "for the unjust," having fulfilled all righteousness, having become a curse for them, having become "obedient unto death, even the death of the cross," it was not possible that he should continue bound by the bands of death. The only reason which ever existed for his dying—to wit, that human guilt might be expiated—existed no longer. Human guilt is expiated; the great atonement has been made; and it is meet that he who was "given," devoted to death as a victim, "for our offences," on account of our sins, should be "raised again for our justification;"[3] that is, I apprehend, on account of that which avails to our justification, his finished work, called our justification, as it is that which justifies us.[4]

[1] Heb. xiii. 20.   [2] 1 Pet. i. 21.   [3] Rom. iv. 25.
[4] "*Our* offences"—the ground of our condemnation—were the procuring cause of his death; "*our* justification," that which justifies us—his obedience unto death—is the procuring cause of his resurrection. This interpretation secures to διά with the accusative the same sense in both clauses, and that sense its proper sense.

(2.) *His ascension to heaven.*

I now proceed to remark, in the next place, that as the result of his penal, vicarious, expiatory sufferings, our Lord ascended to heaven. "He is gone into heaven," says the apostle. When our Lord was raised from the dead, it was not that he might continue to be an inhabitant of this lower world. It was that, in the nature in which he had obtained eternal redemption for all who obey him, he might, on the throne of the universe, preside over the whole train of events by which this everlasting deliverance, in all the variety of its blessings, should be bestowed on those for whom it was procured. He remained on earth long enough to give satisfactory evidence of the reality of his resurrection, and "to give commandments to the apostles whom he had chosen" to wait for the communication of the promised Spirit, and then in his name to "go into all the world," and proclaim to mankind his doctrine and law.

When the forty days appointed for these purposes had elapsed, and the time of his being taken up had come, "He led his disciples out from Jerusalem as far as Bethany, and lifted up his hands, and blessed them; and it came to pass, while he blessed them, he was parted from them, and carried up into heaven." They eagerly gazed after him as he majestically rose, with extended blessing hands, till a cloud received him out of their sight; and "while they looked stedfastly toward heaven as he went up, behold, two men stood by them in white apparel, which also said, Ye men of Galilee, why stand ye gazing up to heaven? this same Jesus, which is taken up from you into heaven, shall so come in like manner as ye have seen him go into heaven."[1]

Such is the sublimely simple account of our Lord's going

[1] Luke xxiv. 50, 51; Acts i. 9-11.

into heaven; but from the intimations of ancient prediction in reference to this event, we cannot doubt that it was accompanied with circumstances of grandeur, too glorious to be made the subject of contemplation to men dwelling in flesh. Beholding it in prophetic vision, at the distance of many centuries, we find the inspired bard exclaiming, "The chariots of God are twenty thousand, even thousands of angels: the Lord is among them, as in Sinai, in the holy place. Thou hast ascended on high, thou hast led captivity captive."[1] "It would seem," as has been remarked,[2] "that the two radiant messengers who appeared to the disciples as they were gazing after their Master with ardent eyes, formed only a small part of his celestial retinue. It would seem that in his train there were thousands and myriads of the chariots or cavalry of God: that legions of the heavenly hierarchies, and a countless multitude of the noblest of created beings, tuned their harps or sounded their trumpets in his praise." It is not an improbable conjecture, though it is nothing more, that "the many saints" who came out of their graves after his resurrection joined him as he ascended, and went with him into heaven, as a proof that he had vanquished sin and death, and become the "first-fruits of them that sleep."

We cannot help attempting to follow him in thought. As he draws near to the heavenly Zion, "the perfection of beauty," "the city of the great King," the habitation of the heavenly Majesty, the tabernacle which God, not man, has pitched; the whole celestial city is moved at his coming, the everlasting gates are flung open for his reception, and "with gladness and rejoicing he is brought, and enters into the King's palace." "God is gone up with a shout, the Lord with the sound of a trumpet. Sing praises to God, sing praises; sing praises to our King, sing praises."

[1] Ps. lxviii. 17, 18.   [2] Balmer.

"Lift up your heads, O ye gates; and be ye lift up, ye everlasting doors; and the King of glory shall come in. Who is this King of glory? The Lord strong and mighty, the Lord mighty in battle. Lift up your heads, O ye gates; even lift them up, ye everlasting doors; and the King of glory shall come in. Who is this King of glory? The Lord of hosts, he is the King of glory."[1]

Where that heaven is which has received our Lord, and which must retain him during "the times of restitution of all things,"[2] where "he must reign till all his enemies become his footstool,"[3] we need not inquire, for it is impossible for us to know; but we are warranted in asserting, that it is a place where all the perfections of the Deity, which can be manifested by means of material grandeur and beauty, are displayed in a degree of which we can form no adequate conception; and that whatever can render a place desirable as a residence to a perfectly holy embodied human mind, with its intellectual faculties and moral dispositions and sensibilities in the highest state of perfection, is to be found there in absolute completeness. The best notion we can form of it is the general one, that it is the place which the eternal Father, the God of infinite power, and wisdom, and righteousness, and love, has prepared as a meet residence for his incarnate Only-Begotten, in whom he is well pleased, after he had on earth finished the work which he had given him to do.

The body in which our Lord rose and ascended was the body in which he had lived and died. It was flesh and blood, as he himself very explicitly states. But "flesh and

---

[1] Ps. xlvii. 5, 6, xxiv. 7-10.
[2] Acts iii. 21 : Ἄχρι χρόνων ἀποκαταστάσεως πάντων. Luke iv. 13 ; Acts xiii. 11 ; Rom. v. 13 ; Gal. iv. 2. In all these passages, ἄχρι seems to signify "during," not "until."
[3] 1 Cor. xv. 25.

blood cannot inherit the kingdom of God." A change seems to have taken place on it on the occasion, similar to that which "in a moment, in the twinkling of an eye," is to pass on the saints who are found alive on the earth at the coming of our Lord, and which also shall take place on them when they are "caught up in the clouds to meet the Lord in the air."[1]

This ascension to heaven, like the resurrection which preceded it, is a result of the penal, vicarious, expiatory sufferings of our Lord. "He that ascended is the same as he that descended;" and it is because he descended to the lowest depths of suffering as our appointed victim, that he ascends to the sublimest heights of celestial honour and felicity as our perfected Redeemer. The entrance within the veil into the holy of holies was closely connected with the offering of the sacrifice for the atonement of the sins of the whole congregation of Israel. The high priest entered there, to present the blood of the sacrifice before God. He could not enter there without having made ceremonial expiation for them by that blood; and it was in consequence of our great High Priest having, by his own sacrifice, "for ever perfected them that are sanctified,"[2] that he passed through these visible heavens, the antitype of the veil under the Mosaic economy, to appear in the true Holy of Holies, in the presence of the divine Majesty, with the tokens of his completed sacrifice, and to plead for the communication of those blessings for which he had paid the price, even his own blood.

(3.) *He is " on the right hand of God."*

Another result of our Lord's penal, vicarious, expiatory sufferings is, His being on the right hand of God, in that heaven into which he entered. The phrase in its complete

[1] 1 Cor. xv. 50, 52; 1 Thess. iv. 17.   [2] Heb. ix. 12, x. 14.

form is, "He sitteth on the right hand of God." This phrase, which occurs frequently in the New Testament, is plainly borrowed from Ps. cx., where Jehovah is represented as saying to Messiah the Prince, David's Lord, " Sit on my right hand, till I make thine enemies thy footstool."[1] The language is plainly figurative. Neither "the right hand of God," nor "sitting" at his right hand, can be literally understood. The figure is, a person sitting on the throne, on the right hand of the sovereign.

Some have strangely held that this is intended to betoken the inferiority of Christ to the Father. It has been said, a person, whom it was intended very highly to honour, was placed on the left hand of the person intending to honour him. But whatever might be the practice among other nations, the right hand was among the Jews undoubtedly the place of honour, and by their customs must their writings be expounded. Others still more strangely have held, that it indicates that, in a certain sense, Christ is superior to the Father. This assertion is absurd and blasphemous. For what saith the Scripture? " The Father hath put all things under his feet. But when he saith all things are put under him, it is manifest that he is excepted who did put all things under him."

The leading idea is common possession, with his Father, of the power and authority and glory of supreme Governor. Paul expounds it to us. Having quoted the text in Ps. cx., " Sit thou at my right hand, until I make thine enemies thy footstool," he draws the conclusion, " He must reign till all his enemies are put under his feet."[2] To use the language of Daniel, " One like the Son of man came with the clouds of heaven, and came to the Ancient of days, and they brought him near before Him. And there was given to him dominion, and glory, and a kingdom, that

[1] Ps. cx. 1.   [2] 1 Cor. x. 25.

all people, nations, and languages should serve him; his dominion is an everlasting dominion, which shall not pass away, and his kingdom that which shall not be destroyed." " The Father judgeth no man; he hath given all judgment to the Son." "He hath put all things under his feet," in giving him a seat at his right hand, on his throne.[1]

While this is undoubtedly the primary idea, there are other and not unimportant secondary ones indicated by this phrase. There are the glory and dignity connected with such power and authority. Sitting on the right hand of God, amid the splendours of the burning throne, he is " crowned with glory and honour." All human, all created glory, when compared with this, grows dim and disappears. And there is also the idea of supreme blessedness: " At thy right hand are pleasures for evermore;" " The King," sitting on Jehovah's right hand, " joys in his strength, and greatly rejoices in his salvation. He hath given him his heart's desire, and hath not withholden the request of his lips. He hath prevented him with the blessings of his goodness, and set a crown of pure gold on his head. His glory is great in his salvation; honour and majesty has he laid on him. For he has made him most blessed for ever; he has made him exceeding glad with his countenance."[2]

There seems, too, in the words, an intended tacit contrast to the posture of the priests even when in the Holy of Holies. They " *stood* ministering" at a humble distance before the emblematical throne of God, the mercy-seat. He " sits down on the throne, on the right hand" of him that sits thereon.[3]

This, like the other things mentioned in the text, is the result of our Lord's penal, vicarious, expiatory sufferings.

---

[1] Dan. vii. 13, 14; John v. 22 ; Ps. viii. 6 : comp. 1 Cor. xv. 27, and Heb. ii. 8, 9.
[2] Ps. xvi. 11, xxi. 1-6.   [3] Heb. x. 11, 12.

These dignities are the purchase of his sufferings, the reward of his toils. It was "for the suffering of death that he was crowned with glory and honour." It was by giving himself a sacrifice that he overcame the enemies of man's salvation; and it was because "he overcame, that he sat down on his Father's throne." And in the Apocalypse, when represented in the midst of the throne and of the four living creatures, he is said to be "a Lamb as it had been slain;" and the song of worship by the redeemed to him is, "Worthy is the Lamb who was slain, and hath redeemed us to God by his own blood."[1]

(4.) *Angels, authorities, and powers, are made subject to Him.*

I have only further to remark, that "the having angels, authorities, and powers, made subject to Him," is the result of the penal, vicarious, expiatory sufferings of our Lord. These words are not perhaps so much the expression of a new thought, as the expansion of the primary idea contained in "is at the right hand of God," which is, as we have seen, supreme dominion. The three words, "angels, authorities, and powers," may either be considered as all descriptive of angelic beings, and as equivalent to all orders of angels—angels both authorities and powers, the same orders that are elsewhere styled "principalities and powers;" or authorities and powers may be viewed as intended to denote the various forms of human authority and power. We are rather disposed to take the first view of the words,—a view which by implication contains the second; for certainly if the highest orders of creatures are made subject to him, all inferior orders must be subjected to him also.

The exalted Mediator, the man Christ Jesus, is the Lord of angels. The command given to them "when the Father

[1] Heb. ii. 9; Rev. iii. 21, v. 6, 12.

is bringing in the first-begotten into the world"—that is, putting him in possession of his inheritance as "heir of all things"—is, "Let all the angels of God worship him,"[1]—a command which we find from the Apocalypse they joyfully obey. He is their King, and they acknowledge him to be so, and do incessantly admire and adore him. They rejoice in his glory, and in the glory and happiness of men through him. They yield him most cheerful obedience, and serve him readily, in the good of his Church and every individual believer, as he deputes and employs them. There are two things intended in these words: Christ's dignity above the angels, and Christ's authority over the angels.[2] He has an essential dignity above the angels. "He has by inheritance obtained a more excellent name than they." 'Created spirits' is their name; the 'only-begotten Son' is his. To which of the angels did he ever say, "Thou art my Son, this day I have begotten thee?" He has also a mediatorial dignity above them. As God-man, he has been "made much better than the angels." "He is Lord of all;" they are servants. Human nature in him is exalted above all angelic nature. "That nature which he stooped below them to take on, 'being made lower than the angels,' he has carried up and raised above them. The very earth, the flesh of man, is exalted in his person above all those heavenly spirits who are of so excellent and pure a being in their nature, and have been from the beginning of the world clothed with so transcendent glory. A parcel of clay is made so bright and set so high as to outshine those bright flaming spirits, those 'sons of the morning,' by being united to the Fountain of Light, the blessed Deity in the person of the Son. In coming to fetch and put on this

---

[1] Heb. i. 6; comp. Ps. xcvii. 9. For illustration of the phrase εἰσαγωγή εἰς τὴν οἰκουμένην, see Ex. vi. 8, xv. 17, xxiii. 23.

[2] Leighton.

garment, he made himself lower than the angels; but carrying it with him at his return to his eternal throne, and sitting down with it there, it is high above them. This they look upon with perpetual wonder, but not with envy or repining. No! Among all these eyes, no such evil eye is to be found. Yea, they rejoice in the infinite wisdom of God in this design, and his infinite love to poor lost mankind. It is wonderful to see him filling the room of their fallen brethren with new guests from earth, yea, such as were born heirs of hell; thrice wonderful to see not only sinful men thus raised to a participance of glory with them who are spotless, sinless spirits, but their flesh in their Redeemer, dignified with a glory so far beyond them. This is that mystery which they are intent in looking and prying into, and cannot, nor ever shall, see the bottom of it, for it hath none. The words intimate not only Christ's dignity above, but his authority over, his angels. They are not only servants, but his servants. He is their Lord, and they worship him. They are under his command for all services in which it pleases him to employ them; and the great employment he assigns them is the attending on his Church, and his particular elect ones. 'Are they not all ministering spirits, sent forth to minister to them who shall be heirs of salvation?'"[1] He who commands angels must control devils. He who is the Lord of angels must be the Lord of all inferior orders of beings, "King of kings and Lord of Lords," "having all power over all flesh," "all power in heaven and in earth."

That this possession of unlimited power and authority, like the resurrection and ascension, is the result of the penal, vicarious, expiatory sufferings of our Lord, is very explicitly stated in Scripture. I shall content myself with quoting two passages. The first is that very remarkable

[1] Leighton. Heb. i. 14.

statement in the Epistle to the Philippians (ii. 5–11) : "Christ Jesus, being in the form of God, thought it not robbery to be equal with God; but made himself of no reputation, and humbled himself, and became obedient to death, even the death of the cross. Wherefore God also hath highly exalted him, and given him a name which is above every name: that at the name of Jesus every knee should bow, of things in heaven, and things in earth, and things under the earth ; and that every tongue should confess that Jesus Christ is Lord, to the glory of God the Father." The other passage I referred to is in the book of Revelation (v. 8–10). It is the song of the redeemed in heaven. Falling down before the Lamb, they exclaim, "Thou art worthy to take the book, and to open the seals thereof," that is, to unfold by accomplishment the decrees of the Eternal, "to receive power, and riches, and wisdom, and strength, and honour, and glory, and blessing ; for thou wast slain, and hast redeemed us to God by thy blood out of every kindred, and tongue, and people, and nation ; and hast made us to our God kings and priests ; and we shall reign on the earth." Thus have I completed my illustrations of the five great topics suggested in this very fruitful passage of Scripture—The illustrious sufferer Jesus Christ, the just One ; His sufferings ; and the nature, the design, and the results of these sufferings.

VI. THE TENDENCY OF THESE TRUTHS RESPECTING THE SUFFERINGS OF CHRIST TO SUPPORT AND ENCOURAGE CHRISTIANS SUFFERING FOR HIS CAUSE.

It only remains that I in a very few words endeavour to show how these topics, as treated by the apostle, are fitted to serve the purpose for which they are brought forward here; that is, to reconcile Christians to sufferings in the cause of Christ, and to give them support and direction under such sufferings.

The subject is a wide and interesting one, but I must confine myself to a hurried sketch of leading thoughts, which you will do well to follow out in your private meditations. My object as a Christian teacher now and at all times should be, not to save my hearers the trouble of thinking, but if possible to compel them to think, and to furnish them with some helps for thinking rightly and usefully.

When involved in suffering, support and direction are obtained by turning the mind to the contemplation of the great and good who have been placed in similar circumstances. It is on this principle that the apostle puts those to whom he wrote in mind, that "the same afflictions to which they were exposed had been accomplished in their brethren who had been in the world;" and that his beloved brother Paul, in the Epistle to the Hebrews, turns the attention of those to whom *he* wrote to "the great cloud of witnesses"—to the power of faith in the hour of trial—with which they were surrounded. There is no example, however, so fraught with instruction and comfort as that of "Jesus, the author and finisher of our faith;" and the points in which that example is instructive and consolatory are finely brought out in the passage before us.[1]

"Even Christ, the just One, suffered." If Christ suffered, should Christians think it unreasonable that they should be called to suffer? "Is it not enough that the disciple be as his teacher, the servant as his Lord?"[2]

And they need not count it strange, though they be harmless and blameless, that they yet suffer. "The just One suffered"—suffered not only though he was just, but because he was just. If they are like Him, they may

[1] 1 Pet. v. 9; Heb. xii. 1, 2. [2] Matt. x. 24, 25.

expect to be treated as he was treated, to "be in the world as he was in the world." If it were otherwise, they would have reason to doubt their discipleship. If the world loved them, it would be strong presumption at least that they were the world's *own*. The hatred of the world and its consequences are among the proofs that Christ has "chosen us out of the world."[1]

To suffer for Christ, to suffer like Christ, is an honourable thing. It is to have fellowship with Christ, the Lord of glory, in that in which his glory was very remarkably displayed.

Christ, the just One, suffered for sins, for sinners,—for our sins, for us sinners. If he suffered to obtain our salvation, should we grudge to suffer to uphold and extend his glory and cause?

If we are *in* him, his sufferings are ours as to their effects: they have expiated our guilt, so that all our sufferings are not penal, but disciplinary—are fatherly chastisements, not wrathful inflictions. Christ has made all sufferings safe and pleasant to his disciples by this one thing, that he suffered once for sins. He has stripped the cross of its worst terrors; he has taken the curse out of it, and made it light to carry and easy to endure. He has taken the poison out of the cup of affliction; and we can take the cup, however bitter, and bless the name of the Lord. He enables us to say, 'Since he has expiated my sin, since he has secured my salvation, deal with me as thou wilt; afflict me how, when, as heavily as it shall please thee; all is well.'

As to sufferings *for* Christ, they are a privilege and honour. "It is given us on Christ's behalf to suffer for his sake."[2]

He suffered "that he might bring us to God." Surely

[1] John xv. 18, 19.   [2] Phil. i. 29.

that is a blessing so great, that, in token of gratitude for it, we should cheerfully do whatever he commands, cheerfully submit to whatever he appoints.

And these our sufferings are, under the influence of his Spirit, one of the means, one of the most powerful of the means, which he is employing, that in our case the design of his death may be realized; that we may be brought to God, made to know him, to enjoy the sweets of his favour and fellowship, "made partakers of his holiness."[1]

His sufferings were severe sufferings—sufferings even to death. Let us not, then, think even "fiery trials" strange. What are the severest of our sufferings when compared with his? Let us not wonder, if we be conformed to our Lord, in continuing to suffer in some form or other while we continue to live.

If we are his, death, as in his case, will put an end to all our sufferings. When he became dead bodily, he was quickened spiritually; and is it not so with his people? Is it not "when they are weak that they are strong?" Out of weakness do they not often wax strong? and "when the outward man perisheth, is not the inward man strengthened day by day?"

As to individual Christian experience, personal suffering is very generally connected with the acquisition of spiritual strength. And in reference to power to do good, to promote the cause of Christ, have not the sufferings of Christians been fully as efficient as their exertions? "The blood of the martyrs was the seed of the Church;" and Christianity as well as Christ may say to her enemies, "Rejoice not against me; when I fall, I shall arise."[2]

Christ's sufferings ended in his resurrection, his ascension, and his celestial dignity, power, and glory. And so will ours, if we be his, and follow in the steps of the ex-

[1] Heb. xii. 10.   [2] 2 Cor. iv. 16; Mic. vii. 8.

ample he has left us in suffering for us. "If we suffer with him, we shall also reign with him." It is the purpose of the Father to conform all his children to the image of "the First-born among many brethren;" first as suffering, then as glorified. "If we suffer with him, it is that we also may be glorified with him." "To him that overcometh he will give to sit with him on his throne, even as he overcame, and has sat down on his Father's throne."

And are these sufferings of the present time, however severe and protracted, "worthy to be compared with the glory which shall be revealed in us" when we shall enter into his joy, see and share his glory, and have even these "vile bodies fashioned like unto his glorious body?" Are they not "light," however heavy? Are they not "but for a moment," however long continued, when looked at in contrast with the "exceeding great and eternal weight of glory" implied in being "with Christ," being "like Christ," in holiness, in felicity, and in glory, for ever and ever?[1] Surely, surely it is better, since such is the will of God, that we should suffer for Christ, like Christ, than that we should not suffer. Paradoxical as they may appear to a worldly mind, strangely as they may sound to a worldly ear, the apostle's judgment was wise, and his exhortation reasonable: "We count them happy who endure, suffering wrongfully." "Count it all joy when ye are brought into divers trials. Yes, blessed is the man that endureth such trials."[2] Here, as in everything else, "good is the will of the Lord"—Christ. So rich in instruction and comfort is the example of Christ to the suffering Christian.

"The example and company of the saints in suffering is very considerable, both for guidance and consolation; but

---

[1] 2 Tim. ii. 12; Rom. viii. 17, 29; Rev. iii. 21; Rom. viii. 18; 2 Cor. iv. 17.
[2] James v. 11, i. 2, 12.

that of Christ is more than any other, yea, than all the rest put together. Therefore, the apostle having, in the eleventh chapter of the Epistle to the Hebrews, represented the former at large, ends on this as the top of them all: 'Looking to Jesus.' There is a race set before us: it is to be a race with patience," or rather perseverance, "and without fainting. Now he tells us of a cloud of witnesses, a cloud made up of the instances of believers who have suffered before us; and the heat of the day wherein we run is somewhat cooled even by that cloud compassing us; but the main strength of the comfort here lies in beholding Christ, eyeing his sufferings, and their issue. The considering and contemplating of Him will be the strongest cordial, will keep you from wearying and fainting by the way."[1]

It is only Christians, in the true sense of that word, that can derive from the sufferings of Christ the advantages which we have now been illustrating. Men, while they continue in their sins, can have neither part nor lot in this matter. They must suffer, for they are men; and "man is born to trouble as the sparks fly upward;" "Man born of a woman is of few days and full of trouble;" but under their afflictions they have none of the supports and consolations which the children of God, the disciples of Christ, derive from the consideration, that "even Christ also suffered for sins, the just for the unjust, that he might bring them to God." Their afflictions are indeed intended to rouse them to serious thought, to tell them they are sinners, to show them what an evil and a bitter thing sin is, and to make them feel how much they need a Saviour; but if these afflictions are not improved for this purpose, they will turn out to have been but the first prelusive drops of the overwhelming storm of divine vengeance.

[1] Leighton.

But why should men continue in sin, in guilt, in depravity; why shut themselves out of all solid comfort under suffering here, as well as all well-founded hope of happiness hereafter, since the great atonement has been made, and is in the word of the truth of the gospel held out to them as the sure ground of hope for eternity? The statements in the text, as a source of direction and support and comfort under affliction, can be of no use to the unbelieving sinner. But he has a very deep interest in these statements, forming as they do the very essence of that gospel, those glad tidings of great joy which are to be made known to all nations, "preached to every creature under heaven." "Christ died, the just for the unjust, that he might bring men to God." We proclaim this as the ground of hope to the perishing sinner, as well as the source of comfort to the suffering saint. "He who knew no sin was made sin, that we might be made the righteousness of God in Him." This is the very truth most sure, "a faithful saying, and worthy of all acceptation." Let the greatest sinner believe this testimony of God concerning his Son, and in the faith of that truth he obtains a saving interest in those penal, vicarious, expiatory sufferings. He obtains "the redemption that is in Christ through his blood, according to the riches" of the divine grace; he is brought to God. And then he will find that the atoning sufferings and death of the Son of God are not only the price of his justification and the ground of his hope, but that they are to him an exhaustless source of powerful and persuasive motive to all the duties of the Christian life, and of abundant and suitable consolation and support amid all the privations and sufferings, the bereavements and sorrows, the struggles and persecutions, in which he may be involved; while he is "in a constant continuance in well-doing," doing and suffering the will of God, seeking to be a follower of those who, through much tribulation, have entered into the kingdom—" who, through faith and patience, inherit the promises;" and seeking especially to tread in the steps of Him who is our pattern as well as our sacrifice, " who, for the joy that was set before him, endured the cross, despising the shame, and is set down at the right hand of the throne of God."[1]

[1] Heb. xii. 2.

APPENDIX TO DISCOURSE XVI.
PART V.

FACTS IN ANTEDILUVIAN HISTORY REFERRED TO BY THE APOSTLE, AND THEIR BEARING ON HIS OBJECT.

"Which sometime were disobedient, when once the long-suffering of God waited in the days of Noah, while the ark was a preparing, wherein few, that is, eight souls, were saved by water. The like figure whereunto even baptism doth also now save us (not the putting away of the filth of the flesh, but the answer of a good conscience toward God), by the resurrection of Jesus Christ." —1 Pet. iii. 20, 21.

The Jewish Scriptures form an important and valuable portion of the volume of inspired truth. To those who lived previously to the gospel revelation, they contained the only authentic and satisfactory account of the divine character and will in reference to man as a fallen creature; they were their sole trustworthy guide to truth, duty, and happiness. They were accordingly highly valued by the wise and pious under the ancient economy. "The law of thy mouth," said the Psalmist,—and he expressed the common sentiments and feelings of the body of the faithful,—"The law of thy mouth is better to me than thousands of gold and silver;" "More to be desired than gold, yea, than much fine gold; sweeter also than honey, yea, than the honey-comb."[1] Even to us, to whom "the mystery which had been kept secret from former ages and generations has been made manifest," the Jewish Scriptures are calculated to answer many important purposes. Though the Mosaic

[1] Ps. cxix. 72, xix. 10.

dispensation "has waxed old and vanished away,"[1] the writings of the prophets have not become obsolete. The pure radiance of apostolical doctrine has not extinguished the dimmer light of ancient history and prophecy. On the contrary, as if borrowing new splendour from the full-risen Sun of righteousness, they cheer us with a brighter and warmer beam than they ever reflected on those who, but for them, must have walked in darkness. In the great edifice of revealed truth, the Old Testament Scriptures are not the scaffolding which, when the building is finished, ceases to be useful, and is removed as an unsightly incumbrance; they are the foundation and lower part of the fabric, forming an important constituent part of "the building of God," and are essentially necessary not only to the beauty, but to the safety, of the superstructure.

It is possible, indeed, to demonstrate the divinity of Christianity and the truth of New Testament doctrine and history on principles which have no direct reference to any former revelation of the divine will; but it is at the same time true, that one of the most satisfactory proofs of these truths is founded on the admission of the divinity of the Jewish sacred books, and consists in the minute harmony of Old Testament prediction with New Testament history and doctrine. "The testimony of Jesus is the spirit of prophecy."

Few exercises are better fitted at once to enlarge the information and strengthen the faith of the Christian than a careful perusal of the Old Testament Scriptures, with a constant reference to Him who is "the end of the law," the substance of all its shadowy ceremonies—to Him of whom "Moses in the law and the prophets did write."

This, however, is by no means the only way in which the Old Testament Scriptures are calculated to minister to

[1] Rom. xvi. 25, 26; Heb. viii. 13.

our improvement. They contain in them an extensive collection of instructions and warnings, counsels and consolations, suited to mankind in every country and age. The man of piety, wherever or whenever he may live, finds in the sacred odes of David at once a fit vehicle for his devotional feelings, and a perfect pattern for his devotional exercises; the maxims of Solomon are found equally suitable for the guidance of our conduct as of that of his contemporaries; and though many of the writings of the prophets bear plain marks of being occasional in their origin and reference, relating to events which, at the time of their publication, excited general interest among the people to whom they were given, yet it is amazing how few passages are not obviously calculated to convey instruction, universal and permanent, fitted to be useful to all men in all time.

Even the historical books of the Old Testament are fitted in a variety of ways to promote the improvement of the Christian, and on this account have strong claims on our attentive study. Like every true history, and indeed in a much higher degree than any other history, they convey to us, in the most engaging form, much information regarding the character and government of God, and respecting the state and dispositions and duty of man. They contain an account of the origin and progress of that system of divine dispensations which found its accomplishment in the redemption of mankind by the death of the incarnate Son of God; an account without which much of the Christian revelation would have been obscure, if not unintelligible. They suggest numerous proofs and illustrations of the characteristic principles of the Christian revelation, and thus at once enable us more fully to understand and more firmly to believe them. The minds of the writers of the New Testament were full of the facts and imagery of the earlier revelation, and they can be but very imperfectly understood—they are constantly in danger of being misunderstood—by those readers who have not, by carefully studying the Old Testament Scriptures, acquired a somewhat similar familiarity with them.

Of the manner in which the New Testament writers employ their familiarity with the Old Testament for the illustration of the subjects which come before them, we have a striking instance in that portion of the interesting paragraph just read, to which your attention is now about to be more closely directed. The paragraph is a statement of the truth with regard to the sufferings of Jesus Christ, in their nature, design, and consequences, made for the purpose of affording instruction and support to his followers when exposed to suffering in his cause. In the course of this statement the apostle refers to certain facts in antediluvian history, recorded in the Old Testament Scriptures, as having a bearing on the facts respecting Jesus Christ which he states, or on the object for which he states these facts. To ascertain distinctly what are the facts in antediluvian history to which the apostle refers, and to show if possible what is his design in referring to them, what bearing they have on the obvious general purpose of the whole paragraph, are the two objects which I shall endeavour to gain in the remaining portion of these remarks.

The passage which is to form the subject of exposition, though not formally, is plainly substantially parenthetical, and is contained in these words: "The spirits in prison sometime were disobedient, when once the long-suffering of God waited in the days of Noah, while the ark was a preparing, wherein few, that is, eight souls, were saved by water. The like figure whereunto even baptism doth also now save us (not the putting away of the filth of the flesh, but the answer of a good conscience toward God), by the resurrection of Jesus Christ."

I. FACTS IN ANTEDILUVIAN HISTORY REFERRED TO BY THE APOSTLE.

The first thing we have to do, then, is to bring before your minds the facts in the history of the antediluvian world, to which the apostle here refers. "The spirits in prison sometime were disobedient, when once the long-suffering of God waited in the days of Noah, while the ark was a preparing, wherein a few, that is, eight souls, were saved by water." I have already endeavoured to show, that the most probable interpretation which has been given to the somewhat remarkable phrase, "spirits in prison," is that which considers it as a descriptive appellation of mankind in their fallen state. "Captives" and "prisoners" are figurative expressions, not unfrequently used in Scripture, to denote the condemned state, miserable circumstances, and degraded character of fallen men. Our Lord having obtained, by his atoning death, a mighty accession, in his official character, to his spiritual life and energy, went, and, through the instrumentality of his apostles, preached with remarkable success to those miserable captives, those spirits in prison, vast multitudes of them becoming obedient to his call.

It had not always been so. Communications of the divine will had often been made in former ages to fallen men, without such effects. In particular, in a very remote age, at a period preceding the general deluge, those "spirits in prison," those condemned criminals, those willing captives of Satan and sin—not, indeed, the same individuals to whom our Lord " came and preached," but individuals of the same race, and therefore properly enough designated by the same name,—had a divine message sent them, and were the subjects of a remarkable manifestation of the divine forbearance: they were almost universally disobedient to this message; and in consequence of their disobedience, they were destroyed in the deluge. A very small minority were obedient, and in consequence of their obedience were saved in the ark, "saved by water." These are the facts respecting the antediluvians, either explicitly stated or necessarily implied, in the words before us.

We have but detached fragments of the history of mankind during the antediluvian period—a period of nearly seventeen centuries. This we know, however, that at the time which our text refers to, they had, with very few exceptions, become decidedly irreligious and excessively depraved. The language of the sacred historian is very striking: "God saw that the wickedness of man was great in the earth, and that every imagination of the thoughts of his heart was only evil continually." "The earth was corrupt," putrid, "before God, and the earth was filled with violence;" and "God looked on the earth, and, behold, it was corrupt: for all flesh had corrupted his way on the earth."[1]

If men were thus irreligious and corrupt, it was not because they had not the means of being otherwise. If the primitive revelation, through the faith of which Abel obtained salvation, was forgotten, disregarded, or perverted, the fault was with mankind. Besides, God never "left himself without a witness, in that he did good, and gave them rain from heaven, and fruitful seasons, filling their hearts with food and gladness." This goodness was calculated, was intended, to bring them to repentance, to change their minds respecting God, whom they had learned to think of as "such an one as themselves." "The heavens," before the flood as

[1] Gen. vi. 5, 11, 12.

well as afterwards, "declared the glory of God, and the firmament showed forth his handy-work." "The invisible things of God were from the creation of the world clearly seen, being understood by the things that are made, even his eternal power and Godhead;" so that, when the antediluvians, having the means of knowing God, "glorified him not as God, neither were thankful," but gave themselves up to work wickedness with all greediness, they "were without excuse." [1]

Nor was this all. It is reasonable to suppose that, during these seventeen centuries, direct divine communications were made to the fallen race. It is certain that "Enoch, the seventh from Adam, prophesied," warning his contemporaries of the destruction which will ultimately overtake the ungodly, saying, "Behold, the Lord cometh with ten thousand of his saints," or holy ones, "to execute judgment on all, and to convince all that are ungodly among them of all their ungodly deeds which they have ungodly committed, and of all their hard speeches which ungodly sinners have spoken against him." [2] Thus had God, by his Spirit, striven with men for more than fifteen hundred years. "Sentence against" men's "evil work was not executed speedily," and the "hearts of men were fully set in them to do evil."

Yet was he not "slack concerning his declaration, as some men count slackness." His wrath loses nothing by sleeping. It becomes fresher by repose. "The impenitent abusers of his patience pay interest for all the time of their forbearance, in the increased weight of the judgment when it comes on them." The end of all flesh was now come before God, and he was about to destroy them "with," or from, "the earth." [3]

[1] Acts xiv. 17; Ps. xix. 1, 2; Rom. i. 19, 20.
[2] Jude 14, 15.   [3] Gen. vi. 13.

But "surely the Lord God will do nothing without revealing his secret to his servants the prophets." There was but one in that generation to whom that name could be given. "Noah had found grace in the eyes of the Lord;" Noah, "by faith, had become an heir of the justification by faith;" he was "a just man, and perfect in his generation, and walked with God." This is the good report he has obtained. "THEE," said Jehovah, that is, *thee* alone, "have I seen righteous before me in this generation."[1] As he testified his regard to Abraham, by telling him of the approaching overthrow of Sodom; so he showed his peculiar favour to Noah, by announcing to him the coming destruction of his contemporaries. He said, "My Spirit shall not always strive with man; yet his days shall be an hundred and twenty years."[2] He shall have an hundred and twenty years of striving with him still. It would seem that Noah was commissioned not only to build the ark, but during its building to announce the approaching deluge, and to call men to repentance. We know that he was "a preacher of righteousness," and that he not only practically by his conduct, but verbally by his preaching, "condemned the world,"[3]—told them of their sins, warned them of their danger.

This is the revelation of the divine will referred to in the text; and as the spirit in the prophets was the Spirit of Christ, THE WORD from the beginning being the great revealer of God, and making his revelations by his Spirit, Christ, who went in spirit to the spirits in prison by his apostles, may be considered as having gone to the same class of persons in spirit by his servant Noah. For one hundred and twenty years Noah proclaimed to a doomed world, "Repent;" as Jonah in after ages proclaimed to

---

[1] Gen. vi. 8; Heb. xi. 7; Gen. vii. 1.
[2] Gen. vi. 3. [3] 2 Pet. ii. 5; Heb. xi. 7.

the doomed city, "Yet forty days, and Nineveh shall be destroyed." Had Noah's preaching been as successful as Jonah's, we have no reason to doubt but that, as in that case, God "seeing their works, that they turned from their evil way, would have repented of the evil he had said he would do to them, and would not have done it."[1] These hundred and twenty years were years of further, years of peculiar trial; the last opportunity to be afforded to that race for escape from final ruin. They were a period during which "God's long-suffering waited;" that is, God waited in the exercise of long-suffering. It was long-suffering, it was patience, which prevented the immediate infliction of the threatened vengeance; for the iniquities of that generation were full. Come the vengeance when it might, it could not come undeserved. But judgment is his "strange work." They shall have one warning more. He is not willing that they should perish.

And there is something in this warning, especially during the closing period of forbearance, peculiarly striking. "Noah, by faith being instructed of the divine oracle concerning things not yet seen, moved with fear, prepared an ark." When we consider the size of the ark, and the time and labour necessary for collecting the animals which were to be saved in it (for we have no reason to think that their gathering together was entirely miraculous), it is obvious that it must have afforded him employment for a considerable period. It was a striking proof that Noah believed his own denunciation. It was an appeal thus, through the eye as well as through the ear, to that wicked, rebellious generation. But they looked on with a thoughtless eye, as well as listened with a careless ear. They were "disobedient." Noah to the men of his generation, like Lot to his sons-in-law, was "as one who mocked." They believed

[1] Jonah iii. 10.

him not. When they saw the ark building, their sentiments probably found language in such words as these: 'What does the old dotard mean? Where does he intend to sail in this strange hulk? He will find some difficulty to launch it.' And when he told them of the coming ruin at the end of one hundred and twenty years, they were likely to say, 'You look far before you! And shall we perish and you only escape? We will take our chance.'

But God will not be mocked. His established law, "Whatsoever a man soweth, that shall he also reap," shall at the appointed time take effect. He is not slack concerning his threatenings any more than his promises, as men count slackness, though he is long-suffering, oh, how long-suffering! Down to the period of the execution of his threatening, these doomed men seem to have been saying, "Where is the promise of his coming? All things continue as they were." "They ate and drank; they married and were given in marriage."

The season of forbearance, long as it was, at last passed away. The ark was finished, and Noah and his family entered into it. "In that same day all the fountains of the great deep," the abyss of subterranean waters, "were broken up, and the windows of heaven were opened," to discharge the immense body of water held in solution by the atmosphere. The rains continued without intermission for forty entire days, and the eruption of subterraneous waters for one hundred and fifty days, until at length the inundation came to its height, and covered all the high hills which were under the whole heaven, fifteen cubits upwards above the highest. "And all flesh died that moved upon the earth, both of fowl, and of cattle, and of beast, and of every creeping thing that creepeth on the earth, and every man." All, with the exception of Noah and his family, had been disobedient, and with that exception all perished.

"The waters covered the enemies of God; not one of them was left."[1]

We pronounce no judgment as to the eternal state of all the antediluvians. It is possible that some of them in a right spirit, amid the rising waters of the deluge, sought mercy; and if they did, who dare say, who dare think, that it was refused them? But whether we look on earth or beyond it, without doubt that day was "a day of the perdition of ungodly men."

While the great body of the spirits in prison in the days of Noah were disobedient, and reaped the fruits of their disobedience, all were not impenitent and unbelieving. Noah was at once believing and obedient. His family were so far obedient, that they availed themselves of the appointed means of deliverance. We have but too good reason to conclude, that, in the best sense of the word, *all* of them were not obedient. They, to the amount of "eight souls," that is, persons—Noah and his wife, and his three sons and their wives—entered into the ark, and were saved by water. "The Lord said to Noah, Come thou, and all thy house—that is, thy family—into the ark. And Noah went in, and his sons, and his wife, and his sons' wives with him, into the ark: and the Lord shut them in. And when the waters increased they bare up the ark, and it was lift above the earth; and when the waters prevailed, and were increased greatly on the earth, the ark went on the face of the waters. And God remembered Noah, and those who were in the ark with him."[2] After five months floating on a shoreless ocean, it rested on the mountain of Ararat; and after having been tenants of this strange mansion for a year and ten days, they, at the command of God, went forth to take possession of a world already

---

[1] Gen. vii. 11, 12, 17-24; Ps. cvi. 11.
[2] Gen. vii. 1, 15, 16, viii. 1, 4.

smiling in vegetable beauty, whose solitudes were soon again to be peopled by the various animal tribes, whose lives had been so strangely preserved amid the general destruction.

These "few, that is, eight souls," are said to have been "saved by water." Various meanings have been attached to these words; some considering them as equivalent to 'saved amid the waters;' others, 'saved notwithstanding the waters;' others, 'saved by being conducted through the waters.' The meaning that the words most naturally suggest seems the true one. They were saved by means of the water. The water which drowned those out of the ark, saved those who were in it. The words of the sacred historian are the best commentary on the apostle's words: "The waters bore up the ark, and it was lift up above the earth, and it went on the face of the waters."[1] As, in consequence of the art of navigation, the ocean, which seemed calculated to separate completely the inhabitants of distant countries, unites them, becoming the great highway of nations; so the waters of the deluge, which were in their own nature fitted to destroy them, by means of the ark saved Noah and his family. Such, then, are the facts of antediluvian history which this passage brings before us.

II. OBJECT OF THE APOSTLE IN REFERRING TO THESE FACTS.

Let us now inquire into the object of the apostle in referring to these facts, and show how they gain that object. It must be acknowledged that the design of the reference is by no means self-evident, or even very readily discernible. It does seem strange, that in the midst of a description of the results of our Lord's penal, vicarious, expiatory suffer-

[1] Gen. vii. 17, 18.

ings, there should be introduced a statement of what took place more than two thousand years before. It is plain, however, to the careful student of the Apostle Peter, that he was accustomed to think of the antediluvian world and the postdiluvian world as of two orders of things which had such strong analogies of resemblance and contrast, as that events in the one naturally suggested to his mind what may be called the corresponding events in the other.

Thus, in the third chapter of his second epistle, he contrasts the two worlds. Of the one he says, "By the word of God, the heavens were of old, and the earth standing out of the water and in the water: whereby the world that then was, being overflowed with water, perished;" and of the other he says, "The heavens and the earth which are now, by the same word are kept in store, reserved unto fire against the day of judgment and perdition of ungodly men." And in the second chapter of the same epistle we find him saying, "God, who spared not the old world, but saved Noah, the eighth person, a preacher of righteousness, bringing in the flood on the world of the ungodly, knoweth" (in this new world) "how to deliver the godly out of temptation, and to reserve the unjust unto the day of judgment to be punished."[1] Both worlds appeared to him peopled by fallen men doomed to punishment, "spirits in prison;" both privileged with a divine revelation, proclaiming danger, and offering deliverance to those spirits in prison; both destined to be destroyed, as a manifestation of the divine displeasure, the first by a deluge of water, the second by a deluge of fire. Taking this view of the subject, it does not seem strange that the mention of Christ, quickened in the Spirit, going and preaching to the spirits in prison by his apostles, as one result of his atoning sufferings, should have suggested to Peter's mind his having in

[1] 2 Pet. iii. 5-7, ii. 5, 9.

his pre-existent state gone in spirit by the ministry of Noah to the same class of persons in the antediluvian world.

But what is the apostle's object in this reference? His primary object is, if we mistake not, that to which we have already alluded: to illustrate by contrast the blessed effects of our Lord's going and preaching to the spirits in prison, after being quickened in spirit. When in the days of Noah he went and preached to them, "they were disobedient," all but universally disobedient, and "few, that is, eight souls," out, it is probable, of many millions, "were saved;" but now, though many are unbelieving and impenitent, still multitudes both of Jews and Gentiles have become obedient to the faith; and before he finishes his preaching to the spirits in prison, much greater multitudes will yet become obedient. "All the ends of the earth shall remember, and turn to the Lord; and all the kindreds of the people shall worship before him. For the kingdom is the Lord's; and he is the governor among the nations." "The kingdoms of this world are become the kingdom of our Lord and his Christ, and he shall reign for ever and ever." And though many shall perish in the deluge of fire, yet still the saved shall not be counted by human numbers. There will be "*nations* of the saved;" and those set free from among the spirits in prison by the word of God, the truth which makes free indeed, shall be " a multitude which no man can number, of all nations, and kindreds, and people, and tongues." [1]

A subsidiary yet still an important object in making the reference, seems to have been to bring these truths before the mind: first, that if Christ's preaching, when "quickened by the Spirit" he comes by the apostolic ministry, is disregarded and disobeyed, a more dreadful destruction will befall the unbelieving and impenitent than

[1] Ps. xxii. 27; Rev. xi. 15, xxi. 24, vii. 9.

overwhelmed the antediluvians, who were disobedient to the revelation made by Noah; and secondly, that there is no escape from the destruction to which we are already doomed, but by availing ourselves now, as then, of the only divinely appointed mode of deliverance. "If they who despised" the preaching of Noah, who was a mere man, and who does not seem to have been a worker of miracles, "died without mercy," receiving in the waters of the deluge "a just recompense of reward," "of how much sorer punishment shall they be thought worthy who have trodden under foot the Son of God, and done despite to the Spirit" in whom he comes to them; "neglecting so great salvation, which at the first began to be spoken to us by the Lord, and was confirmed to us by them that heard him; God also bearing witness, both with signs and wonders, and with divers miracles, and gifts of the Holy Ghost, according to his own will?"[1]

There was no mode of escape from the deluge of water but the divinely appointed ark. It is not improbable that in the day of divine visitation various plans were resorted to. Trees were climbed no doubt, mountains ascended, possibly boats of some kind or other taken to;—all in vain. The whole, with the exception of the eight in the ark, were engulfed in the deep and wide-spreading inundation, agitated with fearful tempest from the air, and heaved up into tremendous billows, by internal commotions shaking the earth. And there is no mode of escape for men from the coming fiery deluge which is to destroy the wicked, but in the redemption that is in Christ. "There is no name given under heaven among men, whereby we must be saved, but the name of Jesus." He, and He only, saves from the wrath to come. To those who reject him, "there remains no more sacrifice for sin, but a certain fearful

[1] Heb. ii. 3, 4.

looking for of judgment, to destroy them as the adversaries of God."[1]

It only remains now that we endeavour to ascertain the object of the apostle's reference in noticing the particular manner in which Noah and his family were saved: they were "saved by water." The water of the deluge was, as we have already explained it, the means of their deliverance. The apostle himself has, in the 21st verse, informed us what is the point he meant to illustrate by this reference, though it must be acknowledged that it is not very easy to extract a clear and definite explanation from his words: "The like figure whereunto even baptism doth also now save us (not the putting away of the filth of the flesh, but the answer of a good conscience towards God), by the resurrection of Jesus Christ."

It is rather remarkable that both those who deny the perpetuity of water-baptism as an ordinance, like that denomination of Christians so estimable on many accounts, the Friends, and those who, like the Papists and Puseyites, insist on the necessity and efficiency of water-baptism for salvation, if administered by properly qualified persons, equally seek in this passage for support to their opposite views; the one class insisting that it teaches that the baptism that saves—Christian baptism—is not that which removes external pollution, that it is not the application of water to the body, nor an external rite at all; the other, that it teaches that baptism, which means here just what it means elsewhere—the religious rite known by that name—does save, is necessary, is effectual to salvation. We shall find that the passage, rightly interpreted, gives no support to either of these equally erroneous, though by no means equally dangerous opinions.

It has been doubted whether the apostle meant to com-

[1] Acts iv. 12; Heb. x. 26, etc.

pare baptism with the water of the deluge, or with the ark, or to compare generally the way in which Christians are saved with the way in which Noah and his family were saved; but when the words are carefully examined, there is no room for these doubts. The translation of the words in our version is strictly literal according to the reading adopted, but it is not very intelligible. To the question, What does the expression, "the like figure whereunto even baptism," mean? I can give no answer. The words may be rendered with perfect accuracy, "which was a type or figure of the baptism which saves us;" that is, which water of the deluge is a type or significant resemblance of baptism which saves us; for that it was a type, in the strict sense of the word, as foreshowing dimly to the antediluvians Christian baptism or its meaning, is a notion utterly without support.

It is, however, right to say that there is another reading which, since the manuscripts of the New Testament have been more carefully collated than they had been when our excellent version was made, has been generally preferred by the most learned and judicious scholars, and which gives this rendering:[1] "which," referring to water, "which also saves us, baptism which corresponds to, or is figuratively represented by, the water of the deluge." It is as if the apostle had said, 'Water saved the family of Noah, and it may be said water also saves us; I refer to baptism, which in this respect resembles the waters of the deluge, both being connected by divine appointment with salvation or deliverance.'

How the water of the deluge was connected with the salvation of Noah's family we have already seen; how baptism is connected with our salvation we are now to inquire;

---

[1] The Textus Receptus gives ᾧ; Griesbach, Scholz, Lachmann, etc., give ὅ.

and the apostle has answered the question both negatively and positively. But before entering on the consideration of his answer, it deserves remark, that the very comparison shows that baptism has but an indirect influence on our salvation; an influence which is emblematized not by the ark, but by the water, which in itself was rather fitted to destroy than to save.

Let us now hear the apostle. He first tells us how baptism does not save: it does not save us, as it is a "putting away of the filth of the flesh." That is the physical effect of the application of water to the body. It removes whatever soils the body, and produces cleanliness; this is all it can do as an external application. This does not, this cannot, save us. The idea that the external rite of baptism can save, can communicate spiritual life, can justify and regenerate, is equally absurd, unscriptural, and mischievous. Moral effects must have moral causes. It has been justly said, "Even the life of a plant, or an animal, far more the life of thought, taste, affection, and conscience, cannot be produced by the use of mere lifeless matter. He who should assert this would be considered as little better than a madman; but is not the statement still more irrational and unintelligible, that the life of the soul, by which it is united to God and secured of salvation, is produced by sprinkling or pouring water on an individual, or by immersing him in it?" A man must be "given up to strong delusions," before he can "believe a lie" like this.

The positive part of the apostle's answer is, however, the most important part of it. Baptism saves us, as it is "the answer of a good conscience towards God, by the resurrection of Jesus Christ." Before entering on the exposition of this statement, which is encumbered with some verbal difficulties, it will, I am persuaded, serve a good purpose to state in the fewest words, to whom, and to what, in the New

Testament, salvation is attributed. God is said to save us. "All things are of him," in the new creation. He "is the Saviour of all men, specially of those that believe."[1] We are said to be saved "by grace," by "God's grace."[2] Christ is said to save us. "All things" in the new creation "are by Him." One of his most common names is "our Saviour." The blood of Christ is said to save us: "Redemption is through his blood." The resurrection of Christ is said to save us: "We are saved by his life."[3] The Holy Spirit is said to save us: "We are saved by the renewing of the Holy Ghost."[4] The gospel is said to save men. The words which Peter was to speak to Cornelius, were words which were to "save him and his family." We are said to be saved by faith: "By grace are ye saved, through faith." "Thy faith," said our Lord, on a number of occasions, "has saved thee." "He that believeth shall be saved."[5] Men are said to be saved by confession of the truth in connection with faith: "With the heart man believes to righteousness," that is, justification; "and with the mouth confession is made unto salvation."[6] Men are said to be saved by baptism in connection with faith: "He that believeth and is baptized shall be saved;"[7] and here "baptism saves us."

Now these statements are all perfectly consistent with each other; and he only understands how sinful men are saved, who sees the meaning and apprehends the consistency of these statements. Here they are in one sentence: God, in the exercise of sovereign grace, saves men through the mediation of his Son, who died as an atoning victim, and rose again to the possession of all power in heaven and earth, that he might save all coming to the Father by him—

---

[1] 1 Tim. iv. 10.   [2] Eph. ii. 4, 5.   [3] Eph. i. 7; Rom. v. 10.
[4] Tit. iii. 5.   [5] Eph. ii. 8; Luke vii. 50, xviii. 42; Mark xvi. 16.
[6] Rom. x. 10.   [7] Mark xvi. 16.

all who, being led by the operation of the Holy Spirit to believe the gospel of salvation, become personally interested in the blessings procured through the mediation of the Son; and wherever men are made really to believe the gospel, they, as the natural result of that faith, and in obedience to the divine command, make a profession of that faith; and in the case of those who in mature life are brought from a false religion to the knowledge and belief of the gospel, the commencement of this profession is baptism, or "the being washed with pure water."

If this statement is understood, there is little difficulty in answering the question, How does baptism save? It is an emblematical representation of what saves us,—the expiatory, justifying blood of Christ; the regenerating, sanctifying influence of the Spirit; and a corresponding confession of the truth thus represented.

Let us look at the apostle's answer, and see if it be not substantially the same as that to which we have been led. I stated to you that there were verbal difficulties. The principal of these are two: the first referring to the meaning of the word rendered "answer;" and the other referring to the connection of the concluding clause, "by the resurrection of Jesus Christ." The word rendered "answer"[1] occurs nowhere else, either in the New Testament or in the Greek translation of the Old Testament. From its etymology, and its use in classic writers, we should say its meaning is "question," not "answer." Many interpreters suppose that there is a reference to an ancient custom of making the baptismal profession in reply to questions put by the administrator, but we have no evidence that this practice existed in the apostle's time; and though it had, the fact would not account for a word meaning "question" being used to signify "answer." Others have rendered it

[1] Ἐπερώτημα.

"inquiry," "application to,"—the application of a good conscience to God for salvation, the sincerely seeking salvation from God. I am persuaded that the word is here employed, as a word of very nearly the same meaning is occasionally in Greek writers, who use a similar dialect with the apostle, —as equivalent to expression, confession, or declaration.[1]

Some interpreters connect the concluding clause with the word *save*—"baptism saves us through the resurrection of Jesus Christ;" others with the phrase, "good conscience towards God;" others with the whole expression, "answer of a good conscience towards God." The second appears to me the most natural mode of connection. What the apostle's words bring before the mind is this: A man has a good conscience; he has obtained this good conscience by the resurrection of Christ; he makes a declaration of this good conscience in his baptism; and it is in this way that the apostle declares that baptism saves.[2]

I had an opportunity some time ago of explaining to you, at some length, what it is to have a good conscience towards God. I stated that a good conscience is just a right and happy state of thought and feeling in reference to our relations and duties to God—confidence in God, love to God; and I showed you that this is obtained by the man's conscience being sprinkled with the atoning blood of Jesus, or, in other words, by his experiencing the power of Christ's atoning blood to pacify the conscience and purify the heart, through the faith of the truth respecting it; and by his being transformed through "the renewing of the mind," produced by "the Holy Ghost shed forth abundantly through Jesus Christ our Saviour."

This good conscience is said to be "by the resurrection

---

[1] See note F.
[2] "Anima enim non lavatione, sed responsione sancitur."—TERTULLIAN, *De Resurrectione Carnis* xlviii.

of Jesus Christ."[1] The resurrection of Christ is the grand proof of the divinity of his mission, and the truth of his doctrine, especially respecting the efficacy of his atoning sacrifice. It is truth regarding these, apprehended in its meaning and evidence under the influence of the Holy Spirit, which produces the good conscience towards God. "I trust in God, seeing he has brought again from the dead our Lord Jesus. I love him who gave his Son for my offences, and who raised him again for my justification."

Of this good conscience, of a mind at peace with God, through our Lord Jesus Christ, a heart with the love of God shed abroad in it, the converted Jew or pagan made a profession when, in obedience to the command of Christ, he submitted to baptism. Thus confessing by an external act what he believed in his heart, that God had raised Christ from the dead, he was saved. In this way, in this way alone, can it be said that "baptism saves us."[2]

Much ingenuity has been discovered in attempting to trace the analogy between the waters of the deluge saving Noah's family, and the water of baptism saving those who in it make an enlightened profession of "a good conscience towards God, through the resurrection of our Lord Jesus Christ." I apprehend we are not to seek anything more than that general analogy which we have already illustrated.

[1] By marking the words "not the putting away of the filth of the flesh, but the answer of a good conscience toward God," as a parenthesis, our translators have disjoined the phrase "by the resurrection of the dead" from "the answer of a good conscience," and connected it with "baptism saves us." Tregelles very justly says that we would find it difficult to read such a passage *aloud* in English, rightly connecting the words. But there are more serious objections to this notation. *Such* a parenthesis is, to say the least, of very rare occurrence; and while it is quite easy to give a clear meaning to the propositions taken singly, 'baptism saves,' and 'the resurrection of Christ saves,' it is difficult to say how baptism saves *by* the resurrection of Christ.

[2] See note G.

The following illustration is at any rate ingenious, and the sentiment it conveys indubitably true and awfully important. "The flood of waters displayed the divine indignation, and executed the threatened vengeance against the wickedness of an ungodly world, while they yet bore up in safety the eight persons enclosed in the ark; so the blood of Christ shed for sin, emblematically represented in baptism, while it has effected the eternal redemption and salvation of all in him, the remnant, according to the election of grace, is at the same time the most awful manifestation of the righteous judgment of God, as well as the surest pledge of its execution against the world which lieth under the wicked one."[1] I have thus concluded my illustrations of this interesting and somewhat difficult passage.

Though I do not think we have been able to clear the difficult passage we have been considering of all its obscurity, I think we have succeeded to a considerable extent; and I am sure we have made it plain enough, that what Paul says of all Scripture given by divine inspiration, is true of this. It is "profitable for doctrine, for reproof, for correction, for instruction in righteousness." I have left myself little time to show you the practical use we should make of it. I shall only notice one very important practical conclusion to which it very directly leads us—the folly and danger of trusting in the mere external rite of baptism, or in anything that is external. Happily *we* are not taught the soul-deluding doctrine of the intrinsic efficacy of the sacraments, as they are called, and of baptismal regeneration as a part of that general dogma. On the contrary, we are taught that "the sacraments become effectual to salvation, not from any virtue in themselves, or in those who administer them, but only by the blessing of Christ, and the working of his Spirit in those who by faith receive

[1] John Walker: *Essays and Correspondence*, vol. ii. p. 107.

them;" and that no baptism saves, except that which is connected with "engrafting into Christ, and partaking of the covenant of grace, and is an engagement to be the Lord's."[1]

But though we are thus taught, and I believe few of us would call this teaching in question, yet there is a natural tendency in the human mind to rest on what is external. Let us beware, then, of supposing that we are safe because we have been baptized, whether in infancy or on our personal profession of faith. The apostle's doctrine respecting circumcision and Judaism is equally true of baptism and Christianity. He is not a true Christian who is one outwardly; neither is that saving baptism which consists merely in the application of water to the body. He is a Christian who is one inwardly, who has the good conscience towards God; and saving baptism is the washing of regeneration, and the renewing of the Holy Ghost. Let all remember, that if they would be saved, enter into the kingdom of God, they "must be born again," "born not of water only, but of the Spirit."[2] And let all who have made profession of a good conscience remember, that where there is a good conscience there will be a good conversation; and that if "a man be in Christ a new creature," he will "put off the old man, who is corrupt in his deeds, and put on the new man, who, after Christ Jesus, is renewed in knowledge and in true holiness." Professing to be saved from the fiery deluge which is coming on the unbelieving, disobedient world, by the blood of Christ represented in baptism, he will show that, by the same precious blood, he is delivered from that world's power, redeemed from "the vain conversation received by tradition from his fathers." Freed from spiritual captivity, he will walk at liberty; and brought into a new world, all old things will pass away, and "all things become new."

[1] *Westminster Shorter Catechism.*   [2] John iii. 1-8.

I cannot persuade myself to close this discourse without dropping a word or two of warning to those " spirits in prison," of whom there are so many in our world, of whom I am afraid there may be some in this assembly, who, though the great Emancipator is present preaching peace and liberty, are yet disobedient, clinging to their chains, and refusing to come forth from their prison-house. I beseech them to consider that the long-suffering of God will not always wait for them, and that the deluge of fire will as certainly come as the deluge of water has come.

Oh, think what must be the issue of this course of yours. " Is it a light matter to you to die in your sins, and to have the wrath of God for ever abiding on you? Think you that it is a light matter to have refused Christ so often, and that after you have been so often requested to receive salvation, after the Lord has followed you with entreaties, hath called so often, 'Why will ye die?' yet wilfully to perish? Would you willingly die in this state? Oh! think, then, he is yet speaking peace; yet waiting, if at length you will return. This is one day more of his waiting and of his speaking to you here; but it may be the last day. For you the flood of fire may come to-morrow. You may die to-night; and as death leaves you, judgment will find you. Oh that ye were wise, and would consider your latter end! Why wear out the day of grace, as careless about Christ, as uncertain about salvation as ever? As you love your souls, be serious in this matter. This was the undoing of the spirits in prison in the days of Noah. They were all for present things; they ate and drank, married and were given in marriage; they were exclusively occupied with things seen and temporal, drowned in them, and that drowned them in a flood. Noah ate and drank too; but his main work was the preparation of the ark. The necessities of life the children of God are tied to. They must give some time and attention to them; but the thing that takes up their hearts, that which the bent of their souls is set on, is an interest in Jesus Christ. All your wise designs are but pleasing madness till this becomes your chief concern also. Others have had your privileges, and abused them; they might have obeyed the gospel, and obtained salvation; but they were disobedient, and are lost, lost for ever. And all they set their heart on has passed away as a shadow; they have nothing of it but the bitter reflection that they sold their souls for a thing of nought."[1]

Will you follow them? You must to the grave, and that soon; but will you follow them to hell? Stop! Consider! Believe, obey the gospel. Now, now is the accepted time. He who listens to this call shall find, amidst the overflowing flood of divine vengeance, in the blessed GOD-MAN, " a hiding-place from the storm, a covert from the tempest," and " shall be safe in that day of evil."

Note A. p. 399.

From the Talmudical writers, it appears that the dead body was not hung by the neck, but by the hands; and that it was hung, not on "a tree" properly called, but ἐπὶ ξύλου, on a piece of timber or stake.—*Mischna*, c. vi.; *Gem. Babyl. Sanhed.* c. vi. fol. 45, col. 2; edit. Amstel. The manner of hanging is thus described by one of these writers: "They fix a stake in the earth, and out of that stake comes a piece of timber; and both the hands placed together are tied, and by them the executioner hangs the body up."—THEOD. DASSOVIUS, *Dissertatio de suspendio hominis lapidibus obruti*, ad Gal. iii. 13; Deut. xxi. 22.

Note B. p. 418.

In bringing about the change referred to, the chief agent employed by Providence has been the Rev. ADAM THOMSON, D.D.,

[1] Leighton.

of Coldstream. Few men have been honoured in a higher degree than this public-spirited minister of Christ. Through his instrumentality, that word of God, which its Author glorifies above all his name,—that word which is able to make men wise unto salvation—which was to a certain extent in this country "bound,"—now runs, has free course, and is glorified. May nothing henceforth stop its course!

Note C. p. 453.

These are well weighed words of the candid and learned Joachim Camerarius, a man every way worthy of being Melancthon's friend: " Est hic unus ex iis locis sacrarum literarum, de quibus pietas religiosa quærere amplius et dubitare quid dicatur, sine reprehensione: et de quibus diversæ etiam sententiæ admitti posse videantur, dummodo non detorqueatur κανὼν τοῦ τὸ αὐτὸ φρονεῖν, id est, religiosa de fide consensio, neque aberretur, ἀπὸ τῆς ἀναλογίας τῆς πίστεως." Luther's remarks, characteristic as they are, do not merit the same eulogium: " Hac tam horribili pœna Petrus Apostolus quoque motus videtur, ut non aliter quam fanaticus loquatur talia verba, quæ ne hodie quidem, a nobis intelligi possunt."—1 Pet. iii. 19, 20. " Mirabile profecto judicium, et vox pæne fanatica."—LUTH.: *Exeg. Opp. Latt.*, tom. ii. p. 221. I do not know that we can make any better apology for the rashness of the great reformer, than to confess with Langé, the worthy father-in-law of the learned and judicious Rambach, " virum optimum aliquid humani passum esse;" and that what he says, " ex affectu potius, quam verbis æstimandum esse."

Note D. p. 454.

Wiclif is uniform in his rendering "made dede *in* fleisch, but made quyk *in* spirit; he cam *in* spirit," etc. So is Tyndale, so far as the repeated mention of spirit is concerned: " Was kylled as pertayning to the flesshe; but was quykened *in* the sprete, *in* which sprete he also went," etc. Cranmer repeats Tyndale, as does the Genevan, with some slight orthographical changes. The Rhemists, in the first part of the rendering, are nearer the truth than any of them: " *Mortified* certes *in* flesh, but quickened *in* spirit; *in* the which spirit," etc.

Contents - Volume III

Original Volume III
Now Appended To End Of This Volume

I. ORDER AND OUTLINE OF DISCOURSES.

DISCOURSE XVII.

EXHORTATION TO HOLINESS BASED ON THE ATONEMENT.

CHAPTER IV. 1-6, pp. 1-69.

PART I. The basis of the exhortation, page 10. PART II. The exhortation, 12. § 1. The particular object to be sought; negative—positive, 12. (1.) Negative, "not to live to the lusts of men," 12. (2.) Positive, "To live to the will of God," 17. § 2. The means for obtaining the practical object; the arming themselves with the thought, "He that suffered in the flesh hath ceased from sin," 22. (1.) The thought explained, 25. (2.) The thought viewed as referring to Christ, 28. (3.) The thought viewed as referring to Christians, 30. (4.) The thought viewed as a piece of Christian armour—the instrumental means of sanctification, 34. PART III. Motives enforcing the exhortation, 46. § 1. Motive drawn from the character of the course against which the exhortation is directed, 47. § 2. Motive drawn from the great design of the gospel revelation, 57. NOTES, 68.

DISCOURSE XVIII.

SOBRIETY AND WATCHING UNTO PRAYER ILLUSTRATED AND ENFORCED.

CHAPTER IV. 7, pp. 70-88.

PART I. The duties enjoined by the apostle, page 71. § 1. Sobriety, 71. § 2. "Watching unto prayer," 76. PART II. Motive urging to sobriety and watching unto prayer: "The end of all things is at hand," 81.

DISCOURSE XIX.

ON THE MAINTENANCE AND MANIFESTATION OF BROTHERLY LOVE.

CHAPTER IV. 8-11, pp. 89-133.

PART I. The maintenance of brotherly love, page 91. § 1. The duty explained, 91. § 2. The duty recommended, 97. PART II. The manifestation of brotherly love, 109. § 1. Christians are to manifest brotherly love by employing their property for each other's good as men, as in ungrudging hospitality, 110. § 2. Christians are to manifest brotherly love, by employing their spiritual gifts for promoting one another's spiritual edification, 119. § 3. Motives to these two manifestations of Christian love, 128. NOTES, 133.

DISCOURSE XX.

DIRECTORY TO CHRISTIANS SUFFERING FOR THEIR RELIGION.

CHAPTER IV. 12-19, pp. 134-179.

PART I. Be not astonished at your sufferings, page 135. PART II. Be not depressed by your sufferings, 141. PART III. Be not ashamed of your sufferings, 154. PART IV. Persevering in well-doing, commit your souls to God under sufferings, 164. NOTES, 176.

DISCOURSE XXI.

THE ECCLESIASTICAL DUTIES OF CHRISTIANS ENJOINED AND ENFORCED.

CHAPTER V. 1-5, pp. 180-282.

PART I. Of the duties of the rulers in the Christian Church, page 182. CHAPTER I. The appellation here given to the rulers in the Christian Church, "elders," 182. § 1. The origin and meaning of the appellation, 182. § 2. Qualifications of Christian elders, 189. § 3. Of the manner in which elders were invested with office, 190. CHAPTER II. Of the duties of Christian elders, 191. § 1. Of the figurative terms in which these duties are described: acting the part of a shepherd and an overseer, 191. § 2. Of the duties themselves, 193. (1.) Instruction, 194. (2.) Superintendence, 200. CHAPTER III. Of the manner in which these duties are to be performed, 205. § 1. "Not by constraint, but willingly," 206. § 2. "Not for filthy lucre, but of a ready mind," 209. § 3. Not as lords of God's heritage, but being ensamples to the flock, 213. CHAPTER IV. Of the motives to these duties, 217. § 1. Motives suggested by the apostle's reference to himself, 218. (1.) He was also an elder, 218. (2.) He was a witness of the sufferings of Christ, 220. (3.) He was a partaker of the glory to be revealed, 224. § 2. Motives from considerations referring to the Church, 226. (1.) It is the flock of God, 226. (2.) It is God's heritage, 227. § 3. Motives from considerations referring to the office-bearers themselves, 229. (1.) The reward of the faithful Christian elder, 229. (2.) The doom of the unfaithful Christian elder, 232. PART II. Of the duties of the members of the Christian Church to their office-bearers, 235. § 1. Preliminary requisites to the discharge of the duty of subjection to elders, 244. (1.) Conviction of the divine authority of church order, 244. (2.) Personal respect for those invested with office, 245. § 2. Subjection to the elders as teachers, 246. § 3. Submission to the elders as superintendents, 249. (1.) Submission to the eldership as a body,

CONTENTS. xi

249. (2.) Submission to the elders as individuals, 252. PART III. Of the duty which all in a Christian church owe to each other: "Mutual subjection," 257. CHAPTER I. Of the mutual subjection which all in a Christian church owe to each other, 259. § 1. What this does not imply, 259. § 2. What this does imply, 261. CHAPTER II. Of the means of performing this duty: "the being clothed with humility," 266. § 1. Humility explained, 267. § 2. The tendency of humility to secure mutual subjection, 270. CHAPTER III. Of the motive urging Christians to cultivate humility, 271. NOTES, 279.

DISCOURSE XXII.

TWO VIEWS OF AFFLICTION AND ITS DUTIES.

CHAPTER V. 6, 7, pp. 283-331.

PART I. First view of affliction, and its duty, page 287. § 1. Affliction is subjection to the mighty hand of God, 287. § 2. Our duty in affliction is to "humble ourselves under the mighty hand of God," 293. (1.) As creatures under the hand of the Creator, 294. (2.) As subjects under the hand of their Sovereign, rebel subjects under the hand of their righteously offended Sovereign, 295. (3.) As children under the hand of their Father, 296. § 3. Motives to humbling ourselves under the mighty hand of God, 298. (1.) It is a part of the humility which God so complacently approves, 298. (2.) It is the hand of God we are called to humble ourselves under, 299. (3.) It is the mighty hand of God we are called to humble ourselves under, 300. (4.) To humble ourselves under the mighty hand of God, is the appointed way of our being in due time exalted, 300. PART II. Second view of affliction and its duty, 307. § 1. Affliction is a state of anxiety and carefulness, 308. § 2. The duty of the Christian under affliction is to "cast all his care on God," 310. (1.) A persuasion that God has power to control what excites our anxiety, 314. (2.) A persuasion that God will employ his controlling power in the best possible way, 315. (3.) A persuasion that he will employ his controlling power in the best possible way for us, 315. § 3. The motive to casting our care on God is, that he cares for us, 318. NOTES, 329.

DISCOURSE XXIII.

THE CHRISTIAN'S GREAT ENEMY; HIS DUTY IN REFERENCE TO HIM, AND HIS ENCOURAGEMENT TO DISCHARGE IT.

CHAPTER V. 8-11, pp. 332-394.

PART I. The Christian's great enemy, page 335. CHAPTER I. Who is he? The Devil, 336. CHAPTER II. What is he? 338. § 1. He is an adversary, their adversary, 338. § 2. He is a subtle adversary, 340. § 3. He is an active adversary, 342. § 4. He is a cruel adversary, 344. § 5. He is a powerful adversary, 345. PART II. The Christian's duty in reference to his great enemy, 349. CHAPTER I. What he must do to his great enemy : Resist him, 349. § 1. He must resist his attacks on himself, 350. § 2. He must resist his attacks on the Christian cause, 352. CHAPTER II. What the Christian is to do that he may resist his great enemy, 354. § 1. He must be sober, 355. § 2. He must be vigilant, 358. § 3. He must be stedfast in the faith, 360. PART III. The Christian's encouragement to perform his duty in reference to his great enemy, 363. CHAPTER I. The encouraging fact : all the brotherhood have sustained and surmounted this struggle, 363. CHAPTER II. The faithful promise, 367. § 1. The encouragement contained in the promise itself, 369. (1.) They shall be made perfect, 370. (2.) They shall be established, 372. (3.) They shall be strengthened, 372. (4.) They shall be settled, 373. (5.) He who does all this for them is God, 376. § 2. The encouragement contained in the adjuncts of the promise, 379. (1.) The God who has promised this is "the God of all grace," 379. (2.) This God of all grace has "called" the Christian "in Christ Jesus," 382. (3.) The God of all grace has called Christians to his eternal glory, 384. (4.) The afflictions are moderate in degree, short in duration, and form a part of the divine plan for their ultimate salvation, 387. PART IV. Conclusion, 390.

DISCOURSE XXIV.

POSTSCRIPT OF THE EPISTLE.

CHAPTER v. 12-14, pp. 395-420.

PART I. Recapitulation, page 397. CHAPTER I. The subject of the Epistle, 398. § 1. The grace of God, 398. § 2. The Christian's duty in reference to this grace: "to stand," 400. CHAPTER II. The form of the Epistle, 402. It is a testimony and exhortation respecting the grace of God, 402. CHAPTER III. The mode of the writing or transmission of the Epistle, 406. PART II. The salutation, 409. § 1. The salutation of the church in Babylon, 409. § 2. The salutation of Marcus, 412. PART III. Exhortation, 413. PART IV. Benediction, 415. NOTES, 419.

II. TABLE FOR FINDING OUT THE EXPOSITION OF ANY VERSE OR CLAUSE OF THE EPISTLE IN THIS VOLUME.

CHAPTER IV.

Ver.
1. Forasmuch then as Christ hath suffered for us in the flesh, 10 ; arm yourselves likewise with the same mind, 22; for he that hath suffered
2. in the flesh hath ceased from sin, 24 ; that he no longer should live the rest of the time in the flesh to the lusts of men, 12 ; but to the

CONTENTS. xiii

Ver.
3. will of God, 17. For the time past of our life may suffice us, 54; to have wrought the will of the Gentiles, 48; when we walked in lasciviousness, lusts, excess of wine, revellings, banquetings, and
4. abominable idolatries, 48; wherein they think it strange that ye run not with them to the same excess of riot, speaking evil of you, 49;
5. who shall give account to him that is ready to judge the quick
6. and the dead, 51. For, for this cause was the gospel also preached to them that are dead, 57; that they might be judged according to men in the flesh, 60; but live according to God in the spirit, 61;
7. But the end of all things is at hand, 81; be ye therefore sober, 71;
8. and watch unto prayer, 76; and above all things have fervent charity among yourselves, 91; for charity shall cover the multitude
9. of sins, 97. Use hospitality one to another without grudging, 110.
10. As every one hath received the gift, even so minister the same one to another, 119; as good stewards of the manifold grace of God,
11. 128. If any man speak, let him speak as the oracles of God; if any man minister, let him do it as of the ability that God giveth, 121; that God in all things may be glorified through Jesus Christ, 129; to whom be praise and dominion for ever and ever, Amen, 130.
12. Beloved, think it not strange concerning the fiery trial which is to
13. try you, as if some strange thing happened unto you, 135; but rejoice, inasmuch as ye are partakers of Christ's sufferings, 141; that when his glory is revealed, ye may be glad also with exceeding
14. joy, 145. If ye be reproached for the name of Christ, 149; happy are ye, 149; for the Spirit of God and of glory resteth upon you, 150; on their part he is evil-spoken of, but on your part he is glo-
15. rified, 151. But let none of you suffer as a murderer or as a thief, or as an evil-doer, 154; or as a busybody in other men's matters,
16. 155. Yet if any man suffer as a Christian, 159; let him not be
17. ashamed, 161; but let him glorify God on this behalf, 161. For the time is come that judgment must begin at the house of God, 165; and if it first begin at us, what shall the end be of them who
18. obey not the gospel of God? 170. And if the righteous scarcely be saved, 167; where shall the ungodly and the sinner appear? 171.
19. Wherefore, let them that suffer according to the will of God, 167; commit the keeping of their souls to him, 168; in well-doing, 172; as unto a faithful Creator, 169.

CHAPTER V.

1. The elders which are among you, 182; I exhort, who am also an elder, 218; and a witness of the sufferings of Christ, 220; and also
2. a partaker of the glory that shall be revealed, 224; feed the flock of God which is among you, 226; taking the oversight thereof, 200; not by constraint, but willingly, 205; not for filthy lucre,
3. but of a ready mind, 209; neither as being lords, 213; over God's
4. heritage, 227; but being ensamples to the flock, 214; and when the chief Shepherd shall appear, ye shall receive a crown of
5. glory that fadeth not away, 229. Likewise, 236; ye younger, 238; submit yourselves unto the elder, 244, 246; yea, all of you be

CONTENTS.

Ver.

  subject one to another, 257 ; and be clothed with humility, 266 ;
for God resisteth the proud, 271 ; and giveth grace to the humble,
6. 275. Humble yourselves, 293 ; therefore, under the mighty hand
7. of God, 287 ; that he may exalt you in due time, 300 ; casting all
8. your care upon him, 308 ; for he careth for you, 318. Be sober,
355 ; be vigilant, 358 ; because your adversary, 338 ; the devil,
336 ; as a roaring lion, 344 ; walketh about, 342 ; seeking whom
9. he may devour, 345 ; whom resist, 350 ; stedfast in the faith, 360 ;
knowing that the same afflictions are accomplished in your brethren
10. that are in the world, 363. But the God of all grace, 379 ; who
hath called us, 382 ; to his eternal glory, 384 ; by Christ Jesus,
383 ; after that ye have suffered a while, 387 ; make you perfect,
11. 370 ; stablish, 372 ; strengthen, 372 ; settle you, 373 ; to him be
12. glory and dominion for ever and ever, Amen, 390. By Silvanus,
406 ; a faithful brother unto you, 407 ; as I suppose, 408 ; I have
written briefly, 404 ; exhorting, 403 ; and testifying, 404 ; that
13. this is the true grace of God, 398 ; wherein ye stand, 400. The
church that is at Babylon, 409 ; saluteth you, and so doth Marcus,
14. my son, 412. Greet ye one another with a kiss of charity, 413.
Peace be with you all that are in Christ Jesus, 415. Amen, 418.

INDEX—
 I. Principal Matters, ... 421
 II. Greek Words and Phrases remarked on, . . . 429
 III. Authors quoted or referred to, ... 431
 IV. Texts of Scripture remarked on, ... 434

EXPOSITORY DISCOURSES.

DISCOURSE XVII.

EXHORTATION TO HOLINESS BASED ON THE ATONEMENT.

" Forasmuch then as Christ hath suffered for us in the flesh, arm yourselves likewise with the same mind: for he that hath suffered in the flesh hath ceased from sin; that he no longer should live the rest of his time in the flesh to the lusts of men, but to the will of God. For the time past of our life may suffice us to have wrought the will of the Gentiles, when we walked in lasciviousness, lusts, excess of wine, revellings, banquetings, and abominable idolatries: wherein they think it strange that ye run not with them to the same excess of riot, speaking evil of you: who shall give account to him that is ready to judge the quick and the dead. For, for this cause was the gospel preached also to them that are dead, that they might be judged according to men in the flesh, but live according to God in the spirit."—1 PET. iv. 1-6.

THE paragraph now read presents us with a very important theme of consideration. It directs us to the practical use which we should habitually make of that great fundamental principle of Christianity, "that Christ, the just One, suffered in the room of the unjust, that he might bring them to God." It teaches us to use it as the most serviceable piece of armour, whether defensive or offensive, that we can employ in the spiritual conflict on which as Christians we profess to have entered; that which in the preceding context is represented as the expiation of our guilt, the price of our pardon, the ground of our hope, being here exhibited as also the means of our sanctification,—the strongest motive, the most cheering encouragement, to "cleanse ourselves from all filthiness of the flesh and spirit, and to perfect holiness in the fear of God,"—to " put off the old man, which is corrupt, and put on the new man, which, after God," that is, in the image of God, "is created in righteousness and true holiness;"[1] or, as the apostle has it here, "to live no longer the rest of our time in the flesh to the lusts of men, but to the will of God."

The words of the text are so obviously and so intimately related to those which immediately precede them, that we cannot help considering the commencement of a new chapter here as injudicious, and as fitted rather to obscure the sense; the natural place for a division being plainly the close of the eleventh verse. The long and somewhat involved sentence which I have read (for it is one sentence), is a following up of the statement which had been made respecting the sufferings of Christ, in their nature, design, and consequences, by an exhortation enforced by two appropriate motives. The exhortation is contained in the second part of the first verse, and in the whole of the second; and the first motive is adduced in the third, fourth, and fifth verses, and the second in the sixth verse. This is clearly the general division of the passage; and even this general view of the construction of the passage will be found useful in guiding our inquiries into its meaning.

Interpreters have been a good deal perplexed, both as to the manner in which the various clauses are connected with each other, and as to the meaning which severally and conjointly they are intended to express. I have never conversed with an intelligent Christian, acquainted merely with our English version of the passage, who has not complained of its obscurity, and acknowledged, that while most, though

[1] Eph. iv. 24. Κατὰ Θεόν.

by no means all, of the expressions seemed clear enough when taken singly, and many of the clauses viewed separately had an obvious meaning, he had failed in his attempts to obtain a consistent and satisfactory view of the whole; and I could not very readily point such a person to any interpretation of the passage where he would find a complete solution of his doubts and difficulties.

I have no doubt the passage has often been read without the perception of any difficulty; but that is only a proof how inattentive many readers of the Bible are to the command of its Author, " He that readeth, let him understand." It is good to observe difficulties; it is the first step towards having them removed. It may be said—I believe it is often thought—an unobserved difficulty can do no harm; but this is a mistake, for it may lead into error: at any rate, it must prevent us from apprehending the truth, and from obtaining from it the practical advantages it is intended to communicate.

There is no difficulty in the first clause, " Forasmuch as Christ hath suffered for us in the flesh," bearing, as it plainly does, on the statements respecting the sufferings of Christ, in their nature, design, and results, contained in the five concluding verses of the preceding chapter,—" That He once suffered for sins, the just for the unjust, that he might bring us to God; and that, having become dead in the flesh, he was quickened in the Spirit, and went and preached to the spirits in prison; and being raised from the dead, is gone into heaven, and, seated at the right hand of God, has angels, and principalities, and powers subjected to him,"—and referring to that statement as the basis on which the apostle is about to place the following exhortation. This is sufficiently plain; but the difficulties immediately commence, and they come in considerable number and close succession.

"Arm yourselves with the same mind." With what mind? If it be answered, with the mind or disposition of Christ, the question returns, But what is said about his mind or disposition in the context? Absolutely nothing. His sufferings are spoken of,—their nature, their design, their results, are particularly referred to; but there is nothing said of his mind, his temper, or disposition. Had the words, " Arm yourselves with the same mind," followed the very similar passage in chap. ii. 21-24,—" Christ suffered for us, leaving us an example, that we should follow his steps; who did no sin, neither was guile found in his mouth; who, when he was reviled, reviled not again; when he suffered, he threatened not, but committed himself to him who judgeth righteously,"—we should at once have seen the connection. The exhortation would have seemed to rise naturally out of the statement, " Forasmuch as Christ has *thus* suffered, arm yourselves with the same mind" when ye are called to suffer. But here the exhortation is not to imitate Christ in suffering, but to make the fact of his having suffered, a piece of armour, offensive and defensive, in our conflicts with our spiritual adversaries.

Then come the words, " For he that suffered in the flesh has ceased from sin; that he no longer should live the rest of the time in the flesh to the lusts of men, but to the will of God." Here are a host of perplexities. Who is this that has " suffered in the flesh, and ceased from sin?" Is it Christ, who in the beginning of the verse is said to have " suffered for us in the flesh?" That certainly is the meaning naturally suggested by the construction; but what can be meant by Christ's ceasing from sin? and, more extraordinary still, what can be meant by his ceasing from sin, " that he should no longer live the rest of his time in the flesh to the lusts of men, but to the will of God?" How could he cease from sin who never began to sin? He never lived any part "of his time in the flesh to the lusts of men." He was always " holy, harmless, undefiled, and separate from sinners;"[1] he always " lived to the will of God." It was " his meat to do the will of him who sent him, and to finish his work."[2] And if " he who suffers in the flesh" be any one who suffers bodily affliction, or any Christian who suffers bodily affliction for Christ's cause,—and it has been supposed to mean all these by different interpreters,—still, we ask, how do any or all of these " cease from sin?" Is bodily affliction a furnace, which uniformly and entirely separates the dross from the precious metal in the human character? Does a man need only to be made sufficiently miserable in order to his becoming sufficiently holy? And were this insuperable difficulty got over, what is meant by a man ceasing from sin, " that he may no longer live to the lusts of men?" Is not that very like an assertion, that he ceases from sin that he may cease from sin? And then, what bearing has this strange declaration on the exhortation, " Arm yourselves with the same mind," of which it seems brought forward as an enforcement?

And then, looking forward to the conclusion of this sentence, the darkness becomes darkness that may be felt. What is the meaning of " the gospel being preached to them who are dead?" what is meant by those dead being " judged according to men in the flesh?" what by their " living according to God in the spirit?" And what connection have these two things with what they seem to be assigned as the reason for—either the general judgment, or Christians avoiding sin and cultivating holiness?

I readily acknowledge, that to some of these questions I cannot give a satisfactory answer; and from the whole sentence, as it stands in our version, it does not seem possible to extract a consistent and pertinent meaning. It is not

[1] Heb. vii. 26.   [2] John iv. 34.

wonderful that some of the most learned and acute interpreters have honestly confessed that they did not understand it. It is more wonderful and less creditable, that many expositors slur over the matter, and leave their readers equally uninformed, so far as they are concerned, as to the existence of difficulties, or the means of lessening or removing them. I do not know that they can all be removed. I am persuaded many of them may.

A few remarks on the meaning of a word or two, and on the construction of one or two clauses, will, I am persuaded, go far to remove all difficulty from the first and second verses, and to make them a clear expression of an obviously just and important thought, of a consistent and pertinent sentiment. The first remark as to the meaning of a word is this—that the term rendered " mind,"[1] which is, to say the least, not its usual meaning, should have been translated in a sense which it very commonly bears—"thought." " Arm yourselves with this same thought." And if you ask what same thought, the first remark as to the construction of the clauses will give a satisfactory answer: the words that immediately follow contain the thought: " He that hath suffered in the flesh hath ceased, or rather, has been made to rest, from sin;"[2] the particle rendered *for*[3] being translated, as it very frequently is, *that*—thus, " Arm yourselves with this same thought, that He who hath suffered in the flesh, has been made to rest from sin."[4] This is the same thought referred to in the commencement of the verse, and more fully brought out in the concluding verses of the preceding chapter.

As to the construction of the words, we have to remark, that the second verse is not to be considered as connected directly with the words which immediately precede it, but with the exhortation, " Arm yourselves with this same

[1] Ἔννοια. [2] Πέπαυται. [3] Ὅτι. [4] See note A.

thought;" and expresses the end to be sought by that means. It is the reply to the inquiry, For what purpose are we to arm ourselves with this same thought? It deserves notice, that there is nothing in the words themselves restricting them either to the first, second, or third person.[1] They are literally, " in order to the no longer living the rest of the time in the flesh to the lusts of men, but to the will of God." There follow in the next four verses two motives, urging compliance with the exhortation: the first contained in the third, fourth, and fifth verses; the second contained in the sixth.

The whole passage, then, stands thus: " Forasmuch as Christ hath suffered for us in the flesh, arm yourselves with this same thought, that He who hath suffered in the flesh has been made to rest from sin." And why arm yourselves with this thought? " that ye may no longer live the rest of your time in the flesh to the lusts of men, but to the will of God." And why not live the rest of your time to the lusts of men, but to the will of God? (1.) " Because the time past of our life may suffice us to have wrought the will of the Gentiles, when we walked in lasciviousness, lusts, excess of wine, revellings, banquetings, and abominable idolatries; wherein they think it strange that ye run not with them to the same excess of riot, speaking evil of you, who shall give account to him who is ready to judge the quick and the dead; and (2.) Because for this cause was the gospel preached to them who are dead, that they might be judged according to men in the flesh, but live according to God in the spirit."

Viewed in this way, the sentence hangs well together, and exhibits a clear, consistent, and important meaning. Its general plan and object thus become apparent, and

---

[1] Εἰς τὸ μηκέτι ἀνθρώπων ἐπιθυμίαις ἀλλὰ θελήματι Θεοῦ τὸν ἐπίλοιπον ἐν σαρκὶ βιῶσαι χρόνον.

first sight beset with so many difficulties, in no ordinary degree rich in Christian doctrine, and law, and motive; "profitable for doctrine, for reproof, for correction, for instruction in righteousness."

I. THE BASIS OF THE EXHORTATION.

The first branch of the subject—THE GREAT PRINCIPLE OF CHRISTIAN TRUTH, "Christ hath suffered for us in the flesh"—which the apostle lays down as the basis of his exhortation, need not detain us long, as we have in our last discourse considered at great length the full announcement of it in the close of the last chapter, on which the more abbreviated statement in the text plainly reduplicates. It is a summary of all that is most peculiar and important in the religion of Christ, a comprehensive epitome of the gospel of our salvation. It is that which Paul first received and first declared to the churches, assuring them that it was that gospel which, if they received it, and kept it in memory, would certainly save the soul.[1] Its import may be thus briefly stated.

Christ, the long promised, divinely appointed, divinely qualified, divinely accredited, divine Saviour, in human nature has endured numerous, varied, violent, severe sufferings, terminating in death.

These sufferings were penal—"for sins," being the execution of the penal sanction of the divine law, the manifestation of the displeasure of God against sin. He was made sin, he became a curse.

These sufferings were vicarious. They were not for his own sins, for he had none, but for the sins of men. "He suffered, the just in the room of the unjust." He "became a curse" in the room of the accursed. "We all like sheep

[1] 1 Cor. xv. 1, 2.

had gone astray: we had turned every one to his own way; and the Lord laid on him the iniquity of us all." "He was wounded for our transgressions, he was bruised for our iniquities, the chastisement of our peace was on him."

These sufferings were expiatory. In them the penalty was not only borne, but borne away. He made an end of sin, by making reconciliation for iniquity. "He took away sin by the sacrifice of himself." "He is the propitiation for our sins," and he is "set forth a propitiation;" and the righteousness of God in the remission of sins is thus declared: "God being just, and the justifier of him who believes in Jesus."

The design of these penal, vicarious, and expiatory sufferings of the divinely appointed, divinely qualified, divinely accredited, divine Saviour, is to bring men to God; to restore ignorant and deluded man to the true knowledge of God, guilty man to the favour of God, depraved man to the image of God, and miserable man to the enjoyment of God; thus making him truly wise, truly good, and truly happy for ever.

Finally, while these sufferings terminated in the death of the incarnate Saviour, they obtained for him as their merited reward, that spiritual power which he exerts through the preaching of the gospel, in giving liberty to the spiritually enslaved, and life to the spiritually dead; and a seat at God's right hand in the Heaven of heavens, angels and principalities and powers being made subject to him. Such is the great truth referred to by the apostle in the words, "Christ has suffered for us in the flesh," and which he lays down as the basis on which he builds an exhortation to universal holiness—"holiness in all manner of conversation."

II. THE EXHORTATION.

That EXHORTATION forms the second division of our subject, to the consideration of which we now proceed. It is contained in these words: "Arm yourselves with this same thought, that He who hath suffered in the flesh has been made to rest from sin, that ye no longer should live the rest of your time in the flesh to the lusts of men, but to the will of God." The exhortation, as I have already had occasion to remark, is twofold. The apostle calls on them to use certain means in order to secure a certain end: to cultivate a particular mode of thinking, that they may follow a particular course of conduct; to arm themselves with an influential thought, that they may perform a difficult work. It will, I believe, subserve the purpose of clear exposition, if we consider the two parts of the exhortation in the inverse order in which they are presented to us in the text: that we first consider the course of conduct which the apostle would have Christians to pursue, and then the means he would have them to employ in order that they may follow that course of conduct.

§ 1. *The particular object to be sought; negative—positive.*

The course of conduct which the apostle would have Christians to pursue, is described in these words: "No longer live the rest of your time in the flesh to the lusts of men, but live[1] the rest of your time in the flesh to the will of God." The exhortation, you perceive, is both negative and positive. It forbids one course of conduct and enjoins another.

(1.) *Negative:* "*Not to live to the lusts of men.*"

The negative exhortation plainly proceeds on the prin-

---

[1] Βιῶσαι. Aptum verbum: non dicitur de brutis.—BENGEL.

ciple, that in the former part of their lives, previously to their conversion, they had been distinguished by a mode of conduct not only different from, but directly opposite to, that by which they ought henceforward to be characterized: they had done what they are now not to do; they had not done what they are now to do; they had lived the former part of their time in the flesh to the lusts of men, and not to the will of God. It is of great importance that Christians should keep habitually in mind their state and character previous to conversion; "that they should often look to the rock whence they were hewn, and to the hole of the pit whence they were dug."[1] It is fitted to hide pride from their eyes, to excite gratitude, to deepen the sense of obligation. To gain these ends, God's ancient people were often put in mind of their humble origin, and their enslaved state in Egypt; and Christians are frequently, directly and indirectly, called on to reflect on the state of error and guilt and condemnation and spiritual enslavement from which they have been delivered. "Once were ye darkness, but now are ye light in the Lord; walk in the light."

"Such were some of you," says the apostle, after giving a list of enormous transgressors: "Such were some of you; but ye are washed, but ye are sanctified, but ye are justified, in the name of the Lord Jesus, and by the Spirit of our God." "In time past," says he, speaking to those who had been, in the great love wherewith the God who is rich in mercy had loved them, quickened together with Christ, and made to sit together in heavenly places in him, "ye were dead in trespasses and sins; ye walked according to the course of this world, according to the prince of the power of the air, the spirit that now worketh in the children of disobedience; among whom also we all had our conversation in time past, in the lusts of our flesh fulfilling the desires

[1] Isa. li. 1, 2.

of the flesh and of the mind, and were by nature the children of wrath, even as others." "Remember," says he, "that at that time ye were without Christ, being aliens from the commonwealth of Israel, and strangers from the covenants of promise, having no hope, and being without God in the world."[1] And here the apostle, not the less impressively because indirectly, reminds the Christians to whom he wrote, that they had spent the former part of their lives in rebellion against God, and in base subjection to his and their enemies.

"The time in the flesh" is an expression just equivalent to the period of our mortal life. During the past part of this life, previous to their conversion, they had lived "not to the will of God, but to the lusts of men." To live to the will of God is to live according to the will of God, to make the will of God the supreme rule and the ultimate reason of our sentiments and conduct. In his unconverted state, no man does this. He is ignorant and misinformed as to the will of God, and no way disposed to seek after more extended or accurate information on this subject. He does "not like to retain God in his knowledge;" and when God presses the truth respecting his will on such a man's notice, he turns away, saying in his heart, "Let me alone;" "Depart from me, I desire not the knowledge of thy will or thy ways." He "walks after the imagination of his own heart."[2] In most cases, in forming a determination as to a course of conduct, the question, 'Is the course resolved on agreeable to or inconsistent with the will of God?' is never put. God is not in all the thoughts. Nor is this the worst of it: for there are cases in which the man is, from circumstances, compelled to admit into his calculations the element of conformity or disconformity with the will of God; and then, instead of giving it its proper place, which is that of supreme control, he deliberately sets it

[1] Eph. v. 8; 1 Cor. vi. 11; Eph. ii. 1, 2, 11, 12.   [2] Jer. xxiii. 17.

aside, and proceeds to choose and to act in direct opposition to what he knows to be the divine will, choosing and doing what he knows God disapproves, and rejecting and refusing to do what he knows God approves. The language of his conduct is that of the rebellious Jews to Jeremiah: "As to the word that thou hast spoken to us in the name of the Lord, we will not hearken to thee; but we will certainly do whatsoever thing goeth forth out of our own mouth."[1]

And while thus not living to the will of God, he is living "to the lusts of men." The lusts of men are just the desires whereby mankind in their fallen state are characterized; some of them sinful in themselves; others of them innocent in themselves, but faulty from excess or misdirection; all of them unfitted for a purpose which they were never meant to answer—to be the regulating principle of conduct. And to live to these desires is just to make them the rule and reason of what we do; to spend life in endeavouring to obtain the gratification of these desires, seeking to conform ourselves to our own natural inclinations; "fashioning ourselves," as the apostle phrases it in the first chapter of this epistle, "according to our former lusts in our ignorance;" forming our character entirely under their influence, and the influence of their objects, present and sensible things, "things seen and temporal;" or seeking to conform ourselves to those desires as reigning in and manifested by others, being "conformed to this world,"—embracing commonly prevalent opinions, regulating ourselves by commonly prevalent maxims, just because they are commonly prevalent,—"walking according to the course of this world;" and, while obstinately refusing to be servants of God in living to his will, basely becoming the slaves of men by living to their lusts. This is a true account of the mode of life of every unrenewed man. It was once the mode of life of those to

[1] Jer. xliv. 16, 17.

whom the apostle is writing. It was once the mode of life of every true Christian. It is the mode of life of vast multitudes of professed Christians still.

But, says the apostle to the strangers scattered abroad, this must be your mode of life no longer. Now that ye are " in Christ," ye have become " new creatures; old things are passed away, all things are become new."[1] You must no more live the rest of your time in the flesh to the lusts of men, but to the will of God. " Worldly desires," whether in yourselves or in others, are not to be the guiding principles of your conduct. You are not, because you desire, or other men desire, a particular object, to set about forthwith to endeavour to obtain it. You are to bring all your own desires, and all the desires of others, viewed as influencing your choice and conduct, before the tribunal of a higher principle; and according to its awards, you are to refuse, or modify, or gratify them. Where they are condemned, they are, as existing in ourselves, to be sought to be weakened and destroyed,—cut off, though apparently useful as a right hand,—pulled out, though felt to be dear as a right eye, and cast from us as an abominable and pernicious thing; and as existing in others, they are not to be complied with, but steadily resisted. And even where they are not sinful in their nature, but merely in danger of becoming exorbitant in their demands, they are never to be permitted to be the guide of our conduct, the controlling power of action. Christians are not to " obey sin by the desires of the body, yielding their members to it as the instruments of unrighteousness." They are not to " make provision for the flesh to fulfil its desires;" on the contrary, they are to " mortify their members that are on the earth;" they are to " crucify the flesh, with its affections and lusts;" they are to " deny themselves;" they are not to be " con-

[1] 2 Cor. v. 17.

formed to this present world," and they are to turn away from them "who walk after their own ungodly desires;" they are to "have no fellowship with the unfruitful works of darkness, but rather to reprove them." They are not to "walk as men," but as Christians; not as "born of the flesh," but as "born of the Spirit."[1]

(2.) *Positive:* "*To live to the will of God.*"

The principle which is to guide their conduct and fashion their character, and which is to control and direct the desires, whether in themselves or others, as principles of their conduct, is "the will of God." They are to live the rest of their time in the flesh "to the will of God," that is, according to the will of God. Not human desire, either in ourselves or others, but divine will, is to be the rule and reason of our conduct.

The will of God is the rule of his own conduct. "He worketh all things according to the counsel of his own will." "He doeth according to his will in the armies of heaven, and among the inhabitants of the earth." His will is the law of all inanimate and irrational being. "He has established the earth, and it abideth. They continue this day according to his ordinance, for all are his servants." This will is the rule and the reason of the conduct of all holy, intelligent beings. The angels that excel in strength, "do his commandments, hearkening unto the voice of his word; they are ministers of his, that do his pleasure."[2] This will should be the rule and reason of the conduct of all intelligent beings.

The will of God can be the rule and reason of the con-

---

[1] Matt. v. 29, 30, xviii. 8; Rom. vi. 12, 13, xiii. 14; Col. iii. 5; Gal. v. 24; Matt. xvi. 24; Rom. xii. 2; 2 Tim. iii. 5; Eph. v. 11; 2 Cor. iii. 3; John iii. 4.

[2] Eph. i. 11; Dan. iv. 35; Ps. cxix. 90, ciii. 20, 21.

duct of intelligent beings, only in the degree in which it is revealed to and known by them. The secret will of God, or what we ordinarily term his decrees, so far as unrevealed, cannot be the guide of our conduct. But when his will becomes apparent in his providential dispensations, then it is our duty to submit to it with unmurmuring acquiescence, however opposed to our natural inclination, saying, "It is the Lord; let him do with us what seemeth good in his sight. The will of the Lord be done. Thy will be done in earth as it is in heaven."[1]

It is however his *will*, as made known in his *word*, that is to be the chief, the paramount rule of our conduct. He has, in the Scriptures of truth, "showed us what is good, and what he requires of us,"—"his good, and acceptable, and perfect will."[2] He has declared to us what is true, and what is right; and it ought to be our habitual endeavour to ascertain what he has declared to be true, that we may believe it; what he has declared to be right, that we may do it. To the question, May we do this? we should reply by the question, Does the revelation of his will permit it?—to the question, Must we do this? by the question, Does the revelation of his will require it? And no amount of opposite influence, from whatever quarter it may come, whether from inclination, or interest, or general opinion, must be permitted to induce us to do what that revelation says we may not do, or to neglect what it says we must do. "What soever we do, whether in word or in deed, we must do it as to the Lord, and not as to men;" acknowledging his authority, seeking his approbation. Regarding ourselves as his property, we must seek to dispose of that property according to his will. Knowing that we are not our own, and therefore not to be regulated by our own will,—not other men's,

[1] 1 Sam. iii. 18; Acts xxi. 14; Matt. vi. 10.
[2] Mic. vi. 8; Rom. xii. 2.

and therefore not to be regulated by their will, but God's—originally his, and anew made his, by being "bought with a price,"—we are to "glorify him," by working that which is well-pleasing in his sight, "in our bodies and in our spirits, which are his." "Whether we live, we are to live to the Lord; whether we die, we are to die to the Lord; whether living or dying," we are to act as His. "Alive unto God, through Jesus Christ our Lord, we are to live to him; yielding ourselves to him as his servants, and our members to him as the instruments of holiness." "For this is the will of God, even our sanctification;" our entire separation in temper, and spirit, and conduct, from "the world lying under the wicked one"—"the Gentiles who know not God."[1]

This view of Christian duty in its two parts, of not living to the lusts of men, and living to the will of God, is quite coincident with many other representations contained in the New Testament;—as when Christians are commanded to "put off the old man, and to put on the new man;" to "cleanse themselves from all filthiness of the flesh and spirit, and to perfect holiness in the fear of God;" to "escape from the corruption that is in the world through lust," and to put on "a divine nature;" to "be not conformed to this world, but so transformed by the renewing of the mind, as to prove what is the good, and acceptable, and perfect will of God;" "to deny ungodliness and worldly lusts, and to live soberly, righteously, and godly in this present world."[2]

It deserves to be noticed in conclusion here, that the phraseology, "to live the rest of your time in the flesh to the will of God," naturally intimates that the course enjoined is to be a persevering one. There is to be no return-

[1] 1 Cor. vi. 20; Rom. xiv. 8, vi. 11, 13; 1 Thess. iv. 3.
[2] Eph. iv. 22, 24; 2 Cor. vii. 1; 2 Pet. i. 4; Rom. xii. 2; Tit. ii. 12.

ing to living to the lusts of men, but a continuing during the whole of the rest of life to live to the will of God,—a constant "continuance in well-doing." Christians "have need of patience,"[1] that is, of perseverance. They must persevere, that having done the will of God, they may obtain the promise. He that turns back, turns back to "perdition."[2]

Let us, my brethren, endeavour to reduce to practice the lesson which has now been given us, of living not to the lusts of men, but to the will of God. To act otherwise is folly and sin in all; but it is doubly sin and folly in those who profess the faith of Christ. Do you not, brethren, profess to have been delivered from the present evil world by Christ's having given himself for you by the will of God? Have you not said that the world is crucified to you by that cross of Christ in which you glory? Have you not said that ye are Christ's? And is it not written, that "they who are Christ's have crucified the flesh, with the affections and lusts?"[3] And while you have denied that you are the world's, ye have declared that ye are the Lord's; and while you have renounced it, ye have avouched Him. You have said, "His we are, and Him we will serve." See, then, that you do not live to the lusts of men who know not God— "worldly lusts." See that you do not make the gratification of your own natural inclinations, in any of their endlessly diversified forms, the object of life. Be not regulated by the love of worldly pleasure, of worldly honour, of worldly power, of worldly wealth. In one word, see that you "love not the world, neither the things that are in the world."[4] See that you do not make present, sensible, apparent good, the great subject of your thoughts, the great object of your affections.

---

[1] Ὑπομονή.—Luke viii. 15; Rom. ii. 7, viii. 25; Heb. xii. 1. "Perseverance" is the ordinary meaning of this word in the New Testament.
[2] Heb. x. 36-39. [3] Gal. v. 24. [4] 1 John ii. 15.

On the other hand, see that you live to the will of Him whom ye have called Master and Lord; and that you may do so, " be ye not unwise, but understanding what the will of the Lord is."[1] Grow in the knowledge of his will; and that you may do so, do his will so far as you know it. " If any man *will* do," that is, is disposed to do, "his will, he shall know of the doctrine, whether it be of God."[2] " The meek," the docile, the obedient, " he will lead in judgment, and the meek will he teach his way." Seek, then, to stand " perfect and complete in all the will of God." Seek to be like Him whose name you bear; who said, " I delight to do thy will; thy law is in my heart." " My meat is to do the will of Him that sent me, and to finish his work." Rest not in profession. Remember the words of our Lord Jesus : " Not every one that saith, Lord, Lord, shall enter into the kingdom of God, but he that doeth the will of my Father who is in heaven."[3]

Guard against the soul-destroying delusion, that it is possible to live both to the lusts of men and to the will of God at the same time. The attempt has often been made; but the thing is impossible. Before it succeed, truth and falsehood, light and darkness, good and evil, must become one. " No man can serve two masters; for either he will hate the one and love the other, or else he will hold to the one and despise the other. Ye cannot serve God and mammon. Love not the world, nor the things that are in the world;" for if ye do, the love of the Father is not in you. " The friendship of the world is enmity with God."

The wisdom of taking the course recommended, is demonstrable already to all whose senses are in any measure " exercised to discern between good and evil." Yet a little while, and it will be made palpable to all mankind. " All

[1] Eph. v. 17. [2] John vii. 17.
[3] Ps. xl. 8; John iv. 34; Matt. vii. 21.

that is in the world, the lust of the flesh, and the lust of the eyes, and the pride of life, is not of the Father, but is of the world. And the world passeth away, and the lust thereof: but he that doeth the will of God abideth for ever."[1]

Our prayer for you, brethren, is, that " the God of peace, who brought again from the dead our Lord Jesus, that great Shepherd of the sheep, by the blood of the everlasting covenant, may make you perfect in every good work, working in you that which is pleasing in his sight." And let this be the prayer of each of you for himself: " Teach me to do thy will, for thou art my God; thy Spirit is good, lead me to the land of uprightness. Quicken me, O Lord, for thy name's sake; for thy righteousness' sake bring me out of trouble: And of thy mercy cut off my enemies, and destroy all them that afflict my soul: for I am thy servant." Yes, say, " Truly, O Lord, I am thy servant, the son of thy handmaid: thou hast loosed my bonds;" and " I will walk at liberty; for I seek thy precepts." " Depart from me, ye evil-doers, for I *will* keep the commandments of my God."[2]

§ 2. *The means for obtaining the practical object; the arming themselves with the thought, " He that suffered in the flesh hath ceased from sin."*

Having thus shown at once the course which Christians ought to avoid and the course which they ought to follow, I now proceed to consider the second part of the second great division of the text—the view which the apostle gives us of the means which Christians must employ to enable

---

[1] Matt. v. 24; 1 John ii. 15-17. "Perdit quod vivit, qui te Deum non diligit; qui curat vivere, non propter te, Domine, nihil est et pro nihilo est; qui tibi vivere recusat mortuus est; qui tibi non sapit, desipit."— AUGUSTINUS.

[2] Heb. xiii. 20, 21; Ps. cxliii. 10-12, cxvi. 16, cxix. 45, 115.

them to avoid the first of these courses, which is natural to all men, and to which the Christian is strongly solicited and urged both from within and without; and to follow the second, which nothing but the new mind, rising out of the belief of Christian truth under divine influence, will induce any man to follow, and to depart from which the Christian is exposed to many and powerful temptations, both internal and external. " Arm yourselves with this thought, that he who has suffered in the flesh has been made to rest from sin." Arm yourselves with this thought, " in order to your no longer living the rest of your time in the flesh to the lusts of men, but to the will of God."

The language here is figurative, but by no means obscure. It very clearly and impressively indicates that the course recommended is a course full of difficulty and obstructions. It is a struggle, a conflict. There are powerful influences, both from within and from without, constantly put forth to induce the Christian to " live his time in the flesh to the lusts of men," and to prevent him from living his time in the flesh to the will of God. This is the great object which his spiritual enemies are constantly endeavouring to gain. " The flesh lusteth against the spirit;" the world, by its allurements and terrors, endeavours to make the Christian " walk according to its course," to " be conformed to it" by living to its " deceitful lusts," and to prevent him from being " transformed by the renewing of his mind, so as to prove the good and acceptable and perfect will of God ;" and this, too, is the great end of all the machinations and assaults, " the wiles" and " the fiery darts" of that powerful and crafty and malignant adversary, the Devil, who is ever seeking to bring back the rescued captives to his debasing slavery, or to retard them in, disable them for, the service of their new Master—the object equally of his terror and his hatred. The Christian must fight his way, and has need of "the armour of righteousness" before and behind, "on the right hand and the left."[1]

The combat is a spiritual one, and the armour must correspond with it. Truth lodged in the mind, by being understood and believed, and meditated on, is the grand means of warfare, both defensive and offensive, with error and sin, and with those malignant spiritual agencies which are constantly endeavouring to lead us into error and sin. It is by arming ourselves with true thoughts, that the Christian is prepared with determined resolution to stand and to withstand. His "good fight" is "the fight of faith;" his sword the word of God; his shield the confidence, and his helmet the hope, which that word believed excites in the soul. "The word of truth" is "the armour of righteousness."

Every part of the doctrine of Christ may be turned to account in the spiritual warfare. In resisting attempts to bring him again into bondage, and in fighting his way forward to perfect holiness and eternal life, there are many *thoughts* which the Christian will find available for armour, both for attack and defence. There is, indeed, no scriptural truth which may not be turned to account in this way; and our blessed Lord has, in his conflict with the great adversary, as recorded in the gospel, set us an example in this respect, that we may follow his steps. The Captain of salvation has there shown his soldiers what their weapons are, and how to use them.[2]

But there is ONE thought which the apostle recommends to the Christians to whom he was writing, as pre-eminently useful as armour in this spiritual conflict. "Arm yourselves with this same thought: He that hath suffered in the flesh has been made to rest from sin." Let this thought sink deep into your hearts by being well understood and firmly

---

[1] Gal. v. 17; Rom. xii. 2; Eph. vi. 11, 16; 2 Cor. vi. 7.
[2] Matt. iv. 3-10.

believed; let it be habitually present to your minds by being often meditated on; and you will find it a most powerful means of enabling you, in opposition to all temptations of whatever kind, during the rest of your time in the flesh, to live not to the lusts of men, but to the will of God. This truth understood, believed, and reflected on, will be found the grand instrumental means, so far as you are concerned, of Christian sanctification.

(1.) *The thought explained.*

To illustrate this part of our subject, it is necessary that we should satisfactorily reply to two questions: What is this thought? And how is it fitted to serve its purpose?

There is the greater need for attending to the first of these questions, as the language is so general as that, taken by itself, it is somewhat equivocal, and even enigmatical. " He that has suffered in the flesh has been made to rest from sin."[1] What is the precise meaning folded up in these words, to which so powerful an energy is ascribed? '

The words have been considered by some interpreters as a statement of the salutary influence of bodily affliction, or external calamity generally, in promoting moral improvement. In their most general sense, that he who sustains bodily or external calamities is made to cease or rest from sin, it is plainly not true without very great limitations. In many cases, affliction, instead of producing cessation from sin, exasperates the depraved principles. The case of Ahaz is no singular one, who " in the time of his distress trespassed yet more against the Lord." When the wrath of God came upon the Israelites, " for all this they sinned still the more."

---

[1] Bengel explains πέπαυται as equivalent to "immunitatem nactus est;" and Winer says, that though usually translated "peccare desiit," it may also be taken passively, "he has rest from sin."—Gram. P. iii. sec. 40, p. 207.

The cessation from sin produced merely by affliction, is but partial and temporary. On another occasion besides that just referred to, "when God slew the Israelites," it is said, "Then they sought him, and they returned and inquired early after God;" but it is added, "yet their heart was not right with him." And it is of these very persons that it is said, "How often did they provoke him in the wilderness, and tempt him in the desert!" Unaccompanied by divine teaching, both by the word and the Spirit, mere affliction will make no man cease from sin. "Blessed is the man whom thou chastenest, and teachest him out of thy law:" this is the afflicted man, the only afflicted man, to whom God gives "rest from the days of adversity."[1] Even limited to the sufferings of the regenerate, the statement is at once exaggerated and inapposite. Afflictions are indeed most useful to true Christians. They "try and purify" them, and "make them white." Their design is, and to a certain extent it is gained, to "make them partakers of the divine holiness;"[2] but surely it cannot be said of every, it cannot be said of any, afflicted Christian in the present state, that he has "ceased from sin:" and though the thought that affliction is designed, and under divine influence is calculated, to mortify sin, is well fitted to reconcile a Christian to suffering, it is difficult to see how it is preeminently fitted to enable him to "live the rest of his time not to the lusts of men, but to the will of God."

The suffering here referred to is not suffering in the flesh generally; it is the kind of suffering that the apostle is speaking of in the text and context: "suffering in the flesh for sin," even unto death. It was thus that Christ suffered in the flesh: he "suffered for sins," and he so suffered as to be put to death, or "become dead in the flesh." I have no doubt the expression, "He that hath suffered in the flesh,"

[1] Ps. lxxviii. 32, 34, 37, 40, xciv. 12, 13.   [2] Heb. xii. 10.

refers to our Lord; but I have as little, that it does not refer to our Lord alone. It is said that He suffered in the flesh "for us," that is, for believers, not only for our benefit, but in our room. He suffered the just in the room of the unjust. When he suffered "for sin," we suffered in him: his flesh was as it were our flesh; and his sufferings in that flesh were as it were our sufferings. If he died in our room, then, according to the apostle's reasoning, we died too, we died in him.[1] "He that has suffered in the flesh," is descriptive of every man who by the faith of the gospel is united to Christ as having died—every man who is "in him."

I apprehend that the apostle intentionally used a considerably indefinite expression, for the purpose of including both Christ and those who are Christ's, very much in the same way as his beloved brother Paul, when—in the sixth chapter of the Epistle to the Romans, verse seventh, illustrating the same subject, the necessary connection between the atonement and the sanctification of those who are personally interested in the atonement—he says, "He that is dead," that is, has died, died for sin, "is free from sin." "This thing," to employ the words of the Apostle John, "is true, in Him and in us." The declaration, He that has suffered in the flesh has, in consequence of his sufferings, been made to rest from sin, is one applicable, and, if we do not much mistake, intended to be applied by the apostle, both to Christ and to Christians. It is true of them both, though with some points of diversity of meaning; and the thought, whether in reference to him or to themselves, is one which is well fitted to promote personal holiness, in leading Christians to avoid all sins, and attend to all duties—not living to the lusts of men, but to the will of God.

This is "the same thought" which the apostle had un-

[1] 2 Cor. v. 14.

folded largely in the close of the third chapter, and briefly referred to in the first verse of this chapter. Christ suffered to death in human nature, as the expiatory victim of our sins, in our room, and we suffered and died in him: we Christians, we believers, being, in consequence of our faith, viewed as identified with him; as having done what he did, as having suffered what he suffered.

Now let us look at the thought, first in reference to Christ, and then in reference to Christians; and let us see how, in both views of it, it is well fitted to "arm" the Christian so that he may no longer live the rest of his time in the flesh to the lusts of men, but to the will of God.

(2.) *The thought viewed as referring to Christ.*

Let us look at the thought in reference to Christ. "He that hath suffered in the flesh," that is, for sins, "has been made to rest from sin." Christ suffered in the flesh for sin; he has been made to rest from sin; and his being made to rest from sin is the consequence of his having suffered in the flesh for sin.

We have had an opportunity, in a foregoing discourse, of directing your attention to our Lord's sufferings in human nature. They began with his birth, and ended only at his death. All these sufferings were sufferings for sin. "God made to meet on him the iniquities of us all;" exaction was made for these iniquities, and He, the appointed victim, answered the exaction. He had no rest after being "made of a woman, made under the law," till in his obediential sufferings to the death he had made full expiation of the sins laid on him.[1]

But having done so, he has obtained rest from sin. On the cross he exclaimed, "It is finished;" and so it was. Sin, armed by the sanction of the law, gave him no rest till

[1] Isa. liii. 6, 7; Gal. iii. 4.

it laid him in a bloody, dishonoured grave; but in doing this, it utterly and for ever lost all power to disquiet him. It could not even retain him in the grave where it had laid him. The debt being fully paid, the surety was set at liberty. He is henceforward a stranger to suffering in all its forms. He *can* no longer suffer, he *can* no longer die. He has entered into his rest; and that "rest is glorious." He is "sitting," the posture of repose, "at the right hand of the Majesty on high; angels and principalities and powers being subject to him." Instead of the incessant toils of his humbled life on earth as the victim of sin, there is the uninterrupted repose of eternity; to the powerlessness of death to which sin reduced him, has succeeded "all power over all flesh, all power in heaven and earth;" in the room of the days of a mortal man, few and full of trouble, has come "length of days for ever and ever;" he who was the man of sorrows and acquainted with griefs, has become "most blessed for ever;" and the soul which was exceeding sorrowful even to death, is "made exceeding glad with Jehovah's countenance."[1]

This rest from sin not only followed the sufferings for sin, but was, properly speaking, their effect. It was by his suffering for sin that he obtained rest from sin. "Having died for sin, he was freed from sin." The reason why death can have no more dominion over him is, that he died for sin *once*, and by that one death completely answered all the demands of law and justice on him as the surety of sinners. The law has nothing further to exact from him; and the immortal state of life, and rest, and power, and dominion, and glory, and blessedness, is to be considered not only as the natural expression of the infinite complacency of Jehovah, "well pleased for his righteousness' sake," delighted with that love of righteousness and hatred of iniquity mani-

[1] 1 Pet. iii. 2; John xvii. 2; Matt. xxviii. 18.

fested in the voluntary, vicarious, penal sufferings of his incarnate Son, for the vindication of his holy, just, and good law, and the restoration to immortal holy happiness of an innumerable multitude of otherwise hopelessly depraved and miserable human beings: it is to be viewed also as the execution of the stipulations of the eternal covenant, that when he had made his soul an offering for sin, he should see his seed, prolong his days, and the pleasure of the Lord should prosper in his hand; he should see of the travail of his soul, so as to be satisfied; he should, through the knowledge of himself, justify many; he should have the great as his portion, the strong for his spoil; because he had poured out his soul unto death, having been numbered with the transgressors, and having borne the sin of many.[1] He who suffered to death in the flesh for sin has been raised from the dead, and exalted to an immortal state of absolute security from suffering, and of the highest enjoyment, and a station of the highest honour and authority; and this resurrection and this exaltation are the results, the effects, of his penal, expiatory sufferings. Such seems to me the import of the thought, "He that hath suffered hath been made to rest from sin," viewed in reference to our Lord.[2]

(3.) *The thought viewed as referring to Christians.*

Let us now look at the thought in reference to Christians. When Christ suffered in the flesh for sins, it was for them, in their room. They of course suffered in him; and it is true in a very important sense, that they, having thus suffered for sin in him, are made to rest from sin.

Christians are very frequently, especially by the Apostle Paul, represented as identified with Christ. In consequence of the faith of the truth respecting his person and work, they are brought into so intimate a relation to him, that they

---

[1] Isa. liii. 10-12.   [2] See note B.

are said to be "in him," one with him. This does not refer to that union of mind and heart, of sentiment, affection, will, and operation, which subsists between Christians and Christ, and which is produced by the Spirit through the instrumentality of the word; that is rather Christ's being in them, than their being in Christ: it is the being so connected with Christ, as that they are treated by God as if what he did and suffered had been done and suffered by them personally. All who are united to Christ by that faith of which profession is made in baptism, are by the apostle represented as united to him in his death, that is, as having died in him; in his burial, that is, as having been buried in him; in his resurrection, that is, as having risen again in him; in his life and glory, that is, as living and reigning in him with God in heaven. "Ye are," says he to the Colossians, "dead," or have died, that is, in Christ; and so, if you live, though you have died, "your life is hid with Christ in God." And of himself he says, what is not peculiar to him as an apostle, but common to him with all Christians, "I am crucified with Christ." When he died, he died *for* them. It was their sins, not his own, that he bore to the tree.[1]

When we say then of Christians, that they have suffered in the flesh for sin, we mean that by a divine constitution they have as deep an interest in Christ's sufferings in the flesh for sin, as if they themselves had undergone them. They are so interested in them as to be made to rest from sin in consequence of them. They are delivered from the condemning power of sin, and they are delivered from the reigning power of sin; and they are delivered from both, not in consequence of their having suffered for sin in the flesh, in their own persons, but in consequence of their having become by faith individually interested in those

[1] Rom. vi. 3-5; Col. iii. 3; Gal. ii. 20.

sufferings for sin in the flesh which were inflicted on the person of their divinely appointed substitute.

Every human being is a sinner, and every sinner is condemned on account of his sin. The curse of God lies on him, and must for ever rest on him, till he become personally connected with him who suffered the just in the room of the unjust. Till then, the sinner can obtain no rest, no security from sin and its penal consequences. Armed with the power of the law, sin keeps fast hold of him, ready at any moment to produce death, casting the body into the grave, plunging the soul into the abyss of perdition.

From this tremendous state all who are in Christ have obtained deliverance. "There is no condemnation to them who are in Christ Jesus;" and the reason is very obvious. They are in him who was condemned in their stead, and suffered that to which they were condemned. They are redeemed from the curse; for the righteous One, their divinely appointed substitute, has become a curse for them. Who can lay anything to their charge? Christ died, died for *them*. "In him they have redemption through his blood, the forgiveness of sins, according to the riches of God's grace." "In him," the beloved One, they are "accepted, being reconciled in the body of his flesh by death." "His blood cleanseth them from all sin." So that they are "dead to the law," to its condemning sentence, "through the body of Christ;" they are "in him made the righteousness of God," in consequence of "Him who knew no sin being by God made sin in their room;" "sinners, ungodly" in themselves, they are "justified freely by His grace, through the redemption that is in Christ Jesus," who is "set forth a propitiation through faith in his blood,"—having been "delivered for their offences, and raised again for their justification."[1] The unbeliever, unconnected with Christ,

[1] Rom. viii. 1-34; 1 John i. 7; 2 Cor. v. 21; Rom. iii. 24, iv. 25.

and therefore unpardoned, is never safe. Guilt, like the avenger of blood, is constantly pursuing him, and at any moment may overtake him and take his life. There is no rest, no peace, no security to the sinner who is not "in him" who has suffered and been made to rest. But he who by faith is "in Christ," has entered the city of refuge and is safe within its walls; and, as our High Priest never dies, to secure his safety he must remain within its walls for ever.

But he who by faith is interested in Christ's suffering in the flesh for sin, as if it had been his own suffering, being indeed suffering in his room, is made to rest from sin, not only in its condemning, but in its reigning power. "Sin shall not have dominion over him" who is in Christ Jesus; for, in consequence of Christ's suffering in the flesh for sin, and his personal interest in his suffering, he is "not under the law, but under grace." He is united to Christ not only as one who was the victim of sin, as one who bore his sins, but to him as one who has borne away his sins; to Christ not only as one who was under the curse, but to Christ as now, for the manner in which he sustained that load, the object of the highest complacency of his Father. He is regarded by God with a complacency like that with which the Saviour is regarded; and that is manifested in the communication of "the spirit of life which is in Christ Jesus," and "delivers him from the law of sin and of death." And this spirit comes not, as "a wayfaring man, to tarry for a night," but to take up his permanent residence in a temple appropriated to him, and which he will in due time make every way suitable for his everlasting dwelling-place.[1]

There is thus absolute security obtained by every person who is by faith united to Christ, and thus personally interested in his suffering in the flesh, of being made completely

[1] Rom. vi. 14, viii. 2.

to rest from sin, of being brought into a state where there shall be no law in the members to war against the law of the mind,—where there shall be no striving of the flesh against the Spirit,—where the Spirit shall rule unopposed, and the law of the mind shall have free course, and be glorified,—where the Christian will no more sigh out, "Wretched man that I am, who will deliver me?" but shall for ever sing, "I thank God," who hath delivered me, completely delivered me, "through Christ Jesus." "Thanks be to God who giveth me the victory."[1] Then will the Christian be made completely to "rest from sin."

That this second kind of rest from sin is as really as the first the fruit of the atonement, the consequence of Christ suffering for sin in the flesh, and our being united to him as our surety and representative, is very clearly stated by the Apostle Paul in these important, but we are afraid very generally misapprehended, or at any rate very imperfectly understood, words: "Our old man was crucified with him, that the body of sin might be destroyed, that henceforth we should not serve sin;"[2] that is, 'In the atoning death of the Son of God, is laid a foundation of absolute security for the complete sanctification of all who are interested in its saving power, by the faith of the gospel.'

(4.) *The thought viewed as a piece of Christian armour—the instrumental means of sanctification.*

Having thus attempted to explain, both in reference to Christ and to Christians, the thought, "He that hath suffered in the flesh has been made to rest from sin," it only remains that we endeavour to show how this thought is fitted to serve the purpose of spiritual armour; or, in other words, how the truth as to the Saviour's accepted atonement, and the interest which believers have in it, is fitted, in opposition

[1] Rom. vii. 24, 25. [2] Rom. vi. 6.

to all opposing influences, to be a prevailing motive to the cultivation of practical holiness, to the "not living the rest of their time in the flesh to the lusts of men, but to the will of God." The subject is a wide and important one. It is not a particularly difficult one; but from its very nature, it requires close attention of mind in order to be distinctly understood.

The thought with which the apostle calls Christians to arm themselves, shows that that holiness in all conversation, that living not according to the lusts of men, but to the will of God, to which he exhorts them, is not an impossible thing. Man is a depraved being; viewed in his relations to God, an entirely depraved being. "In him, that is, in his flesh," in him as he is by nature, "there dwells no good thing."[1] What God requires of him is in the highest degree reasonable, and needs no physical faculty, either intellectual or active, to its performance, which man does not possess. But he labours under a spiritual disinclination to yield that kind and measure of obedience which God requires, most criminal indeed, but still by all but divine influence invincible. And as man is already criminal, has already incurred the divine displeasure, it obviously seems impossible, if some means are not employed to alter man's relations to the divine government, that God, in consistency either with his wisdom, his holiness, his justice, his faithfulness, ay, or his goodness, taking a wide view of the subject, can put forth that influence on the sinner's mind that is necessary to incline him to true holiness; that is, in other words, can confer on the proper object of his judicial displeasure what is the most decided manifestation that a person is an object of his peculiar favour.

The united wisdom and power of men and angels could never have devised and executed a plan for removing this

[1] Rom. vii. 18.

difficulty. But the thought, 'Christ has suffered in the flesh for sins, in the room of sinners, and has been made to rest from sin,'—that thought, if understood, will be found to contain in it distinct intimation, that the apparently insurmountable obstacles in the way of man's compliance with the will of God have been removed. Christ, the only-begotten of God, standing in the room of men, has done what they were bound to do, suffered what they deserved to suffer,—has done more to magnify and make honourable the divine law, than either their unsinning obedience, or their everlasting destruction in consequence of their having sinned, could have done. It thus becomes a just thing in God to justify the ungodly, to pardon sinners, to accept them and treat them as righteous, and to give them his Holy Spirit to quicken their dead, to sanctify their unholy, hearts. Christ's becoming a curse in the room of men thus lays a foundation equally for "the blessing of Abraham," a free and full justification being conferred on men ; and their receiving "the promise of the Spirit through faith," that is, the promised Spirit through believing. An infinite atonement having been offered and accepted, God can, in consistency with the perfections of his character and the principles of his government, pardon the guilty, justify the unrighteous, sanctify the unholy. The divinely appointed Saviour has merit enough to obtain pardon for the guiltiest ; and on the ground of this merit, he is in possession of power and authority enough to send that into the heart of the sinner which will overpower all his natural indisposition to the will of God, and lead him, in opposition to all counteracting influences, to "prove that good, and acceptable, and perfect will."

But this is not all. The thought with which the apostle exhorts Christians to arm themselves, conveys to the mind that understands it the assurance not only that the conformity to the divine will enjoined is something that may be attained, but that it is something that shall most certainly be attained by all believers. It intimates that every believer is actually so interested in the atonement that has been made in his room, by Christ suffering in the flesh for sin, as to have been made to rest from sin. Having suffered in Christ, he has entered with him into his rest. His sins are forgiven. He has received the Holy Spirit, the author of true holiness; and though the powers of evil with which he has to struggle, both within and without, are strong as well as numerous, yet "greater is He" in whom he is, and He "who is in him, than he who is in the world." He is "washed, he is sanctified, he is justified, in the name of the Lord Jesus, and by the Spirit of our God." The condemning power of sin, the want of quickening, sanctifying influences in the heart, keep unbelieving sinners as it were hopelessly bound in the fetters of depravity; but to the believer in Christ "there is no condemnation," and he also has "the Spirit of life in Christ Jesus;" so that in him, "God, by sending his Son in the likeness of sinful flesh, and for sin," that is, as a sin-offering, has "condemned sin in the flesh," has deprived sin of its reigning power over his nature; and thus "the righteousness of the law is fulfilled in him, not walking after the flesh, but after the Spirit,"[1] that is, "not living to the lusts of men, but to the will of God."

From the nature of the case, the security referred to is not a security without reference to the believer's own exertions as an intelligent and moral agent; it is a security that he shall by divine influence be led to use the appropriate means of sanctification, and a security that these means shall not be used by him in vain.

I have only further to remark here, that the thought with

[1] Rom. viii. 3, 4.

which the apostle calls Christians to arm themselves, if understood, brings before the mind the most powerful motives to that disconformity to the lusts of men, and conformity to the will of God, to which he exhorts; motives appealing to all our strongest active principles, to gratitude and love, to hope and fear. This remark admits of very extended illustration. I must confine myself to one or two examples.

How powerfully does "this thought" dissuade from sin in all its forms! In how clear a light does it place the excellence and obligation of the divine law; and the malignant nature, the destructive tendency, and the dreadful effects of moral evil! "The believer," as Archbishop Leighton says, "looking on his Jesus crucified for him, and wounded for his transgressions, and taking in deep thoughts of his spotless innocency that deserved no such thing, and of his matchless love that yet endured it all for him, then will he think, Shall I be a friend to that which was his deadly enemy? shall sin be sweet to me that was so bitter to him, and that for my sake? Shall I ever have a favourable thought of, or lend a good look to, them which shed my Lord's blood? Shall I live in that for which he died, and died to kill it in me?"

How obviously and powerfully is "this thought" calculated to excite and strengthen the love of God, which is the source of all true living to his will! How strikingly are the venerable and amiable excellences of the divine character exhibited in the atonement of Christ, and its blessed effects both to Him and to those who are united to Him! How great the display of divine love in Christ's suffering for sins in our room, and in the rest from sin that is thus secured for us!

How great is the encouragement "this thought" gives to the performance of duty! To borrow again the words of the good Archbishop: "Our burden that pressed us to hell is taken off; our chains that bound us over to eternal death are knocked off. Shall we not walk, shall we not run, in his ways? How heavy, how unsufferable, the burden and yoke of which he has eased us! His yoke is easy, his burden is light! O the happy change! rescued from the vilest slavery, and called to conformity and fellowship with the Son of God."

The thought that brings all this before the mind must be well fitted to arm it against temptation; and powerful in constraining us to live not to ourselves, not to other men, but to God, who hath bought us at so dear a price, that we may glorify him in our souls and in our bodies, which are his.

"This thought" being in our mind, habitually in our mind, is essential to our sanctification. We cannot be sanctified if it be not in our mind; and if it really be habitually in our mind, sanctification is a matter of course.

The Apostle Paul, in the first part of the sixth chapter of the Epistle to the Romans,[1] has cast a flood of light on the subject which we have been considering. I shall give you a summary of his illustration. 'All true Christians are united to Christ, identified as it were with him; united to him both in his death and his resurrection; united to him as having died, and as having risen again to an unending life. His death was a death by sin, for sin—a death penal, vicarious, expiatory. We are united to him in that death. It is as if we ourselves had by death made expiation for our sins. His life is a life conferred on him by God, as a token that he is fully satisfied with the expiation of sin made by his death. We are united to him in that life; God regards us as he regards him. He who is dead, or who has died, that is, by sin,—he who in death has expiated sin,—is free

[1] Rom. vi. 1-14.

from, is justified from, sin. Sin can no longer condemn him. Death, the penalty of sin, can no longer reign over him. It cannot be exacted, for it has been already paid. This is the case with Christ; this is the case with us in Christ.

'Let this thought, then, dwell in your minds. He died once by sin, as the victim of sin. He lives for ever, raised by God as the token of his satisfaction with the sacrifice; and we are united to him both in this death and in this life. We have in him died, been put to death by sin; and we in him have been quickened, and made to sit with him in the heavenly places, made partakers of the favour with which God regards him. And taking these views of your state and relation to God, in consequence of your being by faith united to him as your representative, both in dying and in rising again, " let not sin, therefore, reign in your mortal body, that ye should obey it in the lusts thereof. Neither yield ye your members as instruments of unrighteousness to sin; but yield yourselves unto God, as those who are alive from the dead, and your members as instruments of righteousness unto God; for sin shall not have dominion over you." It reigned unto death over you in the person of your Surety; but it has done its worst to him and to you. He lives, and so do you, with a life of which you can never be deprived,—a holy, happy life, never to be debased by the slavery of sin, but entirely devoted to the service of God.'

Such, if we mistake not, is the substance of the Apostle Paul's statement; and what is it but a somewhat more expanded expression of the sentiment in the passage before us? " Forasmuch as Christ has suffered for us in the flesh, arm yourselves with this same thought, that he who has suffered in the flesh has been made to rest from sin, that ye may no longer live the rest of your time in the flesh to the lusts of men, but to the will of God."

These illustrations have failed of their object, if they have not led us into a just appreciation of Christianity as the most effectual means of morally improving, the only means of spiritually transforming, depraved man, and disclosed to us the secret in which its great strength lies to make men truly holy. The superior efficacy of Christianity, as an instrument of ameliorating the moral condition of mankind, to every other means employed for this purpose, will not be questioned by any enlightened and unprejudiced thinker; but the true cause of this efficacy, and the manner in which it is put forth, are overlooked by most, misapprehended by many, and rightly understood by comparatively few.

The efficacy of Christianity, as a transformer of human character, is attributed by many even of its teachers to the purity, extent, and spirituality of its moral requisitions, and to the plainness with which these are stated, and the energy with which they are enforced in the law, and by the example of Christ. It is impossible to speak too highly of the Christian morality, unless you exalt it, as has often been done, to the disparagement of the atoning sacrifice and quickening spirit of its author; and we willingly admit, that in the formation of a christianly good character, the *law* of Christ occupies an important though still a subordinate place.

But he ill understands the principles of human nature, who expects that a being such as both revelation and experience tell us that man is, wholly depraved, alienated from the life of God, strongly inclined to forbidden indulgence, alike strongly disinclined to the restraints of religious and moral obligation, should merely by a statement and enforcement of duty, however clear and cogent, be made to undergo a radical change in his principles and habits. Who indeed does not know, that the attempt to urge on a person a mode of conduct to which he is strongly disinclined, if you do not at the same time employ appropriate and adequate means for altering the inclination, usually ends in increasing the indisposition it was intended to remove, aggravating the disease it was meant to cure? The morality of Christianity far exceeds any other morality which the world has ever seen. Where is to be found anything to be compared with the Sermon on the Mount, or the moral part of the apostolical epistles? Yet the transforming power of the system does not lie here. The morality of Christianity may be useful in convincing a bad man that he is bad, and in helping a good man to become better; but, constituted as human nature is, it cannot convert a bad man into a good man.

Another class of Christian teachers, in much greater harmony with the principles both of the scriptural revelation and a sound mental philosophy, have held that the power of Christianity to make men new creatures resides in its peculiarities as a doctrinal system: that the clear, well-established disclosures it makes of the grandeur and the grace of the divine character, of the infinite venerableness, and estimableness, and loveliness, and kindness of the Supreme Being,—in the accounts it gives us of the incarnation and sacrifice of his only-begotten Son, and of the inestimably valuable blessings which through his mediation are bestowed on mankind,—when apprehended in their meaning and evidence, that is, when understood and believed, naturally and necessarily produce such a revolution in man's mode of thinking and feeling in reference to God, as naturally and necessarily lead to a revolution in his mode of conduct; and that then, and not till then, the moral or preceptive part of Christianity begins to tell on the amelioration of the character.

These sentiments, especially when connected, as they

usually are, with a persuasion of the necessity of supernatural influence, the influence of the Holy Spirit, to bring the mind and to keep the mind under the moral influence of evangelical truth, appear to us just, so far as they go; but still they exhibit but an imperfect view of the manner in which Christianity produces—what nothing else can—a radical, permanent, ever progressive improvement of the human character, leading a man to " live the rest of his time in the flesh not to the lusts of men, but to the will of God."

Fully to understand this most important subject, it is necessary to recollect that Christianity, in the most extensive sense of the word, is something more than a revelation either of moral or religious truth. It is the development of a divine economy, a system of divine dispensations in reference to a lost world; and it is in these dispensations, the incarnation and sacrifice of the Only-Begotten of God, —dispensations having for their direct object the change of man, the sinner's relation to the Supreme Being as the moral governor of the world,—that the true origin of man's moral transformation is to be found; and it is as a development of these dispensations that the Christian revelation principally conduces to the sanctification of man.

Nothing is more obvious than that a man's state, relations, and circumstances have a powerful influence on the formation of his character. The same individual, if placed in infancy in the state of slavery, or in the state of royalty, would in mature life be distinguished by very different, and in many points directly opposite, dispositions and habits. A certain set of relations and circumstances may be quite incongruous with a certain character; and every species of moral means may be employed in vain to produce that character, till these relations and circumstances are changed. Let a slave receive every advantage of the most accomplished education, if he is not enfranchised there is little probability of his being formed to the generous character of a freeman. Let me know a man to be my enemy, or even suspect him to be so; and no exhibition of his good qualities, though I should be brought to credit them, which I will be very slow to do, can induce me to put confidence in him. Let the relation of hostility be changed into one of friendship, and let me be persuaded of this; and the same moral means which were formerly utterly inefficacious, will produce a powerful effect. These plain, common-sense principles, transferred to the subject before us, lead us into the truth respecting the origin of the transforming, sanctifying influence of Christianity.

The relations of man, as a righteously condemned sinner, are incompatible with a holy character. While man is condemned, and knows that he is condemned, how can he be holy, how can he become holy? How can God consistently bestow the highest token of his complacent regard, the Sanctifying Spirit, on one who is the proper object of his moral disapprobation and judicial displeasure; and how can man love or trust or affectionately obey him whom he knows that he has offended, whom he has reason to consider as his omnipotent enemy? It is by meeting and removing these difficulties that Christianity secures the holiness of man. It is in securing, by a set of divine arrangements, the change of a state of hostility into a state of friendship,— in rendering the pardon and salvation of the guilty consistent with, ay, illustrative of, the perfections of the divine character and the principles of the divine government,—that Christianity lays deep, and broad, and sure, the foundation of man's deliverance not only from misery, but from sin; not only of his endless happiness, but of his moral perfection. In the vicarious sacrifice of the incarnate Son, in his suffering for us in the flesh for sin, the just in the room of the unjust,—so suffering as that he found rest from sin, provision is made for a most happy change in our relations. We united to him, suffering for sin in our room, are made to rest from sin. And in this change of relations is necessarily implied, and indubitably secured, a complete change of moral disposition and habits. It is this which leads to no longer living to the lusts of men, but to the will of God. It is this chief of the works of God, that, like the mainspring or moving power of a complicated piece of machinery, gives resistless energy and unfailing efficacy, in the case of the saved, to the moral influence of the doctrines and precepts of the gospel. The better the connection between the atonement and sanctification is understood, the more firmly it is believed, the more habitually it is meditated on, the greater progress will the individual Christian make in practical godliness; and he who would comply with the apostle's exhortation, to "live no longer the rest of his time to the lusts of men, but to the will of God," must arm himself with this thought, "He that hath suffered in the flesh is made to rest from sin."[1]

The sanctifying efficacy of the atonement is exerted through the faith of the atonement. It is only as known and believed that it can either pacify the conscience or purify the heart. Let all, then, who would make progress in holiness, firmly believe, frequently meditate on, habitually keep in memory, the great topic which we have been attempting to illustrate: the grace of God, manifested in his Son suffering in the flesh for sin in our room. That grace revealed in the gospel, if understood and believed, and meditated on, will do what nothing else can: it will effectually "teach us to deny ungodliness and worldly lusts,

[1] These thoughts on the nature of the sanctifying power of Christianity, are more fully illustrated in the Preliminary Essay to Collins' edition of Maclaurin's Works.

and to live soberly, righteously, and godly in this present world; looking for the blessed hope, even the glorious appearing of the great God and our Saviour Jesus Christ; who gave himself for us, that he might redeem us from all iniquity, and purify unto himself a peculiar people, zealous of good works." If ministers wish to make men holy, let them preach the cross; if Christians wish to grow in holiness, let them look to the cross, and to him who hung on it. It is ours to present to you "this armour;" it is yours, as good soldiers of Christ Jesus, to put it on and prove it. Arm yourselves with this thought, and you shall assuredly put to flight all the armies of the aliens, and be in due time made "more than conquerors through him who loved you."[1]

III. MOTIVES ENFORCING THE EXHORTATION.

The motives to comply with the apostle's exhortation come now to be considered. The duty to which the apostle exhorts Christians is twofold: the no longer living the rest of the time in the flesh to the lusts of men; the living the rest of the time in the flesh to the will of God. And he enforces this twofold duty by two motives: the first bearing chiefly on the negative part of the injunction, drawn from a consideration of the nature of that course which, under the influence of the faith of the gospel, they had abandoned, and which he calls on them henceforward carefully to avoid; the second bearing equally on the negative and the positive part of the injunction, deduced

---

[1] It is most justly remarked by Dr HENRY MORE, that they who do not acknowledge Christ's death as a sacrifice for sin, "by their dry, harsh, and rash reasonings, expunge one of the chiefest powers and choicest artifices of the gospel for the making men good."—*Myst. of Godliness*, Book x. ch. 6.

from a consideration of the great design of the gospel revelation. The first of these motives is stated in the third, fourth, and fifth verses; the second in the sixth. Let us attend to them in their order.

§ 1. *Motive drawn from the character of the course against which the exhortation is directed.*

This, then, is the first motive which the apostle uses to urge Christians not to live the rest of the time to the lusts of men, but to the will of God: "The time past of our life may suffice us to have wrought the will of the Gentiles, when we walked in lasciviousness, lusts, excess of wine, revellings, banquetings, and abominable idolatries: wherein they think it strange that you run not with them to the same excess of riot, speaking evil of you; who shall give account to him who is ready to judge the quick and the dead." The whole of this statement bears on one point—the criminal, disgraceful, dangerous character of that course which the apostle calls on Christians studiously to avoid. The leading ideas are these: To follow that course is to work the will of the Gentiles, the unenlightened heathen, the nations that knew not God. The importance of avoiding that course is manifest from the practices in which those who walk in it indulge, the infatuation under which they labour, and the responsibility under which they lie; and additional force is given to these considerations from the circumstance, that this is a course which Christians themselves once pursued, but which they have through the faith of the truth been led to abandon. Let us endeavour a little more fully to bring out these thoughts, and show how well fitted they are to serve the apostle's purpose, of impressing on the minds of those to whom he wrote a sense of the importance of their not living the rest of the time in the flesh to the lusts of men, but to the will of God.

(1.) The course which he guards them against is that which is characteristic of the Gentiles. It is "the will of the Gentiles." To make "the lusts of men," that is, natural inclination, the rule and reason of conduct, in forgetfulness of, in opposition to, "the will of God," is that which formed the character of the Gentile nations, and made them in a religious and moral point of view the very reverse of what every Christian man must desire to be. The Gentiles are represented in the New Testament as by way of eminence "sinners," as "not knowing God," as "not following after righteousness." The strongest expression for an enormous and uncommon crime is, that it was "not so much as named among the Gentiles;"[1] phraseology intimating that they were familiar with crime in almost every conceivable form. It must be a very strange crime they are unacquainted with, a very shocking one which their moral feelings are revolted by.

We have a few specimens given us here of the kind of conduct by which the Gentiles were generally characterized. They "walked in lasciviousness, lusts, excess of wine, revellings, banquetings, and abominable idolatries;" and we have a complete portrait of Gentile character and manners given us in the close of the first chapter of the Epistle to the Romans, where they are represented as guilty of the most shocking and unnatural crimes,—" filled with all unrighteousness, fornication, wickedness, covetousness, maliciousness; full of envy, murder, debate, deceit, malignity; whisperers, backbiters, haters of God, despiteful, proud, boasters, inventors of evil things, disobedient to parents, without understanding, covenant-breakers, without natural affection, implacable, unmerciful: knowing the judgment of God, that they who commit such things are worthy of death, yet not only doing the same, but taking pleasure in

[1] Gal. ii. 20; 1 Thess. iv. 5; Rom. ix. 30; 1 Cor. v. 1.

those who do them."[1] And in what did this fearful depravity of character and conduct originate? Just in living to the lusts of men, and not to the will of God; allowing natural inclination, unchecked by a regard to the will of God, to be the rule and the reason of action.

In the very fact that the course of conduct forbidden is that by which the Gentiles were characterized, there is couched a strong dissuasive from it. What characterized Gentiles, could not be becoming saints. In the simple phrase "working the will of the Gentiles," you have folded up the principal motive which the Apostle Paul, in his Epistle to the Ephesians, so finely amplifies: "I say therefore, and testify in the Lord, that ye walk not as other Gentiles walk, in the vanity of their mind; having the understanding darkened, being alienated from the life of God through the ignorance that is in them, because of the blindness of their heart: who, being past feeling, have given themselves over to lasciviousness, to work wickedness with greediness. But ye have not so learned Christ; if so be ye have heard him, and been taught by him, as the truth is in Jesus: that ye put off, concerning the former conversation, the old man, which is corrupt according to the deceitful lusts; and be renewed in the spirit of your minds; and that ye put on the new man, which after God is created in righteousness and true holiness."[2]

(2.) The motive suggested by these enormities themselves, to guard against the depraved principle of which all these enormities of the Gentiles were merely the development—the making natural inclination, not the will of God, the rule and reason of conduct,—is greatly strengthened by the view which the apostle takes, in the 4th verse, of the infatuation which characterized those who had given themselves up to its guidance. They were "given up to a reprobate," a

[1] Rom. i. 18-32.   [2] Eph. iv. 17-24.

wrong-judging, "mind."[1] The very faculty of discovering truth from falsehood, and right from wrong, though not destroyed so as that they ceased to be accountable beings, was weakened and perverted. They called, and to a considerable degree thought, in reference to religious and moral subjects, "darkness light, and light darkness; evil good, and good evil; bitter sweet, and sweet bitter." As an evidence of this, "they thought it strange" that they who had "escaped the pollutions of the world, through the knowledge of the Lord and Saviour Jesus, did not run with them to the same excess of riot,"[2] and "spoke evil of them" for those very tempers and habits which ought to have drawn forth expressions of their approbation. They accounted the abandonment of those courses—in which they sought, in which they confidently though vainly hoped to obtain, happiness—arrant folly! And they ran down as irreligious, and despisers of the gods, those who had been "turned from dead idols to serve the living God." They mistook their licentious indulgence for true happiness, and their "abominable idolatries" for true religion. "Their foolish hearts were darkened." What fearful delusion was this! How thankful should Christians be for having been awakened from such a delirious dream, and made soberminded, sound-minded, in their judgments respecting the most important and interesting of all subjects—God's cha-

---

[1] 'Αδόκιμον νοῦν. Rom. i. 29.

[2] Συντρεχόντων ὑμῶν εἰς τὴν αὐτὴν ἀσωτίαν. What a striking illustration of the peculiar appropriateness of the apostle's terms συντρεχόντων and ἀσωτίαν do the following lines from a Roman poet, in reference to the orgies of Bacchus, afford!

> Turba ruunt; mixtæque viris, matresque nurusque
> Vulgusque, proceresque ignota ad sacra feruntur
> Quis furor—
> Femineæ voces, et mota insania vino
> Obscenique greges, et inania tympana.—
>
> OVID, *Met.* iii. 529, etc.

racter and will, and their own duty and happiness! How carefully should they guard against being in any degree again brought under the intoxicating influence of "this present evil world," operating on unbridled natural inclination,—of being in any degree " entangled or overcome" by these deceitful worldly lusts, from which, through the Spirit and word of Christ, they have almost " clean escaped !"[1]

(3.) Another consideration suggested by the apostle as fitted to warn Christians against " living to the lusts of men," is the awful responsibility under which they lie who follow this course. " They must give account to him who is ready to judge the quick and the dead." Men may act as if they were irresponsible; but they cannot make themselves irresponsible. They cannot escape the judgment of God; and though they may make their lusts or their will the rule by which their actions are regulated, they cannot make them the rule by which their actions shall be judged. Their attempts to break the bands that bind them to God are unavailing, except to convert what might have been a silken cord, in the hand of God, to draw them up to heaven, into an iron chain to drag them to the judgment-seat, or adamantine fetters to bind them in the prison of hell. "For God will bring every work into judgment, with every secret thing, whether it be good or whether it be evil." " The Lord hath prepared his throne for judgment. And He shall judge the world in righteousness; he shall minister judgment to the people in uprightness." Before that tribunal all must stand, and " God will render to every man according to his works:" to those " who live to the will of God," " who, in a patient continuance in well-doing, seek for glory, honour, and immortality, he will render eternal life;" but to those "who live to the lusts of men, who work the will of the Gentiles," " who are contentious, and do not

[1] 2 Pet. ii. 19, 20.

obey the truth, but obey unrighteousness, he will render indignation and wrath, tribulation and anguish." " Behold, the Lord cometh with ten thousand of his saints, to execute judgment upon all, and to convince all that are ungodly among them of all their ungodly deeds which they have ungodly committed, and of all their hard speeches which ungodly sinners have spoken against him."[1] Who, with the judgment-seat before him, the account which must there be given, and the fearful results if that account is, that the time in the flesh has been spent in obedience to the lusts of men and the will of the Gentiles, instead of the will of God, would not tremble at the thought of allowing natural inclination or common custom to take the place of divine authority as the controlling and guiding power of life? Such is, I apprehend, the force of the statement contained in the 5th verse as a motive to Christians to avoid living to the lusts of men, working the will of the Gentiles; and it is not easy to estimate the power it ought to have on every mind.

While there can be no doubt that the account here spoken of is the last account at the final judgment, it may be doubted whether that is the judgment which God is here represented as "ready," prepared, just about to execute, on the living and the dead.[2] Eighteen hundred years have nearly elapsed since these words were written, and that judgment has not yet taken place. The whole human race are sometimes divided into the living and the dead, meaning by those terms all who have died, and all who are to be found alive at the coming of our Lord. Thus the apostle declares that "Jesus is ordained of God to be the Judge of the quick," that is, the living, and "the dead;" and Paul orders Timothy to do his official duties "before God and

---

[1] Eccles. xii. 14; Ps. ix. 7, 8; Rom. ii. 6-9; Jude 14, 15.
[2] Τῷ ἑτοίμως ἔχοντι.

the Lord Jesus Christ, who shall judge the quick and the dead at his appearance and kingdom."[1]

But it is difficult to perceive any reason in the passage before us for referring to this division of all mankind, as either dead or living, at the day of judgment. It seems highly probable, that the word "dead," used in the first clause of the next verse as descriptive of persons to whom the gospel is preached, preached when dead, signifies those who are spiritually dead; as there can be no doubt that they who live, spoken of in the second clause, they who "live to God in the spirit," are those who are spiritually alive; and there cannot be a reasonable doubt that the living and the dead spoken of in the fifth verse are the dead and living spoken of in the sixth verse. These remarks would go far to prove that, in the verse before us, the division of mankind here is not into those who shall be naturally dead and those who shall be naturally alive at the coming of our Lord, but into the spiritually dead and the spiritually alive.

On both these classes God was ready, just about, to execute judgment, in the sense of inflicting severe calamities. When we look a little forward in the chapter (ver. 12), we find that a fiery trial was about to try those whom the apostle calls his "beloved"—that is, "the living;" but it was not to be peculiar to them to be thus tried. Suffering was about to fall with still more crushing weight on the "ungodly," "the dead." "The time is come," is just at hand, "when judgment must begin at the house of God"— that is, just in other words, "He is ready to judge the quick," the spiritually alive : but he is ready to judge the spiritually dead too; for the apostle goes on, "If it first begin at us, what shall the end be of them that obey not the gospel of God? and if the righteous, 'the living,' scarcely

[1] Acts x. 42 ; 2 Tim. iv. 1.

be saved," are to be all but destroyed by the awful infliction, "where shall the ungodly and the wicked," 'the dead,' "appear?" The sense of the apostle may, we apprehend, be thus given: These ungodly men, who persist in impenitence, unbelief, and disobedience, must appear before the judgment-seat of a righteous God, who even here makes it evident that he is the Judge of the world, and who is about to inflict calamities which will fall heavily both on his people and his enemies, "the living and the dead."

What the judgment referred to is, it is impossible to say with certainty; some considering it as referring to calamities connected with the overthrow of the ecclesiastical and civil polity of the Jews, which was at hand, and which was the occasion of suffering not only to the Jews of Palestine, but to the Jews of the dispersion; and others considering it as referring to a severe famine, which in the time of the Emperor Claudius visited the region in which the Christians to whom this epistle is addressed resided. To meet such a trial, few things were better fitted to prepare Christians than habitually living to the will of God; and nothing more calculated to make it difficult to bear, than losing the testimony of a good conscience by living to the lusts of men.

(4.) We have not yet, however, exhausted the force of the motive contained in the apostle's statement. In this evil way of living to the lusts of men, working the will of the Gentiles, they had "*once* walked." This they had done "in the time past of their life," that is, in that part of their life which preceded their conversion. It has been a question whether in these words the apostle refers to Christian converts from among the Jews or from among the Gentiles. The churches to which the epistle was addressed were composed of persons belonging to both classes; and therefore it is not wonderful that phrases should be employed, some equally applicable to both classes, some more applicable to the one than to the other. All of them had lived to the lusts of men, all of them had worked the will of the Gentiles. With all of them, natural inclination, uncontrolled by the will of God, had been the rule and reason of their conduct, the forming principle of their character; and in some of them this had led to open and shameless violations of the divine law, which manifested the true nature and tendency of the principles by which all were animated and guided.

The passage before us is very similar to the two following, which show us how it is to be understood. After giving a catalogue of some of the most flagrant violators of the divine law, the apostle says to the Corinthian Christians, "Such were some of you; but ye are washed, but ye are sanctified, but ye are justified, in the name of the Lord Jesus, and by the Spirit of our God." "Ye were dead," says he to the Ephesian Gentile converts, "in trespasses and sins; wherein in time past ye walked according to the course of this world, according to the prince of the power of the air, the spirit that now worketh in the children of disobedience: among whom also we all had our conversation in times past in the lusts of our flesh, fulfilling the desires of the flesh and of the mind."[1]

Now, says the apostle, "the time" spent under such influences, in such practices, "may suffice." We surely have had enough, more than enough, of this. The phraseology is peculiar and very expressive; probably borrowed from the prophet Ezekiel, when he says, in reference to the enormities of the people of Israel, "Let it suffice you of all your abominations."[2] It is a way, with the guilt and disgrace and misery of which we are but too well acquainted. We should never have walked in that way; we have walked too long in it; we have been led to abandon it. Surely we

[1] 1 Cor. vi. 11; Eph. ii. 1-3.   [2] Ezek. xliv. 6, xlv. 9.

will not return to it! Awakened from our dream of delirium, surely we will not again put to our lips the narcotic cup which occasioned it! Recovered from our wanderings in the downward road of ruin, surely we will not again forsake the onward, upward path! Surely the future part of our time should be as exclusively devoted to the will of God, as the former part of it was to "the lusts of men!" We should surely serve HIM who has the highest conceivable claims on our service, as devotedly as we did those who had no claim on our service at all! "We are not debtors to the flesh to live after the flesh." We have greatly overpaid it, which never had any just demand on us. Let us spend no more of our money for what is not bread, but poison; no more of our labour for that which does not profit, but ruins.

The import of the whole illustration here seems to coincide with the striking passage with which the Apostle Paul concludes the sixth chapter of the Epistle to the Romans, of which chapter the passage before us is just a compendium: "Know ye not, that to whom ye yield yourselves servants to obey, his servants ye are to whom ye obey; whether of sin unto death, or of obedience unto righteousness? But God be thanked, ye were the servants of sin; but ye have obeyed from the heart the form of doctrine delivered to you. Being then made free from sin, ye became the servants of righteousness. I speak after the manner of men, because of the infirmity of your flesh: for as ye have yielded your members servants to uncleanness and to iniquity; even so now yield your members servants to righteousness unto holiness. For when ye were the servants of sin, ye were free from righteousness. What fruit had ye then in those things whereof ye are now ashamed? for the end of those things is death." Surely there has been enough, more than enough, of what is so full of guilt and degradation, so fruitful of remorse and shame, which implies such infatuation, and incurs such responsibilities! Surely there should be no more living to the lusts of men, working the will of the Gentiles! It is matter of deep regret that any of our past time, that so much of our past time, should have been so unworthily spent. It will be tenfold folly and sin if any of our future time should be so squandered. So much for the illustration of the first motive.

§ 2. *Motive drawn from the great design of the gospel revelation.*

The second motive is derived from the great design of the gospel revelation, and is brought forward in the sixth verse: "For this cause was the gospel preached also to them that are dead, or even to the dead, that they might be judged according to men in the flesh, but live according to God in the spirit."

The key to the interpretation of this passage, certainly among the most intricate in the whole book of God, seems to lie in its connection. It has been common to seek a connection between these words and those which immediately precede them. I have done so with all the closeness of attention I am capable of, but I have not been able to find it. The statement in this verse is plainly a reason for something previously stated; but I cannot find in these words anything like a reason why God is ready to judge the quick and the dead, or why ungodly, impenitent men must give account to God for their ungodly deeds and hard speeches.

It seems to me that they present another great motive to the duty enjoined in the second verse.[1] Christians are not

---

[1] Ver. 6 stands in closer inner connection with the thought of vers. 1 and 2, than with the intermediate thought in vers. 3-5.—MÜLLER: *Doctrine of Sin*, vol. ii. p. 322.

to live the rest of the time in the flesh to the lusts of men, but to the will of God: first, for the reason contained in the third, fourth, and fifth verses, which we have already illustrated; and secondly, for that contained in this verse, they are not "to live the rest of their time in the flesh to the lusts of men, but to the will of God:" "for, for this cause, the gospel was preached to them who were dead;" that is, the great design of the gospel revelation is just to induce men to make, not the lusts of men, but the will of God, the rule and reason of their conduct.

I have already stated some of the reasons why I consider them who are dead, literally "the dead," to be the spiritually dead, those "dead in trespasses and sins." To translate it, The gospel was preached to those who are now dead, though they were alive when the gospel was preached to them, is to give the words a meaning which they will not bear; and to suppose that they mean, that the gospel has been preached to the dead in the separate state,—the only meaning they can, consistently with the usage of the language, have, if the term dead is understood in its literal sense,—is to suppose them to assert a fact which seems to have no connection with what the apostle is speaking about, and a fact to which there is no reference, except it be in the 19th verse of the preceding chapter, in the whole Bible. That the events referred to in the two passages are the same, I have no doubt. "The spirits in prison" there, and "the dead" here, are the same class of persons; and Christ by the Spirit preaching to the former, and the gospel being preached to the latter, are descriptions of the same event. Both the expressions, "spirits in prison" and "the dead," are figurative expressions. A state of unconversion is often represented as a state of death. "To be carnally minded is death;" the unconverted man "abideth in death;" when he is converted he "passes from death to life;" while he continues in unregeneracy he is "dead in trespasses and sins." Unconverted Gentiles are represented as "dead in the uncircumcision of their flesh."[1]

Now the gospel is preached to men thus dead, destitute of all spiritual life, utterly incapable of spiritual action and spiritual enjoyment, that by means of it they, through the accompanying energy of the Holy Ghost, may be quickened to a new life, manifesting itself in living and acting not to the lusts of men, but to the will of God. Its voice is, "Awake, thou that sleepest, and arise from the dead, and Christ shall give thee light." The revelation of the grace of God, which constitutes the gospel, is mainly intended to teach men "to deny ungodliness and worldly lusts, and to live soberly, righteously, and godly in this present world; looking for that blessed hope, and the glorious appearing of our Lord Jesus Christ, who gave himself for us, that he might redeem us from all iniquity, and purify unto himself a peculiar people, zealous of good works." The design of preaching the gospel is to "turn men from darkness to light, from the power of Satan to God." The knowledge of our Lord Jesus Christ which it communicates, is intended to enable men to "escape the pollutions of the world, and to perfect holiness in the fear of God."[2] Where these ends are not gained, the gospel has been preached in vain. Indeed, in some points of view, it had been better for those whom the gospel leaves still the servants of sin, that it had never been preached to them.

This is obviously a very powerful motive to "live the rest of the time in the flesh not to the lusts of men, but to the will of God." Thus, thus only, can the great benignant purposes of the gospel revelation be answered to the individual. No man continuing unholy can ever obtain

[1] See note C.
[2] Eph. v. 14; Tit. ii. 11, 12; Acts xxvi. 18; 2 Pet. i. 2-4.

the salvation the gospel announces. Just in the degree in which he is sanctified by the truth, does the truth gain its object.

Taking this view of the passage, there would have been no difficulty, had there been no more in the statement than this : " For, for this purpose, viz. that we should no longer live to the lusts of men, but to the will of God," was the gospel preached to "the dead," the unconverted. But there is difficulty, great difficulty, in the words that follow : " that they may be judged according to men in the flesh, but live according to God in the spirit."

The difficulty lies in the first clause, " judged according to men in the flesh ;" for were these words not there, the clause that follows, " that they may live according to God in the spirit," might naturally enough be understood as explanatory of the phrase " for this end," and in this case would be of equivalent signification with the phrase in the second verse, " that we may live to the will of God."

It would serve little purpose to state the various attempts which interpreters have made to extort an apposite meaning out of these words. Their number, and the extravagance of some of them, clearly show that this is a passage " hard to be understood." One learned interpreter[1] states plainly that he does not understand the passage, and therefore lets it alone; and I have, in the course of my inquiries, sometimes been disposed to follow his example.

The following appears to me to be probably the meaning and reference of the words. They seem to describe certain consequences of the gospel being preached with effect to the spiritually dead. The direct design of the gospel being preached to them is, that they may believe it; and the certain effect of its being preached to them if they believe it, as well as its design, is, that believing it, they " no longer

---

[1] Castalio. "Hunc locum non intelligo ; ideoque ad verbum transtuli."

live the rest of their life to the lusts of men, but to the will of God." Such is its designed effect on their character and conduct.

But besides this designed effect on their character and conduct, the gospel, when preached to, believed by, and influential on the spiritually dead, produces certain effects, some of them unfavourable, others of them favourable, on their condition, external or internal. It is to these, I apprehend, the apostle refers, when he speaks of their being " judged according to men in the flesh," but " living according to God in the spirit."

" According to men," that is, plainly, unconverted men (as in the phrase " lusts of men," or the expression " ye are carnal, and walk as men"[1]),—so far as men, unconverted, worldly men, are concerned, they—that is, they who have believed the gospel preached to them when dead—are, by depraved and human agency, " judged," that is, condemned, punished, " in the flesh," in the body or in their external circumstances. " According to God,"—so far as God is concerned, by a holy, divine agency, they " live "—they enjoy true happiness (as the apostle says, " Now we *live* if we stand fast in the Lord"[2])—" in the spirit," in the soul, in the inner man, a happiness suited to the wants and capacities of their higher nature. Had " living according to God in the spirit" been contrasted with " living according to men in the flesh," it would have described character; contrasted with being " condemned or punished according to men in the flesh," it plainly describes condition.

The particle translated " that "[3] not only signifies *in order to,* marking design, but also *so that,* marking effect, as when it is said, " Have they stumbled that they should fall ?"[4] that is, " Have they stumbled so as to fall ?" This seems its force here : " For this end was the gospel preached to

[1] 1 Cor. iii. 3.   [2] 1 Thess. iii. 8.   [3] "Ινα.   [4] "Ινα, Rom. xi. 11.

you when spiritually dead, that believing it ye should abandon sin and follow holiness; and having gained its object, the result has been, ye are persecuted in your external circumstances—your body, your reputation, your outward condition—by men; but ye are happy in your mind—in all your spiritual relations and circumstances—in God."

It was so then. "Men spoke against them as evil-doers," —they "suffered as Christians," "for well-doing," "for righteousness' sake;" but while thus judged, condemned, punished, so far as men were concerned, "in the flesh," they "lived according to God in the spirit." They had a "life hid with Christ in God;" they were happy in their spirits, for "the Spirit of glory and of God rested on them."

Thus were the apostles "judged according to men in the flesh," when they were beaten before the Sanhedrim, and commanded that they should not speak in the name of Jesus; and thus did they "live according to God in the spirit," when "they departed from the presence of the council, rejoicing that they were worthy to suffer shame for his name." Thus were Paul and Silas "judged according to men in the flesh," when, by order of the magistrates of Philippi, they were beaten, and, "after many stripes had been laid on them, thrust into the inner prison, and had their feet made fast in the stocks;" and thus did they "live according to God in the spirit," when "at midnight they prayed and sang praises to God," with a voice so loud and clear that "the prisoners heard them."[1]

And it is so still. Whenever the gospel believed transforms the character, the individual becomes an object of dislike to worldly men; he is "judged according to men in the flesh;" and the manner in which that dislike is manifested depends on circumstances: it may be in silent contempt, in malignant misrepresentation, in spoiling of goods,

[1] Acts v. 40, 41, xvi. 22-25.

in persecution to the death;—and just as certainly does he " live to God in the spirit," obtaining " a peace" in God " which passeth all understanding," which, as the world could not give, it cannot take away; a new life so superior to all that he formerly experienced, that, when he looks back to the time that is past, it appears to him as he had been " dead while he lived."

Materially the same sense may be brought out of the words, giving to " that" its more common sense, " to the end that," by interpreting the passage on the same principle as you must interpret the words, " God be thanked, that ye were the servants of sin; but ye have obeyed from the heart the form of doctrine delivered to you;"[1] that is, God be thanked, that, though you were the servants of sin, ye have obeyed from the heart the form of doctrine delivered to you. So here: " For this cause, that they may give over living to the lusts of men, and begin to live to the will of God, was the gospel preached to the spiritually dead; that they, believing the gospel and yielding to its influence, though persecuted as to their external circumstances by men, may enjoy true spiritual happiness in God."

The only interpretation that can come into competition with this, is that which considers both clauses as referring to the direct and intended effect of the preaching of the gospel; understanding by being " judged in the flesh," the being condemned and punished in reference to that which is depraved in our nature, " the flesh,"—having the body of sin destroyed, the being made to deny self,—" mortifying our members on the earth," taking up the cross,—all which, " according to men," in the estimation of men, unregenerate men, is no better than death; and understanding by " living in the spirit according to God," such an exercise of all their faculties, under the influence of their renewed nature, as in

[1] Rom. vi. 17.

God's estimation deserves the name of life; as if he had said, 'The gospel was preached to the dead in trespasses and sins, that they might become dead to sin, and alive to God, —dead in the sense in which they were alive, alive in the sense in which they were dead;' which is just equivalent to, "that they may no longer live to the lusts of men, but to the will of God." This is Archbishop Leighton's view of the passage, so far as I can understand it; but I do not see how this sense can be brought out of the words without doing violence to them.

The force of the motive may be thus briefly expressed: 'Ye ought to live the rest of the time in the flesh to the will of God, not to the lusts of men, for that was the grand design of the gospel when preached to you "dead in trespasses and sins;" and though by believing the gospel, and yielding yourselves up to its sanctifying influence, you will certainly expose yourselves to the condemnation and persecution of an ungodly world (which, however, can only affect your external condition), you will find far more than a compensation for this in the life, the happiness, which in your spirits you will obtain from God.'

In the very important, but, as we have found, somewhat difficult, paragraph commencing with the 18th verse of the preceding chapter and ending with the 6th verse of this, the great leading features of the divine method of transforming depraved human nature are strikingly delineated. Man has gone astray from God, and is living not to his will, but to his own lusts. He has thus incurred the righteous displeasure of God, and brought on himself the dreadful curse of his holy law. That curse rivets, as it were, the chains of his depravity. He is lost, beyond the power of created wisdom and agency to rescue him. But what man, what angels could not do, God has done. The obedience unto the death of the incarnate Son, the divinely appointed Saviour, the just One, in the room of the unjust, gives full satisfaction to the violated law, and is the propitiation for our sins; securing for *Him* all the power and authority necessary to gain the ultimate ends of his sacrifice. This well-attested record of this mystery of wisdom, righteousness, and love, is the " gospel of our salvation," which, attended by the Spirit, finds its way into the understanding and conscience and affections of men, transforming them by the renewing of their mind, and leading them to live henceforth no more to the lusts of men, but to the will of God; while, at the same time, sinners thus justified and renewed by the grace of God have presented to them motives the most powerful and persuasive to induce them to abstain from every kind of evil, and to cultivate holiness in all manner of conversation; and, amid all the sufferings to which they may be exposed from an evil world, are sustained by the energies of that spiritual life in God, the exhaustless source of peace and joy, which they enjoy by their union to him who died for them in weakness, but lives for ever by the power of God.

It deeply concerns us all seriously to inquire whether we, through the atoning death and restored life of our Lord, have become dead to the world and to sin, alive to God and holiness; whether, under the influence of the truth on these subjects, we are living not as we once did, to the lusts of men, but to the will of God. This is the appropriate evidence, this is the only satisfactory evidence, that the gospel of salvation has come to us not in word only, but in power; that the end for which the gospel is preached to the dead has been gained in us.

Let Christians seek clearer views, more settled convictions, respecting the death of Christ as the great atoning sacrifice, and their own interest in it as not only the price of their pardon, but the means of their sanctification; and let them open their minds and hearts to all those powerful motives, from such a variety of sources, which urge them to live devoted to Him who died devoted for them,—to glorify Him whom they have so long dishonoured,—to deny ungodliness and worldly lusts, and to live soberly, righteously, and godly in the world; constantly seeking more and more disconformity to this world, by being more thoroughly "transformed by the renewing of their minds, and proving the good, and acceptable, and perfect will of God."

And let those who are still running the mad career of thoughtlessness and sin, living not to the will of God, but to the lusts of men, consider, ere it be too late, what must be the end of these things. Men and brethren, allow me to expostulate with you. You "must give account to Him who is ready to judge the quick and the dead." And that account must be given in, not with joy, but with grief. That judgment must be condemnation. Indeed, you are condemned already; and you know it, however you may try to strangle the conviction. God, in his word, condemns you, and your consciences condemn you also. Where is the man who dare say, it is right, it is wise, it is safe, to live to the lusts of men, so foolish, so shameful, so ruinous, and not to the will of God, so wise, so benignant, so reasonable, so advantageous,—to make human inclination rather than divine law the rule of conduct? What has the time past of your life been, but a blank or a blot, guilty inutility or noxious guilt, inglorious inaction or base activity? and how many years have been thus wasted? In many cases, I am afraid, by far the greater part even of a long life.

Surely "the time that is past may suffice." Enough, more than enough, of such madness. Dishonour has received sufficient measure. Close the term of infamy. It is time for fairer days to begin their course. Oh, relinquish those foolish and deceitful lusts to which you have been so long enslaved, and come to Christ, who will bring you to God, that you may know him and love him, and serve him and enjoy him. In him there is spirit and life: dead though you be, he will enable you to live this heavenly life which the apostle enjoins; this life to the will of God, his God and your God, his Father and your Father.

Delay no longer this happy exchange of the slavery of sin for the glorious liberty of the sons of God. Put it off till to-morrow, and it may become impossible. The seal of eternity ere to-morrow may be put on thy thraldom. Thinkest thou that it is irksome to do the will of God? Think that it will be found more than irksome to suffer his wrath for ever. But it is not irksome. Ah, thou knowest not how sweet they find his service who have tried it, and who with one voice cry, "O taste and see that the Lord is good;" "his yoke is easy, his burden is light."

Think not to say within thyself, I will abandon the service of the lusts of men by and by; I will live to the will of God, though not now, yet afterwards. Ah! who can make thee sure of *the will* or of *the afterwards?* And if afterwards, why not now? Hast thou not served sin long enough? May not the time past suffice? Is it not more than enough? He who does not live to God, is "dead while he liveth." He who lives to sin, lives in a dark dungeon, laden with fetters; he who lives to God, dwells in light, walks at liberty. The uncertain wildfires of worldly pleasure, which but light those who follow them to their doom, will soon be extinguished in the blackness of darkness for ever. But he that followeth Christ, in living to the will of God, "shall not walk in darkness, but shall have the light of life." "His path shall be like that of the shining light, which shineth more and more unto the perfect day."[1]

[1] Leighton.

Note A. p. 6.

Amyraut, in his paraphrase, gives the sense very clearly: "Mais encore nous devons armer de cette bonne pensée contre toutes sortes de tentations au mal, 'que celui qui a souffert en cette nature humaine, n'a desormais plus de commerce avec le peché.'" And Gerhard: "" Ὅτι rectius accipitur expositive, exponit enim Apostolus illam cogitationem ἔννοιαν qua nos vult armari: hæc cogitatio erit vobis instar firmissimi scuti et munimenti contra peccatum." Erasmus Schmid's version is: "Eadem cogitatione armamini, *nempe*, quod qui passus est carne destitit a peccato." Beza's version is of the same purport.

Note B. p. 30.

I am aware that the words rendered "hath ceased from sin," have been translated "has caused sin to cease;" bringing out this sense: 'Christ, by suffering in the flesh, has caused sin to cease; has finished transgression, made an end of sin, brought in an everlasting righteousness.' This is a truth, and a truth suggested, as we have seen, by the words; but to make them directly express this, requires very great violence to be done to the original language. The words have also been rendered "has ceased from sin-offering;" bringing out the idea, that his one perfect offering has rendered unnecessary any further sacrifice for sin. This is true too, and, like the other, substantially implied in the statement; but it is to give an unusual meaning to the word "sin," and it is to give the same word two distinct meanings in the same sentence: for certainly "sin," in the first clause of the first verse, does not mean "sin-offering."

Note C. p. 59.

"Propter hoc enim et mortuis, evangelicatus est,—nobis, qui quondam videlicet exstabamus infideles."—Clem. Alex. Adumbrat. ad 1 Ep. Pet. Edit. Pott. Tom. ii. p. 1007.—Apud Beausobre.

"Simplicissime per 'mortuos' quibus Evangelium prædicatum esse Apostolus asserit, intelliguntur spiritualiter, in peccatis, mortui."—Gerhard. "Fieri potest, ut mortuos dixerit infideles

h. e. in anima mortuos. Non cogit apud inferos intelligi."—AUGUST. Ep. xcix. ad Euodium. "De mortuis dicit Apostolus quod judicentur carne. Jam vero naturaliter mortui non habent carnem; ergo intelligitur de hominibus in terra viventibus."—LUTHER. According to Maimonides (More Nevochim), it was a proverb among the Jews: "Impii etiam viventes vocantur mortui."

DISCOURSE XVIII.

SOBRIETY AND WATCHING UNTO PRAYER ILLUSTRATED AND ENFORCED.

"But the end of all things is at hand: be ye therefore sober, and watch unto prayer."—1 Pet. iv. 7.

In the preceding part of this chapter, the apostle presents those to whom he wrote with a general view of Christian duty, as "living not to the lusts of men, but to the will of God;" points out to them the only and effectual means of realizing this view of Christian duty in their own experience —the keeping constantly before their minds the great characteristic truth of the gospel, that the perfect and accepted atonement made by Christ has secured for himself, and for all interested in him, rest from sin; and unfolds to them the powerful motives rising out of the statement he had made of the leading principles of evangelical truth, which urge them to follow the course prescribed to them. In the subsequent context he proceeds to enjoin the cultivation of a variety of particular Christian dispositions, and the performance of a variety of particular Christian duties, which the circumstances in which they were placed peculiarly required. Two of these injunctions, with the special ground on which they stand, lie before us in the verse which we have read as the text of the following discourse.

The subject which these words bring before the mind may be treated in two different ways. We may either illustrate, first, the statement on which the apostle founds his injunctions, "The end of all things is at hand;" and then the injunction built on this statement, "Be sober, and watch unto prayer;" or we may reverse the order, and consider, first, the duties which the apostle enjoins, and then the motive by which he urges to their performance. It does not matter much which of these two plans we adopt; but as a choice must be made, we, upon the whole, prefer the latter.

I. THE DUTIES ENJOINED BY THE APOSTLE.

Let us then proceed to consider the duties which the apostle enjoins. They are—sobriety, and watching unto prayer. "Be sober, and watch unto prayer."

§ 1. *Sobriety.*

The first duty enjoined is sobriety : " Be sober." In the common usage of the English language, the word sobriety is almost exclusively appropriated to denote temperance in drinking, abstinence from the undue use of intoxicating liquors. That this is a Christian duty, there can be no doubt. Drunkenness is enumerated among the works of the flesh, the indulgence in which excludes a man from inheriting the kingdom of God ; and the command is most explicit: "Be not drunk with wine, wherein is excess " And there can be as little doubt that this vice is utterly inconsistent with that virtue which, under the name of sobriety, is in our text, and in so many other passages of Scripture, enjoined.

It is certain, however, that the word *sober* had a much more extensive signification at the time our translation of the Scriptures was made than it has at present ; a signification more in accordance with the sense of the original word of which it is the rendering. The word here rendered sober[1] (for, as we shall immediately see, the word rendered watchful here is often translated sober) is a term which, in its primary signification, refers rather to a physical than to a moral state of the faculties of mind. It signifies to be in the full use of the rational faculties, as opposed to mental alienation or derangement. Thus, it is said of the demoniac who was cured by our Lord, that he was found by his countrymen "sitting, clothed, and in his right mind"[2]—sober, the same word as used here. The Apostle Paul, in his noble reply to the unmanly interruption of the Roman governor, "Paul, thou art beside thyself; much learning hath made thee mad," says, "I am not mad, most noble Festus; but speak forth the words of soberness." My words are the words not of a madman, but of one in full possession of his reason. And, speaking of himself and his apostolic brethren, he says, "Whether we be beside ourselves,"—that is, 'act like madmen in the world's estimation,'—"it is to God," that is, 'from regard to the will of God, from a desire to promote the cause of God;' "whether we be sober,"—that is, 'act cautiously and prudently, like men in the full possession and exercise of all their faculties,'—"it is for your sakes," that is, 'in order to promote your welfare.'[3]

This is the primary meaning of the word, and it is probably with a direct reference to that that the drunkard is considered as specially unworthy of the appellation sober,

---

[1] Σωφρονήσατε. Σώφρων Græcis dicitur cui σῶς φρήν, *mens sana* est, atque adeo qui *mania*, utpote illius contraria, non laborat. Σώφρων, nullis in transversum actus affectibus, recte de rebus judicat, justumque singulis pretium statuit, atque adeo, media incedendo via, nec in excessu, nec defectu impingit: omnia præmeditate suscipit et cum *animi sani* temperie, consequenter illud ipsis Gentibus adeo commendatum: μηδὲν ἄγαν *ne quid nimis* sedulo observat.—SCHRAMM in Tit. i. 8.

[2] Mark v. 15. [3] Acts xxvi. 24, 25; 2 Cor. v. 13.

of a sound mind. The man who indulges in the undue use of intoxicating liquors behaves like an idiot, a person devoid of " discourse of reason ;" and by the continued use of them, he brings himself into a state of madness. Certainly, as Solomon says, the man who allows himself to be deceived by wine, that mocker, " is not wise ;" and he who carefully avoids the habit, so far proves himself to be a man in his right senses, a man of sane mind.

The word, however, though originally significant of a physical state of the rational faculties, is usually employed in the New Testament as descriptive of a moral state of the mind. What is its precise signification will best appear from looking at the passages in which it, and the words derived from it, are employed by the sacred writers. The Apostle Paul exhorts every man "not to think of himself more highly than he ought to think, but to think soberly ;" that is, to think justly, and therefore humbly.[1] The same apostle, in the second chapter of his First Epistle to Timothy, exhorts Christian women, instead of decking themselves with broidered hair and gold, or pearls or costly array, to "adorn themselves with shamefacedness," that is, with modesty ; "and with sobriety,"[2] that is, with prudence or moderation ; and they are required, ver. 15, to " continue in faith, and charity, and holiness, with sobriety," that is, prudence or gravity. In the third chapter of the same epistle, he tells us " a Christian bishop must be sober," wise, prudent, moderate. In his Second Epistle to Timothy, he describes the spirit or disposition which Christians have received from God, as " not the spirit of fear, but of power, of love, and of a sound mind," or sobriety. The spirit of Christianity is not a timid, crouching, time-serving spirit ; it is an energetic, benignant, wise, moderate spirit. In the Epistle to Titus, he states that "a bishop must be sober,"

[1] Rom. xii. 3. [2] 1 Tim. ii. 9.

that is, wise, prudent, moderate; he requires "the aged men to be sober," which is there plainly something different from temperate; he requires the aged women to teach the young women to be "discreet;" and he commands Titus to "exhort the young men also to be sober-minded." In all these instances sobriety is plainly wisdom, prudence, moderation. In the same epistle he also states, that " the grace of God, which brings salvation to all, when understood and believed, teaches men to deny ungodliness and worldly lusts, and to live soberly, righteously, and godly,"—to live wisely in reference to themselves, righteously with regard to their fellow-men, and piously in reference to God.[1] These are all the passages in the New Testament in which the word before us, or those connected with it, are employed; and on considering them, there can be no great difficulty in determining the meaning of the exhortation before us, "Be sober."

Some interpreters consider it an exhortation to prudence —practical wisdom; others to temperance, in the extensive sense in which that word is employed in the New Testament—moderation in all things, the right regulation of our desires and pursuits. I am strongly disposed to think the apostle's exhortation includes both of these things, and perhaps something more. I apprehend it is equivalent to, 'Exercise a sound mind in reference both to "things seen and temporal," and to "things unseen and eternal." "Be not unwise," be not like children; or, if in malice ye be as children, "in understanding be ye men." Take heed not to be imposed on. Beware of mistaking shadows for realities, and realities for shadows. Look at things in their comparative importance, and act accordingly. Be sagacious. Be not content with partial views of the subjects in which you have so deep an interest. Look at all sides of a sub-

[1] Tit. i. 8, ii. 2, 4, 6, 12, 13.

ject. Think before you speak. Reflect before you act. "Walk in wisdom," that is, wisely, both in regard to those who are within, and those who are without; "walk circumspectly, not as fools, but as wise."'

If Christians are thus morally sound-minded, they will discover this in the way in which they think, and feel, and act in reference to this present world. They will show that they have formed a just, and therefore a moderate, sober estimate, both of its goods and evils. They will not inordinately love the one nor fear the other. They will not rate very high its wealth, its honours, or its pleasures. They will be moderate in their desires to possess these, and moderate in their exertions to obtain them; moderate in their attachment to them while they are possessed of them, and moderate in their regrets for them when they are deprived of them. "They who have wives will be as if they had none," knowing that earthly relations, the closest and most endearing, must soon be dissolved; "they who weep as though they wept not," knowing that earthly sorrows, however deep, will soon be over for ever; "they who rejoice as though they rejoiced not," knowing that earthly delights, however exquisite, are shadowy, uncertain, short-lived; "those who buy as though they possessed not," knowing that human possessions are insecure and unsatisfactory, that, "as we brought nothing into the world, we can carry nothing out of it," and feeling that "a man's life consists not in the abundance of his possessions;" "they who use this world as not abusing it," knowing that we must give account to the Supreme Judge for the use of our property; and that, unimportant as wealth is in itself, it is awfully important viewed as connected with eternity. The great truths, that "the fashion of the world passeth away," and that "the things which are unseen are eternal," will be allowed the full influence which a sound, prudent, wise mind perceives they ought to have on the whole of the temper and conduct.[1] This is Christian sobriety.

The substance of the apostle's exhortation, then, is: 'Exercise a sound mind, a mind enlightened and transformed by Christian truth, in reference to both worlds; and exhibit its practical conclusions in your wise and prudent conduct, especially in your habitual moderation in thought, feeling, and action, with regard to " things seen and temporal," the influence of which intoxicates and infatuates the great body of mankind, and makes them act the part of children and fools.'

§ 2. " *Watching unto prayer.*"

The second duty enjoined by the apostle is watching unto prayer. Prayer is well defined in our Shorter Catechism to be, " the offering up of our desires to God for things agreeable to his will, in the name of Christ, with confession of our sins, and thankful acknowledgment of his mercies." This is a primary, essential duty of religion. It is the natural expression of that state of mind and heart, of thought and affection, in which religion consists. It is to religion what breath is to life. It betokens its existence, and it is the means of its continuance. It is very clearly enjoined and very strongly enforced, both by our Lord and his apostles: " Ask, and ye shall receive; seek, and ye shall find; knock, and it shall be opened to you: for every one that asketh receiveth; and he that seeketh findeth; and to him that knocketh it shall be opened." " Men ought always to pray," to continue praying, " and not to faint." " Be careful about nothing; but in everything by prayer and supplication, with thanksgiving, let your requests be made known to God. And the peace of God, which passeth all understanding, shall keep your hearts and minds through

[1] 1 Cor. vii. 29-31.

Christ Jesus." "Continue instant in prayer." "Pray without ceasing." "The effectual fervent prayer of a righteous man availeth much." "Is any man afflicted? let him pray."[1]

This important duty is not, however, that which the apostle here enjoins. His command is not, Pray, but Watch unto prayer. He takes it for granted that they did pray, that they could not but pray; but he is anxious that their prayers should be such as to gain in the highest degree the important ends of prayer. It deserves notice that the word prayer is in the plural form. It is watch unto prayers.[2] Some have supposed that the apostle refers here to the four species of devotional exercise which Paul mentions in his Epistle to Timothy, "supplications, prayers, intercessions, and giving of thanks."[3] John Huss is probably nearer the truth when he finds emphasis in the mode of expression, and says, "Watch unto prayers, not to one, but many; for 'men ought always to pray, and not to faint.'" That prayers are to be offered, habitually offered, the apostle counts certain. He is not a Christian at all who does not pray, habitually pray. But the apostle is desirous that they should "watch unto prayer."

The language is peculiar. What is its meaning? What is meant by watching? what is meant by watching unto prayer?—First, what is meant by watching? This is not the word which is most frequently used to express the idea of watching, as a shepherd does his flock, or a sentinel that committed to his charge. In the original signification[4] it refers to a physical state of the body and mind, rather than

---

[1] Matt. vii. 7, 8; Luke xviii. 1; Phil. iv. 6, 7; Col. iv. 2; 1 Thess. v. 17; James v. 13, 16.

[2] Εἰς τὰς προσευχάς.

[3] 1 Tim. ii. 1. Δεήσεις, προσευχὰς, ἐντεύξεις, εὐχαριστίας.

[4] Νήψατε, not Γρηγορήσατε, as ch. v. 8.

to a moral state of the mind. It is descriptive of that state in which all the faculties are awake and active, as opposed to the state of delusion and stupor which intoxication induces, and answers nearly to our word sober, in the limited sense in which it is often used. It is always, in the New Testament, employed to express a state of mind. What that state of mind is, will best appear in this, as in the previous case, by attending to the comparatively few instances in which the word, and those connected with it, occur in the New Testament. " Awake to righteousness, and sin not; for some have not the knowledge of God: I speak this to your shame;"[1] that is, Shake off the mental delusion and stupor in which the intoxication of error has involved you, that, with clear and excited faculties, you may attend to this most important subject. " Let us not sleep, as do others; but let us watch and be sober,"—the same word as we have here; that is, be wakeful; let us watch, and, that we may watch, let us be wakeful. " Let us who are of the day be sober,"—the same word, be wakeful, " not sleep, as do others."[2] " A bishop must be sober,[3] vigilant," wakeful,—the same word we have here. " The bishops' wives," or the female superintendents, it may be either, " must be," not slanderers, but "sober,"[4]—the same word. It is difficult to see why our translators should have rendered the same word, when used of male superintendents, " vigilant,"—when used of female superintendents, "sober." In both cases wakeful vigilance is the idea: " But watch thou in all things." Keep awake, and be active in the discharge of all thy duties.[5] " Speak the words that become sound doctrine, that the aged men be sober,"[6] vigilant in the margin. The only other places where the word occurs in the New Testament, are in this epistle: " Gird

---

[1] 1 Cor. xv. 34.   [2] 1 Thess. v. 6-8.   [3] 1 Tim. iii. 2.
[4] 2 Tim. iii. 11.   [5] 2 Tim. iv. 5.   [6] Tit. ii. 2.

up the loins of your mind, be sober:"[1] where the idea of wakefulness or vigilance seems better to suit the context than sobriety, either in its stricter or more extended meaning. "Be sober, be vigilant,"[2]—be wakeful, and not only be wakeful, but actively watch. From all these passages it seems plain that the apostle's exhortation is, Be wakeful, be on the alert; look around you; with excited attention actively exert your mind.

But what are we to understand by being watchful, or watching unto prayer? The phrase has received two translations. Be watchful in prayer, that is, while engaged in prayer; or be watchful, in order to prayer. There can be no doubt that they misinterpret the passage who refer it to the vigils or nightly prayers of the ancient Church. This is an interpretation which very properly may take its place alongside of that which would render "repent"[3] by 'do penance.' The primitive Christians were obliged to have their common "prayers," as well as "the doctrine" and "the breaking of bread," during the night, for they durst not assemble during the day. But there does not seem any reference to that here, which was indeed more a matter of necessity than of choice; not a duty in itself, but only in the particular circumstances in which they were placed. All that is included in either of the two renderings mentioned, and something more, is expressed in a translation which, if the words do not demand, they certainly admit: "Be watchful, or watch, in reference to prayer."[4]

---

[1] 1 Pet. i. 13.   [2] 1 Pet. v. 8.   [3] Μετανοεῖτε.

[4] Bishop Jebb considers "watching unto prayer" as = "vigilantly guarding against whatever is unfriendly to devotion,—viewing everything with a reference to the effect it is likely to have on our prayers; this watchfulness respecting not merely things wrong in themselves, but things innocent, useful, laudable. *Perimus* licetis. What was it that kept the guests in the parable from the supper? What, then, is the remedy? are we to renounce these things? By no means, but 1 Cor. vii. 29-31."

Vigilance requires to be exerted in reference to all duties. We need to watch as to the principles in which they originate, the manner in which they are performed, the motives which influence us in performing them, the end we seek to gain by performing them. But there is special need of vigilance in reference to prayer. Christians should be watchful as to proper subjects of prayer, as to fit opportunities for prayer, as to hindrances from and in prayer, as to the proper manner of prayer, and as to the results or consequences of prayer.

The attention of Christians should be actively alive to the circumstances—in the world, in the Church, in the various spheres of relative duty which they occupy, in their own individual experience—which ought to be made the subjects of prayer; and in every case see that what they pray for be agreeable to God's will, something they are warranted to ask, and which he has promised to grant. They should look at everything in this particular aspect, that so "in everything they may in prayer and supplication make their requests known to God."

They should wakefully observe what may be fit opportunities for escaping from the world to hold communion with God, that they may carefully improve them. Thus did David watch unto prayer, when he said, "As for me, I will call upon God, and the Lord shall save me. Evening, and morning, and at noon, will I pray, and cry aloud; and He shall hear my voice."

They should watch against worldliness of mind, and especially against wilful transgressions, remembering that, "if we regard iniquity in our heart, the Lord will not hear us."[1]

They should watch in reference to the manner of prayer when engaged in it; taking care that it be prayer, and not merely saying prayers; that they serve him who is a Spirit,

[1] Ps. lv. 17, lxvi. 18.

with their spirits "in spirit and truth;" that they "present a living sacrifice;" that they yield "rational worship;" that they "pray in the spirit," depending on the promised influence of the Holy Ghost as "the Spirit of grace and of supplications;" that they pray "in faith, nothing wavering; for he that wavereth is as a wave of the sea driven of the wind and tossed—let not that man think that he shall receive anything of the Lord;" that they pray with intense desire, being "instant in prayer;" that they pray in humble submission, saying, "Not my will, but thine be done."[1]

Finally, they should watch in reference to the results of prayer. Like Habakkuk, they should "stand on their watch, and set them upon the tower to see what he will say to them." "I will direct my prayer to thee," says David, "and look up."[2] Christians "should look after their prayers, and hear what the Lord will speak, observe what the Lord will do; that if he grant what they ask, they may be thankful; that if he deny, they may be patient and humbly inquire the cause; that if he defer, they may continue to pray and wait, and not faint. They should look up or look out, as they who have shot an arrow, looking to see how near it has come to the mark. We lose much of the comfort of our prayers for want of observing the returns of them."[3]

II. MOTIVE URGING TO SOBRIETY AND WATCHING UNTO PRAYER: "THE END OF ALL THINGS IS AT HAND."

Let us now, secondly, attend to the motive by which the apostle enforces his exhortation. "The end of all things is at hand;" therefore "be sober, and watch unto prayer."

---

[1] John iv. 24; Rom. xii. 1, λογικὴν λατρείαν; Jude 20; James i. 6, 7; Col. iv. 1; Luke xxii. 42.
[2] Hab. ii. 1; Ps. v. 3.   [3] Matthew Henry.

"The end of all things" is a phrase which, taken by itself, most naturally calls up the idea of the final termination of the present order of things, which is so often mentioned in the sacred writings. A period is fixed when He who established the present mundane system shall proclaim, "It is done;" and the dead shall live, and the living "shall be changed," and all shall be judged; death shall be swallowed up in life, and time be no more, having been lost in eternity: "the heavens and the earth that now are shall be dissolved, the heavens passing away with a great noise; the earth also, and the works that are therein, being burnt up; the very elements melting with fervent heat; and the new heavens and the new earth, wherein righteousness is, and shall dwell," shall take their place. These solemn truths are well fitted to operate as powerful motives on all who believe them, to be sober, and to watch unto prayer. "What manner of persons ought we to be," says the apostle, "in all holy conversation and godliness," "looking for and hastening to the coming of this day of God!" "Wherefore, beloved, seeing that we look for such things, be diligent, that ye be found of him in peace, without spot and blameless." "He who," to use the language of a great writer, "has seen, as through a telescope, the glorious appearance of the Supreme Judge, the solemn state of his majestic person, the splendid pomp of his magnificent and vastly numerous retinue, the obsequious throng of glorious celestial creatures doing homage to their eternal King; the swift flight of his royal guards sent forth into the four winds to gather the elect, and covering the face of the heavens with their spreading wings; the universal attention of all to that loud-sounding trumpet that shakes the pillars of the world, pierces the inward caverns of the earth, and resounds through every part of the encircling heavens; the many myriads of joyful expectants, arising, changing, putting on glory, taking wing, and contending upwards to join themselves to the triumphant heavenly host; the judgment set; the books opened; the frightful, amazed looks of surprised wretches; the equal administration of the final judgment; the adjudication of all to their eternal states; the heavens rolled up as a scroll; the earth and all things therein consumed and burnt up;"[1]—surely that man must be *sober*, deeply, calmly considerate, knowing how present character and conduct is to affect future events; and maintaining a steady restraint and moderation of all his affections and passions in reference to a world the fashion of which is thus to pass away: surely he must watch unto prayer, watch and pray always, that he may be accounted worthy to escape " the perdition of ungodly men," and " stand before the Son of man" in the judgment. This is a powerful motive, fitted to influence the minds and hearts and conduct of all believers in all countries and ages till the end come.

But there are obvious difficulties in this mode of interpretation. " The end of all things is" said to be " at hand;" that is, very near. Now, eighteen centuries have well-nigh run their course since these words were uttered, and the end of the world has not come; nay, when we think of the number and magnitude of the events that must take place before it arrives, we cannot concur with those who are of opinion that it is very soon to take place. " The end is not yet."

To meet and remove this difficulty, it has been remarked by some, that the age of the Messiah is the last age,—that no such great event as the flood, or the giving of the law, or the coming of the Word in flesh, stands between them who live under that age and the end of the world, so that it may be said to be *near* all who live under the gospel

[1] Howe, *Vanity of Man as mortal.*

economy; by others, that it is *near,* if not in the calculations of time, in those of eternity, with him with whom "one day is as a thousand years, and a thousand years as one day;" and by a third class, that as the state of every man is fixed at death, that as death leaves him judgment will find him, the end of all things *to him* is not far off. I must say that these modes of getting over the difficulty do not appear to me to be satisfactory; and that the apostle's obvious design is to intimate that the events referred to in the phrase "the end of all things" were just about to take place.

Their view of the matter is still less satisfactory, who tell us that the apostles really did expect the immediate dissolution of the world. We know there were persons who so misunderstood such statements as that before us; but we find the Apostle Paul, in his Epistle to the Thessalonians, warning them against such a mistake, and telling them that the day of Christ, in the sense of the day of the last judgment, was not at hand.[1] Besides, it is not with what the apostles, exercising their own unassisted judgments, expected, but with what the inspiring Spirit spoke by them, that we have to do.

After some deliberation, I have been led to adopt the opinion of those who hold, that "the end of all things" here is the entire and final end of the Jewish economy in the destruction of the temple and city of Jerusalem, and the dispersion of the holy people. That was at hand; for this epistle seems to have been written a very short while before these events took place, not improbably after the commencement of "the wars and rumours of war" of which our Lord spake. This view will not appear strange to any one who has carefully weighed the terms in which our Lord had predicted these events, and the close connection which the fulfilment of these predictions had with

[1] 2 Thess. ii. 1-3.

the interests and duties of Christians, whether in Judea or in Gentile countries.

It is quite plain, that in our Lord's predictions, the expressions "the end," and probably "the end of the world," are used in reference to the entire dissolution of the Jewish economy.[1] The events of that period were very minutely foretold; and our Lord distinctly stated that the existing generation should not pass away till all things respecting "this end" should be fulfilled. This was to be a season of suffering to all; of trial, severe trial, to the followers of Christ; of dreadful judgment on his Jewish opposers, and of glorious triumph to his religion. To this period there are repeated references in the apostolical epistles: "Knowing the time," says the Apostle Paul, "that now it is high time to awake out of sleep; for now is our salvation nearer than when we believed. The night is far spent, the day is at hand." "Be patient," says the Apostle James; "stablish your hearts; for the coming of the Lord draweth nigh." "The Judge standeth before the door."[2] Our Lord's predictions must have been very familiar to the minds of Christians at the time this was written. They must have been looking forward with mingled awe and joy, fear and hope, to their accomplishment—"looking for the things which were coming upon the earth;" and it was peculiarly natural for Peter to refer to these events, and to refer to them in words similar to those used by our Lord, as he was one of the disciples who, sitting with his Lord in full view of the city and temple, heard these predictions uttered.

The Christians inhabiting Judea had a peculiar interest in these predictions and their fulfilment. But all Christians had a deep interest in them. The Christians of the regions in which those to whom Peter wrote resided, were chiefly

---

[1] Matt. xxiv. 3, 6, 14, 34; Mark xiii. 30; Luke xxi. 32.
[2] Rom. xiii. 11, 12; James v. 8, 9.

converted Jews. As Christians, they had cause to rejoice in the prospect of the accomplishment of these predictions, as greatly confirming the truth of Christianity, and removing some of the greatest obstructions in the way of its progress; such as persecutions by the Jews, and the confounding of Christianity with Judaism on the part of the Gentiles, who were accustomed to view its professors as a Jewish sect. But while they rejoiced, they had cause to "rejoice with trembling," as their Lord had plainly intimated that it was to be a season of severe trial to his friends, as well as of fearful vengeance against his enemies. "The end of all things" which was at hand, seems to be the same thing as the judgment of the quick and the dead, which the Lord was ready to enter on,—the judgment, the time for which was come; which was to begin with the house of God, and then to be executed fully on those who obeyed not the gospel of God—the unbelieving Jews; in which the righteous should scarcely be saved, and the ungodly and wicked should be fearfully punished.

The contemplation of such events as just at hand, was well fitted to operate as a motive to sobriety, and vigilance unto prayer. These were just the tempers and exercises peculiarly called for in such circumstances; and they are just the dispositions and employments required by our Lord when he speaks of those days of trial and wrath. "Take heed to yourselves," says our Lord, "lest at any time your hearts be overcharged with surfeiting, and drunkenness, and cares of this life, and so that day come upon you unawares: for as a snare shall it come upon all who dwell on the face of the whole earth. Watch ye, therefore, and pray always, that ye may be accounted worthy to escape all these things that are about to come to pass, and to stand before the Son of man."[1] It is difficult to believe that the

[1] Luke xxi. 34-36.

apostle had not these very words in his mind when he wrote the passage now before us.

While these exhortations had a peculiar appropriateness to those to whom they were originally addressed, while they received peculiar enforcement from the circumstances in which they were placed, they are plainly exhortations to which Christians in all countries and ages are called to attend, and especially when placed in circumstances similar in any way to those in which they were primarily given. We are obviously placed in such circumstances. There is now, as then, and to a still greater extent, a breaking up of old systems. Dynasties and hierarchies are shaking into dissolution. Society is in one of the great states of transition, which occur but at distant intervals in the history of our race. Seldom has the state of our times been more graphically and justly described than in the words of a living writer : " What times are coming upon the earth we know not; but the general expectation of persons of all characters in all nations, is an instinct implanted by God to warn us of a coming storm. Not one nation, but all; not one class of thinkers, but all,—they who fear, and they who hope, and who hope and fear things opposite; they who are immersed in their worldly schemes, and they who look for some coming of God's kingdom; they who watch this world's signs, and they who watch for the next,—alike have their eye intently fixed on somewhat that is coming; though whether it be the vials of his wrath or the glories of his kingdom, or whether the one shall be herald to the other, none can tell. They who calculate what is likely, speak of it; they who cannot, *feel* its coming. The spirits of the unseen world seem to be approaching to us, and 'awe comes upon us, and trembling, which maketh all bones to shake.' There is 'upon the earth distress of nations with perplexity, men's hearts failing them for fear, and for looking after those things which are coming upon the earth.' Times of trouble there have been before ; but such a time, in which everything, everywhere, tends in one direction to one mighty struggle of one sort,—of faith with infidelity, lawlessness with rule, Christ with antichrist,—there seems never to have been till now." " God warneth us, by the very swiftness with which all things are moving around us, that it is HE who is impelling them. Man cannot impart such speed, nor rouse the winds from the four quarters of the heavens, nor bring men's varying wills into a uniform result ; and therewith he warns us to beware how we attempt to guide what he is thus manifestly governing."[1]

The end of many things seems indeed approaching. Popery, though making convulsive struggles, must ere long expire. Babylon is repairing her battlements, only to make her fall the more signal. The long captivity of Israel is drawing to its close. The Mohammedan delusion is effete. The idols are about to be abolished. The sanctuary is about to be cleansed. Political despotism and ecclesiastical tyranny are doomed. But before the end of these things, what " wars and rumours of wars," what siftings of men and systems ! What struggles, what sacrifices, what sufferings are coming, are at hand ! What need of faith and patience, of dependence and exertion, of caution and vigour ! Never since the destruction of the Jewish economy was there a louder call to Christians to attend to the inspired declarations, " Be sober, and watch unto prayer."

[1] Pusey.

DISCOURSE XIX.

ON THE MAINTENANCE AND MANIFESTATION OF BROTHERLY LOVE.[1]

"And, above all things, have fervent charity among yourselves: for charity shall cover the multitude of sins. Use hospitality one to another, without grudging. As every man hath received the gift, even so minister the same one to another, as good stewards of the manifold grace of God. If any man speak, let him speak as the oracles of God; if any man minister, let him do it as of the ability which God giveth; that God in all things may be glorified through Jesus Christ: to whom be praise and dominion for ever and ever. Amen."—1 Pet. iv. 8-11.

"Holy brethren, partakers of the heavenly calling!" In the sacred services of the forenoon, we have in the most solemn manner recognised the intimate relation in which we stand to each other as Christians. We have declared, that "though many, we are one body, having partaken of one bread," "the bread which came down from heaven, and has been given for the life of the world;" and "having all drunk into one Spirit," "the Spirit of power, and of love, and of a sound mind," which Jesus being glorified has given to all who believe in him. We have, over the instituted emblems of the holy, suffering humanity of our Lord, made the good profession, that we have one God and Father, Jehovah; one Lord and Saviour, Jesus Christ; one faith, the faith of his gospel; one baptism, the baptism of his Spirit; one hope, the hope of his salvation. We have

[1] This discourse was delivered immediately after the administration of the Lord's Supper.

avowed ourselves brethren in Christ, and pledged ourselves to perform all the mutual duties which rise out of a relation so intimate and so sacred.

It cannot, then, be inopportune to direct your attention to an inspired account of some of those duties; and such an account is contained in the paragraph I have just read, which plainly refers to the temper and conduct towards each other by which Christians should be characterized. The whole truth on this subject may be very briefly stated. The entire duty of Christians to each other is summed up in one word—love, brotherly love. The *maintenance* of brotherly love, that is the temper by which Christians should be characterized; the *manifestation* of brotherly love, that is the conduct by which Christians should be characterized.

In the text, both of these are plainly enjoined and powerfully enforced. The maintenance of brotherly love is thus enjoined: "Above all things, have fervent charity among yourselves." And it is thus enforced: "for charity shall cover the multitude of sins." The manifestation of brotherly love is thus enjoined: "Use hospitality one to another, without grudging. As every man hath received the gift, so let him minister the same one to another, as good stewards of the manifold grace of God. If any man speak, let him speak as the oracles of God; if any man minister, let him do it as of the ability which God giveth." And it is thus enforced: "that God may in all things be glorified through Jesus Christ." The *maintenance* and *manifestation* of the love of the brethren, *enjoined* and *recommended*, are thus obviously the substance of the text; and to unfold the meaning of the injunctions, and to point out the force of the recommendations, are the objects I shall endeavour to gain in the following discourse.

I. THE MAINTENANCE OF BROTHERLY LOVE.

§ 1. *The duty explained.*

And first, of the *maintenance* of brotherly love. "Above all things, have fervent charity among yourselves: for charity shall cover the multitude of sins." The injunction first calls for our consideration: "Above all things, have fervent charity among yourselves."[1]

In the ordinary use of language, charity is expressive either of almsgiving, or of that disposition which leads a man to take fully as favourable a view of the character and conduct of other men as facts will justify. In Scripture, however, it is never employed in either of these senses. It is uniformly used as equivalent to the word "love" in its highest sense; and it would have prevented some hazardous misapprehensions and misinterpretations had the original term been uniformly thus rendered. I have had occasion to remark elsewhere, that "there is a love which every man owes to every other man, without reference to his spiritual state or character, merely because he is a man,—a sincere desire to promote his welfare." This is the love which the Apostle Paul, with obvious propriety, represents as "the fulfilling of the law," so far as it refers to our duties to our fellow-men; for he who is under its influence can do no ill to any man; he cannot interfere injuriously with another's personal property or reputation, but on the contrary must, as he has opportunity, "do good to all men." Good-will

[1] The subject of this section has already been considered in Discourses VI., XII., and XV. I have preferred laying myself open to the charge of self-repetition, rather than either, by mere reference to these discourses, giving this discourse a mangled appearance, or, by studiously seeking novelty in the form of expression, running the risk of injuring the substance of the illustration of brotherly love. Similar reasons have led to similar repetitions in other parts of these volumes.

is the essence, indeed the sole component element, of this love.

The love referred to in the text is obviously more limited in its range, and, for that very reason, much more comprehensive in its elementary principles. It is not love towards all men that the apostle here enjoins, but "love among themselves." This affection is called "the love of the brethren," "brotherly kindness," to contradistinguish it from the benevolent regard which should be cherished towards all human beings; for though all men are brethren, as they have one Father, "one God has created them," they are not all brethren in the Christian sense of that expression. The appellation is limited to what has always been a comparatively small class of persons, genuine Christians. The affection spoken of in the text can be exercised only by them: it can be exercised only to them. A man who is unchristian, who is antichristian, in his opinions and temper and conduct, may highly esteem, may tenderly love, a true Christian; but he cannot cherish to him the love which Christians have "among themselves," "brotherly kindness:" he loves him not because he is, but notwithstanding that he is, a Christian. A Christian may love, he ought to love, he does love, all mankind; he desires the happiness of every being capable of happiness; he esteems what is estimable, he loves what is amiable, he admires what is admirable; he pities what is suffering wherever he meets with it: but he cannot extend beyond the sacred pale the love which those within it have "among themselves;" he cannot regard with brotherly kindness any one but a Christian brother. None but a Christian can be either the object or the subject of this benevolent affection. None but a Christian can either be the agent or the recipient in the kind offices in which it finds expression.

This limitation is matter not of choice, but of necessity.

Most gladly would the Christian regard all his fellow-men as fellow-Christians, if they would but allow him to do so, by becoming Christians; but till they do so, it is in the nature of things impossible that he should feel towards them as if they were what they are not. This affection originates in the possession of a peculiar mode of thinking and feeling, produced in the mind by the Holy Spirit, through the knowledge and belief of Christian truth, which naturally leads those who are thus distinguished to a sympathy of mind and heart, of thought and affection, with all who, under the same influence, have been led to entertain the same views and to cherish the same dispositions. They love one another "in the truth, for the truth's sake that dwelleth in them, and shall be with them for ever."[1]

This circumstance, which necessarily limits this principle as to its sphere of operation, gives it a greater intensity and activity in that sphere, as well as much greater comprehension of elementary principles. It includes good-will in its highest degree; but to this it adds moral esteem, complacential delight, tender sympathy. This it does in every instance; but the degree in which these elementary principles are to be found, in individual cases of brotherly kindness, depends on a variety of circumstances; and chiefly on the degree in which he who exercises it, and he to whom it is exercised, approach the completeness and perfection of the Christian character. Every Christian loves every other Christian, when he knows him; but the more accomplished the Christian is, whether the subject or object of brotherly love, the more does he put forth or draw forth its holy, benignant influence.

The end of all love is the good or the happiness of its object, as that happiness is conceived of by its subject. The great end which Christian brotherly love contemplates,

[1] 2 John 2.

is the well-being of its object, viewed as a Christian man; his deliverance from ignorance, and error, and sin, in all their forms and all their degrees; his progressive, and ultimately his complete happiness, in entire conformity to the mind and will of God; the unclouded sense of the divine favour, the uninterrupted enjoyment of the divine fellowship, the being like "the ever-blessed" Holy, Holy, Holy One. It does not overlook any of the interests of its object; but it views them all in reference, in subordination, to the enjoyment of "the salvation that is in Christ, with eternal glory."

This is "the love among themselves" of which the apostle speaks; and his injunction with regard to it is, "Above all things, have fervent love among yourselves." The original word rendered "fervent" is a very expressive one.[1] Its primitive and proper signification is, extensive and wide-reaching; and when applied to love, it describes a benevolent affection, which takes a wide view of the capacities for happiness of its objects, and which seeks its gratification in having all these capacities completely filled; the love expressed in the words of the apostle, "This also we wish, even your perfection;" or in his prayer, "that ye may be filled with all the fulness of God." Nothing short of the perfect holiness, the perfect happiness of its objects, can satisfy it.

This term is also used to signify *intensity*; as when it is said of our Lord, that "being in an agony, he prayed more earnestly." The love which the apostle calls on Christians to maintain, is not cold, not even lukewarm: it is fervent love; an active principle like *fire*; not lying dormant in the mind, but influencing all the powers of action; a love which will make the exertion or suffering necessary to gain its purposes, be readily engaged in and submitted to.

[1] Ἐκτενῆ.

This word, too, is employed to signify *continuance;* as when it is said, that " prayer was made without ceasing for Peter," when Herod had cast him into prison, intending that he should never come out but to his execution. The love here referred to is love that is to last for life, and which even death is not to extinguish. It is an extensive, intense, permanent affection, which the apostle exhorts Christians to maintain towards each other.

The precise import of his exhortation differs somewhat, according to the place you give to the epithet " fervent" in it. If, with our translators, you read, " Have fervent charity among yourselves," the word *have* has the sense of *hold*. He takes for granted that as Christians they were in possession of this fervent love, and his exhortation is to hold it fast. Let not your fervent love wax cold. If, with other interpreters, and fully as much in conformity with the construction of the original text, we read, " Have love among yourselves, *fervent,*" the apostle takes for granted that they had love among themselves; if they had not, they were not Christians at all; and his exhortation to them is, ' See that your love be in extent, in intensity, and in continuance, what it ought to be.' In this case, the passage is exactly parallel with that in chapter i. 22, where he takes for granted, that they had " purified their souls in obeying the truth through the Spirit unto unfeigned love of the brethren ;" and exhorts them to " see that they love one another with a pure heart fervently." The exhortation unites in it both of Paul's exhortations in reference to the same subject: " Be kindly affectioned to one another, in brotherly love;"[1] that is, let your love be intense : and, " Let brotherly love continue;" that is, let your love be permanent.

The only other point in the apostle's injunction to the maintenance of brotherly love that requires illustration, is

---
[1] Rom. xii. 10.

the qualifying phrase, "above all things."[1] Some have supposed that the apostle's object was to call on Christians to show their love to one another before all: 'Before all men, have love among yourselves fervent. Let your mutual love serve the purpose which our Lord meant it to serve. "Hereby," said he, "shall all men know you to be my disciples, if ye have love one to another."[2] Be not ashamed of one another, especially when involved in suffering for Christ. When that "iniquity abounds," let not your love among yourselves "wax cold;" let not these waters quench it, let not these floods drown it.[3] Let it be so fervent, that even the heathen may be constrained to say, "Behold how these Christians love one another!"' We are rather disposed to consider the words as intended to mark the very great importance of this fervent love among themselves, as that without which the great purpose of Christianity could not be gained, either in the individual or in the society, either within the pale of the Christian Church or beyond it; for it is love that "edifies" both the Christian and the Christian Church. He who has love proves that he has faith, for "faith works by love;" and he who has love is sure to have holiness, for "love is the fulfilling of the law." He who loves his brother can do no harm to his brother; he must do him all the good in his power.[4]

Paul's estimate of the comparative value of love was not lower than that of his brother apostle; and his eulogium is the best commentary on the words, "Have charity above all things." "Though I speak with the tongues of men and angels, and have not charity, I am become as sounding brass or a tinkling cymbal. And though I have the gift of prophecy, and understand all mysteries and all knowledge; and though I have all faith, so that I could remove moun-

---

[1] Πρὸ πάντων.   [2] John xiii. 35.   [3] Matt. xxiv. 12.
[4] 1 Cor. viii. 1; Gal. v. 6; Rom. xiii. 10.

tains, and have not charity, I am nothing. And though I bestow all my goods to feed the poor, and though I give my body to be burned, and have not charity, it profiteth me nothing. Charity suffereth long, and is kind; charity envieth not; charity vaunteth not itself, is not puffed up, doth not behave itself unseemly, seeketh not her own, is not easily provoked, thinketh no evil; rejoiceth not in iniquity, but rejoiceth in the truth; beareth all things, believeth all things, hopeth all things, endureth all things. Charity never faileth: for whether there be prophecies, they shall fail; whether there be tongues, they shall cease; whether there be knowledge, it shall vanish away: for we know in part, and prophesy in part. But when that which is perfect is come, then that which is in part shall vanish away. When I was a child, I spake as a child, I understood as a child, I thought as a child; but when I became a man, I put away childish things. For now we see through a glass, darkly; but then face to face: now I know in part; but then shall I know even as also I am known. And now abideth faith, hope, and charity, these three; but the greatest of these is charity."[1] If charity be all and do all this, surely it is not wonderful that Paul should enjoin Christians " above all," or in addition to all other Christian graces, to " put on charity, which is the bond of perfectness,"[2] the perfect bond; and that Peter should exhort them, " above all, to have fervent charity among themselves."

§ 2. *The duty recommended.*

Having thus attempted to unfold the meaning of the apostle's *injunction* respecting the maintenance of brotherly love, let us now endeavour to point out the force of his *recommendation* on this subject: " Have fervent charity

[1] 1 Cor. xiii.   [2] Col. iii. 14.

among yourselves: for charity shall cover the multitude of sins."

I do not know if, in the book of God, there can be found a passage which has been more grossly and dangerously misinterpreted than this. Though certainly not among those passages which are " hard to be understoood," yet by the crafty and self-interested, "the unlearned and unstable," it has been " wrested," it is to be feared, " to their own" and other men's " destruction." Charity has been interpreted as equivalent to almsgiving, the devoting sums of money to benevolent, and what were termed pious purposes; and has been represented as efficacious in covering a multitude of the donor's sins from the eye of the Supreme Judge, on the day when he will finally fix the eternal states of men, securing acquittal where otherwise there must have been condemnation. Or charity has been identified with a disposition the reverse of censorious; and this passage, along with the words of our Lord, " Judge not, that ye be not judged: for with what judgment ye judge, ye shall be judged; and with what measure ye mete, it shall be measured to you again,"[1] interpreted by the sound rather than the sense, has been employed to excite false hopes in the minds of worldly, unbelieving, impenitent men, as if their lenient judgments of their fellow-sinners, whose conduct deserved censure, would plead, and plead successfully, for a lenient sentence to themselves, " in the day of the revelation of the righteous judgment of God."

What a fearful proof of the stupidity and wickedness of fallen man, that, amid the clear light of revelation, such misrepresentations should be made and credited! Surely both the teacher and the taught have given themselves up to strong delusions, before they could make or believe such lies as these. What degrading views of the divine charac-

[1] Matt. vii. 1, 2.

ter and of the divine law must those men have, who think that pardon and ultimate freedom from the penal effects of sin can be secured by anything man can do, much more can be bought with money; or that God will reward what is ordinarily a false judgment on man's part, by another false judgment on His part! Even charity in the true sense of the word, and all its blessed fruits, cannot thus cover sin, cannot obtain the pardon of sin; if for no other reason, for this, that they cannot be the procuring cause of that of which they themselves are the results. The free grace of God exercised in harmony with justice, through the atoning sacrifice of Christ to the believing sinner, can alone cover sin in the sense of forgiveness. The love of God is the sole moving cause, the atonement of the Son the sole meritorious cause, the faith of the gospel, produced by the Holy Spirit, the sole instrumental cause of forgiveness.

Setting aside this monstrous perversion of Scripture, which scarcely deserves even the passing notice we have taken of it, let us inquire what the apostle does mean when he says, that " charity shall cover the multitude of sins;" and endeavour to show how what he means in these words is fitted to operate as a motive to Christians to "have fervent charity among themselves."

It is right to state, that the apostle's assertion is not, that " love shall cover," or, as it is in the margin, " will cover;" but " love covers," not *the* multitude, but " *a* multitude of sins." " Love covereth a multitude of sins." But whose love is it that covers sins? and whose sins are they which love covers? and what is it that love does in reference to sin when it covers it?

Some would interpret " charity," of the love of God or of Christ; and " a multitude of sins," of all the violations of the divine law by those Christians who are exhorted to have fervent love among themselves. 'God has loved you;

his love has led him to forgive you. "He has forgiven the iniquity of his people; he has covered all their sins." Christ hath loved you, and has shed his blood in order that your sins might be forgiven in consistency with justice, in glorious illustration of justice. He has covered your sins with his righteousness; He having been made sin for you, you being made the righteousness of God in him. "Brethren, if God," if Christ, have "so loved you," surely "ye should love one another." This love to you all was fervent love. Should not your love to one another be fervent too? Should not you who have been forgiven, forgive; should you not especially forbear with and forgive your brethren, as God and Christ have forborne and forgiven both you and them?'

This in itself is most important truth, and these are the strongest of all motives to mutual Christian love: yet I think every person must feel, on looking at the passage, that this sense is rather dragged into it than drawn out of it; and it is plain, from the original text,[1] that the love in the second clause is the same as the love in the first clause. "Have fervent love among yourselves; for *love—the* love, *this* love—covereth a multitude of sins." It is, then, the love, the fervent love of the brethren, that covers a multitude of sins, whatever and whosesoever these sins may be, and whatever may be meant by covering them.

The words, "love covereth a multitude of sins," are a quotation from the Old Testament; and it is very possible that, by looking at them in their original connection, we may find some assistance in apprehending more distinctly both their meaning and reference here. They are to be found in Prov. x. 12: "Hatred stirreth up strifes: but love covereth all sins;" that is, a man under the influence of hatred, where there is no offence, where no sin against him creates it, "stirs up strife,"—he provokes, he magnifies, he

---

[1] Εἰς ἑαυτοὺς ἀγάπην ἐκτενῆ ἔχοντες, ὅτι ἡ ἀγάπη, κ.τ.λ.

multiplies offences. He, as it were, invites attack, and he commonly does not invite it in vain. But, on the other hand, love—that is, the man under the influence of benignant principle—" covers all sins;" puts down all strifes and offences, treats them as if they were not, makes them as if they never had been. I think it must be very plain to all, that the sins here referred to are offences committed by one brother against another; and that the assertion of the apostle is, that a brother under the influence of that fervent charity which he has been enjoining will cover these offences, even though there should be many of them,—will, so far as the peace and edification of the brotherhood, whether as individuals or a body, are concerned, really make them as if they had never existed.

If Christians were as much under the influence of love as they ought to be, sins against each other, "offences," would not exist; for " love worketh no ill to his neighbour :" in other words, the man entirely under the influence of love can do no injury to his neighbour. His person, his property, his reputation, his feelings, all his interests, are perfectly safe. The whole law in reference to a Christian brother is summed up in love—" Owe no man anything, but to love one another."[1] If that debt is discharged, our duty is done. Were Christians habitually acting under the power of fervent charity, there would be no sins, no offences to cover. But such a state of things has never yet existed. We have no reason to think it ever will exist in this world. " Offences," says the Master, " must come;" and if they are not met in the spirit of love, they will grow and multiply. The spark will become a flame, and the flame a conflagration.

---

[1] Rom. xiii. 8. Ὀφείλετε is considered by some interpreters as indicative, not imperative, here. This exegesis seems better to suit the apostle's current of thought than the more usual one.

But "love covereth sins." Fervent charity prevents a man from giving any occasion for offence. There is always a want of love in the offending brother—the offence proves this; but had there been more love in the offended brother, and had that love been more plainly manifested, the offence might never have existed. Had there been more Christian, that is, more affectionate, behaviour on the part of him who is offended, there might have been less, there might have been no, unchristian conduct on the part of the offender. Fervent love prevents anything like a handle being given for the unkindly feelings of others to take hold of. A christianly benignant disposition naturally leads a man to give his Christian brethren credit for the same temper which animates himself, and consequently prevents him from being on the look-out for offences. He is unwilling to think that a Christian brother means to injure him, for he has no disposition to injure any brother; and he will gladly admit any reasonable account of a piece of conduct which may wear any unkindly aspect, rather than have recourse to this supposition. This temper makes him overlook much which a man of a less benignant disposition would account offence.

And when offence does present itself in a form so distinctly defined that there is no mistaking it, under the power of fervent love he covers it, inasmuch as he gives no unnecessary publicity to it. He does not conceal from the offending brother that he is aware of what he has done, and that he is sensible of the true character of his conduct. No; as no brother can give another just offence without, in the estimation of that brother, having violated the law of their common Lord, charity, however fervent, does not blind him either to the reality or the magnitude of the fault. Were he deficient in charity, he might be silent to him while eloquent to others respecting the offence. He might cherish hatred to the offender in his heart, bear a grudge against him, and meditate vengeance. But he who loves his neighbour as himself will not so hate his offending brother in his heart; he will not suffer sin on him, he will surely rebuke him. But he will *cover* the sin by, as far as lies in his power, concealing it, till he has used every practicable method to have it covered by hearty forgiveness or penitent acknowledgment; and if he be obliged to discover the offence in the first sense, it is only so far as is necessary in order to having it covered in the second and more important sense.

The offended brother, the man sinned against, if he act under the influence of fervent love, follows the wise advice of the apocryphal sage: " Admonish thy friend; it may be he hath not done it; and if he have done it, that he do it not again. Admonish thy friend; it may be that he hath not said it; and if he have, that he speak it not again. Admonish a friend; for many a time it is a slander, and believe not every tale. There is one that slippeth in his speech, but not from the heart; and who is he who hath not offended with his tongue?"[1] He obeys the law of the Master in heaven. If his brother trespass against him, he goes and tells him his fault by himself alone; and if he hear him, then the fault which he has never divulged has been covered; so far as he is concerned, both concealed and forgiven. It is as if it had not been. But if the offending brother will not hear him, he takes with him one or two more of the brethren, that at the mouth of two or three witnesses everything may be established. If he hear them, then too the sin is covered. It is dismissed from his mind, and from the minds of those who were necessarily informed of it, and they regard their brother as before he had offended. But if he neglect to hear them, the sin, which

[1] Ecclus. xix. 13.

in the sense of concealment can be covered no longer, must be told to the assembly of the elders or of the brethren; and if the offending brother hear them and make due acknowledgment, even then love covers the sin, and receives with cordiality the offending brother. But if he obstinately persist in opposition to the mind of the assembly, then the offence is covered by the offender being removed from the society; his conduct being henceforward viewed as that of a man not connected with the brotherhood—" a heathen man and a publican;" and therefore not likely to be a cause of contention in the Church, nor a scandal or stumbling-block to the world.[1]

Love, where it is fervent, will operate in this way, not only in one instance, but in many instances; not only in the case of one offending brother, but of every offending brother; and not in the case only of one or a few offences, but in the case of many offences, even from the same brother. The course prescribed by our Lord in his law, is just the course which the love produced in the heart by his Spirit, by means of his truth, naturally suggests. "It is impossible," says the Master, "but that offences should come. Take heed to yourselves. If thy brother trespass against thee, rebuke him; and if he repent, forgive him; and if he trespass against thee seven times in a day, and seven times in a day turn again to thee, saying, I repent, thou shalt forgive him." "How oft shall my brother," said Peter, with characteristic forwardness, "sin against me, and I forgive him? till seven times? Jesus saith unto him, I say not unto thee, Until seven times; but, Until seventy times seven."[2] So long as you and he stand in the relation of brothers, love must be ready to cover his sins, however numerous. Such seems to me the meaning of the apostle's statement: "Charity," that is, such fervent

[1] Matt. xviii. 15, 17.   [2] Matt. xviii. 7, 21, 22; Luke xvii. 3, 4.

charity as he had enjoined in the preceding clause, "covers a multitude of sins."

A very few words will suffice for showing the force which this statement has as a motive to the duty which the apostle has enjoined. "Have fervent charity among yourselves, *for* charity covereth a multitude of sins." "Offences must needs come." Brethren will sin against brethren. If these sins are not covered, what is the consequence likely to be? "The beginning of strife is like the letting out of waters." Contentions will be extended and perpetuated. There will be schisms in the body. Individual edification will be materially interfered with. The Spirit of Love will be grieved. The Holy Dove will be driven away. The Church will become impure, schismatical, utterly unfit for answering her great purpose, to exhibit and to extend the religion of love. Biting and devouring each other, Christians will be consumed of each other. Roots of bitterness will spring up and flourish, and the result will be trouble and defilement. There will be envying and strife, confusion and every evil work. Plausibility will be given to the objections of infidels, and men will be deterred from connecting themselves with so suicidal a society, as in this case the Church will prove itself.

This must be the result if sins are not covered, and sins can only be covered by charity, by fervent charity; and though these sins are many (the more pity that it should be so), if there is so much fervent charity among the brethren as to cover them, what is the result? The excellence of Christian truth, the power of divine grace, are just so much the more illustriously displayed in triumphing over the unruly passions and the worldly interests of men. The disjointed yet sound members, reset by the skilful tender hand of enlightened charity, become more firmly united and stronger than ever; and incurably diseased portions of the body, which, if retained in it, would have eaten as does a canker, and diffused languor and weakness through the whole body, are, by the same wise spiritual surgery, amputated; so that, under the influence of truthful love, Christians "grow up to him in all things who is the head;" and "the whole body being joined together and compacted by that which every joint supplieth, according to the effectual working in every part, maketh increase to the edifying of itself in love." The brethren live in peace, and the God of peace manifests his gracious presence in the midst of them. "The churches rest, and are edified; and walking in the fear of the Lord, and in the comfort of the Holy Ghost, are multiplied." The Church becomes pure, and united, and strong, and beautiful in her holy union; and, free from internal quarrels and divisions, prosecutes with ardour and success her holy warfare with the enemies of her Lord and King, while angels look on with delight, and devils with terror.

This would be the effect, were there fervent charity enough among the brethren to cover all sins. Love can do this—ay! love should do this. Nothing but love can do it; no knowledge, no faith, no power of intellect, no energy of exertion, no labours, no sufferings, can effect this without love. Is it wonderful, then, when love can cover a multitude of sins, all sins, and when nothing else can do so, and when by doing so such evils would be avoided and such glorious results secured, that the apostle should use such urgency of persuasion, and call on Christians "above all things to have fervent charity," or to have charity fervent, "among themselves?"

I shut up this part of the discourse by quoting a few passages of Scripture, in which the cultivation of brotherly Christian love is pressed on Christians, praying that the Holy Spirit, who is the Spirit of love, would write them on our hearts, and put them in our inward parts. "A new commandment," says the Master, "a new commandment I have given unto you, That ye love one another; as I have loved you, that ye also love one another. By this shall all men know that ye are my disciples, if ye have love one to another." "Be kindly affectioned one towards another in brotherly love," says one of his holy apostles, " with all lowliness of mind, forbearing one another in love; endeavouring to keep the unity of the Spirit in the bond of peace. The fruit of the Spirit is love, peace, long-suffering, gentleness, goodness"—that is, kindness—"meekness. Live in the Spirit, walk in the Spirit. Grieve not the Holy Spirit of God. Let all bitterness, and wrath, and anger, and clamour, and evil-speaking, be put away from you, with all malice; and be kind one to another, tender-hearted, forgiving one another, even as God for Christ's sake hath forgiven you. Be followers of God as dear children, and walk in love, as Christ also hath loved us. Put on as the elect of God, holy and beloved, bowels of mercies, kindness, humbleness of mind, long-suffering; forbearing one another, and forgiving one another, if any man have a quarrel against any: even as Christ forgave you, so also do ye." "Ye are taught of God to love one another." "The end of the commandment is charity." "Follow after love, patience, meekness." "Let brotherly love continue." "The wisdom that cometh from above," says another apostle, "is first pure, then peaceable, gentle, and easy to be entreated, full of mercy and good fruits, without partiality, and without hypocrisy." "Seeing ye have purified yourselves," says a third apostle, "in obeying the truth through the Spirit unto unfeigned love of the brethren, see that ye love one another with a pure heart fervently. Be of one mind, having compassion one of another; love as brethren." "He," says a fourth, who had a very large measure of the spirit of his Master,—"he that saith he is in the light, and hateth his brother, is in the darkness even until now. He that loveth his brother abideth in the light, and there is no occasion of stumbling in him. Whosoever loveth not his brother, is not of God. We know that we have passed from death to life, because we love the brethren. Whosoever hateth his brother, is a murderer. Hereby perceive we the love of God, that he laid down his life for us; and we ought to lay down our lives for the brethren. My little children, let us not love in word, neither in tongue, but in deed and in truth. This is his commandment, That we believe in his Son Jesus Christ, and love one another, as he gave us commandment. Beloved, let us love one another: for love is of God; and every one that loveth is born of God, and knoweth God. He that loveth not, knoweth not God; for God is love. Herein is love, not that we loved God, but that he loved us, and sent his Son to be the propitiation for our sins. Beloved, if God so loved us, we ought also to love one another. If a man say, I love God, and hate his brother, he is a liar; for he who loveth not his brother whom he hath seen, how can he love God whom he hath not seen? And this commandment have we of him, That he who loveth God love his neighbour also." That we should love one another: this is the commandment which we have received from the beginning, that we should walk in it.[1]

My beloved brethren, "if ye know these things, happy are ye if ye do them." We have much cause to be thankful for that measure of the spirit of love which our Father has been pleased to shed on us as a congregation, through

---

[1] John xiii. 34, 35; Rom. xii. 10; Eph. iv. 3; Gal. v. 22, 25; Eph. iv. 30-32, v. 1, 2; Col. iii. 12; 1 Thess. iv. 9; 1 Tim. i. 5, vi. 11; Heb. xiii. 1; James iii. 17; 1 Pet. i. 22, iii. 8; 1 John ii. 9, 11, iii. 14-16, 23, iv. 7, 11, 20, 21; 2 John 5.

Christ Jesus, and for that peace which is springing out of it. Let us carefully guard against whatever may cool our love or break our harmony. Let us all seek to be kept near Christ, that we may be kept near each other; and let us pray that our love to our Lord, to one another, to all the saints, to all men, "may abound yet more and more in knowledge and in all judgment," and may become more and more effectual in producing personal and mutual edification, and in promoting the prosperity and extension of the kingdom which is not of this world, making us to be of one mind—his mind, of one heart—his heart; a mind all light, a heart all love.

II. THE MANIFESTATION OF BROTHERLY LOVE.

Let us now proceed to the consideration of the apostle's injunction and recommendation of the manifestation of Christian brotherly love. The fervent love which they were to cherish among themselves was to be manifested in performing kind offices to each other as men, and in promoting the spiritual interests of each other as Christians. They were to employ their worldly property in the first of these manifestations of brotherly love, and their spiritual gifts in the second; and the grand motive influencing them in both was to be, that they were stewards, and ought to be good stewards of the manifold grace of God; and "that God in all things might be glorified through Jesus Christ." Let us attend, then, in succession to these two enjoined manifestations of Christian brotherly love, and to the powerful motives by which both are enforced. "Use hospitality one to another, without grudging. As every man hath received the gift, even so minister the same one to another, as good stewards of the manifold grace of God. If any man speak, let him speak as the oracles of God; if any man minister, let him do it as of the ability which God giveth; that God in all things may be glorified through Jesus Christ: to whom be praise and dominion for ever and ever. Amen."

§ 1. *Christians are to manifest brotherly love by employing their property for each other's good as men, as in ungrudging hospitality.*

We observe, then, in the first place, that Christians are to manifest the fervent love which they have among themselves, by employing their worldly property in performing kind offices to each other as men. Of these kind offices we have a specimen in the ungrudging hospitality which is here enjoined: "Use hospitality one to another, without grudging."

The habit of inviting in considerable numbers to our houses and tables, neighbours, acquaintances, and friends, in rank equal or superior to ourselves, and giving them a sumptuous entertainment, is what in our times generally passes by the name of hospitality. Where God's good creatures are not abused, which they often are, as stimulants and gratifications to intemperate appetite, and when these entertainments are not so expensive or so frequent as to waste an undue proportion of our substance and time, and to interfere with the right discharge of the duties of family instruction and devotion, there is nothing wrong in them. I believe we may go a little further, and say that in this case they are fitted to serve a good purpose, in keeping up friendly intercourse among relations and friends.

But they are put out of their place altogether when they are considered as a substitute for the Christian duty of hospitality. It is plain that our Lord did not condemn such meetings, for we find him not unfrequently present at them; but he obviously looked on them as capable of being better managed and turned to more useful purposes than they commonly were among the Jews in his time. "When thou makest a dinner or a supper," said our Lord to one of the chief Pharisees who had invited him to his table, "call not thy friends, nor thy brethren, neither thy kinsmen, nor thy rich neighbours; lest they also bid thee again, and a recompense be made thee. But when thou makest a feast, call the poor, the maimed, the lame, the blind: and thou shalt be blessed; for they cannot recompense thee: for thou shalt be recompensed at the resurrection of the just."[1]

We are certainly not to consider these words of our Lord as a prohibition of convivial intercourse among equals, the entertaining on proper occasions in a suitable manner of our wealthy neighbours, friends, and relatives; but we are to understand that in doing so we are rather complying with an innocent and useful social usage than performing an important Christian duty; and that the proportion of our property devoted to feeding the poor should very much exceed that expended in feasting the rich. What are termed hospitable entertainments, are very generally manifestations of vanity and pride on the part of those who give them. In a very limited degree are they the real expression of even a very low form of benevolent regard to those to whom they are given. The expense at which they are made is not incurred from love to God, regard to his authority, or a wish to promote his glory. Reward from him is altogether out of the question; and the applause, or what is in some instances more relished still, the envy of others, and a similar banquet in return, are the appropriate and the wished-for recompense. It is deeply to be regretted that so many professors of Christianity are in this respect unduly conformed to the word, and lavish on these thankless and profitless entertainments sums which might so

[1] Luke xiv. 12-14.

easily be turned to so much better account in relieving the wants and adding to the comforts of the poor and destitute; or in promoting the glory of God and the highest interests of mankind, by diffusing "the knowledge of salvation through the remission of sins."

But the occasional entertainment of our acquaintances, whether poor or rich, however unobjectionably and even usefully conducted, is not the Christian duty which under the name of hospitality is here and in so many other passages of the New Testament recommended. Hospitality is kindness to strangers, to persons not generally resident in the same place with ourselves, to persons with whom we are not on habits of intimate acquaintanceship; and this kindness is manifested by bringing them to our houses, and furnishing them with suitable entertainment there.

We have this duty strikingly illustrated in the case of Abraham and of Lot, when they "entertained angels unawares." Nothing can be more beautifully simple than the inspired narrative: "And Abraham sat in the door of his tent in Mamre, in the heat of the day; and he lift up his eyes and looked, and, lo, three men stood by him: and when he saw them, he ran to meet them from the tent-door, and bowed himself toward the ground, and said, My lord, if now I have found favour in thy sight, pass not away, I pray thee, from thy servant. Let a little water, I pray you, be fetched, and wash your feet, and rest yourselves under the tree: and I will fetch a morsel of bread, and comfort ye your hearts; after that ye shall pass on: for therefore are ye come to your servant. And they said, So do as thou hast said. And Abraham hastened into the tent unto Sarah, and said, Make ready quickly three measures of fine meal, knead it, and make cakes upon the hearth. And Abraham ran unto the herd, and fetched a calf tender and good, and gave it unto a young man; and he hasted to dress it. And he took butter and milk, and the calf which he had dressed, and set it before them; and he stood by them under the tree, and they did eat." And when two of these illustrious strangers entered Sodom, "Lot, sitting in the gate, rose up to meet them; and bowed himself with his face toward the ground: and he said, Behold now, my lords, turn in, I pray you, into your servant's house, and tarry all night, and wash your feet, and ye shall rise up early, and go on your way. And when they said, Nay, but we will abide in the street all night, he pressed upon them greatly; and they turned in unto him, and entered into his house; and he made them a feast, and did bake unleavened bread, and they did eat."[1] This was ancient hospitality.

In the same spirit we find Jethro saying to his daughters, in reference to the stranger who had assisted them in watering their flocks, "And where is he? why is it that ye left the man? call him, that he may eat bread."[2]

An instance of this virtue, not less interesting, is to be found in the case of the aged "working man" of Gibeah: "Behold, there came an old man from his work out of the field at even. And when he had lifted up his eyes, he saw a wayfaring man in the street of the city: and the old man said, Whither goest thou? and whence comest thou? And he said unto him, We are passing from Bethlehem-Judah toward the side of Mount Ephraim; from thence am I: and I went to Bethlehem, but I am now going to the house of the Lord; and there is no man that receiveth me into his house. Yet is there both straw and provender for our asses; and there is bread and wine also for me, and thine handmaid, and for the young man with thy servant: there is no want of anything. And the old man said, Peace be with thee: howsoever, let all thy wants lie upon me; only

[1] Gen. xviii. 1-8, xix. 1-3.   [2] Ex. ii. 18-20.

lodge not in the street. So he brought him into the house, and gave provender to the asses; and they washed their feet, and did eat and drink."[1]

Kindness to strangers was not only included in the second great command, "Thou shalt love thy neighbour as thyself," but was the subject of express legislation in the Mosaic code. "If a stranger sojourn with thee in your land, ye shall not vex him. But the stranger that dwelleth with you shall be unto you as one born among you, and thou shalt love him as thyself; for ye were strangers in the land of Egypt: I am the Lord thy God. The Levite, because he hath no part nor inheritance with thee, the stranger, and the fatherless, and the widow, which are within thy gates, shall come, and shall eat and be satisfied," at the feast made on the tithe of the increase being set apart, at the end of every third year, "that the Lord thy God may bless thee in all the works of thine hand which thou doest."[2]

In the New Testament, a disposition to entertain strangers is represented as a necessary qualification of a Christian bishop. He must be "given to hospitality," "a lover of hospitality;" and it is mentioned as one of the characteristics of "the widow indeed," that she has "lodged strangers, and washed the saints' feet." And Christians generally are expected to be "given to hospitality," and not to be "forgetful to entertain strangers."[3]

Nor is the duty only enjoined in the New Testament; it is also exemplified. When Lydia was baptized, "she besought Paul and his companions," strangers in Philippi, "saying, If ye have judged me faithful to the Lord, come into my house and abide there; and she constrained them." Mnason from Cyprus, "the old disciple," entertained Paul

[1] Judg. xix. 16-21. [2] Ex. xxii. 21, xxiii. 9; Lev. xix. 33.
[3] 1 Tim. iii. 2; Tit. i. 8; 1 Tim. v. 10; Rom. xii. 13.

and his associates in Jerusalem. Gaius, at Corinth, was so remarkable for his hospitality, that Paul calls him his host, and the host of the whole church; and Philemon refreshed the bowels of the saints, and prepared Paul a lodging.[1]

There can be no doubt that Christians are bound to exercise kindness to strangers generally, though they should not belong to the Christian society. In every way in their power, they ought to " do good to all men, as they have opportunity;" but it is quite plain that the injunction before us has an especial reference to " the household of faith :" " Use hospitality *among yourselves.*" When Christians in the course of their ordinary business went from home, as the means for accommodating strangers were not at all so abundant as in modern times, their brethren in the countries or cities they visited were expected to minister to their wants and convenience. " I commend unto you Phebe, our sister," says the apostle to the church at Rome, not only " that ye receive her in the Lord, as becometh saints," that is, admit her to fellowship with you in the ordinances of religion, but also " that ye assist her in whatsoever business she hath need of you; for she hath been a succourer of many, and of myself also;"[3] that is, Be hospitable to her who has been hospitable to me and many others.

Christians driven from their homes by persecution, were those who had the strongest claims on the hospitality of their more favoured brethren; and next to, or it may be equal to, their claim, was that of those who had devoted their lives to the service of Christ among the heathen. It is in reference to them that the Apostle John speaks to the beloved Gaius: " Beloved, thou doest faithfully," or thou actest the part of a believer, " whatsoever thou doest to the brethren, and to strangers; which have borne witness of

[1] Acts xvi. 14, 15, xxi. 16; Rom. xvi. 23; Philem. 7, 22.
[2] Rom. xvi. 1, 2.

thy charity before the church; whom if thou bring forward on their journey after a godly sort, thou shalt do well: because that for his name's sake they went forth, taking nothing of the Gentiles. We therefore ought to receive such, that we might be fellow-helpers to the truth."[1]

The abundant accommodation which the habits of modern times have secured for strangers sojourning for a season from home, and the extent to which movement from place to place now prevails, makes hospitality, in the same sense and in the same measure as in the primitive times, unnecessary, and indeed impracticable. But Christian morality in its spirit is for all countries and for all ages. It is, like its Author, unchanged and unchangeable. It is a proof that love has waxed cold when Christians are not disposed to pay kind attention to their brethren from other places, who have no claim on their attention but that they are "one with them in Christ."

The prevalence of such an inhospitable spirit is in more ways than one a proof that the purity of Christian communion in these last days has declined from its primitive standard; and it has often seemed to me a token that things are not as they should be among us, when Christians from foreign lands, agents of our christianly benevolent institutions, prosecuting their objects, and office-bearers of the various Christian churches visiting our large cities on business connected with the maintenance and extension of the kingdom of Christ, in so many instances at an expense they can often ill afford, have to take up their abodes for a few days, it may be for a few weeks, in houses of public accommodation, instead of finding an Abraham, a Lot, a Jethro, an old man of Gibeah, a Lydia, a Gaius, or a Mnason, to entertain them; and have sometimes cause to complain, that but for meeting some of the leading men in

[1] 3 John 5-8. See note A.

public, in the prosecution of their objects, they leave those cities as little acquainted with their Christian inhabitants as when they entered them.

Surely Christians should not be behind the Jews in respect to religious hospitality. At the great national Jewish festivals, hospitality was liberally practised so long as national identity existed. On these occasions no inhabitant of Jerusalem considered his house his own. Every house swarmed with strangers, though even this unbounded hospitality could not find accommodation in the houses for all who stood in need of it, and a large proportion of visitors had to be content with such shelter as tents could afford.

The neglected Christian strangers are not the only, are not the principal, sufferers. In receiving *them*, we might have "received angels unawares;" and we should not forget who it is who will one day say, "I was a stranger, and ye took *me* in : I was a stranger, and ye took *me* not in;" and who, when the questions shall be put, When saw we thee a stranger, and took thee in? when saw we thee a stranger, and took thee not in? shall answer, "Inasmuch as ye did it to the least of these my brethren, ye did it to me : Inasmuch as ye did it not to one of the least of these my brethren, ye did it not unto me."[1]

Using hospitality is but one out of many ways in which brotherly kindness is to be manifested in employing worldly substance in performing offices of kindness to our fellow-Christians. The Christian, according to his ability, must be "eyes to the blind, feet to the lame, and a father to the afflicted poor." The Christian law of love confirms the benignant statutes of the Mosaic code : " If thy brother be waxen poor, and fallen in decay with thee, then thou shalt relieve him; yea, though he be a stranger, or a sojourner. Ye shall not rule over one another with rigour. If there

[1] Matt. xxv. 35-46.

be among you a poor man, one of thy brethren, thou shalt not harden thy heart, nor shut thine hand from thy poor brother: but thou shalt open thy hand wide unto him. Beware lest thine eye be evil against thy poor brother, and thou givest him nought, and he cry unto the Lord against thee, and it be sin unto thee: thou shalt surely give him, and thine heart shall not be grieved when thou givest to him. Thou shalt open thine hand wide unto thy brother, to thy poor, and thy needy, in thy land." "If a brother have this world's goods, and see his brother in need," he must not "shut up his bowels of compassion from him;" he must not be contented with saying, Be ye warmed and filled; he must "love not in word, nor in tongue, but in deed and in truth;" he must "give him those things which are needful to the body;" and though community of property is by no means required by the Christian law, though there is no sufficient reason for thinking that it prevailed as a matter of necessity or obligation even in the primitive times,[1] yet where the spirit of primitive Christianity prevails, wherever "the disciples are of one mind and of one heart," they will in effect have "all things common," "doing good" to one another and "to all men as they have opportunity," and valuing worldly property chiefly as affording the means of glorifying God, and promoting the happiness of our fellow-men, and still more our fellow-Christians.

The particular form and measure of hospitality, and other kindred offices of kindness, must depend on circumstances. It must be " as God has prospered us," and " as we have opportunity." It is well observed by Leighton, that " the great straitening of hands in these things is more from the straitness of hearts than of means. A large heart with a

[1] *Vide* Mosheimii "Commentatio" "de vera natura Communionis Bonorum in Ecclesia Hierosolymitana." Diss. ad Hist. Ecclesiast. pertin. Vol. ii. pp. 14, etc.

little estate will do much with cheerfulness and little noise; while hearts glued to the poor riches they possess, or rather are possessed by, can scarce part with anything till they be pulled from all."

In whatever measure these deeds of kindness are done, it is essential that they all possess the quality which the apostle requires in hospitality, that they be " without grudging." " All things" of this kind are to be done " without murmurings." " Every man, according as he hath purposed in his heart, so let him give," so let him act; " for God loveth a cheerful giver,"[1] a cheerful doer. Good offices reluctantly rendered lose more than half their value. It is only when they really embody love that they are acceptable to God; and it is only in the degree in which they appear to embody love, that they are gratifying to their objects. So much for the first way in which Christians are to manifest brotherly love, by employing their worldly property in performing offices of kindness to one another as men.

§ 2. *Christians are to manifest brotherly love, by employing their spiritual gifts for promoting one another's spiritual edification.*

The second way in which they are to manifest their brotherly love, is to employ their spiritual gifts for promoting one another's spiritual interests as Christians: " As every man hath received the gift, even so let them minister the same one to another, as good stewards of the manifold grace of God. If any man speak, let him speak as the oracles of God; if any man minister, let him do it as of the ability which God giveth."

The word " gift"[2] here, and generally in the apostolic epistles, signifies any endowment, it may be natural, or it

---

[1] 2 Cor. ix. 7. [2] Χάρισμα.

may be miraculous, influenced and guided by the Holy Spirit. "The grace of God"¹ is the same as "the gift," only it is descriptive of the aggregate of the gifts; and the endowment and the influence are viewed in the last case as given by God, in the first as enjoyed by man. This grace is termed "manifold,"² to mark the varied forms which the divine gifts, all of them expressive of grace, kindness, take in different individuals. Speaking of the supernatural spiritual gifts, the apostle says what is true of all spiritual gifts: "There are diversities of gifts, but the same Spirit; and there are differences of administration, but the same Lord; and there are diversities of operations, but it is the same God that worketh all in all; and the ministration of the Spirit is given to every man to profit withal."³

The church is viewed as a household, to the various members of which the Divine Master of the family has given various qualifications, by the exercise of which they are mutually to promote one another's improvement and happiness; and thus the improvement and happiness of the whole family is to be secured. These gifts, then, are not to be considered as conferred only or chiefly for the advantage of the individual on whom they are bestowed. They are intended for the good of the whole; and the gifted person is, in the exercise of his gift, not to act as an independent proprietor, seeking his own advantage, and doing what he wills with his own, but as a good steward, turning to the best account, according to the declared will of the Great Householder, a portion of His property, which the individual entrusted with it is expected to use not only for his own good, but for the good of all his brethren.

The meaning of the passage in our version is, I apprehend, somewhat obscured by an attempt to illustrate it. You will observe that the words, "Let him speak," and

---

[1] Χάριτος Θεοῦ.   [2] Ποικίλης.   [3] 1 Cor. xii. 4-6.

" let him do it," are in the italic character, indicating, as you are aware, that there are no corresponding words in the original, but that they are, in the estimation of the translators, necessary to bring out the sense in English; and if the tenth and eleventh verses are two distinct sentences, as they obviously supposed, some such supplement is necessary to bring any sense out of the first part of the latter of the verses; though to bring distinctly out the meaning our translators supposed to be in them, would have required a still larger supplement than that they have inserted. ' If any man speak the oracles of God, let him speak them *as* the oracles of God. If any man act the part of a minister or deacon, let him act the part of a minister, *as* of the ability which God giveth.' These are good advices; and it was only by attending to them that the gifted speakers or ministers could exercise the gift bestowed on them to the advantage of their brethren, and be good stewards of that portion of the manifold grace of God committed to their care.

I apprehend, however, that the two verses are not two sentences, but one, and that no supplement is necessary to bring out the full sense of the apostle. The words in the beginning of the eleventh verse are just an illustration, by examples, of the statement in the beginning of the tenth verse. " Speaking as the oracles of God," " ministering as of the ability which God has given," are just two of " the gifts" bestowed on individuals for the use of the church—two varieties of the " manifold grace of God," which the recipients were to employ " as good stewards." The words may be literally rendered, " According as every man has received the gift, let them minister the same to each other, as good stewards of the manifold grace of God: whosoever speaks, as the oracles of God; whosoever ministers, as of the ability which God hath given him." One man has received the gift of speaking as the oracles of God, the faculty of being useful in teaching and exhorting; he is an inspired teacher. Another has received the gift of ministry, the faculty of being useful in the management of the affairs of the spiritual society, in preserving order, collecting and managing its funds for supporting and extending the ordinances of Christianity, and for relieving the sick, the infirm, and the poor. Whatever faculty any Christian possesses of this kind, or of any other kind, is a gift received from Christ, for the purpose of edifying his body the church, is a portion of his "manifold grace" entrusted to the individual, to be managed faithfully and wisely for the purpose for which it is bestowed.

The passage before us receives illustration from some other passages in the apostolic epistles, which, though not in every respect parallel, obviously relate to the same subject. The first of these passages is to be found in the Epistle of the Apostle Paul to the Romans: "I say, through the grace given unto me, to every man that is among you, not to think of himself more highly than he ought to think; but to think soberly, according as God hath dealt to every man the measure of faith. For as we have many members in one body, and all members have not the same office, so we, being many, are one body in Christ, and every one members one of another. Having, indeed, gifts differing according to the grace given unto us;" as in the passage before us, " having gifts according to the manifold grace of God;" and the gifts spoken of in this passage seem to be precisely the same as those specified in our text, " whether prophecy or ministry."[1] The gift of prophecy seems to be the same thing as the gift enabling a man to "speak as the oracles of God," the gift which fitted for teaching. The gift of "ministry," mentioned in both cases, is the gift, the

[1] Rom. xii. 3-8.

qualification, or class of qualifications, which fit for administration; the first gift being to be exercised in "teaching and exhortation;" the second, in "giving, in ruling or presiding, and in showing mercy."

The second passage I refer to as fitted to throw light on our text, is in the First Epistle of the same apostle to the Corinthians. "Now concerning spiritual gifts, brethren, I would not have you ignorant. There are diversities of gifts, but the same Spirit. And there are differences of administration, but the same Lord. And there are diversities of operations, but it is the same God who worketh all in all. But the manifestation of the Spirit is given to every man to profit withal," that is, to employ for the benefit of his brethren, to use as a steward of the manifold grace of God. "For to one is given by the Spirit the word of wisdom; to another the word of knowledge by the same Spirit; to another faith by the same Spirit; to another the gifts of healing by the same Spirit; to another the working of miracles; to another prophecy; to another discerning of spirits; to another divers kinds of tongues; to another the interpretation of tongues: But all these worketh the selfsame Spirit, dividing to every man severally as he will."[1] The same general division of gifts fitting for teaching, and gifts fitting for administration, may be noticed here. To the first class belong "the word of wisdom, the word of knowledge, prophecy, divers kinds of tongues, and the interpretation of tongues;" to the second, the gifts of "healing and the discerning of spirits;" while the gifts of working miracles, and faith, which seems to mean supernatural confidence and boldness, were gifts which might be usefully employed both in teaching and in administration.

That the design of those various gifts was the mutual edification of Christians and the general advantage of the

[1] 1 Cor. xii. 1-11.

Church, is distinctly stated in what follows : " For as the body is one, and hath many members, and all the members of that body, being many, are one body; so also is Christ. For by one Spirit are we all baptized into one body, and have been all made to drink into one Spirit. For the body is not one member, but many. If the foot shall say, Because I am not the hand, I am not of the body; is it therefore not of the body ? And if the ear shall say, Because I am not the eye, I am not of the body; is it therefore not of the body ? If the whole body were an eye, where were the hearing? if the whole were hearing, where were the smelling? But now hath God set the members every one of them in the body as it hath pleased him. And if they were all one member, where were the body? And the eye cannot say to the hand, I have no need of thee; nor again the head to the feet, I have no need of you. God hath tempered the body together, that there should be no schism in the body; but that the members should have the same care one for another. And whether one member suffer, all the members suffer with it; or one member be honoured, all the members rejoice with it. Now ye are the body of Christ, and members in particular;" that is, every one individually a member of that body.[1]

The third passage peculiarly fitted to illustrate the text, is in the Epistle to the Ephesians. The apostle having exhorted the believers to endeavour to "keep the unity of the Spirit in the bond of peace,"—that is, just to " have fervent charity" among themselves, so that " the multitude of sins" might be covered,—goes on to state the manner in which they, being one body, were connected by having severally diverse gifts fitted and intended for the advantage of the body. "There is one body, and one Spirit, even as ye are called in one hope of your calling; one Lord, one

[1] 1 Cor. xii. 12-27.

faith, one baptism, one God and Father of all, who is above all, and through all, and in you all. But unto every one is given grace according to the measure of the gift of Christ. And he gave some, apostles; and some, prophets; and some, evangelists; and some, pastors and teachers; for the perfecting of the saints, for the work of the ministry, for the edifying of the body of Christ: till we all come in the unity of the faith, and of the knowledge of the Son of God, unto a perfect man, unto the measure of the stature of the fulness of Christ: that we henceforth be no more children, tossed to and fro, and carried about by every wind of doctrine, by the sleight of men and cunning craftiness, whereby they lie in wait to deceive; but, speaking the truth in love, may grow up into him in all things, which is the head, even Christ: from whom the whole body fitly joined together and compacted by that which every joint supplieth, according to the effectual working in the measure of every part, maketh increase of the body, unto the edifying of itself in love."[1]

Viewed in the light of these passages, there is no difficulty in perceiving what are the great principles which our text involves. They are these: that God by Jesus Christ, through the Holy Spirit, communicates to his Church, in manifestation of his sovereign, undeserved, distinguishing favour, those gifts that are necessary to its prosperity as a society, and to the improvement and happiness of its individual members; that this is not done by giving to every member the same gifts, far less an equal measure of the same gifts; that the gifts are manifold or various, suited to serve different purposes, and communicated, too, in diversified measure to different individuals; that these gifts are all communicated for the purpose of being exercised; that the design of these exercises is not only, or so much,

[1] Eph. iv. 3-16.

the advantage of the gifted individual as that of the body at large; and finally, that in the exercise of his gift every person ought to consider himself as a steward who must be faithful, managing the property of another for the specific purposes for which he has been entrusted with it.

He who neglects the gift that is in him is an unprofitable servant. He who converts it into a means of gaining selfish objects, the gratification of his own private tastes, or the purposes of interest or ambition, instead of devoting it to the edification of his brethren, is an unfaithful servant. He who, instead of cultivating and exercising his own gift, attempts to exercise a gift he has not received, and in this way to occupy a field which he is not fitted, and others are fitted, to occupy, is an unwise servant.

These observations are applicable to spiritual gifts, according to the definition already given of them, whether supernatural or not, and whether connected with official station in the Church or not. The reference in the text, as well as in the parallel passages, seems to be to gifts, probably supernatural, connected with the two offices of teaching and ministry, of which all the offices in the primitive Church seem to be represented as varieties; and the command is, of course, to be viewed as addressed primarily to those Christians who occupy official situations in the Church.

The man who, in consequence of a gift conferred on him, and a call addressed to him, " speaks as the oracles of God," officially teaches the doctrines and laws of Christ Jesus, that man is to exercise his gift and perform the duties of his office, not in the way most fitted to gratify his own particular taste, or promote his own reputation for learning, ingenuity, and eloquence, but in the way most fitted for promoting the increase of the Church in knowledge and faith, and holiness and comfort; and if he has a peculiar gift, he is bound especially to cultivate and exercise that gift, whether it be for exposition or exhortation, for the establishment of truth or the exposure of error, for warning the unruly or comforting the afflicted. On the other hand, he who, in consequence of a gift conferred on him and a call addressed to him, "ministers of the ability that God has given," in presiding, superintending, administering the laws of Christ's Church, managing the charities of the Church, performing all the offices indicated by the terms ruling, giving, showing mercy, ought to exercise his gift and perform the duties of his office, not to secure personal influence, to gratify personal vanity, or to promote personal interest, but to advance the great interests of the Church as a spiritual body, and of the individuals constituting its members.

But the *principle* in the text reaches beyond the limits of official station; it is applicable to every individual member of the Church. Every member has a gift; and that gift, whatever it be, is to be exercised not only for his own advantage, but for that of his brethren, as God gives him opportunity. Every Christian is to look not only at his own things, but at the things of others. Christians are to work out each other's salvation, as well as each man his own. Indeed, there is reason to think that that is the reference of the passage in the Epistle to the Philippians now alluded to. Brother is to teach brother. They are to "exhort one another daily;" they are to "bear one another's burdens;" they are to "look diligently, lest any man fail of the grace of God." In the use of the gifts of the private members of a church, wisdom is necessary as well as profitable to direct; but without at all interfering with the peculiar duties or intruding into the peculiar province of official teaching and rule, there is abundant room for the exercise of the gift of each to the common benefit of all;

and there is, questionless, something wanting, something wrong, in all ecclesiastical constitutions which do not, by the regular employment of the gifts of individuals, provide for the common good of all the members of the body of Christ. "I desire none," says the devout prelate so often referred to, "to leap over the bounds of their calling, or rules of Christian prudence, in their converse; yea, this were much to be blamed; but I fear lest unwary hands, throwing on water to quench that evil, have let some of it fall by, upon those sparks that should rather have been stirred and blown up."

§ 3. *Motives to these two manifestations of Christian love.*

Enough has been said in illustration of the duty of the manifestation of Christian love, in the two forms prescribed in the passage before us. Let us say a word or two on the MOTIVES by which the duty is enforced.

There is a motive, and a powerful one, implied in the words, "as good stewards of the manifold grace of God." Neither the temporal goods nor the spiritual gifts of Christians are their own property. Both have been given them, and given not to serve selfish but public ends. They were talents to be traded with, not so much to enrich the individual as to enlarge and improve the Master's property. If they neglect to use them for this purpose, they are unprofitable servants, they waste their Lord's money. An active, wise, faithful use of these gifts, is necessary to their being good stewards. Christians holding office in the Church, and indeed all Christians, should often remember that they must give an account of their stewardship, for they must not always be stewards; and if they do not attend to the command in the text, the account cannot be given in with joy, but with grief, which will be unprofitable to them; whereas, if they do apply their gift, however limited, honestly to its appropriate purpose, their labour shall not be in vain in the Lord. The cordial welcome and its joyful results shall be theirs: "Well done, good and faithful servant, enter thou into the joy of thy Lord." "Thinkest thou," says Archbishop Leighton, "that thy wealth, or power, or wit, is thine, to do with as thou wilt, to engross to thyself either to retain as useless or to use, to hoard and wrap up, or to lavish out; according as thy humour leads thee? No! All is given as to a steward, wisely and faithfully to lay up and lay out, not only the outward estate and common gifts of mind, but even saving grace, which seems most appropriated for thy private good, yet is not wholly for that. Even thy graces are for the good of thy brethren."

The great motive, however, urged by the apostle for manifesting Christian love is, "that in all things God may be glorified through Christ Jesus." In the Christian economy "all things are of God," and all things are "by Christ Jesus." The Christian Church is the new creation; the work of the word and Spirit of God, as was the first creation. Every true member of it is "created anew in Christ Jesus;" and of it, still more emphatically than of the holy nation, which was its type, may it be said, "This people hath He formed for himself." They ought, then, to show forth his praise. When Christians manifest their love to one another in the way enjoined in the text, both the individual improvement of the members and the general spiritual prosperity of the Church as a body, are promoted. Holiness and happiness are diffused. The wisdom, the power, the holiness, and the benignity of God, in the glorious economy of grace, of which the spiritual society, "the Church," is an important element, are illustriously displayed. His authority is visibly acknowledged, his object is visibly gained, when Christians live altogether in holy love. On the other hand, when Christian love is not maintained and manifested, God is dishonoured. A false view is given of his character; and his holy name is blasphemed among the unbelievers, through the unworthy conduct of those calling themselves his people. The taunt is a bitter one, when Christians act a part unworthy their character, 'See how these Christians bite and devour one another! These are the lights of the world! These are the salt of the earth! This is Christianity, and these are Christians!'

A regard to the glory of God, especially as manifested through the mediation of Christ, is the master principle of every true Christian; and it is his prevailing desire that "whether he eat, or drink, he may do all to the glory of God." No motive, then, can be conceived better adapted than this to induce Christians carefully to cultivate, habitually to manifest, brotherly love: without this God cannot be glorified, nay, he must be dishonoured by them; and just in the degree in which they attend to these duties, do they answer the design of their high and holy vocation—the " showing forth the praises of him who hath called them from darkness to light;" the being " to the praise of the glory of him who hath made them accepted in the beloved," whose they are, whom they are bound to serve; " of whom, and through whom, and to whom are all things."

The apostle concludes his exhortation and enforcement of the maintenance and manifestation of brotherly love, by a solemn doxology: "To whom be praise and dominion for ever and ever." If we look merely at the words, it may be doubted whether this ascription of divine honours has a reference to God the Father, or to Jesus Christ. There can be no doubt, that there are similar ascriptions of divine honours to our Lord Jesus in other parts of the New Testament; and that, as He and the Father are one, it is most meet "that all should honour the Son as they honour the Father." At the same time, though Jesus Christ be the nearest antecedent, God the Father is the subject of the preceding statement; and an ascription of divine praise and dominion to HIM seems most naturally to rise out of that statement. It is as if the apostle had said: Seek, by the maintenance and manifestation of brotherly love, to glorify God; for he is worthy of all glory. Praise and dominion are his proper due.

"It is," says Leighton, "most reasonable, his due as God the author of all, not only of all supervenient good, but even of being itself; seeing that all is from him, that all be for him. 'For of him, and through him, and to him, are all things: to whom be glory for ever.' As it is most just, so it is most sweet, to aim at this, that God be glorified. It is the alone worthy design that fills the heart with heavenliness, and with a heavenly calmness; and sets it above the clouds and storms of those passions that disquiet low, self-seeking minds. He is a miserable unsettled wretch who cleaves to himself and forgets God; is perplexed about his credit, and gain, and base ends, which are often broke; and when he attains them, yet they and he shortly perish together. When his estate, or designs, or any comforts fail, how can he look to him whom he looked so little at before? May not the Lord say, 'Go to the gods whom thou hast served, and let them deliver and comfort thee?' Seek comfort from thyself, as thou didst all for thyself. But he that hath resigned himself, and is all for God, may confidently say, 'The Lord is my portion.' This is the Christian's aim, to have nothing in himself, nor in anything but in this tenure: all for the glory of my God,—my estate, family, abilities, my whole self, all I have and am. And as the love of God grows in the heart, this purpose grows;

the higher the flame rises, the purer it is: the eye is daily more upon it; it is oftener in the mind in all actions than before. In common things, the very works of our callings, our very refreshments, to eat, and drink, and sleep, are all for this end, and with a particular aim at it as much as may be. Even the thought of it is often renewed throughout the day, and at times generally applied to all our ways and employments. It is that elixir which turns all into gold, the ordinary works into sacrifices, 'with which God is well pleased.'"

The introduction of this doxology in the midst of his exhortation is a beautiful exemplification of the apostle's piety. We have not a few instances of the same kind in the epistolary writings of his "beloved brother Paul." It were a pleasing proof that we had "obtained like precious faith" with the apostles, and been baptized into the Spirit which was shed forth on them so abundantly, were there in our hearts a fountain of affectionate esteem, grateful admiration, adoring awe of the divine holiness, benignity, and majesty, always ready to gush forth in a stream of praise; " a well of living water, springing up to eternal life." It were indeed, as the devout Archbishop says, "a high and blessed condition to be in all estates in some willing readiness to bear a part in this song, to acknowledge the greatness and goodness of our God, and to wish him glory in all. What are the angels doing? This is their business, without interruption, without weariness, without end. And seeing we hope to partake with them, we should even now, though in a lower key, and not so tunably neither, yet as we may, begin it; and upon all occasions our hearts should often be following in this sweet note or offering at it, 'To him be glory and dominion for ever.'"

Note A. p. 116.

"The care of providing for the support and maintenance of strangers, of the poor, the sick, the old, of widows and orphans, and of those in prison on account of their faith, devolved on the whole Church. This was one of the main purposes for which the collection of voluntary contributions, in the assemblies convened for public worship, was instituted; and the charity of individuals, moreover, led them to emulate each other in the same good work. In particular, it was considered as belonging to the office of the Christian matron to provide for the poor, for the brethren languishing in prison, and to show hospitality to strangers. The hindrance occasioned to this kind of Christian activity, is reckoned by Tertullian among the disadvantages of a mixed marriage. 'What heathen,' says he, 'will suffer his wife to go about from one street to another, to the houses of strangers, to the meanest hovels indeed, for the purpose of visiting the brethren? What heathen will allow her to steal away into the dungeon to kiss the chain of the martyr? If a brother arrive from abroad, what reception will he meet in the house of *the stranger?* If an alms is to be bestowed, storehouse and cellar are shut fast.' On the other hand, he counts it among the felicities of a marriage contracted between Christians, that the wife is at liberty to visit the sick and relieve the needy, and is never straitened or perplexed in the bestowment of her charities. Nor did the active brotherly love of each community confine itself to what transpired in its own immediate circle, but extended itself also to the wants of the Christian communities in distant lands. On urgent occasions of this kind, the bishops made arrangements for special collections. They appointed fasts; so that what was saved, even by the poorest of the flock, from their daily food, might help to supply the common wants."—TERTULL. ad uxorem, ii. 1, 8; de jejunio, c. xii.—NEANDER, Gen. Hist. vol. i. pp. 347–8.

DISCOURSE XX.

DIRECTORY TO CHRISTIANS SUFFERING FOR THEIR RELIGION.

"Beloved, think it not strange concerning the fiery trial which is to try you, as though some strange thing happened unto you: but rejoice, inasmuch as ye are partakers of Christ's sufferings; that, when his glory shall be revealed, ye may be glad also with exceeding joy. If ye be reproached for the name of Christ, happy are ye; for the Spirit of glory and of God resteth upon you: on their part he is evil spoken of, but on your part he is glorified. But let none of you suffer as a murderer, or as a thief, or as an evil-doer, or as a busybody in other men's matters. Yet if any man suffer as a Christian, let him not be ashamed; but let him glorify God on this behalf. For the time is come that judgment must begin at the house of God: and if it first begin at us, what shall the end be of them that obey not the gospel of God? And if the righteous scarcely be saved, where shall the ungodly and the sinner appear? Wherefore, let them that suffer according to the will of God, commit the keeping of their souls to him in well-doing, as unto a faithful Creator."—1 PET. iv. 12-19.

FROM many passages in this epistle, it is obvious that they to whom it was addressed were in adverse circumstances. They had already been exposed to suffering in a variety of forms, in consequence of their profession of the faith of Christ. "They were in heaviness, through manifold temptations;" and it is more than once not obscurely intimated, that the trials in which they had been involved were but the forerunners of more severe persecutions, to which ere long they might expect to be subjected. It was with them a dark and cloudy day, and their sky did not appear to be clearing. The evils they had experienced seemed to be but the prelusive drops of an approaching tempest. The paragraph which is to form the subject of our discourse at this time, contains an inspired directory for those persecuted Christians, amid the increasing difficulties of their situation. The injunctions contained in this inspired directory seem all reducible to the four following: 'Be not astonished at your sufferings;' 'Be not depressed by your sufferings;' 'Be not ashamed of your sufferings;' and, 'Persevering in well-doing, commit the keeping of your souls to God under your sufferings.' Let us shortly attend to these four injunctions in their order, as explained and enforced by the apostle.

I. BE NOT ASTONISHED AT YOUR SUFFERINGS.

The first direction given by the apostle to his suffering brethren is, 'Be not astonished at your sufferings.' "Beloved, think it not strange concerning the fiery trial which is to try you, as though some strange thing had happened to you."

The course of suffering on which these Christians had entered, is figuratively described as a fire or burning, intended to try them. The allusion is to the intense heat of the furnace of the refiner, in which he tests the genuineness and increases the purity of the precious metals. The figurative representation is obviously designed to indicate at once the great severity and the important purposes of the afflictions on which these Christians might reckon with certainty as awaiting them.

These afflictions were to be severe. They are compared, not to the heat of the sun, or of an ordinary fire, but to the concentrated heat of the refiner's furnace; and we know, from authentic history respecting the persecutions to which the primitive Christians were exposed, that this figure does not at all outrun the reality. Calumnious misrepresentation and spoiling of goods, stripes and imprisonments, weariness and painfulness, hunger and thirst, watchings and fastings, cold and nakedness, were to them common trials. The apostle's description of the Maccabean martyrs is equally applicable to the primitive Christians. " Some of them were tortured" in every form which malignant ingenuity could devise; " others had trial of cruel mockings and scourgings, yea, moreover, of bonds and imprisonment: they were stoned, they were sawn asunder, were tempted, were slain with the sword: they wandered about in sheep-skins and goat-skins; being destitute, afflicted, tormented: they wandered in deserts, and in mountains, and in dens and caves of the earth."[1] Well did such sufferings deserve to be termed the burning, " the fiery trial."[2]

The figure is equally significant if we consider it as referring to the design of these sufferings. In this respect, too, they resembled the fire of the refiner's furnace. The design of its intense heat is to test and to purify the precious metals subjected to it. The design of their sufferings is to test the genuineness of profession and the power of principle; and, by separating the precious from the vile, to improve the character both of the Christian society, and of the Christian individuals of which it is composed.

It was not at all unnatural that the primitive Christians, when exposed to such sufferings, should not only feel them to be very painful, but reckon them to be very wonderful; that they should think ' it strange concerning the burning among them, as if some strange thing had happened to them.' Were not they "the children of God through faith in Christ Jesus;" the " sons and daughters of the Lord God Almighty?"[3] Did he not love them? Could he not protect them? Had he not wisdom enough to confound all the plans, power enough to restrain and frustrate all the

---

[1] Heb. xi. 36-38.   [2] Πύρωσις.   [3] Gal. iii. 26; 2 Cor. vi. 18.

efforts, of their enemies? Had he not promised to preserve them from all evil, and to bestow on them every blessing? Was it not strange, in these circumstances, that they should be exposed to suffering at all? doubly strange that they should be exposed to suffering for avowing the relation and performing their duty to him? strangest of all, that they should be exposed to *such* suffering when following such a course?

And if these sufferings seemed strange as coming from God, they must also have appeared strange as coming from men. They were no disturbers of the public peace, no invaders of private rights. They were " blameless and harmless, the sons of God without rebuke;"[1] rendering to all their due, nay, doing good to all as they had opportunity. Was it not strange that they should be the objects of the contempt and dislike of their fellow-citizens, and be treated by their rulers as if they had been egregious malefactors?

Yet, notwithstanding all this, there was abundant reason why the primitive Christians should not think their persecutions strange, however severe. No strange thing, indeed, happened to them. The spirit of Christianity is so directly opposed to the spirit of the world, that the wonder is, not that there has been so much persecution, but that there has not been more. But for the restraints of God's providence on the world, and on him who is its prince and god, Christianity and Christians had long ago been exterminated. " If they were of the world, the world would love its own; but because they were not of the world, even as HE who called them was not of the world, therefore the world hated them as it hated him."[2] Without an entire change in the spiritual character of the world, it could not have been otherwise. It would have been strange indeed if it had not

[1] Phil. ii. 15.   [2] John xv. 18.

hated them. No! "It is not strange that the malignant world should hate holiness, hate the light, hate the very shadow of it: the more the children of God walk like their Father and their home, the more unlike must they of necessity become to the world about them, and therefore become the very marks of their enmities and malice." "There is in the life of a Christian a convincing light, that shows the depravity of the works of darkness, and a piercing heat that scorches the ungodly, which stirs and troubles their consciences. This they cannot endure, and hence rises in them a contrary fire of wicked hatred; and hence the trials, the fiery trials, of the godly."[1]

Nor is this the only reason why Christians should not account sufferings for the cause of Christ, however severe, "strange." They are not only natural, so far as a wicked world is concerned, but they are necessary for them. "It is needful," as the apostle observes above,—"it is needful that ye for a season be in heaviness through manifold temptation." Such seasons of persecution are necessary to the Church as a body. During a period of comparative worldly prosperity, multitudes of worldly men find their way into the communion of the Church; and, just in the degree in which they have influence in it, unfit it for its great purposes both to those within its pale and those without it. A period of uninterrupted external prosperity, if it were not attended with such an effusion of divine influence as the world has never yet witnessed, would soon lead to such secularization of the Church as would destroy the distinction of the Church from the world; not by converting the world, but by perverting the Church; not by making the world Christian, but by making the Church worldly. It is needful that the great husbandman take the fan in his hand, that he may purge his floor, driving off the

[1] Leighton.

chaff, and bringing close together the good grain. "When tribulation for the word's sake ariseth," those who have "no root in themselves are offended," stumbled,—they "go away, and walk no more with Jesus" and his persecuted followers; and it is a good riddance; while, on the other hand, tribulation in the case of those who "have root in themselves," "works patience," endurance. It produces not apostasy, but perseverance.[1] For as persecution purifies the Church, so it improves her true members. They are called by it to a more vigorous exercise of all the principles of the new life; and it is a general law, that exercise invigorates. It is at once an indication of health, and a means of improving it. The Christian in the day of trial quits himself like a man, and becomes strong. His faith, his hope, his patience, his zeal, his humility, are increased exceedingly. "The trial of faith," by these afflictions, "is more precious than the trial of gold." Gold can never be so purified as to become incorruptible; but faith, strengthened by trial, becomes invincible, and will "be found to praise, and honour, and glory, at the appearing of Jesus Christ." Suffering for Christ, in some form and degree or other, seems to be essential to the formation of the Christian character; and that character has usually reached nearest to perfection in those who have had the largest share of that kind of trial.

Another reason why Christians should not think "the fiery trial" a strange thing is, that their Lord met with severe sufferings, "the contradiction of sinners against himself," and that all their brethren who had gone before them have also been severely afflicted. Should they think it strange to be led to heaven in the same road by which He and they had travelled? "The disciple is not above his master, nor the servant above his lord. If they have

[1] Matt. xiii. 6, 21; Rom. v. 3,—ὑπομονή.

persecuted me, they will persecute you." Such afflictions, too, were "fulfilled" in their brethren who had been in the world. Are they better than the apostles, who were " as gazing-stocks to the world, to angels, and to men ?"[1]

There is yet another reason why Christians should never think persecution for Christ's sake, however severe, a strange thing. It is something they should be prepared for; for they have been very plainly taught that they may assuredly expect it in some form or other. " To this they have been called." " In the world ye shall have tribulation." " Marvel not that the world should hate you." " If any man will be my disciple, let him deny himself," forsake all, "take up his cross, and follow me." " All who will live godly must," says the apostle, " suffer persecution." " Through much tribulation we must enter into the kingdom."[2]

Christians, then, in no age of the Church or the world, should count sufferings for the cause of Christ a strange thing. The primitive Christians were especially warned by our Lord, that the season which had arrived when Peter wrote this epistle, the period immediately preceding the destruction of Jerusalem, was to be to his followers a period of peculiarly severe trial. It is in reference to the sufferings of those times he says, " See that ye be not troubled. All these things must come to pass. Lo, I have told you before." The exhortation of Peter is very nearly parallel with that of his brother Paul, in an epistle written about the same time: " Let no man be moved by these afflictions, for yourselves know that ye are appointed thereunto."[3]

---

[1] John xv. 20 ; 1 Cor. iv. 9.
[2] John xvi. 33 ; Matt. xvi. 24 ; Mark viii. 34 ; Luke ix. 23 ; 2 Tim. iii. 12 ; Acts xiv. 22.
[3] Matt. xxiv. 6 ; 1 Thess. iii. 3.

II. BE NOT DEPRESSED BY YOUR SUFFERINGS.

The second direction given by the apostle to his brethren is, "Be not depressed by your sufferings." "Rejoice, inasmuch as ye are partakers of the sufferings of Christ; that, when his glory shall be revealed, ye may be glad also with exceeding joy. If ye be reproached for the name of Christ, happy are ye; for the Spirit of glory and of God resteth upon you: on their part he is evil spoken of (blasphemed), but on your part he is glorified."

In these words the apostle first calls on them generally not to be depressed by their sufferings for Christ, but, on the contrary, to rejoice in them. He gives at the same time very good reasons for his injunction, reasons applicable to all sufferings, of whatever kind, for the cause of Christ; and he then calls on them not to be depressed by a particular form of suffering, that of reproach, which is very much fitted to have this effect; and enforces this exhortation by a very powerful and appropriate motive.

The apostle calls on Christians, for two reasons, not to be depressed by, but to rejoice in, their sufferings for Christ, whatever form they might wear; whether loss of property, reputation, liberty, or life:—First, because, in enduring these sufferings, they are partakers of Christ's sufferings; and secondly, because their fellowship with Christ in his sufferings is, by the divine appointment, connected with fellowship with him in his enjoyments at the revelation of his glory.

1. Christians, in suffering for Christ, are "partakers of the sufferings of Christ." In all their afflictions Christians may be viewed as having fellowship with Christ. When they suffer, they are treading in his steps who was, by way of eminence, a sufferer,—" the man of sorrows and acquainted with grief;" and it is the communication of his

Spirit which enables them to bear their sufferings in the same temper in which he bore his. But there is a peculiar propriety in representing them, when suffering for their attachment to him, as being partakers of his sufferings. The sufferings they then endure are endured in the same cause in which his sufferings were endured—the cause of truth and righteousness, the cause of God's glory and man's happiness. They are inflicted on them just because they are like Him; and they who persecute them would, had they it in their power, persecute him as they persecute them. They stand in his place; they are his representatives. They are " in the world as he was in the world;" and are therefore treated by the world as he was treated by the world. " Therefore the world knoweth not," acknowledgeth not in their true character, "them, because it knew not," acknowledged not, " him" in his true character. They are so identified with him, that he considers what is done to them as done to Him. " He that touches them touches the apple of his eye." " Saul, Saul," said he from the opened heavens, " why persecutest thou ME?" And at last, from the throne of universal judgment, shall he say to those who have cruelly neglected or despitefully used his suffering people, " Inasmuch as ye did it not to one of the least of these my brethren, ye did it not to ME. Inasmuch as ye did it to one of the least of these, ye did it to ME."

Every true Christian, suffering in the cause of Christ, may say with the Apostle Paul, " I fill up that which is behind of the afflictions of Christ in my flesh."[1] We are not to suppose that our Lord left any sufferings to be endured by Paul, or any one else, as the expiation of the sins or the ransom of the souls of his people. These great objects were fully secured by his sufferings " in his own body," " the body of his flesh by death." On the cross, in

[1] Col. i. 24.

reference to them, he said, "It is finished." These sufferings were his personal burden. We partake of them, not in the way of supplementing them by our sufferings, but by becoming sharers of their precious fruits. They are accounted to us as if they had been ours; and we are acquitted, and justified, and saved by them, as a full satisfaction to the demands of the law on us as sinners. The endurance of these expiatory sufferings is something absolutely peculiar to him. We have, we can have, no part nor lot in that matter. The meaning of the apostle plainly is: 'I am so closely connected with Christ, that he regards those sufferings endured by me in his cause, as his sufferings in my body. I know there is a certain measure of such sufferings allotted to me, as to every other Christian. I have undergone already a part of those sufferings; and in the sufferings which I now undergo for the sake of you, Thessalonians, a part of his body, I rejoice to think that I am filling up what remains of the sufferings appointed me, and which I delight in thinking of as the sufferings of Christ in my body.' "The filling up spoken of by the apostle is not the supplementing Christ's personal sufferings, but it is the completing that share allotted to himself as one of the members of Christ—as sufferings which, from the intimacy of union between the head and the members, may be called *his* sufferings. Christ lived in Paul, spoke in Paul, wrought in Paul, suffered in Paul; and in a similar sense the sufferings of every Christian for Christ are the sufferings of Christ."

This is a view of suffering for Christ well fitted to prevent depression and to produce holy joy. "It seems obviously fit," as Leighton says, "that we should follow where our Captain led. It is not becoming that he should lead through rugged, thorny ways, and we pass about to get away through flowery meadows. As his natural body shared with his nead in suffering, so ought his mystical body with him who is their head."

And as this is fit, so it is pleasant. It is good, no less than becoming well. "It is a sweet, joyful thing, to be a sharer with Christ in anything. All enjoyments wherein he is not are bitter to a soul who loves him, and all sufferings with him are sweet. The worst things of Christ are more truly delightful than the best things of the world; his afflictions sweeter than their pleasures, his reproaches more glorious than their honours, and more rich than their treasures. Love delights in likeness and communion; not only in things otherwise pleasant, but in the hardest and harshest things which have not in them anything desirable, but only that likeness. So that this thought is very sweet to a heart possessed with this love. What does the world by its hatred and persecutions and revilings for Christ, but make me more like him, give me a greater share with him in that which he did so willingly undergo for me. 'When he was sought to be made a king, he escaped,' says Bernard," the last of the fathers; "'but when he was sought for the cross, he freely yielded himself.' And shall I shrink and creep back from what he calls me to suffer for his sake? Yea, even all my other troubles and sufferings I will desire to have stamped thus with this conformity to the sufferings of Christ, in the humble, obedient, cheerful endurance of them, and the giving up my will to my Father's. The following of Christ makes any way pleasant; his faithful followers refuse no march after him, be it through deserts, and mountains, and storms, and hazards that would affright self-pleasing, easy spirits. Hearts kindled and actuated by the Spirit of Christ, will follow him whithersoever he goeth."[1]

2. A second reason assigned by the apostle why perse-

[1] Leighton.

cuted Christians should not be depressed by, but rather rejoice in, their sufferings, is, that this fellowship with Christ in his sufferings is, by the divine appointment, connected with fellowship with him in his enjoyments at the revelation of his glory. "Ye are partakers of Christ's sufferings; that, when his glory shall be revealed, ye may be glad also with exceeding joy."

The glory of Christ is the transcendent personal excellence, and official dignity and authority, which belong to the God-man Mediator. Of that glory a partial manifestation is made in the word of the truth of the gospel, and in his administration of that universal empire which he possesses, as well as in his dispensations towards the Church as a body, and towards its individual members, with whom he stands connected in a relation so intimate and peculiar. By those who by his Spirit are led to understand and believe the gospel, and by its light to contemplate the dispensations of his kingdoms of providence and grace, this glory is partially apprehended; and whenever it is so, it casts all other glory into the shade. That which had glory has now no glory, by reason of the glory that excelleth. The Word, who was made flesh and dwelt among men, may be seen in his wondrous works as in a mirror; and all who in them behold his glory, acknowledge that it is a glory worthy of the only-begotten of the Father,[1] and that he is indeed full of grace and truth. And by the believing contemplation of this glory they themselves in their measure become glorious; they are changed into its likeness, made glorious by that which is glorious, converted by glory into glory.[2]

It is, however, but a dim reflection of his glory that reaches this dark earth. His glory, like himself, is "hid with God." The great body of men see it not at all, being destitute of the spiritual organs by which alone it can be

[1] ‘ΩΣ μονογενοῦς παρὰ πατρός. John i. 14.   [2] 2 Cor. iii. 18.

discerned; and even they who see most of it, see at best "through a glass," or by means of a mirror, "darkly;" "they know but in part, they understand but in part."

But this glory is not always to continue so imperfectly manifested in our world to its inhabitants. Out of his heavenly sanctuary he is yet to shine forth gloriously. His "glorious appearance," or the appearance of his glory, is "the blessed hope" of all who believe. At the close of the present order of things he will come "in his own glory, and in the glory of his Father, and in the glory of his holy angels." He will come "in clouds, and every eye shall see him." He will come "in flaming fire, to take vengeance on them that know not God, and that obey not the gospel; and to be glorified in his saints, and admired in all them that believe."[1] He will come to manifest the glories of his power, and wisdom, and righteousness, and grace, removing entirely and for ever the cloud of mystery which hangs over the divine character and dispensations, and manifesting himself at once in all the glories of untarnished holiness and inflexible justice, and infinite, omnipotent, all-wise benignity, as the righteous Judge and the all-accomplished Saviour.

This revelation at once of the glories of his righteousness and grace, shall be a source of the highest satisfaction to all his redeemed ones; and then shall be fully compensated all the privations and sacrifices and sufferings to which they have submitted for his name's sake. Then "shall they rejoice with exceeding joy." "In this last time," when the salvation to which in the present times they are kept by the power of God through faith shall be revealed, and in the revelation of which shall be revealed the glory of Christ the Saviour, "they shall rejoice with a joy that is unspeakable and full of glory."

[1] 2 Thess. i. 7-10.

And they shall have good cause thus to rejoice; for when He who is their life appears, is manifested, they shall also appear or be manifested in glory. His glorious appearing, and their manifestation as the sons of God, by their entering on full possession of all the privileges of divine sonship, shall be contemporaneous. He shall appear in glory, and they shall be "like him, seeing him as he is." "When the Son of man shall come in his glory, and all the holy angels with him, when he shall sit on the throne of his glory, and before him shall be gathered all nations," he will make those who have been partakers of his sufferings exceeding glad in the fellowship of his glory. Having reunited their glorified spirits to their once mortal but now immortal bodies, he shall place them at his right hand as his honoured friends, and shall say to them in the presence of the assembled universe of intelligent beings, "Come, ye blessed of my Father, inherit the kingdom prepared for you from the foundation of the world." And then "they shall go into life eternal;"[1] and "conquerors, more than conquerors," through his love, sit down with him on his throne, even as he, when he had overcome, sat down with his Father on his throne, and shall "reign in life" with him for ever and ever. Such are the blessings which await all the faithful at the coming of the Lord; and there is reason to conclude that the measure of the enjoyment and glory of individuals will correspond to the measure of labour and sufferings submitted to in his cause.

This is a consideration well fitted not only to prevent depression of mind under suffering however severe, but to fill the heart with holy triumph, and enable the Christian to glory in such tribulation as is connected with so glorious a hope, counting it indeed " all joy to be" for Christ's cause " brought into manifold temptations." Well, as the pious

[1] Matt. xxv. 31-46.

Archbishop says, may Christians " rejoice in the midst of all their sufferings, standing upon the advanced ground of the covenant of grace, and by faith looking beyond this moment, and all that is in it, to that day wherein the crown of everlasting joy, that diadem of beauty, shall be put upon their head, and when sorrow and mourning shall fly away. Oh, that blessed hope! How soon will this pageant of the world that men are gazing on, these pictures and fancies of pleasures and honours, falsely so called, vanish and give place to the real glory of the sons of God, where the blessed First-born among many brethren shall be seen appearing in full majesty, as the Only-begotten of the Father, and all his brethren with him, beholding and sharing his glory, having 'come out of great tribulation, and washed their robes and made them white in the blood of the Lamb.'" Believing that if we suffer with him it is that we may be glorified together with him, we cannot but " judge that the sufferings of the present time are not worthy to be compared with the glory that is to be revealed in us;" so that we may well rejoice amid these sufferings, especially as we know that "these light afflictions, which are but for a moment, are working out for us a far more exceeding and eternal weight of glory."[1] There is something more than mere sequence here. "We are partakers of his sufferings; that, when his glory is revealed, we may rejoice with exceeding joy."

Having thus enforced the general exhortation not to be depressed by, but to rejoice in, sufferings for Christ, of whatever kind, from a consideration of the nature of these sufferings, as sufferings in which they have fellowship with Christ, and of the design and certain issue of such sufferings, the bringing of them into the fellowship of the Saviour's glory and joy, the apostle next calls their atten-

[1] Rom. viii. 17, 18; 2 Cor. iv. 17, 18.

tion to a particular form of suffering, in its own nature peculiarly fitted to depress the mind, "reproach," and shows that even it is a proper ground not of depression, but of exultation. "If ye be reproached for the name of Christ, happy are ye,[1] for the Spirit of glory and of God resteth on you; on their part he is evil spoken of, but on your part he is glorified."

Reproach was one of the most common and most severe of the trials of the persecuted primitive Christians. And few things are more fitted to break the heart; as the Psalmist, in the person of the Messiah, says, "Reproach hath broken my heart; I am full of heaviness."[2] Their "names were cast out as evil." They were "accounted as the filth of the world, and the offscouring of all things;" and they were thus reproached for being Christ's,—for bearing his name, and professing his religion,—for believing its doctrines, for cherishing its hopes, for observing its institutions, for obeying its laws. On this account they were represented as despisers of the gods, enemies of the commonwealth, haters of mankind, the accomplices or the dupes of an impostor, deceived or deceivers, dreaming enthusiasts or designing villains.

Now, says the apostle, be not discouraged by all this contumely. If you are really—what these men call you—Christians, you are truly happy, and are possessed of a true inward honour and glory, of which all their malignant abuse can in no degree deprive you. "The Spirit of glory and of God resteth on you;" that is, the Spirit of glory, *even* the Spirit of God, resteth on you; or, the Spirit of God resteth on you as the Spirit of glory.

There can be no doubt that the reference here is to the

[1] Here, as at ch. iii. 14, there is an evident reference to the Sermon on the Mount. Matt. v. 11.
[2] Ps. lxix. 20.

Holy Ghost, personally the divine author of our salvation, so far as it is an inward transformation. The appellation, "the Spirit of glory," may be considered as equivalent to the glorious Spirit of our Lord Jesus Christ; as "the Lord of glory" means our glorious Lord Jesus Christ.[1] But it seems more probable that the Holy Spirit is here termed the Spirit of glory, to indicate that he is the author of true glory and honour. Unbelieving men reckoned the primitive Christians despicable and dishonourable, and called them so in their reproaches. But were they indeed so? No, by no means. The Spirit of God, who is the fountain of true honour, rested on them, and by his influence formed them to a character which was the proper object, not of contempt, but of approbation and admiration to all good and wise intelligent beings.

It is as if the apostle had said, 'You are really honourable, and your honour is not of a kind of which these reproaches can deprive you. They count you fools; but the Spirit of wisdom and good understanding rests on you, and makes you wise unto salvation : he gives you a sound mind, and makes you of good understanding. They count you weak, and contemn you for your imbecility in the sight of the Lord; but he makes you "strong in the Lord, and in the power of his might;" he is in you "the Spirit of power," as well as "of a sound mind." They reckon you mean, but he gives you true dignity and grandeur of character; he makes you "great in the sight of the Lord," and decks you with ornaments becoming your dignity as kings and priests unto God, even your Father. Is not the consideration of what he has made you more than sufficient to neutralize the painful effects of all that they can call you? If he has made you wise, what though they call you fools? If he has made you strong, what though they call you

[1] James ii. 1.

weak? If he has made you illustrious, what though they should represent you as despicable? His bearing witness with your spirits that you are indeed the sons of God, "and if sons then heirs, heirs of God and joint-heirs with Christ Jesus," is surely more than enough to counterbalance all their false and malignant reproaches.' Such seems to be the import of the motive which the apostle employs to induce Christians to rise above the disheartening influence of reproach for Christ, and even to rejoice in it. If you are Christians indeed, you have a real abiding honour, springing from the Spirit of God, who is the Spirit of glory resting on you, dwelling in you, which their reproaches can in no degree affect.

The meaning and reference of the concluding words of the 14th verse, "On their part he is evil spoken of, but on your part he is glorified," are somewhat doubtful. They may mean, what from their rendering our translators obviously supposed they did mean, This Spirit of glory which exists in you is evil spoken of, or blasphemed, by those men who reproach you for the name of Christ, who load you with abuse because you are Christians. He made you what you are as Christians, and in reproaching you they indeed blaspheme him. They who mock at Christians, as Christians, play at a dangerous game. The time is coming when the Son of God will say, "Inasmuch as ye did it to them, ye did it to me;" and the Spirit of God will say, 'In reproaching them you blasphemed me, in ridiculing my work you poured contempt on my person.' Let the men of the world take care. What they think but a jest, may prove a very serious affair. The Jews thought they were putting to death a poor unfriended Nazarene: it turned out that they crucified the Lord of glory. The enemies of vital Christianity may think they are only running down a set of wrongheaded enthusiasts: it may turn out they are coming very near the sin "that hath no forgiveness, neither in this world nor in that which is to come." It is as if the apostle had said, Their reproaches are more against the Spirit that animates you than against you.

But while *they* blaspheme him, *you* glorify him; and surely it is very meet that it should be so. Christians should honour the Holy Spirit, who makes them honourable. They should show forth his praises, giving visible form to his inward work, by proving themselves to be under his influence as "the Spirit of love, and of power, and of a sound mind." This is the best way of meeting the reproaches of men against ourselves as Christians, and against the Spirit by whom, as Christians, we are animated and guided. Let us show what manner of spirit we are of; that it is indeed the Spirit of glory that rests on us,—a Spirit which makes "pure, then peaceable, gentle, and easy to be entreated,"—a Spirit which leads us to think on and to practise "whatsoever things are true, whatsoever things are honest, whatsoever things are just, whatsoever things are pure, whatsoever things are lovely, whatsoever things are of good report."[1]

While this is important truth, and while the words in themselves may be considered as well enough fitted to convey it, I am rather disposed to go along with those interpreters who consider the *verbs* here as used impersonally, and think the apostle expresses this sentiment: On their part there is evil-speaking, blasphemy, reproach; but on your part there is glory, true honour. They reproach, indeed, but ye are not dishonoured. The Spirit of glory rests on you, and therefore all their reproaches cannot rob you of true honour, cannot make you really contemptible. You are what the Spirit of God has made you, not what

[1] James iii. 17; Phil. iii. 8.

they represent you. What a comfort is this to a calumniated Christian, and how well fitted to enable him in patience to possess his soul, amid calumnious reproaches and cruel mockings!

There is a question which naturally enough is suggested by what has been said. Since we all, with scarcely an exception, profess the religion of Christ, have we ever been exposed to suffering on account of our religion? Is the fiery trial a strange thing to us? Have we never been "partakers of the sufferings of Christ?" never been exposed to "the reproach of Christ?" If we have not, I am afraid there is something wanting, something wrong. The world and Christianity are substantially the same things they were in the primitive times; and though the world may take other ways of showing its hatred and contempt of Christianity and Christians now than it did then, that hatred and contempt still exist unmitigated, and will find a way to manifest themselves when they meet with their appropriate objects. But it is not everything called Christianity that the world hates; it is the Christianity of the New Testament. It is not the name, it is the thing. There is much that is called Christianity which the world does not at all dislike; it is its own work. There are many called Christians who are of the world, and the world loves them. A woe is denounced on the Christian man of whom all men speak well; and if we have in no way incurred the hatred of an ungodly world, we have reason to fear, that though we have the name, we have not the thing. It is a faithful saying, "Every one who will live godly must suffer persecution." We are not to court persecution: if we are consistent Christians, we will not need to do so. It will come of its own accord. The world will be consistent in its hatred, if Christians are but consistent in their profession and conduct. Let us take care that we do not sinfully shun it. Let us hold fast the faith and profession of the gospel, to whatever privations and sufferings this may expose us. Let us part with everything rather than the Saviour and his truth, the testimony of a good conscience, and the hope, through grace, of rejoicing with exceeding joy at the appearing of his glory; let us show how highly we value him and his gospel, by the cheerfulness with which we submit to such trials as attachment to them may bring on us.

III. BE NOT ASHAMED OF YOUR SUFFERINGS.

The third direction given by the apostle to his persecuted brethren is, Be not ashamed of your sufferings in the cause of Christ. "Let none of you suffer as a murderer, or as a thief, or as an evil-doer, or as a busybody in other men's matters. Yet if any man suffer as a Christian, let him not be ashamed; but let him glorify God on this behalf."

The apostle proceeds on the principle, that there are sufferings which are indeed disgraceful; that it is a possible thing that Christians may expose themselves to such sufferings, which in their case must be doubly disgraceful; that it is the duty of Christians carefully to guard against rendering themselves liable to such sufferings; that there are sufferings to which Christians may be exposed, merely because they are Christians, merely because they profess the faith, obey the laws, observe the institutions of Christ; and that such sufferings, however disgraceful in their own nature, and in the estimation of men, are no proper ground of shame to those who meet with them; but, on the contrary, should be subjects of gloriation and thanksgiving to God.

When suffering is just punishment, it is always disgraceful. Crime in all its forms is a shameful thing, something base and unworthy; and so must punishment be, which proclaims the man a criminal, which at once publishes the fact that he has been guilty, and brands him with public reprobation on account of his guilt. It is shameful to commit murder, and therefore it is shameful to suffer as a murderer. It is shameful to commit theft, and therefore it is shameful to suffer as a thief. It is shameful to violate any law of man established by competent authority, which is not opposed to the law of God, that is, to be an evil-doer, a malefactor in the eye of the law; and therefore it is shameful to be punished for such a violation as an evil-doer or malefactor. When such punishments have been incurred, the person subjected to them ought to be ashamed; and when they are not felt to be shameful by the criminal, it is a proof of most deplorable obtuseness of moral apprehension and feeling.

Nor are sufferings which are the punishment of violation of positive public law the only sufferings which are of a shameful kind. All suffering which is the effect of improper conduct is shameful, just in proportion as the conduct which has produced it is shameful. There are many very improper acts or habits which are not, and cannot be, the subject of public law, lying beyond or below its sphere, which yet naturally bring down on those characterized by them appropriate, and it may be severe, punishment. For example, "the busybody in other men's matters," whether his intrusive interference originate in mere impertinent curiosity or in worse motives, is likely to suffer by exclusion from respectable society, by general contempt, and it may be in even more substantial forms; and his sufferings, whatever they may be, are disgraceful sufferings—sufferings of which he ought to be ashamed.

By many interpreters, I am aware that the "busybody" here is considered as equivalent to "the seditious person," who in a private station plots against the existing order of society, meddling with things too high for him, and who consequently is naturally enough classed along with the murderer and the thief, as drawing down on himself deserved punishment from the hand of violated law; but I think it more likely that the apostle meant to warn Christians against exposing themselves, not only to shameful suffering as violators of public law, but to shameful suffering originating in impropriety of behaviour of whatever kind.[1]

It may seem strange that the apostle should caution those to whom he wrote, and whom he had represented as "elect according to the foreknowledge of God the Father, through sanctification of the Spirit, unto obedience and sprinkling of the blood of Jesus Christ; as begotten again to a living hope; as the heirs of an incorruptible, undefiled, unfading inheritance, reserved in heaven for them," to which they were "kept by the power of God through faith;" as having "tasted that the Lord is gracious;" as "a chosen generation, a royal priesthood, a holy nation;"—it may seem strange that he should have thought it needful to caution such persons against exposing themselves to the penalties which the law denounces against theft and murder, or even to the minor punishments society inflicts on the pragmatical intermeddler.

It may be supposed that the apostle meant not so much to warn those to whom he wrote against murder, theft, and impertinent intrusion in other men's matters, as against affording even the shadow of an occasion for their being punished for these or similar crimes and improprieties by their enemies, who were disposed to speak evil of them, and to punish them as malefactors. "By well-doing they were to seek to put to silence the ignorance of foolish men;" and

[1] See note A.

their conduct was to be so harmless, and blameless, and circumspect, that when charged before the tribunals with such crimes, their adversaries should find it impossible to substantiate their charge, and difficult even to give anything like plausibility to it; so that the result might be, that, instead of their being visited with the shameful punishment of murderers and thieves, "they who spoke evil of them as of evil-doers, should be made ashamed of falsely accusing their good conversation in Christ;" or if their enemies, as they often did, should, without evidence and against evidence, proceed to punish them, that it might be made manifest to all that it was not for crimes which might be alleged, but which had not, could not be, proved against them, but simply for their being Christians, that they were punished.[1]

This, however, is not by any means the only passage in which Christians are cautioned against very gross sins. Exhortations to Christians, in the apostolic epistles, not only proceed on the principle that there were false professors in the primitive churches, who might discredit their profession by unholy conduct, but on the principle that in the truly converted man, that is, "in his flesh, dwelleth no good thing;" and that, but for the restraining influence of the Spirit and providence of God, there is scarcely any violation of the divine law into which remaining depravity, stimulated into active operation by powerful temptation, may not hurry him. To use the words of an old Scottish expositor, "Except Christians employ Christ's Spirit to apply that virtue which he hath purchased by his death, for the changing of their nature, and mortifying of the love of sin in their hearts, and study watchfulness in their carriage,

---

[1] It was a glorious thing for Christianity when its apologists could appeal to the heathen, and say, "De vestro numero carcer exæstuat. Christianus ibi nullus, nisi aut reus suæ religionis aut profugus."— MINUCIUS FELIX.

they will readily break out in those abominations for which even heathens would justly put them to suffer: for this direction of the apostle's does import, that except Christians did watch and pray, and make use of Christ's death for mortification of sin within them, to which duties he had stirred them up before, they were in hazard to break out in the sins here mentioned, and so be put to suffer as murderers, thieves, evil-doers, and busybodies in other men's matters." [1]

These practices referred to by the apostle were shameful in themselves, shameful by whomsoever committed; but it is obvious they were peculiarly shameful in Christians. It was disgraceful for a heathen to suffer for such causes; what, then, must it have been for a Christian thus to suffer? Sin is hateful in every man, additionally hateful in a professor of Christianity; nowhere so hateful as in the heart and life of a child of God. It is not wonderful, then, that the apostle should say, "Let none of you suffer as a murderer, or as a thief, or as an evil-doer, or as a busybody in other men's matters." By exposing himself to punishment for the violation of the laws, a Christian would draw down discredit not only on his own character, but on the Christian cause, giving occasion to the enemies of the Lord to blaspheme. He would destroy his own inward peace, and, by making shipwreck of character, render it scarcely possible that he should ever have it in his power to repair in any good measure the injury he had done to the worthy name.[2]

It ill becomes such persons to complain of their sufferings, but it well becomes them to be ashamed of them, and especially to be ashamed of their cause. Nothing is more deplorable than to find men bearing the name of Christ, after involving themselves in suffering by their imprudence

[1] Nisbet.   [2] "Martyrem facit non poena sed causa."—AUGUSTIN.

and sin, exposing themselves to the penalties of the law, or drawing down odium on themselves and reproach on religion, by their conceited officiousness or impertinent intermeddling; instead of being ashamed of their conduct, actually taking credit for it; pleasing themselves with the thought that they are persecuted for righteousness' sake, when they are only suffering for their faults; and imputing that to the malice of their enemies which is but the natural result of their own folly and wickedness. It becomes such persons to blush and weep, to retire as much as may be from the public gaze, and "to walk softly all their years."

But however carefully and successfully the primitive Christians might avoid all such disgraceful sufferings, discreditable to themselves and injurious to their religion, sufferings they were not likely to escape—sufferings of another kind. Though they should violate no civil law which was not in direct opposition to the divine law; though they should "live quiet and peaceable lives," minding their own business, and not intermeddling with what did not concern them; and though they should act so circumspectly that even their enemies, watching for their halting, could find nothing which they could plausibly represent as a violation of law, or an undue interference with the affairs of others; yet still they were likely, ay, they were sure, to meet with sufferings—it might be very severe sufferings; sufferings in their external form of a very shameful and degrading character—just because they were Christians;[1] just because they made a consistent profession of the faith of Christ, acknowledging him as their teacher and Lord, observing his institutions and obeying his laws. Though, as in the case of Daniel, no occasion might be found against them on other grounds, an occasion would be found against them "concerning the law of their God."[2]

[1] See note B. [2] Dan vi. 5.

Such were the sufferings inflicted on the apostles and first teachers and professors of Christianity, of which we have a record in the Acts of the Apostles; sufferings for the infliction of which, in some cases, no cause was even alleged but that they were Christians; and in others where, though other causes were alleged, this was indeed the true reason. The time was come of which our Lord had spoken, when his followers were to be "hated by all nations"[1]—both by the Jews and the Gentiles—" for his name's sake," just because they were Christians.[2] To be a Christian, was a sufficient reason with the Jews why a man should be cast out of the synagogue; and with the Romans, why he should be treated as a criminal. At a somewhat later period we find an imperial edict, that of Trajan, which seems to have been intended rather to mitigate the severity of the treatment to which Christians, as Christians, had been exposed, requiring that, though Christians were not to be officially sought after, such as were accused and convicted of an adherence to Christianity were to be put to death;[3] their Christianity, apart from everything else, being considered as a capital offence.

And if thus, as Christians, they were exposed to sufferings so serious in the shape of legal inflictions, it is quite plain that, in the ordinary intercourse of life, they must have been liable to an endless variety of annoyances, living in the midst of men who, whether Jews or heathens, regarded their religion with sentiments of abhorrence and contempt. These sufferings were in many cases, in their own nature, of a degrading character. Christians were, as the apostle expresses it, "shamefully entreated." The punishments inflicted were such as were commonly inflicted on the vilest criminals, on felons and slaves. Stripes and the cross, punishments which could be legally inflicted on no

[1] Matt. xxiv. 9. [2] See note C. [3] Plinii Epp. ix. 97, 98.

Roman citizen, fell to the lot of many of them, from the hands of the magistrate; and from the great body of their fellow-citizens they received " cruel mockings;" their names were cast out as evil, and they were treated by them " as the filth of the world, and the offscouring of all things." [1]

But of sufferings of this kind, however ignominious in their own character, however fitted to express the contempt of those who inflicted them, and excite the shame of those who endured them, they were not to be ashamed. They were not to count them really dishonourable. In truth, they were not. The most ignominious treatment, when it is unmerited, reflects dishonour not on him who innocently endures, but on him who unjustly inflicts it. To profess what we believe to be true, and to do what we believe to be right, to refuse to give either explicit or tacit approbation of what we account false and wrong, to acknowledge obligations to a divine benefactor for favours of inestimable value, in the manner which that divine benefactor enjoins, can never be dishonourable. No contumely poured on Christians could in the slightest degree affect the truth or excellence of Christ's doctrine and law; nor, supposing the divine origin of these, could such calumnies for a moment occasion any reasonable doubt as to the wisdom and rectitude of the conduct of those who had embraced that doctrine and submitted to that law. The disgrace plainly lay with the authors, not with the victims, of such shameful oppression and cruelty. The persecutor, not the persecuted, had reason to be ashamed of the sufferings inflicted on Christians as Christians.

But the apostle exhorts the persecuted Christians not only not to be ashamed of such sufferings, but to " glorify God on this behalf." They are to consider these ignominious sufferings as indeed an honour and a privilege, and

[1] Heb. xi. 36; 1 Cor. iv. 13.

they are to thank God for them, and while under them to act such a part as will glorify him; their sense of the honour done to them being expressed not in words only, but in cheerful submission to these sufferings, and in patient and heroic endurance of them. They are to reckon it a proper subject of thanksgiving, that to them "it is given, on behalf of Christ Jesus, not only to believe but to suffer for his sake," and to "rejoice that they are counted worthy to suffer shame for his name." They should account it a token of the confidence reposed in them by their divine Leader, when he places them, as it were, in the fore ranks in the battle, and calls on them to "suffer great things for his name's sake." They should rejoice in the opportunity thus given them of showing their gratitude to him who for them "endured the cross and despised the shame;" who, in the cause of their salvation, "gave his back to the smiters, and his cheeks to them that plucked off the hair, hid not his face from shame and spitting, but set his face as a flint," and amid all contumelies "held fast the confidence and rejoicing of his hope," that he should not ultimately be ashamed.[1]

They should be thankful for these sufferings, as fitted to promote their personal spiritual improvement both in holiness and in comfort; such "tribulations working *patience*," that is, leading to perseverance, not to apostasy; such "patience working experience," that is, such perseverance leading to *proof* both of the reality and the strength of the principles of the new life; and such "experience working hope,"—such proof strengthening the hope of eternal life, by showing that it is indeed founded on the gospel really believed, and will prove a hope which shall never make ashamed.[2] Well may Christians glory in such tribulations—

[1] Acts v. 41; Phil. i. 29; Acts ix. 16; Heb. xii. 2; Isa. l. 6, 7.
[2] Rom. v. 3-5.

tribulations fitted and intended to have, secured of having, such glorious results.

Still further, and finally, they should glorify God on account of such sufferings, because their tendency, when endured in the right spirit, was greatly to advance the cause of Christ. "The blood of the martyrs is the seed of the Church." Persecution very generally "has fallen out" to the furtherance of the gospel. The patient, joyful endurance of most cruel and contumelious wrongs by Paul and Silas, probably was highly influential in producing the conversion of the Philippian jailor. The faith and patience of the martyrs amid their sufferings, more impressively than all their eloquence, declared the power of divine grace and the efficacy of the gospel; made the torturers ashamed, and induced beholders to take share with those who were tortured. This consideration had great influence on Paul's mind, enabling him to glory in his sufferings as a Christian, and to glorify God on their behalf. " I rejoice in my sufferings for you," says he to the Colossians, " and fill up that which is behind of the afflictions of Christ in my flesh for his body's sake, which is the Church ;" and in the Epistle to Timothy, " I *endure*"—patiently, joyfully suffer—" all things for the elect's sake, that they may also obtain the salvation that is in Christ, with eternal glory."[1]

Christians in every country and in every age are bound to regulate themselves by the direction we have been endeavouring to illustrate. From a regard to the honour of their religion and their Saviour, they are bound carefully to avoid everything which may justly bring on them contempt or punishment, knowing that Christ has entrusted the reputation of his religion to their care ; and that its character is so identified with theirs, that the one cannot be injured without affecting the other ; while at the same time

[1] Col. i. 24 ; 2 Tim. ii. 10.

they are never, under the influence of a false shame, to shrink from suffering for professing the faith and obeying the law of their Lord, however ignominious a form that suffering may wear, ever bearing in mind his impressive declaration, " Whosoever shall be ashamed of me and my words in this adulterous and sinful generation, of him also shall the Son of man be ashamed, when he cometh in the glory of his Father with the holy angels." " Whosoever shall confess me before men, him will I confess also before my Father and the holy angels."[1] He who counts these faithful sayings, will not be ashamed of suffering as a Christian. He will be disposed to say with the apostle, " I suffer trouble as an evil-doer, even unto bonds:" "nevertheless I am not ashamed; for I know whom I have believed, and am persuaded that he is able to keep that which I have committed unto him against that day."

IV. PERSEVERING IN WELL-DOING, COMMIT YOUR SOULS TO GOD UNDER SUFFERINGS.

The last direction which the apostle gives to persecuted Christians is, " Persevering in well-doing, commit the keeping of your souls to God under your sufferings." " For the time is come when judgment must begin at the house of God: and if it first begin at us, what shall the end be of them that obey not the gospel of God? And if the righteous scarcely be saved, where shall the ungodly and the sinner appear? Wherefore, let them that suffer according to the will of God commit the keeping of their souls to him in well-doing, as to a faithful Creator."

A careful reader will see that these three verses are very closely connected; that the statements in the 17th and 18th verses are the foundation on which the directions

[1] Matt. x. 32; Luke xii. 8.

in the 19th are based, or the motives by which they are enforced. The statement is twofold: Severe afflictions are awaiting the professors of the faith of Christ, and still more tremendous evils are impending over those who believe not the gospel, or who apostatize from the faith. And the direction is twofold also: Commit your souls to God, that ye may be enabled to sustain those severe afflictions; and do this in well-doing, in a constant continuance in well-doing, in a perseverance in the faith, profession, and practice of Christianity, that you may escape those tremendous evils. Such seems the connection of the apostle's thoughts.

"The time is come when judgment must begin at the house of God; a time in which the righteous shall scarcely be saved: therefore, let them who suffer by the will of God commit the keeping of their souls to him, as to a faithful Creator." The "house of God," in Old Testament language, would signify either the temple of Jerusalem; or—understanding the word figuratively as equivalent to family, a sense in which it is so often used—the Israelitish people. In the language of the New Testament, it signifies the Christian Church, Christians. "Know ye not," says the apostle, "that ye are the temple of God?" "His house are we, if we hold fast the confidence and the rejoicing of the hope stedfast to the end." It denotes them who obey the gospel of Christ, as contradistinguished from the unbelievers or the apostates, who do not obey the gospel of Christ.[1] "The righteous" is obviously just another appellation for the same individuals, and describes their character as opposed to the wicked, "the ungodly, and the sinner." The words then signify: 'A period is arrived, or is just at hand, when a very severe trial of Christians, a trial of some continuance, is about to com-

[1] 1 Cor. iii. 16; Heb. iii. 6.

mence; when judgment, or rather *the* judgment,[1] shall begin at the house of God.'[2]

There seems here a reference to a particular judgment or trial, that the primitive Christians had reason to expect. When we consider that this epistle was written within a short time of the commencement of that awful scene of judgment which terminated in the destruction of the ecclesiastical and civil polity of the Jews, and which our Lord had so minutely predicted, we can scarcely doubt of the reference of the apostle's expression. After having specified wars and rumours of wars, famines, pestilences, and earthquakes, as symptoms of "the beginning of sorrows," our Lord adds, "Then shall they deliver you up to be afflicted, and shall kill you: and ye shall be hated of all nations for my name's sake. They shall deliver you up to councils and to synagogues, and ye shall be beaten; and ye shall be brought before rulers and kings for my sake: Ye shall be betrayed both by parents, and brethren, and kinsfolk, and friends; and some of you shall they cause to be put to death. And then many shall be offended, and shall betray one another, and shall hate one another. And many false prophets shall rise, and deceive many. And because iniquity shall abound, the love of many shall wax cold: but he that shall endure to the end shall be saved. Except the Lord had shortened those days, no flesh should be saved; but for the elect's sake, whom he hath chosen, he hath shortened the days."[3]

---

[1] Τὸ κρίμα.

[2] There seems here an allusion to Ezek. ix. 6, "Slay utterly old and young; and *begin at my sanctuary.*" Green, in his Gram. of the New Testament, would place the ἐστι, which must be supplied, not before ὁ καιρὸς, but before ἀπὸ τοῦ οἴκου τοῦ Θεοῦ, and would translate, "for the season of the commencement of judgment is from the house of God." It was a common opinion among the Jews, that national punishments always commence with the just and godly.—See Schœtgen and Wetstein.

[3] Matt. xxiv. 9-13, 22.

This is *the* judgment which, though to fall most heavily on the holy land, was plainly to extend to wherever Jews and Christians were to be found, " for where the carcase was, there were the eagles to be gathered together ;" which was to begin at the house of God, and which was to be so severe, that the " righteous should scarcely," that is, not without difficulty, " be saved." They only who stood the trial should be saved, and many would not stand the trial. All the truly righteous should be saved; but many who seemed to be righteous, many who thought themselves to be righteous, would not endure to the end, and so should not be saved; and the righteous themselves should be saved, not without much struggle, exertion, suffering—" saved as by fire." Some have supposed the reference to be to the Neronian persecutions, which by a few years preceded the calamities connected with the Jewish wars and the destruction of Jerusalem.

Now, on entering on this scene of severe trial, they who were to " suffer according to the will of God"—a phrase marking the origin of their sufferings rather than the manner in which they were sustained; nearly equivalent to, ' on account of the divine will,' that is, on account of their doing the divine will—are enjoined to " commit the keeping of their souls to God, as to a faithful Creator." To commit their souls, that is, themselves, into the hands of God, to be kept by him, is just under a deep sense of their own incapacity to meet and sustain the trial in a way glorifying to God and advantageous to themselves—to resign themselves entirely to the guidance of God's providence, and word, and Spirit, in the expectation that he will make their duty obvious to them in circumstances of doubt and perplexity; and, when their duty is made plain to them, enable them at all hazards to perform it, trusting not to their own understanding, but to the divine wisdom; relying not on their own energies, but on the power of God; trusting that he will indeed keep that which they commit to him; protect them from all real evil; allow them to be exposed to no unnecessary, no useless suffering; lay on them no load of labour or suffering which he will not enable them to sustain; "not suffer them to be tried above what they are able to bear, but with the temptation give them a way of escape;" "deliver them from every evil work, and preserve them unto his heavenly kingdom."[1]

This is obviously the general meaning; but there is something peculiar and emphatic in the phrase, "Commit the keeping of your souls to him." They were to commit the care of their bodies, their lives, their reputation, their property, their relations, to God, with a distinct understanding that they may be called on by him to part with them all; and well pleased to part with them all, in the assurance that their souls are safe in his keeping—safe in life, safe in death, safe for ever,—" bound in the bundle of life with the Lord their God."[2]

He who thus commits the keeping of his soul to God, is ready for all trials, however severe. Such a person will be "anxious about nothing;" and while "in everything, by prayer and supplication, he makes his requests known to God," his need shall be supplied according to God's glorious riches; and "the peace of God, which passeth all understanding, shall keep his heart and mind through Christ Jesus."[3]

The persecuted Christians are encouraged thus to commit the keeping of their souls to God, by the consideration that he is "a faithful Creator." He is their Creator. He not only is the "Father of their spirits" and the former of their bodies, as he is of the spirits and bodies of all men, but He has "of his own will begotten them by the word of truth,

[1] 2 Tim. iv. 18. [2] 1 Sam. xxv. 29. [3] Phil. iv. 6, 7.

through the resurrection of Christ Jesus from the dead, so that they are a kind of first-fruits of his creatures." They are not only his creatures, but his " new creatures,"—his " workmanship created anew unto good works."[1] To whom should they commit the keeping of their souls but to him? They are his property; more his than their own. He is able to take care of them. He who made them can preserve them. Conservation does not require greater power than creation. And he is disposed to take care of them. He hates none of his creatures; he loves all his new creatures with a peculiar, an unchangeable, an eternal love. Looking at him as their Creator, they may well be persuaded that he is able and that he is willing to keep that which, in obedience to his own command, they have committed to him.

And then he is not only a Creator, but "a faithful Creator."[2] He is faithful to fulfil the expectations of support and protection, which the very relation of Creator is fitted to excite in the mind of an intelligent loyal creature. The new creature cannot but have an expectation, that he who has given it true life will preserve it, will never let it perish. This is an instinct of the new nature; and " he will fulfil the desire of them that fear him, he also will hear their cry and save them." " The Lord preserveth all them that love him." Besides, he has given to them as his creatures, his new creatures, " exceeding great and precious promises." We will quote a few of them: " In six troubles God shall deliver thee; in seven no evil shall touch thee. He shall cover thee with his feathers, and under his wings shalt thou trust; he shall give his angels charge concerning thee, to keep thee in all thy ways. The Lord is thy keeper, the Lord shall preserve thee from all evil, the Lord shall

---

[1] Heb. xii. 9; James i. 18; Eph. ii. 10.
[2] "The relation of Creator implies *omnipotent* love; the attribute of faithful *eternal* love declared in his promises."—BATES.

preserve thy soul. When thou passest through the waters, I will be with thee, and the flood shall not overflow thee: when thou passest through the fire, thou shalt not be burnt, neither shall the flame kindle on thee. I give unto my sheep eternal life, and they shall never perish; neither shall any one pluck them out of my Father's hand. Neither death, nor life, nor angels, nor principalities, nor powers, nor things present, nor things to come, nor height, nor depth, nor any other creature, can separate" those created anew in Christ Jesus " from the love of God which is in Christ Jesus their Lord." " Faithful is he who hath promised, who also will do it." " He is not a man, that he should lie; nor the son of man, that he should repent: hath he said it, and shall he not do it? hath he promised it, and shall he not make it good?" " All these promises are yea, amen, in Christ Jesus, to the glory of God by us."[1]

Nothing but this committing unreservedly the keeping of the soul to God as a faithful Creator, could meet the exigencies of the case, and fit for so severe and complicated a trial. This only would enable the persecuted Christian so to endure the trial, as to " obtain the crown of life which the Lord hath promised to those who love him."

Connected with the statement, that severe trials were awaiting Christians, the apostle makes an impressive announcement of the dreadful doom of " those who obey not the gospel of God." The beginning of the judgment was to come on the house or family of God; the end of it on them who obey not the gospel of God. The first drops were to fall on the former, the collected tempest on the latter: the first were to be chastened, severely chastened; but on the last was to come " wrath to the uttermost." The first were to be " saved as by fire," the others were to be

[1] Job v. 19-25; Ps. xci., cxxi. 7, 8; Isa. xliii. 2; John x. 28-30; Rom. viii. 38, 39; 1 Thess. v. 24; Num. xxiii. 19; 2 Cor. i. 20.

" destroyed with an everlasting destruction;" the one getting into a place of safety with difficulty, the other finding no place of shelter from the " fiery indignation which was to devour the adversaries" of God. This is more strongly expressed in the interrogative form than it could be by any direct affirmation. " What shall the end be? Where shall they appear?"

It may be right to remark in passing, that the 18th verse is a quotation from the Greek version of the 31st verse of the eleventh chapter of the book of Proverbs. Our English version, which is an accurate rendering of the Hebrew text, gives a meaning which seems at first altogether different. " Behold, the righteous shall be recompensed on the earth: much more the wicked and the sinner." Though these words may, and probably do mean, ' Even really good men are chastened for their sins; and if so, surely the wicked and the sinner shall be punished with a severity suited to the heinousness of their guilt,'—a sentiment not materially different from that in the passage before us; at the same time this does seem an instance in which the inspired writer merely uses the words of the Greek translation of the Scriptures, as the vehicle of his own thoughts, without any particular reference to their meaning and bearing in the place from which they are borrowed.

If we have not misapprehended altogether the meaning of this paragraph, the direct reference in these words is to the tremendous evils which came upon the Jewish opposers of Christianity very soon after these words were written. These were " the days of vengeance," days in which there was "such affliction as had not been from the beginning of the creation which God created till that time, neither shall be."[1] Nor are we called to limit these words to the calamities which befell the unbelieving and impenitent

[1] Mark xiii. 19.

Jews in their own land and other lands, dreadful as we know, from the authentic narrative of their own historian Josephus, these were. These to them were not "the end" of the judgment. They were foreshadowing symbols of that everlasting destruction in the world to come, which awaited them, along with all who, like them, "obey not the gospel of God," but, in opposition to all the means used for reclaiming them, continue ungodly and sinners.

As the statement concerning the severe trial to which Christians were to be exposed is made the basis of the exhortation, "Commit the keeping of your souls to God, as unto a faithful Creator;" so this statement respecting the perdition of ungodly men seems to us to be the basis of the exhortation, " Commit the keeping of your souls to God *in well-doing.*" It is evident that "to suffer for well-doing," as referred to at the 20th verse of the second chapter, is just equivalent to suffering as a Christian, suffering on account of the consistent profession of the faith of Christ. And the "patient continuance in well-doing," in which Christians are "to seek for glory, honour, and immortality," is plainly just the persevering faith of the doctrines and practice of the duties of Christianity. The persecuted Christians were to continue in well-doing. They had done well in embracing the gospel, denying themselves, and becoming followers of Christ; and they must persevere in doing well, by holding fast their profession.

Should they not thus persevere in well-doing, but, under the power of terror and shame, abandon the cause of Christ, making "shipwreck of faith and a good conscience," they would make a miserable exchange of circumstances. They must in this case take their place among the ungodly and sinners, who obey not the gospel of God. However severe the trials of Christians may be, they are nothing compared with the punishment which awaits the impenitent and unbelieving. Even in this world, some of the apostates of that age, in seeking to escape the persecution to which Christians were exposed, involved themselves in still more dreadful calamities. They who in Jerusalem remained faithful to Christ, following his command, left the doomed city, embracing an opportunity very wonderfully offered to them, and so were saved—saved with difficulty; while the apostates continued, and perished miserably in the siege and sack of that city.

In the times of the severest persecution, it is men's wisdom, by embracing the gospel, to cast in their lot with the afflicted people of God. That is the only way of escaping evils immeasurably more dreadful than any which the malignant ingenuity of earth or hell can inflict on the saints; and it is absolute madness to purchase security from persecution, and all that this world can bestow, at the price of apostasy: " for he who turns back, turns back to perdition." Since, then, trials so severe were awaiting the Church of God, and destruction so awful was impending over those ungodly men and sinners who, either by impenitence or apostasy, were disobedient to the gospel of God, how appropriate and how powerfully enforced the injunction of the apostle, " Wherefore, let them that suffer according to the will of God commit the keeping of their souls to him in well-doing, as to a faithful Creator!"

The two injunctions are most intimately connected. It is only he who is continuing in well-doing, that in the day of severe trial can commit the keeping of his soul to God, as to a faithful Creator; and it is only he who commits the keeping of his soul to God, as to a faithful Creator, that in the day of severe trial will continue in well-doing. All others will become weary in well-doing under persecution; and silently withdraw from, or openly renounce connection with, the oppressed persecuted Church of Christ.

There are two general principles of a practical kind, and of very general application, naturally suggested by what we have said, to which I would call your attention for a moment before we conclude.

They who obey the gospel may count on varied, and it may be severe trials, previously to their obtaining "the salvation that is in Christ with eternal glory;" and they who obey not the gospel can reasonably count on nothing but everlasting perdition.

They who obey the gospel are as sure of salvation as the love and power, the faithfulness and wisdom, of God can make them. The righteous—those "justified freely by God's grace through the redemption that is in Christ Jesus," those sanctified by the Spirit through the truth—shall certainly be saved. When it is said they are "scarcely saved," the reference is not to the uncertainty of their being saved, but to the difficulties and trials they may experience in the course of their being saved. All Christians are not tried as the Christians to whom Peter wrote, the Christians at the close of the Jewish dispensation; but all Christians meet with afflictions, and meet with afflictions because they are Christians; all suffer, and all suffer as Christians. We must never think ill of a cause merely because it is persecuted, nor indulge dark thoughts respecting the spiritual state and prospects of men merely because they are very severely afflicted. The absence of trial is a worse sign than what we might be disposed to think the excess of trial. "If ye are without chastisement, of which all are partakers, then are ye bastards, and not sons."[1] But it is not exposure to trial, it is the endurance of trial in "a patient continuance in well-doing," that is the characteristic mark of those who obey the gospel of God. Let Christians, then, not wonder at their trials, however severe. Let them not

[1] Heb. xii. 8.

count strange even the fiery trial, as if some strange thing had happened to them; and let them seek, by rightly improving their trials, to convert them into proofs of saintship and means of salvation.

They who obey not the gospel of God can reasonably count on nothing but unmixed misery, everlasting perdition. "If judgment begin at the house of God, what shall the end be of those who obey not the gospel of God? and if the righteous scarcely be saved, where shall the ungodly and the sinner appear?" These words most strikingly bring before our minds both the severity and the certainty of the punishment which awaits the wicked. If even the children of God, the objects of his peculiar love, are severely chastened for their faults in this season of divine forbearance, what can those who are the objects of his moral disapprobation and judicial displeasure expect, but the unmitigated punishment of their sin, under an economy which is the revelation of his righteous judgment, where justice is to have free course and to be glorified? If the trials to which the righteous are exposed are so varied and severe, that, though saved, they are "saved so as by fire," saved with difficulty, with a struggle, after "a great fight of affliction," what shall be the state of those who are not to be saved at all—not saved, but destroyed with an everlasting destruction from the presence of the Lord, and the glory of his power? If even children are so severely chastened, how shall hardened rebels be punished? "If these things are done in the green tree, what shall be done in the dry?" Oh that men who obey not the gospel of God, could be but induced to lay these things to heart! If they continue disobedient to the gospel, there is no hope; for there is no atoning sacrifice, no sanctifying Spirit, no salvation, but the sacrifice, the Spirit, the salvation revealed in the gospel.

But why should they not obey this gospel? Is it not "a

faithful saying, and worthy of all acceptation?" Oh, why will they reject the counsel of God against themselves? If they continue to reject this counsel of peace, they must perish; but there is no necessity of rejecting this counsel of peace, but what originates in their own unreasonable, wicked obstinacy.

I conclude, in words full of comfort to the first of those classes of whom I have been speaking, and full of terror to the second. May God carry them home with power to the hearts of both! "The Lord knoweth how to deliver the godly out of temptations, and to reserve the unjust unto the day of judgment to be punished." "The Lord is not slack concerning his declaration, as some men count slackness; but he is long-suffering to usward, not willing that any should perish, but that all should come unto repentance." "He that, being often reproved, hardeneth his neck, shall suddenly be destroyed, and that without remedy."[1]

Note A. p. 156.

It must be admitted that there is a strange disparity between "the busybody," and "the thief," and "the murderer." It is an ingenious conjecture, but nothing more, of Dr Mangey, that a very early transcriber may have written ἀλλοτριοεπίσκοπος, which appears in all existing manuscripts, for ἀλλοτριοεπίκλοπος, "a purloiner of other men's property." There is more weight in Bishop Barrington's suggestion: "This caution probably owed its origin to the temper and conduct of the Jews at this period. They were peculiarly fond of intermeddling in the public councils and concerns of other bodies of men." Josephus, *de Bell. Jud.* lib. ii. c. xviii. § 7, 8, gives an excellent comment on this apostolical prohibition. He relates that his countrymen, "needlessly mixing with the Greeks assembled at Alexandria on their own affairs, and acting the part of spies, greatly suffered for it." This took place A.D. 66, just about the time this epistle was written.—*Vide* Bowyer's *Conjectures*, pp. 603–4.

[1] 2 Pet. ii. 9, iii. 9; Prov. xxix. 1.

Note B., p. 159.

"'The disciples,' we are told, 'were called *Christians* first in Antioch' (Acts xi. 26): a notice curious and interesting, all would acknowledge, even as everything must have interest for us which relates to the early days of the Church. Some perhaps would see in it nothing more; and yet if we question this notice a little closer, what vast amounts of history it contains, and is ready to yield up to us; what light it throws on the whole development of the apostolic Church, to know where and when this name was first imposed on the faithful! I have said 'imposed;' for 'Christians' was clearly a name which they did not give to themselves, but received from their adversaries, however afterwards they learned to accept and to glory in it as the highest title of honour. For it is not recorded that they 'called themselves,' but 'were called,' Christians first at Antioch; nor do we find the name anywhere in Scripture, except on the lips of those alien from, or opposed to, the gospel (Acts xxvi. 28; 1 Pet. iv. 16). And as it was a name imposed by adversaries, so among those adversaries it was plainly the heathen, and not the Jews, who gave it; for these would never have called the followers of Jesus of Nazareth, 'Christians,' or 'those of Christ,' the very point of their opposition to Him being, that He was *not* the Christ, but a false pretender to the name.[1]

Starting then from this point, that 'Christians' was a title given to the disciples by the heathen, let us ask ourselves what we may learn from it. At Antioch they first obtained this name—at the city, that is, which was the headquarters of the Church's missions to the heathen, in the same sense as Jerusalem had been the headquarters of those to the seed of Abraham. It was there, and among the faithful there, that a conviction of the world-wide destination of the gospel arose; there it was first plainly seen as intended for all kindreds of the earth. Hitherto the faithful in Christ had been called by their enemies, and indeed often were still called, 'Galileans,' or 'Nazarenes,'—both names which indicated the Jewish cradle in which the gospel had been nursed, and that the world saw in its followers no more

[1] Tacitus (*Annal.* xv. 24) confirms these conclusions: Quos *vulgus* . . . Christianos appellabat.

than a Jewish sect. But it was plain that the Church had now, even in the world's eyes, chipped its Jewish shell. The name 'Christians,' or 'those of Christ,' while it told that Christ and the confession of Christ was felt even by the world to be the sum and centre of this new faith, showed also that the heathen comprehended now, I do not say what the Church would be, but what it claimed to be,—no mere variation of Judaism, but a society with a mission and destination of its own. Nor will the thoughtful reader fail to observe that the imposing of this name on believers is by closest juxtaposition connected in the sacred narrative, and still more closely in the Greek than in the English, with the arrival at Antioch and the preaching there of that apostle who was God's appointed instrument for bringing the Church into the recognition of its destination for all men. As so often happens with the rise of a new name, the rise of this marked a new epoch in the Church's life, that it was entering upon a new stage of its development. Before we dismiss this word, let us note a much smaller matter, yet not without its own interest. The invention of this new name is laid by St Luke—so, I think, we may confidently say—to the credit of the Antiochenes. Now the idle and witty inhabitants of Antioch were famous in all antiquity for the invention of nicknames; it was a manufacture in which they particularly excelled. And thus it was exactly the place, where beforehand we might have expected that such a name, being a nickname or little better in the mouths of those that devised it, should have first come into being."—TRENCH : *On the Study of Words.*

NOTE C. p. 160.

Christians were persecuted just because they were Christians. The words of Tertullian are remarkable: " Non scelus aliquod in causa, sed nomen Christianus, si nullius criminis reus, nomen valde infestum." Not less remarkable are the words of Pliny to Trajan (Epistt. x. 97): " Cognitionibus de Christianis interfui nunquam ; ideo nescio quid et quatenus aut puniri soleat, aut quæri. Nec mediocriter hesitavi *an nomen ipsum, etiamsi flagitiis careat,* an flagitia cohærentia nomini puniantur. Interim in iis qui ad me tanquam Christiani deferebantur hunc sum secutus modum. Interrogavi ipsos an essent Christiani? **Confitentes** iterum et tertio interrogavi, supplicium minatus. Perseverantes duci jussi; neque enim dubitabam, qualecunque esset quod faterentur, pervicaciam certe et inflexibilem obstinationem debere puniri. Fuerant alii similis amentiæ, quos, quod cives Romani essent, annotavi in urbem remittendos." "It seems," as Lord Hailes observes, "that Pliny did not know what inquiries ought to have been made, and therefore he limited *his* to two words, 'Christianus es?' It required but other two, such as 'Ego quidem,' or 'Ita sane,' and the cause was judged and the culprit despatched to execution. Blessed era in which, without any captious question as to flaws in the indictment, exceptions to the verdict, or motion for arrest of judgment, a trial for life might be begun, carried on, and brought to a comfortable issue, by the pronouncing of about twenty letters! and what mighty obligations did not the primitive Christians owe to their equitable and intelligent judges, who by a single and simple interrogatory relieved them from the delays and suspense of a long trial!"—*Disquisitions concerning the Antiquities of the Christian Church*, chap. iv. p. 100. "Your religion is illegal—*non licèt esse vos*, was the reproach commonly cast on Christians, without reference to the *contents* of their religion."—NEANDER, *Memorials of Christian Life*, Part i. chap. iii.

DISCOURSE XXI.

THE ECCLESIASTICAL DUTIES OF CHRISTIANS ENJOINED AND ENFORCED.

"The elders which are among you I exhort, who am also an elder, and a witness of the sufferings of Christ, and also a partaker of the glory that shall be revealed: feed the flock of God which is among you, taking the oversight thereof, not by constraint, but willingly; not for filthy lucre, but of a ready mind; neither as being lords over God's heritage, but being ensamples to the flock: and when the chief Shepherd shall appear, ye shall receive a crown of glory that fadeth not away. Likewise, ye younger, submit yourselves unto the elder. Yea, all of you, be subject one to another, and be clothed with humility: for God resisteth the proud, and giveth grace to the humble."— 1 PET. v. 1–5.

IN the preceding portions of this epistle the apostle has instructed those to whom he wrote in many of their religious and moral duties as individuals, and also in many of their duties as members of domestic and civil society. In the paragraph which comes now before us, he writes to them that they "may know how they ought to behave themselves in the house of God." He gives them a directory for their conduct, as office-bearers or private members of a Christian church. The duties of office-bearers in the Church to those committed to their charge, and the duties of the members of the Church, both to their office-bearers and to each other, are here very succinctly stated, and very powerfully enforced.

With regard to the office-bearers of the Church, here termed "the elders," the whole of their duty is represented as consisting in acting the part of shepherds and overseers of that portion of the flock or family of God committed to their care; the temper or disposition in which this duty must be discharged is described, both negatively and positively—" not by constraint, not for filthy lucre, not as lords of God's heritage," but " willingly, of a ready mind, as ensamples to the flock;" and to secure a conscientious performance of this duty, besides employing his personal influence with them, as being himself " also an elder, and a witness of the sufferings of Christ, and a partaker of the glory which shall be revealed," the apostle turns their attention to the peculiar character of the Church as " the flock" and " heritage of God," and to the rich reward which shall be conferred on the faithful under shepherds and overseers by the chief Shepherd and Overseer at his " glorious appearing," and their " gathering together to him."

With regard to the members of the Church, who, with a reference, we apprehend, to their office-bearers being termed " elders,"[1] are described by the correlative appellation " younger,"[2] or juniors,—just as, if the office-bearers had been termed fathers, they would have been termed children, —their duty to their office-bearers is described under the general word " submission."

The duty of all connected with the Christian Church, whether as officers or private members, is enjoined under the expression, mutual subjection. Humility is enjoined as necessary in order to the right discharge of all these classes of duties ; and the cultivation of this disposition, so requisite to the prosperity and good order of the Church, is recommended by a strong statement, couched in the language of Old Testament scripture, of the peculiar complacency with which God regards the humble, and the contemptuous reprobation with which he regards the proud. Such is a brief analysis of the paragraph, which we shall find of use in guiding our thoughts in our subsequent illustrations.

[1] Πρεσβύτεροι.   [2] Νεώτεροι.

The peculiar duties of the rulers in the Christian Church, the peculiar duties of the members of the Christian Church, and the duties common to both,—these are the important topics to which in the sequel your attention will be successively directed.

I. OF THE DUTIES OF THE RULERS IN THE CHRISTIAN CHURCH.

And first, of the duties of the rulers in the Christian Church. For the right illustration of this part of our subject, it will be requisite that we consider, first, the appellation here given to those who rule in the Christian Church, and to whom that appellation properly belongs; secondly, the duty which they are required to perform; thirdly, the manner in which that duty ought to be performed; and lastly, the motives by which the performance of this duty in this manner is enforced.

CHAP. I. THE APPELLATION HERE GIVEN TO THE RULERS IN THE CHRISTIAN CHURCH: "ELDERS."

§ 1. *The origin and meaning of the appellation.*

The appellation here given to the rulers in the church, those who were to act the part of shepherds to it as the flock of God, the part of overseers to it as the family of God, is that of "elders," or presbyters, which last term is just the Greek word with an English termination. "The elders, or presbyters, who are among you, I exhort." The word in its literal signification describes the persons to whom it is given as of comparatively advanced age. As rule ought to be committed only to those who are characterized by knowledge and wisdom; as, in ordinary circumstances, these are not to be expected in a high degree in very young persons, since both qualifications are generally understood to be of somewhat difficult acquirement and slow growth; as in the simplest form of human government, the domestic, the elder members of the society are the ruling members in it; and as, where the ruling orders in civil society are elective, they are generally chosen from among those of at least mature age, it is not at all wonderful that the appellation, primarily significant merely of superior age, should have been very generally employed to denote superior dignity and authority.[1] The Hebrew ordinary civil rulers are termed "the elders of Israel." The assembled magistrates of Rome were termed the senate or meeting of elders, and its individual members senators. In some of the most extensively spoken continental languages, the title expressive of dignity and rule, and which we would render by the word lord, actually signifies just elder;[2] and the English term "alderman," descriptive of municipal authority and power in many cities, is just an antiquated form of the words "elder man."

It has been the opinion of some of the most judicious and learned students of the history of apostolical and primitive Christianity, that the constitution of the Christian Church was, under apostolic guidance, "modelled for the most part after that religious community with which it stood in closest connection, the Jewish synagogue; such modifications, however, taking place as were required by the nature and design of the Christian community, and the new and peculiar spirit by which it was animated."[3] In this case it would have

---

[1] Οὐ μόνον τὴν πρὸς τὸ ὂν πίστιν αὐτῷ μαρτυροῦσιν οἱ χρήσιμοι, τὴν βασιλίδα τῶν ἀριτῶν ἀλλὰ καὶ πρῶτον αὐτὸν ἀπέφηναν πρεσβύτερον.—Τὸν δὲ φρονήσεως καὶ σοφίας, τῆς πρὸς τὸν Θεὸν πίστεως ἐρασθέντα λέγοι τις ἂν ἐνδίκως εἶναι πρεσβύτερον παρωνυμοῦντα τῷ πρώτῳ.—Philo. Πρεσβυτέρους merito et sapientia dici, non ætate.—Isidor. Hispalens. Carpzov. Sac. Ex. in Ep. ad Heb. p. 500.

[2] Señor, seigneur, of which our own respectful compellation "Sir" is a contraction.

[3] Vitringa, Whately, Neander.

been strange if the designation of the managers of the affairs of the Jewish synagogue, "elders," had not been transferred to the superintendents of the Christian Church. And we cease to wonder that we have no particular account of the formal establishment of the office of elders, it being very probable that the existing order of things in the synagogues for religious instruction and discipline, which had been originally organized by inspired men, was silently, and without the formality of express legislative enactment, transferred, under apostolic superintendence and with apostolic sanction, to the meetings of the disciples, the churches of Christ.

With the exception of "the deacons," a term signifying ministers or servants, who obviously as deacons had no part in the government of the Church, "the elders" appear to be the only ordinary set of office-bearers in the apostolic and primitive churches. In an inspired account of the constitution of the Christian Church, we are informed, when her only Lord and King ascended on high, "he gave"—that is, he appointed, and qualified, and commissioned—"some apostles, and some prophets, and some evangelists, and some pastors and teachers, for the perfecting of the saints, for the work of the ministry, for the edification of the body of Christ." [1] The office of the apostles was altogether peculiar, and they who filled it were intended for the benefit of the Church in all ages. They were the accredited messengers of Christ. They had his mind.[2] He spake by them, and wrought by them; and though they have long left this world, in their inspired writings they are still in the Church, according to the promise of their Lord, "sitting on thrones, judging the twelve tribes of the spiritual Israel;" and in the same writings they are still "going into all the world, proclaiming the gospel;" and their Lord by his Spirit is with them, and will continue to be with them till the end of the

[1] Eph. iv. 11, 12.   [2] 2 Cor. ii. 16.

world. The prophets necessarily disappeared when the prophetic spirit was withdrawn. The evangelists seem not to have been properly office-bearers in the Church, but messengers from the Church to the world lying under the wicked one; and the missionary, in the later ages of the Church, seems to fill a place similar to that occupied by the evangelists in the primitive age. The pastors and teachers—which terms do not seem to denote two distinct classes of men, but two functions of the same general class—appear to be the only permanent ordinary office-bearers appointed for the putting and keeping in fit order, for that is the meaning of the word rendered "perfecting the saints,"—those sanctified in Christ Jesus, called to be saints, the disciples, the brethren,—for the work of the ministry, for the edifying of the body of Christ; and, as we shall see by and by, these pastors and teachers were just the same persons who are here called elders.[1]

In another inspired account by the same apostle of the constitution of the Christian Church, we are informed that "God hath set some in the Church,—first, apostles; secondarily, prophets; thirdly, teachers; after that, miracles; then gifts of healing, helps, governments, diversities of tongues."[2] Here it is plain that the apostles, the prophets, the workers of miracles of various kinds, do not belong to the permanent order of the Church. Fact has decided that question. "Helps," or helpers, seem plainly the deacons; while the teachers and the governments are just the same class of persons as the pastors and teachers, their two different functions of instruction and rule being mentioned in an inverse order in the two cases.

[1] It is by no means meant to throw any doubt on the permanence of the order of deacons. They obviously, however, were not intended to be "rulers" in the Church.
[2] 1 Cor. xii. 28.

As this order of men received the appellation of elders on the same ground as rulers have generally been designated by some such title,[1] and as occupying in the church materially the same place as the Jewish elders did in the synagogue; so, from the great design of their appointment, they are not unfrequently termed bishops, which is an anglicized Greek word, disguised in this way in our version of the New Testament, there is reason to believe, to serve a purpose, and an unworthy one, but which means neither more nor less than our English word "overseers;" by which word indeed, to serve a purpose too, and the same one, it is in one or two cases rendered. That the only bishops known in the New Testament are the same class of persons who are termed elders, may be made very plain in a very few words. Paul, on his journey from Macedonia to Jerusalem, sent from Miletus, and called the elders of Ephesus; and when these elders had come, he exhorted them to "take heed to all the flock over which the Holy Ghost had made them overseers, bishops." Paul, writing to Titus, states that he had left him in Crete, to "ordain elders in every city." He enumerates the qualifications of an elder, and then adds, "for a bishop," or overseer, "must be blameless," etc.[2] If this does not identify the bishop with the elder, what can do it? Suppose a law pointing out the qualifications of a sheriff were to say: A sheriff must be a man of good cha-

---

[1] Πρεσβύτερος, id est, senior, est nomen quod tribuitur Ministris Ecclesiæ, sive quia olim Ministri Ecclesiæ plerumque deligebantur, qui jam essent grandioris ætatis: sive potius quia Ministri Ecclesiæ moribus senes referre debent, iisque is tribuendus honor, qui senibus tribui solet; ita igitur nomen non est ætatis sed officii et dignitatis.—SUICER.

[2] Acts xx. 17, 28; Tit. i. 5-7. Ἐπειδὴ λανθάνει τοὺς πολλοὺς ἡ συνήθεια, μάλιστα, τῆς καινῆς διαθήκης, τοὺς ἐπισκόπους πρεσβυτέρους ὀνομάζουσα, καὶ τοὺς πρεσβυτέρους ἐπισκόπους, σημειωτέον τοῦτο ἐντεῦθεν (Acts xx. 17, 28) καὶ ἐκ τῆς πρὸς Τίτον ἐπιστολῆς καὶ ἐκ τῆς πρὸς Τιμόθεον πρώτης.—Πρεσβυτέρους καὶ τοὺς ἐπισκόπους, καὶ ὁ τῶν πράξεων βίβλος οἶδε λεγομένους. In hunc loc.—ŒCUMENIUS.

PART I.] DUTIES OF THE OFFICE-BEARERS. 187

racter, great activity, and resolute spirit, for it is highly necessary the chief magistrate of the county should be of unspotted reputation; would it be possible to come to any other conclusion than that, in the eye of the Legislature, the sheriff and the first magistrate of the county were just two names for the same officer? How inconsistent would it be to say to a captain: In appointing sergeants you must appoint only men of such qualifications, specifying them, and then add, for these are the proper qualifications for a general or field-marshal! But we need not go further than the text in search of the identification of the Christian elder, and the apostolic bishop, and the apostolic pastor: "The elders I exhort: Act the part of pastors to the flock; shepherd them, acting the part of bishops or overseers."[1] The elders, in other words, are exhorted to act the part of good pastors, good bishops.[2]

The whole care of a Christian church, as a spiritual

[1] Ποιμάνατε ἐπισκοποῦντες. Presbyter quicunque (Petro teste) est veri nominis episcopus.—BLONDELL.

[2] "All the attempts that have been made for the discovery in the writings of the apostles of some traces of inequality among the πρεσβύτεροι (from which *presbyter* and priest) and the ἐπίσκοποι break down entirely alike before ideas and words, before the general tenor and the details. Even were these attempts a little less fruitless, it would be a powerful argument at once against the Roman system, that so laborious a search must be made for its germs, without finding in the whole New Testament a single formal mention of a true inequality between bishops and presbyters. But not even the germs are to be found there: wherever men may fancy they have found them, close at hand there is something that destroys them. The words priest and bishop, elder and overseer, are perpetually used there the one for the other."—*Bungener's History of the Council of Trent*, translated by Scott, p. 378. "Constat nomina illa *episcopi, pastoris, presbyteri*, nomina fuisse tempore apostolorum, officii ejusdem."—HOBBES: *Lersiathan*, cap. 42. JEROME'S words in his note on Tit. i. 7 are characteristically acerb: "Idem est ergo presbyter, qui episcopus; et antequam diaboli instinctu studia in religione fierent, et diceretur in populis: 'Ego sum Pauli, ego Apolli, ego autem Cephæ, communi presbyterorum concilis ecclesia gubernabatur.'"

society, including instruction, superintendence, and discipline, was committed to these elders, though it is very probable that in the primitive churches, as among us, there were authorized public teachers who were not elders, and had no share in the management of any church.

It is plain there was a plurality of such elders in every church. These formed the eldership or presbytery of that church. In the church of Jerusalem, when met for government, we find just the apostles, extraordinary officers, the elders, ordinary officers, and the brethren or church members who listened to their deliberations, and to whom their decision seemed good. We know there were deacons in that church; but their office was not rule, and therefore they are not named. The church of Philippi, which was set in order by the apostle, was composed of " the saints in Christ Jesus," the private members; " with the bishops," overseers; elders, who ruled; and " the deacons," who served.[1]

While the entire spiritual charge of the church was committed to the presbytery or meeting of elders, what we are in the habit of calling the session, there is evidence, not that the elders were divided into a pastor or pastors who only taught, and bishops who ruled; but that, while all the elders severally and in a body superintended and ruled, there were some of these elders " who laboured in word and doctrine," devoting themselves chiefly to the exposition and enforcement of the doctrine and law of our Lord Jesus.

It is comparatively a modern, at any rate it is not a New Testament usage, to apply the term " pastor" exclusively to those teaching elders; that term naturally expressing the whole work of the Christian eldership, and, like the kindred term " bishop," being given in the New Testament to Christian elders indiscriminately. But that such a distinc-

[1] Phil. i. 1.

tion as that between elders who taught and ruled, and elders who only ruled, existed from the beginning, is made probable by the reasonableness and almost necessity of the arrangement, and its obvious tendency to secure the gaining in the best way and in the greatest degree the ends of the Christian eldership; and appears to me proved by the passage in the First Epistle to Timothy, v. 17, of which, after all that has been said for the purpose of reconciling it to the episcopal or independent order of church polity, I am disposed to say, with Dr Owen, that " on the first proposal of this text, that ' the elders who rule well are worthy of double honours, especially those who labour in word and doctrine,' a rational man who is unprejudiced, who never heard of the controversy about ruling elders, can hardly avoid an apprehension that there are two sorts of elders; some of whom labour in word and doctrine, and some who do not so."[1]

§ 2. *Qualifications of Christian elders.*

With regard to the qualifications which are necessary for filling the office of a Christian elder, we have full information in the Epistles of Paul to Timothy and Titus. " This is a true saying," says he, in his First Epistle to Timothy, iii. 1, " If a man desire the office of a bishop," an overseer, an elder, in the Christian Church, " he desireth a good work. A bishop then must be blameless, the husband of

---

[1] " Si omnes duplici honore sint digni qui bene præsunt maxime ii qui laborant in sermone et doctrina" perspicuum est, fuisse aliquos qui non (sic) laborarunt. Nam si omnes fuissent tales, sensus fuisset absurdus, sed μάλιστα ponit discrimen. Si dicerem omnes academici qui bene student sunt duplici honore digni maxime ii qui laborant in studio theologiæ, vel immo non omnes incumbere studio theologiæ, vel insulse loquor. Quamobrem fateor illum esse sensum maxime genuinum quo pastores et doctores discernuntur ab aliis qui solum gubernabant, Rom. xii. 8, de quibus ambobus legimus, 1 Tim. v. 17.—WHITAKER.

one wife, vigilant, sober, of good behaviour, given to hospitality, apt to teach; not given to wine, no striker, not greedy of filthy lucre; but patient, not a brawler, not covetous; one that ruleth well his own house, having his children in subjection with all gravity; for if a man know not how to rule his own family, how shall he take care of the house," the family, " of God? Not a novice," a late convert, " lest, being lifted up with pride, he fall into the condemnation of the devil. Moreover, he must have a good report of those who are without; lest he fall into reproach and the snare of the devil." "Ordain elders," says he to Titus, " in every city, as I had appointed thee. If any be blameless, the husband of one wife, having faithful children, not accused of riot, or unruly. For a bishop must be blameless, as the steward of God; not self-willed, not soon angry, not given to wine, no striker, not given to filthy lucre; but a lover of hospitality, a lover of good men, just, holy, temperate; holding fast the faithful word as he hath been taught, that he may be able by sound doctrine both to exhort and to convince gainsayers." These are qualifications which are requisite in all elders, though some of them may be required in a higher degree in those who are called to labour in word and doctrine.

§ 3. *Of the manner in which elders were invested with office.*

With regard to the manner in which the elders were invested with these offices in the apostolic Church, we have comparatively little information. We know that Paul and Barnabas ordained elders in every church which was gathered by their ministry;[1] and that Titus was enjoined by Paul to ordain elders in every city where the gospel had taken root.[2] But we should undoubtedly err, were we concluding that these offices were appointed by the apostles

[1] Acts xiv. 23.   [2] Tit. i. 5.

or evangelists, whatever their authority might be, without consulting the brethren. When we reflect on the nature and design of a Christian church, and take into consideration the probable method of electing an apostle in room of Judas, and the distinctly recorded facts respecting the election of the deacons, we cannot doubt that the elders were elected by the brethren from among themselves, and presented by them to the apostles, evangelists, or other church rulers, who, with fasting, prayer, and laying on of hands, solemnly set them apart to the discharge of the functions of the office to which they had been chosen; thus in the most impressive way intimating their conviction of their fitness for the office, and their cordial acknowledgment of them as fellow-labourers, and commending them to the special care and blessing of their common Lord. So much for the elders to whom the apostle here addresses so solemn and affectionate an exhortation.

CHAP. II. OF THE DUTIES OF CHRISTIAN ELDERS.

§ 1. *Of the figurative terms in which these duties are described: acting the part of a shepherd and an overseer.*

Let us now, in the second place, attend to the duty which is here enjoined on these elders. They are enjoined to "feed the flock of God, and to take the oversight of it." The two words employed to describe the elder's duty, are suited to the two figurative representations here given us of the objects of their care. If viewed as the flock of God, they are to feed, or rather, as the word properly signifies, they are to act the part of shepherds to them. If viewed as the property of God or the family of God, they are to act the part of overseers in reference to them. The Israelitish people are often in Scripture termed "the flock of God," and their rulers appointed by him their shepherds; they are represented also as the peculiar property and as the family of God, and their rulers as overseers, tutors, governors, appointed by the Father. The Christian Church is the antitype of the Israelitish people. The whole body of believers are the flock of God, the property of God, the family of God; for in the new economy all things are of God by Christ Jesus. We are Christ's, Christ is God's. Jesus Christ, who laid down his life for the sheep, is the Great Shepherd, the Chief Shepherd, whose own the sheep are. To him is committed the care of the property which was purchased, redeemed to God, by his blood; and he, as the Son, is entrusted with the management of the whole family called by his name. He is the shepherd, and bishop or overseer, of their souls.[1] Christian elders are here represented as under shepherds, subordinate overseers; and their duty to that portion of the flock of God committed to their care is what the apostle here refers to.[2]

It has, I believe, been very generally supposed by interpreters, that the expression rendered "feed" refers solely to instruction; and that rendered by "taking oversight," to discipline and government. If the term "feed" adequately represented the force of the original term, there might be a good deal said for this mode of interpretation; for, no doubt, knowledge is mental food, and instruction is spiritual feeding. But the truth is, the word signifies, generally, act the part, discharge the duty, of a shepherd, and is ordinarily, when used in a figurative sense, significant of ruling, being applied to

[1] John x. 11-14; Heb. iii. 6; 1 Pet. ii. 25.
[2] The apostle gives the elders the charge which the Chief Shepherd had given him on a very memorable occasion (John xxi. 15-17). That scene was always in his mind (2 Pet. i. 14). It is remarked by Stanley (*Serm. and Essays on the Apost. Age*), that "there is no part of the New Testament, with the exception of John x., where the image of the Shepherd is so prominently brought forward as in the First Epistle of Peter."

kings.¹ To procure and administer food to the flock is an important part of the shepherd's duty, but it is not his only duty: he must strengthen the diseased, and heal the sick, and bind up the broken, and bring again that which was driven away, and seek that which was lost. He must go before them, and guide them, and govern them. The whole duties of the Christian eldership are included in shepherding the flock; and equally extensive is the other figurative representation of the elder superintending, that is, taking care of. If it refer to property, how can such a property, consisting of immortal minds, be taken care of? Must not instruction, putting them in the way of taking care of themselves, be a part of the overseer's work? and if it refer to a family, must not the good steward, tutor, and overseer, the ruler over his master's family, not merely superintend the conduct of the household, keep them at their proper work, out of mischief, away from danger, but "give to every one his portion of meat in due season?"² The first term does not, then, exclusively refer to instruction; nor the second to superintendence and government. They are two figurative representations, each of them embracing the whole compass of the duty of the eldership of a Christian church.

§ 2. *Of the duties themselves.*

The whole of the duties of the Christian eldership do, however, naturally enough range themselves under the two heads of instruction and discipline, or superintendence and government; and to these in their order I wish very briefly to call your attention.

---

¹ Ποιμαίνω is a word much more comprehensive in its meaning than βόσκω. Ποιμήν is applied to Kings, Eurip. Phœn. 1157; Hom. Il. i. 263; Xen. Mem. iii. 1, 2. *Vide* Casauboni Exercitt. Anti-Baron. xvi. § 133. Χριστὸς ποιμήν, ὅτι ἡμᾶς νέμει.—CHRYSOSTOM. Olshausen justly remarks that ποιμαίνειν includes both κυβέρνησις and διδασκαλία.

² Luke xii. 42.

(1.) *Instruction.*

First, then, Christian elders are to act the part of shepherds and overseers to those under their care, by providing and administering instruction to them. It is an important part of the shepherd's duty to find wholesome nourishing pasture for his flock. It is an important part of the duty of the overseer of the family to see that every member of it be furnished with a sufficient portion of suitable food. "The truth as it is in Jesus," the doctrine and the law of Christ, serve in the spiritual economy a purpose analogous to that which food does in the animal economy. Suitable wholesome food must be eaten and digested, in order to health and bodily growth, and indeed to the continuance of animal life; and divine truth must be understood and believed, and thus become influential on the intellect and conscience and affections, in order to the continuance of spiritual life, and to the healthy exercise of the functions of the new creature. The private members of the Church, as well as the ministers of Jesus Christ, are "nourished up by the words of faith and good doctrine," whereunto they attain; and the "new-born babes grow" by "the sincere milk of the word," which the instincts of their new nature lead them to desire.

Regularly and effectually to meet this exigence is one leading object of the Christian eldership; and where suitable provision is not made for securing the growing intelligence of the members of a Christian church, there must be, on the part of the eldership, most blameable neglect of duty. When the disciples come together on the first day of the week to observe the ordinances, the ordinance of "doctrine" or teaching must be attended to; and the assembled brethren must be taught to hold fast and observe all things, whether doctrine, law, or institution, which the Lord has commanded them. On these occasions the elders who labour in word and doctrine should be prepared, after close study and fervent prayer, to present to their brethren a clear and impressive exhibition of the meaning, evidence, and practical bearing of some of our Lord's doctrines, or a perspicuous and practical explanation and enforcement of some of our Lord's laws, having a reference to what they know to be the necessities and capacities of their audience; taking care not to confine themselves to a few topics, to descant on which may be peculiarly easy to themselves and palatable to their hearers, but endeavouring as much as possible to bring out in the course of these exercises, so far as they have discovered it, " the whole counsel of God;" and withholding nothing that can be profitable, whether it may be pleasing or otherwise. When we consider how much the great body of Christians, belonging to the classes whose time is chiefly devoted to obtaining the necessaries and comforts of life for themselves and families, must be dependent on the instructions received on the Lord's day for their knowledge of Christian truth, the importance of Christian teachers endeavouring on such occasions to communicate the largest possible amount of distinct impressive instruction, both doctrinal and practical, must appear great indeed.

The Christian preacher, if he is really wise, when teaching the people knowledge, will give good heed to his doctrine, that it be wholesome and nourishing, and, if possible, palatable. He will seek to find out, first, true and important thoughts, and then plain acceptable words; and he will endeavour that his words be as goads, entering readily, and as riveted nails when they have entered, sticking fast.[1] The teaching elder ill discharges this, his highest duty, who satisfies himself with commonplace statement or empty

[1] Eccles. xii. 13.

declamation; or who spends the hours devoted to Christian instruction in metaphysical discussions, and " questions that profit not." It has been well said, " To preach, to show the extent of our learning or the subtlety of our wit, to blazon them in the eyes of the people with the beggarly accounts of a few words which glitter, but convey little light and less warmth, is a dishonest use of sacred time; it is not to preach the gospel, but ourselves:" it is not to feed, but to starve, our hearers.

It is the duty of the Christian teaching elder not only thus to teach publicly on the Lord's day, but also, as God gives opportunity, to teach " from house to house," taking such opportunities for presenting Christian truth in a form more familiar than befits the character of public instruction, and more suited to the circumstances of the individuals addressed. It seems to me also, that a Christian eldership are but following out the spirit of the injunction in the text, when they endeavour to secure, and earnestly recommend for the perusal of those under their care, the use of a collection of really good and appropriate books, fitted to promote the knowledge of Christian truth, the cultivation of Christian feeling, and the performance of Christian duty, by enabling their readers better to understand the Bible.

The use of all appropriate means, especially the preaching of the word, for securing that the brethren under their care grow in accuracy and extent of Christian knowledge, must ever be considered by the Christian eldership as the fundamental part of their duty. The church is the school of Christ, and the elders are the schoolmasters. The maxim, that ignorance is the mother of devotion, is utterly inapplicable to the religion of Christ. Knowledge is necessary in order to faith; and a well-instructed Christian mind is the only soil in which can grow and flourish the fair flowers and the rich fruits of devout feeling and holy conduct, "which are by Christ Jesus to the praise and glory of God."

The duty of instructing the brethren lies with peculiar weight on the teaching elder. It is his business, his appropriate work, to which above all things he must give himself, and to which he must endeavour to make all things subservient. Whatever may be cursorily done, this must be done carefully; and he must "study to prove himself a workman that needs not to be ashamed, rightly dividing the word of truth." At the same time, every Christian elder, though not called to labour in word and doctrine, ought to endeavour to promote the instruction of the brethren. Every elder, or bishop, should be "apt to teach;" both able and disposed to communicate Christian instruction to his brethren. Indeed, till "the earth be full of the knowledge of the Lord as the waters cover the sea," it is the duty of every Christian man "to teach his neighbour, and every man his brother, saying, Know the Lord." And the Christian elder, whose ordinary and principal business is to superintend and govern, is not only warranted, but bound, to turn to account his intercourse with the brethren in discharging his appropriate functions, for directly as well as indirectly endeavouring to promote their progress in that knowledge of God and our Lord Jesus Christ, through which, and through which alone, grace, mercy, and peace can be multiplied to them,—through which, and through which alone, they can become the holy, happy, active, useful persons that all members of a Christian church ought to be.

This duty of instruction must be performed to *all* the flock. The command of the chief Shepherd is not only, "Feed my sheep," but "feed my lambs;"[1] and there does seem something wanting in a Christian church where pro-

[1] John xxi. 15-17.

vision is not made, and made by the elders, directly or indirectly, personally or by guiding and superintending the exertions of others, for the instruction of the younger branches of the family. The instruction of Christian children is the appropriate work of Christian parents, and is never likely to be so efficiently performed as by them; but it seems plain, that not only is it the duty of Christian elders, in their work of superintending and governing, to see that parents discharge their obligations in this respect, but also, by a system of religious training, common to all the children connected with the Church, not to supersede, but to assist and supplement, parental instruction.

In these remarks I have been preaching chiefly to two individuals : " my true yoke-fellow, who serves with me as a son in the gospel of Jesus Christ," and myself. The next department of the discourse will be directed to the brethren of the eldership who rule, though they do not labour in word and doctrine. But if those illustrations of the law of Christ in reference to elders serve, as I hope they will, their proper purpose in us and in them, the congregation are likely to be fully as much the better for them, as for any sermons they have ever heard addressed more directly to themselves. The importance and the difficulty of rightly instructing a Christian congregation, especially such a congregation as this, consisting of so many individuals, placed in such a variety of circumstances, and possessed of such a variety of capacities and tastes for religious mental training, are, I trust, justly estimated by your ministers; and it is our earnest wish, " by the manifestation of the truth, to commend ourselves to every man's conscience in the sight of God." We would not willingly conceal nor corrupt any portion of the doctrines or the laws of our Lord. We wish to preach Christ, the sole authoritative teacher and law-giver, the sole atoning Saviour, the sole sovereign Lord;

"warning every man, and teaching every man in all wisdom, that we may present every man perfect in Christ Jesus." "Being allowed of God to be put in trust with the gospel, we would so speak, not as pleasing men, but God, who trieth the hearts." Sensible of the importance of rightly dividing the word of truth, we would "give attendance to meditation and to reading," as well as to exhortation and doctrine; we would "shun profane and vain babblings, and speak the things, and only the things, that become sound doctrine;" in our teaching "showing incorruptness, and sound speech that cannot be condemned."[1]

Help us, brethren, with your prayers. Pray for us, that our understandings may be more and more opened, that we may understand the Scriptures; that, being more thoroughly and extensively taught of God ourselves, we may be the better fitted for teaching you. "Brethren, I beseech you, for the Lord Jesus' sake, and for the love of the Spirit, that ye strive together with us in your prayers for us; that our minds and hearts may be more and more filled with the truth, and the love of it; and that utterance may be given us, that we may open our mouths boldly, to make known the mystery of the gospel; that the word of the Lord may have free course and be glorified among us;"[2] that we may speak it as it ought to be spoken, with firm faith and melting affection. It is your interest as well as ours, that you should be thus employed. "Were people much in the duty of prayer for their teachers, not only would the ministers be the better for it; the people themselves would receive back their prayers with much gain into their bosom. They would have the returned benefit of it, as the vapours that go from below fall down again upon the earth in sweet showers, and

---

[1] 2 Cor. iv. 2; Col. i. 28; 1 Cor. i. 23; 2 Cor. iv. 5; 1 Thess. ii. 4; 1 Tim. iv. 13, 15; 1 Tim. vi. 20; Tit. ii. 1, 8.
[2] Rom. xv. 30; Eph. vi. 19; Col. iv. 3; 2 Thess. iii. 1.

make it fruitful. If there went up many prayers for ministers, their doctrine would drop as the rain, and distil as the dew, and the sweet influence of it would make fruitful the valleys, the humble hearts receiving it."[1] And we pledge ourselves to reciprocate your friendly supplications. " God forbid that we should sin against the Lord by ceasing to pray for you." Daily will we " bow our knees unto the Father of our Lord Jesus Christ, of whom the whole family in heaven and in earth are named," that the gospel may come to you " not in word only, but in power, with the Holy Ghost, and much assurance;" "that the God of our Lord Jesus Christ, the Father of glory, may give to you the spirit of wisdom and revelation in the knowledge of him; that the eyes of your understanding being enlightened, ye may know what is the hope of his calling, and what the riches of his inheritance in the saints, and what is the exceeding greatness of his power in them that believe," transforming them by the renewing of their mind, purifying their hearts by faith, filling them with all joy and peace in believing; and " that he would grant you, according to the riches of his glory, to be strengthened with might by his Spirit in the inner man; that Christ may dwell in your hearts by faith; that ye, being rooted and grounded in love, may be able to comprehend with all saints what is the breadth, and length, and depth, and height, and to know the love of Christ, which passeth knowledge, being filled with all the fulness of God."[2]

(2.) *Superintendence.*

I proceed to remark, in the second place, that Christian elders are to act the part of shepherds and overseers to those under their care, by *superintending* and *governing* them. The shepherd has but imperfectly done his work when he

---

[1] Leighton. [2] Eph. i. 17-19, iii. 16-19.

has procured for, and administered to, his flock wholesome nourishment. He must watch over them; he must not allow either wolves or goats to mix with them, and, should such find their way among them, he must use appropriate means to get rid of them; he must endeavour to prevent the sheep from straying, and, when they do wander, he must employ every proper method to bring them back; he must endeavour to preserve them from the attacks of disease, and administer suitable preventives and medicines for prevailing maladies; and even at personal hazard he must protect them from those beasts of prey who go about seeking to devour them. The overseer or steward has but imperfectly done his duty, when he has secured that the children are furnished with suitable instruction. It is his business to see that they pay a proper attention to the instruction prepared for them, and make due improvement. He must look to the formation of their character and the direction of their conduct. He must take care that they are neither idle nor mischievous; that they are kind to each other, and dutiful to all. Both the shepherd and the overseer must be superintendents and governors. In like manner, the furnishing the flock and family of God with an abundance of wholesome spiritual nourishment, though, as we have seen, one most important part of the duty of Christian elders, is by no means the whole of it. The elders are not only to "speak the word of God" to their charge: they are to " have," hold, or exercise, " rule over them;" they are to " care" for them, to " watch for their souls."[1]

The duties of rule or superintendence which devolve on Christian elders may be considered in reference either to the Christian society over which they are placed viewed as a body, or to the individual members of that body. The fundamental part of this duty, so far as the society is con-

[1] Heb. xiii. 7, 17, 24; 1 Tim. iii. 5, v. 17.

cerned, and without a careful performance of which the other duties, whether to the society or to its members, can only be very unsatisfactorily discharged, is to take care that it be composed of the right materials. How could a shepherd manage a flock composed of swine as well as of sheep? or how could an overseer manage a family into which aliens, " strange children," were continually intruding themselves? Nothing can be plainer from the New Testament than this, that though Christian churches are the grand means for converting the world, the apparent conversion of the worldling must precede, not follow, his admission into the church. The great ends to be gained by Christian churches, whether in reference to their Lord, as living manifestations of his truth, and holiness, and grace; or in reference to their members—their edification in knowledge, faith, love, and Christian excellence and usefulness generally; or in reference to the world lying under the wicked one—their conviction and conversion,—will be secured just in the degree in which these societies are formed of men who really know and believe the truth, and have felt its transforming efficacy. The churches of Christ must be churches, that is, assemblies, societies of saints, " separated persons," " devoted persons," " sanctified persons;" separated from the present evil world, devoted to the service of God and his Son, sanctified by the influence of the Holy Ghost. Such are the designations given the members of the Church in the apostolic epistles: " Beloved of God, called to be saints, sanctified in Christ Jesus, calling on his name, brethren, faithful, elect," that is, selected " by a spiritual separation to the obedience of faith, and sprinkling of the blood of Jesus Christ, men that have obtained like precious faith with the apostles."

The office-bearers are " stewards of the mysteries of Christ." It is their business " to take the precious from the vile." They are builders of the temple of the Lord, which ought to be composed of " living stones," of precious materials; and they must take care that the materials they employ in building it up be not " wood, hay, and stubble," but " gold, silver, and precious stones." [1] Christian elders should admit none to the communion of the church except those who make an intelligent and credible profession of the faith,—who, in the judgment of an enlightened charity, are Christians in the only true sense of that word; and should, as in every church will be the case, persons be admitted who are not what they appear to be, when the real character is developed, the elders ought, in the exercise of an impartial discipline, to exclude them from a place they should never have occupied; and by continuing to occupy which, while their characters remain unchanged, they can only do injury to all the interests which the Christian Church is meant to subserve.

Christian elders are to seek to promote this healthy state of a Christian church, not only by careful admission and discipline, but by such a clear and faithful exhibition of the holy doctrines and laws of Christ, and by keeping the society so actively engaged in the great object of their association, the promoting each other's edification, and the advancing the cause of Christ in the world, as will make ungodly men little desirous, while they continue ungodly, to enter such a society; and if, by a mistake on either side, they have entered it, will make them soon feel that they can be comfortable in it in no other way than by imbibing the spirit and submitting to the law of its great Founder.

It is the duty of Christian elders not only thus to endeavour that the society be composed only of right members, but in all their meetings to preside among them; keeping before them the law of Christ; taking care that they " continue stedfastly " in the observance of Christian insti-

[1] Jer. xv. 15; 1 Cor. iii. 12-15.

tutions, keeping the ordinances committed to them by the apostles, "holding the traditions" as taught in the Scriptures, "the apostles' doctrine, and fellowship, and in breaking of bread, and in prayers;" that they do all things as a body which Christ Jesus has commanded them, and that they do them all " decently, and in order."

But the Christian elders must not only thus shepherd the flock of Christ, oversee the family of God, viewed as an organized body, but they must act the part of shepherds and overseers to the individuals of which that flock and family are composed. This is indeed necessarily implied in the right discharge of their duty to the society as a society; for how can a society be kept pure but by its members being such as they should be; and how can this be secured but by superintending and watching individual conduct? The spiritual shepherd must "look well to his flock, and know the state of his herd." How otherwise can he "strengthen the diseased, heal the sick, bind up that which is broken, and bring again that which is driven away?" how is he to "warn the unruly, to comfort the feeble-minded, and to support the weak?"[1] It is the duty of the Christian elder not impertinently to intrude into private affairs, but carefully and affectionately to watch the whole conduct of those under his care, and to administer caution, encouragement, advice, comfort, rebuke, and exhortation, as circumstances require; and to do all this as an under shepherd, an appointed overseer, in the name of Him who, counting him trustworthy, has put him into this ministry.

In thus taking care of the house of God by ruling it, Christian elders are never to forget the true nature of their rule: they are "men under authority." They are not arbitrary despots, they are not even constitutional lawgivers; they are but constituted administrators of the law of the

[1] Ezek. xxxiv. 4; 1 Thess. v. 14.

one Master who is in heaven. The flock is to be managed according to the revealed will of the great, good Proprietor-Shepherd, whose own the sheep are. The family is to be governed according to the distinctly declared mind of the one Father who is in heaven.

But Christian elders, as well as those under their care, are to remember that they are *rulers* under him, that they must take their orders from him, that they are accountable to him, that the sheep are not to dictate to the shepherds, nor the children to the tutors and governors. If Christian elders seek to please even the members of the church in any other way than by pleasing them for their good for edification, by declaring and executing the law of Christ, they will prove that they are not the servants of Christ, but the servants of men. The authority of Christian elders, though subordinate and deputed, is real authority; so that, in the right discharge of their official duties, " he that despiseth them, despiseth not man, but God." He that contemns the humblest subordinate magistrate, regularly appointed and acting within the limits of his delegated authority, is guilty of disobedience to the supreme power. Such is a short view of the duty of Christian elders, as shepherds of the flock, overseers of the family of God; duty included under the two heads, instruction, and superintendence or government.

CHAP. III. OF THE MANNER IN WHICH THESE DUTIES ARE TO BE PERFORMED.

Let us now, in the third place, turn our attention to the account which the apostle gives of the manner in which these duties should be performed. In discharging their duties, Christian elders are not to act " by constraint, but willingly; not for filthy lucre, but of a ready mind; neither as being lords over God's heritage, but being ensamples to the flock."[1] We shall consider shortly, in their order, these characteristics of the right mode of performing the duties of the Christian eldership.

§ 1. *"Not by constraint, but willingly."*

Christian elders are to shepherd the flock, and superintend the family of God, "not by constraint, but willingly." Some have supposed that these words refer rather to the flock or family than to the shepherds or overseers; that they describe rather the means to be employed than the temper to be cherished by Christian elders; that they intimate that the flock of Christ are to be ruled, not by *force*, but by *persuasion*; that they are to be drawn, not driven; and that the Christian shepherds are to take as beacons, not examples, those Jewish shepherds who "with force and with cruelty ruled"[2] the sheep of the Lord. This is unquestionably truth, important truth; but it cannot be brought out of the apostle's words without using violence. The three double clauses, all of them, obviously refer to the state of the mind of the Christian elder in the discharge of his duty. Even some of those interpreters who have seen this clearly, have yet fallen into a slight misapprehen-

---

[1] "Dum pastores ad officium hortari vult, tria potissimum vitia notat, quæ plurimum obesse solent: pigritiam, scilicet, lucri captandi cupidatem et licentiam dominandi. Primo vitio opponit alacritatem aut voluntarium studium: secundo liberalem affectum: tertio moderationem et modestiam qua seipsos in ordinem cogant."—CALVIN.

[2] Ezek. xxxiv. 4. "Though most expositors apply μὴ ἀναγκαστῶς ἀλλ' ἑκουσίως to the bishop's willingness to his work, yet Dr Hammond applieth it to the bishop's manner of guiding the flock, as not constraining them by force, nor using violence in an active sense. And whether these words prove this or not, other scriptures, and the nature of the case, prove that bishops have no power of corporal force, but of ruling by God's word, and that none but volunteers are capable of church privileges, and communion, and pastoral conduct."—RICHARD BAXTER.

sion as to the precise meaning and reference of the words before us. From not noticing that these words are equally connected with both the figurative injunctions of the duties of the Christian elder, and from being more occupied with the sound than the sense of the phrase, "taking the oversight," it has been common to consider these words as describing exclusively the temper in which the office of the eldership should be undertaken, not the disposition in which its duties should be habitually performed. It is obvious, however, that it refers to "feed the flock of Christ," as well as to "taking the oversight;" and it is equally obvious, that the word rendered "taking the oversight" does not refer to a person's entering on the eldership, though very applicable to such a person, but to persons who are elders; and might have been still more literally rendered, "superintending them;"[2] that is, not so much undertaking, as exercising, superintendence.

The passage has often been quoted to prove, that no man should be compelled by ecclesiastical authority to take office in the Church generally, or to take office in a particular church; but its bearing on this subject, though important, is indirect. The meaning is, that a Christian elder should perform his duties, not reluctantly, as something that he is obliged to do, but cheerfully, as something that he delights to do; not as a task to a hard master that he must perform, but as an honourable and delightful service, which carries its reward in the satisfaction it affords. The more the Christian elder is constrained by a regard to the authority of Christ, a sense of his grace, and the love of the brotherhood, to the discharge of these duties, so much the better; but these are species of constraint that not only do not interfere with, but necessarily imply, willinghood.[2] It is

[1] Ἐπισκοποῦντες.
[2] Necessitas incumbit, 1 Cor. ix. 16. Sed hujus sensum absorbet lu-

true of duty generally, and eminently true of the duties of the Christian eldership, that they have no value in the estimation of God, and are little likely to be effectual for answering their object, unless they proceed from a willing mind; unless, as the apostle expresses it in the Epistle to Philemon, they are, "not as it were of necessity, but willingly." The duties of the eldership must be performed not "grudgingly or of necessity; for God loveth a cheerful" doer as well as a cheerful "giver."[1] A Christian elder, if he is what he should be, will be very thankful that God has given him a place in his house at all; and though sensible of the difficulties of his duties, and his unfitness for their right discharge, he will be still more grateful that he has been honoured with office there. He will be disposed to adopt the apostle's words, "I thank Christ Jesus our Lord, who has enabled me, for that he counted me trustworthy, faithful, putting me into the ministry;" and to say with the Psalmist, "What shall I render to the Lord for this benefit?" The spirit of the under shepherd should be that of the chief Shepherd, who, when called according to his covenant engagement to lay down his life for the sheep, was "not rebellious, neither turned away back," but said, "Lo, I come;" "I have a baptism to be baptized with; and how am I straitened till it be accomplished!"[2] "There may be," as Archbishop Leighton says, " in a Christian elder, very great reluctance in engaging and adhering to the work, from a sense of the excellence of it, and his unfitness; and the deep apprehension of those high interests, the glory of God and the salvation of souls; and yet he

---

bentia. Id valet et in suscipiendo et in gerendo munere. Non sine reprehensione sunt pastores, qui, si res integra sit, mallent quidvis potius esse.—BENGEL.

[1] Philem. 14; 2 Cor. ix. 7.
[2] 1 Tim. i. 12; Isa. l. 5; Ps. cxvi. 12, xl. 7; Luke xii. 50.

enters and continues in it with this willingness of mind, with most single and earnest desires of doing all he can for God and the flock of God; only grieved that there is in him so little suitableness of heart, so little holiness and acquaintance with God for enabling him to it; but might he find that, he were satisfied; and in attendance upon that, goes on and waits, and is doing according to his little skill and strength, and cannot leave it; is constrained indeed, but all the constraint is love to Jesus, and for the sake of the souls He hath bought; a constraint far different from the constraint here discharged; yea, indeed, that very willingness which is opposed to that other constraint."

§ 2. "*Not for filthy lucre, but of a ready mind.*"

Christian elders are to shepherd the flock, and superintend the family of God, not "for filthy lucre, but of a ready mind;" as well as "not from constraint, but willingly." The former clause, as we have just seen, is equivalent to—not reluctantly, but cheerfully. This seems equivalent to—not in a self-interested, mercenary disposition, but in a disinterested spirit of gratitude to God and love to the brethren.

There is nothing wrong in a Christian elder, who devotes his time and talents to the promotion of the good of the church over which he is placed, receiving, from the church's justice and gratitude, their sense of his claims on them, and their obligations to him, temporal support. It is the command of the apostle, "Let him who is taught, communicate to him that teacheth in all good things." It is the ordination of our Lord, "that they who preach the gospel should live of the gospel," just as "they who ministered at the altar lived by the altar." "Who goeth a warfare any time at his own charges? who planteth a vineyard, and eateth not of the fruit thereof? or who feedeth a flock, and eateth not of the milk of the flock? Say I these things as a man? or saith not the law the same also? For it is written in the law of Moses, Thou shalt not muzzle the mouth of the ox that treadeth out the corn. Doth God care for oxen? or saith he it altogether for our sakes? For our sakes, no doubt, this is written, that he who ploweth should plow in hope; and that he that thrasheth in hope should be partaker of his hope. If we have sown unto you spiritual things, is it a great thing if we shall reap your carnal things?"[1] These passages seem to refer to the teaching elder, whose whole attention is to be directed to reading and meditation in private, and to "word and doctrine," both "publicly and from house to house;" but it is plain that the elders who rule, if they are in circumstances in which they cannot devote the time necessary to the service of the church, without injustice to themselves and families, are equally entitled to support. This is implied in the injunction, "Let the elders who rule well be counted worthy of double honour," obviously not excluding the honour of voluntary support, "especially those who labour in word and doctrine."

But while all this is true, it is not less true that the duties of Christian elders must be performed "not for filthy lucre." No man must convert the Christian eldership into a trade, in this way "making gain of godliness." Even with those elders who are entirely dependent on their labours, who have no source of income but the effect of the authority and grace of Christ on the minds and consciences and hearts of those to whom they minister, the principle must be, "Freely ye have received, freely ye give." And wherever sacred duties are performed from a regard to worldly gain, in whatever form,—whether in the form of fixed stipend, or occasional gifts, or increased respectability

[1] 1 Cor. ix. 7-11.

of character and worldly influence, leading to success in worldly business,—there is fearful desecration. The apostle obviously lays much stress on this point. In his First Epistle to Timothy (iii. 3) he says, a bishop must "not be greedy of filthy lucre, not covetous;" and in his Epistle to Titus (i. 7) he repeats the declaration. Such repeated warnings were not more than the case required. There has been too much of this in every age of the Church, and the evil is not unknown even in our own times; nor is it confined within the limits of richly endowed churches, where its existence, if not less criminal than elsewhere, is less wonderful. It is a most deplorable thing when a regard to secular interest is allowed to interfere either with the declaration of Christian doctrine or the administration of Christian discipline; when professed Christian teachers "prepare war against him that putteth not into their mouths,"[1] and "teach things that they ought not for filthy lucre's sake, through covetousness, with feigned words, making merchandise of their people, having hearts exercised to covetous practices, serving not the Lord Jesus Christ, but their own belly;"[2] and when the rulers of the Church, from secular considerations, prefer one before another, and do anything in the administration of discipline by partiality; when "the watchmen are greedy dogs that can never have enough, all looking to their own way, every one for his gain from his quarter;" and when Malachi's question is an appropriate one, "Who is there among you that would shut the doors for nought? neither do ye kindle the fire on my altar for nought."[3] Balaam's resolution should be formed and kept, not only as it was by him, in the letter, but as it was not by him, in the spirit. "If Balak would give me his house full of silver and gold, I cannot go beyond the

[1] Mic. iii. 5.   [2] Tit. i. 11; 2 Pet. ii. 3, 14; Rom. xvi. 18.
[3] Isa. lvi. 11; Mal. i. 10.

word of the Lord my God, to do less or more." Yet it is very delightful to perceive that so many of our ministers are men who, with the same talents and education and effort, might have secured for themselves far higher secular advantages than they possess, or ever can expect to possess, as Christian elders. And the disinterestedness of many of our Christian elders who rule, but do not labour in word and doctrine, in not only cheerfully giving their unpaid and often ill-estimated labour to the churches, but, in addition, being patterns to the believers in liberally giving of their substance to promote the support and extension of the cause of Christ, makes it very evident that they shepherd the flock, that they superintend the family, of God, "not for filthy lucre, but of a ready mind." The Christian elder, when he becomes old and grey-headed, should be able to say with Samuel, "Behold, here I am; witness against me before the Lord; whose ox have I taken? or whose ass have I taken? or whom have I defrauded?" or with Paul, "I have coveted no man's silver or gold;" "I seek not yours, but you."[1]

Disinterestedness, in opposition to mercenariness, should characterize the labours of the Christian elder. Regard to the divine glory; gratitude for the divine grace; love to the Saviour who died, and to those for whom he died; eager desire that his name may not be blasphemed through the inconsistent conduct of those who are called by it, and that it may be glorified in the holiness and happiness of his blood-bought heritage, and in bringing down the people in subjection to him, making them "willing in the day of his power:" these are the principles which should preside in the mind and heart of the Christian elder, and make him alert and cheerful in all the duties, however burdensome, of his official calling; producing a forwardness of mind far

[1] Num. xxii. 18; 1 Sam. xii. 3; Acts xx. 33; 2 Cor. xii. 14.

superior to what the stimulus of covetousness can create. Yes, as the good Archbishop says, "it is love, much love, which gives much unwearied care and much skill in this charge. How sweet is it to him that loves to bestow himself, 'to spend and be spent,' upon his service whom he loves! Jacob, in the same kind of service, endured all, and found it light by reason of love, the cold of the nights and the heat of the days seven years for his Rachel, and they seemed to him but a few days because he loved her. Love is the great endowment of a shepherd of Christ's flock. He says not to Peter, Art thou wise, or learned, or eloquent? but, 'Lovest thou me? lovest thou me? lovest thou me?' Art thou of a ready mind? 'Feed my sheep: feed my lambs.'"

§ 3. *Not as lords of God's heritage, but being ensamples to the flock.*

Christian elders are to shepherd the flock and oversee the children of God, "not as lords of God's heritage,[1] but being ensamples to the flock." These duties are to be performed not in a proud, overbearing spirit. They are duties of *rule*, and therefore there is a temptation to pride in performing them. But the elders are to remember that, though they are rulers in, they are not lords over, the family of God. The Son alone is lord over his own house. We proclaim not ourselves lords, says the Apostle Paul; "we preach Jesus *the* Lord," the only Lord, the One Master and Proprietor. There were rulers in Israel; but Jehovah alone, in the highest sense of the word, was Israel's king. The soil was his, and so were the people. Of the spiritual Israel, Jehovah-Jesus is the proprietor and lord. He is Lord of all: he is our Lord, and we are all brethren. For

[1] Presbyteri postea dominatum sumserunt. Unde ex *Seniore* factus est *Signore*, in Italia presertim.—BENGEL.

the good of the whole, some of the brethren are called by him to rule under him, to administer his laws; but this lays no foundation for claiming to be lords of their faith. "The bride is the bridegroom's;" the Church is the Lord's. The Church does not belong to the elders, but the elders to the Church. "All things are *yours*, and ye are Christ's, and Christ is God's." "Diotrephes, who loveth to have the pre-eminence," is the beacon, not the model, for Christian elders.

The Christian elder, even when he must "come with a rod," as but too often is necessary, should come "in love, and in the spirit of meekness." How beautifully did Paul, though in authority and success and gifts "not behind the very chiefest of the apostles," exemplify his beloved brother Peter's precept! He did not conduct himself as a lord over God's heritage. He disowned all claim to personal lordship over their faith. He sought not glory, but, when he might have used authority as an apostle of Christ, was "gentle" among the disciples, "even as a nurse cherisheth her children." And the servant of the Lord in every age must not be overbearing and ambitious: "he must not strive, but be gentle to all men, apt to teach, patient; in meekness instructing those who oppose themselves." He must never forget the words of the Master, "Ye know that the princes of the Gentiles exercise dominion over them, and they that are great exercise authority upon them. But it shall not be so among you: but whosoever will be great among you, let him be your minister; and whosoever will be chief among you, let him be your servant; even as the Son of man came not to be ministered unto, but to minister, and to give his life a ransom for many."[1]

Instead of acting as if they were lords of God's heritage, Christian elders are to perform their duties "as ensamples

---

[1] Matt. xx. 25-28; Luke xxii. 25, 26. *Vide* note A.

to the flock." In the careful discharge of their duty to those under their care, they are to teach them by example to perform the duties which they owe them and their Lord. By being dutiful to their people, they are to teach their people to be dutiful to them. By being obedient to Christ, they are to teach them to be obedient to him. And it deserves notice, that all the duties Christian elders are called on officially to discharge, are duties which the Christian brethren are substantially called on to perform. They are to " exhort one another daily while it is called to-day;" they are all of them to " look diligently, lest any man fail of the grace of God." And the graces which are required in the Christian life, are just those which must be manifested in the right discharge of pastoral duty.[1]

A Christian elder cannot neglect duty, cannot commit sin of any kind, without doing more harm than a common church member; and no kind of neglect or fault is likely to exercise a more malignant influence than those which refer to official obligations. The Christian elder, therefore, should seek to be " an example to the believers in word, in conversation, in charity, in spirit, in faith, in purity; showing himself a pattern of good works." What a blessed influence is the holy character and conduct of Christian elders calculated to diffuse through the church! In certain cases they should readily waive undoubted rights, that they may be the better able to give a needed example. They should imitate Paul: " Yourselves know," says he to the Thessalonians, " how ye ought to follow us: for we behaved not ourselves disorderly among you; neither did we eat any

---

[1] " Ea debet esse Pastoris vita ut non solum quicquid loquitur, sed etiam quicquid agit, sit auditorum doctrina."—GERHARD. "Monstrosa res est gradus summus et animus infimus; sedes prima et vita ima; lingua magniloqua et vita otiosa; sermo multus et fructus nullus; vultus gravis et actus levis; ingens auctoritas et nutans stabilitas."—BERNARD.

man's bread for nought; but wrought with labour and travail night and day, that we might not be chargeable to any of you: not because we have not power, but to make ourselves an ensample unto you to follow us."[1] How happy is it when they can say, "We beseech you, be followers of us, as dear children; be followers of us, even as we also are of Christ!" After a Christian elder has said to those under his care, "Whatsoever things are true, whatsoever things are honest, whatsoever things are just, whatsoever things are pure, whatsoever things are lovely, whatsoever things are of good report; if there be any virtue, and if there be any praise, think on these things," what a powerful enforcement is it to the exhortation, when the eloquence of a holy example, more persuasive than words, is felt in the heart of every hearer, saying, "Those things which ye have both learned, and received, and heard, and seen in me, do: and the God of peace shall be with you!"[2]

The two parts of the clause under remark throw light on each other. The elder who lords it over his brethren, is not, cannot be, "an *ensample*" to the flock. He is the very reverse of an ensample. He exemplifies the temper which they ought most carefully to avoid. And, on the other hand, if the elder acts as an ensample to the flock, he cannot lord it over them. The domineering elder cannot be an exemplary elder, and the exemplary elder cannot be a domineering elder. Nothing sits so gracefully on the ruler in the Christian Church as kind condescension. Nothing is more unbecoming in him than overbearing haughtiness. The Master is the great model. "Ye call me Master and Lord: and ye say well; for so I am. If I then, your Lord and Master, have washed your feet, ye also ought to wash one another's feet. For I have given you an example, that

[1] Acts xx. 34, 35; 2 Thess. iii. 7.   [2] Phil. iv. 8, 9.

ye should do as I have done to you. Verily, verily, I say unto you, The servant is not greater than his lord; neither is he that is sent greater than he that sent him. If Christian elders know these things, happy will it be for themselves and for the churches if they do them." [1]

Such is the temper in which the duties of Christian elders should be performed; not reluctantly, but cheerfully; not mercenarily, but disinterestedly, from love to God and love to the brethren; not ambitiously, to display or establish superiority and rule, but humbly, for the purpose of setting an example of Christian obedience; [2] not to glorify themselves, but to edify the brethren.

CHAP. IV. OF THE MOTIVES TO THESE DUTIES.

It still remains for us on this part of our subject to attend to the motives by which the apostle urges Christian elders to discharge their duties in this manner. These motives are derived from considerations referring personally to the apostle—" I exhort you; I who am a fellow-elder, a witness of the sufferings of Christ, and a partaker of the glory that shall be revealed;" from considerations referring to the Church—it is "the flock of God," "God's heritage;" and from considerations referring to the office-bearers themselves—if they perform their duties in this way, "when the chief Shepherd appears, they shall receive a crown of glory, which fadeth not." Let us shortly endeavour to bring out the force of the motives arising from these three sources.

---

[1] John xiii. 13-17.
[2] "Tres sunt ministerii ecclesiastici pestes, ἀεργία, αἰσχροκερδεία et φιλοπρωτεία."—GERHARD.

§ 1. *Motives suggested by the apostle's reference to himself.*

(1.) *He was also an elder.*

And first, let us consider the motives suggested by the apostle's reference to himself. "The elders who are among you I exhort, who am also an elder, and a witness of the sufferings of Christ, and a partaker of the glory which shall be revealed."[1] I exhort, says Peter; and who was he? "An apostle of Jesus Christ,"—one of those so specially commissioned by Christ Jesus to act the part of ambassadors in his room, who is the great ambassador from God, as that when they exhorted it was "as though God did beseech men" by them; to whom he had said, "As the Father hath sent me, so I send you: whatsoever ye bind on earth is bound in heaven; whatsoever ye loose on earth is loosed in heaven: he that receiveth you, receiveth me; and he that receiveth me, receiveth him that sent me: he that despiseth you, despiseth me; and he who despiseth me, despiseth him that sent me;" to whom the Son of man, on sitting down on the throne of his glory, gave twelve thrones, on which they should sit and judge, rule the twelve tribes of the spiritual Israel; who, along with the inspired prophets, are the foundation on which the Church is built, and whose names are represented in the Apocalypse as engraved

[1] "The Greek words are more expressive of equality than the English: 'The presbyters among you,' he says, not 'I their arch-presbyter command,' but, 'I their fellow-presbyter exhort.' And to what does he exhort them? To 'feed the flock of God, acting the part of overseers, not of lords of God's heritage.' Was it not, however, as under shepherds that they were to feed and guide the Christian community? Who, then, was the chief shepherd? This also we learn from his works. It was not Peter himself. It was Jesus Christ, his and their common Master. Nothing here of that arrogant and imperious style which his pretended successors so soon assumed, and so injuriously fastened upon him."—CAMPBELL: *Lect. on Ecc. Hist.* xvii.

on the jewelled foundations of the New Jerusalem. An exhortation from such a quarter was equivalent to a command. He that rejected the apostles, "rejected not men, but God, who had given them his Spirit;" while they spoke as apostles, Christ, and God in Christ, spoke by them. An apostolical exhortation is equivalent to a divine command.[1]

The apostles, though possessed of this authority, made no unnecessary display of it. It was generally acknowledged by the churches; and though they sometimes found it requisite to "command," as well as to exhort, in the name of the Lord Jesus, yet for the most part, "though they might be much bold in Christ" to enjoin that which was convenient, they "rather, for love's sake, besought" those whom they addressed. The injunction lost none of its intrinsic authority from the form it took; and, while more agreeable to him who gave, was not likely to be less influential on those to whom it was given. Peter not only uses the word exhort instead of command, but, instead of using the official appellation which was peculiar to the highest order of church officers, apostle, he employs that of "elder," which in its most general acceptation includes all church rulers. He does not take the name which distinguishes him from, but that which identifies him with, those whom he addresses.

Peter speaks of "the wisdom given to his beloved brother Paul;" and it is plain he himself had been made partaker of the same spirit of wisdom and of love. "I am," says the venerable apostle, 'I am a co-presbyter, a fellow-elder. I know what it is to have a charge in the house of God. I have felt the responsibilities arising out of the command to feed the sheep, to feed the lambs of the great, good Shepherd. I know the duties of the Christian pastor; I know

[1] 2 Cor. v. 20; Matt. xvi. 19, xviii. 18; Matt. x. 40; John xiii. 20; Matt. xix. 28; Eph. ii. 20; Rev. xxi. 14.

his difficulties; I know his temptations; I know his joys; I know his sorrows. I know the heart of the Christian elder. The exhortation comes from one who can, who does, thoroughly sympathize with you.'[1]

The kindly condescending address of the apostle was calculated to give additional force to his exhortation; and its peculiar form is surely intended to teach elders, especially old elders, men who have been long in office in God's Church, to use the influence which, if they have in any measure rightly discharged their duty, they must have acquired, in exhorting their fellow-elders, especially those younger than themselves, to diligence and fidelity in the duties of their common offices. "The duty of mutual exhorting, which lies on each Christian to another, is little known amongst the greater part; but surely pastors should be, as in other duties so in this, eminent and exemplary in their intercourse and converse, saying often one to another, 'Oh, let us remember to what we are called, to how high and heavy a charge! to what holiness and diligence! How great the hazard of our miscarriage, and how great the reward of our fidelity!'—whetting and sharpening one another by those weighty and holy considerations." It is peculiarly becoming in old Christian elders to say to their young brethren, especially when the exhortation is enforced by a protracted course of faithful services to Christ and his Church, "Take heed to the ministry which ye have received of the Lord, that ye fulfil it." Such exhortations, given in the right spirit, seldom fail of doing good.

(2.) *He was a witness of the sufferings of Christ.*

To give further weight to his exhortation, the apostle not

[1] "Est autem eximia modestia, quod se συμπρεσβύτερον, ipse nominat, quem caput et principem apostolorum postea confinxerunt, et vicedeum adeo."—SEMLER.

only calls himself a fellow-elder, but " a witness of the sufferings of Christ." " The sufferings of Christ," which the ancient prophets are in the first chapter (ver. 11) represented as witnesses of, as testifying about, are not, as I endeavoured to show when explaining that part of the epistle, the personal sufferings of our Lord, but the "sufferings until Christ," or "the sufferings in reference to Christ," as the words literally signify,—" the sufferings of the present time," to which for a season it is needful that Christians be exposed,—as contrasted with the glory which is to follow, the salvation laid up in heaven, the grace to be brought to Christians at the revelation of our Lord Jesus. And some have supposed that the phrase " sufferings of Christ" has the same meaning here, and that the apostle expresses the same sentiment as the Apostle Paul to the Thessalonians, when he says, " We told you before that we should suffer tribulation." There can be no doubt that Peter as well as Paul, when confirming the souls of the disciples, and exhorting them to continue in the faith, did testify, that " through much tribulation they must enter into the kingdom."[1] We find him doing so in this epistle, and this was in itself a good reason why he should exhort the office-bearers to a conscientious performance of their duties; for that, important at all times, becomes doubly so in a time of trial. But the expression here is not the same as that in the first chapter, and seems varied to show that it refers to Christ's personal sufferings, and not to the sufferings of his body, the Church, till he comes.

Of these sufferings Peter was " a witness." These words may signify that the sufferings of Christ were a principal subject of Peter's testimony as an apostle. The apostles, after they received power through the Holy Ghost coming upon them, were, according to their Master's appointment

[1] Acts xiv. 22.

and prediction, " witnesses unto him both in Jerusalem, and in all Judea, and in Samaria, and unto the uttermost parts of the earth." And wherever they went, the cross was the great theme of their testimony. The Messiah they proclaimed was the crucified Messiah, " a stumbling-block to the Jews, foolishness to the Greeks; but to the called, whether Jews or Greeks, the power of God, the wisdom of God." Peter, judging of his ministry from his discourses recorded in the Acts of the Apostles and in this epistle, had, as well as Paul, " determined to know nothing among" his converts " but Jesus Christ and him crucified." He too could say, " God forbid that I should glory, save in the cross of our Lord Jesus Christ, by which the world is crucified to me, and I to the world."[1]

It appears to me, however, more natural to understand the words, "a witness of the sufferings of Jesus Christ," in their most obvious sense as equivalent to, I saw Jesus Christ suffer. It is as if he had said, ' He who addresses you, and calls on you to be faithful to Christ, and to the Church purchased by his blood, knows well how strong are his claims on *you*, how strong is his regard for *them*. With these eyes I have seen the Eternal Word, the Lord of glory, a poor, destitute, afflicted, tormented, despised, dying, dead man. I heard his groans in Gethsemane. I saw his "sweat, as it were great drops of blood, falling to the ground." I saw him betrayed by one of his disciples, Judas. I saw him deserted by them all. I saw him insulted and abused before the high priest. I saw how deeply he felt, and how tenderly he forgave, my base denial of him.' And as we can scarcely persuade ourselves that Peter and the other apostles were not witnesses of the last scene of suffering, it is as if he said, ' I saw him affixed, like a felonious slave, to the cross. I heard the wail of agony, " My God, my

[1] 1 Cor. i. 23; Gal. vi. 14.

God, why hast thou forsaken me!" I heard, though I then understood it not, the mysterious parting cry, "It is finished." Having witnessed all this, is it wonderful that HIS words who thus suffered for me, for you, for the flock committed to our care,—that his words, "Lovest thou me? feed my lambs; Lovest thou me? feed my sheep? Lovest thou me; feed my sheep,"—should be continually sounding in my ears, continually weighing on my heart, and that I should with deep earnestness exhort you to do that which he so impressively commanded me to do?'

"These, indeed, are things that give great weight to a man's words, make them powerful and pressing, 'a witness of the sufferings of Christ.' The apostles had a singular advantage in this, that they were eye-witnesses;[1] and Paul, who wanted that, had it supplied by a vision of Christ at his conversion. But certainly a spiritual view of Christ crucified is generally, I will not say absolutely, necessary to make a minister of Christ. It is certainly very requisite for the due witnessing of him, so to preach the gospel as one 'before whose eyes Jesus Christ had been evidently set forth crucified.' Men commonly read and hear, and may possibly preach, of the sufferings of Christ as a common story, and in that way it may a little move a man and wring tears from his eyes; but faith hath another kind of sight of them, and so works another kind of affection. By the eye of faith to see the only-begotten Son of God, as stricken and smitten of God, bearing our sorrows and wounded for our transgressions; Jesus Christ the righteous, reckoned among the unrighteous and malefactors; to see him stript naked, and scourged, and buffeted, and reviled, and dying, and all for us: this is the thing that will bind upon us most strongly all the duties of Christianity and of

[1] Αὐτόπται.

our callings; and best enable us, according to our callings, to bind them upon others."[1]

(3.) *He was a partaker of the glory to be revealed.*

But still further to add cogency to his exhortation, the apostle styles himself " a partaker of the glory that shall be revealed." The glory here spoken of is obviously " the glory of Christ," a state of dignity and happiness contrasted with his suffering state. ' I am not only a witness of his sufferings, but a partaker of his glory which is to be revealed.' Some have supposed that in these words there is a reference either to our Lord's transfiguration or to his resurrection state; as if Peter had said, ' I witnessed and shared his sufferings, and I have witnessed and shared too his glory. I was " with him in the holy mount, when he received from God the Father honour and glory." I, though fearing, entered with him into the cloud of glory, from the midst of which came the voice, " This is my beloved Son, in whom I am well pleased." And I too " companied with him" after his resurrection, when God had " raised him from the dead, and given him glory." I am one of those on whom he breathed and to whom he said, " Receive ye the Holy Ghost;" and of whom he also said, " The glory thou hast given me I have given them." That glory is as yet in this state veiled. It is " hid with Christ in God," but it will by and by be manifested.'[2]

It seems to me more natural to consider the glory here referred to as the glory of Christ in the celestial state. That glory at present is concealed, and shall continue so till the close of the present state of things. The glories of the holy of holies are hidden from this outer court of the temple by the veil of these visible heavens, through which our Lord has passed. But this veil shall by and by be

[1] Leighton.   [2] 2 Pet. i. 16-18; John xvii. 22.

rent asunder, and all the splendours of the inner sanctuary burst on the sight of an amazed world. "Christ, the life of his people, shall appear"[1]—be manifested to be what he is, and they his people shall be manifested with him in glory. The day of his manifestation as the Son of God shall be the day of their manifestation as the sons of God. He shall be "glorified in his saints, and admired in all them that believe;" and they shall be glorified in him, admired in him.[2] His glories shall be displayed; and it shall be made to appear that the glory which his Father has given him he has given to his people.

Of this participation in the revealed glories of Christ, Peter was so persuaded in reference to himself, that he speaks of himself as already a "partaker of the glory that shall be revealed." Having the spirit of faith, he was confident, "knowing that he that raised up the Lord Jesus would also raise up him by Jesus," and that he should be for ever "with him where he is," beholding and sharing his glory, so far as the thing is possible, being "glorified together with him."[3] But the words are so chosen as naturally enough to convey, in addition to this thought, that he should be a partaker of the glory of Christ at the time of its revelation, the idea that even now, amid all the imperfections and sorrows of the present state, Peter considered himself as a partaker of the glory of Christ—that glory now concealed, but one day to be manifested. He considered himself as "planted together with Christ," not only "in the likeness of his death," but also "in the likeness of his resurrection;" as having fellowship with him not only in his death, but also in his life,—"sitting with him," reigning with him "in the heavenly places;"[4] already

[1] $\varphi\alpha\nu\epsilon\rho\omega\theta\tilde{\eta}$. [2] Col. iii. 4; 2 Thess. i. 10.
[3] 2 Cor. iv. 14; John xvii. 24; Rom. viii. 17.
[4] Rom. vi. 5; Eph. ii. 6.

a partaker, though in far inferior measure, of that holiness and happiness, in the enjoyment of the divine favour and conformity to the divine image, in the perfection of which Christ's glory consists. Peter was, and every Christian in the measure of his faith is, thus even here " a partaker of the glory which is to be revealed."

The bearing of this statement as a motive on the apostle's exhortation, is manifest when you look forward to its close, where he points to the crown of glory, which, when the chief Shepherd comes, that is, at the time of the revelation of his glory, shall be conferred on the faithful under shepherds. The exhortation of a man who, under the influence of the spirit of faith, believes, and therefore speaks, and who, when speaking of the future rewards of the faithful minister, speaks of something of which he has already the earnest, and of the full enjoyment of which he is completely assured, is plainly fitted to be peculiarly impressive and persuasive. It is as if he had said, "I speak what I do know. I testify what I have seen."

§ 2. *Motives from considerations referring to the Church.*

Let us now look at the motives derived from considerations referring to the Church. Feed the Church; it is the flock of God. Superintend the Church; it is the heritage of God.

(1.) *It is the flock of God.*

The Church is the flock of God, and every true member of it is one of his sheep. This is one of the figurative expressions by which Jehovah's peculiar property in and care for ancient Israel is often expressed. "Ye, my flock, the flock of my pasture, are men, and I am your God, saith the Lord God."[1] Like most expressions of the kind, it is employed

---
[1] Ezek. xxxiv. 31.

in an extended and elevated sense to describe the peculiar relation in which the true spiritual Church stands to God. They are his peculiar property, separated from the rest of mankind, saved from destruction by the good Shepherd laying down his life for them; protected by his peculiar providence, and blessed with the tokens of his special love. The good Shepherd, who laid down his life to save them from destruction, took it again to complete their salvation: " He gathers the lambs in his arms, and carries them in his bosom;" "He feeds them, and causes them to lie down. He seeks that which was lost, and brings again that which was driven away; and binds that which was broken, and strengthens that which is sick." Hear what he himself says: "I give unto my sheep eternal life, and they shall never perish; neither shall any pluck them out of my hand. My Father, who gave them me, is greater than all; and none can pluck them out of my Father's hand."[1] Should not we count it a great honour, and feel it a most responsible trust, to have those who stand in so close a relation to God, and in whom he takes so peculiar an interest, committed to our care? Should we not care for those for whom he cares? Should we not watch for those for whom his Son died?

(2.) *It is God's heritage.*

Substantially the same ideas with regard to the Church are suggested by its being termed God's heritage. The term here used has a reference to the manner in which the Israelites obtained their possessions, which were heritages transmitted from generation to generation. It is borrowed from the fact that these possessions were originally fixed by lot, so that lot and possession are often in Scripture convertible terms. Like the former figure, it is often used to

[1] Isa. xl. 11; Ezek. xxxiv. 11-14; John x. 28.

express Jehovah's peculiar relation to Israel: "The Lord's portion is his people; Jacob is the lot of his inheritance;"[1] and both designations are transferred to the spiritual Church under the new economy. Christians are called "the purchased possession," the peculiar property of God, "the chosen generation, the holy nation, the peculiar people."[2] To be employed to take care of his ancient people was a great honour. To be the king of Israel was greater honour than to be king of Egypt, Assyria, or Babylon. How far above all pagan legislators stands Moses the servant of the Lord! How low the rank of heathen sages compared with that of Hebrew prophets! The most honourable and responsible situation man can occupy, is that of a teacher and ruler in that spiritual family of which God is the head, Jesus Christ is the elder brother, and holy angels the willing ministers. Should not God's most valued property be well cared for? Should not the education of his children be well attended to? Is there not great honour involved in the charge being entrusted to us? Must there not be high responsibility incurred by our undertaking it? Such seems the force of the motives derived from a reference to the Church.

It is but right to remark, before leaving this particular, that the precise meaning of the expression rendered "God's heritage" is somewhat doubtful. You will observe the word *God's* is in italics, which, as you know, indicates that there is no term answering to it in the original. The word is in the plural—the lots or possessions. Not lording it over "the lots."[3] The term lot or possession in the singular is applied to the Church, as the lot or possession of Jehovah; but nowhere else in the plural. This has led some to suppose that it refers to the possessions, the property, of the Church; not treating the Church property as if it were

[1] Deut. xxxii. 9.　　[2] Eph. i. 18; 1 Pet. ii. 9.　　[3] See note B.

their own, as if they were the proprietors of it. There is no reason to think that at this early period the churches had anything like fixed property; and there is no proper contrast in this case between the two obviously antithetic clauses of the sentence. It is a much more probable opinion that considers the lots or possessions as referring to the separate flocks of different elders or elderships:[1] not lording it over the (or their) lots or possessions, the flocks allotted to them by the great Shepherd, but showing them an example. In this case, the motive folded up in the phrase is, You have had a specific work assigned you by the great Shepherd. Each has his appointed sphere of labour. Let the labourers see that their own vineyard be well kept, and their own flock be well shepherded. Yet a little while, and the great Husbandman will take account of his servants, and then woe to the unprofitable, double woe to the unfaithful, servant!

§ 3. *Motives from considerations referring to the office-bearers themselves.*

It only remains now that we attend a little to the motives derived from a reference to the office-bearers themselves. The words of the apostle express much; they suggest more. They describe the reward of the faithful Christian elder; they dimly shadow forth the punishment of the unfaithful Christian elder.

(1.) *The reward of the faithful Christian elder.*

The words describe the reward of the faithful Christian elder: "He shall receive a crown of glory, which fadeth not away, when the chief Shepherd shall appear." Jesus Christ is the *chief* Shepherd; he is *the* Shepherd of the

---

[1] "*Cleros* non vocat clericos, sed particulares ecclesias, quibus singuli essent per sortem vel electionem præfècti."—PAREUS.

sheep, the good Shepherd, the great Shepherd, the proprietor Shepherd, whose own the sheep are; the Shepherd of the shepherds as well as of the sheep. He is even now really present in his Church. The faithful Witness did not lie when he said, "Lo, I am with you alway." "Where two or three are gathered together in my name, there am I in the midst of them."[1]

His presence, however, is spiritual, not bodily. The heavens have received him, and we see him no more. But when he disappeared, the most explicit declarations were given that he should reappear. "I will come again," said he himself, "and receive you to myself; that where I am, there ye may be also." "This same Jesus," said the angels to the apostles, when they stood gazing up towards heaven, in the clouds of which their Lord had just disappeared,— "This same Jesus, who is taken up from you into heaven, shall so come in like manner as ye have seen him go into heaven."[2] This reappearance, which is to be a glorious manifestation of what he is both essentially and officially, a revelation of his glory, is a leading subject of the apostolic testimony, and has been all along the great object of the Church's hope. Their "blessed hope" is, and has all along been, "the glorious appearing of Him who is the great God and their Saviour."[3] The day of his coming is to be the day of their "gathering together to him."

When He shall come, he shall come in his character of the chief Shepherd, to collect his flock together, and to conduct them all in a body into the heavenly fold. One purpose of his coming shall be to take account of his under shepherds, and to render to them according to their work. To the faithful, laborious servant, who has affectionately and wisely shepherded and superintended, fed and guided, the flock committed to him, not grudgingly, but cheerfully;

[1] Matt. xxvii. 20, xviii. 20.   [2] Acts i. 10, 11.   [3] Tit. ii. 13.

not mercenarily, but disinterestedly; not ambitiously, seeking to be a lord, but humbly, striving to be an ensample; "he will then give a crown of glory which shall never fade."

The language is figurative, but the meaning is plain. He will visibly reward his faithful services, by bestowing on him a large measure of the highest kinds of happiness and honour of which his nature is capable; blessings which shall endure for ever, and for ever retain undiminished their power to satisfy their possessors. In what the peculiarity of the rewards of the faithful Christian elder shall consist, we can form but inadequate and indistinct ideas. There is much, however, to lead us to believe that a portion, and probably no small portion of it, is to consist in witnessing the holy happiness of those to whose spiritual interests he ministered on earth; and to know most certainly that to his labours and instrumentality their happiness has been owing. Such is the view which the apostle's words naturally lead us to take when he calls the Philippian Christians his "joy and his crown;" and when to the Thessalonians he says, "What is our hope, or joy, or crown of rejoicing? Are not even ye in the presence of our Lord Jesus Christ at his coming? for ye are our glory and our joy."[1]

The Christian pastor will, according to his measure, be admitted into the joy of his Lord when he sees the travail of his soul and is satisfied. This is an exceeding great and a peculiarly appropriate reward; a reward which will be enjoyed just in proportion as the individual Christian pastor has been filled with the spirit of his office, and discharged its duties. What a high, what a holy satisfaction, to know that we have efficiently co-operated towards the accomplishment of the favourite purpose of Deity, to reconcile all things to himself by Jesus Christ; that we have

[1] Phil. iv. 1; 1 Thess. ii. 19.

been the means of saving souls from death, of covering multitudes of sins, of increasing the joys of angels, of ministering to the satisfaction of Him who loved us, and washed us from our sins in his own blood! What a reward!

To borrow the words of the holy Leighton, "It is a crown of glory, pure, unmixed glory, without any ingrediency of pride or sinful vanity, or any danger of it; and a crown that fadeth not, formed of such flowers that wither not; not a temporary garland of fading flowers, as all here are. Though made of flowers growing in a rich valley, their glorious beauty is fading; but this is fresh and in perfect lustre to all eternity. May they not well trample on base gain and vain applause, that have this crown to look to? Joys of royal pomp, how soon do they vanish as a dream! But this day begins a triumph and a feast that shall never either end or be wearied of. All things here, even the choicest pleasures, cloy, but satisfy not. Those above shall always satisfy, but never cloy. What is to be refused in the way to this crown? All labour for it is sweet. And what is there here to be desired to stay our hearts, that we should not most willingly let go, to rest from our labours and receive our crown? Was ever any man sad that the day of his coronation drew nigh? In that day when he on whose head are many crowns shall bestow many crowns, there will be no envy, no jealousies; all kings, each having his own crown, and each rejoicing in the glory of another, and all in HIS, who that day shall be all in all."

(2.) *The doom of the unfaithful Christian elder.*

These words of the apostle, while they describe the final destiny of the faithful Christian pastor, naturally suggest the awful truth respecting the Christian elder who has not fed the flock of God, who has not superintended aright his heritage. What is to become of him who has done his work by constraint, not willingly, for filthy lucre, not of a willing mind, who has lorded it over God's heritage, and has not been an ensample to the flock : shall he be crowned ? No; he has not " striven," or, at any rate, " not striven lawfully." The doom of the unprofitable, the doom of the unfaithful servant, will be his. Expelled from the family of God, he will be " cast into outer darkness; there shall be weeping and gnashing of teeth." His portion is with the hypocrites, a class peculiarly hateful to Him who desires truth in the inward part; with the perfidious, who have broken their engagements both to God and to man. And it is his fit place; for the honour of God, the cause of truth, the interests of souls, were put into his hands : he accepted the trust, and basely betrayed them all. In the prison of hell, with " the basest, the lowermost, the most dejected, most underfoot and down-trodden vassals of perdition,"[1] must he have his everlasting abode. "This pertaineth to him as the portion of his cup." What Christian elder can think of these things, can realize them to his mind, without having new nerve given to his resolution to be " faithful to him who has appointed him;" " faithful to death," that he may " obtain the crown of life," and escape the brand of everlasting shame and contempt; that he may be greeted with the invitation, " Well done, good and faithful servant," " come up hither;" instead of meeting the heart-withering denunciation, " Depart, depart, I never knew you ?" You called me Lord; but I never considered you as my servant, for I knew you were not.

Thus have I brought to a close my illustrations of the first part of this paragraph, that part of it which refers to the duties of the office-bearers of the Christian Church to those committed to their care. But ere proceeding further,

[1] Milton.

I would press on my own mind, and on the minds of my brethren in the eldership in this congregation, the solemn considerations which, in the illustration of this passage of Scripture, have been placed before us. Let us remember that this word of exhortation is as really addressed to us as it was to those to whom the epistle was originally written. Let us humble ourselves under the consciousness how very imperfectly we have discharged the inestimably important duties of our most responsible situation. Let us cast ourselves on our Master's kindness, for the forgiveness of all that has been wanting and wrong in our official conduct; and while in our inmost hearts saying, "Who is sufficient for these things?" let us, undiscouraged though not unwarned by our former failures, cherish an ever-growing resoluteness of determination, by his grace, to be "stedfast and unmoveable, always abounding in the work of our Lord," assured that our labours shall not be in vain in the Lord.

Holy brethren, partakers of this high vocation, elders, suffer the words of exhortation from one who also is an elder. They shall be the words of the holy apostles of our common Lord: "I charge you before God, and the Lord Jesus Christ, and the elect angels, that ye take heed to yourselves, and to all the flock over which the Holy Ghost has made you overseers. Hold the mystery of faith in a pure conscience. Be examples to the believers in word, in conversation, in charity, in spirit, in faith, in purity. Let no man despise you. O men of God, flee pride, strife, evil surmisings, perverse disputings, and that love of money which is the root of all evil. Follow after righteousness, godliness, faith, love, patience, meekness. Fight the good fight of faith; lay hold on eternal life. Hold fast the form of sound words. Hold fast what you have attained; let no man take your crown. I give you charge in the sight of God, who quickeneth all things, and before Christ Jesus, who before Pontius Pilate witnessed a good confession, that ye observe these things, without preferring one before another, doing nothing by partiality. Keep this commandment without spot, unrebukeable, until the appearing of our Lord Jesus Christ: which in his times he shall show, who is the blessed and only Potentate, the King of kings, and the Lord of lords; who only hath immortality, dwelling in the light which no man can approach unto; whom no man hath seen, neither can see: to whom be honour and power everlasting. Amen."[1]

II. OF THE DUTIES OF THE MEMBERS OF THE CHRISTIAN CHURCH TO THEIR OFFICE-BEARERS.

I go on now to call your attention to the view which the text gives us of the duties of the members of Christian churches towards their office-bearers. This is contained in the first clause of the 5th verse: "Likewise, ye younger, submit yourselves to the elder." Before proceeding further, however, it will be proper that I endeavour to satisfy you that these words are indeed an injunction of the duties of church members to their office-bearers, and not, as many have supposed, of the duties of the young to the aged. Were we merely looking at the words, without taking into consideration the connection in which they are introduced, this last mode of viewing them would probably be that which would first occur to every reader. But it requires only a little reflection to see, first, that the connection by no means leads us to expect here an injunction of the duties of the young to the aged, and that the language by no means obliges us thus to understand it; and secondly, that

[1] 2 Tim. iv. 1; Acts xx. 28; 1 Tim. i. 19, iii. 9, iv. 12; Tit. ii. 15; 1 Tim. vi. 11, 12; 2 Tim. i. 13; Rev. iii. 11; 1 Tim. vi. 13-16.

the connection does lead us to expect an injunction of the duties of the private members of the Church, as contradistinguished from the office-bearers; and, still further, that while there is nothing in the language which is inconsistent with this mode of interpretation, there is something which cannot be satisfactorily explained on any other supposition.

There can be no doubt that the first four verses of the chapter refer to the duties of Christian office-bearers; and as little, that the injunction in the 5th verse has a close connection with the injunctions contained in these verses,—a connection intimated by the connective particle "likewise;"[1] a word which seems to intimate that the duties enjoined are correlative, or, at any rate, belong to the same general family of duties. In enjoining domestic duties, after stating the duties of servants, the apostle says, "*Likewise*, ye wives, be in subjection to your own husbands;" and after stating the duties of wives, he says, "*Likewise*, ye husbands, dwell with your wives according to knowledge, giving honour unto the wife, as unto the weaker vessel, and as being heirs together of the grace of life; that your prayers be not hindered."[2] The word certainly leads you to expect the injunction of some kindred, some ecclesiastical duty, not the injunction of a duty belonging to an entirely different class.

It is the ordinary practice of the apostles, a practice plainly dictated by the proprieties of the case, to enjoin the duties rising out of mutual relations in succession: thus, "Wives, submit yourselves to your own husbands; husbands, love your wives." "Children, obey your parents; fathers, provoke not your children to anger." "Servants,

---

[1] Ὁμοίως manifeste ostendit eosdem hic significari presbyteros: sicut antea Petrus de presbyterorum erga suas oves, sic nunc de ovium erga suos προιστῶτας officio disserit: quamobrem etiam recte Syrus interpres addidit affixum *vestris*.—BEZA.

[2] 1 Pet. iii. 1, 7.

be obedient to them that are your masters; masters, do the same thing to them."[1] When, therefore, we meet with an injunction to elders to do their duty to a certain class clearly defined, and then find a certain class, not quite so clearly defined, called on to do their duty to elders, we naturally conclude that the objects of the first exhortations are the subjects of the second, and not some other class altogether.

Had the office-bearers been represented as spiritual fathers, and had the injunction run thus, 'Fathers in Christ, carefully superintend and instruct the family of God committed to your care;' and been followed by the command, 'Likewise, ye children, be submissive to the fathers;' would not every one at once have seen that, in the latter clause, it was not the duty of children to their parents that was enjoined, but that of spiritual children to their spiritual fathers—in other words, of the members of the Church to the office-bearers of the Church?

It seems very unnatural, without a strong reason, to suppose the elders of the 5th verse to be a different class of men from the elders of the 1st verse;[2] and if they are the same class, it seems strange that young persons alone should be called on to perform to them a duty which is owing to them by all to whom they stand in official relation. Besides, had the apostle meant to enjoin the duties of the young to the old, he would have used some other word for the old than that which he has just used to express office. Still further, the duty enjoined is one due to all official elders, from their office; and not due to any old man, merely from his age. It is not submission, but respect, that is due from the young to the old. "Thou shalt rise up before the hoary head, and honour the face of the old man, and fear thy God; I am the Lord."[3]

[1] Eph. v. 22, 25, vi. 1, 4, 5, 9; Col. iii. 18-22, iv. 1.
[2] Πρεσβύτεροι.   [3] Lev. xix. 32.

We consider ourselves, then, as not only warranted, but shut up, to interpret "the younger," or the juniors here, as a general name for the ordinary church members, as contradistinguished from their elders, in the same way as they are termed sheep, or a flock, when their office-bearers are termed shepherds; scholars, or disciples, when they are termed teachers; and as John the elder speaks of his converts as his children, "I have no greater joy than to hear that my children walk in truth."[1] I am not aware of the designation "younger" being used in any other part of the New Testament in the sense which it seems to bear here, though there is a passage where it is employed in a somewhat analogous way: "He that is greatest among you, let him be as the younger; and he that is chief, as he that doth serve."[2]

That the younger here are those who stand in some relation to the presbyters or elders just mentioned, is so evident, and its reference to the young in age is so unnatural,[3] that we find a number of commentators supposing that the term refers to the six inferior orders of clergy,[4] as they were called, after the simplicity of the primitive Christian polity was departed from; and that submission referred to their duties to the bishops. The use of such an expression for church members was natural in the primitive times, when their official elders were generally not young men, certainly not young Christians; it being matter of statute that the elders should not be novices, but tried men, old disciples; so that the great body of the church members were both naturally and spiritually their juniors. Indeed still, in ordinary cases, the great body of the members of a church are younger than their elders.

On the supposition that the younger, the juniors, are the

---

[1] 3 John 4.   [2] Luke xxii. 26.
[3] See note C.   [4] Salmeron.

private members of the Church, the whole passage has a character of close connection and complete consistency. We have first the duties of the office-bearers; then the duty of the private members of the Church to their office-bearers; and then the duty of all connected with the Church, whether officers or private members, clearly stated and powerfully enforced. The duties enjoined are just the duties belonging to those who respectively occupy those ecclesiastical relations. On the other supposition all is disjointed. An injunction of the duties of Christian pastors is followed by an injunction of the duties of the young to the old; and this followed by an injunction of the duty which every man owes to every man. And the duties enjoined in the two last cases are not those which we expect: for though the young are bound to respect the aged, they are not bound to submit to them; and though every man is to be kind and just to every other man, every man is not bound to be subject to every man; though there is an important sense in which every Christian man should be subject to every other Christian man, every church member to every other church member. Even Leighton, who follows the common mode of interpretation, acknowledges that the words have "some aspect to the relation of those that are under the discipline and government of the elders." The good Archbishop was forgetful of the wise saying of Dr Owen: "If Scripture have more meanings than one, it has no meaning at all." If the younger means the members of the Church, it cannot mean the young properly so called.

Having thus ascertained that the injunction before us is an injunction to church members to perform their duty to their office-bearers, let us proceed now to inquire into the meaning of the injunction. What is the duty of church members to their office-bearers, as here described? The duty here enjoined is substantially the same as that enjoined by the Apostle Paul, in his Epistles to the Thessalonians and Hebrews: " We beseech you, brethren, to know, or acknowledge, them which labour among you, and are over you in the Lord, and admonish you; and to esteem them very highly in love for their work's sake." " Obey them that have the rule over you, and submit yourselves; for they watch for your souls, as they who must give account; that they may do it with joy, and not with grief: for that is unprofitable for you."[1]

It is quite plain from these passages, that obedience and submission are required from church members to their office-bearers. It is unhappily too certain, that much mischief has been done, and much good prevented, by church officers assuming a power and authority that do not belong to them, but to the one Lord, and encroaching on the liberties which every Christian possesses in unalienable right, by virtue of the gift of this one Lord; and by church members impiously permitting such an usurpation, and tamely submitting to such encroachments on their privileges. But it is just as unhappily notorious, that much mischief has been done, and much good prevented, in the Christian Church, by anarchy as well as tyranny: by church members refusing to obey them that are over them in the Lord, and by church officers allowing themselves to be denuded of the authority with which their Master has clothed them, and without the exercise of which the great and salutary ends of their office cannot be gained.

A Christian church is a very free society; but they mistake the matter who consider it as a democracy. It is a monarchy, administered by inferior magistrates, chosen by their fellow-subjects, who are to execute the King's laws, being guided solely by his word, and neither by their own

[1] 1 Thess. v. 12, 13; Heb. xiii. 17.

judgment or caprice, nor by the opinions and will of those whom they govern. Christ is the Lord, and he administers his government by officers appointed according to his ordinance, and regulated by his laws. It is of great importance, both to the office-bearers and private members of a Christian church, that they have distinct scriptural views on this subject, that the former may not exact what they have no right to, and that the latter may not refuse what, by the law of Christ, they are bound to give.

It is an elementary principle in the Christian polity, that the office-bearers of every Christian church should be chosen by the members of that church. No man should become an office-bearer in the Christian Church, but thus by the suffrage of his brethren; and every individual, in joining a Christian church which has office-bearers, by doing so chooses them as his ecclesiastical superiors. Pastors and teachers are Christ's gifts.[1] The Holy Ghost constitutes all true ecclesiastical overseers;[2] but he does this, not by miraculous interposition, but by endowing them with the suitable qualifications, and inclining their brethren to call them to the exercise of these gifts. The primitive Church elected their own officers. The apostles ordained them, but those ordained by them were chosen by the brethren.[3]

The power of election was with them, and continued to be so till the Church became so corrupted as scarcely to deserve the name. So important is this consideration, in my apprehension, that I could not plead for obedience or submission as an ecclesiastical duty from Christian men in their social capacity, to a person imposed on them from without, either by civil or ecclesiastical authority. Non-intrusion is the fundamental principle of the administrative polity of the Christian Church. Where a man, claiming rightly or wrongly the character of an elder in Christ's

[1] Eph. iv. 11.   [2] Acts xx. 28.   [3] Acts vi. 3, 4.

Church, is not chosen explicitly or implicitly by me to be over me in the Lord, I am not bound to submit to him as my pastor.

Even to those elders whom the members of a church have explicitly or implicitly chosen to be their elders, the obedience due is obedience within certain clearly defined limits. It is only in the discharge of the duties of their office that they are to be submitted to; and even in the discharge of these duties, they are to be submitted to only as far as they administer the law of the one Lord. It is not to the arbitrary will of your elders that you are bound to submit. It is to them declaring and executing the will of Christ.[1] "Pastors" (that is, elders), says Mr Fuller, "are that to a church which the executive powers or magistrates of a free country are to the people at large—the organs of the law. Submission to them is submission to the law." If elders teach doctrine inconsistent with the doctrine of Christ, or enjoin anything inconsistent with his law, they are not to be submitted to, but on the contrary opposed,—opposed to the face, for they are to be blamed. But when the Christian eldership keep themselves within the proper bounds of their office, it is the duty of all private members of the society to submit to and obey them; and they cannot do otherwise without disturbing the peace of the society, interfering with the edification both of themselves and of their fellow church members, and drawing down upon themselves that disapprobation with which the one Lord, who is the author of order and not confusion, must regard all who resist his ordinances.

[1] "This power" (the power given to church officers) "is wholly ministerial, without domination, without coaction; and, therefore, one of the requisites of a bishop is—'he must be no striker:' he has no arms put into his hands for this purpose; the ecclesiastical state being furnished 'auctoritate suadendi magis quam jubendi potestate.'"—JER. TAYLOR, *Ductor Dubitantium.*

The truth on the subject of church authority has never been better stated than by the learned and judicious Dr Owen: "The obedience due to church rulers is not a blind, implicit obedience. A pretence hereof has been abused to the ruin of the souls of men; but there is nothing more contrary to the whole nature of gospel obedience, which is our reasonable service. It has respect unto them in their office only, and while they teach the things which the Lord Christ hath appointed them to teach: when they depart from these, there is neither obedience nor submission due to them. Wherefore, in the performance of these duties, there is supposed a judgment to be made of what is enjoined or taught by the word of God. Our obedience unto them must be obedience to God. On these suppositions their word is to be obeyed, and their rule submitted to, not only because they are true and right materially, but also because they are theirs, and conveyed from them unto us by divine institution."[1]

Keeping these general remarks in view, let us proceed to consider a little more particularly what is included in that submissive obedience which the Christian people, according to the law of the Lord, owe to the office-bearers whom they themselves have chosen. And here, with a reference to the view taken of the official duties of the eldership in a former part of this discourse, I shall show, in succession, how the members of the Church are to submit themselves to the elders teaching, and to the elders superintending or governing. But before entering on this illustration, I have to solicit your attention for a moment to two things which may be considered as necessary prerequisites, in order to any individual rightly discharging his duty to the eldership in either of these aspects. These are, first, a reverence for church government as an ordinance of Christ; and secondly,

[1] *Owen on the Hebrews*, vol. iv. p. 260. Fol. ed.

a respect for the persons who, in the church of which the individual is a member, are invested with office.

§ 1. *Preliminary requisites to the discharge of the duty of subjection to elders.*

(1.) *Conviction of the divine authority of church order.*

To fit a man for the right discharge of the duty here enjoined, it is not necessary that he should be persuaded that every arrangement in the church with which he is connected is of divine authority; but it is of great importance that he should be persuaded that the Christian Church is a divine, not a human institution; and that its office-bearers, properly chosen, are authorized by its divine Head to execute his laws and administer his ordinances. Without such a conviction, ecclesiastical obedience, as a religious duty, is impossible. The individual may comply with the arrangements as expedient; but he must feel himself at liberty, whenever he thinks them inexpedient, which is nearly equivalent to whenever he feels them to be inconvenient, to decline compliance with them. A Christian church is a voluntary society, inasmuch as no man can lawfully be compelled either to enter into its fellowship or to continue in it; but it is not a voluntary society, either in the sense that a Christian man can, without impropriety, continue unconnected with it, or, having connected himself with it, is not bound to submit to the laws of its Lord and King, administered by office-bearers appointed according to his revealed will.

A great deal of the insubordination which prevails in Christian churches originates in the want of just views and settled convictions on this point. It is certainly true of ecclesiastical government, in a higher sense than of civil government, that it is " of God;" and that " he who resists it," in the performance of its legitimate functions, "resists the ordinance of God, and receives to himself condemnation." And this holds good, whatever form ecclesiastical government may assume, provided only the rights of Jesus Christ as the Head of the Church, and the privileges of his people, the members of it, are secured.

(2.) *Personal respect for those invested with office.*

Inferior in importance to this, but only inferior to it, is the second prerequisite to the right discharge of the duty of submission or obedience to church officers: A personal respect for the individuals invested with office. To discharge the duties of civil obedience without this, is difficult. Without this, to discharge the duties of ecclesiastical obedience, is impossible. No man ought to become a member of a church where the office-bearers, as a body, do not command his respect for their personal qualifications. He sports with his own edification if he does so. Nor ought he to continue a member of a church where, as a body, they forfeit their claims on his respect. This is obvious; for how, in this case, can he have Christian fellowship with them?

In churches, in any good measure rightly constituted, the office-bearers are likely to be men worthy of esteem for their own sake, as well as for their work's sake. If they are not, it must reflect much discredit on those who placed them in a situation so prominent and so responsible; a station which men of low Christian attainments, and doubtful spiritual character, cannot occupy without dishonour to Christianity, and injury to the edification of the Church. This consideration ought to have a powerful effect on the minds of church members in electing office-bearers, and of Christians fixing on a particular religious society with which permanently to connect themselves. They ought to see to it that the elders of the church they belong to be such men, as that nothing in their private character and deportment shall throw obstacles in the way of the discharge of the duty due to them as public officers; but that, on the contrary, the respect which they cannot but feel for their worth as Christian brethren, shall make it a very easy thing to render to them the honour and submission due to them as Christian elders.

§ 2. *Subjection to the elders as teachers.*

Let me now a little more particularly consider what this honour and submission is, in reference to the two great departments of the elders' official duty, explained in a former part of this discourse: Teaching and superintendence. And first, of the submission which church members owe to their elders as teachers. Now, church members are certainly not bound to believe everything their elders teach, nor to do everything they enjoin; nay, they are not bound to believe anything they teach, merely because they teach it —to do anything they enjoin, merely because they enjoin it. But they are bound to submit to their teaching, both by regularly and conscientiously waiting on their instructions, and by receiving these instructions in the candid, humble spirit of discipleship.

Attendance on, and attention to, his teaching, is what every Christian teaching elder is entitled to from those under his care. It is the duty of the Christian teacher to "wait on his teaching."[1] The Christian teaching elder who, without a very sufficient reason, is not in his own place when the church assembles to observe the ordinances of Christ, among which attention to the doctrine of the apostles is one of the most important, is in fault. He ought to be there, prepared to expound and enforce the doctrine and law of the Lord, like a householder with a well-furnished store, out of which he is ready to distribute "things

[1] Rom. xii. 7.

new and old," "to give to each of the household his portion in due season." But the same authority which requires the elders to be present to teach, requires the brethren to be present to be taught. The pulpit must not only be filled, but in every case where there is not a sufficient reason for absence, filled by its proper occupant; and so ought the pew. Regular attendance on the public instructions of the teaching elders is the fundamental part of submission to them. If you do not hear your own elders, how can you be taught by them so as to be "obedient to them in the Lord?" And it is of importance that there should be attendance at the hour as well as on the day of public instruction. Punctuality as well as regularity should be attended to. It should be said of every Christian assembly as of Peter's congregation in the house of Cornelius, when the minister rises to address them, "They are *all* present before God, to hear all things that are commanded him of God."[1]

The remark respecting attendance on the instruction of the elders applies not only to their public teaching, but also to their ministrations from house to house. It is obviously the duty of the church members, so far as it is practicable, to afford the elders an opportunity of giving them those instructions more appropriate to their individual character and circumstances, which it would be unsuitable to communicate in public addresses.

But there must be attention as well as attendance; church members must show their submission to their elders' teaching, not only by a regular personal waiting on their instructions, but also by giving them the ready attention and the respectful consideration they deserve. They are to listen, and to listen not in the temper of captious critics, but of humble docile disciples; as persons who are come to learn the doctrine and law of the Lord, and who consider the

[1] Acts x. 33.

teaching eldership as his appointed ordinance for bringing and keeping this doctrine and law before their mind. It is one of the many advantages of a stated ministry, that they who have placed themselves under it are in a great measure freed from temptation to indulge in that critical mode of hearing, in which the hearer acts the part rather of the judge than of the disciple; seeking to form an opinion respecting the powers of the mind, the orthodoxy of the doctrine, or the qualities of the style and manner of the preacher, rather than to derive spiritual improvement. The church member, in listening to the teacher whom he has chosen, with whose character and qualifications he is satisfied, with whose style and manner he is familiar, is, no doubt, to judge of the accordance of what he hears with the divine infallible exhibition of the doctrine and law of Christ, like one whose spiritual senses are exercised to discern good and evil; but he is to come, expecting to hear nothing reprehensible, disposed to give a candid consideration to everything that is said, anxious to hear what God the Lord will say to him, and expecting to hear this through the medium of his own elders, the instructors of his own unbiassed choice, the divinely appointed organs of instruction, and determined to "receive with meekness the word," which, if "engrafted" into him, will indeed "save his soul."

Instead of taking offence when the elder in teaching comes very close to his conscience, the church member should readily and thankfully receive "the reproof" which gives "wisdom;" and, instead of rising in inward rebellion against the preacher, should accept the warning and rebuke which through his instrumentality is administered by his Master and ours. The church member who treats the instructions of the elders in an opposite spirit violates the law in the text, forgets his place in the body of Christ, and throws almost invincible obstacles in the way of their usefulness and his own edification. It is a just observation of Mr Fuller, "If men attend preaching merely as judges of its orthodoxy, they will receive no advantage to themselves, and may do much harm to others. It is the humble Christian who hears that he may be instructed, corrected, and quickened in the ways of God, who will obtain that consolation which the gospel affords."

§ 3. *Submission to the elders as superintendents.*

It only remains now that we say a few words on the duty of submission due by church members to their elders as superintendents, as those who are "over them in the Lord," who "have the oversight of them," who "have the rule over them." And here I will, first, attend to the submission which is due to the eldership in their corporate capacity, and then to that which is due to individual elders when performing their duties as superintendents.

(1.) *Submission to the eldership as a body.*

Submission to the eldership as a body, or to the session, as we call that body, has a reference to the two great functions that body has to perform: the preservation of external order in the society, and the exercise of spiritual discipline in the society. It is plain that in such a society as a Christian church, there are certain arrangements with respect to the time and place of meeting, and the order and minor circumstances of the services, that must be made and attended to. It belongs to the eldership to make such regulations, and it is the duty of the members of the church to observe them. These arrangements may not in every case seem to individual members to be the best; they may not be the best. It is quite right in private members to suggest to the elders what they think would be an improvement; but it is for the elders to judge of such things; and their judgment, in every case where conscience is not concerned, should be submitted to. If this be not attended to, there can be no such thing as order in a church.

The other form of submission to the eldership, submission to them as the administrators of the discipline of the society, requires somewhat more extended illustration. The admission of members into the body, the dealing with such members as have violated the laws of the society, and the exclusion of obstinate offenders from the society, are important official duties of the eldership. In the right discharge of these functions the members of the society have a deep interest, and every member of the church should show that he is aware of this. The province of the members is not, however, directly to do these things; but to furnish, where they have it in their power, the means to the eldership to do them to the best advantage. It is their duty, when they are aware that individuals are applying for admission into the society, to give their elders any information which may help them to a right decision in a question of vital importance to the body; and in the same way, when offences occur, after having used in vain the means appointed by our Lord (Matt. xviii.) for having them removed privately, to bring the subject before the assembly of the eldership, and to give them all the assistance in their power to have it properly disposed of. Every member of a church is bound "to look diligently lest any fellow church member fail of the grace of God; lest any root of bitterness springing up trouble the body, and many be defiled."[1]

In the decisions of the eldership as to admission, discipline, and exclusion, it is the duty of the members of the Church to acquiesce, except in cases where they have satisfactory evidence that the law of Christ has not been rightly

[1] Heb. xii. 15.

administered; and even where they may suppose that this has been the case, they are not to take it on them to judge and condemn those whom they themselves have elected to judge in such matters; far less are they to blazon their view of the matter before the Church, least of all before the world. They are respectfully to remonstrate with the eldership; and if they cannot obtain satisfaction, they are to apply to those larger associations of elders which, under the name of presbyteries and synods, our church polity, in harmony, as we think, with the great leading principles of order laid down in the New Testament, provides; and if even then they cannot obtain satisfaction, if the matter is of such importance as to require it, after giving testimony against what they consider as a violation of the law of Christ, they should peaceably retire from the society. For private members of the Church to counterwork the eldership in the legitimate discharge of their functions—to attempt, by producing popular commotions, to overawe their deliberations, or interfere with and overthrow their judgments, is plainly inconsistent with everything like good order, and directly opposed to that submission here enjoined by the supreme authority in the Church.

Before leaving this part of the subject, I must say a word or two as to the duty of submission which a member of the church owes to the eldership when he himself unhappily becomes a subject of discipline. Such a person, though innocent, may, through mistake, or even through malignity, be regularly brought before the session as an accused person. In such circumstances, the individual concerned is not to refuse to submit the case to trial. He is not to behave as if he thought the eldership were acting an unkind part to him, in doing what they are imperatively bound to do, to examine every question connected with the purity of the body, regularly brought before them; he is to furnish them with the means of vindicating his character and that of the body, if he has been unjustly accused; and if he have really committed a fault, he is readily to acknowledge it, not carping at every mistake that may have been committed either by his accusers or judges, but by confession, penitence, and reformation, putting it in the power of the elders, with as little delay as possible, to restore him.

It is a very hazardous thing for offending members of a church not to submit themselves to their elders, when, in the impartial administration of the wise and benignant law of Christ, they are endeavouring to heal their backslidings, and wipe off the stain their conduct has cast on the worthy name, and remove the stumbling-block it has cast before both the Church and the world. It is no light matter to set at nought the authority of an assembly of elders met in the name of Christ, and intelligently and honestly administering his laws. A deeper solemnity hangs over such an assembly, however humble in worldly rank may be its members, than over the highest court which refers merely to the affairs of this world. He that despiseth them, despiseth their Lord; and he who despiseth him, despiseth also Him who sent him.

(2.) *Submission to the elders as individuals.*

A very few remarks on the duty of submission due from the church members to the individual elder, in discharging his functions of superintendence, shall conclude these discussions. It is the duty of the elder to watch for the souls of those placed under his more immediate superintendence, to see that those duties on which their church membership is suspended be carefully performed. I refer to such duties as attendance on public worship, the religious government and education of their families, the maintenance of family worship, etc. It is also their duty to see that they be generally acting as becometh saints; walking so as to please God, and adorning the doctrine of God our Saviour in all things.

To enable himself to perform these duties, the elder must seek a more intimate acquaintance with those under his care than the mere common intercourse of society can give; and must make inquiries which from a stranger would be justly counted intrusive and impertinent. The inquiries of the elder should be kindly taken, as originating in a desire to preserve a good conscience to himself, and to promote the highest interests both of the individual and of the society. And when he finds it necessary to exhort, and warn, and even rebuke privately, all this proceeding from a regard to Christ's law, and being indeed but an execution of it, is to be met in a becoming spirit, not submitted to as a hardship, but received as a privilege. The proper discharge of these private duties of the elder, and the meeting them in a right spirit, would mightily promote the edification of the body, and most happily lighten the disciplinary labours of the eldership.

"It has long appeared to me," says that wise and good man Andrew Fuller, "that there are some species of faults in church members, which are not proper objects of church censure, but of private pastoral admonition" by the elders; "such as spiritual declension, hesitation on important truth, occasional neglect of religious duties, worldly anxieties, and the early approaches to any evil course. A faithful elder,[1] with an eye of watchful tenderness, will perceive the first symptoms of spiritual disorder, and by a timely hint will counteract its operations." The church member may be aware that this is very self-denying work to the elder, who would much rather visit him with the smile of affectionate

[1] Pastor is Mr F.'s word; but, we have seen, pastor and elder are synonymous.

congratulation than with a countenance which says, 'My child, I stand in doubt of you.' And they ought not to render that disagreeable but important part of his work more disagreeable, by manifesting an irritable and resentful disposition, but receive the warning and the reproof which Christian love dictates, and which Christian law requires, with candour, and even gratitude. "Correction may be grievous to him that forsaketh the way, but he that hateth reproof shall die."[1]

Such is a short view of the duty of church members to their office-bearers, as here enjoined by the apostle. It is indeed what Archbishop Leighton terms it, just "the obedience due to the discipline of God's house. This is all we plead for on this point. And know, if you refuse it, and despise the ordinance of God, he will resent the indignity as done to him. And oh that all that have that charge of his house upon them would mind his interest wholly, and not rise in conceit of their power, but wholly employ and improve it for their Lord and Master; and look on no respect to themselves as for themselves desirable, but only so far as is needful for the profitable discharge and advances of the work in their hands. What are the differences and regards of men? How empty a vapour! and whatsoever it is, nothing is lost by single and entire love of our Lord's glory, and total aiming at that. Them that honour him He will honour, and those that despise Him shall be despised."

I shall conclude this part of the subject by briefly illustrating the argument by which the apostle, in the Epistle to the Hebrews, enforces compliance with an injunction of parallel meaning. "Obey them that have the rule over you, and submit yourselves: for they watch for your souls, as they that must give account; that they may do it with

[1] Prov. xv. 10.

joy, and not with grief: for that is unprofitable for you."[1] Think of the work in which they are engaged; think of the character which they bear in performing it; think of the effect which your obedience or disobedience will have on the manner in which this work will be performed; and think of the influence which the manner in which their work is performed will have on your own interests.

Think of the work of your elders. They watch, they watch for you, they watch for your souls. They watch: their work requires constant solicitude; they must be ever on the alert, to observe danger and to prevent evil. They watch for you. Your best interests are the object of their solicitude. They are not watching for their own emolument or fame, but for your happiness. Others are watching against you; they are watching for you. Satan is watching you as a wolf the sheep-fold, to steal and to destroy: your elders watch, as faithful shepherds, to protect and save you. The world is watching you with a malignant eye, waiting for your halting: your elders are watching, with the solicitude of parents, to keep you from falling. They watch for your souls—for that which is, of all you possess, most precious. Surely those who are benevolently engaged in a work so full of solicitude, and labour to promote your highest interests, should not be counteracted by you, as they will be if you be not subject to them in the Lord.

Then think of the character they bear in doing this work. They watch as "they who must give account." They are commissioned and responsible. What they do, they do by the authority of him who has appointed them. Do not resist them in their proper work, as you would not offend Him; and remembering that they must give account to him, recollecting what a stake they have in the matter, do not wonder that they should hazard offending you by the

[1] Heb. xiii. 17.

discharge of their duty, rather than run the risk of being ashamed before Him at his coming, as they must be if they act not the part of faithful watchmen.

Consider, still further, the effect which your submission or non-submission is likely to have on their discharge of their work. If you do not submit yourselves, they will perform their work with grief. There are few bitterer sorrows than that of a faithful elder, labouring among a people who counteract his attempts to promote their spiritual improvement. Even Moses, one of "the elders, who by faith received a good report," when the Israelitish people were disobedient and rebellious, was tempted to wish that God would kill him out of hand rather than continue to cause him to see his wretchedness.[1] Slothful, selfish, cold-hearted, cavilling, conceited, contentious congregations, have broken the spirit of many a faithful minister of Christ, and made him go mourning to the grave.

And if you do submit yourselves, they will perform their work "with joy." They will have a holy satisfaction in it. Their work will be their reward. Their hearts will be lifted up in the ways of the Lord. The joy of the Lord will be their strength. All good Christian elders can say with John the elder, "We have no greater joy than to see our children walk in truth."

And then, finally, think of the influence which the manner in which the work is performed will have on your own interests. If it is performed with grief, that will be unprofitable for you. The labours of a disheartened spiritual teacher or superintendent are not likely to be effective. Even where there is the highest degree of spiritual holy principle, the hands will wax feeble when the heart is discouraged; and the blessing of the great Master is not likely to be imparted when his commands are disregarded, and his

[1] Num. xi. 15.

servants misused. On the other hand, if your elder's work is performed "with joy," it will be "profitable" to you. He will be enabled to do all his work in the most satisfactory way. His best affections will be strongly drawn out to those who rightly estimate his labours, and show a regard to the law of the Lord; and he will pray for you, and preach to you with double fervour and impressiveness. Seeing of the travail of his Master's soul, and of his own, he will be satisfied; and he will become more and more desirous that those in whom the good work is going forward, under his instrumentality, may grow in all holy attainments; he will become ingenious in devising and unwearied in executing plans for their spiritual improvement; and the great Head of the Church, regarding with a benignant smile the affectionate laborious eldership, and the docile obedient church, will pour out on them in rich abundance of the selectest influences of his grace, and bless them, and make them blessings. Happy elders! Happy church! In their experience is verified the ancient oracle, "Then shall thy light break forth as the morning, and thine health shall spring forth speedily; and thy righteousness shall go before thee: the glory of the Lord shall be thy rereward. And the Lord shall guide thee continually, and satisfy thy soul in drought, and make fat thy bones: and thou shalt be like a watered garden, and like a spring of water, whose waters fail not."[1]

III. OF THE DUTY WHICH ALL IN A CHRISTIAN CHURCH OWE TO EACH OTHER: "MUTUAL SUBJECTION."

There still remains to be considered the duty which all in a Christian church, whether office-bearers or private members, owe to each other, as stated by the apostle in

[1] Isa. lviii. 8, 11.

these words, "Yea, all of you be subject one to another, and be clothed with humility: for God resisteth the proud, and giveth grace to the humble."

It has been supposed by some interpreters, that these words are not to be considered as having any particular reference to Christians in their ecclesiastical relations, but as an injunction referring to all the relations of human life; and that the subjection one to another required, is either that mutual kindly consideration of each other's interests, and that readiness to submit to inconvenience to promote these interests, which is required by the law, "Whatsoever ye would that men should do to you, do ye even so to them," and which is equally due in all the relations of society, from all to all; or that the apostle meant to intimate, that not only in the ecclesiastical relation, but in all the relations of life, subjection to superiors is a Christian duty: that not only is the church member to be subject to the church ruler, but the member of the state to the state ruler, the member of the family to the family ruler; the wife to the husband, the child to the parent, the servant to the master; that, in one word, wherever the relation of inferior and superior is established by God, there the duty of subjection finds place, as in Ephesians v. 21, where the general command, "Submit yourselves to one another," is followed and illustrated by the particular injunctions, 'Wives, submit yourselves to your husbands; children, obey your parents; servants, be obedient to your masters.' Either of these important moral truths might, without violence, be brought out of the words before us, viewed by themselves; but considered as a part of a closely connected paragraph, there can be no reasonable doubt, that the term "all of you" refers to the elders and to the juniors just mentioned, the office-bearers and members of the church; and that the duty enjoined is a duty equally owing by the elders to each other, by the members to each other, and by the elders and members to each other.

It may be of use in enabling you to perceive the precise import and bearing of the apostle's words, to remark, that their literal rendering is, " But let all of you, being subject one to another, be clothed with humility; for God resisteth the proud, but he giveth grace to the humble." As if he had said, 'While it is the duty of church officers to exercise the rule with which Christ has invested them, and for church members to yield the obedience which Christ has enjoined on them, there is a kind of mutual subjection which all church members owe to all church members; which all church officers owe to all church officers; ay, which all church officers owe to all church members; in order to the discharge of which, it is necessary to cherish and display that humility which is in a remarkable degree the object of the divine approbation.'

There are obviously three topics which the apostle's words bring before the mind, and which must be successively considered:—1. The duty which all connected with the Christian Church, whether as office-bearers or members, owe to each other — mutual subjection; 2. The means which are necessary to the discharge of this duty—the being clothed with, that is, the cherishing and manifesting humility; and 3. The motive urging the use of this means, its being the object of the peculiar approbation of God— "God resisteth the proud, and giveth grace to the humble."

CHAP. I. OF THE MUTUAL SUBJECTION WHICH ALL IN A CHRISTIAN CHURCH OWE TO EACH OTHER.

§ 1. *What this does not imply.*

Let us first, then, inquire, What is that MUTUAL SUBJECTION which the apostle here enjoins on all Christians, whether office-bearers or private members. It is so plain as scarcely to require to be noticed, that the subjection here required is by no means the same thing, though expressed by the same word, as the submission which, in the preceding clause, the juniors are enjoined to yield to the elders, the church members to the church rulers. It is obvious that church members are not bound to submit, to be subject, to their fellow church members, as they are to their elders; still less, if possible, can elders be bound to submit or be subject to the members, as the members are to be to them. This is obviously impossible; and to attempt it, were just in other words to annul church government, and to introduce all the disorders of ecclesiastical anarchy.

Nor does the command before us enjoin anything that in any degree involves in it a compromise of conscientious conviction respecting truth or duty. Christians must not submit to each other by taking each other's conscience as a guide in matters of faith or duty. Every man must give account of *himself* to God; and, so far as fellow-men or fellow-Christians are concerned, every man must think, inquire, judge, act, for himself. " One is our Master, even Christ."

The Christian elder must not, in teaching or administering the law of Christ, fashion his conduct in subservience to the views and wishes of those committed to his care. He must speak what he knows to be true, because it is Christ's doctrine, whatever they may think of it. He must do what he knows to be right, because it is Christ's law, whatever they may think of it. He must not in this way be a servant of men, even of Christian men. Were he to serve men in this way, he could not be a servant of Christ. Were he to serve them in this way, he would disserve them in a more important way.

No Christian man must submit, in matters of conscience,

to be led by another; to avow or conceal what he wishes him to avow or conceal; to do or to refrain from doing what he wishes him to do or refrain from doing. Instead of being thus subject to one another when any such submission is sought, either on the part of fellow church members or of church office-bearers, we are not to give subjection to such usurpation, "no, not for an hour." Our submission to one another is to be submission "in the fear of God."[1]

§ 2. *What this does imply.*

The mutual subjection referred to obviously implies a distinct recognition of, and a sacred regard to, our mutual rights as Christians and church members. Every encroachment by elders on the rights of church members, every encroachment by church members on the rights of their elders, every encroachment by church members, either individually or collectively, on each other's rights—and there has been a great deal too much of all these kinds of encroachment in the history of Christianity—is inconsistent with this mutual subjection. Every Christian man, official or unofficial, is to be yielded to, submitted to, in the exercise of his legitimate rights. This is most reasonable; it is absolutely necessary to the peace of the society; and, if carefully and uniformly attended to, would go very far to secure that peace.

This regard for mutual rights must be connected with a

---

[1] "When the apostle (Eph. v. 21) says, 'Submit yourselves one to another in the fear of God,' it is as though he said, 'Do not submit yourselves one to another *except* in the fear of God.' This limit of submission arises out of the very same principle which forms the motive of submission; the same expression serves to designate the reason of the precept and its limitation. We cannot sacrifice our own will to that of our brethren in the spirit of the text, beyond what is consistent with the glory of God, the public good, justice, and the rights of others."—VINET.

just, and, because a just, a high estimate of the honour due to Christians as Christians. No man will ever perform well the duties of civil life who has not learned to "honour all men,"—to honour man as man, and to see that the circumstances which distinguish one man from another are as nothing when compared with those which distinguish all men from the lower creation. In like manner, the higher a Christian estimates those privileges which are possessed by all Christians as Christians, and those spiritual characteristics which belong to every Christian, and which can belong to none but a Christian, the better will he be prepared to perform the duty here enjoined. Every Christian, just because he is a Christian, in relation and character a child of God, will be an object of his respectful affection; and he will find it impossible intentionally to treat him unjustly, contemptuously, or unkindly.

The disposition to mutual submission is greatly strengthened by that generous appreciation of the personal Christian excellences of those with whom we are associated in church fellowship, to which Christian principle naturally leads. Christians should be eagle-eyed towards each other's good qualities, "in honour preferring one another," each "esteeming others better than themselves."[1] When this state of mind prevails, "being subject to one another" follows as a matter of course. There is a disposition to oblige, a backwardness to occasion pain. While there is a mutual teaching, admonition, and exhortation, there is a mutual submission to instruction, admonition, and exhortation. And while a brother does not so hate his brother in his heart as to "suffer sin" on him, his brother reproved says by his conduct, "Let the righteous smite me, it shall be a kindness; and let him reprove me, it shall be an excellent oil, which shall not break my head." Even Archippus, the

[1] Rom. xii. 10; Phil. ii. 3.

office-bearer, will be subject to him, whether an official or only a Christian brother, who in the right spirit says to him, "Take heed to the ministry, which thou hast received of the Lord, to fulfil it."[1] There is a kindly yielding to each other in matters which do not involve conscience ; and there is a serving one another in love, a readiness to submit to labour and inconvenience to promote one another's true happiness. Instead of insisting on having everything our own way, we have a satisfaction in pleasing every one his neighbour to his edification. We not only "bear with the infirmities" of our brethren : we bear their infirmities, not pleasing ourselves. We "forbear one another in love," and "let no man seek his own, but every man another's wealth."[2]

Such was the temper and conduct of the great apostle of the Gentiles. Though free from all, he became the servant of all. He most willingly both spent and was spent to promote the welfare of his brethren; and declares that he would neither eat flesh nor drink wine while the world stood, if by this means his brother were likely to be offended or made weak. "Who was weak, and he was not weak? who was offended, while he did not burn? To the weak he became as weak, that he might gain the weak. To the Jew he became a Jew, that he might gain the Jew; to them who were under the law as under the law, that he might gain them who were under the law; to them who were without law, as without law, not being without law to God, but under the law to Christ, that he might gain them without law. He became all things to all men, that he might gain some."[3] Nor was this disposition in him confined to fellow-Christians; he was willing to be thus subject

[1] Ps. cxli. 5 ; Col. iv. 17.
[2] Rom. xv. 2 ; Eph. iv. 2 ; Col. iii. 13 ; 1 Cor. x. 24.
[3] 1 Cor. ix. 20, 21.

to every man, if that might but promote his happiness, secure his salvation.

Such was the temper and conduct of the great apostle's infinitely greater Lord and Master, and ours. He, though "Lord of all," became "the servant of all." Amid his disciples, he was as "one who served." "The Son of man," said he,—and the whole of his life was an illustration of the saying,—"The Son of man came not to be ministered unto, but to minister, and give his life a ransom for many."[1] Never was the lesson here given by the apostle so strikingly taught and so powerfully recommended as in the conduct of our Lord in that memorable night in which he was betrayed, of which we have so touching a narrative in the evangelical history: "Now, before the feast of the passover, when Jesus knew that his hour was come that he should depart out of this world unto the Father, having loved his own which were in the world, he loved them to the end. And there was a strife among the disciples, which of them should be accounted the greatest. And supper being ended, 'or rather being come,' Jesus knowing that the Father had given all things into his hands, and that he was come from God, and went to God; he riseth from supper, and laid aside his garments; and took a towel, and girded himself, 'clothing himself with humility.' After that he poureth water into a basin, and began to wash the disciples' feet, and to wipe them with the towel wherewith he was girded. So after he had washed their feet, and had taken his garments, and was set down again, he said unto them, Know ye what I have done to you? The kings of the Gentiles exercise lordship over them; and they that exercise authority upon them are called benefactors. But ye shall not be so. But he that is greatest among you, let him be as the younger; and he that is chief, as he that doth

[1] Matt. xx. 28.

serve. For whether is greater, he that sitteth at meat, or he that serveth? is not he that sitteth at meat? but I am among you as he that serveth. Ye call me Master and Lord: and ye say well; for so I am. If I, then, your Lord and Master, have washed your feet, ye also ought to wash one another's feet. For I have given you an example, that ye should do as I have done unto you. Verily, verily, I say unto you, The servant is not greater than his lord; neither he that is sent greater than he who sent him. If ye know these things, happy are ye if ye do them."[1]

This kind of mutual subjection, readiness to serve one another, should characterize all the members of the Church in their conduct to one another; but it should be especially prominent in the character and conduct of the office-bearers of the Church. They ought never to forget, that though they are over their brethren in the Lord in one sense, in another they are not their lords; Christ Jesus is the Lord; they are their "servants for Jesus' sake."[2] Our Lord, aware of the tendency of superiority of rank to produce arrogance, warns his official servants against this hazard. "Be not ye called Rabbi: for one is your Master, even Christ; and all ye are brethren. Neither be ye called masters: for one is your Master, even Christ. But he that is greatest among you shall be your servant."[3] The same truth is suggested by the peculiar form of expression in the passage before us. "Ye juniors, submit yourselves to the elders" in the discharge of their official functions; "but"[4] this is not the only kind of submission that is required in the Church—among Christians: "let all of you," whether elder or younger, seniors or juniors, official rulers or private members,—"let all of you be subject one to another."

[1] John xiii. 1-17; Luke xxii. 24-27.　　[2] 2 Cor. iv. 5.
[3] Matt. xxiii. 8, 10, 11.　　[4] Δί.

Mutually do service; and let him who is most esteemed in the Church be the readiest to serve.

CHAP. II. OF THE MEANS OF PERFORMING THIS DUTY: "THE BEING CLOTHED WITH HUMILITY."

Let us now, in the second place, consider the means by which Christians are to be enabled thus to be subject to one another. It is by being "clothed with humility." "Let all of you, being subject one to another, be clothed with humility."[1] The idea plainly is: Cherish and manifest humility; that will dispose and enable you to be subject one to another. But there is something peculiarly beautiful and instructive in the manner in which the idea is brought out. The apostle, in the Epistle to the Colossians, calls on Christians to "put on," among other Christian virtues, "humbleness of mind,"—the same word rendered here "humility,"—as necessary to their "forbearing one another, and forgiving one another," which are just particular forms of being subject to one another.[2] The figure there is just the general one common in all languages. The cultivation and display of a disposition is represented as the putting on and wearing a garment. But there is more in the phrase before us. The word rendered "Be clothed" is a remarkable one, occurring nowhere else in Scripture. It is borrowed from a piece of dress worn by servants when they were doing menial offices,—a kind of apron fastened by strings, a piece of dress which at once intimated their station, and fitted them for the performance of its duties.[3] The apostle calls on Christians, viewed as servants to each other, to put on humility as this piece of dress, to tie it on;

---

[1] What a contrast does this exhibit to the Horatian "virtute mea me involvo!"

[2] Col. iii. 12.   [3] See note D.

just as he calls on them, as soldiers of the Captain of salvation, to put on faith as a breastplate, and hope as an helmet. Cultivate humility, which will mark you as mutual servants, and fit you for mutual service. And it is difficult not to entertain the thought, that our Lord on the occasion already adverted to, putting on the towel like the servant's apron, and tying it around him, the visible emblem of his humility, and his readiness under its influence to serve, was before the apostle's mind; and that he then remembered the words of the Lord Jesus, words he was not likely to forget, "I have given you an example, that ye should do as I have done to you." All that is necessary here in the way of illustration, is shortly to show what that humility is which the apostle enjoins, and then in a few words to point out how it fits Christians for being "subject one to another."[1]

§ 1. *Humility explained.*

Humility, or, as the same word is elsewhere rendered more literally, "humbleness of mind," "lowliness of mind," is expressive of a low because a just estimate of ourselves—of our nature, of our character, of our condition, of our deserts.

The humble man has just, and therefore lowly, views of his own nature, as a *creature* infinitely inferior to, entirely dependent on, God; greatly inferior to angels, belonging to the lowest order of God's intelligent offspring; and, as a *sinner*, the proper object not only of the judicial displeasure of God, but of the moral disapprobation of all good and wise intelligences; inexcusably guilty, thoroughly depraved, righteously doomed to "everlasting destruction;" who, if saved at all, must owe his salvation to the riches of free grace, sovereign mercy.

The humble man has also just, and therefore lowly, views

[1] Col. iii. 12; Phil. ii. 3.

of his own individual character. He is sensibly impressed with the heinousness and aggravation of his own sins; he feels his own heart to be deceitful above all things, and desperately wicked; he knows that in him, that is, in his flesh, dwells no good thing. If his inward and outward man, his character and conduct, have been brought into any measure of conformity to the mind and will of God, he is aware that, so far as he is a new creature, he is "God's workmanship, created in Christ Jesus unto good works;" that "by the grace of God he is what he is;" that the work of renovation is very imperfect in him; that there is still very much wanting, very much wrong; and that, while he has much for which to be thankful, he has much of which to be ashamed, nothing of which to be proud.

And not only does the humble man form a low estimate of his nature generally, and of himself individually, when he tests human nature and his own character and conduct by the law of God, but he cherishes a humble opinion of himself, intellectually, morally, spiritually, in comparison with others. His tendency is to notice the excellences rather than the faults of others; while he looks at his own faults rather than at his excellences, and "in lowliness of mind he esteems others better than himself." He knows his own deficiencies and faults much more extensively and thoroughly than he can know those of other men; and the charity which always accompanies true humility, leads him to attribute what seems to be good in other men to the best principle which can reasonably be supposed to have produced it; while it leads him, from his necessary ignorance of their motives, to make allowances for their defects and failings, which he cannot make for his own. Humility does not lead a man to overlook or disclaim what God has done in him or by him, but it leads him to give all the glory to Him to whom it is due; and while he cannot but see that God has made him to differ from others, and be deeply grateful for this, he at once feels that it is God alone who has done this; and is so sensible of the manner in which he has counterworked the divine operations for his sanctification, that he is very ready to believe and acknowledge, that any other person blessed with his helps and advantages would have greatly surpassed him in his attainments. When he thinks of what he is in comparison of what he ought to have been, in comparison of what he might have been; when he thinks of what others with far inferior advantages have attained to, and recollects that whatever is spiritually good in him has been put into his heart by the invincible but not unresisted efficacious operation of the Holy Ghost, he not only feels that he ought to lie very low before God, but that, even in reference to his fellow-men, he has nothing to boast of.

Humility has been well described as consisting in "the not being deluded with a false conceit of what we have not, not puffed up with a vain conceit of what we really have, nor affecting to be esteemed by others, either in their imagining us to be what we are not, or discerning us to be what we are."[1] Humility will not make us unconscious of what is good in us, but it will make us beware of imagining that to be good which is not, or that which is good to be better than it is; and it will constantly keep before the mind, that whatever good is in us has been put into us, is not so much ours as God's, the gift of his grace, the work of his Spirit, and thus make the very consciousness of our sanctification, instead of puffing us up, a means of deepening the conviction that no flesh may "glory in his presence," but that "he who glorieth must glory in the Lord."[2] Such is the humility with which the apostle exhorts all Christians to be clothed, that they may be all subject one to another.

[1] Leighton.   [2] 1 Cor. i. 29-31.

§ 2. *The tendency of humility to secure mutual subjection.*

I have already adverted to the peculiar force of the expression, "Be clothed." The command does not refer so much, if at all, to the manifestation of this disposition in demeanour and language, but rather to the cherishing of it in the heart, to the maintaining of it in all circumstances, as that which fits a Christian for being subject to his fellow-Christians, by serving them in love, like the servant who fastened his serving robes about him as necessary for the proper discharge of his duty as a servant. Humility is to the Christian, as the servant of all his brethren, what the appropriate dress for service was to the servant in common life. A proud, self-conceited man is not disposed, is not qualified, for serving others. He is continually making demands on others for service. It is their duty in his estimation to serve him, not his to serve them. A haughty mind ill comports with becoming all things to all men, pleasing our neighbour to his edification, in love serving each other, bearing one another's burdens, and so, in one word, fulfilling the law of Christ: just as a gaudy dress, a rich flowing robe, does not suit, is at once incongruous and inconvenient in, one that serves. On the other hand, the humble-minded man is ready to serve, feels honoured in being permitted to do any office which can promote the honour of his Lord in the welfare of his brethren. Like the plainly, suitably-attired servant, he is like his work, and fit for it. He is ready to loose the latchets of his Lord's sandals, and to wash his brethren's feet.

The importance of humility, in order to the discharge of those offices which are so closely connected with the peace and spiritual prosperity of a church, is very strikingly manifested in the following exhortations of the Apostle Paul: "Be like-minded, having the same love, being of one accord, of one mind. Let nothing be done through strife or vainglory; but in lowliness of mind let each esteem other better than themselves. Look not every man on his own things, but every man also on the things of others. Let this mind be in you, that was in Christ Jesus," the disposition to humble himself that he might serve others. " Put on, therefore, as the elect of God, holy and beloved, bowels of mercy, kindness, humbleness of mind, meekness, longsuffering; forbearing one another, and forgiving one another, if any man have a quarrel against any."¹

CHAP. III. OF THE MOTIVE URGING CHRISTIANS TO CULTIVATE HUMILITY.

The only other topic in the text which requires consideration is the motive employed by the apostle to urge Christians to cultivate that humility which was so necessary to their mutually serving each other. " Be clothed with humility: for God resisteth the proud, and," or rather but,² " giveth grace to the humble." The leading idea is, ' Humility is the object of the approbation of God, and pride of his disapprobation; and he makes this very manifest in his dispensations respectively to the proud and to the humble.' As to any disposition or action, the first question with every man ought to be, the first question with a Christian will be, What is the estimate God forms of them; what effect will the cultivation of the one and the performance of the other have on my relations towards him? And the resolution of that question ought to have more influence with every man, with every Christian will have more influence, than all other things taken together, as to his checking or cherishing the disposition, following or avoiding the course of conduct. This matter is very clear as to pride and humility: " God

¹ Phil. ii. 2-5; Col. iii. 12, 13.   ² Δί.

resisteth the proud, but giveth grace to the humble." This is a quotation from the book of Proverbs (iii. 34), according to the Greek version in common use at the time: in our version, which is a literal rendering of the Hebrew original, it runs thus, " Surely he scorneth the scorners, but giveth grace to the lowly."

"God resisteth the proud." He sets himself to oppose them. It is impossible, in the nature of things, that God should not disapprove of pride, for it is a disposition which, just in the degree in which it prevails, unfits a man for his duty to God and to man, makes him a rebel to the one and an oppressor to the other; and in any view we can take of it, it counteracts God's design to glorify himself in making his creatures happy. The divine disapprobation against pride is strongly marked in an endless variety of ways. It is deeply impressed on the constitution of man as God's work, whether you consider the misery it inflicts on its subjects, or the disapprobation and dislike it produces in all who witness it. An apocryphal writer has said, " Pride was not made for man."[1] It may be with equal truth said, Man was not made for pride. It is a disposition he cannot indulge without making himself unhappy. They sadly err who " count the proud happy." There is harmony in all God's works, and, to make man happy, his disposition must correspond to his condition : a proud being, who is at the same time a dependent being, entirely dependent on God, to a great extent dependent on his fellow-men, must be miserable. His whole life is a struggle to be and to appear to be what he is not, what he never can be.

The disapprobation of pride by God is evident, not only in his having so constituted man as that the proud man cannot be happy, but in his so constituting man as that the proud man is the natural object of disapprobation and

[1] Ecclus. x. 18.

dislike to all other men. No class of men are more disliked than proud men. And how could God more distinctly mark his disapprobation of pride, than by constituting human nature so, that the display of pride should excite in, and draw forth from men, sentiments directly opposite to those which the proud man wishes? He seeks admiration, he meets with contempt. No one really wishes to gratify the proud, and his mortification affords general satisfaction.

In the ordinary course of his providential dispensations, God so often shows his opposition to pride, that it has become a proverb, that "a haughty spirit goeth before a fall;" and he has sometimes departed out of his usual mode of procedure, and miraculously shown how much he disapproves of haughtiness in man. Nebuchadnezzar, the proud king of Babylon, walked in the palace of his kingdom; and as he walked, he spake and said, "Is not this great Babylon, which I have built for the house of the kingdom, by the might of my power, and for the honour of my majesty?" How strikingly and effectually did God resist this proud man, and show that He, the King of heaven, all whose works are truth, and his ways judgments, is able to abase those who walk in pride! While the word was in the king's mouth, there fell a voice from heaven, "O king Nebuchadnezzar, to thee it is spoken, The kingdom is departed from thee: and they shall drive thee from men, and thy dwelling shall be with the beasts of the field: they shall make thee to eat grass as oxen, and seven times shall pass over thee, until thou know that the Most High ruleth in the kingdom of men, and giveth it to whomsoever he will. The same hour was the thing fulfilled upon Nebuchadnezzar; and he was driven from men, and did eat grass as oxen, and his body was wet with the dew of heaven, till his hairs were grown like eagles' feathers, and his nails like birds' claws." Take another example: "Upon a set day Herod, arrayed in royal apparel, sat on his throne, and made an oration. And the people gave a shout, 'It is the voice of a god, and not of a man.' And immediately the angel of the Lord smote him, because he gave not God the glory: and he was eaten up of worms, and gave up the ghost." [1]

The plan of salvation through Christ is so framed as strikingly to show that "God resisteth the proud." No man can become a partaker of its blessings who does not "deny," renounce, "himself." It is only as a being deserving, capable of deserving, nothing but punishment, and deeply sensible of this, that any man can obtain the pardon and peace, the holiness and comfort, of the Christian salvation. "The rich" in their own estimation are "sent empty away."[2] Men, who are all naturally proud, must be "converted, and become" humble "like little children," else they cannot enter into the kingdom of heaven. And just in that degree in which pride prevails, even in a regenerate man, will he fail to enjoy the consolation that is in Christ. The declarations of Scripture on this subject are very explicit: "Pride and arrogancy do I hate. The Lord knoweth the proud afar off. The lofty looks of men shall be humbled, and the haughtiness of man shall be bowed down; and the Lord alone shall be exalted. For the day of the Lord of hosts shall be upon every one that is proud and lofty, and upon every one that is lifted up, and he shall be brought low."[3] "God," to borrow the words of Archbishop Leighton, "singles out pride as his great enemy, and sets himself in battle-array against it, as the word is.[4] It breaks the ranks of men in which he hath set them, when they are not subject, as the word is before;[5] yea, it not only breaks rank, but rises up in rebellion against God, and

---

[1] Dan. iv. 29-33; Acts xii. 21-23. [2] Luke i. 53.
[3] Prov. viii. 13; Ps. cxxxviii. 6; Isa. ii. 11, 12. [4] Ἀντιτάσσεται.
[5] Ὑποτασσόμενοι.

doth what it can to dethrone him and usurp his place. Therefore he orders his force against it; and so be sure, if God be able to make his part good, pride shall not escape ruin. He will break it, and bring it low; for he is set upon that purpose, and will not be diverted."

While God thus resists the proud, "he giveth grace"—that is, he shows favour—"to the humble." Humility is the object of his approbation, and he shows this by his conduct to those who are characterized by it. A humble state of mind, as in accordance with truth, and calculated to promote the true happiness both of the individual who cherishes it, and of all with whom he is connected, must be the object of the divine approbation; and we have just to reverse the representation given of the manifestation of the state of the divine mind, in reference to the proud, to see how he shows favour to the humble. He does so in the quiet and peace of mind which, from the very constitution of human nature, humility produces; and in the comparative freedom from ill-will, and enjoyment of the esteem and good wishes of others, which from the same constitution it secures. The more deeply a man realizes his insignificance as a creature, and his demerit as a sinner, his guilt and depravity and helplessness, the more readily does he embrace the gospel of God's grace, "the word of the truth of the gospel," and in it obtain possession of all heavenly and spiritual blessings. It is the man who knows and believes that he is a fool, that is made wise; the man who has no hope in himself, that obtains "good hope through grace;" the man who sees and feels that he is nothing but sin, that is "made the righteousness of God in Christ;" the man who loathes himself, that is "sanctified wholly in the whole man—soul, body, and spirit." It is the man who most feels his own weakness, that is most "strengthened with all might in the inner man," and experimentally understands the spiritual paradox, "When I am weak, then am I strong." It is a remark, by one who was very intimately acquainted with the hidden life, "It is undoubtedly the secret pride and selfishness of our hearts that obstructs much of the bounty of God's hand, in the measure of our graces and the sweet embraces of his love, which we should otherwise find. The more that we let go of ourselves, still the more should we receive of himself. Oh, foolish we, that refuse so blessed an exchange!"[1] The passages of Scripture in which God declares his approbation of humility, and his delight in the humble, are very numerous. "Though the Lord be high, he has respect to the lowly. He forgets not the cry of the humble, he hears their desire; he prepares their hearts, he causes his ear to hear. Thus saith the high and lofty One who inhabits eternity, whose name is Holy, I dwell in the high and holy place, with him also that is of a contrite and humble spirit, to revive the spirit of the humble, and to revive the heart of the contrite ones." And this is the declaration of him who came to reveal the character and will of his Father, and who was himself meek and lowly in spirit: "Whosoever shall exalt himself shall be abased; but he that shall humble himself shall be exalted. Blessed are the poor in spirit; for theirs is the kingdom of heaven."[2]

Leighton's paraphrase on "God giveth grace to the humble" is characteristically beautiful. "He pours it out plentifully on humble hearts. His sweet dews and showers slide off the mountains, and fall on the low valley of humble hearts, and make them pleasant and fertile. The swelling heart, puffed up with a fancy of fulness, has no room for grace, is not hollowed and fitted to receive and contain the graces that descend from above. And again, as the humble

[1] Leighton.
[2] Ps. cxxxviii. 6, x. 12, 17; Isa. lvii. 15, lxvi. 2; Matt. xxiii. 12, v. 3.

heart is most capable, as emptied and hollowed out it can hold most; so it is most thankful, acknowledges all as received. But the proud cries all is his own. The return of glory that is due for grace, comes most freely and plentifully from a humble heart. God delights to enrich it with grace, and it delights to return to him glory. The more he bestows on it, the more it desires to honour him withal; and the more it doth so, the more readily he still bestows more upon it. And this is the sweet intercourse between God and the humble soul. This is the noble ambition of humility, in respect of which all the aspirings of pride are low and base. When all is reckoned, the lowliest mind is truly the highest; and these two agree so well, that the more lowly it is, it is thus the higher; and the higher thus, it is still the more lowly."

Surely this is a powerful motive for the cultivation of humility. What so much to be feared as God's disapprobation, and what so much to be desired as his favour? The command, "Be ye clothed with humility," has great additional force from the consideration that this was the chosen garb of our Lord and King, and chosen by him as that in which he could both best serve his Father and his people. Surely, to use the words of an old divine, "it is meet that we should remember that the blessed Saviour of the world hath done more to prescribe, and transmit, and secure this grace than any other, his whole life being a great continued example of humility,—a vast descent from the glorious bosom of his Father to the womb of a poor maiden, to the form of a servant, to the miseries of a sinner, to a life of labour, to a state of poverty, to a death of malefactors, to an untimely grave, to all the intolerable calamities which we deserved; and it were a good design, and yet but reasonable, that we should be as humble in the midst of our calamities and base sins, as he was in the midst of his fulness of the Spirit, great wisdom, perfect life, and most admirable virtues."[1]

And while the thought, that it is only by thus putting on humility that Christians can be mutually subject to and serve each other, and thus promote the peace and prosperity of the Church on earth, should be felt as a powerful incentive to grow in this grace; we should remember also that the cultivation of this grace is a necessary preparation for the holy delights of the Church above. They to whom, on that day when men's destinies shall be finally fixed, the universal Judge will say, "Come, ye blessed of my Father," are those who can scarcely recognise their own actions in those eulogized by him.[2] And the exercises of heaven are such as only the humble can engage in with satisfaction. They fall down on their faces there before the throne, and him who sits on it; they cast their crowns at his feet. The only worthiness they celebrate is the worthiness of the Lamb that was slain; and the whole glory of their salvation is ascribed to him, of whom, and through whom, and to whom are all things. "Salvation to our God which sitteth upon the throne, and unto the Lamb." We must be formed to the temper of heaven, if we would be sharers in its joys. We must have the same mind in us as is in the holy angels and the spirits of the just made perfect, if we would be admitted to their society, and participate in their delights. Were we to carry pride with us to heaven, it would soon cast us out again, as it did the angels who kept not their first estate. Let us then earnestly covet a large measure of this heavenly temper. Let it be our constant prayer, that the Spirit of all grace would so bring the truth before our minds, and keep it there, respecting our condition and character as creatures and sinners, sinners lost by their own inexcusable guilt, saved solely by the sovereign grace of God, as that

[1] Jeremy Taylor.   [2] Matt. xxv. 37-39.

every rising of undue self-complacency may be repressed, and that we may be enabled to "walk worthy of the vocation wherewith we are called, with all lowliness and meekness; with long-suffering, forbearing one another in love, endeavouring to keep the unity of the Spirit in the bond of peace." Oh, how happy the church, where all the elders and all the members are habitually under the influence of Christian humility! May that blessing, through the grace of him who is exalted to be "Head over all things to his Church," be increasingly ours! And to his name be all the glory.

Note A. p. 214.

How different was the spirit which animated those who pretended to be Peter's successors, appears strikingly in a remarkable story told in the Clementine Homilies: "Peter, wishing to establish in a bishopric, Zaccheus, who was backward to accept of it, cast himself at his feet, and entreated him to administer τὴν ἀρχήν—the princedom. 'I would readily do,' said Zaccheus, 'whatever a prince ought to do; but I am afraid to bear the name, because it exposes to so much envy as to be dangerous.' Peter consented that Zaccheus should not take the name prince; but he gave him all the authority of one. Καὶ σοῦ μὲν ἔργον, said he, κελεύειν· τῶν δὲ ἀδελφῶν ὑπείκειν καὶ μὴ ἀπείθειν. 'It is your business to command; and as to the brethren, it is theirs to submit to and obey you.'" It is universally admitted that the Clementine Homilies are forgeries; but they are very authentic evidences of the spirit of the Roman Church at the time of their production. The bishops are there represented as Δυνασταὶ, βασιλεῖς, δεσπόται, κύριοι. How strangely does all this contrast with the words of the One Master: "Call no man master on earth: be not ye called masters!"—*Hom. Clem.* iii. 63, 64, 66, p. 646.

Note B. p. 228.

"Τῶν κλήρων plurale: singulare gregis. Ποίμνη μία—Grex unus sub uno Pastore principe Christo: sed κλῆροι portiones multæ, pro numero locorum et antistitum."—Bengel. This view throws light on the whole passage. Among the nomadic tribes wealth consisted almost entirely in flocks and herds. The great proprietors were just shepherds on a great scale. Ἀρχιποιμένες, ποιμένες ὧν εἰσὶ τὰ πρόβατα ἴδια.[1] The whole ποίμνη belonged to them; but under them there were ποιμενες, each of whom had his own κλῆρος. The Ἀρχιποιμὴν was often absent; but, on his coming to see his flocks, he would notice the manner in which the under shepherds had treated *his* property, and deal with them accordingly.

"Vetustus quidem fuit ille loquendi modus, ut totum ordinem ministrorum clerum vocarent: sed utinam Patribus nunquam venisset in mentem ita loqui: quia quod toti Ecclesiæ Scriptura communiter tribuit, minime consentaneum fuit ad paucos homines restringere."—Calvin.

"Clerus temporibus Apostolorum erant plebeii, quod apparet ex prima Petri Epistola majestuosa."—Scaliger.

"Cleros vocat non diaconos aut presbyteros, sed gregem qui cuique fortè contigit gubernandus; ne quis existimet, Episcopis in Clericos interdictum dominium, in ceteros esse permissum. Et presbyteros hîc Episcopos vocat. Nondum enim increverat turba sacerdotum; sed quot erant Presbyteri, totidem erant Episcopi."—Erasmus.

"Olim populus Israeliticus κλῆρος, sors, sive patrimonium Dei, Deut. iv. 20, ix. 29. Nunc populus Christianus; cujus singulæ partes ut fieri solet ἐν ὁμογενέσει idem nomen participant."—Grotius.

"Κλήρους hereditates vocat Ecclesias singulas, quibus singuli pastores præficiuntur."—Suicer.

"All believers are God's clergy."—Leighton.

It deserves notice, that it is a verb derived from κλήρους which is used, Acts xvii. 4, to describe the association of the believers with Paul and Silas at Thessalonica—προσεκληρώθησαν. Our translators have preserved the reference in their version "consorted."

[1] John x. 12; Gen. xlvii. 6; 1 Sam. xxi. 7.

"Κλήρους multi Latinorum interpretantur clericos; veruntamen longe probabilius est, per cleros intelligi gregis dominici portiones, quæ singulis Episcopis pascendæ ac regendæ velut sortito obtigerunt, juxta id quod Cyprianus dicit, Ecclesiam esse unam, cujus singulas portiones singuli Episcopi in solidum tenent."—Estius.

Vater takes a singular view of the meaning of the term here: "Κλήρων plurali numero, non nisi, Acts i. 26, eodemque forsan significatu et hic." In this case κατακυρεύειν τῶν κλήρων would signify arbitrarily to overrule the votes, to disregard the will of the church, when manifested by their giving forth their κλήρους.

Note C. p. 238.

A word of similar meaning (Νεανίσκοι) is apparently used in the New Testament to signify common soldiers, Mark xiv. 51, as well as in the profane Greek (Polyb. iv. 16, iii. 62). A similar usage prevails in the Latin language, as to the word of corresponding meaning (Juvenis). We find the same thing in the Hebrew language: Abraham's armed servants are called "the young men" (נערים), Gen. xiv. 24. We have the same use of the word, Jos. ii. 1; 2 Sam. ii. 14; Gen. xviii. 7; Ps. cx. 3. "The word 'young' possesses, in the Christian usage of various languages, the sense of 'lay.' See Bolten."—Steiger.

"Νεώτεροι hic non videntur esse natu minores; nam opponuntur doctoribus, sed potius auditores et discipuli, eodem fere sensu, quo, Luc. xxii. 26, ὁ μείζων et ὁ νεώτερος sibi opponuntur."—Rosenmüller.

"Νεώτεροι opponuntur πρεσβυτέροις et ex lege oppositionis intelligendi sunt omnes reliqui qui exceptis Presbyteris ecclesiam constituerent."—Küttner.

Schotanus, though obviously very averse, "a communi Doctorum sententia discedere videri," states very distinctly, and defends very successfully, what appears to me the true meaning:
—"Hic per *juniores* intelligimus totam ecclesiam. Id autem probamus (1) ex repetitione verbi *presbyteri;* (2) ex collatione in verbis: *similiter;* (3) quia summissionem regimini opponit; (4) quia passim Apostoli quando agunt de officiis in quibus mutuus est respectus, solent utrumque urgere. Si autem quis dicat nomen illud *juniores* repugnari, respondemus—nequequam.

Nonne Apostolus Paulus totam Ecclesiam Galaticam 'filiolos' vocat, Gal. iv. 19, et hæc ratio est, quia tum temporis præcipue Ecclesiæ præficiebantur qui provectioris ætatis erant."

"Per juniores autem hoc loco maxime intelligitur Grex qui pendet à pastoribus, quia pastores et presbyteri, maxima ex parte, electi fuerunt ex senioribus ætate, et proinde maxima pars gregis constabat ex junioribus."—AMESIUS. "Sicut nomen, senior, præfectum significat, etiam si ætate sit minor, ita nomen, junior, sive adolescens, recte interpretante Beda, subditum omnem, tametsi ætate superiorem designat."—HESSELIUS.

NOTE D. p. 266.

"Κόμβος nodus vinculum quo illigabantur manicæ præsertim in vestitu servorum."—BENGEL. Grotius gives the following quotation from Pollux, lib. iv., which is quite to the point:— Τῇ τῶν δούλων ἐξωμίδι καὶ ἱματίδιόν τι προσκεῖται λευκὸν, ὃ ἐγκόμβωμα λέγεται. Putting on the ἐγκόμβωμα, was preparing in a becoming manner to act as a servant—assuming the appearance and preparing for the duties of the servile state. "'Εγκόμβωμα vestis humilis et servorum erat: qui cum breves tunicas quas ἐπωμίδας vocant gestarent, super has ἐγκόμβωμα induere solebant; palliolum vilissimum sed candidum; quod et ἐπίβλημα, ut observant antiqui, dicebant."—HEINSIUS, *Sac. Exercit.* p. 577.

DISCOURSE XXII.

TWO VIEWS OF AFFLICTION AND ITS DUTIES.

"Humble yourselves therefore under the mighty hand of God, that he may exalt you in due time; casting all your care upon him; for he careth for you."
—1 PET. v. 6, 7.

THERE are few practical questions of deeper and more extensive interest than, How should we conduct ourselves amid the afflictions of life so as to be best sustained under them, most improved by them, and soonest and most certainly delivered from them? This is a question which concerns us all; for however we may differ in other points of view, here we all occupy common ground. We are all sufferers. It is not less universally true that "man is born of a woman," than that he is "born to trouble." It is certain, too, that affliction, though in all forms in itself an evil, is far from being an unmixed evil; that by means of it, men, constituted and circumstanced as they are, may be made wiser and better, and ultimately happier, than they could have become without it. "It has been good for me that I have been afflicted," says the Psalmist. "Chastisement yieldeth peaceable fruits,"[1] says the apostle. And there is "a great cloud of witnesses" of the wisest and the best, in every age, all of whom have set to their seal that this testimony is true.

It is, however, just as certain that there have been many sufferers who could not truly make the Psalmist's declaration

[1] Job xiv. 1; Ps. cxix. 71; Heb. xii. 11.

their own. It has *not* been good for them that they have been afflicted. They were bad when affliction seized them; they did not improve under its grasp; and now that it has let them go, they are worse than ever. Indeed, the waters sent forth from the fountain of affliction seem in themselves poisonous as well as bitter. The infusion of a foreign ingredient into them appears to be necessary to make them salutary, or even safe. Their effects are usually powerful; but they often aggravate rather than mitigate moral disease.

The different effects of affliction on different individuals depend mainly on their being or their not being under the influence of the Holy Spirit; and that is chiefly manifested in the views they entertain of affliction, and in the dispositions they cherish under affliction,—two things which are very closely connected with each other. The influence of affliction on the mind and character of a man who considers his sufferings as the effect of blind chance or unintelligent necessity, or of intelligent but malignant power, and who is inconsiderate, or proud, or fretful, or desponding under them, must be very different from its influence on the mind of a man who considers his sufferings as proceeding from the appointment and inflicted by the agency of the infinitely powerful, wise, righteous, and benignant Sovereign of the universe,—as tokens of displeasure against sin, yet means of reclaiming sinners,—as important parts of God's mysterious economy for making foolish, depraved, miserable man, wise, and good, and happy; and who cultivates a thoughtful, submissive, prudent, devout, patient, hopeful disposition under them.

The moral effect of affliction on an irreligious or superstitious mind cannot but be mischievous, though it will vary with the variety of character and circumstance, and take the form, in one case, of stupid insensibility; in another, of querulous fretfulness; in another, of hopeless despondency; in another, of hardened impiety. It will in every such case drive men from God, not draw them towards him. It will make them worse and more miserable, not better and happier; it will fit them for hell, not for heaven.

On the other hand, the moral effect of affliction in a mind enlightened with heavenly truth, and a heart pervaded by holy influence, must be in a very high degree advantageous. Every principle of the new life,—such as faith, hope, penitence, patience, humility, self-sacrifice,—is exercised and strengthened; and the result is, increased conformity in mind and will, and choice and enjoyment, with the all-wise, the all-holy, the all-benignant, the ever-blessed God. Who would not wish that his afflictions might have this result? We must be chastened; that is a settled point. "To each his sufferings, all are men."[1] Who would not tremble to be so chastened as to be destroyed with the world?. who would not desire to be so chastened as to be made partakers of God's holiness? It is this book that alone can so instruct us in the true nature of afflictive dispensations, and in the right way of dealing with these dispensations, as that it may be secured that in our case the last, and not the first, result shall be realized. We must go to the school of revelation in order to learn how to behave ourselves in the school of affliction so as to obtain improvement there; and a most instructive lesson of this kind may be derived from that interesting passage of inspired Scripture which has been read as the subject of discourse. May the great Teacher, who makes all whom he teaches apt to learn, enable us so to improve it as that " his rod and reproof," when he sees meet to subject us to them, may more than ever " give wisdom!"

These words present us with two interesting views of affliction,—first, as a state of subjection to the mighty hand

[1] Gray.

of God; and secondly, as a state of anxiety and carefulness,—and with two corresponding views of the duty of the Christian under affliction, each accompanied with its appropriate motive. In the first view of affliction, the Christian is to humble himself under the mighty hand of God; and he is to do this because humility is well-pleasing to God, because it is the hand of God, the mighty hand of God, that he is under, and because doing so is the appointed way to be exalted in due time ; and in the second view of affliction, the Christian is to cast all his cares on God, and he is to do this because God cares for him. This is the outline I mean to fill up in the remaining part of the discourse ; and in doing this, I shall not first consider the two views of affliction, then the two views of the duty of the Christian under affliction, and then the two views of motive urging to the performance of these duties; but I shall successively, as the apostle does, take up each connected view of affliction, duty, and motive.

Before entering on this, however, it may be proper to say a word or two on the manner in which these two verses are connected with the immediately preceding context. In the close of his directory respecting ecclesiastical duties, the apostle recommends the cultivation of humility as necessary to that mutual subjection by which all in Christian fellowship, whether office-bearers or private members, whether elders or juniors, should be distinguished ; calling them to put it on as their appropriate dress when in love they served each other ; and he strengthens his recommendation by quoting an Old Testament oracle, in which God's complacent approbation of the humble, and his indignant reprobation of the proud, are strongly expressed. " God resisteth the proud, and giveth grace to the humble." And in proceeding to offer them some advices suited to those circumstances of persecution and trial to which, by the appointment of God, and through the direct and indirect agency of the great adversary the devil, they were already exposed, and were likely soon to be still more exposed, he naturally, in so high a recommendation of humility as a disposition peculiarly pleasing to God, finds a ground for enjoining on them the cultivation and display of this virtue in reference to their afflictions viewed as the work of God's hand: "God resisteth the proud, and giveth grace to the humble. Humble yourselves *therefore* under the mighty hand of God." The quotation from the Old Testament is brought forward as a motive to enforce equally the injunction that precedes it, and the injunction that follows it.

I. FIRST VIEW OF AFFLICTION, AND ITS DUTY.

§ 1. *Affliction is subjection to the mighty hand of God.*[1]

The first view here given us of a state of affliction is, that it is a state of subjection to the mighty hand of God. The words of the apostle are equivalent to, Being in affliction, ye are under the mighty hand of God; humble yourselves under it. "The hand of God," like "the arm of the Lord," is a figurative expression for the power of God in action, as men put forth their power by their arm and hand. He is said to have brought his people from Egypt "by strength of hand;" that is, by the exertion of power. It is said, "None can stay his hand," none can prevent or control the exertion of his power. When Job expresses a wish that by an act of divine power he might be destroyed, he says, "Oh that it would please God to let loose his hand, and cut me off;" and speaking of the power of God as the efficient cause of all things, he says, "The hand of the Lord hath done this, in whose hand is the soul of every living thing, and the breath of all mankind."[2] The epithet

[1] *Vide* note A. [2] Job. vi. 9, xii. 10.

"mighty" is added to suggest the idea of great, resistless energy.

To have the hand of God on a person, to be in his hand, or under his hand, does not necessarily indicate being in a state of affliction. It merely means that the power of God is exercised with regard to that person. Jehovah is said by Moses to "love his people;" and in a parallel case he adds, "All his saints are in thy hand," protected by thy power. "The hand of our God," says Ezra, "is upon all them for good that seek him; but his power and his wrath is against all them that forsake him. The hand of our God was upon us, and he delivered us from the hand of the enemy." The powerful inspiring influence of the Holy Spirit is described as the hand of the Lord being on the prophets, in the cases of Elijah and Ezekiel. But the phrase is very often used in a more specific sense, as descriptive of the power of God put forth for punishment or chastisement. It is said, "the hand of the Lord was heavy on the men of Ashdod," when he visited them with a severe judgment. "The hand of the Lord is on thy cattle," said Moses to Pharaoh, when he announced the plague of murrain. "Have pity on me," says Job, "Have pity on me, O my friends, for the hand of God hath touched me." "Day and night," says the Psalmist, "thy hand was heavy on me. Thine arrows stick fast in me; thy hand presseth me sore."[1] "Let me not fall into the hand of man, but into the hand of the Lord," said David, when called to choose whether war, or famine, or pestilence was to be the punishment of his sin. Some interpreters consider the phrase before us, "under the mighty hand of God," as merely referring generally to the being entirely at the disposal of God, completely in his hand;

---

[1] Deut. xxxiii. 3; Ezra viii. 22, 31; 1 Kings xviii. 46; Ezek. i. 3; 1 Sam. v. 11; Ex. ix. 3; Job xix. 21; Ps. xxxii. 4, xxxviii. 2; 1 Chron. xxi. 13.

but the use of the epithet mighty, and the contrast of the depressed state of the person *under* the mighty hand of God, with the state of elevation promised him if the temper of his mind should properly correspond with his circumstances, as well as the succeeding context, all convince me that the apostle had in his eye " the manifold trials," " the afflictions," to which, as a part of the Christian brotherhood in the world, those to whom he wrote were exposed. The thought which he wished to bring strongly before their mind is this: ' Those afflictions to which you are exposed are the result of the divine appointment and agency.' Let us shortly illustrate that thought; it is an important one.

" Affliction cometh not forth of the dust; trouble doth not spring from the ground." They " come down from above;" they " come forth from Him who is wonderful in counsel, and excellent in working."[1] There are many who think and feel in reference to afflictive dispensations, as the Philistines of old did, when they said, " A chance hath happened us." But there is neither blind chance nor unintelligent necessity in God's world. " He worketh all things according to the counsel of his own will." No event occurs apart from his plan, and the execution of his plan. " His counsel stands, and he doth all his pleasure."[2]

The doctrine of providence, a particular providence (for it is not very easy to understand what is meant by a general providence as opposed to a particular one), is supported by numerous and powerful arguments, deduced from rational principles, as well as from the declarations of inspired Scripture. Admit the wisdom, the power, and the omnipresence of the Divine Being, and you cannot consistently deny his providence. " Are not two sparrows," says our Lord, " sold for a farthing? yet one of them shall not fall

[1] Job v. 6 ; James i. 17 ; Isa. xxviii. 29.
[2] 1 Sam. vi. 9 ; Eph. i. 11 ; Isa. xlvi. 10.

on the ground without your Father: even the hairs of your head are all numbered."[1] Can He who cares for sparrows, and numbers the hairs of our head—can he be inattentive to, or unconcerned in, what so closely concerns the honour of his character, and the highest interests of his people, as their afflictions?

The agency of God in the afflictions of his people is not only deducible from, or more properly involved in, the doctrine of his universal providence; but it is taught in the most explicit terms which language can furnish: "Shall there be evil," that is, suffering, affliction in any form, "in a city, and the Lord hath not done it?" "I am the Lord, and there is none else; there is no god besides me. I form the light, and create the darkness; I make peace, and create evil. I, the Lord, do all these things." "The Lord killeth, and maketh alive: he bringeth down to the grave, and bringeth up. The Lord maketh poor, and maketh rich: he bringeth low, and he lifteth up." "See now that I, even I, am he, and there is no god with me. I kill, and I make alive; I wound, and I heal: neither is there any who can deliver out of my hand." "He maketh sore, and bindeth up; he woundeth, and his hands make whole." The person accidentally killed, as we phrase it, is by Moses said to be "delivered by God into the hands" of the person who unintentionally deprived him of life.[2]

And we are to consider those afflictions as proceeding from the hand of God, not merely when there appears to us no intermediate agent, whether physical or intelligent, as in the case of sudden death or unaccountable accident; but whatever be the immediate occasion,—whether they occur from the operation of what we call natural causes, in

---

[1] Matt. x. 29, 30.
[2] Amos iii. 6; Isa. xlv. 7; 1 Sam. ii. 6; Deut. xxxii. 39; Job v. 18; Ex. xxi. 13.

the course of the established order of things, or from the agency of intelligent beings, human, angelic, or infernal,— they are to be considered as coming forth from him "of whom, and through whom, and to whom are all things."[1] The miraculous slaughter of Korah, Dathan, and Abiram, for whose punishment the Lord "made a new thing," and the death of those who through disease or old age were cut off in the wilderness, were equally the works of the Lord. Wars which spring from human passions, and are carried on through human instrumentality, equally with the famine and the pestilence, are numbered among the works of God; and their ravages are "desolations which he makes in the earth."[2] When adversity mingles its bitter ingredients in our cup, whatever these ingredients are, let us never forget that it is God who puts that cup into our hand. It matters not whether our affliction springs from those disastrous visitations in which the agency of man has no part, and over which it has no control, like that mysterious blight which has lately turned into rottenness so large a portion of the produce of our fields and the food of the people; or arises from the improvidence, the injustice, or the cruelty of human beings; in either case it forms a part of the administration of Him whose kingdom ruleth all. Job spoke like a philosopher as well as a saint,—his words were those of wisdom as well as of piety,—when, after the Sabeans had carried away his oxen, the fire of God falling from heaven had consumed his sheep, the Chaldeans had robbed him of his camels and murdered his servants, and a great wind from the wilderness had buried his children in the ruins of his eldest son's house, he said, "It is the Lord." The lightning and the tempest, the Sabeans and the Chaldeans, he considered, and rightly, as the instruments (the human beings the guilty instruments) of the execution of

[1] Rom. xi. 36.   [2] Ps. xlvi. 8.

God's most holy and righteous appointment. "The Lord," said he, "gave, and the Lord hath taken away; blessed be the name of the Lord."[1] And He of whose faith and patience Job's afford but a faint resemblance, amid his unparalleled sufferings, proceeding in a great measure directly from the malignant agency of men and devils, looked beyond Judas and his band, Caiaphas and the chief priests, the denial of Peter and the flight of the disciples, Pontius Pilate and the Roman soldiers, the prince of darkness and his hosts, to Him whose high and holy determination all these were unconsciously and most wickedly carrying into accomplishment, and with meek reverence and devout submission said, "The cup which my Father hath given me, shall I not drink it?"[2]

This important principle, that our afflictions are the work of God, seems the principal truth intended to be taught by the representation before us; a truth, the apprehension of which is absolutely necessary to the deriving of any spiritual advantage from affliction. A conviction of this will persuade us that our afflictions are not the effect of caprice or of cruelty; that they are the result of design, wise design, benignant design,—sent to serve a purpose, a holy and benevolent purpose.

The words, however, seem further to indicate, what we are very ready to forget, that in affliction God is very near us. He is always so, ever at our right and left hand, intently looking on us; but in affliction, to rouse us to the fact of his nearness, he, as it were, lays his hand on us; and we are stupid indeed if we still continue inapprehensive of his presence.

Affliction, as a laying God's hand on us, intimates not only that he is near us, but that he is actually dealing with us: he has business with us, he has to do with us, and we

---

[1] Job i. 21.   [2] John xviii. 11.

have to do with him. He has accounts to settle with us; he is not satisfied with us; we are not what he would have us to be. If we were, he would not indeed let us alone—that were a dreadful evil; but he would interfere only to give new proofs of his love in new gifts of his grace: his hand would never be on us for chastisement; it would be on us only for good. He does not afflict willingly. If he gives us a blow, assuredly we deserve it. We have provoked it. It comes from a reluctant hand.

Still further, in the case of God's own people—and it is of them the apostle is speaking—affliction, viewed as laying his hand on them, is a manifestation of kind interest in them. He has not given them up; He means to make something of them; He smites because he loves them; He "chastens them for their profit." It is not the stroke of a cruel one; it is not the hand of the destroyer. To vary the figure, affliction with them is as "the refiner's fire, and the fuller's soap." "He sits as a refiner and purifier of silver; and he shall purify them and purge them as gold and silver, that they may offer to the Lord an offering of righteousness."[1]

§ 2. *Our duty in affliction is to "humble ourselves under the mighty hand of God."*

Having thus considered the Christian's state of affliction as a state of subjection to God's chastening hand, let us now consider the corresponding view the apostle gives of their duty: Christians are to "humble themselves under the mighty hand of God." The command is equivalent to "Despise not the chastening of the Lord." Rebel not against it, fret not under it, murmur not at it, call not in question either Jehovah's right, or the manner in which he asserts it. Beware of doubting the wisdom, or the righteousness, or the kindness of the visitation. "Be still, and

[1] Heb. xii. 10; Mal. iii. 3.

know that *He* is God." "Glorify the Lord in the fires." "Sanctify the Lord God in your heart." "Hear the rod, and Him who has appointed it."[1] The whole truth on this subject may be comprehended in the threefold injunction: Humble yourselves under the mighty hand of God, as creatures under the hand of their Creator; as subjects under the hand of their Sovereign; as children under the hand of their Father.

(1.) *As creatures under the hand of the Creator.*

Christians in affliction should humble themselves as creatures under the hand of their Creator. Pride, impatience, murmuring, and rebellion under affliction, which all flow from pride, are absolutely monstrous in a creature under the hand of the Creator. What is the creature but what the Creator has made him? What has he but what God has given him? Is not he and all that he has far more the Creator's property than his own? Is he not, must he not be, ought he not to be, entirely dependent on, submissive to, Him who made him? "Hath not the potter power over the clay?" "Shall the clay say to him who fashioned it, What makest thou? or the work to him who formed it, Thou hast no hands?" "Shall the axe boast itself against him that heweth therewith? or shall the saw magnify itself against him that shaketh it? as if the rod should shake itself against them that lift it up, or as if the staff should lift up itself, as if it were no wood."[2] In affliction we feel the touch of that hand which made us, and which can easily turn us to dust again. Surely, in these circumstances, it is meet to acknowledge that we are " nothing, less than nothing, and vanity," before him " who was, and is, and is to come, the Almighty;" " of whom, and through whom, and

[1] Ps. xlvi. 10; Isa. xxiv. 15, viii. 13; Mic. vi. 9.
[2] Rom. ix. 22; Isa. xlv. 9, x. 15.

to whom are all things." We should even wonder that he takes so much notice of us as to send us salutary afflictions. "Lord, what is man, that thou takest knowledge of him! or the son of man, that thou makest account of him! that thou shouldest visit him every morning, and try him every moment?—man who is like unto vanity; whose days are as a shadow that passeth away."[1]

(2.) *As subjects under the hand of their Sovereign—rebel subjects under the hand of their righteously offended Sovereign.*

Christians should humble themselves in affliction as subjects under the hand of their Sovereign, as rebel subjects under the hand of their righteously offended Sovereign. If creatures should be humble just because they are creatures, sinful creatures are tenfold bound to be humble. In the being sinners, everything base and degrading is necessarily included. There is no folly like sin, no baseness like sin. Affliction is intended to bring sin to remembrance. We should never forget our guilt and depravity, and the state of condemnation and debasement into which they have brought us; but in the day of affliction we should especially say, "I remember my faults this day:" I lay my hand on my mouth, my mouth in the dust, unclean, unclean. I have no ground of complaint, I can have none. I deserve no good. I deserve all evil. "It is of the Lord's mercies I am not consumed."[2] Does it not become rebels justly doomed to death, spared by the clemency of their insulted, injured sovereign, yet bearing ever on them distinct marks of their crime, and both of his unmerited clemency and just displeasure—does it not become them to be humble? Deep self-abasement is the becoming temper in him who knows that he has incurred the righteous displeasure of

[1] Ps. cxliv. 3, 4. [2] Lam. iii. 22.

God by innumerable, unprovoked violations of the law that is holy, just, and good; and that in him, that is, in his flesh, dwells no good thing. Deep self-abasement is the temper which becomes him at all times, and especially when he is under the mighty hand of God. However severe the afflictions, why should he murmur? Why should he complain? "A man for the punishment of sins;" a man punished, but punished far less than his iniquities deserve? "Surely it is meet to be said unto God, I have borne chastisement, I will not offend any more: that which I see not, teach thou me; if I have done iniquity, I will do so no more." The language of his heart should be, "Righteous art thou, O Lord, when I plead with thee." "Behold, I am vile; what shall I answer thee, O thou Preserver of men?" "I have sinned, I have committed iniquity, I have done wickedly, I have rebelled by departing from thy precepts and from thy judgments. O Lord, righteousness belongeth to thee, but to me confusion of face, because I have sinned against thee."[1] Thus does it become the sinner, under the mighty hand of God, to "sit alone and keep silence, to put his mouth in the dust, if so be there may be hope." This kind of humbling a person's self is just as becoming the converted as the unconverted man. It will for ever continue a fact that he has broken God's holy law, and had a thoroughly depraved nature; and the recollection of these facts, which affliction is intended to recall to the mind, should for ever hide pride from the Christian's eyes.

(3.) *As children under the hand of their Father.*

But the Christian stands to God in the relation not only of a creature to the Creator, not only of a subject to his Sovereign, but also of a child to his Father. This is the

[1] Lam. iii. 39; Job xxxiv. 31, 32; Jer. xii. 1; Job xl. 4, vii. 20; Dan. ix. 5, 7.

peculiar relation in which the Christian stands to God; and in this relation he ought, in the season of affliction, to "humble himself under the mighty hand of God." Of all men, it least becomes the Christian to question the wisdom or righteousness or kindness of the divine afflictive dispensations, to be fretful or unsubmissive under the mighty hand of God. He knows the character of him who inflicts chastisement; he knows how richly he deserves chastisement; he knows how much he stands in need of chastisement; he knows the true nature and design of chastisement; and therefore he ought to be distinguished by the humility of reverence, the humility of acquiescence, the humility of gratitude. He should humbly acknowledge the right of him who inflicts: he has done nothing but what he has a good right to do. He should humbly acknowledge that the affliction was not uncalled for: he has got nothing but what he deserves; and that, however heavy, it might have been much heavier, without affording him cause either of surprise or complaint. And he should humbly acknowledge his obligations to his Father in heaven, both for afflicting him, and afflicting him in measure; for sending the very afflictions, in kind and degree, which infinite wisdom saw he needed, and which infinite faithfulness secures shall serve their purpose. I cannot conclude this part of the subject better than in the words of the apostle in his Epistle to the Hebrews, when he bids them not forget "the exhortation which speaketh unto them as to children, My son, despise not thou the chastening of the Lord;" that is, in other words, Humble yourself under his mighty hand. "For whom the Lord loveth he chasteneth, and scourgeth every son whom he receiveth. If ye endure chastening, God dealeth with you as with sons; for what son is he whom the father chasteneth not? But if ye be without chastisement, whereof all are partakers, then are ye bastards, and not sons. Furthermore, we have had fathers of our flesh which corrected us, and we gave them reverence: shall we not much rather be in subjection unto the Father of spirits, and live?"[1]

§ 3. *Motives to humbling ourselves under the mighty hand of God.*

The motives which either implicitly or explicitly are here urged by the apostle for Christians thus humbling themselves under the mighty hand of God, come now to be considered. They are the following:—

We ought thus to humble ourselves under the mighty hand of God, for this is just a particular form of that humility which God so complacently approves, and the opposite of which he so indignantly condemns. "God resisteth the proud, but giveth grace to the humble. Humble yourselves *therefore*," for this reason, "under the mighty hand of God." We should humble ourselves under the hand of God, just because it is the hand of God. We should humble ourselves under the mighty hand of God, because it is the *mighty* hand of God. Finally, we should humble ourselves under the mighty hand of God, because this is the appointed way of being exalted in due time.

(1.) *It is a part of the humility which God so complacently approves.*

We should humble ourselves under the mighty hand of God, for this is the course of which God complacently approves; while the opposite is a course which he indignantly condemns. "He giveth grace," he manifests favour, towards those who humble themselves under his mighty hand; while he resists, he treats as enemies, those who despise his chastening, and rebel under the rod. This is a

[1] Heb. xii. 5-9.

most powerful motive. What makes anything duty but its being according to the will of God made known to us; what makes anything sin but its being opposed to the will of God made known to us? Besides, the conscious possession of the cordial love, the complacent approbation of the greatest and wisest and best Being in the universe, arising out of constant manifestations of his favour, is the highest happiness a creature can enjoy. It is the essence of the happiness of holy angels and the spirits of the just made perfect. On the other hand, to be resisted, opposed, treated as an enemy by him, is the greatest evil a creature can be exposed to; it is the essence of the miseries of devils and lost human beings.

(2.) *It is the hand of God we are called to humble ourselves under.*

We should humble ourselves under the hand of God, just because it is the hand of God. We should be humble in reference to God, because he is *God,* infinitely great, wise, and holy; because he is our Creator, our Governor, our Judge, our Father; because we are entirely dependent on him; because we are pensioners on his bounty; because we have incurred his displeasure, and are completely at his mercy. Humility should therefore be our habitual temper towards God; but when we are visited with affliction, when his hand is on us, these truths are more directly and powerfully presented to the mind. We are brought near God. He who despises the chastisement of the Lord, as it were insults the Sovereign at a personal interview. He defies the Almighty even when he appears whetting his sword and bending his bow. "He stretcheth out his hand against God, and strengtheneth himself against the Almighty. He runneth on him, even on his neck, on the thick bosses of his buckler."[1]

[1] Job xv. 26.

(3.) *It is the mighty hand of God we are called to humble ourselves under.*

Christians ought to humble themselves under the hand of God, for that hand is mighty; mighty to smite still harder, if the strokes given do not serve their purpose; mighty to deliver from, as well as to inflict, evil. There is no striving with success against him. As Archbishop Leighton says, "It is a vain thing to flinch and struggle, for he doth what he will; and his hand is so mighty, that the greatest power of the creature is nothing to it; yea, it is all indeed derived from him, and therefore cannot do any whit against him. If thou wilt not yield, thou must yield; if thou wilt not lead, thou shalt be pulled and drawn: therefore submission is your only course."

(4.) *To humble ourselves under the mighty hand of God, is the appointed way of our being in due time exalted.*

Finally, Christians should humble themselves under the mighty hand of God, for this is the appointed way to their being exalted. "Humble yourselves under the mighty hand of God, that ye may be exalted." That humility leads to exaltation, as pride to degradation, is a sentiment often expressed in Scripture. "Before honour is humility." "A man's pride shall bring him low: but honour shall uphold the humble in spirit." "He that exalteth himself shall be abased; but he that humbleth himself shall be exalted."[1] In the providential dealings of God, as recorded in his word, we have many very remarkable instances of humbling a person's self under the mighty hand of God leading to deliverance from calamity, and restoration to prosperity. When the princes of Israel, on the desolations occasioned by the invasion of Shishak, king of Egypt,

[1] Prov. xv. 33, xxix. 23; Luke xiv. 11.

"humbled themselves, and said, The Lord is righteous," "the Lord saw that they had humbled themselves;" and he said, by his prophet Shemaiah, "They have humbled themselves; therefore I will not destroy them, but I will grant them some deliverance." When their prince, king Rehoboam, "humbled himself, the wrath of God turned from him: also in Judah things went well." When the king of Nineveh and his people humbled themselves under the mighty hand of God lifted up to smite them, "He repented of the evil he had said he would do to them," and the impending stroke was averted. When Hezekiah "humbled himself for the pride of his heart," in the matter of the Babylonian ambassadors, the threatened wrath of the Lord came not on him. When Manasseh was, for his enormous transgressions, "bound with fetters and taken to Babylon, he in affliction besought the Lord his God, and humbled himself greatly before the God of his fathers, and prayed to him; and he was entreated of him, and heard his supplication, and brought him again to Jerusalem into his kingdom. Then Manasseh knew that the Lord he was God." When even Ahab, to whom "there was none like, who did sell himself to do wickedness in the sight of the Lord," humbled himself, Jehovah said to Elijah, "Because he humbleth himself before me, I will not bring the evil in his days." And to notice but one other instance, when Nebuchadnezzar, who for his pride was bereft both of his reason and of his power, employed the first effort of returning intelligence in humbling himself under the mighty hand of God, "the glory of his kingdom, his honour and brightness, returned to him: he was established in his kingdom; and excellent majesty was added to him."[1]

[1] 2 Chron. xii. 7, 12; Jonah ii. 5-10; 2 Chron. xxxii. 26, xxxiii. 12; 1 Kings xxi. 29; Dan. iv. 34-37.

This part of the divine government is beautifully described by Elihu: To "hide pride from man," "he is chastened also with pain upon his bed, and the multitude of his bones with strong pain: so that his life abhorreth bread, and his soul dainty meat. His flesh is consumed away, that it cannot be seen; and his bones which were not seen stick out. Yea, his soul draweth near to the grave, and his life to the destroyer. If there be a messenger with him, one among a thousand, to show unto him His," that is, God's, "uprightness; then he is gracious to him, and saith, Deliver from going down to the pit; I have found a ransom. His flesh shall be fresher than a child's: he shall return to the days of his youth. He shall pray to God, and he shall be favourable to him; and he will see his face with joy. He looketh upon man; and if any say, I have sinned, and perverted that which was right, and it profited me not; he will deliver his soul from going into the pit, and his life shall see the light. Lo, all these things worketh God oftentimes with man, to bring back his soul from the pit, to be enlightened with the light of the living." "If men be bound in fetters, and be holden in cords of affliction; then he showeth them their work, and their transgressions wherein they have exceeded. He openeth also their ear to discipline, and commandeth that they return from iniquity. If they obey and serve him, they shall spend their days in prosperity, and their years in pleasure; but if they obey not, they shall perish by the sword, and they shall die without knowledge."

Nor is the Psalmist's description less striking and instructive: "Such as sit in darkness, and in the shadow of death, being bound in affliction and iron; because they rebelled against the words of God, and contemned the counsel of the Most High: therefore he brought down their heart with labour: they fell down, and there was none to help. Then they cried unto the Lord in their trouble, and he saved them out of their distresses. He brought them out of darkness and the shadow of death, and brake their bands in sunder. Oh that men would praise the Lord for his goodness, and for his wonderful works to the children of men! For he hath broken the gates of brass, and cut the bars of iron in sunder. Fools, because of their transgression, and because of their iniquities, are afflicted: their soul abhorreth all manner of meat; and they draw near unto the gates of death. Then they cry unto the Lord in their trouble, and he saveth them out of their distresses. He sent his word, and healed them, and delivered them from their destructions. Oh that men would praise the Lord for his goodness, and for his wonderful works to the children of men! And let them sacrifice the sacrifices of thanksgiving, and declare his works with rejoicing."[1]

The Christian's humbling himself under the mighty hand of God always leads to his exaltation. Frequently, the affliction, having served one of its leading purposes, which was to humble him, and make him humble himself before God, is removed, and prosperity comes in the room of adversity. At other times, though the affliction may not be removed, or though it may be one of those irreparable losses we so often meet with, the heaviness, the painful depression which it occasioned, is removed.

Humility brings in its train patience, long-suffering, and hope; and even though not delivered from suffering, he who has humbled himself under the mighty hand of God, is so lifted up by that hand as to "joy in tribulation." "His heart is lifted up in the good ways of the Lord." The Christian who, while he could not humble himself, could not bring his mind to God's mind, his will to God's

[1] Job xxxiii. 17-29, xxxvi. 8-12; Ps. cvii. 10-22.

will, was tossed as in a sea of trouble, is no sooner enabled to humble himself under the mighty hand of God, to kiss the rod, to say, "Even so, Father, for so it seems good in thy sight," than the storm is turned into a calm; and, it may be, amid unabated external suffering, he has perfect peace, submitting himself to God, staying himself on God.

It is the purpose of God ultimately to exalt his people far above the reach of evil, in all its forms and in all its degrees. The humble, patient suffering of his will, equally with active, persevering doing of his will, is the appointed way to that final exaltation; and the degree in which the people of God are to be exalted, will be proportioned to their attainments in holiness, among which, humbling themselves under his mighty hand occupies an important place. This is an exercise that not only precedes, but prepares for, that exaltation to which it is his purpose to raise them.

The exaltation promised as the result of humbling ourselves under the mighty hand of God, is said to be exaltation "in due time." When the affliction has served its purpose, "when they shall confess their iniquity," says Jehovah, in reference to his cast-off people; when their uncircumcised hearts shall be humbled, "and they accept of the punishment of their iniquity, then will I remember my covenant." "In due time,"—in God's time. "Not thy fancied time," as Leighton says, " but his own wisely appointed time. Thou thinkest, I am sinking; if he help not now, it will be too late. He can let thee sink still lower, and yet bring thee up again. He doth but stay till the most fit time. 'He waiteth to be gracious.' Doth he wait, and wilt not thou? If he should see fit to keep us under a cloud all our days on the earth, what then? it is but a moment of wrath, to be succeeded by an endless lifetime in his favour: it is but sorrow for a night, and in the due time comes joy in the morning; that eternal morning without clouds, to which no night succeeds for ever."[1] So much for an illustration of the apostle's view of the Christian's state of affliction as a state of subjection to the mighty hand of God, and of the corresponding view of his duty in this state, and the motives which urge to its performance.

These remarks have been addressed almost exclusively to the people of God. But I cannot conclude this part of the subject without expressing my sympathy with those irreligious men who are under the mighty hand of God, and of offering them a word of counsel. It is an awful thing to be under the mighty hand of God, while we are lying under the curse of his holy law. Such a person is in the grasp of an almighty hand, which can, and which, unless a change take place in his spiritual state and character, will, cast him into hell. All he suffers now, is nothing in comparison to what he shall suffer for ever and ever. The bed of sickness, languishing, and pain, are ill to bear. How will it be with you when you must make your bed in hell? God's hand is heavy now. What will it be then? He lays it on you *now*, irreligious sufferers, that he may not require to lay it on you *then*. For he has no pleasure in your death. Alas! how often does "God speak once, yea twice, yet man regardeth it not." Even when he lays his hand on men, few say, " Where is God my Maker?" They do not pray to *him* when they are constrained to " howl upon their beds." Oh that they were wise![2] "Hear the rod." Its voice to every thoughtless sufferer is, 'Humble thyself; acknowledge thy guilt, thy depravity, thy helplessness, and cry for mercy. Submit to the will of God.' There is no

---

[1] Ps. xxx. 5.—"Non omnes intelligunt, quod scriptum est a Davide, Ps. xxx. 5. Quid igitur dicit? Nisi vehementer fallor hoc dicit: 'Benevolentia ipsius diu durat:' Contrarium illius quod præcedit 'momentum in ira ejus.' Affine est quod in Latio usitamus, ætatem vivere, pro, diu vivere."—DRUSIUS.

[2] Job xxxiii. 14, xxxv. 10; Hos. vii. 14.

hope for thee but in this. Submit to his will, as to the way of salvation through his Son; as to the requisitions of his law, holy and good; as to the dispensations of his righteous and wise providence. Humble yourselves in submission to this will of God, and all will yet be well with you, well with you for ever. No affliction will then be intolerable. Every affliction will produce sweet and salutary fruit, fruit to holiness, and the end will be everlasting life. But what will be the consequence if you do not humble yourselves under his mighty hand; if you do not unreservedly submit to the overtures of his mercy, to the injunctions of his law, to the appointments of his providence?

Take the truth in the forcible words of a divine of a former age: "His hand, to which ye will not submit, is a mighty, an almighty, hand. 'Have ye an arm like God? or can ye thunder with a voice like him?' He whose will you oppose is incontrollably powerful. His will must prevail one way or other, either with your will or against it; either so as to bow and satisfy us, or so as to break and plague us: for 'my counsel,' saith he, 'shall stand, and I will do all my pleasure.'[1] As to his dispensations, we may fret, we may wail, we may bark at them; but we cannot alter or avoid them. Sooner may we by our moans check the tides, or by our cries stop the sun in his course, than divert the current of affairs, or change the state of things established by God's high decree. What he layeth on, no hand can remove. What he hath destined, no power can reverse. Our anger, therefore, will be ineffectual; our impatience will have no other fruit than to aggravate our guilt and augment our grief. As to his commands, men may lift up themselves against him; they may fight stoutly; they may in a sort prove conquerors; but it will be a miserable victory, the trophies whereof will be erected in hell, and

[1] Isa. xlvi. 12.

stand on the ruins of their happiness: for while they insult over abused grace, they must fall under incensed justice. If God cannot fairly procure his will of men in the way of due obedience, he will surely execute his will upon them in the way of righteous vengeance; if we do not surrender our wills to the overtures of his goodness, we must submit our backs to the strokes of his anger. He must reign over us, if not as over loyal subjects to our comfort, yet as over stubborn rebels to our confusion; for this, in that case, will be our doom, and these will be the last words God will deign to spend upon us: 'Those, mine enemies, which would not that I should reign over them, bring them hither and slay them before me.'"[1]

"Enter into the rock, and hide thee in the dust, for fear of the Lord, and for the glory of his majesty. The lofty looks of man shall be humbled, and the haughtiness of men be bowed down; and the Lord alone be exalted." "Hear ye, and give ear; be not proud: for the Lord hath spoken. Give glory to the Lord your God, before he cause darkness, and before your feet stumble on the dark mountains, and, while ye look for light, he turn it into the shadow of death, and make it gross darkness. What wilt thou say when he shall punish thee?"[2] To all, then, whether saints or sinners, when visited with calamitous dispensations of providence, we proclaim, "Humble yourselves under the mighty hand of God, that he may exalt you in due time."

II. SECOND VIEW OF AFFLICTION AND ITS DUTY.

Let us now contemplate, for a little, affliction in the second view here given us of it—as a state of anxiety and carefulness; the appropriate duty of the Christian in this

[1] Barrow.   [2] Isa. ii. 10, 11; Jer. xiii. 16, 21.

state—casting all his care on God; and the motive for performing this duty—God cares for him.

§ 1. *Affliction is a state of anxiety and carefulness.*

Let us then, for a little, consider affliction as a state of carefulness; a state fitted to excite painful anxieties and fears. When the afflicted Christian is called to cast all his cares on God, it is obviously supposed that he has cares, many cares, distressing cares, cares which he feels that he cannot himself bear. The life of man, the life of the Christian man, even in its most prosperous state, is not without its cares and anxieties. Its enjoyments are at once imperfect and uncertain. Man has by no means all the things necessary to his happiness, nor any one of them in the measure in which he feels to be desirable: so that he naturally wishes for what he has not; and his wishes, in proportion to their ardour, and the difficulties which seem to lie in the way of their being gratified, become painful anxieties. Besides, the tenure by which he holds most of these things is very precarious: they may soon, they may suddenly, be diminished, or entirely withdrawn from him; so that, if the mind is not under the influence of that thoughtlessness which blinds it to all possible or probable hazard, or of that enlightened religious principle which raises it above the fear of such hazards when distinctly discerned, even a life of prosperity would seem necessarily to be a life of carefulness. But while every situation in human life may afford occasion for carefulness, there can be no doubt that the season of affliction is peculiarly calculated to excite painful anxieties. The mind gets into an anxious state; everything assumes a dark, discouraging, alarming aspect. 'How am I to sustain present evils, or how am I to escape from them? How am I to avert apparently coming evils? and if they cannot be averted, How am I to endure them?' These are questions which force themselves on the suffering mind; and most sufferers will readily acknowledge that the fruitless attempt to get satisfactory answers to them has often greatly aggravated the pressure of external calamity, and that the anxieties occasioned by affliction have been felt to be a more insupportable burden than the affliction itself.[1]

The case of affliction which the text naturally brings before the mind, that of a Christian exposed to persecution on account of his religion, is one which is calculated to be peculiarly fertile in harassing cares and perplexing anxieties. 'Spoiled as I am already, or am likely soon to be, of my goods, how am I to meet my engagements, and provide things honest in the sight of all men? What is to become of my family, to provide for whom is one of the most clearly enjoined, strongly enforced, of Christian duties? How am I to be enabled to sustain the sufferings to which I am likely to be exposed? How am I to be enabled distinctly to see my duty? How am I to be enabled determinedly to do my duty? I am afraid I shall not be able to stand in the evil day. I am afraid my faith will fail, and that I shall make shipwreck of a good conscience; and then, what will be the fearful result of this to the cause of truth? How will its enemies exult! How will its friends be ashamed! What will be the more fearful result of this to my own weak, guilty soul? The anguish of an outraged conscience, the frown of an insulted Saviour; and all this for ever!' And anxieties of this kind could not be confined to the individual's own case; they naturally extended to the whole brotherhood, and to the great cause. This is

---

[1] This state of mind is very beautifully described by the poet:
"Magno curarum fluctuat æstu,
Atque animum nunc huc celerem nunc dividit illuc,
In partesque rapit varias, perque omnia versat."—VIRGIL.

the case, I apprehend, more immediately in the apostle's view; and it is easy to see that persons placed in these circumstances were likely to have anxieties, many anxieties, oppressive anxieties. But it is obvious that affliction in all its forms is a natural source of painful carefulness to all, even to the Christian. The questions, How shall I be strengthened to endure those afflictions? how shall I be enabled to conduct myself aright towards God and man under them? am I ever to be delivered from them? and if so, how? and if not, what are likely to be their consequences to me and to others?—these are inquiries which are involuntarily pressed on the consideration of the mind, and it becomes careful and troubled, perplexed and fearful, oppressed and downcast.

§ 2. *The duty of the Christian under affliction is to " cast all his care on God."*

The duty of the Christian under the pressure of affliction, viewed in this aspect, is to "cast all his care on God." The language is figurative, strongly figurative. These harassing cares and anxieties are represented as a burden, which is felt to be oppressively heavy; and the sinking sufferer is represented as so transferring them to God as to obtain relief from their painful pressure. The figure is still more fully brought out in the passage in the Old Testament Scriptures here referred to, " Cast thy burden upon the Lord, and he shall sustain thee."[1] Casting our cares on God, is descriptive of such actings of the mind towards God as shall have an effect in giving it a relief, analogous to that ease of body which the transference of a load to another person procures to him who was previously bent down by it. The figurative expression "cast," not lay, seems to intimate that the duty enjoined is one that

[1] Ps. lv. 22.

requires an effort; and experience tells us it is no easy matter to throw off the burden of carefulness. To describe the state of mind indicated by this figurative expression, and show how the Christian is to find his way into it, are the objects I have in view in the following observations.

To think rightly on this subject, it is of primary importance that we have distinct ideas respecting the true nature of those cares, *all* of which the afflicted Christian is called on to cast on God. There are cares and anxieties which originate in cherishing false views as to what is necessary and conducive to happiness in ourselves and others; and in unlawful, inordinate desires, corresponding with these false views. There are very many such cares and anxieties in the world. Indeed, they are all but universal. "Surely every man walketh in a vain show; surely they are disquieted in vain."[1] Men are anxious to obtain what, if they thought and felt rightly, they would never have desired; and that is the object of fear which, were they not blinded by passion or false views of interest, would occasion no alarm, but rather be the object of hope. This is the character of the greater part of the worldling's anxieties, and it is the character also of but too many of the Christian's. These cares are not to be cast on God: they are to be cast away from us. We are not to go to him in the hope that he will gratify such desires, disappoint such fears, realize such hopes. To ask Him to do this, were to insult him. If we take them to him at all—and we cannot do better—it ought to be as his enemies and ours, to slay them before his face.

There are other cares which we are not warranted to cast on God, for another reason. God has laid them on us, and he expects that we shall bear them. God would have his people without carefulness, in the sense of painful, useless anxiety. But he would not have them without thoughtful-

[1] Ps. xxxix. 6.

ness, in the sense of considerate reflection. We are bound to exercise those faculties God has given us for discovering what is truth and what is falsehood, what is right and what is wrong, what is good and what is evil. We are not to resign ourselves to mental inactivity, and to expect that, in some miraculous way without our own agency, God is to lead us unto truth, and preserve us from error; show us what is duty, and what is sin; give us what is fitted to make us happy, and defend us from all that is fitted to injure us. It is in the eager, I had almost said anxious, employment of our faculties as intelligent beings, on the revelation which God has made of his will, in his word and in his providence, that we are to expect to find out what is the course of conduct we should follow in any particular case; and it is in the persevering diligent employment of our faculties as active beings, carrying into effect the conclusion to which we have arrived, that we are to expect to obtain the desired results. We are warranted to look up to him for the aids of his good Spirit both in our inquiries and in our exertions. But we are not to expect him to do that directly which his infinitely wise plan and our real interests equally require should be done by us. The apostle does not mean to encourage inconsideration, indolence, or presumption, when he enjoins Christians to cast all their cares on God. It has been well said, "We must not cast our work on God, and presume that he will save us in the way of sloth and carnal indulgence; on the contrary, we are commanded to 'work out our own salvation with fear and trembling.'" It is only in "well-doing" that we can "commit the keeping of our souls to God."[1]

The cares and anxieties spoken of here have a reference to what properly belongs to God, what lies beyond the range of human agency. All a Christian's cares of this

[1] Phil. ii. 12; 1 Pet. iv. 19.

kind, whether in a state of affliction or otherwise, whether respecting secular or spiritual things, the body or the soul, time or eternity, must refer, I apprehend, either to duties or to events.

As to duties, the Christian is apt to be anxious and careful about the discovery of what is duty, and the discharge of what is known to be duty. In regard to the first, he is carefully to use the means God has appointed for discovering his duty. He is to read his Bible; he is to attend to the aspect of providence; he is to compare the one with the other; he is to ask the guidance of the Spirit; he is to guard against false biases; he is to see that his eye be single, that his whole body may be full of light: but he is not to be anxious as if, doing all this, he shall yet be left in darkness, and allowed to fall into error or sin. He is to cast all such cares on the Lord. They refer to his work, and he has pledged himself to do it; and we may be assured he will not fail to do as he has said.

But the Christian may be anxious also about the performance of known duty. In this case he is carefully to guard against temptations to neglect duty; but he is not to indulge in any anxiety as to whether he will be enabled, trusting in God, to perform any duty, however difficult, to which God may be pleased to call him. That is God's concern; why does he burden himself with it? He will look after the accomplishment of his own promise, " My grace is sufficient for thee, and my strength shall be perfected in weakness;" and let the Christian, in the full assurance of this, with an earnest, determined, but unanxious mind, set about the performance of the difficult, perhaps at the time apparently impossible, work.

As to events, they, properly speaking, belong entirely to God. Man proposes; God disposes. To man some events seem desirable, others undesirable; and, so far as we are concerned in the matter, we are to use such lawful means as seem to us best fitted to further events which, with the widest and most accurate view we can take of them, seem to be desirable; and when we have done this, anxiety should cease. Our care should be cast upon God, who "worketh all things according to the counsel of his own will," whose "work is perfect," "most honourable and glorious."[1] This is the duty of the Christian respecting all the events of time, and all the events of eternity, both in reference to himself individually, and to all with whom he is connected; with regard to the Church, and with regard to the world. Respecting *duty*, we ought to cast on him all our care and anxiety as to skill to discover it, and strength to perform it; respecting *events*, we ought to trust him with them entirely.

In order to thus casting our cares on God, there are plainly required three things: 1. A persuasion that God has complete control in reference to those things which excite our anxiety; 2. A persuasion that he will use this control in the best manner, abstractly considered; and 3. A persuasion that he will use this control in the best possible manner, so far as we are concerned.

(1.) *A persuasion that God has power to control what excites our anxiety.*

I could not get rid of painful anxiety by casting it on God, if I did not believe he could sustain it. What lies at the very foundation here, is the conviction that God is Sovereign of the universe, uncontrolled and uncontrollable, "whose kingdom ruleth over all," "who can do everything," " whose arm none can stay, to whom none dare say, What doest thou?" whose ends his enemies further by opposing them, who "makes their wrath to praise him, and who restrains the remainder thereof."[2]

[1] Eph. i. 11; Ps. cxi. 3. [2] Ps. ciii. 19, lxxvi. 10; Dan. iv. 35.

(2.) *A persuasion that God will employ his controlling power in the best possible way.*

But though I had entire conviction of the divine power, I could not cast my care, all my care, on him, unless I believed that his power was guided by wisdom and righteousness, and influenced by benignity. A belief in the existence of a being possessed of infinite power, if I were not sure that this being is possessed of infinite wisdom and righteousness, would increase, not diminish, my anxieties. But the clear apprehension that He who has all things under his control is perfect in knowledge, infinite in wisdom, glorious in holiness, plentiful in justice, and full of kindness, must persuade me that his management of everything must be the best possible.

(3.) *A persuasion that he will employ his controlling power in the best possible way for us.*

It might be thought that this conviction of absolute intellectual and moral perfection, in combination with almighty power, should be quite enough to enable me, quite enough morally to compel me, to cast all my care on God; that in the presence of such convictions, anxieties of every kind would cease. But no! I am a sinner. I have offended this infinitely powerful and wise and excellent Being, and the very excellence of his nature may render certain those events, anxiety about which can only be quieted by an assurance that they never shall take place. I must be persuaded that this control which he possesses will be exercised not only in the best possible way in the abstract, but in the best way for me. In other words, I must know and believe him to be my friend. I must know that he is " pacified towards me for all the iniquity which I have done." I must believe his own testimony, that he has no pleasure in my death; that he is "in Christ reconciling the world to himself;" that "for the great love wherewith he loves us, he blesses us with all heavenly and spiritual blessings." I must, on the faith of his testimony, lay hold of his promise, and believe that to me, trusting in him, he will do all that he has said, make all things work for my good, and bestow on me "the salvation that is in Christ with eternal glory."

Wherever there is, and in the degree in which there is, the possession of this threefold persuasion, we learn to cast our cares on God; and we find that, by doing so, we are relieved of them. When we are thus "anxious about nothing, but in everything by prayer and supplication make our requests known to God, the peace of God, which passeth all understanding, keeps our hearts and minds by Christ Jesus." It is then, in believing prayer, that the afflicted, anxious Christian is to cast his cares on God.

"This is the way," as good Leighton says, "to walk contentedly and cheerfully homewards, leaning and resting all the way on him who is both our guide and our guard, our wisdom and our strength, who hath us and all our good in his gracious hand. The more tender and weak we are, the more tender will he be of us, the more strong will he be in us. He feeds his flock as a shepherd, and the weakest he is most careful of. They go in his arms and bosom, and it is easy for the feeblest so to go."

In reference to events, the more completely we rid ourselves of all anxiety, we act the more reasonably and wisely. It is entirely his province to manage them. If we meddle with it—and we are constantly meddling with it—we displease him, and disquiet ourselves. This sin carries its punishment in its bosom. "If thou wilt," says the pious prelate, "be struggling with that which belongs not to thee, and poising at that burden which is not thine, what wonder, yea, I may say, what pity, if thou fall under it? Is it not just, if thou wilt do for thyself, and bear for thyself what thy Lord calls for to bear for thee, is it not just that thou feel the weight of it to thy cost?"

There is just one other thought to which I would solicit your attention before closing this part of the subject. The Christian must beware of laying his cares on any but God. He must cast all his cares on God. He may seek the sympathy and the advice of his fellow-Christians; but he must never cast his cares or place his confidence on them. They cannot bear the burden. They are obliged to cast their own cares on God. "Cursed is the man that trusteth in man, and maketh flesh his arm." He well understood the blessed art of casting all his care on God, who said, "My soul, wait thou only on God; for my expectation is from him. He only is my rock and my salvation; he is my defence; I shall not be moved. In God is my salvation and my glory: the rock of my strength, and my refuge, is in God. Ye people, place your confidence in him continually; pour out your heart before him: God is a refuge for us. Surely men of low degree are vanity, and men of high degree are a lie; to be laid in the balance" with God, as the object of confidence, "they are altogether lighter than vanity." [1]

Finally, here, in the right state of mind under affliction, the two things recommended by the apostle must be con-

[1] Ps. lxii. 5-9.—Hengstenberg very justly remarks that the words "Pour ye out your heart before him—God is a refuge for us"—are, as to sense, quite parallel to that before us.—Arndt gives the meaning of "pour out"—'completely empty your heart of all that is distressing it'—pour it *out* before the Lord! What a beautiful example have we of "pouring out the heart before God," "casting all care on him," in Ps. cxlii. 1-5! Hannah, too—1 Sam. i. 10-17—shows us what the mental exercise is, expressed by these significant figures; and her experience shows how "he on whom we cast our cares" "cares *for* us," and relieves us of our cares.

joined: "Humbling ourselves under the mighty hand of God," and "casting all our cares upon him." Our self-abasement must not lead to despondency, but to deeper dependence, greater confidence; and our reliance on God, and consequent ease of mind, must not be presumptuous. A sense of sin must not prevent the use of privilege, and a continuous enjoyment of privilege must not diminish self-abasement.

§ 3. *The motive to casting our care on God is, that he cares for us.*

It is time now that I proceed to turn your attention to the motive by which the apostle urges the Christian to cast all his care on God: "Casting all your care on God; for he careth for you." And here I shall very briefly state the evidence of this truth, that God cares for his people; and then show how the belief of this truth should lead them to cast their care on him.

It is quite obvious that the apostle is not here speaking of the general providential care which God has of men as his creatures, but of the peculiar care which he has of those who are in a peculiar sense his children, his people, his inheritance, his purchased possession. He cares for them in another way than he does for the world. On those who are elect according to the foreknowledge of God, by a spiritual separation, and who are made obedient to the truth and sprinkled with the blood of Jesus, are bestowed peculiar "heavenly and spiritual blessings;" to them who have obtained like precious faith with the apostles, are given "exceeding great and precious promises." It is the care of God for this peculiar people, that I mean to establish as a ground why this peculiar people should cast all their care on him.

It deserves notice that the word "careth" in this last

clause is a word of a very different meaning from that used in the first clause, though rendered by the same English word.[1] The word in the first clause denotes painful anxiety; in the second, kind interest. It is said, "The hireling fleeth when the wolf cometh; for he careth not for the sheep." It is said Judas "cared not for the poor."[2] "He cares for you" is equivalent to 'He takes a kind interest in you.'

Now that God does, must, take a peculiar and most benignant interest in his people, will be very plain, if we attend for a moment to the peculiar relation in which he stands to them, the peculiar works he has done for them, the peculiar privileges he has bestowed on them, and the peculiar "exceeding great and precious promises" he has made to them.

What is the relation in which God stands to them? He is their God and Father; they are his people and children, in a sense quite peculiar. They were "predestinated to the adoption of children;" and when he called them out of the world, by the power of his Spirit attending the invitation of his word, he said, "I will be a father to you, and ye shall be my sons and daughters." "Behold," may "this chosen generation, this holy nation, this peculiar people," say, "Behold what manner of love the Father hath bestowed on us, that we should be called the sons of God!"[3] The title is not an empty name. There is great force in the apostle's argument, "If children, then heirs."[4] If you stand in the relation of children to God, you may be sure of the treatment of children. Is it possible that our Father in heaven should not care for his children? "If ye, being evil," says our Lord, "know how to give good gifts to your children; how much more shall your Father in heaven give good

---

[1] Μέριμναν—Μέλει.   [2] John x. 13, xii. 6.
[3] Eph. i. 5; 2 Cor. vi. 17, 18; 1 John iii. 1.   [4] Rom. viii. 17.

gifts to them that ask him?" "Like as a father pitieth his children, so the Lord pities them that fear him. He knoweth our frame; he remembereth that we are dust."[1]

What has God done for, what has he given to, his peculiar people? He "chose them before the foundation of the world." He "commended his love to them, in that, while they were yet sinners, Christ died for them." He "spared not his Son, but delivered him up" "for their offences, and raised him again for their justification," and set him at his own right hand, that, ever living to make intercession for them, he might be "able to save them to the uttermost." For them he poured out the Holy Ghost in his miraculous and inspiring influence, and diffused his gospel and established his ordinances throughout the earth. This is a specimen of what he has done for them. And what has he given them? He has "blessed them with all heavenly and spiritual blessings;" he has bestowed on them "redemption in Christ through his blood, according to the riches of his grace;" he has made them "accepted in the Beloved;" he has conferred on them "an inheritance incorruptible and undefiled, and that fadeth not, reserved in heaven for them," while he keeps them by his power, through faith, unto salvation; he has given them the Holy Scriptures as the charter, and the Holy Spirit, in his sanctifying and comforting influences, as the "seal" and the "earnest," of their inheritance; he has sent forth his angels, who excel in strength, as "ministering spirits, to minister to them as heirs of this great salvation;" he has delivered them from the "present evil world," and from the power of the wicked one, and given them "everlasting consolation and good hope through grace." Surely he who has done all this for them, and given all this to them, does, must, care for them. For these "gifts and callings are without repentance." He

[1] Matt. vii. 11; Ps. ciii. 13, 14.

"rests in his love," and is "the same yesterday, to-day, and for ever."[1]

Still further, what has he promised them, or rather, what has he not promised them, which could show his care for them? He has promised that he will "withhold no good thing from them;" that "it shall be well with them;" that "their desire shall be granted," and that "their hope shall be gladness." He has declared that theirs is the world, and that they "shall inherit all things;" and promised to "supply all their need according to his riches in glory by Christ Jesus." He has a promise which meets every anxiety which can arise in their hearts. Are they anxious as to strength to perform duty? He says, "My grace is sufficient for you." "God will work in you to will and to do of his good pleasure." "I will strengthen them in the Lord, and they shall walk up and down in my name." Are they anxious as to guidance in difficulty? "I will lead the blind in a way that they know not; I will make darkness light before them." "I will instruct thee, and teach thee in the way that thou shouldest go." Are they afraid of falling before their spiritual enemies, and ultimately coming short of eternal life? He who is the Father's substantial image says, "I give to my sheep eternal life, and they shall never perish; neither shall any pluck them out of my hand. My Father, which gave them me, is greater than all; and none can pluck them out of my Father's hand." "God, who is faithful, will not suffer you to be tempted above what ye are able to bear; and will with the temptation also make a way of escape, that ye may be able to bear it." "Satan shall be bruised under your feet shortly." And as to events: Are they anxious about affliction? "He shall

[1] Eph. i. 4; Rom. v. 8, viii. 32, iv. 25; Heb. vii. 25; Eph. i. 3, 6, 7; 1 Pet. i. 4, 5; Eph. i. 13; Ps. xci. 11; Heb. i. 14; Gal. i. 4; 2 Thess. ii. 16; Rom. xi. 29.

deliver thee in six troubles, in seven no evil shall touch thee." "When thou passest through the waters, I will be with thee; and through the rivers, they shall not overflow thee. When thou walkest through the fire, thou shalt not be burnt; neither shall the flame kindle on thee." "All things shall work together for good to them that love God." In every situation in life fitted to excite anxiety, there are appropriate promises which I cannot stop to enumerate. To his people, when in poverty, in famine, bereaved of relations, spoiled of their possessions, misrepresented and calumniated, promises singularly suited to their circumstances are made; all proving that he cares for them, that "in all their afflictions he is afflicted," and that "they who touch them, touch the apple of his eye."[1]

Are they anxious about death, and about what is to follow death? He shows that he cares for them by promising, that when they "walk through the valley of the shadow of death, he will be with them; his rod and his staff, they shall sustain them." "He will swallow up death in victory." "I will ransom them from the power of the grave; I will redeem them from death. O death! I will be thy plagues: O grave! I will be thy destruction." "This corruptible shall put on incorruption, and this mortal must put on immortality; and death shall be swallowed up in victory." The Saviour shall come from heaven, and "change these vile bodies, and fashion them like unto his own glorious body;" and they "shall be caught up in clouds to meet the Lord in the air, and they shall be for ever with the Lord." "He who testifieth these things is a

---

[1] Ps. lxxxiv. 11; Eccles. viii. 8; Isa. iii. 10; Ps. cxlv. 19; Prov. x. 24, 28; 1 Cor. iii. 22; Rom. iv. 13; Rev. xxi. 7; Phil. iv. 19; 2 Cor. xii. 9; Phil. ii. 13; Zech. x. 12; Isa. xlii. 16; Ps. xxxii. 8; John x. 28, 29; 1 Cor. x. 13; Rom. xvi. 20; Job v. 19; Isa. xlii. 2, lxiii. 9; Rom. viii. 28; Zech. ii. 8.

true and faithful witness." He cannot be deceived; he cannot deceive. "He is not a man, that he should lie." He means all he says; he can and will do all he promises.[1]

Does he not, then, care for his people? Do not the relations he has assumed towards them, the works he has performed for them, the privileges he has bestowed on them, and the promises so exceeding great and precious that he has made about them and to them, abundantly prove the assertion in the text, "He cares for them?"

It will not require many words to show, that this truth, so abundantly demonstrated, is a most powerful and appropriate motive to the Christian's casting his care, all his care, upon God. Why should he allow the burden that so oppresses and depresses him, that so interferes both with his duty and with his comfort, to remain on him? He knows very well that these anxieties can be of no use to him; they refer to matters that he cannot control. His anxieties, however intense, do not bring him one whit nearer the object of his hope, or remove him one whit further from the object of his fear. But, to obtain relief from anxiety, I must not only be convinced that my anxiety is useless. A conviction of this, if I do not see some way of getting rid of the evils which occasion it, will but fix the burden more firmly on me. But the Christian who knows that God cares for him, knows that his anxieties are not only useless; they are needless. God, who has the entire management of those matters which excite his anxieties, God cares for him. And who is this who cares for the Christian? He is the all-wise, "the only wise God," who never can be deceived as to what is the Christian's true interest, and who knows how to make "all things work together for good." He never can fall into any mistake as

[1] Ps. xxiii. 4; Isa. xxv. 8; Hos. xiii. 14; 1 Cor. xv. 53-57; Phil. iii. 20, 21; 1 Thess. iv. 17.

to what is good for his people, nor as to the means best fitted for securing this good to them. Then he is God Almighty, the all-powerful God. "Whatsoever he pleaseth, that doeth he in heaven, in the earth, and in all deep places." He never can want power to execute what his wisdom deems to be best for those he cares for. When a Christian is "afraid of a man that shall die, and of the son of man who shall be made as the grass," surely it is in momentary forgetfulness that He who cares for him is "the Lord his Maker, who stretched forth the heavens, and laid the foundations of the earth; the Lord God who divided the seas, whose waters roared; the Lord of hosts is his name." Then he is God, ever present, omnipresent; nothing can overtake you in his absence. The connection in the parallel passage in Phil. iv. 5, 6, deserves to be marked. "The Lord is at hand; be careful for nothing." Then still further: He is "the God of all grace;" "the Father of mercies." He who cares for you, has his wisdom and power influenced and guided by infinite love, infinite love to you. Hear his own words, which are as true in reference to every one of his people individually, as in reference to their collective body, the Church: "Can a woman forget her sucking child, that she should not have compassion on the son of her womb? yea, she may forget; yet will not I forget thee." This love will keep wisdom ever wakeful, power ever active, in reference to the true interests of its objects. Is not anxiety, then, on the part of the Christian, a very needless, and therefore a very unreasonable thing? Surely it is very unwise in him not to cast his care on God.[1]

But it is worse than unwise; it is ungrateful and undutiful. When God says, 'Leave these matters which you cannot manage to my management,' if we refuse, what is it

[1] Ps. cxxxv. 6; Isa. li. 12, 15, xlix. 15.

but to insult our divine Benefactor by discovering doubts of his sincerity, or of his wisdom, or of his power? Whether would the ingratitude or the folly of the Levite of Mount Ephraim have been greater, if he had met the generous invitation of the hospitable old man of Gibeah, "Let all thy wants lie on me, only lodge not in the street," with a sullen refusal? And when the greatest and best of all beings says to us, who are but dust and ashes, 'Let all your wants lie upon me'—wants we well know we cannot supply, but he can—where shall we find words to describe the baseness and the absurdity of putting away from us so generous, so needed a boon? Is it a fitting return for all his kindness, to insist on keeping hold of a burden from which he is willing to release us, when getting rid of that burden is necessary to enable us to yield him the cheerful, ready, joyful service he so well deserves? Surely when he says, 'I would have you without carefulness, that you may serve me without fear in righteousness and holiness all the days of your lives,' the sense of his kindness and the desire of his glory should equally lead us to comply with the command, "Cast all your care on God." Indeed, wherever the proposition, 'God, the infinitely powerful, wise, and benignant Sovereign of the universe, cares for me, is interested in my welfare, and has pledged himself to secure it,' is understood and believed, in the degree in which it is understood and believed, it does, it must, banish carefulness and anxiety from the mind. Here, as in so many other cases, it is with a man according to his faith. Oh, how happy, oh, how holy, should we be! how easy should labour be, how light affliction! could we but, believing that God cares for us, "cast all our care on him," saying, "I am poor and needy; but the Lord thinketh on me! Thou art my help and deliverer, O my God!"[1]

[1] Ps. xl. 17.

Thus have I turned your attention to affliction as a state calculated to excite anxiety and carefulness; to the afflicted Christian's duty in reference to this view of affliction—to cast all his anxieties on God; and to the motive urging him to this course—God cares for him.

This is the duty of the Christian at all times, and the motive is equally powerful in all circumstances. The inward ear of the Christian should ever be open to these words of the great Master, so full of wisdom, so full of love: "Take no thought; be not careful," anxious "for your life, what ye shall eat, or what ye shall drink; nor for your body, what ye shall put on: Is not the life more than meat, and the body than raiment? Behold the fowls of the air; for they sow not, neither do they reap, nor gather into barns; yet your heavenly Father feedeth them. Are ye not much better than they? Which of you, by taking thought," by anxiety, "can add one cubit to his stature," or, as it has been explained, "one moment to his life? And why take ye thought for raiment? Consider the lilies of the field, how they grow: they toil not, neither do they spin; and yet I say unto you, that even Solomon, in all his glory, was not arrayed as one of these. Wherefore, if God so clothe the grass of the field, which to-day is, and to-morrow is cast into the oven, shall he not much more clothe you, O ye of little faith? Therefore take no thought, be not anxious, saying, What shall we eat? or what shall we drink? and wherewithal shall we be clothed? (for after all these things the Gentiles seek), for your heavenly Father knoweth that ye have need of all these things. But seek first the kingdom of God and his righteousness, and all these things shall be added to you. Fear not, little flock; it is your Father's good pleasure to give you the kingdom."[1]

There is a class, a large class of men, and it is very likely

[1] Luke xii. 22-32.

there are some of them here, to whom I can address neither the exhortation nor the encouragement in the text in the true sense—that which I have endeavoured to bring out to you; to whom I dare not say, Cast your care, all your care, ay, any of your care, on God; to whom I cannot say, God cares for *you* in the way in which he cares for his own, for them who know and love him; for those I refer to are none of his. His creatures they are, but his disobedient creatures; his subjects, but his rebellious subjects: they are not his children, they are not his people. There are men whose anxieties are all engaged about worldly, many of them about sinful, objects. Even with their very low notions of the divine character, they themselves would be ashamed to take their cares and anxieties to God in prayer, and try to cast them on him. They feel that it would be to insult him to do so. Their inward feeling is, the less God hears of such things the better. They are cares he would never take off their hand, and undertake for. And though there is a sense in which God's mercies, God's " tender mercies, are over all his works," in which he cares for all; yet, with regard to those who are living in unbelief and disobedience, it is quite plain that, remaining in that state, what they have to depend on is not pledged covenant love. Their dependence, if they have any, must be a presumptuous dependence on insulted kindness, or severely tried patience and long-suffering. Such persons are proper objects of deep sympathy, shutting themselves out, as they do, from all rational support and consolation, amid the anxieties and perplexities and sorrows of life. Oh that we could awaken even one such person to carefulness about that of which he has no care—the salvation of the soul; to anxiety about that regarding which he is not at all anxious,—the miseries of eternity! Oh that we could hear him, like Ephraim, bemoaning himself, and saying, " What is a man profited if he gain the whole world, and lose his own soul? Who can dwell with devouring fire? who can dwell with the everlasting burnings? How shall I come before the Lord? How shall I stand before this holy Lord God? Oh how shall I escape, or how shall I endure the wrath to come? What, what must I do to be saved?" Then when he is beginning to despair, we should begin to hope of him. Then should we say, with all the intensity of earnestness we could throw into our language and voice,—for however desirable such anxiety is, in comparison of stupid inconsideration or presumptuous confidence, its continuance is not a desirable thing; the sooner it is removed, if aright removed, the sooner it is got quit of, if safely disposed of, the better,—then we should say, Poor overburdened one, cast thy care on God, the God of salvation. He cares for thee, he alone can release thee. In the belief of the truth respecting his gracious character, manifested in consistency with, in glorious illustration of, his immaculate holiness and infinite justice in the atoning death of his Son, the just One, in the room of the unjust, you may obtain, you shall obtain, relief at once from a burden of guilt, which will certainly, if unremoved, sink your soul to hell, as well as from a burden of anxiety which, if unremoved, may lay your body in an untimely grave. And in getting relief from that anxiety, a foundation is laid for getting relief from all anxieties; and henceforward we could with unfaltering voice address to him the words of the text, in all the blissful immeasurable breadth and depth of meaning which belongs to them: "Cast all your care on God, for he cares for you." Oh that it may be so with some poor thoughtless sinner, anxious about everything but that about which, above all other things, he has cause to be anxious! Amen.

Note A. p. 287.

The following views of affliction, in a work not likely to come into the hands of many of my readers, discover so deep and accurate an acquaintance with human nature, Scripture doctrine, and religious experience, that I count on thanks for giving them a place here:—

"That supposed greatness of soul which considers suffering as a plaything, upon which one should throw himself with manly courage, is not to be met with on the territory of Scripture; upon that, everywhere, appear faint, weak, and dissolving hearts, finding their strength and consolation only in God. This circumstance arises from more than one cause.

"I. Suffering has quite another aspect to the members of God's Church than to the world. While the latter regard it only as the effect of accident, which one should meet with manly courage, the pious man recognises in every trial the visitation of an angry God, a chastisement for his sins. This is to him the real sting of the suffering, from which it derives its power to pierce into the marrow and bone. 'Rightly to feel sin,' says Luther, 'is the torture of all tortures.' He who considers suffering in that light cannot, without impiety, attempt to cast it to the winds. He must regard it as his duty to allow it to go to his heart; and if this is not the case, even that must become again the object of his pungent sorrow. To make light of tribulations is all one, in the reckoning of Scripture, with making light of God.

"II. The tenderer the heart, the deeper the pain. Living piety makes the heart soft and tender, refines all its sensibilities, and consequently takes away the power of resistance which the world possesses from the roughness of its heart. Many sources of pain are opened up in the Christian which are closed in the ungodly. Love is much more deeply wounded by hatred than hatred itself; righteousness sees wickedness in a quite different light from what wickedness itself does; a soft heart has goods to lose which an hard one never possessed.

"III. The pious man has a friend in heaven, and on that account no reason to be violently overcome by his sorrow. He permits the floods of this quietly to pass over him, gives nature its free spontaneous course, knowing well that, besides the natural principle, there is another also existing in him, which always unfolds its energy the more, the more that the former has its rights reserved to it, that according to the depths of the pain is the height of the joy which is derived from God—that every one is consoled after the measure in which he has borne suffering—that the meat never comes but from the eater, and honey from the terrible. On the contrary, whosoever lives in the world without God, he perceives that for him all is lost, when he is lost himself. He girds himself up, gnashes at his pain, does violence to nature, seeks thereby to divert himself, and to gain from nature on the one side what it abstracts from him on the other; and thus he succeeds in obtaining the mastery over his pain, so long as God pleases.

"IV. The pious man has no reason to prevent himself and others from seeing into his heart. His strength is in God, and so he can lay open his weakness. The ungodly man, on the other hand, considers it as a reproach to look upon himself in his weakness, and to be looked upon by others in it. Even when smarting with pain inwardly, he feigns freedom from it so long as he can.

"What is the proper place of sufferings, is manifest from the consequence to both classes. The pious man, while he regards all suffering as a punishment, takes that as the means of leading him to repentance, and derives from it the fruit of righteousness. He, on the other hand, who looks upon suffering merely as the sport of accident, thereby deprives himself of all blessing from it; and while in this respect he is not the better for his suffering, he is decidedly the worse in another. He therefore only throws himself on his own resources, only raises himself above his suffering, awakening as much as possible the fancy of his own worth, dignity, and excellence; and in the same proportion that he calls pride into exercise, his love decays, hardness becomes his inseparable companion, so that he in reality feeds upon his own fat, and quenches his thirst with his own heart's blood; and the question here also is applicable, 'What shall it profit a man if he should gain the whole world and lose his own soul?' But suffering, when borne with faith, serves to free the heart of its natural hardness, to make it soft, and open it to love.

"Finally, it is possible, even at so dear a cost, to find consolation out of God only for smaller sufferings. While nothing can happen amiss to the righteous, however much may befall him of evil—for he strengthens himself in God, whose power is infinite—the man who trusts in himself bears up only so long as 'fate,' or, in truth, he who sends the affliction, permits. Every moment he may be precipitated into the abyss of despair. He who never fainted, who used to mock at the faintings of believers, and to speak in a contemptuous tone of the 'plaintive psalms,' must then feel utterly undone. Human strength, and whatever besides he can summon to his aid, is still but a limited resource; it finds its proper antagonist only in what wounds the heel, and gives way when the resistance is too strong and violent to be contended with on feigned ground. Nothing is better fitted to show the insufficiency of all human power in the struggle against suffering, than the valuable confession of King Frederick II., who spared no cost to elevate this power, and whose great and mighty soul certainly did the utmost that can generally be accomplished in that field. He says, among other places in the *Ep. to D'Alembert*, sec. 12, p. 9: 'It is unhappy that all who suffer must flatly contradict Zeno; as there is none but will confess pain to be a great evil.' P. 12: 'It is noble to raise one's self above the disagreeable accidents to which we are exposed, and a moderate stoicism is the only means of consolation for the unfortunate. But whenever the stone, the gout, or the bull of Phalaris mix in the scene, the frightful shrieks which escape from the sufferers leave no doubt that pain is a real evil.' Again, p. 16: 'When a misfortune presses us, which merely affects our person, self-love makes a point of honour to withstand vigorously this misfortune; but the moment we suffer an injury, which is for ever irreparable, there is nothing left for us in Pandora's box which can bring consolation, except, perhaps, for a man of my advanced years, the strong conviction that I must soon be with those who have gone before me (*i.e.* in the land of nothingness). The heart is conscious of a wound. The Stoic freely confesses, 'I should feel no pain, but I do feel it against my will; it consumes, it lacerates me; an internal feeling overcomes my strength, and extorts from me complaints and fruitless groans.'"—HENGSTENBERG: *Commentary on the Psalms*, vol. i. 90–92.

DISCOURSE XXIII.

THE CHRISTIAN'S GREAT ENEMY—HIS DUTY IN REFERENCE TO HIM, AND HIS ENCOURAGEMENT TO DISCHARGE IT.

"Be sober, be vigilant; because your adversary the devil, as a roaring lion, walketh about, seeking whom he may devour: whom resist stedfast in the faith, knowing that the same afflictions are accomplished in your brethren that are in the world. But the God of all grace, who hath called us unto his eternal glory by Christ Jesus, after that ye have suffered a while, make you perfect, stablish, strengthen, settle you: to him be glory and dominion for ever and ever. Amen."—1 Pet. v. 8-11.

THERE is perhaps no article of revealed truth which has been more generally ridiculed by infidels, and probably for that reason more frequently attempted to be explained away by philosophizing Christians, than the doctrine of the existence and agency of evil spirits. That among professed Christians highly absurd notions on this subject have been entertained, and to a certain extent are still entertained, I am not disposed to question; but surely revelation cannot be fairly charged with the errors and absurdities of those who profess to believe it, unless it can be satisfactorily proved that it gives sanction to these errors and absurdities.

In the present instance it will be no difficult task to show that no such sanction is afforded, and that in the doctrine of the existence and agency of evil spirits, as taught in the Holy Scriptures, there is nothing irrational or ridiculous. For what is their doctrine on this subject? It may be thus briefly stated: 'There exists a numerous race of unembodied intelligent beings, occupying a higher place than man in the general scale of existence, who have lost the moral integrity in which they were created, and who, though under the control of the Supreme Providence, are constantly engaged in an attempt, by a variety of methods, and particularly by influencing in a malignant manner the minds of men, to uphold and extend the empire of evil in the universe of God.' Now, what principle of reason, what appearance in nature, what well-established fact, what declaration of Scripture, is contradicted by this doctrine? I know of none. Let us look at the subject a little more closely.

That there should be morally imperfect, that is, wicked creatures, in a world which owes its origin and continued existence to an all-perfect Being, infinite in power and wisdom, holiness and benignity; and that a being, capable of moral judgment, and possessed of free agency, should refuse the greatest good and choose the greatest evil, are mysterious facts, for which no man can fully account, but of which surely no rational man can seriously doubt. Every man has their evidence, alas, but too abundant, around him and within him. Man certainly is a depraved intelligent being; and if it be certain that there are depraved embodied spirits, it would be difficult to prove that there cannot be depraved unembodied spirits.

The mode in which these immaterial agents influence human character and conduct and destiny, may safely be acknowledged to be inexplicable; but the fact that they do possess and exert such influence is not on this ground, if supported by appropriate and adequate evidence, incredible. The mode in which one human mind influences another, though no sane person can doubt of the fact, is involved in equal mystery. It is not more wonderful, nor on sufficient evidence more difficult to be believed, in some points of view it is less so, that one spiritual being should act on another without the intervention of bodily organs, than that by certain conventional sounds conveyed to the ear, or certain arbitrary characters presented to the eye, the thoughts and feelings of one embodied spirit should be communicated to another embodied spirit, and become the instruments of altering opinion, exciting desire, stimulating to action.

The agency of the evil spirits on the human mind is no more inconsistent with the freedom of human action than the influence exerted by objects presented to the mind by the senses, or by the reasonings and persuasions of our fellow-men; and to him to whom nothing can be difficult, since the resources of his power and wisdom are infinite and inexhaustible, there can be no more difficulty in overruling the agency of devils than in overruling the agency of wicked men, to the promotion of the great ends of his righteous and benignant government.

These remarks go no further, and were intended to go no further, than to show that the doctrine of the existence and agency of evil spirits is not, abstractly considered, an absurd tenet; that the attempt to put it down by ridicule is altogether unworthy of men who lay claim to the honourable appellation of philosophers, lovers of wisdom; and that there is no necessity to have recourse to metaphor and allegory to explain away those passages of Scripture which, in their obvious and literal sense, explicitly teach this doctrine.

The evidence of the existence and agency of evil spirits is to be sought for in the Holy Scriptures. It is entirely a matter of supernatural revelation; and I have no hesitation in asserting, that such evidence is to be found there in such abundance and explicitness, that an unprejudiced reader, who believes the authenticity and inspiration of the sacred volume, and interprets its declarations on the principles which he applies to written language generally, will find it as difficult to doubt of the existence and doings of such a being as Satan or the devil, and his subordinate agents, as of the existence and doings of such men as Moses and Samuel, Peter or Paul.

The passage before us is one, out of a multitude, which clearly proves the existence and wide extent of malignant spiritual agency; and, in common with the most of such passages, shows that this doctrine is, like the doctrines of revelation generally, not a mere matter of curiosity or speculation, but calculated and intended to exert a powerful and a salutary influence in forming the character and guiding the conduct of Christians during their present disciplinary and preparatory state. The fact is distinctly asserted, that the "devil, their adversary, as a roaring lion, walketh about, seeking whom he may devour." This assertion is made that they may be induced to resist him; and that, in order to their successfully resisting him, they may be sober and watchful, and stedfast in the faith; and they are encouraged, under the sufferings in which the attempts of their powerful, and crafty, and cruel, and active adversary may involve them, by the consideration that such sufferings have been the common lot of the faithful in all ages, that they have been enabled to endure them, and in due season have been delivered from them, and by the promise of a divine support under and a glorious triumph over them. To these interesting topics, then, it is my intention to turn your minds in the remaining part of the discourse: The Christian's adversary; the Christian's duty in reference to this adversary; and the Christian's encouragement while engaged in performing this duty.

I. THE CHRISTIAN'S GREAT ENEMY.

Let us first, then, consider the statement made respecting the Christian's adversary: "Your adversary, the devil, as a roaring lion, walketh about, seeking whom he may devour." There are two questions which here require attention: Who is this adversary? and what is here stated in reference to him?

CHAP. I. WHO IS HE? THE DEVIL.

To the first question, Who is this adversary? the answer is, He is "the devil." The word translated devil properly signifies accuser, slanderer, calumniator, and is given to the chief of evil spirits as an appropriate designation. The same being is termed "Satan," a word of similar meaning with Devil, signifying enemy or accuser; "the Wicked One," to mark his depravity generally, and especially his malignity; "Belial," a term signifying low, abject, describing both his character and situation; "the Tempter;" "the god and the prince of this world;" "the Chief of the demons;" "Beelzebub," the lord of the flies; "the Prince of the Power of the Air;" "Apollyon," the destroyer; "he that hath the power of death;" "the Great Dragon;" and "the Old Serpent."[1]

With regard to this very remarkable being, our information, all of course derived from revelation, though very limited, is abundantly distinct. He is a being of the angelic order, formed, as all intelligent beings were, and must have been, in a state of moral integrity, who, at a period anterior to the fall of man, in consequence of violating the divine law, in a manner of which we are not informed, was, along with a large number of other spirits, who, it would appear, in consequence of being seduced by him, were partakers of his guilt, cast out of heaven, his "original abode," placed in a state of degradation and punishment, and reserved to deeper

[1] 1 Chron. xxi. 1; Job i. 6; Eph. vi. 16; 2 Cor. vi. 15; Matt. iv. 5; 1 Thess. ii. 5; 2 Cor. iv. 4; John xii. 31; Matt. xii. 24; Eph. ii. 2; Rev. ix. 11; Heb. ii. 14; Rev. xii. 3, 9.

shame and fiercer pains "at the day of the revelation of the righteous judgment of God." Through his malignity and falsehood, man, who was innocent, became guilty; man, who was holy, became depraved; man, who was happy, became miserable; man, who was immortal, became liable to death.

Over the minds of the human race, while they continue irregenerate, he exercises a very powerful, though not physically irresistible influence, "working in the children of disobedience," and "leading them captive at his will;" and even over their bodies he has in many instances exercised a malignant power. He exerts himself, by his numerous agents, infernal and human, in counteracting the divine benignant plan for the salvation of men. Error, sin, and misery, in all their forms, are ultimately his work; his animating principle is hatred of God, and his leading object the maintenance and extension of the power of evil.

During that period of holy light and happiness, the millennium, to which the Church and the world have so long looked forward with eager desire, his power and opportunities to do evil will be greatly diminished, if not entirely taken away. In the period immediately preceding the general judgment, he will again manifest his unchanged hostility to the benignant designs of God respecting man; and when the "mystery of God is finished," will, along with those angels and men who have chosen him for their leader in preference to God, be cut off for ever from all intercourse with the unfallen and restored part of the intelligent creation, and "punished with everlasting destruction from the presence of the Lord, and the glory of his power."

CHAP. II. WHAT IS HE?

§ 1. *He is an adversary—their adversary.*

Let us now inquire, in the second place, what is said of this extraordinary being in the passage before us. He is the Christian's adversary: "your adversary the devil." He is "the adversary;" the friend of none, the enemy of all. Enmity, malignity, is the very element of his moral being. He hates God, and men, and holy angels; and the only tie apparently existing between him and his subordinate agents, is a common enmity against God, and all that is God's. He is the adversary of all men. He has deeply injured the race; and he does not pity, but hate, those whom he has injured. "Murderer," manslayer, is his name from the beginning.[1]

But he is peculiarly the adversary of that portion of mankind who have been led by the good Spirit to revolt from his usurped dominion, to place themselves under the guidance of the Captain of the Lord's host, and to become fellow-workers under him in the accomplishment of his great enterprise, which is "to destroy the works of the devil." Both as individuals and as a body, true Christians are the objects of the peculiar enmity of the evil one. This is the truth which is taught us in the Apocalypse, when we are told that "the dragon persecuted the woman who was clothed with the sun, and had the moon under her feet, and upon her head a crown of twelve stars; being wroth with her, and making war with the remnant of her seed, which keep the commandments of God, and have the testimony of Jesus Christ." "They were," as Archbishop Leighton says, "once under his power; and now, being escaped from him, he pursues them, as Pharaoh with all his forces, as a

[1] John viii. 44. 'Ανθρωποκτόνος.

prey that was once in his den, and under his paw; and now that it is rescued, he rages and roars after it." His object is the destruction of the Christian cause,—the cause of truth and holiness, of God's glory and man's happiness; and therefore he cannot but be the adversary of those who seek to promote that cause. He exerts himself, by craft or violence, to induce them to abandon that cause, by doing which their sharing his destruction would be secured; or if he cannot succeed in this object, he endeavours to make as miserable as he can in this world, those whom he knows he will have no opportunity of tormenting in the next.

Of the manner in which their adversary manifests his enmity to them, we have a very picturesque account in these words, "As a roaring lion, he walketh about seeking whom he may devour." Under the influence of inflamed malignity, which will not let him rest, compared to the lion's appetite for blood, sharpened by hunger, he, in the exercise of his power and craft, both of which are indicated by the figure, the lion being at once strong and wily, is constantly endeavouring to do them mischief. It is highly probable that the apostle had immediately in his eye the attempts which the wicked one was then making, by means of his agents both infernal and human, to produce those fearful persecutions on the part of the Roman pagan empire, by which the faith and patience of the saints were so severely tried, by which multitudes were induced to make shipwreck of faith and a good conscience; turning back to perdition, becoming his prey, body and soul, for ever. And multitudes more, who were faithful to the death, and obtained a crown of life, were "by the devil cast into prison, and suffered tribulation;" "they had trial of cruel mockings and scourgings: they were stoned, they were slain by the sword; they wandered about in sheep-skins and goat-skins; being destitute, afflicted, tormented; they wandered in deserts and in mountains, and in dens and in caves of the earth." While I have little doubt that this is the immediate reference of the words, they bring before the mind certain general truths respecting our great spiritual enemy, of which it is of great importance that Christians in all countries and ages should be habitually mindful. They lead us to think of him as subtle, active, cruel, and powerful.

§ 2. *He is a subtle adversary.*

This passage leads us to think of our great adversary as subtle. The lion, like all other beasts of prey, is endowed with a high degree of sagacity, to enable it to discover and surprise its prey. When David would convey to our minds an idea of the cunning of his enemies, he compares them to the lion. "He sitteth in the lurking-places of the villages: in the secret places doth he murder the innocent: his eyes are privily set against the poor. He lieth in wait secretly as a lion in his den: he lieth in wait to catch the poor: he doth catch the poor, when he draweth him into his net. He croucheth, and humbleth himself, that the poor may fall by his strong ones."[1] The figure naturally thus suggests the idea of subtlety. This is one of the leading thoughts, too, suggested when the devil is represented as the old serpent: for "the serpent was more subtle than any beast of the field which the Lord God had made."

Subtlety is one of the most striking characters of our great spiritual enemy. He originally belonged to that order of beings whose wisdom is proverbial—"wise as an angel of God;" and when he lost his moral purity, we have no reason to think he lost his intellectual energy. It took a new direction, but with unabated force. From the change of its object, it ceased indeed to deserve the name of wisdom. The appropriate appellation henceforward was

[1] Ps. x. 8-10.

craft or subtlety. We have a melancholy proof of his cunning, in the method he followed in his successful attempt to deceive the mother of mankind. With what consummate address does he whet her curiosity, quiet her fears, and flatter her vanity, till he has accomplished his great purpose—the ruin of our race! Ever since he obtained that victory over our first parents, he has been engaged in tempting their children; and the experience of nearly six thousand years added to his natural cunning must have rendered him expert indeed in the art of deceiving that he may destroy. Accordingly, we find the apostle terming those suggestions by which he endeavours to lead men astray from God, "the wiles," the devices "of the devil."[1]

He has no power indeed of obtaining directly a knowledge of the human heart. That is the peculiar prerogative of Him who made it. "I the Lord search the heart, I try the reins."[2] But he carefully observes our conduct, and shrewdly draws conclusions respecting our prevailing dispositions. His temptations are regulated by the information he thus obtains. He suits the snare to the habits of the bird he means to entrap. He draws the voluptuary into the way of iniquity by the lure of pleasure, the avaricious by the promise of gain, the ambitious by the prospect of glory. He goes round about his victims, that he may espy where is the quarter in which they are weakest, or least afraid of attack, that he may assault them there. He takes advantage of everything in their temper, age, and condition, to give effect to his suggestions.

He keeps himself as much as possible out of view, and manages his approaches so as that, when danger is at length apprehended, there is scarce a possibility of escape. He even occasionally transforms himself into an angel of light, and employs as his instruments, often while they

[1] Rev. xii. 9; Gen. iii. 1; Eph. vi. 11.   [2] Jer. xvii. 10.

themselves are unaware of it, the very persons from whom we would have been the last to suspect any hazard.

Sometimes he gets possession of the citadel of the heart as it were by storm, without allowing opportunity or time for repelling the assault. At other times he proceeds by sap and mine; and, without alarm to the conscience, effects his nefarious purpose. But it were endless to enumerate all the subtle devices by which Satan endeavours to disturb the peace and retard the progress of the saint—to prevent the repentance and to secure the destruction of the sinner. Enough has been said to show that the figure chosen by the sacred writer is in this respect a significant one; and that the lion, in his arts for securing his prey, is a truly but an imperfectly descriptive emblem of " him who beguiled Eve through his subtlety," and has deluded and is deluding so many millions of her sons into those ways of error and sin which lead down to the chambers of eternal death.

§ 3. *He is an active adversary.*

But our great spiritual enemy is not only subtle; he is also active. The lion ranges far and near in quest of his prey. The lion of hell is here represented as walking about, seeking whom he may devour. " Whence comest thou?" said Jehovah to Satan, when he, as the accuser of the brethren, appeared in the midst of the sons of God. " Whence comest thou?" The answer was, " From going to and fro through the earth, and from walking up and down in it."[1] The malignant exertions of the wicked one seem to be unintermitted. Languor and fatigue appear to be feelings to which he is a stranger. In the book of Revelation he is represented as " accusing the brethren before God day and night."[2] He is probably the more

[1] Job i. 7. [2] Rev. xii. 10.

assiduous in his labours of malignity, as he knows that the period for his active exertions is limited. We cannot doubt that he is aware of the doom that awaits him; that, after a fixed term of ages, he is to be cast into the lake of fire, in the abyss of woe, and kept there under chains, which no created power can, which the uncreated power will not, unloose for ever. He has nothing approaching to satisfaction but in propagating sin and misery; and he knows that this is to come to a close. "The devil is come down among men, having great wrath, knowing that his time is short," or limited.

In realizing to our minds the activity of our great spiritual foe, we are not to think of him merely as an individual. No doubt he is a very active being; but this is not all. He is the chief and prince of unnumbered depraved spirits, who own his authority, prosecute his designs, and obey his commands. Their name is legion; for there are many of them. This gives him a species of ubiquity, and enables him to do what no individual created power and activity could accomplish.

His operations are often really continued when they seem to be intermitted. The mode of conducting them is changed, but the work is not abandoned; and if he does suspend them for a season, it is but that he may recommence them with a greater probability of success. This remark holds both with respect to those who are yet his willing slaves, and to those who have escaped from under his thrall. "When the unclean spirit goeth out of a man, he walketh through dry places seeking rest, but finding none. Then he saith, I will return again to my house from whence I came out; and when he is come, he finds this empty, swept, and garnished. Then goeth he, and taketh with him seven other spirits more wicked than himself, and they enter in and dwell there: and the last state of that man is worse than the first."[1] We have an instance of his returning to renew his attack with redoubled violence on those over whom he has no power, in the case of our Lord. We read, after the temptation of forty days in the wilderness, that "the devil departed from him;" but it was only in that form, and but "for a season."[2] He was still going about him, seeking an occasion to make an attack on him; and we find him in the hour of exhaustion and sorrow springing on his victim, and by his infernal assault drawing forth from the lips of him who was embodied patience and fortitude those awful words, as if all he had experienced of diabolical attacks hitherto were unworthy of notice, "This is your hour and the power of darkness."

§ 4. *He is a cruel adversary.*

Cruelty is another feature in the character of our great spiritual enemy, which the statement in the text brings before the mind. The lion is a stranger to pity. Like most ravenous beasts, he seems to have satisfaction in inflicting pain. The bleating of the lamb whom he is about to devour awakens in him no relentings, and he regards not the agonies he occasions to the bleeding, mangled sufferer. Equally ruthless is the great murderer from the beginning, the great destroyer of human souls. He appears to have a savage satisfaction in producing misery. The lion, when he tears to pieces the quivering limbs of the slaughtered kid, has an enjoyment altogether separate from the gratification of the desire to destroy. He satisfies the painful cravings of hunger, and obtains nourishment for his body. But the destroyer of human innocence and peace, the devourer of souls, derives no advantage, can derive no advantage, knows that he can derive no advantage, from the miseries which he inflicts, the ruin which he occasions. On

[1] Matt. xii. 43-45. [2] Luke iv. 13.

the contrary, every malignant act deepens his guilt, and will aggravate his future condemnation; and he cannot but be aware of this. Yet so deeply is the desire of diffusing misery rooted in his nature, that though conscious that in yielding to it he is but rendering his miserable condition more miserable, " treasuring up to himself wrath against the day of wrath, and revelation of the righteous judgment of God," he still, day and night, restlessly seeks for opportunities of making the good bad, and the bad worse, the happy miserable, and the miserable more miserable.

§ 5. *He is a powerful adversary.*

The only other idea suggested by the figurative description of our great spiritual enemy is, that he is a being of formidable power. Solomon informs us that the " lion is the strongest among beasts,"[1] and I believe modern naturalists hold that there is no animal of the same size which possesses so much muscular power. The devil belongs to an order, the angelic, which excels in strength; and though we know his powers are restrained by the divine providence, we have no reason to think that his moral depravation produced any diminution of his physical energy. The tempest which overwhelmed the family of Job in the ruins of the house of their elder brother, and the fearful effects produced both on the bodies and the minds of those individuals who were the subjects of demoniac possession, prove both what he can do, and would do, if not restrained by a superior power. To what extent he can and does employ physical agents, what are commonly termed the powers of nature, in executing his malignant designs, we cannot tell. This we know, that the Scripture representations naturally lead us to think of Satan as not weak, but powerful. He is emblematized in the parable by

[1] Prov. xxx. 30.

"the strong man;" and the apostle obviously estimates those unseen opponents, of whom the devil is the leader, as far more formidable foes than the most powerful human enemies.

We need, according to him, *divine* strength and heavenly armour to resist such enemies. " Be strong," says he, " in the Lord, and in the power of his might. Put on the whole armour of God, that ye may be able to stand against the wiles of the devil: for we wrestle not against flesh and blood, but against principalities and powers, against the rulers of the darkness of this world, against spiritual wickedness in high places."[1] So much for illustration of the apostle's statement respecting the Christian's great spiritual enemy, so subtle, so active, so cruel, so powerful.

That part of our subject which we have attempted to illustrate, is replete with important practical instruction.

What a striking view does the contrast of the original and the present character and employment of the devil, give us of the malignant nature and tremendous power of moral evil! He who is now the worst and the most miserable of created beings, was once one of the best and the happiest. He who now prowls about the universe, " a fugitive and a vagabond," restless and miserable everywhere, had his first abode in the region of perfect purity, near to the throne of the Eternal; and instead of, as now, going about seeking how he can waste and destroy the best part of God's works, his constant employment and delight was to celebrate the praises and do the commandments of Jehovah, hearkening to the voice of his word. And what has effected the fearful change? What has converted the angel into the devil? It was sin; that only evil in God's universe in which there is no good; that evil, the depths of whose malignity no created mind can sound. Man in his fallen state compared with man in his primeval state, earth in its present state

---

[1] Matt. xii. 29; Eph. vi. 11-13.

compared with paradise, strikingly show that it is an evil and a bitter thing to depart from God; but still more striking is the illustration we have of this most important truth, when we contrast the accursed fiend with the holy angel, and the bottomless pit and the fiery lake with the palace of the great King, the Lord of hosts, and the rivers of pleasure that are at his right hand for evermore.

How disgraceful and miserable must be the condition of those who are the slaves of this subtle, active, cruel, powerful, depraved intelligence, in turns the instruments of his detestable designs and the victims of his insatiable cruelty! And this is the situation of all unconverted men, whether they are aware of it or not. They are of their father the devil; and his lusts—the things he desires and delights in—they willingly abuse their powers and degrade their nature in doing. They are "taken captive by him at his will."[1] He is their successful tempter now. He will be, if mercy prevent not, their unrelenting tormentor for ever. Oh that they were aware of the horrors of their situation, that they saw its debasement, that they felt its wretchedness, that they realized its dangers!

How grateful should we be to HIM who came to destroy the works of the wicked one, and to deliver men from his usurped dominion and baleful power! The house of the strong man has been entered by one stronger than he. The prey has been taken from the mighty, and the captive of the terrible one delivered. The greatness of the blessing, apart from the manner in which it was procured, calls for lively gratitude; but the claims of our Deliverer are felt to be tenfold strong, when we recollect that He, the only-begotten, the Holy One, of God, submitted to be tempted of the devil, to have the moral sensibilities of his holy nature shocked and tortured by his loathsome suggestions, that we

[1] 2 Tim. ii. 26.

might be delivered from his power, and be taught by the example of "the Captain of our salvation" how to conduct the conflict with the enemy, so as to become more than conquerors through him who loved us. Blessed, ever blessed be he who came in the name of the Lord to bruise the head of the old serpent, and who, through the merit of his atonement and the power of his Spirit, enables the most feeble and timid of his people to "tread on the lion and the adder," and to "trample the young lion and the dragon under foot."

Let Christians rejoice that, if a subtle, cruel, active, and powerful enemy is continually prowling about, the eye of infinite wisdom and love rests ever on them, the arm of never-tiring omnipotence is ever around them to protect and defend them. The lion of hell is a chained lion, a muzzled lion, to Christians. He may alarm, but he shall never devour them. His chain is in the hand of his conqueror and their Lord.

It was very natural for Peter to put his brethren in mind of their great enemy. He must have often thought of the words of our Lord Jesus, "Simon, Simon, Satan hath desired to have thee, that he may sift thee as wheat; but I have prayed for thee, that thy faith fail not."[1] His experience is full of warning and encouragement. It proves that if Christians are not cautious, though the lion of hell shall not be permitted to devour them, he may inflict wounds of which they will bear the marks till the close of life; and it finely illustrates our Lord's declaration, "I give unto my sheep eternal life, and they shall never perish; neither shall any pluck them out of my hand." Neither their own heedlessness, nor the malignity of their infernal foe, shall be able to accomplish their destruction. Let him, then, that is born of God, "keep himself, that the wicked one touch him not;" and let his joy, that he has a better keeper than

[1] Luke xxii. 31.

himself, even the keeper of Israel, who never slumbers nor sleeps, not produce security, but encourage vigilance. God keeps his people, not without, but through their own watchfulness.

Finally, let all of us who have reason to hope that we have been emancipated from the powers of the wicked one, in our humble station co-operate with our great Deliverer in rescuing our fellow-men from the degrading bondage, from the destroying power of his and our great enemy; and while the children of the devil are so clearly proving themselves to be so, by imitating him in going about seeking whom they may destroy, let us prove our connection with him whom we claim as our Lord and Master, by going about doing good, endeavouring to pluck the brand from the burning, to pull the prey of the lion of hell from his devouring jaws, to seek and to save what is in extreme hazard, through the craft and activity, the power and cruelty of the wicked one, of being lost, lost for ever.

II. THE CHRISTIAN'S DUTY IN REFERENCE TO HIS GREAT ENEMY.

Let us now consider the apostle's account of the Christian's duty in reference to his great spiritual adversary. His duty is to resist him; and in order effectually to resist him, to be sober, to be watchful, to be stedfast in the faith.

CHAP. I. WHAT HE MUST DO TO HIS GREAT ENEMY: RESIST HIM.

The attacks of our great spiritual enemy naturally divide themselves into two classes,—those which are made on the Christian as an individual, and those which are made on the Christian cause. It is the duty of the Christian to resist both.

§ 1. *He must resist his attacks on himself.*

Temptation to sin is the manner in which the evil one attacks the individual Christian. Sometimes these temptations are direct, oftener they are indirect; but all temptation to sin, like all sin itself, may be considered as directly or indirectly the work of the devil. It is much more a matter of curiosity than of use, to seek to distinguish accurately the temptations which come immediately from the wicked one, from those in presenting which to the mind he employs intermediate agencies. But it is of great importance to remember, that all solicitations to sin, from whatever quarter they come, are in accordance with his will, and, if not resisted, will contribute to the gaining of his object in warring against the soul. Of all suggestions of this kind, we may say both that they come not, they cannot come, from above; they do, they must, come from beneath. Of some of them we may say, they are "earthly;" of others, they are "sensual;" of all, they are "devilish."

Generally speaking, it is the duty of the Christian carefully to keep out of the way of temptation, to avoid everything which can be avoided in consistency with duty, which may afford an opportunity to the great enemy or his agents to assail him with solicitations to sin. It is madness to hold parley with him, or uncalled on to provoke him to combat. Such unnecessary tamperings, such self-confident conflicts, generally end in sin and shame.

But the adversary will not let the Christian alone, and the path of duty is a path that sometimes, indeed ofttimes, leads into temptation. When the Christian is attacked, he must not flee, he must not yield himself up into the hands of his enemy; he must resist, he must oppose him. He must not comply with his solicitations. Like that good spiritual soldier of ancient times, he must say, "How can I do this great wickedness and sin against God?" or, like the Captain of salvation, he must with the shield of faith quench all the fiery darts of the wicked, repelling his reiterated suggestions by, "It is written, it is written," and in holy indignation bidding him "get behind him."[1] He must not allow himself to deliberate on a proposal which involves in it the denial of truth, the neglect of duty, or the commission of sin, by whatever plausibilities and apparent advantages it may be recommended, but immediately, and with abhorrence, reject it.

Non-compliance with the suggestions of the wicked one is, however, but a part of the Christian duty of resistance. The Christian must oppose the wicked one. He must not merely stand on the defensive; he must attack the enemy, he must quit himself like a man, and so fight as to turn to flight the alien and his armies. He must so resist the devil as that he shall flee from him. In plain words, he must make solicitations to sin occasions and means of progress in holiness. For example, when tempted to fretfulness under affliction, instead of yielding to the temptation, he must "glorify God in the fires," by more than ever possessing his soul in patience, and counting it all joy to be brought into manifold tribulation. When tempted to be ashamed of Christ or his cause, he must seize that opportunity of making his conduct proclaim more loudly than ever, "God forbid that I should glory, save in the cross of our Lord Jesus Christ." When tempted to penuriousness in supporting the cause of Christ, he must give more cheerfully, and if possible more plenteously, than ever. When tempted to be "weary in well-doing," he must feel this as a powerful reason why he should be "stedfast and unmoveable, always abounding in the work of the Lord." When tempted to associate with the worldly and ungodly, he

[1] Matt. iv. 4, 7, 10.

should take an opportunity of showing that in the "saints that are in the earth, and the excellent, is all his delight." When tempted to draw very near the borders of criminal indulgence, let him not even stand still where he is, but retire still further from the appearance of evil, and carefully keep off "the debateable land." When the evil one tempts to unfrequency or carelessness in secret prayer, let it be felt as a reason why he should seek to realize more and more, in his own experience, what it is to "pray in the spirit," to "pray always, with all prayer and supplication, and to watch thereunto with all perseverance." Let temptations to carelessness produce increased vigilance, and to indolence increased diligence. Let attempts to make us neglect the assembling of ourselves together, lead to more conscientious attendance on public religious services, and more undivided attention in them. In one word, let all his endeavours to lead us in the way of sin, end in our further advancement in the opposite way of holiness. This is the way to turn the artillery of the wicked one against himself. Nothing is so well fitted to mortify that old adversary, as to find that the very means he employs to produce our apostasy and ruin are converted into the occasion of our establishment in the faith, our advancement in holiness, and our fitness for heaven. So much for the resistance which the Christian is to make to the attacks of his great spiritual enemy, directed immediately against himself as an individual.

§ 2. *He must resist his attacks on the Christian cause.*

But the Christian is to resist not only these attacks; he is to resist also the attacks which his adversary the devil is constantly making on the cause of Christ. He is constantly engaged in endeavouring to corrupt the truth as it is in Jesus; to introduce and maintain and extend error, and superstition, and fanaticism, and schism, and bigotry, and disorder, and impurity, in the churches of Christ, and to oppose the exertions which are making to diffuse the knowledge and the influence of " the grace and truth which came by Jesus Christ." The Christian is to fight against Satan not only in his own heart, but in the Church and the world. There is a battle-field without as well as within. He is carefully to avoid everything which may in any way prove, however unintentionally, co-operation with the lawless one in his nefarious designs; and by all proper methods he must endeavour to counteract him.

He must, however, take care not to attempt what has been too frequently attempted—to vanquish the wicked one by weapons borrowed from his own armoury. He must not repel force by force, false argument by false argument, railing by railing. In such conflict the devil is sure to overcome; indeed, the very employment of these weapons is a proof that he has already, to a certain degree, overcome. In this warfare, Christians must remember that " the weapons of their warfare are not carnal, but mighty through God to the pulling down of strongholds, and bringing into captivity every high thought that exalteth itself against the knowledge of God." Their motto must be, " Not by might and power, but by God's Spirit. By pureness, by knowledge, by long-suffering, by kindness, by the Holy Ghost, by love unfeigned, by the word of truth, by the power of God, by the armour of righteousness on the right hand and the left." This is the manner in which the apostle teaches us to carry on our warfare for the cause of Christ against the cause of the devil. " The servant of God must not strive, but be gentle to all men, apt to teach, patient; in meekness instructing those who oppose themselves, if God peradventure will give them repentance to the acknowledging of the truth, and that they may deliver themselves out of the snare of the devil, who are taken captive of him at his will."[1]

Christians are not to stand looking idly on when the wicked one, by ignorance and error, and superstition and profligacy, is consummating the eternal perdition of men by millions. No, they are to "rise up for God against the evil-doer; they are to stand up for Him against" his armies, "the workers of iniquity." As "the armies of heaven, clothed in fine linen, white and clean,"[2] they are to follow on their white horses him whose name is the Word of God, faithful and true, who, clothed in a vesture dipped in blood, rides forth prosperously on his white horse, "in righteousness, judging and making war, conquering and to conquer." Like Him, wherever they are, according to the facilities afforded by their circumstances, they are to be constantly engaged in destroying the works of the devil. Thus, then, are Christians to resist their adversary the devil.[3]

CHAP. II. WHAT THE CHRISTIAN IS TO DO THAT HE MAY RESIST HIS GREAT ENEMY.

The apostle not only enjoins this duty of resistance; he also instructs Christians how they are to be enabled to perform it. If they would successfully resist the devil, either in their own hearts or in the Church and the world, they must "be sober, vigilant, and stedfast in the faith." Let us shortly explain these exercises, and show how necessary

[1] 2 Cor. x. 4; Zech. iv. 6; 2 Cor. vi. 6-8; 2 Tim. ii. 24-26.
[2] Rev. xix. 11-14.
[3] The motives to resistance are strongly put by Tertullian: "Stat conflictus conspector, Agonothetes, Deus vivus est: Xystarches, Spiritus Sanctus: Epistates, Christus Jesus; Corona, æternitatis brabium angelicæ substantiæ, in cœlis politia, gloria in secula seculorum."—*Lib. ad Martyr.* iii.

they are, and how well fitted they are to enable the Christian to resist his adversary the devil.

When we read these words, we feel that the injunctions contained in them have already been given; the first of them more than once. The reiteration of such precepts in so short an epistle, teaches a lesson both to ministers and people, both to the teachers and the taught. It says to the first, "For you to say the same things should not be grievous," for to the second "it is safe," ay, it is necessary. "Precept must be on precept, line upon line; here a little, and there a little." "It were easy," says Archbishop Leighton, "to entertain men's mind with new discourse, if our task were rather to please than to profit: for there be many things which, with little labour, might be brought forth as new and strange to ordinary hearers. But there be a few things which it chiefly concerns us to know and practise, and these are to be more frequently represented and pressed. This apostle, and other divine writers, drew from too full a spring to be ebb of matter; but they rather choose profitable iterations than unprofitable variety, and so should we." Yet we shall find that, though substantially the same exhortations are repeated, it is always with a peculiar adaptation to the connection in which they occur. They are not mere repetitions; they are examples of the application of general principles or precepts to particular cases. It is obviously so in the instance before us.

§ 1. *He must be sober.*

The word here translated "be sober," is the same which, in the seventh verse of the preceding chapter, is rendered "be vigilant." Its proper signification is to be abstinent from, or temperate in the use of, wine or other intoxicating drinks. It designates a state directly the reverse of a state of intoxication. The word may be understood either literally or figuratively. If understood literally, we are here taught that temperance, in reference to intoxicating drinks, is necessary in order to our resisting the devil. And certainly nothing can be more obviously true than this. The natural tendency of intoxicating drinks is to diminish the power of conscience and reason, and to increase the power of the lower principles of our nature, animal appetite and irascible feeling. It increases the strength of what needs to be restrained, and weakens the strength of what is fitted and intended to restrain. It delivers the man, in one point of view, bound hand and foot, so far as resistance is concerned, into the devil's hands; and, in another, presents him a willing soldier, appropriately armed for his service. An intoxicated man would be ill fitted to take care of himself if exposed to the attacks of subtle, powerful beasts of prey; and he is certainly not better fitted to guard himself against that crafty and active, strong and cruel spiritual enemy, who is here represented as prowling about like a roaring lion. While this is undoubtedly true and highly important, as the corresponding term "be vigilant," that is, wakeful, is plainly to be understood in a figurative sense, we apprehend the expression before us must also be interpreted figuratively; an interpretation which substantially includes the literal meaning, while it includes much more.

"Things seen and temporal," the pleasures, the riches, the honours of this world, are apt to intoxicate the mind. Men under their supreme influence are regulated more by imagination and appetite than by conscience and reason. What is present and sensible occupies the whole mind. What is unseen and future is overlooked and forgotten, and treated as if it had no existence. Time is everything, eternity is nothing. This is mental intoxication; and sobriety, in opposition to this, is just the sound estimate which enlightened conscience and reason form of the comparative value of things seen and unseen, things temporal and eternal, with a habitual state of feeling and action corresponding to this estimate.

He is sober who reckons that the ever-enduring holy happiness, which can be found only in possessing the favour and being conformed to the image of God, is of more true value to man than all else which the created universe contains; that the certainty of attaining the greatest earthly good is too dearly purchased by the slightest hazard of losing this happiness; that no sacrifice, no suffering, is to be much counted on if necessary in order to its attainment; and that what has no tendency to secure this, cannot be a matter of very much importance to a being like man. Such a man shows a mind free from intoxication. He judges of things as they really are. His maxims are obviously the words of truth and soberness. God is more excellent than the creature. The soul is more valuable than the body. Heaven is better than earth, far better than hell. Time is shorter than eternity.

The man who is thus sober is prepared for resisting the devil in both the ways illustrated above. The devil is "the god of this world," and all his power is derived from it. The sum of what he has to say in the way of temptation is, 'All earthly good is delivered to me, and to whomsoever I will I give it. All earthly evil is in my power, and on whomsoever I will I inflict it.' It is by the hope of worldly good, or the fear of worldly evil, that he prevails on men to neglect duty and to commit sin. But the truly sober man has his spiritual senses too well exercised to believe either the implied or the express falsehood. He knows that God has not relinquished the government of the world, or so committed it into the hands of his great enemy, as that he has the disposal either of the good or the evil of life; and though it were otherwise, he knows that there is a more valuable good which compliance with his suggestions would forfeit—a more dreadful evil to which compliance with his suggestions would expose him. So far as he is influenced by this sober judgment, he "keeps himself, and the wicked one toucheth him not." And the same sober judgments of the value of the soul, and of the importance of eternity, naturally lead to strenuous persevering exertions to resist the devil in his attempts to introduce error and superstition into the Church, and to perpetuate ignorance, idolatry, and wickedness in the world.

§ 2. *He must be vigilant.*

But that Christians may effectually resist their adversary the devil, the apostle calls on them to be not only sober, but "vigilant."[1] The literal meaning of the word is in opposition to falling asleep, to keep awake as shepherds do when watching their sheep by night, or sentinels when keeping watch on the walls of a city; it indicates a state of watchfulness in opposition to a state of sleep or drowsiness. Some would interpret the words literally; and it is on this ground, among others, that Roman Catholics prescribe watching as well as fasting as a means of spiritual advantage, and of successfully resisting our ghostly adversaries.

There can be no reasonable doubt, however, that here, and wherever else in the New Testament watching is prescribed as a general Christian duty, the word is used figuratively. A state of security, inattention, and inactivity, is naturally emblematized by a state of sleep; and a state of consciousness of existing hazards, attention to them,

---

[1] "Our adversary, the devil, goes about day and night; therefore, by day νήψατι, be sober, and by night γρηγορήσατι, be watchful."—BISHOP JEBB.

and active employment of the means to escape them, by a state of watching or wakefulness.

To be watchful, with a reference to the resistance of the evil one, implies that the individual is aware of the existence and reality of the hazards to which, from malignant spiritual influence, his highest interests are exposed; that he is on the alert to notice all the movements of the subtle, active, cruel, and powerful foe; and that, not ignorant of or inattentive to his devices, he looks around him, walks circumspectly, aware that in any quarter the enemy may make his appearance; and that he so disguises himself and varies his form, that it requires spiritual sagacity in its most awakened state to detect him; and finally, that when he does discover him ready to deceive or to devour, to delude or destroy, he is ready, broad awake, in full possession of his spiritual faculties, prepared to employ the proper means for counter-working him and disappointing his nefarious purposes.

It is not enough that a man be sober, that is, not intoxicated, round whom a powerful crafty beast of prey is prowling. He must be wakeful. However sober, if he fall asleep, he is in imminent hazard of being dangerously wounded, if not devoured. Indeed, he is not acting like a sober man, if in these circumstances he allows himself to fall asleep. In like manner, the Christian must not only have a just estimate of the transcendent importance of things unseen and eternal, but his spiritual senses must be habitually exercised; the eyes of his mind "must look right on, and his eyelids look straight before him." He must "ponder the path of his feet," and especially "keep his heart with all diligence; for out of it are the issues of life."[1] He must, like a watchful sentinel, take good heed that through none of the external senses—the gates, as

[1] Prov. iv. 23, 25, 26.

Bunyan represents them, of the good town Mansoul—the great adversary, under any disguise, find his way to the citadel of the heart. He must be watchful, for his enemy is so.

The influence which this vigilance is calculated to exert on the resistance of the wicked one in his attack both on us as individuals and on the cause of Christ, is so obvious, that I may safely leave you to follow out this train of thought in your private meditations.

§ 3. *He must be stedfast in the faith.*

The third and principal means by which Christians are to be enabled to resist the great adversary, is the being "stedfast in the faith." We call that the principal means; for it is as necessary to the right use of the other means as to the gaining of the common end,—as necessary to the being "sober and vigilant," as to "the resisting of the devil."

The apostle takes for granted that the persons whom he addressed were "believers." They were "in the faith;" and he calls on them to be "stedfast in the faith." Had he been speaking to unconverted men, the first thing he would have called on them to do, would have been to believe; for, till they believed, they could neither see their danger, nor use the means which were necessary for their safety. They to whom he writes had believed the truth respecting their natural condition as the willing helpless slaves of the wicked one, bound in the fetters of guilt and the cords of depravity. They had believed the truth respecting Jesus the great deliverer, who by the blood of his covenant had made provision for the deliverance of the "prisoners out of the pit in which there was no water;" who "proclaims liberty to the captive, and the opening of the prison to them who are bound;" who takes the prey from the mighty, and delivers the captive of the terrible one. They had believed that those who refuse to be released by him, must, along with their enslaver, be shut up under everlasting chains in the prison of hell, and that they who accept of the freely offered deliverance shall, under the protection and guidance of their redeeming Lord, be preserved, amid all the attempts of their former oppressors to bring them again into slavery, and ultimately placed by him in circumstances of perfect holy happiness, while Satan shall be for ever bruised under their feet.

It is the belief of these things that has sobered their minds, and roused them to spiritual vigilance. This has wakened them, and it is this only that can keep them awake; and for this purpose they must be " stedfast in the faith." They must hold fast the truth as it is in Jesus.

It is not enough that they have believed; they must continue believing. The truth and its evidence must be habitually before their minds. Everything depends on that. They are safe "if they keep in memory what has been preached to them;" not otherwise. The truth works effectually towards the resistance of the wicked one, but only in him who believes it, and only in the degree in which he believes it. It is faith that makes the Christian strong for combat. Let him lose sight of the truth and its evidence, and, like Samson shorn of his locks, he is weak as another man. Whenever he staggers through unbelief, he becomes powerless in resisting the great adversary. It is he only who puts on "the whole armour of God" that can "stand in the evil day;" but it is the believer alone who can put on and wear and wield that armour. It is the girdle of truth believed that can alone gird up the loins of the mind. The breastplate is the righteousness which is of God by faith. The well-roughed shoes, of the preparation of the gospel of peace, which are necessary to enable the spiritual soldier to stand firm in the slippery field of temptation, can be worn only by them who believe that gospel. The shield, which enables him to "quench all the fiery darts of the wicked one," is the shield of faith. The hope, which is "the helmet of salvation," can grace no brow but the brow of the believer, for hope rests on faith; "the sword of the Spirit, which is the word of God," can be wielded only by the arm of the believer; and the prayer which is necessary to secure the right and the effectual use of all those pieces of spiritual armour, is the prayer of faith.

Had our first parents been stedfast in faith, they had never fallen. They became the prey of unbelief in the shape of doubt, before they became the victims of the devil. God said, "Ye shall surely die;" they doubted him. The devil said, "Ye shall not surely die;" they believed him, and then were befooled and enslaved by him. It was by being stedfast in faith that the great Captain of our salvation successfully resisted the wicked one, and blunted all his fiery darts. To them all he presented the shield of faith in a specific divine declaration, and the most envenomed of them fell harmless at his feet. By faith all the elders who have "received a good report" turned to flight the alien armies of their infernal as well as mortal enemies; and still is it true, and it will continue true till the last spiritual conflict has taken place on earth, "This is the victory that overcometh the world," and the god of the world, "even our faith."[1] Here, as in the former case, I leave it to yourselves to follow out more fully the manner in which stedfast faith operates in enabling Christians to resist the adversary in his attacks on themselves individually, and on the great cause of their Lord and King.

[1] 1 John v. 4.

III. THE CHRISTIAN'S ENCOURAGEMENT TO PERFORM HIS DUTY IN REFERENCE TO HIS GREAT ENEMY.

It only remains that we briefly attend to the encouragement which the Christian has amid the sufferings in which his struggles with his spiritual enemies may involve him. That encouragement is derived from two sources—an undoubted fact and a faithful promise: an undoubted fact—the same struggle has been sustained and surmounted by all the brotherhood; and a faithful promise—"The God of all grace, who hath called them unto his eternal glory by Christ Jesus, after they have suffered a while, will make them perfect, stablish, strengthen, settle them." Let us attend to these encouragements in their order.

CHAP. I. THE ENCOURAGING FACT: ALL THE BROTHERHOOD HAVE SUSTAINED AND SURMOUNTED THIS STRUGGLE.

And first, let us consider the encouraging fact. "Knowing this," says the apostle, "that the same afflictions are accomplished in your brethren who are in the world." It has been questioned whether the sufferings here spoken of refer to the inward sufferings occasioned by the temptations of the wicked one, or to the outward sufferings, the persecutions which spring out of the influence of the wicked one on the minds of his slaves and their enemies. I do not think that it is necessary, or even proper, to confine it to either. It refers to sufferings growing out of the machinations and agency of their great spiritual adversary, of whatever kind. The apostle states that "the same afflictions"—afflictions of the same kind arising from the same cause—"were accomplished in their brethren," literally, 'in their brotherhood,' "in the world."

Some have thought that these words contain in them but little to support under suffering, and have applied the words of a heathen moralist: "It is but poor consolation that I am one of many sufferers." But if we look at the words carefully, we shall find that they are replete with encouragement.

Sufferers are very apt to think their case quite singular; others have been tried, but none tried as they are; and the Apostle Paul shows his knowledge of human nature when he says to the Corinthians, "There hath no temptation taken you but such as is common to man." Your sufferings are not peculiar. It is unreasonable to complain of what is so common a lot. It were pusillanimous to sink under what so many are suffering and have sustained.

But the consolation here given is of a higher kind than this. These sufferings are characteristic of the brotherhood to which you belong. Every member of that brotherhood is a partaker of them. He who is the "first-born of the many brethren" experienced the temptations of the devil and the persecutions of wicked men; and in their sufferings all the younger branches of the holy family have fellowship with Him. You could not belong to that brotherhood if you were entire strangers to their afflictions.[1] "If ye were of the world, the world would love its own," and the god of this world would not so attack you; "but because ye are not of the world, but chosen out of the world," therefore the world and its prince harass and abuse you. It is one of the family badges: "If ye are without such chastisements," of which all the children, all the brotherhood, are partakers, "then are ye bastards, and not sons."[2] Would you willingly part with the characteristic privileges

---

[1] "Erras si putas, unquam Christianum persecutionem non pati."—HIERONYMUS.
[2] John xv. 19; Heb. xii. 8.

of the brotherhood, in order to obtain exemption from their characteristic sufferings? Besides, as these sufferings are common to the brotherhood, you may be assured of that cordial sympathy which lightens suffering, and that "fervent prayer which avails much."

Then there is some peculiarity in the phrase " are accomplished," are fulfilled. It is not said they are endured by, but they are accomplished or fulfilled in. This peculiar mode of expression leads us to think of these sufferings as appointments which must be fulfilled. No chance has happened to you. "This hath come forth from Him who is wonderful in counsel and excellent in working." Satan and his agents are but doing to you as they did to your Lord, " what God's hand and counsel beforetime determined to be done." These temptations and persecutions are a part of the manifold trials to which, for a season, it is needful that you be subject; for " they who would live godly in this world must suffer persecution." Your Lord has assured you, that " in the world ye shall have tribulation;" and his apostle, that " through much tribulation ye must enter the kingdom." These are sufferings to which ye are appointed and called. These are sufferings appointed to every Christian, as a member of the body of Christ, and they must be accomplished. They are a part of the discipline by which the brotherhood on earth are to be made fit for joining the brotherhood in heaven.[1]

And then, what encouragement and consolation is there in the thought, that these afflictions, as they must for wise and benignant reasons be endured by the whole brotherhood while they are in the world, are to be *accomplished* here! The brotherhood who are with their Father and their elder Brother in heaven, are completely beyond the reach of temptation and persecution. Satan is bruised

[1] Isa. xxviii. 29; Acts v. 28, xiv. 22; John xvi. 33.

under their feet. They are made more than conquerors. The helmet has been exchanged for the crown that fadeth not away; the sword of conflict for the palm of victory; and the cry, "I am oppressed, undertake for me," for the shout, "Salvation to our God and the Lamb for ever and ever." "To him that loved us and washed us from our sins in his blood, and hath made us kings and priests to God and his Father, to him be glory and dominion for ever and ever."

And where they are, their brethren on the earth will ere long be. Is it not meet that we should endure with patience and fortitude on earth, since such rest and enjoyment are prepared for us in heaven? The phrase, brotherhood on earth, naturally leads the mind to the brotherhood in heaven. There is to be the permanent abode of the *whole* brotherhood. "The gathering together" at the coming of the Lord is to be there. "Faithful is he who hath promised, who also will do it:" "In my Father's house are many mansions," accommodation for all the brotherhood; "if it had not been so, I would have told you. I go to prepare a place for you; and if I go, . . . I will come again, and receive you to myself, that where I am there ye may be also."[1] He became perfect through the accomplishment of his sufferings; and so, in a sense suited to our case, must we become perfect through the accomplishment of our sufferings. At the very utmost, we are not to be long in the world where our afflictions are to be accomplished, finished: we are to be for ever in the better world, where the glorious results which infinite wisdom and kindness have wrought out by these afflictions, will continue unfolding themselves to our growing astonishment and delight throughout eternity.

Thus are all these afflictions accomplished *here*. The brotherhood who have passed the Jordan of death, and entered into the heavenly Canaan, are for ever secure from

[1] 2 Thess. ii. 1; John xiv. 2.

the attacks of the wild beasts that roam the desert through which we are passing, and from all the afflictions which flow from these attacks. The old serpent shall never find his way into the restored paradise; and thither all the brotherhood are tending. Yet a little while and they shall all be there, safe and happy together, in their Father's house for ever. This is surely great encouragement, abundant consolation.

CHAP. II. THE FAITHFUL PROMISE.

Let us now turn our attention to the still more explicit encouragement suggested by the faithful promise contained in the 10th verse; for, on careful inspection, it will be found to be a promise. The 10th verse is very generally considered as a prayer on the part of the apostle, that Christians might, amid their struggles and sufferings, be " made perfect, stablished, strengthened, settled." There can be no doubt that was his wish and prayer for them; but a closer consideration of the words convinces me that this verse is not a prayer, but a promise; not a request that God would confer certain most valuable and appropriate blessings on tempted, struggling, afflicted Christians, but a declaration that he will bestow them.

I think most careful readers of the Bible must have felt disappointed, that after so very graphic a view had been given of the dangers and struggles of the Christian, all that should have been said for his encouragement and comfort is, " The same afflictions are fulfilled in your brethren that are in the world." The rendering given by our translators of the 10th verse is not literal; indeed, from the text from which they translated, no strictly literal intelligible version could have been given. By the slightest of all changes, the putting one vowel in the place of another,[1]—a change

[1] ι instead of α.

which the inquiries of critics have found not only to be authorized but required,—the original passage is freed from all difficulty, and the encouragement administered to the tempted, struggling, afflicted believer, is as abundant and complete as we could expect or desire; indeed, "above all that we could ask or think." Literally rendered, the words thus amended are, "But the God of all grace, who hath called *us*," or "*you*, unto his eternal glory [1] by or in Christ Jesus, after ye have suffered a while, shall make you perfect, strengthen, stablish, settle you." It is as if he had said: Such afflictions, rising out of the attacks of the wicked one, must be endured by you; for they are the result of divine appointment,—an appointment reaching to and fulfilled in all your brotherhood in the world. But be not discouraged: "The God of all grace, who has called you unto his eternal glory by Christ Jesus, after ye have suffered a while, shall make you perfect, stablish, strengthen, settle you." The Christian, watching against the wiles, struggling against the assaults of the lion of hell, and suffering under the effects of his attacks, and their resistance, has need of abundant support and encouragement and consolation, and assuredly he has got it here.

There is strong consolation *in the promise itself*. "God shall make you perfect, stablish, strengthen, settle you," notwithstanding, nay by means of, these very afflictions. And then, what superadded encouragement and comfort is there *in the adjuncts of the promise*, in the manner in which the promise is given! For who promises? "The God of all grace;" "the God who has called you;" "the God who has called you unto his eternal glory in Christ Jesus;" "the God who has called you to this glory after ye have suffered a while." Is there not in every one of these considerations a new and most exuberant fountain of spiritual

[1] Ἐν Χριστῷ Ἰησοῦ.

encouragement and joy opened to the Christian warrior, from which he may draw most refreshing draughts when fatigued by his conflicts with his great adversary, "faint yet pursuing?" Well may he, like the Captain of his salvation, "drink of the brook in the way, and lift up the head" for renewed conflict or untiring pursuit. Let us first, then, look at the matter of the promise, and then at the manner in which it is given.

§ 1. *The encouragement contained in the promise itself.*

Let us look at the promise: " God shall make you perfect, stablish, strengthen, settle you." The general meaning of the promise obviously is: God shall, notwithstanding, and even by means of these afflictions, promote your spiritual improvement, and add to your real happiness. All the figurative expressions are well fitted, and, with the exception of one of them,[1] frequently employed in the New Testament, to denote spiritual improvement and growth in holiness and comfort; and it has been supposed by many interpreters, that it is to no purpose to look for any specific meaning in each of these terms. They consider the promise as just a declaration, that through the preaching of God's word, the influence of his Spirit, and the overruling power of his providence, these afflictions should work together for their good, in the most extensive sense of the word, for making them really and, in the end, completely holy and happy, in entire conformity to the holy, holy, holy, ever-blessed One. We are disposed to think, however, that the apostle seldom heaps up words merely for the sake of emphasis, and that, in the passage before us, every one of the figurative expressions presents us with a distinct phase, as it were, of the blessings which God bestows on his people, under the afflictions, and by means of the afflictions, which

[1] Σθενώσει is one of the ἅπαξ λεγόμενα.

are connected with the assaults of the great adversary on them, and their resistance to these assaults.

It has been ingeniously supposed, that there is but one image in the whole passage, and that the different figurative expressions are connected representations of its different parts. Christians are supposed here, as in many places of the New Testament, to be represented as "God's building," "a holy temple,"[1] and the whole of their Christian improvement is termed their "edification" or building up. They are "settled," or the foundation is laid; then they are "strengthened," strong beams are fixed and massy pillars raised; then they are "stablished," the building is roofed and protected from the injuries of the weather; and finally, they are "perfected." Everything within and without is so fashioned, as to become a meet habitation for God through the Spirit. There is ingenuity enough here; but it is plain, if that had been the apostle's figure, the order of the expressions would have been reversed. The four expressions seem plainly to bring four distinct and unconnected figurative representations before the mind. Let us endeavour to ascertain their precise meaning.

(1.) *They shall be made perfect.*

God promises, first, that he will "make" Christians struggling with their great adversary "perfect." The word translated "make perfect" properly signifies to make fully ready, to put in full order, to complete. It is used of fitting nets by mending them for being employed, and of the wickedness of the wicked fitting them as "vessels of wrath" for being destroyed.[2] This is its meaning, when the apostle prays "the God of peace, who brought again from the dead our Lord Jesus, that great Shepherd of the sheep,

---

[1] 1 Cor. iii. 9; Eph. ii. 21, 22; 1 Pet. ii. 5.
[2] Matt. iv. 21; Rom. ix. 22.

by the blood of the everlasting covenant," to make Christians " perfect in every good work to do his will," [1]—that is, to fit them, by supplying what was wanting in them, for doing God's will in the performance of every good work; and when the Messiah, our High Priest, who must have somewhat to offer, is introduced as saying, " A body hast thou prepared (the same word as here) me," made ready for, fitted for me; and when the worlds are said to be " framed (the same word) by the word of God," prepared, fitted for the purpose they were meant to serve.[2] In the passage before us, viewed as a promise to those who were called to conflict with an adversary, with whom in themselves they were very ill able to cope (and such general words must almost always be modified in their meaning and limited in their reference by the context), its meaning plainly is: God will, by supplying all your defects, fit you for the conflict to which you are called. He will by his word and Spirit qualify you for all that you shall be called on to do and suffer in the combat. His grace shall be sufficient for you. He does not send you unarmed to the field of combat. He gives you the whole armour of God,[3] " that ye may be able to stand against the wiles of the devil." He gives you the girdle of truth, the breastplate of righteousness, the sandals of the preparation of the gospel of peace, the helmet of salvation, and the sword of the Spirit, which is the word of God; and he not only lays them down before you, but by his Spirit he enables you to put them on, and teaches you so to prove the various parts of this celestial panoply, as that in the day of battle you may turn them to good account in the combat with the alien and his armies. He will give you all the wisdom, all the courage, and all the energy that are necessary for successful conflict. This promise seems addressed to the Christian looking forward to the combat.

[1] Heb. xiii. 21.   [2] Heb. x. 5, xi. 3.   [3] Eph. vi. 13-18.

The succeeding ones seem to refer to him when engaged in it.

(2.) *They shall be established.*

The second promise is, that God will "stablish" them. To stablish is to keep firm and stedfast. The Christian is afraid that he shall fall before his enemies,—that he shall not be able to keep his ground,—that he shall lose courage,—that he shall be turned back, with shame to himself and disgrace to his Lord and his cause,—that he shall prove an apostate,—that he shall not be able to hold fast the faith and its profession,—that he shall find it difficult to stand, far more to withstand,—that he shall make "shipwreck of faith and a good conscience," and, instead of being crowned as a victor, shall be put to shame as a recreant and castaway; but God meets these not unnatural apprehensions with the promise—I will stablish thee, I will keep thee from falling. The promise in the Second Epistle to the Thessalonians (iii. 3) seems quite parallel with this: "The Lord is faithful who shall stablish you, and preserve you from evil," rather from the evil one.[1] It is just the evangelical version of the Old Testament oracle: "Fear thou not; for I am with thee: be not dismayed; for I am thy God: .... I will help thee; yea, I will uphold thee with the right hand of my righteousness." He will "put his law into their hearts;" and then, notwithstanding all the attempts of their spiritual enemies, "they shall not depart from him."[2]

(3.) *They shall be strengthened.*

The third promise is, God will "strengthen" you. In the day of spiritual conflict he will enable them not only to stand, but to withstand; not only to keep their ground, but to press forward; not merely to defend themselves, but to

---

[1] Τοῦ πονηροῦ.   [2] Isa. xli. 10; Jer. xxxii. 40.

attack their enemies. "Out of weakness they shall" so "wax strong," as to "turn to flight the armies of the aliens." He will, by the effectual operation of his Spirit, through the instrumentality of his word, render the very efforts of their enemies to subdue them the means of calling forth into action a power of which they themselves were before unconscious, so as to compel them to say, with a new feeling of the depth of truth contained in the words, "When I am weak, then I am strong." Thus does "he give power to the faint, and to them who have no might he increaseth strength;" so that, though "even the youths faint and be weary, and the young men utterly fall," they, "waiting on the Lord, renew their strength; they mount up with wings as eagles; run, and are not weary; and they walk, and are not faint."[1] Thus it is, that amid the infirmities of his people "the power of Christ rests on them." They are made "strong in the Lord and in the power of his might;" and they "go in the strength of the Lord God, making mention of his righteousness, even of His only." "In the Lord, in whom they have righteousness, they also have strength."

(4.) *They shall be settled.*

The fourth and last promise is, "God will settle you." The word rendered "settle" is equivalent to make to rest securely, as a building on its foundations. The idea is, The design of these attacks of Satan is to drive you from the foundation, Jesus, and the truth as it is in Jesus; but God will render all these attempts ineffectual by his preparing you for them, stablishing you, and strengthening you under them, and, by enabling you to stand and withstand, he will make them the means of fixing you firmer on that foundation than ever. Such afflictions, instead of pro-

[1] Isa. xl. 29-31.

ducing apostasy, produce perseverance. "We glory in tribulation," that is, suffering in the cause of Christ, produced by the influence of the adversary,—"knowing that tribulation worketh patience," that is, perseverance, increased attachment to the Saviour and his cause. Satan desires to have Christians that he may sift them, and scatter them to the winds of heaven; but through the grace of the Father and the prayers of the Son their faith fails not, and to their own increased comfort and confirmed hope, by this very sifting they are proved to be not chaff, but the Lord's wheat, which is to be "gathered into his garner, while the chaff is burned with fire unquenchable." These afflictions both prove the soundness of the foundation, leading the Christian more narrowly to examine it, and prove, too, that he is really built on the foundation. The Christian who is enabled to triumph over temptation is stronger than if he had never been tempted; and there is no such firm believer as he who has battled with and fairly overcome, through Him who loves him, all the doubts which the father of lies, and that most skilful sophister, the evil heart of unbelief under his influence, can suggest to the mind. This is the great object of God, to settle his people on the foundation, the rock, Christ. "This," to borrow some of the beautiful thoughts of Leighton, " is the only thing that perfects and strengthens us. There is a wretched natural independency in us. We are apt to rest on something in ourselves. When we do so, we build castles in the air, imagining buildings without a foundation. A battle with our spiritual enemies will show us there is no safe footing there. If we do not seek firmer ground, we shall assuredly fall. Never shall we find safety, heart-peace, and progress in holiness, till we are driven from everything in ourselves, to make him all our strength, 'our rock, our fortress, our buckler, the horn of our salvation, and our high tower,'—to do nothing, to attempt nothing, to hope for nothing, but in him. Then shall we find his fulness and all-sufficiency, and be 'more than conquerors through him who hath loved us.' Few things in Christian experience are more employed by God to bring his people into this state of settledness on the rock Christ than the afflictions rising out of the assaults of the evil one, and that resistance to these assaults which are accomplished in the whole Christian brotherhood in the world. Thus can God bring good out of evil; strengthen faith by what was meant to overthrow it; increase the holiness and comfort of his people by what was meant to involve them in guilt and depravity and misery; make the wrath of devils as well as men to praise him, while he restrains the remainder thereof. 'He shall deliver them out of the mouth of the lion;' ay, 'he shall deliver them from every evil work,' every mischievous device, every malignant attempt of their adversary or his agents, earthly or infernal, 'and preserve them unto his heavenly kingdom.'"

Such appears to be the import of the promise; such seems to be the perfecting, stablishing, strengthening, settling, of which the apostle speaks. To use the words of the pious and learned Bengel, "He shall perfect (that no defect may remain in you), he shall stablish (that ye may be guilty of no backsliding), he shall strengthen (that ye may overcome every adverse power), and thus he shall settle you:" establish you more firmly than ever on the foundation, by those very means which were intended to remove you from it, and to convert into an unsightly heap of ruins all the holy dispositions and all the glorious hopes which, like a stately edifice, "polished after the similitude of a palace," rested on that foundation.

(5.) *He who does all this for them is God.*

This perfecting, and stablishing, and strengthening, and settling, are just what the Christian needs when called to combat, "not with flesh and blood, but with the rulers of the darkness of this world, with spiritual wickedness in high places;" and the assurance of obtaining it is well fitted to encourage and comfort him. But to realize this encouragement and consolation, he must "know and be sure" who it is that hath promised thus to perfect, and stablish, and strengthen, and settle. Such a promise from the most accomplished of men, from the highest of angels, from all good men and all good angels together, would sound like bitter mockery; but it is God who, by the mouth of his holy apostle, declares that he will perfect and stablish, strengthen and settle, the Christian combating with his subtle, active, cruel, and powerful spiritual adversary. And deeply as he feels how much is wanting in him for the conflict; how ready, how sure, if left to himself, to turn back in the day of battle; how powerless he is in the grasp of the strong man, the terrible one; how much in danger, so far as depends on anything in himself, of being permanently moved from his stedfastness, and torn from that rock of salvation on which the whole fabric of his holiness and spiritual enjoyment and hopes rests: this is enough to sustain and encourage him.

HE can do all that he has here promised. He is infinite in power; and infinite, too, in wisdom. No enemy so powerful but he can restrain and subdue him; no enemy so crafty but he can circumvent and disappoint him. No Christian so weak but he can make him strong; no Christian so foolish but he can make him wise. Is anything too hard for the Lord? To the Christian struggling with his spiritual foes, with a heart failing for fear and an arm falling down with weariness, is addressed the words of the prophet: "Why sayest thou, O Jacob, and speakest, O Israel, My way is hid from the Lord, and my judgment is passed over from my God? Hast thou not known, hast thou not heard, that the everlasting God, the Lord, the Creator of the ends of the earth, fainteth not, neither is weary? there is no searching of his understanding."[1] There is no situation in which, in resisting your adversary, you can be placed, however full of painful exertion, anxiety, and suffering, in which he cannot give support, from which he cannot give deliverance.

Then he is disposed to do all that he has promised. He is "rich in mercy;" he is "ready to forgive." The love that dictated the promise secures the accomplishment. "If ye, being evil, know how to give good gifts to your children, how much more shall your Father in heaven"—who is not evil, who is good, only good, good continually, infinitely benignant, whose nature as well as name is love,—how much more shall he "give good gifts to his children" when they ask them? But this truth, so richly fraught with encouragement, will come more fully before us when we come to speak of the adjuncts of the promise, or of the manner in which it is given.

Finally, here, he who gives the promise will most assuredly perform it. He can do it; for he is infinitely powerful and wise: he is disposed to do it; for he is infinitely kind and compassionate: he will do it; for he is inviolably faithful. He can do all things, but he cannot lie. Nothing is impossible with him but the denying himself. "He is not a man, that he should lie; neither the son of man, that he should repent: hath he said, and shall he not do it? hath he spoken, and shall he not make it good?" No: "heaven and earth shall pass away;" we know they shall

[1] Isa. xl. 27, 28.

pass away; "but one iota, one tittle" of his declarations, "shall not pass till all be fulfilled."[1] As certainly as God is powerful and wise, merciful and faithful, so certain is it that he will not abandon the Christian resisting the subtle, active, powerful, cruel adversary of his soul; but will "make him perfect, stablish, strengthen, settle" him, by the very means which were intended for his spiritual ruin, thus "disappointing the devices of the crafty one, taking the wise in his own cunning, and turning the counsel of the froward headlong,"[2]—saving the poor from the mouth of the devourer, and rescuing them out of the hand of him who is mightier than they.[3]

Such is the promise; and is it not full of encouragement to the Christian amid the privations, and exertions, and sufferings to which the resistance of his great adversary may expose him? Is it not well fitted to fill his heart with that joy of the Lord which is the strength of his people; to make him thank God, and take courage, saying, "If God be with me, who can be against me? Rejoice not against me, O mine enemy: though I fall, I shall arise; though I sit in darkness, the Lord shall be a light to me. Greater is he who is with me than all that can be against me. Greater is he that is in us than he who is in the world."[4]

[1] Num. xxiii. 19; Matt. v. 18. [2] Job v. 12.

[3] There is much emphasis given to the promise by the insertion of the pronoun αὐτὸς between the nominative ὁ Θεὸς πάσης χάριτος and the verbs belonging to it, though it is not noticed in our version. It was just a thing for Bengel to notice. "Αὐτὸς, ipse—vos tantum vigilate et resistite hosti: reliqua Deus præstabit. Conf. אן Josh. xiii. 6; conf. 1, ej. cap." Forster, in his elaborate work, *On the Apostolical Authority of the Epistle to the Hebrews*, supposes that the insertion of αὐτὸς marks reference to ch. xiii. 20, 21 of that epistle, to which he conceives that Peter refers in his second epistle (iii. 15, 16).

[4] Rom. viii. 1; Mic. vii. 8; 1 John iv. 4.

§ 2. *The encouragement contained in the adjuncts of the promise.*

But even this is not all the encouragement and comfort which this passage is fitted to administer to the struggling Christian warrior. The adjuncts of the promise have the same character with the promise itself; its manner as well as its matter is full of consolation. This is the next subject which calls for our consideration. What encouragement to him who resists the adversary, to reflect that He who has given to him such "exceeding great and precious promises" is "the God of all grace," the God "who has called him," "called him to his eternal glory in or by Christ Jesus," called him to this glory "after he has suffered a while!" These are fruitful themes, respecting which our meditation should be profitable as well as sweet, on which "our hearts should indite a good matter, and our tongues be as the pen of a ready writer."

(1.) *The God who has promised this is "the God of all grace."*

The first consolatory and encouraging consideration here brought forward is, that the God who has promised these blessings is the "God of all grace." The proper signification of grace is kindness, the disposition to communicate happiness; but the term is also often employed to denote those actions or gifts in which this disposition is manifested. In both of these closely related significations of the word, God is the "God of all grace."

He is the all-gracious God. His name is "the Lord, the Lord God, merciful and gracious, long-suffering, and abundant in goodness and truth." His nature as well as his name is love. "Fury," malignity, passion, "is not in him;" and from the benignity of his nature, he is "keeping mercy for thousands, forgiving iniquity, transgression, and sin." "This is his name, and this is his memorial to all generations." From his perfect holiness he cannot but hate sin, and punish the sinner " who goes on in his trespasses;" but he has "no pleasure in the death of the wicked." On the contrary, He " wills him to turn from his evil ways, that he may live," be saved ; while he is "ready to forgive," and " delights in mercy," in reference to those who, by the faith of the truth, are " in Christ Jesus." Every obstacle which prevents the manifestation of his love to them is removed. " As a father pities his children, he pities them." " A woman may forget her sucking child, she may not have compassion on the son of her womb ;" but he never can forget them, and he can never remember them but with loving-kindness and tender mercy. And he rests in his love to them. He is " Jehovah, who changes not ;" " the same yesterday, to-day, and for ever." " The mountains shall depart, and the hills be removed ; but God's loving-kindness shall not depart from them, neither shall the covenant of his peace be removed" by the Lord God, " who has mercy on them."

Is this his character? Then assuredly, amid all their afflictions, his children, " the brotherhood," may have " abundant consolation and good hope." If he has the power—and who can doubt that ?—he must sustain, and comfort, and deliver. He can never allow them to become the prey of His and their adversary, who, "like a roaring lion, goeth about, seeking whom he may devour." " He cannot deny himself;" and if he cannot do this, he cannot but " deliver them out of the mouth of this lion,"—he cannot but deliver them " from every evil work, and preserve them to his heavenly kingdom."[1] Being " the all-gracious God," he will assuredly " make them perfect, stablish, and strengthen them."

[1] Ex. xxxiv. 6, 7 ; Ezek. xviii. 23, 32 ; Isa. liv. 10 ; 2 Tim. iv. 18.

God is also the God of all grace in the sense of benefit. He is the author and bestower of all true happiness. When he is termed "the God of all consolation," the meaning is, all true comfort comes from him, and he bestows on his people abundance of all they need. When he is termed "the God of peace," the meaning is, that he is the author and bestower of true peace. So, when he is called "the God of all grace," the meaning may be, all blessings come from him; He is their ever-full, ever-flowing fountain, and to his people he communicates them, in all the variety and abundance that their wants can require or their capacities receive. He "blesses them with all spiritual and heavenly blessings." What can he want, all whose need the God of grace, of all grace, promises to supply, "according to his glorious riches?" He can, he will, fit for the combat; he can, he will, sustain during the conflict; he can, he will, make victorious in the conflict; he can, he will, reward after the conflict. If there be any necessary blessing not included in "all grace," then the struggling Christian might have some cause to despond; but when Jehovah, "God Almighty" (rather all-sufficient), says, I am "the God of all grace," and "my grace is sufficient for thee," well may he "glory in tribulation," "count it all joy to be brought into manifold temptations," and sing with the apostle, "I have all, and abound; having nothing, I possess all things; I am complete in him. Most gladly will I glory in my infirmities, that the power" of the God of all grace "may rest on me: though troubled on every side, I am not distressed; though perplexed, I am not in despair; though persecuted, I am not forsaken; though cast down, I am not destroyed."[1] The God of all grace has pledged his word and oath to me that I shall want no good thing; and what would I have, what could I have more?

[1] 2 Cor. i. 3; Eph. i. 3; Col. iv. 19; Gen. xvii. 1; 2 Cor. xii. 9.

(2.) *This God of all grace has "called" the Christian "in Christ Jesus."*

A second consoling and encouraging consideration is, this God of all grace has called the Christian in Christ Jesus. The "called" is one of the distinguishing denominations of true Christians: in its fuller form, "the called of Christ Jesus," "the called according to God's purpose and grace," "the called who obtain the promised eternal inheritance;" and their calling is designated "a high calling," "a holy calling," a "calling not according to works, but according to God's own purpose and grace, given us in Christ Jesus before the world began." All mankind are called to God's service; and all mankind, to whom revelation comes, are "called" by God to the enjoyment of his favour, as well as to obedience to his will; but in the case of the great majority, they are "called" in vain, ineffectually called. They will not listen to the call; they very imperfectly understand it; they obstinately refuse to obey it. And were it not that the sovereign kindness of God accompanies in certain cases the call of providence and revelation with the effectual operation of his Spirit, the outward call with the inward call, this would be universally the case with mankind. All would continue in a state of ignorance, unbelief, disobedience, and alienation from God. All men would always be what all by nature are—"without God in the world."

But in the case of "a multitude that no man can number," God, in the exercise of his sovereign mercy, accompanies the call of his word and providence with the special influence of his Spirit; so that the calling is not in vain, but effectual. "It comes not in word merely, but in power, with the Holy Ghost, and much assurance." The sinner hears the call of the God of all grace; he understands it, he believes it, he is sweetly constrained to comply with it. This calling is the same thing which the apostle styles "election according to the foreknowledge and purpose of God," by which Christians are spiritually separated from the rest of mankind, and put in possession of the blessings which flow from the shedding of the blood of sprinkling, which "speaketh better things than that of Abel." This "effectual calling," which is one of the characteristic blessings of the Christian salvation, and is the gate by which we enter into the enjoyment of all the rest, is well described in our Shorter Catechism as " a work of God's Spirit, whereby, convincing us of our sin and misery, enlightening our minds in the knowledge of Christ, and renewing our wills, he doth persuade and enable us to embrace Jesus Christ, as he is freely offered to us in the gospel." "This is a call," as Leighton beautifully says, "that goes deeper than the ear, a word spoken home to within, a touch of the Spirit of God on the heart, which hath a magnetic power to draw it, so that it cannot choose but follow, and yet freely and sweetly chooses to follow; doth most gladly open to let in Jesus Christ, and his sweet government, upon his own terms; takes him, and all the reproaches and troubles that can come with him; and well it may, seeing, beyond a little passing trouble, abiding eternal glory."

This calling is said to be "in Christ Jesus," that is, either 'persons standing in a peculiar relation to Christ Jesus, identified as it were with him, are its subjects;' or, "through Christ Jesus," through his mediation, in consequence of his atonement, by his Spirit and word. It is probably the last of these that is here the apostle's idea. Men are called by the Father through the Son. This fundamental blessing was enjoyed by those to whom the apostle wrote. The God of all grace had called them out of darkness into his marvellous light; out of subjection to sin, and the world, and the god of this world, into the glorious liberty of his children. The communication of this blessing is a proof that God loves with a special love the individual on whom it is conferred; and a distinct intimation, that all the other blessings of that salvation, of which this is a constituent part, shall in due time be bestowed. The fact of their being called by the God of all grace, involves in it satisfactory evidence that their spiritual adversary shall not ultimately prevail against them, that their afflictions cannot be permanent, and that they shall be made conducive to their final salvation. Listen to the Apostle Paul's development of this argument: "We know that all things"—he is referring to the afflictions which are accomplished in the brotherhood in this world—"We know that all things work together for good to them that love God; who are the called according to his purpose. For whom he did foreknow, he also did predestinate to be conformed to the image of his Son, that he might be the first-born among many brethren. Moreover, whom he did predestinate, them he also called; and whom he called, them he also justified; and whom he justified, them he also glorified. What shall we then say to these things? If God be for us, who can be against us?"[1] Can the wiles or the ferocity of the roaring lion, the fraud or the fury of the great adversary, accomplish OUR ruin, who are the called, the called of the God of all grace?

(3.) *The God of all grace has called Christians to his eternal glory.*

A third consolatory and encouraging consideration is, that "the God of all grace has called the Christian to his eternal glory." The phrase, "called unto God's eternal glory," may either signify, called in order eternally to promote the glory of God, or called to enjoy or participate in the eternal glory of God. In either case, the words

[1] Rom. viii. 28-31.

express a truth, and a truth well fitted to comfort and encourage Christians while struggling with their spiritual enemies.

The calling of the Christian, and the conferring on him all the blessings of the Christian salvation which grow out of it, have for their ultimate object, like everything else in the new creation as in the old, the manifestation of God, the illustration of his excellence, the display of his glory. This idea is very finely brought out by the apostle, in the first chapter of his Epistle to the Ephesians: "The God and Father of our Lord Jesus Christ hath blessed us with all spiritual blessings in heavenly places in Christ; according as he hath chosen us in him before the foundation of the world, that we should be holy and without blame before him in love : having predestinated us unto the adoption of children by Jesus Christ to himself, according to the good pleasure of his will, *to the praise of the glory of his grace,* wherein he hath made us accepted in the Beloved : in whom we have redemption through his blood, the forgiveness of sins, according to the riches of his grace; wherein he hath abounded towards us in all wisdom and prudence; having made known to us the mystery of his will, according to his good pleasure, which he hath purposed in himself: that, in the dispensation of the fulness of the times, he might gather together into one all things in Christ, both which are in heaven and which are on earth, even in him : in whom also we have obtained an inheritance, being predestinated according to the purpose of him who worketh all things according to the counsel of his will; that we should be *to the praise of his glory,* who first trusted in Christ. In whom ye also trusted," or rather have received an inheritance, " after that ye heard the word of truth, the gospel of your salvation : in whom also, after that ye believed, ye were sealed with that Holy Spirit of promise, which is the earnest of our inheritance," both ours and yours, " until the redemption of the purchased possession, *to the praise of his glory*."[1] Were the Christian to be allowed to fall a prey to his spiritual enemies, his calling, instead of being to God's eternal glory, would give cause to the adversary to speak reproachfully, saying, "The Lord was not able to bring them into the land which he had promised them." But Jehovah is determined, even through means of those babes and sucklings whom he calls, to perfect praise to himself, and to " still the enemy and the avenger." He has called them to be his people, and " formed them for himself, and they shall show forth his praise." His power, and wisdom, and faithfulness, and kindness, shall be illustriously displayed in the salvation of all the called ones. " His counsel shall stand, and he will do all his pleasure."[2] This is truth, important truth; truth naturally enough expressed by the words, and truth well fitted to encourage and strengthen the Christian when conflicting with his great adversary.

Yet we are inclined to think the other view of the words expresses the apostle's thought. He has called them to a participation of his eternal glory. The glory of God sometimes signifies the approbation of God. Thus the Jews are said to " receive honour (the same word) one of another, and not to seek the honour that cometh from God only." Thus all are said to " have sinned and come short of the glory of God;" and believers, justified through believing, are represented as "exulting in the hope of that glory," that approbation, of which they had come short, and in which true glory and happiness consist. Here, as in some other places, there can be little doubt that " the glory of God " is the celestial blessedness; but still it is the celestial blessedness in a particular aspect. The glory of God is that which

[1] Eph. i. 3-14.
[2] Num. xiv. 16 ; Ps. viii. 2 ; Isa. xliii. 21, xlvi. 10.

makes God glorious; his eternal glory, that which makes him eternally glorious. Now, what is it which makes God glorious? His own inherent excellences, especially his moral excellences, his righteousness and benignity; in one word, his holiness. He is "glorious in holiness." Now, the grand ultimate object of the calling of the Christian is, that he, to the highest degree of which his nature is capable, may be made a partaker of God's holiness, which is his glory. He is called to the fellowship as well as predestinated to be conformed to the image of God's dear Son, who is the "brightness of his glory and the express image of his person." It is the purpose of God in calling him, and in giving him the adoption of sons to which he has been predestinated, that he shall be holy as He, the holy, holy, holy One, is holy, perfect as he is perfect. It is his purpose, that in the kingdom of their Father, "the Father of lights," his called ones shall shine forth radiant with his light, glorious in his glory; and in the only sense in which eternity can be truly predicated of them, or of anything that belongs to them, that their glory shall be eternal, that "they shall shine as the brightness of the firmament, and as the stars for ever and ever." Now, no assault from Satan, no calamities, no afflictions, can prevent this glorious consummation; nay, all their afflictions will be found to have been but disciplinary means of preparing them for this grand result of all the divine dispensations to them—the making them "partakers of his holiness," which is his glory.[1]

(4.) *The afflictions are moderate in degree, short in duration, and form a part of the divine plan for their ultimate salvation.*

A fourth consolatory and encouraging consideration suggested, is derived from the peculiar character of the

[1] 1 Cor. i. 9; Rom. viii. 29; Heb. xii. 10.

afflictions to which the brotherhood are exposed: they are comparatively moderate in degree and short in duration; they form a part of the divine plan resulting from divine appointment; and they are closely connected with the great end of their calling—their coming to a participation in the glory of God. The God of all grace has called you to his eternal glory "after ye have suffered a while," or a little. These words, "after ye have suffered a while," have been closely connected by some with the clause that follows: "After ye have suffered a while, make you perfect, stablish, strengthen, settle you." The laws of the language would warrant either mode of connection; but it is plain that the promise is not one which is not to be fulfilled till Christians have suffered a while. The first promise refers to preparation for suffering, the two next to help under suffering, the last to the happy result of suffering. God calls his people to participate in his eternal glory, but not to participate in it "till they have suffered a while," or a little. The word may refer either to time or degree. In either case, a truth, and a consolatory one, is expressed. The afflictions to which the brotherhood are exposed in this world are comparatively moderate in degree. They are often heavy when compared with those of other men, and are often felt as heavy by those who bear them, making them breathe out, "I am oppressed; undertake for me." They are always lighter than they easily might be,—always lighter than strict justice would require them to be. Everything to a sinner, short of the severest suffering he is capable of, is mercy. God does not, however, "suffer them to be tempted above that they are able, but will with the temptation also make a way of escape, that they may be able to bear it;" and especially they are moderate when compared with the "far more exceeding and eternal weight of glory" which is to follow them.

They are limited in duration. Seasons of very severe affliction are not ordinarily of long duration; they bear usually but a small proportion to the whole of human life. How inconceivably small a proportion do they bear to the eternity of coming glory! Surely, then, whether he look on their measure or their period, their degree or their duration, the Christian may well "reckon the sufferings of the present time not worthy to be compared with the glory which shall be revealed in him."

Then these afflictions are a part of the divine plan. It is as much a part of the divine plan to put them in possession of the fellowship of his eternal glory after they have suffered a while, as to put them in possession of it at all. "It is the Father's good pleasure to give them the kingdom;" but it is equally the Father's good pleasure that "through much tribulation they enter into that kingdom." It is his determination that they "shall reign with Christ;" but it is equally his determination that they "shall first suffer with him."[1]

And finally, here, this connection, though an appointed one, is not an arbitrary one. The glory not only comes after the sufferings, but it is in some sense the result of them. Afflictions are, under the divine blessing, appropriate means of sanctification; of forming the character which fits for the holy happiness of heaven, "that prepared place for a prepared people." The truth on this subject is strikingly stated by the apostle from his own experience: "Though our outward man perish, yet the inward man is renewed day by day. For our light affliction, which is but for a moment, worketh for us a far more exceeding and eternal weight of glory; while we look not at the things which are seen, but at the things which are not seen: for the things which are seen are temporal; but the things

[1] Luke xii. 32; Acts xiv. 32; Rom. viii. 17.

which are unseen are eternal." "Who would refuse to suffer a while, a little while, anything outward or inward He sees fit? How soon shall this be over, past and overpaid in the very entry, the beginning of that glory that shall never end!"[1]

IV. CONCLUSION.

It now only remains that we shortly illustrate the concluding clause of the verse, which is very generally considered as a doxology. The words are, "To him be glory and dominion for ever and ever, Amen." The word *be* is inserted by our translators, who consider the clause as an ascription of glory and dominion to God. The word *is* might as well have been inserted, in which case it is an assertion that glory and dominion belong to God. Had the preceding verse been a prayer or a thanksgiving, the words would likely have been meant as a doxology; but following a promise, they seem to state something corresponding to the promise. " His is the glory for ever and ever," and therefore he can confer on his people that glory to which he has called them, after they have suffered a while. He has not only an essential glory peculiar to himself, and of which no creature can participate: He has a communicable glory,—" the riches of his glory," as the apostle expresses it, by the bestowing of which on others he can make them glorious. He is "the Father of glory," as well as the God of all grace, who can give not only grace, but also glory. And as "glory for ever and ever" belongs to Him who has "called Christians to his eternal glory after they have suffered a while," so "dominion" (a word denoting both power and authority) "for ever and ever" belongs to Him, who, as the God of grace, promises that he

[1] Leighton. 2 Cor. iv. 16, 17.

will make perfect, stablish, strengthen, and settle his people. He has power and right to do whatever pleases him, and therefore can do what he has said. "His is the greatness, and the power, and the glory, and the victory, and the majesty: for all in the heaven and in the earth is his; his is the kingdom, and he is exalted as head above all. Both riches and honour come of Him, and he reigneth over all; and in his hand is power and might; and in his hand it is to make great, and give strength to all." He who has glory for ever and ever, can give to his called that fellowship of his eternal glory which he has promised; and he whose is the dominion, the power, and the authority for ever, is "of power to establish his people according to the gospel and the preaching of Jesus Christ." He is "able to do exceeding abundantly above all that we can ask or think, according to the power that worketh in us." He can "make them perfect in every good work to do his will, working in them that which is well-pleasing in his sight." He is "able to keep them from falling, and to present them faultless before the presence of his glory with exceeding joy."[1] It deserves notice that the apostle concludes his epistle as he began it, by turning the minds of those to whom he wrote to God, and to the same features in the divine character—those which make him a fit object of our love and dependence—his kindness and his might. In the beginning he speaks of Him as the God of abundant mercy, who has power to keep his people for the inheritance he has destined for them, and for which he is preparing them; and here he speaks of Him as the God of all grace, whose is the dominion, to whom all the power and authority rightfully belong.

The apostle adds an emphatic "Amen"—a word, in reference to statement, expressive of firm faith; in reference to

[1] 1 Chron. xxix. 11, 12; Jude 24.

promises, of confident hope and ardent desire. In the first instance it is equivalent to, 'It is most certainly so; this is the very truth most sure.' In the second, 'I trust it shall be so; I desire that it may be so.' Such, then, is the comfort and encouragement by which the apostle seeks to strengthen the brotherhood amid the afflictions which must be accomplished in them in the world.

If anything extrinsic could add force to the sentiments expressed in these words—sentiments so instinct with life, so fitted to impart spiritual vigour to the exhausted spirit of the Christian, worn out with watching the wiles and resisting the attacks of his great adversary—it is to be found in the circumstances of him who uttered them. "Truth," such truth, "from his lips prevails with double sway." The word of warning, the word of instruction, the word of promise, the word of encouragement, come all with peculiar force from the lips of him to whom, on a most memorable occasion, the Master said, " Simon, Simon, Satan hath desired to have you, that he may sift you as wheat. But I have prayed for thee, that thy faith fail not; and when thou art converted, strengthen thy brethren."

He speaks the things which he knew, he testifies what he had seen and felt. He had disregarded the Master's warning, and the consequence had been shameful discomfiture in his conflict with the great enemy; aggravated sin, followed by deep penitence, and confirmed attachment to the cause of Christ. He had found how faithful he is who had promised, and how able he is to do as he had said. He had preserved him from apostasy when on its very brink; and notwithstanding the partial success of his spiritual adversary, he had " stablished, strengthened, settled" him,— " set him on a rock, and established his goings."

How emphatic the warning, " Your enemy, the devil, goeth about, like a roaring lion, seeking whom he may devour," from him who had experienced both his wiles and his ferocity, and would bear about with him the scars of his wounds while he lived!

How forcible the injunction, " Resist the devil," and, that you may do so, " Be sober, and wakeful, and stedfast in the faith," from him who, notwithstanding repeated warnings, did not watch and pray, and therefore entered into temptation, and fell before it, and whose failure in faith had brought him so near destruction and despair—had made him fall into sin, and but for the God of all grace would have made him fall into perdition!

How consoling and encouraging the promise, " The God of all grace, who hath called you unto his eternal glory by Christ Jesus, shall make you perfect, stablish, strengthen, settle you; His is the glory and the dominion for ever and ever," from him whom the God of all grace, in the person of his Son, had so " out of weakness made strong,"—so strengthened in the faith as to make him one of the chief pillars of the Church while he lived; and when he died, enabled him to glorify God, confessing, amid the protracted tortures of a peculiarly cruel martyrdom, the Master whom once he had thrice denied!

We cannot help thinking that the Saviour's words, "When thou art converted, strengthen thy brethren," were ringing in the apostle's ears when he wrote these words. And certainly never were addressed to the tempted, struggling, worn-out, afflicted Christian soldier, words more full of warning, instruction, consolation, and encouragement. They have, by the accompanying power of the Spirit of Jesus, strengthened many a brother. They have been " words in season" to many a tempted, afflicted, perplexed, downcast, weary heart; and will continue to be so as long as these afflictions continue to be accomplished in the brotherhood in the world.

Oh may we, my brethren, through their means, be made humble and cautious, vigilant and believing, "stedfast and unmoveable," rooted and built up in Christ, strengthened with all might, according to his glorious power, unto all patience and long-suffering with joyfulness; giving thanks to the Father, who hath made us meet to be partakers of the inheritance of the saints in light, who hath delivered us from the power of darkness, and hath translated us unto the kingdom of his dear Son; so that, full of the strength which is the result of the joy of the Lord, glorying in tribulation, and rejoicing in hope of the glory of God, we may "walk worthy of the Lord unto all pleasing, being fruitful in every good work, and increasing in the knowledge of God."[1] "Consider what has been said, and the Lord give you understanding in all things."

[1] Col. i. 10-13.

DISCOURSE XXIV.

POSTSCRIPT OF THE EPISTLE.

"By Silvanus, a faithful brother unto you (as I suppose), I have written briefly, exhorting and testifying that this is the true grace of God wherein ye stand. The church that is at Babylon, elected together with you, saluteth you: and so doth Marcus my son. Greet ye one another with a kiss of charity. Peace be with you all that are in Christ Jesus. Amen."—1 Pet. v. 12-14.

"All Scripture is given by inspiration of God," and "all Scripture," too, "is profitable, for doctrine, for reproof, for correction, for instruction in righteousness; that the man of God may be perfect, throughly furnished unto every good work." In the mines of Peru there are veins of peculiar riches, and even their rubbish is valuable. In the Holy Scriptures there are portions of peculiar importance, excellence, and usefulness, but there is nothing trivial, nothing valueless in them. The superficial thinker may indeed find it difficult, it may be impossible, for him to derive instruction or improvement from many passages of Scripture, and may on this account rashly call in question their divine origin, or indulge in reflections against the divine wisdom, for allowing such passages a place in the inspired volume; but it is his own imbecility, or ignorance, or inattention, that is wholly to blame: for it may be safely affirmed, that there is no passage of Scripture respecting which the pious, diligent, docile inquirer cannot easily see that it may have served, or may yet serve, some important and useful purpose; and that there are very few from which, after serious consideration, he cannot draw for himself lessons which may be turned to account for the guidance of his conduct and the improvement of his character.

To be able to extract from what have been called the barren, from what ought to be called the less exuberant, passages of Scripture, the instruction, and warning, and reproof, and consolation which they are intended and fitted to communicate, is a talent which every Christian should be desirous of acquiring, as, without the possession and employment of it, a considerable part of those Scriptures which are "able to make men wise to salvation," will be utterly useless to him; and it is not one of the least important duties of a public teacher of Christianity, to instruct his audience in the best way of extracting spiritual improvement from this class of Scripture passages : on the one hand guarding them against that passion for allegory which leads men to make the plainest statements of the sacred writers the vehicle of the dreams of their own imagination, thus converting a divine oracle into a human figment; and, on the other, showing how important purposes are served by what at first sight may seem inappropriate and unnecessary statements, and how replete such passages, when viewed in their connection and design, often are with religious and moral instruction.

The subject of to-day's discourse, the postscript of the First Epistle of the Apostle Peter, belongs to the class of Scripture passages of which we have been speaking. It is not indeed to be compared, in point of intrinsic importance, deep personal interest, and extensive usefulness, with the admirable doctrinal and practical discussions by which it is preceded, and which for a considerable time past have not unpleasantly nor unprofitably, I trust, formed the subject of our consideration, when we have come together on the first day of the week, to wait on the "doctrine of the apostles;" but it is far indeed from being unimportant, uninteresting, or useless. And if it want many of the attractions which belong to them, it will be found to have attractions peculiar to itself. It is with the word as it is with the works of God. "There is one glory in the sun, and another glory in the moon, and another glory in the stars; for one star differeth from another star in glory." Let us look at the passage a little more closely, that we may perceive its meaning and ascertain its use.

It obviously forms a postscript to the epistle, which, as a doctrinal and hortatory address, is most appropriately and gracefully concluded in the 11th verse. This postscript is occupied with recapitulation, salutation, exhortation, and benediction. The recapitulation is contained in the 12th verse; the salutation in the 13th; the exhortation in the first clause, and the benediction in the last clause, of the 14th. Let us attend to them briefly in their order.

I. RECAPITULATION.

It has been supposed by some interpreters of high name that the 12th verse has in it nothing recapitulatory, and that the epistle referred to in it is not that which the apostle had just finished, but one that he had sent to the same churches on some former occasion. This supposition is an entirely gratuitous one. It is not required by the words, though, were it otherwise supported, the words might easily be reconciled with it. But there is no trace in Scripture or in ecclesiastical history of the apostle having written such an epistle; and there is satisfactory evidence that he did not write it, for he terms an epistle which he subsequently addressed to these churches, his *second* epistle: "This second epistle, beloved, I now write unto you; in both which I stir up your pure minds by way of remembrance."

The recapitulation refers to three things: the *subject* of the epistle, and the duty of Christians in reference to it; the *form* of it, a testimony and an exhortation, and a brief testimony and exhortation; the testimony that "the grace of God," which is the great subject of the epistle, is "the true grace of God," and the exhortation to stand, with regard to that grace; and finally, the *mode* of writing or transmitting the epistle, "By Silvanus, a faithful brother."

CHAP. I. THE SUBJECT OF THE EPISTLE.

§ 1. *The grace of God.*

"The grace of God" properly signifies the kindness, the free favour of God, as a principle in the divine mind; but is often employed to signify the deeds of kindness, the gifts and the benefits, in which this principle finds expression. It has been common to interpret the phrase here as equivalent to the gospel, the revelation of God's grace; and the apostle has been considered as affirming that the doctrine which those he was writing to had embraced, and to which they had adhered,—to use the Apostle Paul's phrase, "which they had received, and in which they stood,"—was the true gospel. But I doubt if the gospel is ever called "the grace of God" in the New Testament; and I equally doubt whether the words, thus understood, are an accurate statement of what this epistle actually contains. There are just two other passages in the New Testament in which "the grace of God" has been supposed to be a designation of the gospel. After stating the message of mercy which the ministers of reconciliation are called to deliver, the apostle in his Epistle to the Corinthians says, "We beseech you that ye receive not the grace," or this grace, "of God in vain."[1] The reference here is no doubt to the gospel; but the meaning of the phrase, "the grace of God," is plainly just this divine favour, this benefit which so expresses, and, as it were, embodies the divine grace. And in the Epistle to Titus, the same apostle states, that "the grace of God, bringing salvation to all," has been manifested, or has " appeared, teaching" those who apprehend it "to deny ungodliness and worldly lusts, and to live soberly, righteously, and godly in the present world."[2] The grace of God is often said to mean here the gospel, but the gospel is the manifestation, the revelation of this grace; and the truth taught in this passage is, that the free, sovereign mercy of God, when it is apprehended by the sinner, is the true principle of holiness in his heart and life. Let a man but really believe the grace of God, know it in truth, and he can be an ungodly, immoral man no longer. And as there is no satisfactory evidence that "the grace of God" is, properly speaking, a synonym for the gospel; so, on the other hand, if we read this epistle carefully, we shall not find that the sum of it is a testimony that the gospel, as received and held by the churches addressed, was the true gospel. That question is never mooted, but obviously throughout taken for granted. It would be a correct account of the Epistle to the Galatians, that it is a testimony that the gospel preached to them by the apostle was, in opposition to that preached to them by the Judaizing teachers, the true gospel; but the character of *this* epistle is in no degree controversial. What "the grace of God" in the passage before us means, will be most satisfactorily ascertained by inquiring what it means in the epistle of which it is represented as one of the great subjects. In the 10th verse of the first chapter the apostle speaks of "the grace" of which the ancient prophets prophesied as to come

[1] 2 Cor. vi. 1.   [2] Tit. ii. 11, 12.

to Christians; and in the 13th verse of that chapter, of "the grace which was to be brought to them at the revelation of Jesus Christ." That grace is obviously the Christian salvation in its heavenly and spiritual blessings, enjoyed partially on earth, fully in heaven. This grace is a leading subject of the epistle. The specific nature and transcendent glory and excellence of those blessings, in which the grace of God is manifested, are declared. Christians are represented as " elect, according to the foreknowledge of God;" spiritually separated from the world; sprinkled with the blood of Jesus Christ; begotten to a lively hope, to an inheritance incorruptible, undefiled, and that fadeth not away; as having tasted that the Lord is gracious, by being constituted a chosen generation, a spiritual temple, a royal priesthood, a holy nation, a peculiar people; as having 'salvation,' complete deliverance from all evil, laid up for them in heaven, where it is ready to be revealed in the last time, while they are kept for it by the power of God through faith, and on receiving which at the revelation of the Lord Jesus they will be glad with exceeding joy, rejoicing " with a joy that is unspeakable and full of glory." This is " the grace of God" concerning which the apostle here says he had given a testimony in the epistle which he has just closed.

§ 2. *The Christian's duty in reference to this grace:* "*to stand.*"

The other subject of the epistle, according to its author, is the Christian's duty in reference to this grace of God. At first sight, the words in which we think the duty of Christians in reference to the grace is very briefly but very comprehensively summed up, the words rendered by our translators "in which ye stand," seem merely to be a part of the testimony respecting " the grace of God," and to denote rather the Christian's privilege than his duty; just as when the Apostle Paul says, "By faith ye have entrance into this grace wherein ye stand."[1] But the two expressions are not the same. The phrase before us is literally "into which," which may mean, in reference to which, or until which, but which cannot mean strictly *in* which.[2] It deserves notice, that the apostle speaks of having exhorted in the epistle; but, as the words are ordinarily understood, there is no subject of exhortation referred to. In some ancient manuscripts the reading is not "ye stand," but "stand ye;"[3] expressive not of an assertion, but of a command or exhortation. If that reading be adopted—and it has been by some learned men—then the meaning is, "in reference to which grace of God," or until which grace of God is fully brought unto you, "stand ye." This most certainly is the sum and substance of the duty enjoined on Christians in this epistle: the standing firm amid all temptations in the faith and practice of Christianity with a reference to the grace of Christ, as persons who have already been made partakers of it, as persons who hope to be made partakers of it in far larger measure, and to obtain full participation of it through "standing." As the whole doctrinal subject of the epistle is the grace of Christ, so the whole practical subject of the epistle is the duty of Christians in reference to that grace; and the whole of that duty may be summed up in one word, "stand." The whole practical part of the epistle is just the development of the first exhortation: "Wherefore," that is, seeing ye have received these promises and hopes, "gird up the loins of your mind, be sober, and hope to the end, for the

---

[1] Rom. v. 2.

[2] Εἰς never can mean ἐν; as "motion towards" can never be identified with "rest in."

[3] Στῆτι. Lachmann.

grace that is to be brought unto you at the revelation of Jesus Christ: as obedient children, not fashioning yourselves according to the former lusts in your ignorance; but as he which hath called you is holy, so be ye holy in all manner of conversation." This is a favourite compendium of Christian duty with the Apostle Paul.[1]

CHAP. II. THE FORM OF THE EPISTLE.

It is a testimony and exhortation respecting the grace of God.

The apostle notices not only the subjects of the epistle, but the *form* in which he has treated them. His statements with regard to the grace of God take the form of a "testimony." His statements with regard to the Christian's duty take the form of "an exhortation:" "I have written, exhorting and testifying that this is the true grace of God, in reference to which do ye stand." We would naturally have expected, from "exhorting" coming before "testifying," that the sum of the exhortation should have preceded the sum of the testimony. But it is a common peculiarity in Hebrew composition, of which we have many instances in the New Testament, after dividing a subject into two parts, to take up the second part first, and then revert to the first. It would be more according to the usage of modern language to say, "Testifying that the grace of God, which ye as Christians enjoy, is the true grace of God, and exhorting you to stand in reference to this grace."

The testimony in the epistle respecting the grace of God which they enjoyed, that is, the blessings of the Christian salvation, is, that it is the true grace of God. The sum of that part of the epistle that is occupied with doctrine is just: Ye Christians are the *true* spiritual people of God, of whom the Jews, his ancient external people, were types; and the

[1] 1 Cor. xvi. 13; Gal. v. 1; Eph. vi. 14; Phil. iv. 1; 2 Thess. ii. 15.

blessings you enjoy are the true spiritual blessings, of which the external blessings of the ancient economy were the types. To use the language of John, " They, out of the fulness of him who is the Only-begotten of God, the revealer of him in whose bosom he was from the beginning, who is full of grace and truth, true grace, had received grace for," in the room of " grace," the blessings of the new dispensation in the room of the blessings of the old; " for the law," which was a grace, a favour, and a great one, "was given by Moses, but the grace and truth," the true grace, the great manifestation of the love of God in the blessings of a spiritual and eternal salvation, " came by Jesus Christ."[1] This, says Peter, is " the grace that is come to you," and " this is the true grace of God."

The apostle's declaration on this subject takes the form of a testimony. Not a demonstration on abstract principles, not a statement of his own individual opinion, but the declaration of a testimony with which, in common with his apostolic brethren, he had been " put in trust" by God. " The grace" to be brought to the true people of God under the Messiah, was " a mystery, kept secret from former ages and generations;" " as it is written, Eye hath not seen, nor ear heard, neither have entered into the heart of man, the things which God had prepared for them that love him." That was " the wisdom of God in a mystery, the hidden wisdom, which God had ordained before the world, unto the glory" of his people under the last and best dispensation of his grace. " But God revealed these things" unto his holy apostles " by his Spirit, and they, having received the Spirit which is of God, and having the mind of Christ, testified the things which he revealed to them, not in words taught by man's wisdom, but in words taught by the Holy Ghost."[2]

[1] John i. 16, 17.   [2] Rom. xvi. 25; 1 Cor. ii. 7, 9, 13.

As the declaration respecting truth took the form of "testimony," so the declaration with regard to duty took the form of "exhortation." The practical part of the epistle is not a dry system of ethics, but a warm exhortation, showing Christians what it is to stand, how they were to be enabled to stand, and why they should stand.

The apostle further notices, that the testimony and the exhortation contained in this epistle were a brief testimony and exhortation : " In few words exhorting and testifying." Here, as well as in the Epistle to the Hebrews, where the apostle says, at the close of the comparatively long Epistle to the Hebrews, "I have written a letter to you in few words," we apprehend the reference is rather to the condensation than to the brevity, strictly so called, of the compositions. This is not a short epistle, and the Epistle to the Hebrews is one of the longest in the New Testament; but there is no unnecessary diffuseness, no waste of words; and on this account, as well as higher ones, Peter's letter, like Paul's, is " weighty and powerful." In our illustrations of the epistle, we have had abundant opportunities of observing in how few words Peter wraps up pregnant thoughts, exhibits far-reaching views.

What the apostle represents as the characteristics of his epistle, are equally those of the apostolic epistles generally. They are occupied with brief, condensed testimonies and exhortations respecting the grace of God, and the duty of Christians in reference to that grace. And as the apostles' discourses, recorded in the Acts of the Apostles, are the models which Christian ministers should follow in preaching the gospel to the world lying under the wicked one, so their epistles are the models which they should follow in teaching the doctrine and the law of Christ to the churches of the saints, to " them who have believed through grace." Every Christian teacher's system of instruction should embrace in it a clear, distinct statement of the true grace of God, of the exceeding great and precious blessings of the Christian salvation; he should conduct his people throughout the length and breadth of the goodly heritage assigned them even here below; and he should often take them up as it were into an exceeding high mountain, and, teaching them to apply the prospective glass of the gospel to the eye of faith, show them the glories of the kingdom which awaits them in the land that is far off. If he does not do this, he is not a minister of the gospel at all. And his system should equally embrace in it a clear statement and a powerful enforcement of the duties which lie on Christians, as partakers of the grace of God in truth. And his doctrinal preaching must all wear the form of "a testimony," a declaration, of what God the Lord says, of what is the mind of Christ, of what the Holy Ghost has declared,—not of human conjectures and reasonings, but of divine revelations; and his practical preaching must all have the form of exhortation, —not occupying the mind with ethical disquisitions and questions, but pressing home clearly announced divine injunctions on the conscience and the heart. The testimony and the exhortation must go together, and be presented as closely connected,—the one the foundation, the other the building. The grace, the true grace, must be declared, in order that they who believe in Christ may be careful to maintain good works. It is also very desirable that all this should be done briefly, "in few words;" that is, that the teaching, though plain, should be condensed. The time afforded for Christian teaching is necessarily very limited, and many Christians have few means of Christian instruction besides public teaching. It is therefore a matter of great importance that the discourses of a Christian minister should contain as much matter as can be brought into them, without overtasking the minds of the hearers.

CHAP. III. THE MODE OF THE WRITING OR TRANSMISSION OF THE EPISTLE.

The only other thing in the recapitulatory part of the postscript that requires attention, is the mode of the writing or of the transmission of the letter: "By Silvanus, a faithful brother unto you, as I suppose, I have written." In the Acts of the Apostles, and in the epistles of Paul, we read of a person of this name. In the epistles he is always termed Silvanus; in the Acts his name is always contracted into Silas. Some have supposed, from the last name and Tertius, the one a Hebrew, the other a Latin word, having the same signification, that he is the person who performed the office of amanuensis to Paul when writing to the Romans.[1] All that we know of him with certainty is, that he was a distinguished "teacher and prophet" in the church of Jerusalem, "a chief man among the brethren;" that he was associated along with Barsabas, surnamed Judas, and sent with Paul and Barnabas to the Gentile churches in Antioch, Syria, and Cilicia, to carry those letters of the apostles, elders, and brethren, which contained their decision of the question respecting the obligation of the law on Christian Gentiles which had been referred to them; that on the disagreement between Paul and Barnabas, he accompanied the former on his journey through Asia Minor to Macedonia; that he remained behind at Berea for a short time, when Paul was obliged to flee from that place, but rejoined the apostle at Corinth; and that he is mentioned along with Timothy by the apostle in the inscription of the Epistles to the Thessalonians. It would appear that he had

[1] Acts xv. 22, 27, 34, 40, xvi. 25, xvii. 7, 10, 15; 2 Cor. ii. 19; 1 Thess. i. 1; Rom. xvi. 22; Burmanni Exercitationes, p. 161; Wolfii Curæ, 2 Cor. i. 19; Walchii. Miscellan. Exercitatt. ii. p. 39; Capelli Spicileg. p. 97; Witsii Meletem. Leid. p. 99; Hilleri Onomasticon, p. 680.

gone, it may be sent by Paul, into the Parthian empire, where Peter seems to have been when he wrote this epistle; for the tradition that this is another person of the same name has no foundation.

It has been made a question whether Silvanus was Peter's amanuensis in writing the epistle, or his messenger in carrying it into Asia Minor and the adjacent regions. The expressions are applicable to either case, and it is quite possible he might be both. Had he meant to remain with Peter, it is likely his salutation would have been given as well as Mark's, and the phraseology is that commonly used in reference to the bearers of the apostolic letters.

Peter describes Silvanus as a " brother." All men are brothers. " Have we not one Father? hath not one God created us?" " for we are all *his* offspring."[1] All Christians are brothers. " One is your Father, and ye are all brethren," says our Lord: " holy brethren," as the apostle has it, " partakers of the heavenly calling." All Christian office-bearers are brothers. Thus Peter speaks of his beloved brother Paul.[2] It is in this last sense probably that Peter here uses the appellation. We know that Silas was a teacher and a prophet, and we know that, when the whole Church are called " saints," the office-bearers are distinguished by being called " brethren."[3] The word " faithful," the epithet given to Silvanus, sometimes signifies believing, sometimes trustworthy, sometimes distinguished by fidelity. I have no doubt it was applicable to Silvanus in all these shades of meaning. As the word is connected with " to you," for it is not " I wrote to you," but " a faithful brother to you," I think it likely that it was meant to convey the two last ideas,—a minister of Christ who has proved himself trustworthy by his faithful discharge of duty to you.

[1] Mal. ii. 10; Acts xvii. 28.
[2] Matt. xxiii. 8; Heb. iii. 1; 2 Pet. iii. 15.   [3] Phil. iv. 21, 22.

The parenthetical words rendered "as I suppose"[1] do not imply the idea of uncertainty, as our English word 'suppose' does. It is the word the apostle uses when he says, "We *conclude* that a man is justified by faith, and not by works of the law;" "I *reckon* the sufferings of the present time not worthy to be compared with the glory that shall be revealed;" "Abraham *accounted* that God was able to raise the dead."[2] There was no doubt in any of these cases, and we have no cause to think there was any doubt here either. It is, "I have sent my letter by Silvanus; and the reason why I have done so is, that I have perfect confidence in his fidelity, and know that he has approved himself a faithful minister of Christ on your behalf." The apostles were accustomed to send their letters, not by ordinary messengers, but by individuals of known and accredited character. Paul sent the Epistles to the Ephesians and Colossians by Tychicus; the First Epistles to the Corinthians and Thessalonians by Timothy; the Second to the Corinthians by Titus; the Epistle to Philemon by Onesimus; the Epistle to the Romans by Phebe, a deaconess. Thus two objects were gained: the apostles were assured that the epistles would be delivered, and the churches assured that the epistles were not surreptitious. It is a piece of Christian wisdom to employ men in engagements for which they are peculiarly fitted. Silvanus, intimately acquainted with the churches to whom the apostle wrote, was far better fitted to be his messenger than an equally good and gifted man who was a stranger to them. Silvanus bringing the letter would be to them abundant proof of its authenticity. And it is exceedingly becoming in men who, like Peter, are pillars in the Church, men of long standing and high influence, to comfort the hearts and increase the usefulness of their younger brethren, by, on proper occa-

---

[1] Ὡς λογίζομαι.   [2] Rom. iii. 28, viii. 18; Heb. xi. 19.

sions, proclaiming the confidence they have in them, and the esteem with which they regard them; and, on the other hand, nothing is more unworthy than for one of Christ's servants, through little jealousies, to withhold from another all the support which the seasonable expression of merited good opinion is calculated to communicate. So much for the recapitulation.

II. THE SALUTATION.

The salutation contained in the 13th verse is in these words: "The church that is at Babylon, elected together with you, saluteth you; and so doth Marcus my son." To salute is to kiss or embrace: here it plainly means to cherish and express cordial affection, of which a salute is the token.

§ 1. *The salutation of the church in Babylon.*

You will notice that the words "church that is" are printed in italics, intimating that there is nothing in the original to answer to them. The text literally rendered is, "She at Babylon, co-elect, saluteth you." It has been a question among interpreters, whether the person here mentioned is a real or figurative person, an individual or a society. Some have supposed that it refers to some Christian woman, perhaps of the name of Suneklekta, the Greek word rendered "elected together with you," probably of great worth and usefulness, and perhaps rank and wealth, resident at Babylon, well known for her good works—one like John's "elect lady;" though some have supposed that she and her elect sister were sister churches, and their children the church members. Others have supposed that it was Peter's "sister-wife," that is, Christian wife, whom we know from the Apostle Paul he was accustomed to "lead about" with him in his apostolic labours, and who was at this time residing in Babylon, and that Marcus, mentioned immediately after, was not Mark the evangelist, but their son. Either of these suppositions, no doubt, may be true; but the probability seems on the side of the view taken by our translators, and by the great body of interpreters in all ages. "She at or in Babylon, co-elect," seems to be the Christian society there.

It has been disputed whether Babylon is to be understood mystically or literally here: whether it means Rome, which in the Apocalypse is called Babylon; or Jerusalem, which, now apostate, better deserved that name than her own, or the city in Chaldea, so well known both in profane and sacred history. In the absence of anything like evidence on the other side, we must hold that whatever Babylon may signify in a book full of symbols, here it must be interpreted just as we do Pontus, Galatia, Cappadocia, Asia, and Bithynia. Our own city is sometimes called Athens, from its situation, and from its being a seat of learning; but it would not do to argue that a letter came from Edinburgh because it was dated from Athens. It is remarkable that the Roman Catholics, who are very shy of admitting that Rome is the Babylon of the Apocalypse, generally hold that it is referred to here. The reason is, that if Babylon do not mean Rome here, there is nothing in Scripture that can be made to look like evidence for the fact, on which the whole enormous fabric of the papal supremacy is built, that Rome was at any time the residence of Peter. So far from being able to prove that the Pope is the legitimate successor of Peter in a universal episcopate, of which Rome, the capital of the world, was the appropriate seat, there is no evidence in Scripture that he was ever in that city; and all that ecclesiastical history makes in some measure probable is, that he came there to suffer martyrdom. Surely those who can believe such things, on such evidence, are given up to strong delusions.

Allowing Babylon to be the proper name of the place referred to, it has been questioned whether it refers to the city generally known both in profane and sacred history by that appellation, or Seleucia, a city in its neighbourhood, on the other side of the Tigris, which is said sometimes to have received its name, or a small garrison town in Egypt known by this appellation. The first opinion is the more probable one, for there is no reason to think that at this time Babylon, though greatly dilapidated, was a mere heap of ruins; though I think it very likely that the word does not refer exclusively to the city, but to the region known as Babylon or Babylonia.[1]

It is the elect dispersion of Babylonia sending their kind regards to the co-elected dispersion of Pontus, Galatia, Cappadocia, Asia, and Bithynia. They, having "obtained like precious faith," were " holy brethren, partakers of the heavenly calling," co-elect, equally with them "elect according to the foreknowledge of God, spiritually separated, obedient to the faith, and sprinkled with the blood of Jesus Christ." Genuine Christians of the most distant countries ought to cherish the kindest affections towards each other, and avail themselves of every proper opportunity of expressing them. And Christian ministers should gladly stir the sacred flame, and give facilities for its manifestation. Apostolical influence was always employed in this way. Alas, how often has clerical influence been put forth in the opposite direction! The leaders of Christ's people have often made them to err, to wander from the path of catholic unity and love, and kept them wandering. " Blessed are the peacemakers."

[1] See note A.

§ 2. *The salutation of Marcus.*

But the apostle transmits the cordial good wishes not only of the church in the region where he was sojourning to their brethren in Pontus, Galatia, Cappadocia, Asia, and Bithynia, but also the kind remembrances of an individual Christian man and minister: "So doth Marcus, my son." We know Peter was married, and ecclesiastical tradition declares that he had children;[1] but we have no evidence that he had sons, or that any of his sons were in the Christian ministry. On the other hand, we do know that there was a very intimate connection between Peter and John Mark. We find Peter going to his mother's house as to his ordinary abode in Jerusalem, after having been miraculously delivered from prison; and all antiquity represents Mark's Gospel as written from information received from Peter,—a tradition carrying with it great probability, as none of the Gospels has more of that circumstantiality which a narrative coming from an eye-witness naturally possesses; and whatever does Peter credit is rather cast into the shade, while his faults are very plainly stated.[2] There is nothing remarkable in Peter calling Mark his son, especially as it is likely he was the means of his conversion. Paul calls Onesimus his "son, begotten in his bonds," and Timothy his "own son in the faith."[3] "Marcus my son" is equivalent to, who is to me instead of a son, or, as Paul has it in reference to Timothy, "who serves with me as a son in the gospel."[4] It does not appear that at this time Mark had ever seen the churches to which Peter wrote; but,

---

[1] Clemens Alexandrinus; Stromata, Lib. iii.

[2] Origen (Eus. H. E. vi. 25) declares that he had learned from tradition that Mark wrote the second Gospel ὡς Πέτρος ὑφηγήσατο αὐτῷ.

[3] Philem. 10; 1 Tim. i. 2.

[4] Μάρκον δὲ υἱὸν κατὰ πνεῦμα καλεῖ, ἀλλ' οὐ κατὰ σάρκα.—ŒCUMENIUS.

though strangers in the flesh, they were dear to him in the Lord. That Christian minister has not the proper spirit of his office, who does not cherish an affectionate regard for every Christian church, for every Christian man, throughout the world.

III. EXHORTATION.

We come now to the exhortation contained in this postscript: "Greet ye one another with a kiss of charity." These words may be understood generally as an exhortation to mutual love, and to all proper expressions of it: 'See that ye love one another, and show that ye love one another;' and in this general sense they embody an injunction obligatory on all Christian churches in all countries and in all ages. But there is no reason to doubt that the apostle meant the churches he addressed to understand and comply with the injunction in the plain literal meaning of the words. Salutation by kissing was the ordinary way of expressing friendly affection in those countries and in that age; and the command is not more strange than if the apostle, addressing a church in our country and times, were to say, 'Give to each other the right hand of fellowship.' We find similar advices given to other churches:[1] "Salute one another with a holy kiss;"[2] "Greet ye one another with an holy kiss;"[3] "Greet all the brethren with an holy kiss."[4] That the apostle meant the members of the churches, on receiving this epistle, to salute one another, is certain; that he meant that at allt heir religious meetings they should do so, is not improbable.

That he meant to make this an everlasting ordinance in all Christian churches, though it has sometimes been asserted,

[1] Rom. xvi. 16. [2] 1 Cor. xvi. 20.
[3] 2 Cor. xiii. 12. [4] 1 Thess. v. 26.

has never been proved, and is by no means likely. That the practice prevailed extensively, perhaps universally, in the earlier ages, is established on satisfactory evidence. "After the prayers," says Justin Martyr, who lived in the earlier part of the second century, giving an account in his *Apology* of the religious customs of the Christians, "after the prayers we embrace each other with a kiss." Tertullian speaks of it as an ordinary part of the religious services of the Lord's day; and in the *Apostolical Constitutions*, as they are termed, the manner in which it was performed is particularly described. "Then let the men apart and the women apart salute each other with a kiss in the Lord." Origen's note on Rom. xvi. 16 is: "From this passage the custom was delivered to the churches, that after prayer the brethren should salute one another with a kiss." This token of love was generally given at the Holy Supper. It was likely, from the prevalence of this custom, that the calumny of Christians indulging in licentiousness at their religious meetings originated; and it is not improbable that, in order to remove everything like an occasion to calumniators, the practice, which, though in itself innocent, had become not for the use of edifying, was discontinued.

Some Christian societies still retain the practice, and even insist on it as a term of communion. We have no objection to the first; but we must protest against the second. Surely this is not one of the points on which the peace of the Church should be disturbed or her communion broken. They who observe it should not condemn them that observe it not; and they who do not observe it should not despise them who observe it. "Let each be fully persuaded in his own mind." In both cases, if they are sincere, they will be accepted of the Lord. The grand matter is the cultivation of mutual love; the mode of expressing it—

unless there be distinct proof, which, we apprehend, there is not, that it has been fixed by apostolical authority for the Church in all ages—is a matter of very inferior importance. It seems, like every external thing not essential, not expressly enjoined as a law to the churches, a thing of time and place, depending on the manners of the age or country, like the wearing or the not wearing long hair at Corinth. A kiss of charity is equivalent to a kiss not of mere form, but expressive of real Christian affection.[1] But though the external *mode* of expressing Christian love be a matter comparatively unimportant, the importance of cherishing this affection, ay, and of expressing it too, cannot be exaggerated. "The entertainment, and increase, and expression of Christian love is not optional, but obligatory; the very stamp and badge of Jesus Christ upon his followers." And the members of the same Christian church should especially cultivate mutual brotherly affection, and on all proper occasions manifest it, by readily and cordially recognising one another as brethren.

IV. BENEDICTION.

It only remains now that we say a word or two on the parting benediction, "Peace be with you all that be in Christ Jesus. Amen." It is the all but uniform practice of the apostles both to begin and end their epistles with prayers and benedictions. Peter began his epistle with the prayer, "Grace unto you, and peace be multiplied;" and he ends with the prayer, "Peace be with you all that are in Christ Jesus." The apostles exemplified their own precepts, to "pray always," to "pray without ceasing." To pray for Christian brethren is one of the most natural modes of expressing Christian affection; as Christians are "taught

[1] See note B.

of God[1] to love one another," they are also taught of God to pray for one another.

"Peace" is a word expressive of whatever is necessary to happiness. Peace be to you, is just equivalent to, May you be happy. When the man is happy, the mind is tranquil. The unhappy man has a disturbed, unquiet, agitated mind. The import of the wish, "Peace be with you," depends on the views of the person who utters it. In the mouth of a well-informed Christian it means, May you have all the happiness which flows from possessing, and knowing that you possess, that favour of God which is life, that loving-kindness which is better than life; from the conscience being sprinkled with the blood of atonement; from the heart being renewed by the Holy Ghost; from the mind being fixed in the belief of the truth; from the faith of the exceeding great and precious promises; from the hope of the salvation that is in Christ with eternal glory. May you "want no good thing." May you "be kept in perfect peace." May "the peace of God keep your hearts and minds through Christ Jesus." May "the Lord of peace himself give you peace always by all means."[2] This prayer the apostle presents for *all* the elect strangers, as being "in Christ Jesus,"—so closely related to Christ Jesus as to be, as it were, identified with him, having fellowship with him in his death, his resurrection, his new life, his honours, his happiness; living in him, animated by his spirit, walking in him, sustained by his grace, imitating his example, regulated by his laws, being his living images, his "epistles seen and read of all men."

This is an expression of the love of a Christian man to Christian men, and is a wish that they may enjoy in abundance Christian happiness. It is they only who are in Christ Jesus that can enjoy the peace which the apostle

---

[1] Θεοδίδακτοι.   [2] Phil. iv. 7; 2 Thess. iii. 16.

here invokes. There is no peace of this kind to them who are not in Christ Jesus. To all who are not in him there is condemnation: "There is no peace, saith my God, to the wicked." It is they who believe in Christ, and who are thus united to him, that can enter into peace. To quote once more the devout Archbishop, from whom I part with reluctance as from a pious accomplished friend, who has been my instructive and delightful companion during my leisurely journey through this most fertile region of the world of inspiration, and to whom I am much indebted for turning my attention to some of its more recondite beauties, and for gathering for me, and for you, some of its sweetest flowers and richest fruits: "They that are in Christ are the only children and heirs of true peace. Others may dream of it, and have a false peace for a time, and wicked men may wish it to themselves and to one another, but it is a most vain hope and thought; but to wish it to them who are in Christ Jesus hath good ground. All solid peace is founded on him, and flows from him." All who are in Christ have peace. "Being justified by faith, they have peace." But the apostle's prayer is, that their peace may be multiplied, preserved, increased; that their peace may be as a river, and their happiness as the waves of the sea; that they may grow in holy happiness till they become perfectly happy, because perfectly holy; having the peace of God, because having the purity of God; "peace, quietness, assurance for ever."

The peculiar expression, " Peace be with you all who are in Christ Jesus," seems to intimate that there might be among them some who were not in Christ Jesus. It was so in the primitive age as well as now. All were not in Christ who bore his name. To those men continuing in that state, there is, there can be, no peace, no true peace. They may, they do say, Peace, peace to themselves; but the Christian minister dares not say, Peace to them. He wishes—oh how eagerly!—their salvation; but he expects this only in the destruction of their false peace. His call to them is, "Let sinners in Zion be afraid;" and his prayer to God is, that he may disturb their peace, shake them with salutary terror, chase them out of all the "refuges of lies" in which they are so apt to seek and find shelter, and never allow them to be at peace, till, "being justified by faith, they have peace with God through our Lord Jesus Christ;" and that they may never know what hope is till they "have fled for refuge to lay hold on the hope set before them in the gospel."

The apostle concludes his benedictory prayer with the emphatic Hebrew word *Amen*, expressive at once of desire and expectation. 'May it be so.' 'It shall be so.' He could not but wish it; for he loved them: and he could not but expect it; for it is one of those promises which "are all yea and amen in Christ Jesus to the glory of God by us." "The Lord will bless his people with peace."[1]

And now, brethren, I have finished these Expository Discourses on this important and interesting part of divine truth. It is more than sixteen years since I commenced them. Of those who witnessed their commencement, many are in another, not a few of them, I doubt not, in a better world. We must soon go to them in the grave. Oh, let us see that we also go to them in heaven. It is in a very high degree improbable that I shall ever deliver to you again so long a series of discourses; a solemn reflection both to me and to you. It says to me, "Make full proof of thy ministry;" it draws to a close: "work while it is called to-day; the night cometh when no man can work." "Prepare to meet thy God." "The Judge standeth before

[1] 2 Cor. i. 30; Ps. xxix. 11.

the door." Make up thy account; thou canst not long continue a steward. And to you it says, "To-day, if ye will hear my voice, harden not your hearts. Now is the accepted time; now is the day of salvation."

My work in composing and delivering these discourses, and yours in listening to them, are over; but there remain the improvement which ought to be made, and the account which must be given. The first will, I trust, follow; the second certainly shall. It is by attending to the first that we shall be prepared for the second. For this, as for all means of religious improvement, we must ere long give account. Oh that it may be given with joy, and not with grief! "The Lord grant" that both the teacher and the taught may, notwithstanding all that has been wanting and wrong in the manner in which they have performed their respective parts,—" the Lord grant that we may find mercy of the Lord in that day."[1] Amen.

Note A. p. 411.

"Explodatur figurata, admittatur literalis expositio."—Pearson, *de Succ. Rom. Episc.*

"Babylona proprie accipio pro celebri illa Assyriæ urbe."—Beza. "Babylon hic haud dubiè est urbs illa Chaldææ ubi Petrus circumcisionis Apostolus prædicavit. Nulla enim est causa, cur Romæ nomen dissimularet."—Pareus.

"Cur Babylon in Italia potius aut in Egypto, quam in Mesopotamia, sit quærenda, causam non video."—Wetstein.

"Multi ex veteribus Romam ænigmatice putarunt notari. Hoc commentum Papistæ libenter arripiunt, ut videatur Petrus Romanæ Ecclesiæ præfuisse. Neque enim deterret eos infamia nominis, modo sedis Apostolicæ titulum prætexere ipsis liceat; nec Christum magnopere curant, modo Petrus ipsis relinquatur.

[1] 2 Tim. i. 18.

Quinetiam, modo retineant Cathedram Petri nomen, suam Romam in profundis inferis collocare non recusabunt. Atqui vetus illud commentum nihil habet coloris."—CALVIN. There is historical evidence that Seleucia was built out of the ruins of ancient Babylon, and was known in the apostolic age under its name.—CONDER: *Literary History of the New Testament*, p. 177.

NOTE B. p. 415.

"Osculo sancto, osculo vero, osculo pacifico, osculo columbino, non subdolo, non polluto."—BEDA. "Non adulatoria sicut Absolon osculabatur populum, non simulatorio sicut Joab Amasam, non proditorio sicut Judas Dominum, non impudico sicut mulier adultera juvenem, sed osculo sancto, quod est caritatis signum et ejus fomentum."—LYRA. "Osculo, non suavio quod voluptatis est, sed osculo quod religionis; osculo caritatis, osculo sancto, osculo in Domino Jesu: quale prisco ecclesiæ ritu, cum super cœnam Dominicam, tum die Paschatis festo, tum in ordinationibus sacris, pie olim et pudice dabatur et reddebatur."—BENTLEY.

"The fraternal kiss with which every one, after being baptized, was received into the community by the Christians into whose immediate fellowship he entered—which the members bestowed on each other just before the celebration of the communion, and with which every Christian saluted his brother, though he never saw him before—was not an empty form, but the expression of Christian feelings; a token of the relation in which Christians conceived themselves to stand to each other. It was this indeed which, in a cold and selfish age, struck the pagans with wonder: to behold men of different countries, ranks, stages of culture, so intimately bound together; to see the stranger who came into a city, and by his letter of recognition (his 'Epistola formata'), made himself known to the Christians of the place as a brother beyond suspicion, finding at once among them, to whom he was personally unknown, all manner of brotherly sympathy and protection."—NEANDER: *Gen. Hist. of the Christ. Relig. and the Church*, TORRY'S Translation, vol. i. sec. iii. p. 347.

INDEX.

I.—PRINCIPAL MATTERS.

AFFLICTION, two views of, iii. 283; its duties, 293; motives to the performance of them, 298; is a state of carefulness, 308.

Amen, import of, iii. 418.

Angels, subjection of, to Christ, ii. 487; is the result of his expiatory sufferings, 489; study the final happiness of Christians, i. 100.

Antediluvian history, facts in, ii. 502; object of the apostle in referring to, 509;—revelations, 505;—worlds, analogies of post-diluvian and, 510.

Apostles, characteristic features of, i. 14; had no successors, 16.

Ascension of Christ to heaven the result of his expiatory sufferings, ii. 484.

Atonement, the, connection of sanctification with, i. 156; fellowship with God obtained through, ii. 443; exhortation to holiness based on, iii. 1.

Babes, new-born, illustration of the figure, i. 191.

Babylon, the church in, iii. 409.

Baptism, the deluge was a type of, ii. 513; how it saves, 515.

"Bearing sins," meaning of the phrase, ii. 178.

Bishop, meaning of the term, ii. 187.

Blessings of salvation, God is the author of, i. 51; originate in the abundant mercy of God, 56; are of vast magnitude, 58; proper method of acknowledging, 59.

Brotherhood, the, who are, ii. 94; have a common character, 96; common education, 97; common residence, 97; common inheritance, 97; fellowship of, 99; Christians must show their love of, 103; by joining it, 104; by regular attendance, 104; by endeavouring to preserve its purity, 105; by seeking its peace, 106; by their prayers, 108; duty to a particular brotherhood, 109; duty of Christian brotherhoods to other Christian brotherhoods, 111; address to those who do not belong to, 114.

Brotherly love, illustrated, i. 165; objects and elements of, 166; distinctive characters of, 168; recommended, 174; by the mutual relation of Christians, 175; by the common character of Christians, 178; the maintenance of, explained, iii. 91; and recommended, 97; manifestation of, by employing property, 110; by employing spiritual gifts, 119; motives to the manifestation of, 128.

Called to show forth the praises of God, Christians are, i. 312; what is this calling? 315; who is its author? 316; what is the design of it? 316; show them forth passively, 317; and actively,

319; address to those who are not among the called, 323;—out of darkness, Christians are, 325.
Calumnies against the Christians, Note, i. 371.
"Ceased from sin," meaning of the phrase, iii. 22. See *Flesh*.
Cephas, meaning of the name, i. 8.
Character, common, of Christians, a motive to brotherly love, i. 178.
Christ, meaning of the term, ii. 381; is the foundation of the spiritual temple, i. 257; is the great object of his people's affections, i. 64.
Christian salvation, grandeur, excellence, and security of, a motive to Christian duty, i. 137.
Christians, present and future state of, contrasted, i. 61; as to the absence and presence of Christ, 64; as to trials and their results, 70; as to expectation and enjoyment, 74; as to sorrows and joys, 76; the final happiness of, is the subject of Old Testament prophecy, 83; and of apostolical preaching, 93; and of angelic study, 100; mutual relation of, 175; common character of, 178; state and character of, described generally, 189; and under the figure of new-born babes, 191; exhortation to, 199; dissuasive, 200; persuasive, 207; the two parts are closely connected with each other, 222; peculiar privileges of, 241; miserable condition of, previously to their obtaining those privileges, 246; manner in which they were obtained, 252; are called living stones, 272; a holy priesthood, 274; and a chosen generation, 279; have obtained mercy, 336; are the servants of God, ii. 13.
Church, Christian, constitution of, iii. 240; is the flock of God, 226; and God's heritage, 227.
Civil government, nature and design of, i. 376; is called a "creature," not an "ordinance,"

380; subjection to, 383; how limited, 387; Christ's commandment concerning, 389; Christ's example concerning, 391.
"Coming to Christ," meaning of the phrase, i. 252.
Conjugal duties of Christians, ii. 191; of wives, 195; of husbands, 222. See *Husbands* and *Wives*.
Conscience, a good, what it is, ii. 351; must be sprinkled by the blood of Christ, 356.
Consolation, the epistle abounds in, i. 4.
Conversation, meaning of the term, i. 117; a good, in Christ, explained, ii. 360.
Courtesy enjoined, ii. 279; origin of the term, 280; not to be confounded with artificial polish of manners, 283; commensurate with our social relations, 285; consistent with truth and integrity, 285; enjoined by the highest authority, 287; enforced by the example of Christ, 287; Abraham, 288; Sarah, 288; Paul, 290.
"Covereth a multitude of sins," the phrase explained, iii. 99.
Cruelty of the devil, iii. 344.

Darkness, Christians are called out of, i. 325; what it is, 327; illustrated by the midnight darkness of Egypt, 326.
Dead, the spiritually, who are, iii. 58; the gospel is preached to, 59.
Deluge, the, was a type of baptism, ii. 513; state of mankind previous to, 503.
Desire of the milk of the word described, i. 219.
Devil, the, iii. 336; is an adversary, 338, subtle, 340; active, 342; cruel, 344; powerful, 345; the Christian's duty in reference to, 349; to resist his attacks on himself, 350; and on the Christian cause, 352; what the Christian is to do that he may resist,

354; encouragement to perform this duty, 363.
Doxology, iii. 130.
Dress, duty of Christian wives in reference to, ii. 200.
Duties of Christians to each other, ii. 247; union of sentiment, 248; union of feeling, 257; brotherly kindness, 259; to mankind generally, 265; pity, 265; courtesy, 279; to give a reason of the hope that is in them, 331; to maintain a good conscience and a good conversation, 351.
Duty, Christian, i. 105; general view of, 111; particular view of, 115; means for the performance of, 118; determined resolution, 119; moderation, 122; hope, 126; fear, 132; motives to the performance of, 136.

Ecclesiastical duties enjoined, iii. 180.
Elder, faithful, reward of, iii. 229; unfaithful, doom of, 232.
Elders, origin and meaning of the appellation, iii. 182; divided into the teaching and the ruling, 188; qualifications of, 189; manner of investing with office, 190; are called shepherds and overseers, 191; duties of, 193; instruction, 194; superintendence, 200; manner of performing their duties, 205; not by constraint, 206; not for filthy lucre, 209; not as lords of God's heritage, 213; motives suggested by the apostle's reference to himself, 218; drawn from considerations referring to the church, 226; and to the office-bearers themselves, 229.
Elect, meaning of the term, i. 18; stone, 265. See *Foundation.*
Election, double sense of the term in Scripture, i. 282.
"End of all things," meaning of the phrase, iii. 82.
Enemy, great, of the Christian, who he is, iii. 336; what he is, 338.

Envy, warnings against, i. 202.
Epistle, First, of Peter, character of, by Leighton, i. 2; Erasmus, Grotius, and Bengel, 3; authenticity and genuineness of, 3; resemblance to Paul's Epistles, 3; holds an intermediate place between those of Paul and James, 5; abounds in consolation, 4; date, 5; object, 6; to whom addressed, 17; salutation, 23; references to the Old Testament in, 25; postscript, iii. 395; recapitulation, 397; form, 402; subject, 398; mode of writing or transmission, 406; salutation, 409; benediction, 415.
Epistolary part of Scripture, advantages of, i. 2.
Equity of God, a motive to Christian duty, i. 145.
Evangelists, their office, iii. 185.
Evidence of Christianity, importance of a knowledge of, ii. 344.
Evil-speaking, warnings against, i. 202.
Exaltation of Christ, ii. 475; his resurrection, 476; ascension to heaven, 481; sitting on the right hand of God, 484; placed over angels, 487.
Example of Christ, how far binding on us as a pattern, ii. 167.
Exhortation to Christians, dissuasive, i. 200; persuasive, 207; to seek spiritual growth, 208; to desire the sincere milk of the word, 216;—to holiness, based on the atonement, iii. 1; not to live to the lusts of men, 12; to live to the will of God, 17.
Expiatory sufferings of Christ, the design of, ii. 182; effects of, 185; connection of sanctification with, i. 156.

"Fadeth not away," meaning of the phrase, i. 40.
Faith, obedience of, i. 21.
"Faithful Creator," import of the expression, iii. 168.

Fear of God, a means of Christian obedience, i. 132; the foundation of, ii. 115; produced by the faith of the gospel, 122; how manifested, 123; the best means of guarding against the fear of man, 316.

Fellowship with God explained, ii. 443; obtained through the atonement, 444.

Fervently, meaning of the term, i. 169.

"Flesh, he that hath suffered in the," iii. 22; the thought explained, 25; viewed as referring to Christ, 28; as referring to Christians, 30; as a piece of Christian armour, 34.

Fleshly lusts, abstinence from, i. 356; what they are, 356; what must be done in order to abstain from, 358; to indulge in, incongruous in a child of God, 367; how they war against the soul, 368.

Flock of God, the church is the, iii. 226.

Foreknowledge of God, i. 20.

Foundation of the spiritual temple, the, Jesus Christ is, i. 257, 264; is a corner-stone, 265; is chosen, 265; is precious, 266; was rejected by men, 267; is a living stone, 268.

Free, Christians are, ii. 1; in reference to God, 2; to man, 7; to the powers and principles of evil, 10; they are to act as, 19, 20, 25, 32.

Freedom, the Christian's duty to guard against the abuse of, ii. 37; in reference to God, 40; to man, 46; to the powers and principles of evil, 51.

Friendly temper or behaviour, a, described, i. 168.

Generation, a chosen, why Christians are called, i. 279.

"Gifts," meaning of the term, iii. 119.

Glory of God, a regard to, the highest motive to duty, iii. 129; of Christ, 145.

God, the author of all saving blessings, i. 51; as the God and Father of our Lord Jesus Christ, 54; abundant mercy of, 56; holiness of, a motive to Christian duty, 141.

Gospel, the, is preached to the spiritually dead, iii. 59.

Grace of God, the, one great subject of the epistle, iii. 398.

Grotius, ingenious conjecture of, i. 380.

Growth, spiritual, is progressive sanctification, i. 213; resemblance of, to the growth of a child, 214; motives to, from the state and character of Christians, 227; from having tasted that the Lord is gracious, 232.

Guile, warnings against, i. 201.

Happiness, final, of Christians, the subject of Old Testament prophecy, i. 83; of apostolical preaching, 93; of angelic study, 100.

"Healed by Christ's stripes," meaning of the phrase, ii. 185.

Heritage of God, the church is the, iii. 227.

History, Old Testament, uses of, ii. 499.

Holiness, exhortation to, based on the atonement, iii. 1; motives to, drawn from the character of the will of the Gentiles, 47; from the great design of the gospel revelation, 57.

Holiness of God, the, a motive to Christian duty, i. 141.

"Holy nation," meaning of the phrase, i. 295.

"Holy One," import of the appellation as applied to God, ii. 322.

"Holy priesthood," meaning of the phrase, i. 274.

Holy Scriptures, fulness of, ii. 369; difficulties of, 449; not systematic, but miscellaneous in their form, i. 1.

Honour due to all men, ii. 75; not to be confined to the brotherhood, 76; nor to classes, 81; foundation of, 82; evil consequences of the want of, 84; motives from the example of God, 88; and of Christ, 89.
"Honour the king," what is implied in, ii. 125; its foundation, 127; its limits, 128.
Hope, Christian, ground of, i. 43; how produced, 44; connected with the faith of the gospel, 46; why called living, 47; connected with the resurrection of Christ, 49; a means of Christian obedience, 126; the profession of, is positively enjoined, ii. 338; "maketh not ashamed," and why, i. 48.
Hospitality, what it is not, iii. 110; what it is, 112; of the primitive Christians, 114.
"House of God," meaning of the phrase, iii. 165.
Humility enjoined, ii. 295; explained, iii. 267; tendency of, to secure mutual subjection, 270; motives to, 271.
Husbands, Christian, duties of, ii. 222; motives to the discharge of, 235.
Hypocrisy, warnings against, i. 202.

"Incorruptible," meaning of the term, i. 39.
Inheritance of God's children, i. 36; free gift of, 38; security of tenure, 38; excellence of, 39; living hope of, 42.
"Inner man of the heart," import of, ii. 204.
Instruction one of the duties of Christian elders, iii. 194.
Intoxicating liquors, tendency and effects of, iii. 72.

"Kingdom of priests," meaning of the appellation, i. 290.

Law, difference as a covenant and a rule, ii. 41.

Light, marvellous, Christians are called into, i. 328; of knowledge, 328; of purity, 329; of rational joy, 330; why termed God's light, 331.
"Live according to God in the spirit," meaning of the phrase, iii. 61.
"Living stone," meaning of the phrase as applied to Christ, i. 268.
"Living stones," meaning of the phrase as applied to Christians, i. 255, 272.
"Loins of the mind," girding up of, i. 119.
Love, brotherly. See *Brotherly Love*.
"Lusts of men, not to live to," meaning of the phrase, iii. 15.
Lusts, fleshly. See *Fleshly Lusts*.

"Maketh not ashamed," i. 48.
Malice, warnings against, i. 200.
Manifestation, of brotherly love, iii. 109; of the fear of God, ii. 123.
Mankind, state of, previous to the deluge, ii. 503.
Marcus, notice of, iii. 412.
"Marry in the Lord," meaning of the phrase, ii. 210.
"Marvellous light." See *Light*.
Means for performing Christian duty. See *Duty*.
Members of the church, duties of the, to their office-bearers, iii. 235; subjection to the elders as teachers, 246; submission to them as superintendents, 249; duties to each other, 257.
Mercy, of God, the moving cause of saving blessings, i. 56; Christians have obtained, 336; address to those who have obtained, 340; and to those who have not obtained, 340.
"Mighty hand of God," meaning of the expression, iii. 287; duty of humbling ourselves under it, 293; motives to do so, 298.
Milk, why spiritual truth is com-

pared to, i. 218; of the word, what it is, 216; how we grow by it, 218; what it is to desire it, 219.
Miserable condition of Christians, previously to obtaining their peculiar privileges, i. 246.
Misery of those who refuse to come to Christ, i. 342.
Moderation, a means of Christian obedience, i. 122.
Morality, Christian, bearing on the evidences of Christianity, i. 376.
Motives to the performance of Christian duty, i. 136; from the grandeur, excellence, and security of the Christian salvation, 137; from the holiness of God, 141; from the strict equity of God, 145; from the provision made for sanctification in the sacrifice of Christ, 152; to spiritual growth, 227; to holiness, iii. 46. See *Holiness*.
Mutual relation of Christians, i. 175.
Mutual subjection the duty of church members, iii. 259; what this implies, 261; what it does not imply, 259.

Nation, a holy, why Christians are called, i. 295.
Noah, his character, ii. 505; his preaching, 505.

Obedience, Christian, i. 111; means for the performance of, 118.
Obedience, the duty of servants, ii. 144; its limits, 144.
"Obedience of faith," meaning of the phrase, i. 21.
"Obtained mercy," Christians have, i. 336.
Old Testament prophecy as to the final happiness of Christians, i. 83; Enoch, 86; Job, 87; Psalms, 87; Isaiah, Daniel, Hosea, and Malachi, 88; was imperfectly understood by the prophets themselves, 89.
"Ordinance of man," meaning of the phrase, i. 380.

Partakers of the sufferings of Christ, in what sense Christians are, iii. 141.
Pastor, meaning and reference of the appellation, iii. 185.
Patient suffering, Christians are called to, as a part of conformity to Christ, ii. 159; as a great end of Christ's expiatory sufferings, 175.
Peace, meaning of the term, i. 24.
Peculiar people, a, why Christians are called, i. 303.
"People of God," meaning of the term, i. 332.
Persecution, good effects of, iii. 136; duties of Christians under, ii. 298; motives, 304; Christians are called to this course, 304; blessing which attends, 308; tendency of the course recommended to secure from suffering, 310.
Perseverance necessary, iii. 19.
Peter, history and character of, i. 7-14.
"Pilgrims and strangers," force of the appellation as applied to Christians, i. 366.
Pitiful, Christians are enjoined to be, ii. 265; for the spiritual wants of men, 270; for their temporal wants, 271.
Pleasantness of the service of God, ii. 64.
Postscript of the epistle, iii. 395.
Power of God, i. 41.
Power of the devil, iii. 345.
"Precious stone," meaning of the phrase, i. 266.
Present expectation and future enjoyment of Christians contrasted, i. 74.
Priesthood, a holy, why Christians are called, i. 274.
Principles, doctrinal, in which all Christians are agreed, ii. 250; practical, in which all Christians are agreed, 251.
Privileges, peculiar, of Christians, i. 270; obtained by believing the truth about Christ, 281.

INDEX. 427

Profession of Christian hope positively enjoined, ii. 331.
Provision made for sanctification in the sacrifice of Christ, i. 152.
Pure heart, a, Christians are required to love one another with, i. 168.

"Quick and dead," meaning of the phrase, iii. 51.
Quotations from the Old Testament, principles on which they are made, ii. 318, 375.

References to the Old Testament in the epistle, i. 25.
Regeneration, baptismal, absurdity of, ii. 515.
Rejected by men, Christ was, i. 267.
Relation, influence of, on character, iii. 43; mutual, of Christians, a motive to brotherly love, i. 175.
Relief and United Secession Churches, union of, ii. 135.
Reproaches cast on Christians, iii. 149.
Resemblance of this epistle to Paul's epistles, i. 3.
Resolution, a means of Christian duty, i. 119.
Resurrection of Christ, the, connection of Christian hope with, i. 49; evidences of, ii. 477; importance of knowing these evidences, 479; the result of his expiatory sufferings, 476.
Revelation, divine, connection with the atonement, ii. 415; analogy of, to the sun, ii. 191.
"Right hand of God," meaning of the phrase, ii. 485.
Rulers in the Christian church, duties of, iii. 182.

Sacraments, efficacy of, doctrine of Westminster Assembly respecting, ii. 520.
Sacrifice of Christ, the intrinsic worth of, i. 159; the subject of divine appointment, 160; has been actually offered, 161; has answered the purpose for which it was intended, 161; motives derived from, to the performance of Christian duty, 152.
Salutation of the epistle, i. 23; the practice of the primitive churches, iii. 414, 420.
Salvation, the Christian, described, i. 30.
Sanctification obtained through the sacrifice of Christ, i. 156; "of the Spirit," meaning of the phrase, i. 21.
Sanctify, the meaning of the term, ii. 322.
"Saved by water," meaning of the phrase, ii. 509.
Scriptures, holy, fulness of, ii. 369. See *Holy Scriptures*.
Servants of God, Christians are, ii. 13; their duty to act as, 53; address to those who are not, 67.
Servants, Christian, duties of, ii. 140; in general, 144; of a particular class, 150; motives to the discharge of the duties of, 151; from its being acceptable to God, 151; from a consideration of Christ's sufferings, 158; who suffered, 160; for us, 161; with patience, 163.
Service of God, the, is reasonable, ii. 63; pleasant, 64; highly honourable, 65; advantageous, 66.
"Show forth God's praises," Christians are called to, i. 312. See *Called*.
Silvanus, notice of, iii. 406.
Sobriety, meaning of the term, iii. 71; a means of resisting the devil, 355.
Sonship, divine, i. 33; descriptive of relation, 34; of character, 34; obtained by faith, 35.
"Spirit of Christ," why he is so called, i. 84.
"Spirits in prison," who are meant by, ii. 462.
"Spiritual house," meaning of the phrase as applied to Christians, i. 273.

"Sprinkling of the blood of Jesus Christ," i. 22; on the conscience, ii. 356.
State and character of Christians described, i. 186; a motive to spiritual growth, 227.
Stedfastness in the faith, one means of resisting the devil, iii. 360.
Stewards, in what sense Christians are, iii. 125.
"Stone, living." See *Living Stone*.
Stripes of Christ, what it is to be healed by, ii. 185.
Subjection due to Christian elders as a body, iii. 249; as individuals, 252.
Subtilty of the devil, iii. 340.
Sufferings of Christ, their nature, ii. 396; were penal, 397; vicarious, 399; expiatory, 403; their design, 409; to bring men to the knowledge of God, 411; to favour with God, 424; to likeness to God, 437; to fellowship with God, 443; an encouragement to Christians suffering for his cause, 490; in what manner Christians are partakers of, iii. 141.
Sufferings, for Christ, directory under, iii. 134; not to be astonished at, 135; not to be depressed by, 141; not to be ashamed of, 154.
Sufferings undeserved, Christians need not wonder when they meet with, ii. 170; should be careful that they are undeserved, 171; should submit to, in a meek spirit, 173.
Superintendence, one of the duties of Christian elders, iii. 200.

"Taste that the Lord is gracious," meaning of the phrase, i. 234.
Temple, the spiritual, Jesus Christ is the foundation of, i. 257.
Times, peculiar character of the, iii. 87.
Trials of Christians contrasted with their results, i. 70.

Tribute, civil, payment of, obligatory on Christians, i. 386.
Truth and integrity, courtesy consistent with, ii. 284.

Unbelief, malignity and ill desert of, i. 347.
"Undefiled," in what sense the inheritance of Christians is said to be, i. 39.
Undeserved sufferings. See *Sufferings*.
Union of sentiment, the duty of Christians, ii. 248; of feeling, the duty of Christians, 257.

Vicarious, the sufferings of Christ were, ii. 399.
Vigilance, importance of, iii. 80; one means of resisting the devil, 358.

"War against the soul," meaning of the phrase, i. 368.
Warnings against malice, i. 200; guile, 201; hypocrisy, 202; envy, 202; evil-speakings, 202.
"Watching unto prayer," meaning of the phrase, iii. 77.
"Weaker vessel," the woman is, meaning of the expression, ii. 229.
Will of God, the, is the rule of his own conduct, iii. 17; as made known in his word, is the chief rule of our conduct, 18.
Witness of the sufferings of Christ, Peter was, iii. 220.
Wives, Christian, duties of, ii. 195; subjection, 196; chaste conversation coupled with fear, 199; adorning themselves with inward ornaments, 200; motives to the performance of, 208; probability of converting the husband, 208; example of holy women, 215.

Younger, meaning and reference of the term, iii. 238.

INDEX. 429

II.—GREEK WORDS AND PHRASES REMARKED ON.

'Αγαλλιᾶσθε, i. 62.
'Αγαπῶντι, ii. 114.
'Αγιάζω, ii. 322.
'Αγιασμῷ πνεύματος, i. 21, 27.
'Αδόκιμον νοῦν, iii. 50.
'Αληθεύοντες, i. 172.
'Αλλοτριοεπίσκοπος, iii. 176.
'Αμάραντος, i. 40.
'Αμίαντος, i. 39.
'Αμώμου, i. 160.
'Αναγκαστῶς, iii. 206.
'Ανακόλουθον, i. 245.
'Αναστροφή, i. 117.
'Ανθρωποκτόνος, iii. 338.
'Αντιτάσσεται, iii. 274.
'Απειθοῦντες, i. 345, 354.
'Από, ii. 70.
'Απολογία, ii. 341.
'Απώλεια, i. 76.
'Αρετάς, i. 316.
'Αρτιγέννητα, i. 220.
'Ασθενεστέρῳ, ii. 224.
'Ασπίλου, i. 160.
'Ασωτίαν, iii. 50.
Αὐτοθυσία, i. 276.
Αὐτόπται, iii. 223.
Αὐτός, iii. 378.
''Αφθαρτος, i. 39.
''Αχρι, ii. 483.

Βεβαιότερον, i. 92.
Βιῶσαι, iii. 12.

Γάλα λογικόν, i. 208, 217.
Γνῶσιν, ii. 225.

Δί, iii. 265, 271.
Διά, i. 42; ii. 480.
Διασπορά, i. 19.
Δικαιοσύνη, ii. 70.

'Εγκόμβωμα, iii. 282.
'Εθανατώθητε, ii. 459.
''Εθνος, i. 302.
Εἰ, i. 145.
Εἰ δέον ἐστί, i. 77.
Εἴπερ, i. 232.
Εἰσαγάγῃ εἰς τὴν οἰκουμένην, ii. 488.

Εἰς σωτηρίαν, i. 207.
'Εκλεκτοί, i. 27.
'Εκλογήν, i. 18.
'Εκουσίως, iii. 206.
'Εκτενῆ, iii. 94.
'Εκτενῶς, i. 169.
'Ελεύθεροι, ii. 70.
'Ελπίδα ζῶσαν, i. 47.
'Ελυτρώθητε, i. 155.
'Εμψύχους, i. 273, 354.
'Εν, i. 42.
''Ενδυσις ἱματίων, ii. 200.
''Εννοια, iii. 6, 68.
'Εν ᾧ, ii. 462.
'Εξουσία, i. 281.
''Επαθεν, ii. 160.
'Επερωτᾶσθαι, ii. 527.
'Επερώτημα, ii. 517, 526.
'Επί, ii. 177.
'Επικάλυμμα, ii. 38.
'Επισκοποῦντες, iii. 187, 207.
'Εσόπτρου, i. 70.
'Ετοίμως ἔχοντι, iii. 52.

Ζῶντας, i. 273.
Ζωοποιηθείς, ii. 454, 460.
Ζῶσαν, i. 47, 49.

Θανατωθείς, ii. 454, 459.
Θεοδίδακτοι, i. 173; ii. 261; iii. 416.
Θρασύδειλος, i. 354.

'Ιλαστήριον, ii. 402.
''Ινα, i. 51; iii. 61.

Καί, ii. 380.
Κακία, i. 200; ii. 38.
Καλήν, i. 362.
Καρπός, i. 329.
Κατὰ Θεόν, iii. 2.
Καταλαλιάς, i. 203.
Κατήργηνται, ii. 70.
Κλῆροι, iii. 280.
Κοινωνικά, ii. 101.
Κόμβος, iii. 282.
Κτίσις, i. 380.

Λαὸς εἰς περιποίησιν, i. 304.

Λογικὴν λατρείαν, i. 218; iii. 81.

Ματαίας, i. 154.
Μέλει, iii. 319.
Μέριμναν, iii. 319.
Μετανοεῖτε, iii. 79.
Μετάνοια, ii. 415.
Μέχρι, ii. 180.

Νεανίσκοι, iii. 281.
Νεώτεροι, iii. 181.
Νήψατε, iii. 77.

Ὁμοίως, iii. 236.
Ὁμόφρονες, ii. 248.
Ὅτι, iii. 6, 68.
Ὀφείλετε, iii. 101.

Παρακαλῶν καὶ ἐπιμαρτυρῶν, i. 4.
Παρακύψαι, i. 101.
Παρεπιδήμοις, i. 19, 366.
Παροίκους, i. 366.
Πατροπαραδότου, i. 154.
Πέπαυται, iii. 6, 25.
Περιποίησις, i. 76.
Πέτρος, i. 8.
Πίστις, i. 76.
Πνεῦμα, i. 79; ii. 454, 464.
Ποικίλης, iii. 120.
Ποιμάνατε, iii. 187, 193.
Ποίμνη, iii. 280.
Ποῖον, i. 90.
Πολίτευμα, i. 117.
Πρεσβύτεροι, iii. 181, 186, 237.
Πρὸ πάντων, iii. 96.
Πρόγνωσις, i. 27.
Προέθετο, i. 161.
Προσεκληρώθησαν, iii. 280.
Προσκόπτουσι, i. 354.
Πρόφασιν, ii. 39.
Πύρωσις, iii. 136.

Σαρκί, ii. 454.
Σαρκικῶς, ii. 459, 465.

Σθενώσει, iii. 369.
Στῆτε, iii. 401.
Στρατεύονται, i. 368.
Συμπαθεῖς, ii. 249.
Συμπρεσβύτερον, iii. 220.
Συντρεχόντων, iii. 50.
Σῶμα, i. 79.
Σωτηρίαν ψυχῶν, i. 76, 79.
Σωφρονήσατε, iii. 72.

Τὰ παθήματα εἰς Χριστόν, i. 85, 104.
Τὰ παθήματα τοῦ Χριστοῦ, i. 86, 104.
Ταπεινόφρονες, ii. 280.
Τελείως, i. 127.
Τετυπωμένα, ii. 101.
Τιμή, i. 271.
Τιμιώτερον, i. 73.
Τίνα, i. 90.
Τὸ κρίμα, iii. 166.
Τοῦ ἀγαθοῦ, ii. 310.

Ὑπακοῆς, i. 112.
Ὑποδείγματα, ii. 357.
Ὑπομονή, iii. 20, 139.
Ὑποτασσόμενοι, iii. 274.
Ὑποστολή, i. 76.

Φανερωθῆ, iii. 225.
Φιλάδελφοι, ii. 260.
Φιλανθρωπία, ii. 89.
Φιλόφρονες, ii. 280.
Φιμοῦν, i. 394.
Φωτός, i. 329.

Χάρις παρὰ Θεῷ, ii. 152.
Χάρισμα, iii. 119.
Χάριτος, iii. 120.
Χριστός, ii. 382.

Ψυχή, i. 79.

Ὦ, ii. 514.
Ὡς λογίζομαι, iii. 408.

III.—AUTHORS QUOTED OR REFERRED TO.

Achilles Tatius, vol. i. page 220.
Alshech, i. xxix.
Amesius, iii. 282.
Amyraut, i. 27 ; iii. 68.
Anderson, Christopher, ii. 418.
Aristotle, i. 233 ; ii. 84.
Augustine, i. 371 ; ii. 133-5 ; ii. 187, 525-6 ; iii. 22, 69, 158.

Balmer, ii. 443, 444, 482.
Barnes, i. 4-5.
Barrington, Bishop, iii. 176.
Barrow, ii. 90 ; iii. 306-7.
Bates, ii. 83 ; iii. 169.
Baxter, i. 211, 219, 224 ; ii. 166, 213, 226, 344, 368, 458 ; iii. 206.
Beausobre, i. xxv, xxvii ; ii. 526 ; iii. 68.
Beda, i. 271, 313 ; iii. 420.
Bengel, i. xxv, xxviii, xxxvi, xxxvii, 3, 41, 49, 79, 83, 154, 160, 220, 255, 272, 366, 368 ; ii. 152, 225, 309, 463 ; iii. 12, 25, 207-8, 213, 280, 378.
Benson, i. xxxiii, 63.
Bentley, ii. 337 ; iii. 420.
Bernard, iii. 215.
Beza, i. xxv, xxx, xxxi, xxxiii, 27, 275 ; iii. 68, 236, 419.
Binney, ii. 297.
Bishops' Bible, i. xxix.
Black, Dr, ii. 178.
Blair, i. 184.
Blondell, iii. 187.
Bolten, iii. 281.
Bowyer, iii. 176.
Bullinger, i. xxxvii.
Bungener, iii. 187.
Bunyan, iii. 360.
Burke, i. 304.
Butler, ii. 346, 352.
Byfield, i. 27.

Cæsarius, ii. 167.
Calvin, i. xxvi, 104, 145, 276 ; ii. 46 ; iii. 206, 280, 419-20.
Camerarius, i. xxxiii ; ii. 524.
Camero, ii. 180.

Campbell, i. 16 ; iii. 218.
Capellus, i. 354 ; ii. 375.
Carpzov, i. xxix, xxxii ; iii. 183.
Casaubon, ii. 165 ; iii. 193.
Castalio, i. xxv, xxvi, xxxi, xxxii ; iii. 60.
Chrysostom, i. 4, 8, 393 ; ii. 129, 376 ; iii. 193.
Cicero, i. 217.
Clarius, i. 63.
Clemens Alexandrinus, ii. 214-15 ; iii. 68, 412.
Clemens Romanus, i. 13.
Clementine Homilies, iii. 279.
Conder, iii. 420.
Coverdale, i. xxvi, xxvii, xxix, xxxii, xxxiii, xxxvi, xxxvii.
Cowper, i. 311, 369 ; ii. 3, 33, 86, 217, 320, 330, 356, 358.
Cranmer, i. xxvii, xxix, xxxvi, xxxvii ; ii. 524.
Culverwell, ii. 70-1.
Cyprian, ii. 101.

Dassovius, ii. 523.
De Wette, i. 6.
Deylingius, i. xxxiv.
Dick, ii. 27.
Douglas, ii. 43.
Drusius, ii. 201 ; iii. 305.

Erasmus, i. 3, 175 ; iii. 280.
Estius, ii. 165 ; iii. 281.
Euripides, iii. 193.
Eusebius, i. 6, 13, 371 ; ii. 101 ; iii. 412.

Fawcett, Joseph, ii. 85-6.
Felix, Minucius, iii. 157.
Fleetwood, Bishop, ii. 143.
Forster, iii. 378.
Frederick II., iii. 331.
Fry, Caroline, ii. 230.
Fuller, iii. 242, 249, 253.

Gataker, ii. 238-9.
Geneva Version, i. xxxii, xxxiii ; ii. 524.

INDEX.

Gerhard, i. 271; ii. 19; iii. 68, 215, 217.
Glas, John, i. 297.
Gray, i. 348; ii. 469; iii. 285.
Green, iii. 166.
Griesbach, i. xxviii, xxxv, xxxvi, xxxvii, xxxviii; ii. 514, 526.
Grotius, i. 3, 27, 73, 217, 380; ii. 461-2, 464; iii. 280, 282.

Hailes, Lord, iii. 179.
Hall, Robert, i. 361; ii. 86, 87, 256.
Hammond, i. xxvii, xxix, xxx, xxxvi, xxxvii.
Harrington, i. 385.
Harwood, i. xxvi.
Heinsius, iii. 282.
Hemmingius, i. 354.
Hengstenberg, ii. 322-3; iii. 317, 329-31.
Henry, Matthew, i. 171; ii. 293; iii. 81.
Hesselius, iii. 282.
Herodian, i. xxxi.
Hesychius, i. xxxvi.
Hieronymus, iii. 364.
Hildebertus, ii. 136.
Hobbes, iii. 187.
Homer, iii. 193.
Hooker, i. 387; ii. 53.
Horsley, ii. 525.
Hottinger, i. 145.
Howe, i. 259, 321; ii. 132-3, 310, 411; iii. 82-3.
Hug, i. 5, 6.
Hume, i. 348.
Huss, John, i. 203, 235; ii. 160; iii. 77.

Isidore Hispalensis, iii. 183.

Jaspis, i. xxvii.
Jay, ii. 65, 197, 199, 206, 214, 227, 236, 237.
Jebb, iii. 79, 358.
Jerome, iii. 187.
Jortin, ii. 135, 284.
Josephus, ii. 39; iii. 176.
Justin, i. 371.
Juvenal, ii. 354.

Kelly, ii. 171.

Kitto, i. 5, 16.
Knapp, i. 84.
Knatchbull, i. xxvi.
Küttner, ii. 459; iii. 281.
Kypke, i. 354.

Lachmann, i. xxviii, xxix, xxxv, xxxvi, xxxvii, xxxviii; ii. 318, 514, 526; iii. 401.
Lactantius, i. 13.
Lange, ii. 524.
Lapide, i. xxvii, 257.
Le Bas, ii. 418.
Le Clerc, i. 104.
Leighton, i. 2, 19, 30, 40, 48, 74, 91, 93, 125, 132, 135, 144, 149, 152, 205, 206, 236, 237, 266, 269, 277, 279, 283, 317, 330, 361, 367, 369-70, 373; ii. 18, 73, 85, 137, 153, 156, 164, 175-6, 198, 202, 203, 207, 232, 232-4, 235, 254, 274, 286, 302, 304, 308, 315-16, 324, 326-7, 347, 348, 361, 363, 367-8, 430, 459, 468, 470-1, 488, 489, 494-5, 522-3; iii. 38, 39, 64, 67, 128, 129, 131, 132, 138, 143, 144, 148, 199-200, 208, 213, 223-4, 232, 239, 254, 269, 276, 280, 300, 304, 316, 338, 355, 374, 390, 417.
Le Moyne, i. 273.
Luther, i. 63, 104, 217; ii. 36, 45, 48, 524; iii. 69.
Lyra, ii. 200; iii. 420.

Mackintosh, i. ix.
Maclaurin, ii. 123, 416-17.
Maclean, i. 134.
Maimonides, iii. 69.
Mangey, iii. 176.
Martyr, Justin, iii. 414.
Matthæi, i. xxxv; ii. 526.
Matthews, i. xxvi, xxvii, xxix, xxxii, xxxiii, xxxvi.
Michaelis, i. 5, 6, 17, 353.
Middleton, ii. 526.
Miles, Dr Henry, i. x.
Mill, i. xxviii.
Milton, ii. 45, 281, 469; iii. 233.
Mischna, ii. 523.
Mons Version, i. xxix, xxxiv.
More, Hannah, ii. 292-3.
More, Dr H., iii. 46.

Morus, i. 39.
Morus, A., i. 354.
Mosheim, iii. 118.
Müller, iii. 57.
Neander, i. 7, 27, 275; ii. 83, 101, 126, 527; iii. 133, 179, 183, 420.
Nisbet, ii. 189; iii. 157-8.
Nösselt, i. 6.

Œcumenius, xxxvii, 63, 380; ii. 213, 462; iii. 186, 412.
Olney Hymns, ii. 93.
Olshausen, ii. 42; iii. 193.
Origen, iii. 412, 414.
Ovid, i. 354; iii. 50.
Owen, Dr John, i. 274, 276; iii. 189, 239, 243.

Paley, i. 390; ii. 479.
Pareus, i. 62, 63, 75; iii. 229, 419.
Pearson, ii. 391, 394; iii. 419.
Peirce, ii. 149.
Philo, iii. 183.
Plato, ii. 208.
Pliny, iii. 160, 178.
Polyænus, i. xxxi.
Polybius, ii. 249; iii. 281.
Pope, ii. 332.
Pott, i. 63; ii. 525.
Purver, i. xxvii.
Pusey, iii. 87-8.

Racine, ii. 321.
Raphelius, i. xxxi; ii. 249.
Rhemists, i. xxx, xxxiii, xxxvi, xxxvii; ii. 524.
Robinson, i. xxvi, xxxi, xxxiv; ii. 177.
Rosenmüller, i. 145; ii. 450; iii. 281.

Salmeron, iii. 238.
Sanderson, ii. 14, 27, 43-5, 47, 51, 69, 90.
Scaliger, iii. 280.
Scapula, i. xxviii.
Schleusner, i. xxxvi.
Schmid, E., i. xxvii, xxxvi; iii. 68.
Schoetgen, i. xxxii; ii. 464; iii. 166.
Scholz, i. xxxvii, xxxviii; ii. 514, 526.
Schotanus, i. 27, 28; iii. 281.

VOL. III.

Schott, i. 6, 14, 17.
Schramm, iii. 72.
Scott, i. 212-13; ii. 311-12.
Semler, i. 27; iii. 220.
Sherlock, i. 380.
Simon, Father, ii. 165.
Stanley, i. 18; iii. 192.
Steiger, i. xxxvii, 5, 18; iii. 281.
Stennet, ii. 144, 228.
Storr, i. 26; ii. 454.
Suicer, iii. 186, 280.
Symmachus, i. 277.
Symonds, i. xxviii, xxxi, xxxiii.
Syrus, P., ii. 198.

Tacitus, iii. 177.
Targum, i. xxix.
Taylor, Jeremy, ii. 125, 240; iii. 242, 277-8.
Tennyson, ii. 206.
Tertullian, i. 275; ii. 370, 371, 518; iii. 133, 178, 354, 414.
Theile, ii. 318.
Theophylact, i. xxxvii, 63.
Thomson, Dr Adam, ii. 523.
Tischendorf, ii. 318.
Torry, iii. 420.
Townley, ii. 418.
Tregelles, ii. 318, 519.
Trench, iii. 177-8.
Tyndale, ii. 524.

Usher, ii. 136.

Vatablus, i. xxv, 63.
Vater, xxix; iii. 281.
Vinet, i. 386; ii. 339, 342, 347, 377; iii. 261.
Virgil, i. 354; iii. 309.
Vitringa, iii. 183.
Voltaire, i. 348.
Vulgate, i. xxvi, xxvii, xxix, xxx, xxxii, xxxiv, xxxv, xxxvi, 63; ii. 165, 475.

Wakefield, i. xxxi, xxxii.
Walker, John, ii. 520.
Warburton, i. 384.
Wardlaw, i. 173; ii. 269, 407.
Watson, i. 215.
Watts, i. 288; ii. 129.
Wesley, Charles, ii. 113.

2 E

Westminster Confession, i. 173, 253; ii. 110.
Westminster Shorter Catechism, i. 253, 315; ii. 521.
Wetstein, i. xxix, 26; ii. 526; iii. 166, 419.
Whately, i. 386; ii. 452; iii. 183.
Whitaker, iii. 189.

Wiclif, i. xxx, ᛫xxxi, xxxiii, xxxiv, xxxvi, xxxvii; ii. 418, 524.
Winer, i. 42, 104; ii. 527; iii. 25.
Wolzogenius, ii. 525.
Wynne, i. xxxiii.

Xenophon, iii. 193.

IV.—TEXTS OF SCRIPTURE REMARKED ON.

Gen. xviii. 15,	vol. ii.	page 220
xxxi. 42,	ii.	321
Ex. iv. 22,	i.	33
xiii. 19,	i.	371
xviii. 11,	i.	314
xix. 6,	i.	290, 295
Josh. xiii. 6,	iii.	378
2 Sam. i. 26,	ii.	261
xxiii. 3,	ii.	384
2 Kings vi. 15-17,	i.	45
Job xxix. 11-16,	ii.	271
Ps. iv. 3,	i.	283
viii. 4-6,	i.	87
x. 8-10,	iii.	340
xvi. 3,	i.	180
xix. 8,	ii.	450
xxx. 5,	iii.	305
xxxiv. 8,	i.	234
xxxiv. 19, 20,	ii.	384
lv. 22,	iii.	310
cvi. 4, 5,	i.	311-12
cxviii. 22,	i.	255, 352
Prov. iii. 34,	iii.	272
x. 12,	iii.	100
xi. 31,	iii.	171
xxiv. 11, 12,	ii.	270
xxvii. 8,	ii.	226
Isa. viii. 11-13,	ii.	317
viii. 13,	i.	135
viii. 14,	i.	˙255, 353
x. 3,	i.	371
xiii. 3,	i.	300
xxviii. 16,	i. 244, 255, 345	
xl. 6, 7,	i.	176
liii. 11,	ii.	388
liv. 11-14,	i.	263
lviii. 7, 10,	ii.	272
lx. 13,	i.	263
lxii. 11,	i.	302
Isa. lxvi. 8,	vol. i.	page 334
Jer. xxii. 6,	ii.	388
Ezek. ix. 6,	iii.	166
Dan. ix. 2, 3,	i.	90
Hosea ii. 23,	i.	336
xi. 11,	i.	326
xiv. 2,	i.	277
Micah iv. 1,	i.	263
Hab. iii. 4,	i.	317
Mal. iii. 16,	i.	304
Matt. iv. 4, 7, 10,	iii.	351
v. 3,	ii.	460
v. 44-48,	i.	229
vii. 6,	ii.	342
xxv. 34-36,	ii.	272
Luke i. 68,	i.	372
i. 80,	ii.	460
iv. 13,	ii.	483
vi. 36,	ii.	265
viii. 15,	iii.	20
x. 21,	ii.	460
xx. 20,	i.	201-2
xxiii. 4,	ii.	162
John i. 16, 17,	iii.	403
iii. 36,	i.	34
vi. 35,	i.	252
vii. 17,	iii.	21
vii. 33, 34,	i.	62
viii. 39,	ii.	218
xii. 24, 32,	ii.	461
xii. 27, 28,	i.	322
xv. 8,	i.	229
xv. 19,	i.	19, 283
xxi. 18, 19,	i.	13
Acts i. 26,	iii.	281
iii. 21,	ii.	483
viii. 22,	ii.	38
xiii. 11,	ii.	483
xv. 14,	i.	283

INDEX.   435

Reference	vol.	page	Reference	vol.	page
Acts xxviii. 10,	ii.	231	2 Cor. ii. 16,	iii.	184
Rom. i. 4,	i.	49	vi. 1,	iii.	398-9
i. 29,	iii.	50	vi. 14,	ii.	210
ii. 10,	i.	74	vii. 15,	ii.	149
ii. 14, 15,	ii.	352	Gal. iii. 13,	ii.	393
iii. 25,	i.	161	iii. 13, 14,	i.	157
iii. 25,	ii.	402	iii. 24,	i.	104
iv. 25,	i.	50, 162	iv. 2,	ii.	483
v. 2,	ii. 333; iii.	401	v. 5,	ii.	333
v. 5-10,	i.	48	v. 13,	ii.	37
v. 13,	ii.	483	Eph. i. 3-5,	i.	18
vi. 1-14,	iii.	39	i. 4-6,	i.	283
vi. 14,	i.	112	i. 12, 13,	ii.	333
vi. 14,	iii.	33	i. 14,	i.	304
vi. 16, 17,	i.	21	ii. 12,	i.	42
vi. 17,	i.	219	ii. 12,	ii.	332
vi. 20,	ii.	70	ii. 13-17,	ii.	465
vii. 4,	ii.	459	iii. 10,	i.	101
vii. 24,	i.	77	iv. 3-16,	iii.	125
viii. 3, 4,	iii.	37	iv. 11, 12,	iii.	184
viii. 5,	ii.	249	iv. 15, 16,	i.	172
viii. 17,	i.	36	iv. 25,	i.	230
viii. 17,	iii.	319	iv. 32,	ii.	265
viii. 23-25,	i.	75	v. 1,	i.	229
viii. 28-31,	iii.	384	v. 8,	i.	329
viii. 33,	i.	52, 285	v. 25,	ii.	194
xi. 11,	iii.	61	Phil. i. 1,	iii.	188
xii. 1,	i.	217	i. 9, 11,	i.	212
xii. 3,	iii.	73	ii. 3,	ii.	249
xii. 3-8,	iii.	122	ii. 6-8,	i.	234
xii. 9,	i.	168	ii. 12,	ii.	149
xii. 10,	ii.	265	ii. 12,	iii.	127
xiii. 8,	iii.	101	ii. 15,	i.	229
xiii. 8-10,	i.	166	iii. 14,	i.	140-1
xiv. *passim*,	ii.	31	iii. 15,	ii.	253
xiv. 6,	ii.	252	iii. 20, 21,	i.	75-6
xiv. 13,	ii.	48	iv. 5, 6,	iii.	324
xvi. 13,	ii.	292	iv. 6,	ii.	329
1 Cor. i. 26-29,	i.	14	Col. i. 24,	ii.	172
iii. 8,	i.	150	i. 24,	iii.	142
iii. 16,	iii.	165	iii. 1-5,	ii.	53
v. 1,	iii.	48	iii. 9,	i.	230
vii. 39,	ii.	210	iii. 12,	iii.	266
ix. 7-11,	iii.	210	1 Thess. i. 4,	i.	285
ix. 21,	i.	112	i. 5,	i.	94
x. 16,	i.	245	iii. 3,	iii.	140
xii. 12-27,	iii.	124	iv. 14,	i.	87
xii. 28,	iii.	185	v. 8,	ii.	333
xiii. 12,	i.	67	2 Thess. i. 6,	i.	232
xiv. 20,	ii.	38	ii. 1-3,	iii.	84
xv. 34,	iii.	78	ii. 13,	i.	29
xv. 35,	i.	62	iii. 3,	iii.	372

Reference	Vol.	Page	Reference	Vol.	Page
1 Tim. ii. 9,	vol. ii.	page 201	Heb. xi. 6,	vol. i.	page 252
v. 17,	ii.	231	xi. 7,	ii.	149
Titus i. 5-7,	iii.	186	xii. 22-24,	i.	273-4
i. 8,	iii.	74	xiii. 17,	iii.	255
ii. 4,	ii.	194	xiii. 21,	iii.	371
ii. 11, 12,	iii.	399	James ii. 1,	iii.	150
iii. 2-8,	ii.	277	ii. 17,	i.	47
iii. 7,	ii.	333	2 Pet. i. 5,	ii.	220
iii. 8,	i.	236	i. 19,	i.	92
Heb. i. 6,	ii.	488	i. 20,	i.	90
ii. 5-9,	i.	88	1 John iii. 1,	iii.	319
iii. 6,	ii. 338; iii.	165	iii. 9,	ii.	12
iv. 1,	i.	134	iii. 14,	i.	181
v. 8,	ii.	397	iii. 24,	i.	68
vi. 11, 12,	i.	131	iv. 18,	i. 132; ii.	138
x. 5,	iii.	371	3 John 5,	iii.	115
x. 36,	i.	139	Jude 14,	i.	87
x. 39,	i.	76	Rev. xi. 5,	i.	62
xi. 3,	iii.	371	xxi. 3,	i.	263

THE END.

www.ingramcontent.com/pod-product-compliance
Lightning Source LLC
Chambersburg PA
CBHW071147230426
43668CB00009B/869